Applied Social Research

A Tool for the Human Services

Applied Social Research

A Tool for the Human Services

NINTH EDITION

DUANE R. MONETTE

THOMAS J. SULLIVAN
Northern Michigan University (Emeritus Professor)

CORNELL R. DeJONG
Northern Michigan University (Emeritus Professor)

TIMOTHY P. HILTON
Northern Michigan University

Australia • Brazil • Japan • Korea • Mexico • Singapore • Spain • United Kingdom • United States

BROOKS/COLE
CENGAGE Learning

Applied Social Research: A Tool for the Human Services, Ninth Edition, International Edition

Duane R. Monette, Thomas J. Sullivan, Cornell R. DeJong and Timothy P. Hilton

Executive Editor: Mark Kerr

Senior Acquiring Sponsoring Editor: Seth Dobrin

Assistant Editor: Naomi Dreyer

Editorial Assistant: Nicole Bator

Managing Media Editor: Elizabeth Momb

Senior Brand Manager: Elisabeth Rhoden

Senior Market Development Manager: Kara Kindstrom

Design, Production Services, and Composition: PreMediaGlobal

Manufacturing Planner: Judy Inouye

Rights Acquisitions Specialist: Thomas McDonough

Cover Image: James Lauritz/Getty Images

© 2014, 2011 Brooks/Cole, Cengage Learning

CENGAGE and CENGAGE LEARNING are registered trademarks of Cengage Learning, Inc., within the United States and certain other jurisdictions.

ALL RIGHTS RESERVED. No part of this work covered by the copyright herein may be reproduced, transmitted, stored or used in any form or by any means graphic, electronic, or mechanical, including but not limited to photocopying, recording, scanning, digitizing, taping, Web distribution, information networks, or information storage and retrieval systems, except as permitted under Section 107 or 108 of the 1976 United States Copyright Act, or applicable copyright law of another jurisdiction, without the prior written permission of the publisher.

> For permission to use material from this text or product, submit all requests online at **www.cengage.com/permissions**.
> Further permissions questions can be e-mailed to **permissionrequest@cengage.com**.

International Edition:

ISBN-13: 978-1-285-16232-4

ISBN-10: 1-285-16232-3

Cengage Learning International Offices

Asia
www.cengageasia.com
tel: (65) 6410 1200

Brazil
www.cengage.com.br
tel: (55) 11 3665 9900

Latin America
www.cengage.com.mx
tel: (52) 55 1500 6000

Australia/New Zealand
www.cengage.com.au
tel: (61) 3 9685 4111

India
www.cengage.co.in
tel: (91) 11 4364 1111

UK/Europe/Middle East/Africa
www.cengage.co.uk
tel: (44) 0 1264 332 424

Represented in Canada by Nelson Education, Ltd.
www.nelson.com
tel: (416) 752 9100 / (800) 668 0671

Cengage Learning is a leading provider of customized learning solutions with office locations around the globe, including Singapore, the United Kingdom, Australia, Mexico, Brazil, and Japan. Locate your local office at: **www.cengage.com/global**

For product information and free companion resources:
www.cengage.com/international
Visit your local office: **www.cengage.com/global**
Visit our corporate website: **www.cengage.com**

Printed in the United States of America
1 2 3 4 5 6 7 17 16 15 14 13

To my mother,
Thanks for everything.

To Nancy,
Who accepted my fleeting presence.

To Susan,
From where the sun now stands, we shall commute no more forever.

To Samantha,
For picking up the tab when I decided on an academic career.

Brief Contents

Chapter 1 Research in the Human Services 1
Chapter 2 The Logic of Social Research 19
Chapter 3 Ethical Issues in Social Research 49
Chapter 4 Issues in Problem Formulation 76
Chapter 5 The Process of Measurement 102
Chapter 6 Sampling 130
Chapter 7 Survey Research 160
Chapter 8 Analysis of Available Data 195
Chapter 9 Field Research and Qualitative Methods 219
Chapter 10 Experimental Research 256
Chapter 11 Single-System Designs 289
Chapter 12 Evaluation Research 315
Chapter 13 Scaling 344
Chapter 14 Data Analysis I: Data Preparation and Presentation 370
Chapter 15 Data Analysis II: Descriptive and Inferential Statistics 398
Chapter 16 Analysis of Qualitative Data 426
Chapter 17 Writing for Research: Grant Proposals and Report Writing 453

APPENDIX A: A GUIDE TO LIBRARY USE AND INFORMATION RETRIEVAL 477
APPENDIX B: GENERATING RANDOM NUMBERS 491
GLOSSARY 494
REFERENCES 503
NAME INDEX 527
SUBJECT INDEX 535

Contents

PREFACE xxix
NEW TO THE NINTH EDITION xxxiv
ACKNOWLEDGMENTS xxxviii

1 Research in the Human Services 1

Research in the Human Services 3

   Goals of Research 3

   Applications of Research 4

   Evidence-Based Practice 6

   Diversity and Research: The Impact of Diversity and Difference on Research 8

Parallels and Linkages Between Research and Practice 8

   Steps in Conducting Research 8

   Steps in Practice Intervention 10

The Plan of the Book 12

Review and Critical Thinking 15

   Main Points 15

   Important Terms for Review 15

   Critical Thinking 15

   Exploring the Internet 16

   For Further Reading 16

   Class Exercises for Competency Assessment 17

2 The Logic of Social Research 19

Sources of Knowledge 20
   Tradition 20
   Experience 21
   Common Sense 22
   Journalism 22
   Science 23
   Scientific Practice 25

Theories in Research and Practice 26
   What Is a Theory? 26
   The Functions of Theories 28

Concepts and Hypotheses 30
   Defining Concepts 30
   Developing Hypotheses 32
   Concepts and Operational Definitions among Minority Populations 33

Perspectives on Science 34
   Deduction versus Induction 34
   Types of Explanations 35
   Paradigms in Science 38

Cause-and-Effect Relationships 41

Review and Critical Thinking 45
   Main Points 45
   Important Terms for Review 45
   Critical Thinking 46
   Exploring the Internet 46
   For Further Reading 47
   Class Exercises for Competency Assessment 47

3 Ethical Issues in Social Research 49

The Minority Experience: The Need for Ethical Standards 50
Ethical Issues 54
   Informed Consent 54
   Deception 56
   The Right to Privacy: Anonymity and Confidentiality 57
   Harm, Distress, and Benefit 61
   Sponsored Research 62

Scientific Misconduct and Fraud 64
Scientific Advocacy 65
Protecting Vulnerable Clients 66
Withholding Treatment for Research Purposes 67

Codes of Ethics 71
Review and Critical Thinking 71
Main Points 71
Important Terms for Review 72
Critical Thinking 72
Exploring the Internet 73
For Further Reading 73
Class Exercises for Competency Assessment 74

4 Issues in Problem Formulation 76

Selecting a Research Problem 77
Personal Interest 77
Social Problems 77
Testing Theory 78
Prior Research 78
Program Evaluation and Policy Implementation 78
Human Service Practice 80
Minorities in Research: The Political Context of Problem Selection 80

Shaping and Refining the Problem 82
Conceptual Development 82
Review of the Literature 83
Units of Analysis 85
Reactivity 89
Qualitative versus Quantitative Research 89
Cross-Sectional versus Longitudinal Research 91

Feasibility of a Research Project 92
Time Constraints 93
Financial Considerations 94
Anticipating and Avoiding Problems 95

Review and Critical Thinking 98
Main Points 98
Important Terms for Review 98

Critical Thinking   98

Exploring the Internet   99

For Further Reading   99

Class Exercises for Competency Assessment   100

5 The Process of Measurement   102

Ways of Measuring   103

From Concepts to Indicators   103

Techniques of Measuring   105

Positivist and Nonpositivist Views of Measurement   106

Levels of Measurement   109

Nominal Measures   110

Ordinal Measures   110

Interval Measures   110

Ratio Measures   111

Discrete versus Continuous Variables   113

Evaluating Measures   113

Validity   113

Reliability   117

Measurement with Diverse Populations   121

Errors in Measurement   122

Random Errors   122

Systematic Errors   123

Improving Validity and Reliability   123

Choosing a Measurement Device   126

Review and Critical Thinking   126

Main Points   126

Important Terms for Review   127

Critical Thinking   127

Exploring the Internet   127

For Further Reading   128

Class Exercises for Competency Assessment   129

6 Sampling   130

The Purpose of Sampling   131

Sampling Terminology   132

Populations and Samples   132

Sampling Frames 132
　　　Learning From Experience: Poor Sampling Frames 134
　Probability Samples 135
　　　Simple Random Sampling 135
　　　Systematic Sampling 136
　　　Stratified Sampling 136
　　　Area Sampling 138
　　　Estimating Sample Size 139
　Nonprobability Samples 145
　　　Availability Sampling 146
　　　Snowball Sampling 147
　　　Quota Sampling 147
　　　Purposive Sampling 148
　　　Dimensional Sampling 149
　Sampling with Diverse Populations 151
　A Note on Sampling in Practice 153
　Review and Critical Thinking 156
　　　Main Points 156
　　　Important Terms for Review 157
　　　Critical Thinking 157
　　　Exploring the Internet 158
　　　For Further Reading 158
　　　Class Exercises for Competency Assessment 159

7 Survey Research 160

　Designing Questions 161
　　　Closed-Ended versus Open-Ended Questions 161
　　　Wording of Questions 164
　Questionnaires 166
　　　Structure and Design 167
　　　Response Rate 168
　　　Checking for Bias Due to Nonresponse 172
　　　An Assessment of Questionnaires 172
　Interviews 174
　　　The Structure of Interviews 174
　　　Contacting Respondents 176
　　　Conducting an Interview 177

    Diversity and the Interview Relationship   181
    An Assessment of Interviews   182
Telephone Surveys   183
Online Surveys   186
Focus Groups   187
Practice and Research Interviews Compared   189
Review and Critical Thinking   191
    Main Points   191
    Important Terms for Review   192
    Critical Thinking   192
    Exploring the Internet   192
    For Further Reading   193
    Class Exercises for Competency Assessment   194

8   Analysis of Available Data   195
Statistical Data   196
    Sources of Statistical Data   196
    Using Statistical Data   200
Content Analysis   203
    Coding Schemes   204
    Units of Analysis   205
    Manifest versus Latent Coding   206
Issues in Content Analysis   207
    Validity   207
    Reliability   208
    Level of Measurement   208
    Sampling   210
Assessment of Available Data Analysis   211
    Advantages   211
    Disadvantages   213
    Using Available Data in Research on Minorities   214
Review and Critical Thinking   216
    Main Points   216
    Important Terms for Review   216
    Critical Thinking   216
    Exploring the Internet   217
    For Further Reading   217
    Class Exercises for Competency Assessment   218

9 Field Research and Qualitative Methods 219

Characteristics of Qualitative Methods 220
  Contextual Approach 220
  Grounded Theory Methodology 221
Field Research 222
  Participant Observation 222
  Unobtrusive Observation 227
Steps in Field Research 229
  Problem Formulation 229
  Selecting a Field Setting 229
  Entering the Field 230
  Developing Rapport in the Field 230
  Becoming Invisible 231
  Attitude of the Researcher 231
  Observing and Recording in the Field 233
  Exiting the Field 234
Recording Observations in Field Research 234
  Qualitative Observation: Field Notes 234
  Quantitative Observation: Coding Sheets 236
Other Qualitative Methods 239
  In-Depth Interviewing 239
  Case Studies, Life Histories, and Narratives 240
  Focus Groups 241
Issues in Observational and Field Research 242
  Sampling 242
  Validity and Reliability 244
  Reactivity 246
  Observational and Field Research on Diverse Populations 247
Assessment of Field Techniques and Qualitative Methods 248
  Advantages 248
  Disadvantages 249
Observation in Human Service Practice 250
Review and Critical Thinking 251
  Main Points 251
  Important Terms for Review 252
  Critical Thinking 253

Exploring the Internet 253

For Further Reading 254

Class Exercises for Competency Assessment 254

10 Experimental Research 256

The Logic of Experimentation 257

Causation and Control 257

Matching and Randomization 259

Internal Validity 261

Experimental Designs 265

Preexperimental Designs 266

True Experimental Designs 266

Quasi-Experimental Designs 272

Modes of Data Collection in Experiments 276

External Validity 277

Reactive Effects of Testing 277

Unrepresentative Samples 278

Reactive Settings 278

Multiple-Treatment Interference 280

Enhancing the External Validity of Experiments 281

Lack of Minority Participation and Analysis 281

Assessment of Experiments 282

Advantages 282

Disadvantages 283

Review and Critical Thinking 285

Main Points 285

Important Terms for Review 286

Critical Thinking 286

Exploring the Internet 286

For Further Reading 287

Class Exercises for Competency Assessment 287

11 Single-System Designs 289

The Clinical Research Model 290

The Clinical Research Process 292

Identify Problems 292

Establish Goals 292

Select a Single-System Design 293
Establish and Measure the Baseline 293
Introduce Treatment 296
Assess Treatment Effects 297
Types of Single-System Designs 300
Single-Treatment Designs 300
Specialized Designs 305
Generalizability of Single-System Designs 308
Assessment of the Clinical Research Model 310
Advantages 310
Disadvantages 312
Review and Critical Thinking 312
Main Points 312
Important Terms for Review 313
Critical Thinking 313
Exploring the Internet 313
For Further Reading 313
Class Exercises for Competency Assessment 314

12 Evaluation Research 315

What Is Evaluation Research? 316
Why Evaluate? 316
Evaluation Research and Basic Research 316
The Politics of Evaluation Research 318
Types of Evaluation Research 319
Formative Evaluation Research 319
Summative Evaluation Research 321
Evaluability Assessment and the Logic Model 321
Specification of Variables 323
Measuring Variables 324
Evaluation of Minorities in Evaluation Research 325
Designs for Evaluation Research 326
Nonpositivist Approaches to Evaluation 332
Cost–Benefit Analysis 333
Cost-Effective Analysis 337

Improving Utilization of Evaluation
   Research   338
Review and Critical Thinking   340
   Main Points   340
   Important Terms for Review   341
   Critical Thinking   341
   Exploring the Internet   341
   For Further Reading   342
   Class Exercises for Competency
      Assessment   342

13 Scaling   344

Advantages of Scaling   345
   Improved Validity   345
   Improved Reliability   345
   Increased Level of Measurement   345
   Increased Efficiency in Data Handling   346
Developing Scales   346
   Sources of Scale Items   346
   Characteristics of Scale Items   347
Scaling Formats   349
   Likert Scales   349
   Thurstone Scales   352
   Semantic Differential Scales   354
   Guttman Scales   356
   Multidimensional Scales   360
Avoiding Response Bias   361
   Sources of Response Bias   361
   Reducing Response Bias   362
Scaling in the Human Services   363
Review and Critical Thinking   366
   Main Points   366
   Important Terms for Review   367
   Critical Thinking   367
   Exploring the Internet   367
   For Further Reading   368
   Class Exercises for Competency Assessment   368

14 Data Analysis I: Data Preparation and Presentation 370

Preparation for Data Analysis 371

    Coding Schemes 371

    Preparing and Using a Codebook 376

Data Entry 376

    Raw Data Entry 376

    Data Cleaning 377

    Creating New Variables 378

Data Distributions 379

    Types of Data Distributions 379

    Constructing Frequency Distributions 381

Graphical Display of Data Distributions 385

    Bar Graphs 385

    Histograms and Frequency Polygons 386

    Pie Charts 387

Contingency Tables 388

    Bivariate Relationships 388

    Multivariate Analysis 390

Review and Critical Thinking 395

    Main Points 395

    Important Terms for Review 395

    Critical Thinking 395

    Exploring the Internet 396

    For Further Reading 396

    Class Exercises for Competency Assessment 397

15 Data Analysis II: Descriptive and Inferential Statistics 398

Considerations in Choosing Statistics 399

    Level of Measurement 399

    Goals of the Data Analysis 400

    Number of Variables 401

    Properties of the Data 401

    Audience 402

Descriptive Statistics 402

    Measures of Central Tendency 403

    Measures of Dispersion 404

   Measures of Association 405
   The Normal Distribution 408
  Inferential Statistics 411
   Probability Theory 412
   Sampling Distributions 413
   Statistical Hypothesis Testing 414
   Statistical Procedures 417
  Review and Critical Thinking 422
   Main Points 422
   Important Terms for Review 423
   Critical Thinking 423
   Exploring the Internet 423
   For Further Reading 424
   Class Exercises for Competency Assessment 424

16 Analysis of Qualitative Data 426

  Goals of Qualitative Data Analysis 427
  Data Reduction and Analysis 429
   Codes and Coding 429
   Reflective Remarks and Memos 435
   Contextualizing Strategies 436
  Displaying Data 438
   Narrative Text 438
   Visual Displays 439
  Conclusions and Verification 441
  Using Computers in Qualitative Research 445
   Coding and Retrieving Data 446
   Data Analysis and Hypothesis Testing 447
   Conceptualization and Theory Building 447
  Review and Critical Thinking 449
   Main Points 449
   Important Terms for Review 450
   Critical Thinking 450
   Exploring the Internet 451
   For Further Reading 451
   Class Exercises for Competency Assessment 452

17 Writing for Research: Grant Proposals and Report Writing 453

The Grant-Funding Process 454
    Federal Government Funding Sources 454
    State Government Grants 455
    Private Funding Sources 456
    Learning about Funding Opportunities 457

Grant Proposal Planning 458
    Proposal Development as a Process 458
    Identifying the Topic 459
    Needs Assessment 459
    Specifying the Organization's Mission 460
    Developing a Program 460
    Targeting a Funding Source 461
    Contacting and Visiting Funding Sources 462

Writing the Grant Proposal 463
    Appearance and Writing Style 464
    Components of the Proposal 465
    Submitting the Proposal 467

Writing a Research Report 468
    Consideration of the Audience 468
    Organization of the Report 470
    The Process of Writing 472

Review and Critical Thinking 473
    Main Points 473
    Important Terms for Review 474
    Critical Thinking 474
    Exploring the Internet 474
    For Further Reading 475
    Class Exercises for Competency Assessment 475

APPENDIX A: A GUIDE TO LIBRARY USE AND INFORMATION RETRIEVAL 477

Organization of the Library 478
    Library Departments 478
    Accessing Library Materials and Other Information 479

Books   479
- *The Classification System*   479
- *The Library Catalog*   481

Periodicals   482
- *The Classification System*   482
- *Journals Important to the Human Services*   483

Online Databases   484

Reference Books for the Human Services   487

Government Documents   487

Information Literacy and Critical Thinking Skills   489

For Further Reading   489

APPENDIX B: GENERATING RANDOM NUMBERS   491
GLOSSARY   494
REFERENCES   503
NAME INDEX   527
SUBJECT INDEX   535

Research in Practice

1.1 Practice Effectiveness: "Scientific Practice" as a Challenge to the Human Services   7

1.2 Practice Effectiveness: Practice Competencies and Social Research   13

2.1 Practice Effectiveness: Providing Services to Gays and Lesbians   27

2.2 Practice Effectiveness: Social Theory and Burnout among Social Workers   36

3.1 Practice Effectiveness: Sex Offenders as Participants   63

3.2 Program Evaluation: Vulnerable Clients at Risk   68

4.1 Policy Planning and Development: Current Policy Implementation as a Source of Research Problems   79

4.2 Behavior and Social Environments: Feminist Research Methods: Do Males and Females Have Different "Voices"?   90

5.1 Behavior and Social Environments: Controversies in Measuring Violence against Women   108

5.2 Assessment of Client Functioning: Both Research and Practice Require Valid and Reliable Measurement   124

6.1 Policy Planning and Development: An Area Sample Using Address-Based Sampling in a National Children's Health Study   141

- **6.2** Behavior and Social Environments: Using Nonprobability Samples to Study Hidden Populations 150
- **7.1** Behavior and Social Environments: Surveys as an Evidence-Based Foundation for Practice Delivery 173
- **7.2** Assessment of Client Functioning: Merging Quantitative and Qualitative Measures 178
- **8.1** Program Evaluation: Evaluating Outpatient Substance Abuse Treatment Services Using an Agency Database System 199
- **8.2** Policy Planning and Development: Hazards in Estimating the Crime Problem from Available Data 202
- **9.1** Behavior and Social Environments: The Complete Participant Role in a Prison 226
- **9.2** Policy Planning and Development: Field Research to Inform Policy on Homeless Children in Diverse Cultures 242
- **10.1** Program Evaluation: Matching and Randomization in a Community-Level Alcohol Prevention Experiment 264
- **10.2** Program Evaluation: Field Experiments on Police Handling of Domestic Violence Cases 270
- **11.1** Practice Effectiveness: Evidence-Based Practice through Single-System Designs 301
- **11.2** Practice Effectiveness: A Multiple-Baseline Evaluation of Treating Panic Disorder 306
- **12.1** Program Evaluation: Evidence-Based Evaluation: The Effectiveness of Programs to Reduce Recidivism 330
- **12.2** Program Evaluation: A Nonpositivist Evaluation of a Juvenile Gang Intervention Program 334
- **13.1** Program Evaluation: Developing a Scale to Measure Intimate Justice 350
- **13.2** Assessment of Client Functioning: Rapid Assessment Instruments 364
- **15.1** Program Evaluation: Designed for Failure: Statistical Power in Human Service Research 418
- **16.1** Behavior and Social Environments: Technology Advances the Analysis of Qualitative Interviews 448

Information Technology in Research

Chapter 1	Digital Technology and Research in the Human Services 14
Chapter 3	Ethical Challenges in Internet-Based Research 70
Chapter 4	Searching the Literature: Lessons from Evidence-Based Practice 96
Chapter 5	Computerized Data Collection: Enhancing Researcher–Practitioner Collaboration 125
Chapter 6	Sampling in a Cell Phone World 154
Chapter 7	Survey Design and Data Collection 190
Chapter 8	Access to Statistical Available Data 215
Chapter 9	Handheld Computers in Field Research 251
Chapter 10	Computer Applications in Experimental Research 284
Chapter 11	Computer-Aided Single-System Data Analysis 310
Chapter 12	Online Interviews and Focus Groups in Evaluation Research 339
Chapter 13	Measurement Issues in Online Research 365
Chapter 15	Statistical Software 422

Eye on Ethics

Chapter 4	The Ethics of Selecting and Conceptualizing Research Problems 84
Chapter 5	The Ethics of Measuring Shameful, Harmful, or Deviant Behavior 117
Chapter 6	Ethical Issues with Respondent-Driven Sampling 152
Chapter 7	Ethical Use of Cell Phones in Survey Research 186
Chapter 8	Information Technologies and Ethical Research 212
Chapter 9	The Moral Complexity of Research Work in Field Settings 232
Chapter 10	Deception and Informed Consent in Experiments 280
Chapter 11	Protecting Human Subjects and Single-System Designs 309
Chapter 12	The Ethics of International Research with Abandoned Children 327
Chapter 13	Revictimizing Victims through Research 360
Chapter 14	Out of Sight, Out of Mind: The Ethics of Data Editing 379
Chapter 15	Thou Shalt Not Lie (or Even Mislead) with Statistics! 414
Chapter 16	When the Truth Hurts—Seeing Unflattering Data 442
Chapter 17	Ethical Issues in Publishing Research 469

About the Authors

Duane R. Monette is recently deceased, after a 30-year career as a member of the sociology and social work faculty of Northern Michigan University. His areas of expertise included criminology, deviance, and statistics and research methods. He published some of his research on deviance and crime in the journal *Sociology and Social Research*. For many years, he was the lead faculty member in directing the program in research methods and statistics at NMU. An avid sports fan and long-time member of the NMU Athletic Council, Dr. Monette developed a popular Sociology of Sport course. Dr. Monette received his undergraduate education at Luther College and his doctorate from the University of Iowa.

Thomas J. Sullivan is Professor Emeritus of Sociology and Social Work at Northern Michigan University, after more than three decades as a faculty member at the university. He specializes in social psychology, research methods, applied sociology, and medical sociology. He earned his undergraduate degree in sociology from San Francisco State University and his MA and PhD in sociology from the University of California at Santa Barbara. He is the author of *Sociology: Concepts and Applications in a Diverse World,* 8th ed. (Allyn & Bacon, 2009); *Introduction to Social Problems,* 9th ed. (Allyn & Bacon, 2012); *Methods of Social Research* (Wadsworth/Cengage Learning, 2001); and *Applied Sociology: Research and Critical Thinking* (Allyn & Bacon, 1992). He has published articles in *Social Science and Medicine* and the *Humboldt Journal of Social Relations*. His applied work has focused on evaluation research of social service delivery in elementary schools and of teen pregnancy prevention and intervention services. He has served in various elected and appointed positions for the American Sociological Association, the Society for Applied Sociology, and the Midwest Sociological Society.

Cornell R. DeJong is Professor Emeritus of Sociology and Social Work at Northern Michigan University, after four decades as a faculty member at the university. He specializes in intimate partner violence, research methods, and social work field education. He earned an undergraduate degree in psychology from Calvin College and an MSW from the University of Michigan. He completed additional advanced work in research methodology and social welfare at the University of Wisconsin–Madison. As a program evaluation consultant, he has conducted studies of Head Start, community mental health, schools, and substance abuse prevention. He has held social work practice positions in both corrections and mental health. He has over 10 years' experience conducting and evaluating domestic violence group services for men who batter. Professional memberships include the National Association of Social Workers and the Council on Social Work Education.

Timothy P. Hilton is an Associate Professor and Social Work Program Director at Northern Michigan University. He has more than 10 years of social work practice experience in the areas of welfare and work, policy analysis, and program evaluation. He earned his undergraduate degree from Boston College in sociology and psychology, and his master's and PhD degrees in social service administration from the University of Chicago. His research is primarily qualitative and covers several areas, including: homelessness, low-wage work, prisoner reentry, substance abuse treatment, and child protective services. He has published in the *Journal of Ethnographic and Qualitative Research*; the *Journal of Public Administration, Research and Theory*; and the *Social Service Review*. He is also a contributing author in a forthcoming book entitled *Race, Ethnicity and the Prison System—Critical Perspectives* (ABC-CLIO Publishers), which will highlight his research on Native Americans transitioning from prison to reservations.

Preface

The social sciences and the human services confront an important challenge in the twenty-first century. Human service programs in today's environment must demonstrate a need for their services, document the quality of the services they deliver, explicate a theoretical knowledge base for the services, and show evidence for the effectiveness of those services. These expectations mean that human service professionals must be able to apply social science research methods to practice problems, because it is those research methods that will provide convincing evidence of these needs, quality, and effectiveness.

Students who are new to the human service field often are unaware of research's contribution to human service delivery. A common question that we hear from our own students is this: "I want a career where I can help people. Why do I need to study research methods?" We know that building a convincing case for the connection between research and practice in the human service curriculum cannot be done in just a paragraph of an introduction, nor can it be accomplished in the first lecture of a semester. Sustaining student interest requires that the connection between research and practice be a constant theme throughout the textbook and the course. Our goal, from the first edition through this ninth one, has been to present the methods of social science research within the context of human service practice. Research is unquestionably a demanding subject, but consistently seeing the connections between research and human service practice can instill enthusiasm based on its utility and relevance.

One of our most rewarding experiences in writing this textbook and in teaching research has been to witness student uncertainty about its relevance dissipate with the discovery of new knowledge and the mastery of new ideas. It is our desire to emphasize the connections between research and practice and encourage more students to share that positive growth. Having engaged in both practice and research ourselves, we are convinced that each enterprise has much to offer the other, and we hope readers will share our enthusiasm for uncovering the parallels and linkages between them.

The original combination of authors of this text was selected to enhance their interdisciplinary contributions from a variety of social science and human service disciplines. The passage of time has, of course, taken its toll on this team, so we have added a new author to this ninth edition: Dr. Timothy Hilton, who has degrees from Boston College and the University of Chicago (see his biography preceding this Preface). His expertise in human service research, practice, and education will ensure that this ninth edition—and future editions—will retain the same quality and focus as the preceding eight editions. With Dr. Hilton on the team, our professional experience now includes direct provision of human services, conduct of human service evaluation research, and consultation to help practitioners design and evaluate service. As teaching faculty, we instruct students in basic research methods, practice evaluation, program evaluation, and direct human service practice methods.

As is the case with allies in any human enterprise, disputes, tensions, and disagreements occur among the authors over the exact relationship between research and practice—the nature and extent of the parallels and linkages between them. But these disagreements fade in significance when we observe the accumulation over the years of excellent projects where research and human service practice work together to advance both research and practice goals. We have incorporated many of these projects into this revision of the text. As with earlier editions, our goal has been to prepare a book that is useful both to those in human service departments who integrate research into students' practice education and to social scientists who emphasize the applied dimension of social science methods.

The special theme of this book, then, is that many parallels and linkages exist between social research and human service practice. We outline these ideas in the first chapter and carry this theme through the remainder of the book. This textbook is primarily an introduction to social research as it relates to the human services. As such, we have presented all the topics of scientific research that are important for such an introduction; but we have offered a challenge as well—we hope students will learn that social research has many parallels with human service practice and that understanding these parallels will make them better practitioners as well as social scientists. The challenge also is to recognize the ways in which the two can be linked—by incorporating research activities into practice, and by shaping practice settings into research opportunities.

FEATURES

A number of special features in this book are designed to help develop an appreciation for social research and its importance to the human services.

Research in Practice and Evidence-Based Practice: Almost every chapter includes at least one boxed feature titled *Research in Practice,* in which we discuss some special examples where research and practice have been linked. In this way, we emphasize the theme of the book and encourage students to consider the many ways in which this linkage can be achieved. In this feature and elsewhere we give considerable attention to *evidence-based practice,* which is an approach to practice that has gained popularity throughout the health and human service professions. Evidence-based practice stresses reliance on empirical research to make decisions about practice approaches. This emphasizes the importance of researchers and practitioners collaborating in the design, delivery, and evaluation of human services. A new, expanded introduction to evidence-based practice is now included in Chapter 1, and the approach is integrated into many parts of the text.

Information Technology in Research: In the twenty-first century, what are broadly called information technologies (IT), or computer-mediated communications technologies (CMCT), have become an integral part of both research and human service practice. This goes beyond what we traditionally called "computers" (a twentieth-century technology). Today, the technologies include such things as cell phones, iPods, and PDAs, as well as the online e-world. All these modern technologies need to be understood for two reasons: First, they are integral tools in the research process. Second, their capabilities and impact on social life force us to adapt the research process to conduct valid and reliable research. So we include a feature titled *Information Technology in Research,* and have expanded its scope to reflect these new developments. Many chapters include this boxed feature, and some chapters also discuss these issues as a part of the text.

Eye on Ethics: A boxed feature titled *Eye on Ethics* is used to emphasize the centrality of ethical issues in scientific research. It appears in every chapter following Chapter 3 (the ethics chapter) and enables us to explore additional ethical issues. It also encourages students to see that ethics is not a discrete topic to be covered once during the semester, but rather an issue integral to research that must be addressed on a continual basis.

Impact of Diversity and Difference on Research: Earlier editions gave recognition to the need for human service workers to be knowledgeable about the special needs and problems of women and minorities. In this edition, we have expanded that focus, to be consistent with the CSWE Accreditation Standards, to focus more broadly on *diversity and difference.* To this end, we have addressed in most chapters some special considerations in research methods as they apply to groups that are diverse or different—whether the difference is founded in gender, minority status, or some other characteristic.

Coverage of Both Qualitative and Quantitative Approaches: Throughout the book we emphasize the diversity of research methods that are applicable to the human services. Qualitative methods are increasingly recognized for their capacity to address the richness and complexity of human behavior that one encounters in the human services. At the same time, quantitative methods offer the human service professional the means to summarize data, to use precise measurement tools, and to generalize from study samples to larger populations. Our purpose is not to champion one approach over the other, but rather to encourage use of the full range of research methods in the search for knowledge to inform the human services.

Review and Critical Thinking: In order to give students a more effective way of reviewing and testing themselves on the material in a chapter, we have designed the end of each chapter as a *Review and Critical Thinking* section, which includes six parts: *Main Points, Important Terms for Review, Critical Thinking, Exploring the Internet, For Further Reading,* and *Class Exercises for Competency Assessment.*

Critical Thinking: The *Critical Thinking* section will encourage students to consider how the material on research methods learned in a chapter can serve as a foundation for thinking critically about issues and information in the human service practice and policy realms, as well as in their everyday lives. This will support the emphasis in the CSWE Accreditation Standards calling for content on critical thinking in human service curricula. (CSWE Educational Policy 2.1.3 in the Accreditation Standards calls for social work practitioners to "apply critical thinking to inform and communicate professional judgments," and in doing so, use the "principles of logic, scientific inquiry, and reasoned discernment.") This new feature will also serve as another way for students to review the content of the chapter.

Exploring the Internet: We encourage students to go beyond the boundaries of what can be provided in a textbook by exploring additional resources available on the World Wide Web. The Internet has become an increasingly important adjunct to all kinds of research and practice delivery tasks. In every chapter, a feature called *Exploring the Internet* suggests some specific websites that we personally have found valuable.

For Further Reading: Each chapter includes a brief, annotated list of books that students will find useful for pursuing chapter topics in greater depth.

Class Exercises for Competency Assessment: Each chapter ends with a set of exercises in which we present some problem or setting in human service practice and ask the student questions about it. The questions are designed to test the student's comprehension of the material in the chapter and promote critical thinking about social research and its application to human service practice. Because academic programs in the human services, such as social work, emphasize competency-based preparation for practice, we have designed the exercises to serve as a means of assessing those key competencies. The Council on Social Work Education, in its 2008 Educational Policy and Accreditation Standards, provides a listing of 10 such core competencies, and we describe the ones relating to research in Research in Practice 1.2 in Chapter 1. With each exercise, we designate which competencies are relevant to that exercise. These exercises can be used as a context for class discussion or they can serve as out-of-class assignments.

Appendix on Library Use and Information Retrieval: We have included an appendix in which we discuss how to use the library and online information retrieval technologies, focusing specifically on the special needs of students in the human services. Although many college students will be familiar with some of this by the time they take a research methods course, some may find they have a weakness in this area that can be strengthened by studying the appendix. Even those who are familiar with the library and information retrieval will find some new and useful information relevant to the human services.

ANCILLARY MATERIALS

Several ancillary materials are also available with this textbook. You can access these materials by creating a free account at http://login.cengage.com, or by contacting your Cengage Learning representative (visit http://sites.cengage.com/RepFinder or call 1-800-354-9706).

Instructor's Manual with Test Bank The Instructor's Manual with Test Bank, available electronically on the Instructor Resource Site, includes chapter-by-chapter test items, suggested lecture topics, and class discussion topics.

PowerPoint Slides Microsoft PowerPoint lecture slides for each chapter assist you with your lecture by providing concept coverage of all topics covered in the text.

Website The book-specific website offers students a variety of study tools and useful resources such as glossaries, flashcards, and quizzes. For instructors, an instructor's manual, test banks, and presentation slides are available for download. Students can access this site via the "Free Study Tools" link on the book's page on http://cengagebrain.com, while instructors can create an account and login at http://login.cengage.com.

New to the Ninth Edition

In approaching this revision of *Applied Social Research,* we have done our best to balance two goals—namely, to add new material and additional features on the one hand and to retain the content and style that has served instructors and students so well in past editions. New and exciting studies that illustrate the principles of social science research are continuously appearing in the literature. We've used some of these to update *Research in Practice* illustrations and to update and add some new *Information Technology in Research* sections. Advances in computer technology and use of the Internet have transformed not only how research is conducted but also how we access and use research, and these changes are reflected throughout this new edition. The perspective of the student—the ultimate consumer of the book—was foremost in our minds as we reviewed each chapter. Where the same point could be made with less elaboration, we've been more concise. Some illustrations have been modified to eliminate confusion, and some content has been reordered to enhance comprehension.

MAJOR CHANGES

Four major changes have been made in the ninth edition:

1. **Core Competencies in the Human Services.** The Council on Social Work Education (2008) specifies a series of core competencies that social work professionals should exhibit. Other human service professionals would also aspire toward these competencies. While these competencies were addressed in the eighth and earlier editions of this text, we have expanded on it in this edition by specifying more clearly and completely how research methods training contributes to the student's mastery of a number of these competencies. In particular, we do the following:

a. From the list of five focal areas discussed in Chapter 1, we have dropped "needs assessment," since this is more of a specific research method than a CSWE competency. In its place, we have added the focal area "policy planning and development." This is one of the CSWE competencies (2.1.8). While this topic was discussed in previous editions, adding it to the list of focal areas links it more clearly with the core competencies and gives it more prominence as something to which professionals attend. Three of the Research-in-Practice sections that are new to this edition have been labeled as focusing on the policy planning and development focal area.

b. At the end of each chapter, in the section labeled "Class Exercises for Competency Assessment," each exercise discussed is explicitly labeled as linked to one or more of the core competencies. So as students and instructors use these exercises, they can direct their focus toward the competencies we felt the exercise most clearly represented (or discuss what other competencies might be related to that exercise).

c. In Chapter 1, Research in Practice 1.2 is completely rewritten to discuss the six core competencies that, in our judgment, most closely link with research. This provides the student and the instructor with a framework to assess, throughout the book, how social research ties in to the core competencies.

d. Other features of this text are also included as core competencies by the CSWE: Eye on Ethics inserts (competency 2.1.2), Critical Thinking sections (competency 2.1.3), and the Diversity and Difference sections (competency 2.1.4). Where these features are introduced and discussed, they are explicitly linked to the CSWE competencies.

2. **Diversity and Difference.** To make this edition more consistent with the CSWE Educational Policies standards, we have changed the feature that focused on special research issues relating to minorities and women to cover a broadened emphasis on "diversity and difference." Difference can relate to gender or minority status, but it can also stem from social class, ethnicity, and many other factors. This broader characterization provided by the CSWE standards enables us to address difference in the many forms it might take.

3. **The Logic Model.** In Chapter 12, the section on "Evaluability Assessment" has been completely rewritten and now includes a lengthy discussion of logic models, including a new figure to serve as an outline of the process. Logic models provide a framework for determining whether a program can be evaluated and how to evaluate it, and the chapter now offers a more complete picture of the whole cycle of planning and evaluating programs and policies.

4. **Practitioner-Researcher Interviews.** To personalize the issue of practitioners-as-researchers for students, we have prepared five new Research-in-Practice inserts based on interviews with human service practitioners who have conducted research as a part of their practice

(RIPs 4.1, 7.1, 8.1, 9.2, and 16.1). These are intended to encourage students to recognize that it is not just academics with doctoral degrees who do research; rather, human service practitioners at many educational levels and in many practice settings are involved in research endeavors.

CHAPTER-BY-CHAPTER SUMMARY OF CHANGES

To assist the professor in making the transition to this new edition, we list the significant changes made in each chapter. In addition, in every chapter, the following changes are made: Each class exercise is now linked to at least one core competency.

Chapter 1. The "needs assessment" focal areas has been replaced with the "policy planning and implementation" focal area (see above). The section on "Special Issues: Research on Minorities and Women" has been relabeled and rewritten with the broader focus on "diversity and difference" (see above). Research in Practice 1.2 is new, being an introduction to the CSWE core competencies (see above).

Chapter 4. Research in Practice 4.1 is new, based on an interview with a practitioner-researcher (see above). Table 4.1 still contains a summary table of a literature review, but we have redone it based on current research on homelessness. Table 4.3 still contains a budget for an interview study, but now it is a hypothetical budget, which enables us to present budget elements in a way that is more comprehensible for students.

Chapter 5. Research in Practice 5.2 is new, although still focused on the same point that practitioners need valid and reliable measurements as much as do researchers. It focuses on a measurement device that students in the human services may well be familiar with—the APA's *Diagnostic and Statistical Manual*. Practitioners who use the DSM depend on it being a valid and reliable tool for measuring mental disorder, and the DSM has been revised over the years in hopes of making it more valid and reliable. The DSM provides a better vehicle for making these points than the Goal Attainment Scale used in the previous editions.

Chapter 6. The part of the section on "Sampling Frames" that discusses sampling frames for household-based surveys has been extensively updated and rewritten to focus on various forms of "address-based sampling." The section on "A Classic Sampling Disaster" has been relabeled "Learning From Experience: Poor Sampling Frames," which provides a more accurate description of the material. The section also has been shortened by eliminating the material on the poor response rate in the survey, and devoting attention only to the issue of poor sampling frames. Research in Practice 6.1 is new and provides a more contemporary example of multi-stage sampling, and one that is more directly germane to the human services. The "Information Technology" section has been updated considerably with new research on the impact of cell phones on sampling and survey research.

Chapter 7. Research in Practice 7.1 is new, based on an interview with a practitioner-researcher (see above). Figure 7.1 has been redone, using a more contemporary research project on homelessness. The section on "Minorities and the Interview Relationship" has been relabeled "Diversity and the Interview Relationship," and it has been extensively updated and rewritten based on new research that became available. Table 7.4 has been redone based on a hypothetical budget for a survey so it is easier for the student to understand and directly comparable to the budget presented in Table 4.3.

Chapter 8. Research in Practice 8.1 is new, based on an interview with a practitioner-researcher (see above).

Chapter 9. Table 9.1 and Figure 9.1 have been replaced with a new and more simplified table and figure that will be easier for students to understand. The related text about coding and coding sheets has been rewritten to take this change into account. Research in Practice 9.2 is new, based on an interview with a practitioner-researcher (see above).

Chapter 10. Figure 10.2 has been replaced with an updated time-series design using data showing the impact of "stand your ground" laws on justifiable homicide rates. The associated text has been rewritten to reflect this change. The "Information Technology" insert has been substantially updated and rewritten.

Chapter 12. The section on "Evaluability Assessment" has been completely rewritten and now includes a lengthy discussion of logic models, including a new figure to serve as an outline of the process. Logic models provide a framework for determining whether a program can be evaluated and how to evaluate it, and the chapter offers a more complete picture of the whole cycle of planning and evaluating programs and policies. In the section on "Alternatives to Randomized Experiments," the gun-control example of a time-series design has been replaced with the impact of "stand your ground" laws on justifiable homicide rates (elaborated in Chapter 10, Figure 10.2).

Chapter 14. The sections from "Coding Schemes" through "Raw Data Entry" have been heavily revised to take into account changes in technology as well as higher levels of knowledge about these issues on the part of students today. This results in shortening the sections considerably.

Chapter 16. Research in Practice 16.1 is new. It discusses some of the features available in qualitative data analysis when using some of the newest applications.

Of course, we have updated recommended readings with new publications, and we have incorporated recent citations from the literature to illustrate key points. New content and reorganization of material are identified in the *Instructor's Manual*.

Acknowledgments

This book began as an idea born from our own experience teaching research methods to future professionals in social work, criminal justice, education, health care, and other human service areas, as well as students in various social science disciplines. We became convinced that existing books contained significant shortcomings and that a better textbook could be prepared for students in these fields. Over the years we hope that, with each revision, we have come closer to the ideal of helping students discover the linkages and parallels between practice and research. Those students who have passed through our courses played a major role in shaping our thoughts and the content of this text. Their criticism, frustration, questioning, and desire to learn have motivated us to revise and improve with each edition. We owe them much.

We are indebted to the many social scientists, social workers, and other researchers who reviewed earlier editions of this book and provided important suggestions on how to improve it. We also were guided in preparing this ninth edition by some additional reviewers. For their insightful comments and helpful suggestions, we wish to thank the following reviewers: Morgan Mulenga, Providence College; Tim Bower, Keuka College; Kathryn McKinley, Buena Vista University; Jong Choi, California State University Bakersfield; Spencer Baker, Hampton University; John Ridings, University of Illinois at Chicago; Matthew Miller, University of Maryland; Kristina Hash, West Virginia University; Dale Weaver, California State University, Los Angeles; Dara Bergel, Shippensburg University; Sister Kathleen Cooney, Ursuline College; James A. Forte, Salisbury University; Richard W. Griffin, Ferris State University; Kendra J. Garrett, School of Social Work, College of St. Catherine and University of St. Thomas; Teresa G. Laird, Northeastern State University; David Carlson, Campbellsville University; Margaret A. Herrick, Kutztown University of Pennsylvania; Carmen V. Negron, New York City College of Technology CUNY; James E. Rollin, Addis Ababa University, Graduate School of Social Work; Melissa W. Burek,

Bowling Green State University; Bibhuti K. Sar, Kent School of Social Work, University of Louisville; Lisa E. Cox, The Richard Stockton College of New Jersey; Catalina Herrerías, University of Oklahoma; Adele Crudden, Mississippi State University; Kimberly Carter, Washington University; Karen Castellanos-Brown, University of Maryland, Baltimore; Bibhuti K. Sar, Kent School of Social Work, University of Louisville; and Mary Ann Jones, Silver School of Social Work, NYU.

As authors, we have been gratified to see our interest in and enthusiasm for applying research to practice rewarded with demand for a ninth edition. Such longstanding success could not have been achieved without the support and understanding of some very special people who have tolerated our preoccupation, coped with our irregular schedules, and inspired us when the task seemed dreary. We dedicate this book to you.

Chapter 1

✴

Research in the Human Services

Research in the Human Services
   Goals of Research
   Applications of Research
   Evidence-Based Practice
   Diversity and Research: The Impact of Diversity and Difference on Research

Parallels and Linkages between Research and Practice
   Steps in Conducting Research
   Steps in Practice Intervention

The Plan of the Book

Review and Critical Thinking
   Main Points
   Important Terms for Review
   Critical Thinking
   Exploring the Internet
   For Further Reading
   Class Exercises for Competency Assessment

This book is about the use of research in the human services. The term **human services** refers to activities with the primary goal of enhancing the relationship between people and societal institutions so that people may maximize their potential and alleviate distress. At the broadest level, the human services include formal systems such as government welfare programs, mental health services, child development and family support programs, addiction prevention and intervention programs, and correctional services of the justice system. At the federal level, many of these programs are funded and administered through the U.S. Department of Health and Human Services (DHHS). Likewise, *department of human services* or a similar label designates the agency that administers financial assistance and intervention programs at the state level. In addition to public organizations, many charitable and nongovernmental organizations deliver supportive and ameliorative services, ranging from foster care for children to meals programs for the elderly. All these programs may be included under the umbrella term *human services*. More recently this term has come to mean not merely a collage of programs, but an organized system. Defined this way, the human services comprise a coordinated or integrated set of programs that are designed to work together across agency and professional boundaries, enabling people to cope with problems and thrive in our complex society. There is an emphasis on working in teams and in collaborative relationships across disciplines.

Research is increasingly essential to the delivery of human services and to the professionals who are mandated with the responsibility of making the delivery of these services effective, efficient, and responsive to human needs. Consider the following actual case:

> Two months after giving birth to a baby boy, a young mother kills her infant son and disposes of the body by dumping it in the trash. Through a routine visit by a public-health nurse, the tragedy is discovered. In the course of the investigation, it is learned that the mother had made threatening remarks about the child while she was still in the hospital. The local community is outraged. Why was the mother allowed to leave the hospital with the child? Why was there no police intervention? Where was the local community mental health agency? The various human service agencies of the community are called on to do something to make sure that similar events will not happen again.

Do something. But what? The answer to that question begins with asking more questions. How common is infanticide? Are there predictive factors, such as particular mental conditions, that can identify individuals who are at risk of such behavior? What interventions are effective in helping them? Besides focusing on the individual person, human service professionals also might have questions about the community system. Is a breakdown in inter-agency communication a contributing factor? How might hospital procedures be improved? Are changes needed in our society's health care policy? If our community develops a prevention program, how will we know it's working? Asking and answering questions such as these is what applied social research is all about. For the human service professionals who are charged with taking action in this case, the challenge is to access, organize, and evaluate the knowledge that research has generated, and then use this scientific evidence as the basis for making practice decisions.

Thus, numerous linkages exist between research and human service practice. By linkages, we mean that research can contribute to the goals of practice, just as properly conducted practice can contribute to the goals of research. Because research provides the means for understanding the problems with which professionals work and the means for evaluating change, practitioners in human services are certain to encounter the need to understand, apply, and, in some cases, even conduct research in carrying out the goals of their professions. Some would go further and argue that the link between research and practice is even more intimate—namely, that there can be (and should be) a fruitful merger of the two. In fact, the notion that scientific research and human service practice are totally distinct enterprises is gradually disappearing (Gibbs, 2003; Kirk & Reid, 2002). Two reasons explain this.

First, strong parallels are now recognized between the conduct of research and the conduct of practice. By parallels, we mean that the two endeavors have some similar structures, follow some similar processes, and use some similar techniques. Practitioners can benefit by incorporating into practice some of the techniques that are used in research. Both research and practice, for example, are based on observation, but the observations of practitioners often are characterized as being unstructured and intuitive. Some of the more precise and structured observational techniques (discussed in Chapters 7 and 9) that researchers use can be adapted for practice purposes.

Second, properly conducted practice intervention can provide scientifically valid knowledge about human behavior and the effectiveness of intervention. For example, practitioners can scientifically assess the effectiveness of their interventions if those interventions are organized in a manner that researchers call *single-system design* (discussed in Chapter 11), which parallels the scientific experiment.

The purpose of this book is to introduce students in the human services to social research logic, methods, and design. We do this by emphasizing the parallels and linkages between research and practice. Because research and practice are intertwined, human service professionals need training in the techniques of social research as much as they need to know about group processes or theories of personality. In some situations, human service providers will *consume* social research as they apply the findings of research to practice intervention. Therefore, they need to understand the logic of research and be able to assess critically the procedures of research to decide whether research findings can be introduced into practice, and if so in what fashion. Human service workers are also called on to *collaborate* with researchers who are conducting studies involving agency services, data, or clients. In some cases, human service professionals also are expected to *conduct* social research as part of their overall intervention strategy so they must know how to design and carry out scientifically valid research projects.

RESEARCH IN THE HUMAN SERVICES

Goals of Research

The word *research* is applied to many activities: the student who browses in the library for a few hours; the social worker who, while visiting clients about other issues, makes a mental note of some of their social characteristics; the parole officer who routinely inquires about a parolee's family life as part of an intake interview. All these people might claim to be doing research. Yet the term, as it is commonly used in the social and behavioral sciences, has a considerably more precise meaning, according to which none of these activities would be considered as scientific research. This is not to say that these activities are unimportant. They may have a variety of uses. Social research, however, has specific goals that can be achieved only by using proper procedures.

Social research is the systematic examination (or reexamination) of empirical data, collected by someone firsthand, concerning the social or psychological forces operating in a situation. Three major elements characterize this definition. First, social research is *systematic*—that is, all aspects of the research process are carefully planned in advance, and nothing is done in a casual or haphazard fashion. The systematic nature of research is at the core of the scientific method, which is discussed in detail in Chapter 2. Second, social research involves the collection of *empirical data*—that is, information or facts about the world that are based on sensory experiences. As such, it should not be confused with philosophizing or speculating, which lack the empirical base of research. Third, social research studies *social and psychological factors* that affect human behavior. Biological, physiological, nutritional, or other such factors would be a part of social research only to the extent that they affect, or are affected by, social and psychological factors.

Research in the human services generally focuses on one or more of the following goals: description, prediction, explanation, or evaluation. **Descriptive research** has as its goal *description*, or the attempt to discover facts or describe reality. Descriptive research, for example, might deal with questions such as these: What are people's attitudes toward welfare? How widespread is child abuse? How many people avail themselves of the services of home health care workers? Some descriptive research efforts are quite extensive. For example, the National Center for Health Statistics (NCHS) and the Centers for Disease Control and Prevention (CDC) collect voluminous amounts of data each year to describe the health status of Americans.

Predictive research focuses on *prediction* or making projections about what may occur in the future or in other settings. Insurance companies, for example, make use of sophisticated actuarial schemes to predict the risks involved with insuring people or property. Based on past descriptive research concerning deaths and injuries, they can project how long people with certain characteristics are likely to live or the degree of likelihood that they will suffer injuries. Such projections also can be made by the NCHS. For example, the NCHS can project that infants and children with particular social characteristics will have an increased likelihood of being undernourished or suffering from infectious or parasitic diseases. Armed with this information, it is possible to devise preventive health care programs that are targeted at the high-risk groups.

Explanatory research involves *explanation* or determining why or how something occurred. Explanatory research, for example, would go beyond describing rates of juvenile delinquency or even predicting who will engage in delinquent acts. Explanatory research would focus on *why* certain people become delinquents. The goal of explanation may appear to be quite similar to that of prediction, but there is a difference: One can make predictions without an accompanying explanation. Insurance companies, for example, make actuarial predictions based on past statistical associations, but often without knowing why those associations occurred.

Evaluation research focuses on *evaluation* or the use of scientific research methods to plan intervention programs, to monitor the implementation of new programs and the operation of existing ones, and to determine how effectively programs or clinical practices achieve their goals. Evaluation research can also determine whether a program has unintended consequences, desirable or undesirable. In the past few decades, a vast array of social programs has emerged—relating to poverty, child development, crime, alcoholism, delinquency, and the like—that attempts to ameliorate undesirable social conditions. As competition over funds for such programs has increased (especially in the past decade), program directors often must justify and defend their programs in terms of cost-effectiveness. Thus, evaluation research has become an often integral part of human service programs.

Applications of Research

Some social research is called **basic research** (or **pure research**) in that its purpose is to advance knowledge about human behavior with little concern for any immediate, practical benefits. Many sociologists and psychologists conduct basic research. Research in the human services, however, is more likely to be **applied research**—that is, research designed with a practical outcome in mind and with the assumption that some group, or society as a whole, will gain specific benefits from it. Thus, explaining juvenile delinquency to social workers, probation officers, and the police is important because it can lead to programs intended to alleviate delinquency in a community. Although we distinguish between basic and applied research, it is important to recognize that the line between the two is vague and, in fact, that pure research can have applications in the human service field just as applied research can advance our knowledge of human behavior.

So the focus of this book is primarily on applied social research and, especially, on the linkage of social research with the human services. Human service fields such as social work or criminal justice focus on two important issues—practice and policy—and research can be utilized in each of these areas to produce more effective outcomes. Human service practice involves the direct provision of services to clients, such as individuals, families, or other groups, to assist them in dealing with some difficulties. Human service policy involves working through the political, governmental, and legal systems to establish programs, laws, administrative procedures, and other interventions that will deliver desired outcomes to individuals or groups. While not every human service activity falls into one of these two categories, practice and policy constitute the bulk of human service work.

To make these distinctions between basic and applied research and between human service practice and policy more concrete, it is useful to identify five focal areas or applications where research is used in the human services: understanding human functioning in social environments, policy planning and development, assessment of client functioning, program evaluation, and practice effectiveness evaluation. We do not claim that this is the only way to divide the human service field or that our list of areas of application is exhaustive. These five categories, however, are a helpful aid as we analyze the links between research and practice. Here, we review each area briefly. Then, each Research in Practice insert in this and subsequent chapters will emphasize one of these focal areas.

Behavior and Social Environments. Human service providers do many things: link people to resources they can use, enhance people's coping abilities, improve the operation of social systems, and participate in the development of social policy, to name only a few. All these activities rest on an understanding of the behavior of the people to whom services are provided and on a comprehension of the social environment in which they function. Social research can provide much of this knowledge. For example, an agency providing services to teenagers can turn to research on adolescents in American society for a better understanding of the problems facing their clients. Although this research may be conducted without any particular practice or policy goals in mind, it can still be applied in both realms.

Policy Planning and Development. Human service professionals gain direction from policies that are intended to advance the well-being of individuals, families, and society as a whole. Human service policy involves working through the political, governmental, and legal systems to establish programs, laws, administrative procedures, and other interventions that will deliver desired outcomes to individuals or groups. Policies can be thought of as a set of rules that govern what types of resources will be available to people to assist them in achieving goals, maximizing potential, and alleviating distress (Herrick, 2008). So, for example, a few years back, most states changed their laws to make welfare a temporary, time-limited support for people. One could receive payments for, say, a lifetime maximum of five years. So research can be conducted to discover the positive and negative consequences of such a policy. This research can help policymakers in the original development of the policy as well as in deciding whether to change or eliminate the policy after it has been in operation for some time. In this way, social research can be used to help develop, evaluate, and, if necessary, change policies.

Assessment of Client Functioning. In the provision of human services, assessing the level of functioning of clients is often necessary. What kind of communication problems exist in a family? How capable is a teenage parent in dealing with the stresses of motherhood or fatherhood? How skilled is a person in negotiating a job interview? Practitioners often make such assessments, but the danger is that they will be made unsystematically. The past 20 years have seen extensive development of systematic and, in some cases, quantitative assessment tools that can be used for both research and practice tasks. The results of these assessment tools can be compared at different times to see if any change or improvement has occurred. Examples of such client assessment tools can be found in Sheafor and Horejsi (2012).

Program Evaluation. The term *policy* refers to broad directions or goals whereas the term *program* refers to the organized delivery of services to people or groups. Programs represent the implementation of a policy or policies whereas policies determine what programs will exist and what they will look like. In the past few decades, many large, ambitious, and expensive programs intended to cope with social problems and provide services to individuals have been developed. Along with the growth of these programs has emerged an increasing concern over their results: Do they achieve their intended goals? These programs are costly, and some evaluation is needed to assess whether resources are, indeed, being used effectively. Equally important, a program that fails to achieve its goals leaves a problem unsolved or an effective service undelivered. *Program evaluation* is the use of scientific research techniques to assess the results of a program and evaluate whether the program, as currently designed, achieves its stated goals (Rossi, Lipsey, & Freeman, 2004). It is crucial that human service providers understand when program evaluation is called for and when it is possible to conduct an effective evaluation. In addition, many practitioners likely will find themselves participating in programs that include evaluation as one of their goals. (Given the close link between policy and program, there is much overlap between the two: Program evaluation is often a part of a policy evaluation.)

Practice Effectiveness Evaluation. Whereas program evaluation focuses on the assessment of entire programs or policies, the concern of human service professionals often is considerably more specific—namely, "Is what I am doing right now with this particular client working?" For this reason, practitioners are often disenchanted with the utility of evaluation research as a direct aid to helping clients. In recent years, however, major advances have occurred in the ability of research to answer professionals' questions about the efficacy of intervention efforts on specific clients. One such advance is a form of research called *single-system design*, in which practitioners devise a way to repeatedly measure the occurrence of a problem and monitor the behavior of a single client, group, family, or larger system for a period of time. Intervention then begins, and the behavior is again monitored. Comparison between the baseline and intervention periods permits the practitioner to make more accurate assessments of progress than the informal assessment on which human service professionals traditionally have relied. Through such careful monitoring of behavior and measuring of intervention effects, human service workers not only can enhance their own effectiveness, but also can contribute to the development of an intervention technology that others can successfully apply.

Obvious similarities exist between program evaluation and practice effectiveness research. For example, both are concerned with the effectiveness of certain practices. The difference, however, is in the scope of the efforts. Program evaluation focuses on complete programs, whereas practice effectiveness emphasizes the assessment of some particular aspect of a practice situation in a way that will not necessarily affect the entire program.

Evidence-Based Practice

A theme that underlies many recent developments in the human services, and shows great promise for linking practice and research, is encapsulated by the term **evidence-based practice**: "the conscientious, explicit, and judicious use" of the best evidence in making decisions about human service assessment and intervention (Sackett, et al., 1997, p. 2). According to this approach, the "best evidence" is knowledge that has been gained via the scientific research process. Research in Practice 1.1 discusses some of the issues involved in the development of evidence-based practice in the human services. As the insert shows, this approach has been called a number of different things over the years by different practitioners, although "evidence-based practice" seems to have emerged as the most widely used designation. The evidence-based approach is inherently critical, which means that it is always questioning whether particular practices or policies are effective. Just because a practice method has been routinely used in the past does not mean it is necessarily effective. Just because a practice method has worked with clients with certain characteristics (e.g., based on age, race, or gender) does not mean it will work on other clients. The evidence-based practitioner constantly questions the efficacy of methods, and the primary yardstick used in resolving these questions is the evidence provided by scientific research (Mullen, Bledsoe, & Bellamy, 2008).

This approach has emerged, in part, because there is now a growing body of research evidence—some of it basic and some of it applied—that can provide guidance to human service practitioners and policy makers. In the past century, researchers in the social sciences and human services have developed more sophisticated research techniques and have used them to produce a large and complex body of knowledge about human social and psychological behavior. This body of knowledge now provides human service practitioners and policy makers with scientifically grounded evidence about what works and what doesn't. So it is much more feasible today—than it was, say, 50 years ago—to base practice and policy on scientific evidence.

Another reason for the emergence of the evidence-based approach is that some startling criticisms of human service practice surfaced a few

Research in Practice 1.1 — Practice Effectiveness: "Scientific Practice" as a Challenge to the Human Services

Four decades ago, the Health Research Group, one of Ralph Nader's public citizen organizations, aimed a challenge in the direction of the human services (Adams and Orgel, 1975). The group suggested that people seeking help from human service professionals should demand a written contract at the outset of the relationship specifying the conditions of the therapy, the goals of the intervention, and even the site at which the therapy would take place. The group also suggested that the contract specify the character of the practitioner–client relationship, especially regarding the empirical evidence showing what kind of relationship would enhance the achievement of the client's goals. Underlying these recommendations was a demand for a high degree of *accountability* on the part of the helping professions. In the intervening decades, these demands for accountability have become louder and broader in scope, as illustrated by a number of developments (Cournoyer & Powers, 2002):

- The emergence of managed care systems that drive much human service practice and reward use of interventions shown to be effective by research.
- The empowerment of consumer groups, such as Nader's Health Research Group, and a proposed interprofessional Clients' Bill of Rights that includes the right to "be informed about the options available for treatment interventions and the effectiveness of the recommended treatment" (Joint Initiative of Mental Health Professional Organizations, 2003).
- The establishment of accreditation standards by such organizations as the Council on Social Work Education that require schools to prepare social workers to "use practice experience to inform research, employ evidence-based interventions, evaluate their own practice, and use research findings to improve practice, policy, and social service delivery" (Council on Social Work Education, 2008, p. 5).

These demands for accountability have motivated human service professionals in such fields as psychology, social work, criminal justice, and nursing to begin defining the human services as *scientific* disciplines (Goldfried & Wolfe, 1996; Rosen, 1996; Turnbull & Dietz-Uhler, 1995). These professionals now use terms such as "scientific practice," "scientist practitioner," and "evidence-based practice." In the field of community mental health, Abraham Jeger and Robert Slotnick (1982) developed what they called a behavioral–ecological approach to the delivery of mental health services. In presenting this approach, they argued that research should be viewed as an integral part of treatment. Over the ensuing decades, this idea has continued to receive support. For example, integrating research with practice served as the organizing theme of an entire special issue of the journal *Education and Treatment of Children*. In one of the articles, Alisa Bahl and colleagues (1999) discussed treating behavioral problems in children using what they called a data-driven approach. They advocated collecting data not only before and after treatment, but also throughout the course of treatment itself. To illustrate this point, they discussed how they employed Parent–Child Interaction Therapy to treat a 6-year-old boy with oppositional defiant disorder. They employed parent and teacher reports, observation during clinic sessions, and parental monitoring during each daily home practice session. The case illustrates the importance of using research procedures not only for the advancement of knowledge, but also as an enhancement of service delivery.

On a similar note, the National Association of Social Workers (NASW) Code of Ethics (2008) emphasizes the responsibility of professionals to employ empirical knowledge in practice and to contribute to the advancement of professional knowledge through research. The section on evaluation and research in the NASW Code of Ethics includes the following points:

- Social workers should monitor and evaluate policies, implementation of programs, and practice interventions.
- Social workers should promote and facilitate evaluation and research to contribute to the development of knowledge.
- Social workers should critically examine and keep current with emerging knowledge relevant to social work and fully use evaluation and research evidence in their professional practice.
- Social workers should educate themselves, their students, and their colleagues about responsible research practices.

In each chapter, we will set aside separate space entitled "Research in Practice" where we will discuss particular instances in which research and practice have been linked. In this fashion, students in the human services can gain a deeper understanding of the many ways in which this linkage might be achieved.

decades ago that concluded that such practice is not very effective at achieving its goals—or at least that we don't have much proof that it is effective, other than the claims of the practitioners themselves. In response, in the intervening decades, human service researchers and practitioners focused their attention on producing research that would provide such proof. The resulting collaboration of researchers and practitioners has produced a body of research that provides us with evidence about what is effective in practice and what isn't.

Evidence comes in many different forms, of course. The observations that a practitioner makes of a single client in her office is "evidence," as is the complex statistical analysis done on the observations of thousands of people in a highly controlled experimental study. So a central part of the evidence-based approach is to critically evaluate research studies to determine how much confidence we have in their conclusions, and thus whether we want to use them as evidence in particular practice or policy settings. The purpose of this text is to provide students in the human services with an introduction to research methods so that they are in a better position to understand and participate in this critical evaluation. Although an understanding of research methods in general certainly contributes to becoming a more effective human service practitioner, we will link research methods specifically with evidence-based practice in a number of chapters where the linkage is especially relevant. In addition, we have enhanced the focus on this critical perspective by including a brief section toward the end of each chapter titled "Critical Thinking." There we suggest some ways in which the material in a particular chapter can be a guide for critical thinking and analysis in practice and policy realms, as well as in one's everyday life.

Diversity and Research: The Impact of Diversity and Difference on Research

Human service professionals recognize that diversity and difference—whether they arise from variations in race, ethnicity, gender, or something else—are powerful influences on people and social life. Diversity and difference can lead some groups to suffer disproportionately from the problems that human service workers attempt to alleviate, such as poverty, inequality, or discrimination. So human service practice devotes special attention to diversity and difference. Issues of diversity and difference also need to be addressed when conducting research in the human services. Because of the position of minorities in society, conducting research that produces accurate and complete data on them can be a challenge. In fact, in some circumstances, the standard research methods used in human service research result in misleading and, in some cases, outright false conclusions regarding a minority. In those circumstances the research methods need to be modified.

This problem is sufficiently important to human service research that we devote special attention to it throughout the book. In each chapter, where relevant, we point out particular ways in which problems or biases in research on minorities can occur and provide strategies for overcoming them. The goal is to create a sensitivity to the fact that research methods can have built-in biases when focused on particular minority groups, and that care must be exercised to detect and avoid this.

PARALLELS AND LINKAGES BETWEEN RESEARCH AND PRACTICE

Although scientific research is different in many respects from human service practice, important parallels exist between the two. In fact, researchers and practitioners use many of the same strategies in approaching their problems. After reviewing the steps in conducting research, we will point out parallels that can be found in practice.

Steps in Conducting Research

Although each research project is unique in some fashion, some general steps characterize virtually every project. The research process can be divided into six identifiable stages: problem formulation, research design development, data collection, data analysis, drawing conclusions, and public dissemination of results.

Problem Formulation. The first step in conducting social research is to decide on the problem to research. When first encountering the issue of problem formulation, students commonly question its importance. So many problems exist that it would appear to be a simple matter to select one on which to conduct research. However, such a casual view of scientific problem formulation is erroneous. For example, some problems about which we might desire answers are not scientific questions at all, and no amount of research will answer them. Other problems, though possibly interesting and intriguing, might prove to be impractical from a methodological, ethical, or financial standpoint.

Another element of problem formulation is to shape a concern into a specific researchable question. Such global concerns as "the state of the modern family" are far too broad to be considered as research problems. They need to be narrowed down to specific issues for which empirical data can be gathered, such as: What is the divorce rate? How does it compare with the divorce rate of previous years? Do children who are raised in single-parent families exhibit poorer social development than children who are raised in two-parent families? As the initial step in research, developing a researchable problem is highly important. (In Chapter 4 we outline the many issues involved in this process.)

Research Design Development. Having successfully established a researchable problem, we must develop a **research design**, which is a detailed plan outlining how observations will be made. This plan is followed by the researcher as the project is carried out. Research designs always address certain key issues such as who will be studied, how these people will be selected, and what information will be gathered from or about them. In fact, the research design spells out, in considerable detail, what will occur during the following stages of the research process. (Chapters 7 through 12 describe the different kinds of research designs and issues that must be considered in their development.)

Data Collection. A part of any research design is a description of what kinds of data will be collected and how this will be done. The data collected at this stage constitute the basic information from which conclusions will be drawn, so great care must be exercised in this step.

Two aspects of data collection, *pretests* and *pilot studies*, illustrate just how careful scientists are about this. The **pretest**, as the name implies, is a preliminary application of the data-gathering technique to determine its adequacy. It certainly would be risky and unwise to jump prematurely into data gathering without first knowing that all the data-collection procedures are sound. For example, if our study were a needs assessment of homemakers to determine how many would make use of occupational training services, we would choose a small group of homemakers and collect the same data from them that we plan to collect in the final project. A pretest is, in a sense, a trial run—and unless we are very good or very lucky, some modifications in the data-collection technique are likely to be required based on the results of the pretest. After these modifications are made, the technique is pretested again. Additional pretests are always desirable after any modifications in the data-gathering technique to assess whether the modifications handle the problems encountered in the previous pretest.

In some cases, it may even be necessary to do a **pilot study**, which is a small-scale trial run of all the procedures planned for use in the main study. In addition to administering the data-gathering instrument, a pilot study might include such things as a test of the procedures for selecting the sample and an application of the statistical procedures to be used in the data-analysis stage.

It is this kind of care in data collection that improves the validity of the data collected and bolsters confidence in the conclusions drawn.

Data Analysis. As with data collection, data analysis is spelled out in the research design and can be the most challenging—and interesting—aspect of a research project. It is challenging because data in raw form can be quite unrevealing. Data analysis is what unlocks the information hidden in the raw data and transforms it into something useful and meaningful. During data analysis, researchers learn whether their ideas are confirmed or refuted by empirical reality. In this step, researchers often make use of statistical tools that can range from simple percentages to complex statistical tests, which require much training to understand and master. These statistics aid in communicating the findings of the researchers to others. Once a researcher has learned the special language and interpretations of statistics, he or she can be more effective in communicating research findings in a clear, concise manner than when using conventional English. (Chapters 14, 15, and 16 review some of the basic data-analysis and data-manipulation techniques that are used in social research.)

Drawing Conclusions. The next step in conducting social research is to draw some conclusions from the data analysis. The form this takes depends partly on the goals of the research project. A descriptive study, for example, simply presents what was found, possibly in a summarized form to make it more easily understood. Predictive and explanatory research, on the other hand, usually have hypotheses, or statements of what the researchers expect to find, presented before the data are collected. In this case, a major element of drawing conclusions is to assess how much support exists for the hypotheses. The support that the data provide for the hypotheses can range from strong to weak to none, and researchers have an obligation to those who might use their research to accurately represent the strength of their findings. Finally, in evaluation research, drawing conclusions usually involves making a judgment about the adequacy and effectiveness of programs and any changes that might improve conditions.

Often, research discovers some things that do not relate directly to any specific hypothesis or even things that are completely unanticipated. When drawing conclusions, researchers should make note of the implications of any findings that are of sufficient importance to warrant mention. When complete, the conclusions should clearly indicate what has been learned by conducting the research and the impact of this new knowledge.

Public Dissemination of Results. Research findings are of little value if they remain the private property of the researchers who produce them. A crucial stage of social research is the public dissemination of findings by publication in a book or professional journal or through presentation to a professional organization. This shares the newly created knowledge with those who can put it to use or build on it in future research. In fact, public dissemination of knowledge is a major mechanism for scientific advancement. (As we discuss further in Chapters 2 and 3, public dissemination makes it possible for others to reanalyze or replicate the research and confirm the findings or identify cases of error-filled, biased, or fraudulent research.)

Steps in Practice Intervention

Just as the research process can be organized as a series of steps, the process of human service practice also often is conceptualized as a series of stages. In fact, the stages of practice intervention demonstrate the parallels and linkages between practice and research (see Figure 1.1).

Problem Assessment. In much the same way that social researchers must decide on the problem to research, practitioners must specify the precise problem with which they are concerned, factors that might contribute to the problem, and which aspects of the problem will be given priority. In problem formulation, researchers make judgments concerning the feasibility of researching a particular phenomenon. Likewise, in problem assessment, practitioners must pose answerable questions. The initial step in evidence-based practice involves crafting questions for searching electronic databases so the relevant information can be retrieved. A well-formed question describes the client, course of action, alternate courses of action, intended result, and whether effective intervention is possible.

Formulation of an Intervention Strategy. Just as researchers develop a research design, practitioners develop a strategy for intervention that will be effective in alleviating the problem specified during the

Stages of Social Research	Steps in Human Service Practice
Problem formulation	Problem assessment
Research design development	Formulation of an intervention strategy
Data collection	Implementation
Data analysis	Evaluation
Drawing conclusions	Closure
Public dissemination of results	Documentation and dissemination

FIGURE 1.1 Parallels between Human Service Practice and Social Research

assessment stage. Whereas researchers choose among a variety of research methods, practitioners choose among a variety of intervention strategies such as crisis intervention, behavior modification, or vocational training. Just as researchers may use more than one research technique over the course of a project, practitioners also may use more than one intervention strategy in attacking a problem. Tracking down the research studies and other data that will help one to evaluate intervention strategies requires access to relevant electronic databases and specialized skills in their efficient use. In addition to general web-searching tools and library databases, databases that relate specifically to medicine and human service practice are being developed to aid in the access and use of practice-related studies. As you will learn through the course of studying research methods, however, all research results are not of equal value. Some research designs generate more convincing evidence of causation than others. Determining how valid and useful the results of any given study are must be approached in a systematic way so that so-called best evidence receives more weight than results of other studies. At this stage, the practitioner must organize the results, consider conflicting findings, and determine which practice interventions show the most promise.

Implementation. Following the development of the research design, researchers proceed to put it into practice. In a similar fashion, practitioners implement the intervention strategies outlined during the preceding stage. Normally, researchers' activities are limited to data collection; they do not attempt to change the people they are studying. Practitioners, on the other hand, may collect data as a part of the implementation stage, but they are concerned primarily with the effectiveness of the intervention strategy in creating some changes in clients or in the systems that affect them.

Evaluation. Once researchers have collected their data, they analyze it to determine what their study has found. Similarly, evidence-based practice evaluates the effectiveness of the intervention strategy that was implemented during the preceding stage. Were the goals of the plan achieved? What were the costs of the strategy? Were any undesirable side effects brought about by the intervention? Which aspects of the intervention process seemed to be most important in producing the change that resulted? The evidence-based model emphasizes the employment of single-system designs and other systematic assessment strategies in contrast to the more casual observation that is associated with traditional practice. The results of these systematic assessments can help shape future research studies and may serve as evidence in their own right for guiding practice decisions.

Closure. Termination of intervention is an important part of the helping process. The extent to which the intervention has been effective must be determined, as well as the degree to which the goals of the intervention cannot be—and possibly will never be—achieved. Researchers may make suggestions for future research, which might be helpful in further clarifying the relationships found in the study. Likewise, practitioners might suggest other sources of help that the client could use to cope with any problems left unresolved by the intervention. In other words, for both researchers and practitioners, the conclusion is a time to review what has been accomplished and look forward to directions and alternatives for the future.

Documentation and Dissemination. We have made the point that both the process and the results of research must be carefully documented; the same can be said for human service practice. At a minimum, this stage includes meeting agency requirements for record keeping and case documentation, such as preparing treatment plans and case-closing reports. Although such agency-mandated reporting may serve a useful quality-control function, practitioners also have a responsibility to share with others the knowledge gained from their practice. This may take the form of case conferences within the agency, workshop presentations, or formal articles published in appropriate journals. As a consequence of subjecting practice to the scrutiny of supervisors and peers, deficits are identified, intervention techniques refined, and advances made in the delivery of human services.

By this point, you should be gaining an appreciation for the parallels and linkages between social research and human service practice. The parallels involve the similarities between the activities of researchers and those of practitioners. The linkages involve the contributions that research can make to practice endeavors, and vice versa. Research in Practice 1.2 elaborates on this by suggesting how social research is an aspect of the core competencies that have been identified as being at the center of one human service field, namely social work.

THE PLAN OF THE BOOK

This first chapter has discussed the extent to which research is fundamental to the delivery of human services. The remainder of the book discusses how research is applied to the human services. Chapters 2 through 6 present some of the important issues that underlie research, including the role of hypotheses and theories, and ethical problems that researchers are likely to confront. We also address the issue of how to formulate a research problem and select a scientifically sound sample on which observations will be made.

With Chapter 7, we begin the first of five chapters on specific research methods. Chapter 7 covers *survey research*, which is a widely used data-collection technique based on obtaining people's responses to questions. In Chapter 8, we discuss the use of *available data* in research. Though not used as commonly as surveys, available data can be helpful to human service researchers. For example, the records kept by prisons, hospitals, or social service agencies would fall into the category of available data that could be used for research. Chapter 9 presents *field research* and *observational methods*, which involve the direct observation of people's behavior, often in the natural settings where people lead their everyday lives. This also is a common research technique in the human services, because human service practitioners typically make observations of the everyday lives of clients during the course of intervention. In Chapter 10, we discuss *experiments*, which are research techniques designed to assess the effect of one factor on another. Although human service providers only occasionally may conduct conventional experiments, they often are in a position to carry out *single-system research*, the topic of Chapter 11. Single-system research involves assessing the impact of some factors on the feelings or actions of a client, and it derives its basic logic from the experimental designs discussed in Chapter 10.

The remaining six chapters focus on issues that may have to be addressed irrespective of which specific research method is used in a particular study. *Evaluation research*, discussed in Chapter 12, refers to assessing how well a particular policy, program, or practice achieves its goals. This has become an increasingly important element in the human services, and evaluation researchers often use some—or all—of the five research techniques discussed in the preceding chapters. In Chapter 13, we analyze

> **RESEARCH IN PRACTICE 1.2**   **Practice Effectiveness: Practice Competencies and Social Research**
>
> The evidence-based approach described in this chapter has been embraced by many fields, including medicine, nursing, psychology, and social work. As this approach to practice has evolved over the decades, the professional organizations in these fields have identified the core competencies that professional practitioners in these fields should possess, and they have established means of assessing how well students have learned these competencies. In social work, for example, the Council on Social Work Education (2008) developed a set of standards that are used to evaluate college programs in social work. The CSWE Educational Policy and Accreditation Standards (EP) delineate 10 core competencies that students should develop as part of their education. Some of these competencies have to do with social research and research-related skills and activities. One of the goals of this book is to demonstrate the ways in which research is an integral part of these competencies. This will further promote the major themes of this book, namely that there are significant parallels and linkages between social research and human service practice.
>
> We will focus on the six competencies that, in our judgment, have the most direct parallels and linkages to research. They are presented here, with a brief description of how and where they are addressed in this book and with their identifying number (EP number) in the CSWE Educational Policy list.
>
> 1. **[Ethics]** An obligation to engage in *ethical human service practice* (EP 2.1.2). An entire chapter in this book (Chapter 3) is devoted to ethics in research, and every subsequent chapter has a boxed feature titled "Eye on Ethics" that explores ethical issues relating to the topic of each chapter.
> 2. **[Critical Thinking]** Use of *critical thinking* in professional human service work (EP 2.1.3). Every chapter ends with a section titled "Review and Critical Thinking" in which one section ("Critical Thinking") explores how the research process discussed in that chapter can assist in the development of critical thinking skills.
> 3. **[Diversity]** The engagement of *diversity and difference* in research and practice (EP 2.1.4). Most chapters have a section titled "Diversity and Research" in which we discuss how various dimensions of diversity and difference may influence the research process, and the uses to which research results may be put.
> 4. **[Research & Practice]** Use of *research-informed practice* and *practice-informed research* (EP 2.1.6). This is an underlying, general theme of this whole book, and we will explicitly address it in many places.
> 5. **[Policy Practice]** Engage in *policy practice* to deliver effective social work services (EP 2.1.8). One of the focal areas used in this book is "policy planning and development," so some of the Research in Practice sections will be devoted to showing how research is used to shape and evaluate human service policies. Also, Chapter 12 is on program evaluation, which is an integral part of policy planning and development.
> 6. **[Evidence-Based Evaluation]** Utilize *evidence-based interventions* and *evaluate intervention effects* (EP 2.1.10). Three of the focal areas ("assessment of client functioning," "program evaluation," and "practice effectiveness evaluation") address these issues directly, so many of the Research in Practice sections focus on this. Also, Chapter 11, Single-System Designs, is devoted to the assessment of individual clients and interventions.

how to develop *indices* and *scales*, which are measuring devices that derive a single composite score from a number of other scores that measure something of interest. Chapters 14 through 16 offer an introduction to *data analysis* or what to do with numerical and non-numerical data once they are collected. Chapter 17 is an introduction to the *grant-seeking process*, or how to find financial support for research, including how to write grant proposals and research reports.

Computers and various forms of electronic technologies have now become an integral part of the research process. In recognition of this, we have included in most chapters an insert titled

> ## INFORMATION TECHNOLOGY IN RESEARCH
>
> ### Digital Technology and Research in the Human Services
>
> The computer, probably more than any other single invention, stands as a symbol of technological progress in the late twentieth and early twenty-first centuries. Computers now pervade all areas of society, including the human services. A few decades ago, computer applications in the human services were limited to accounting and bureaucratic record keeping. In the field of research, computers were used mostly to store data and conduct statistical analysis on that data. By the twenty-first century, however, information technologies (IT) or computer-mediated communications technologies (CMCT) have become an integral part of virtually all social life and human service activities and taken us far beyond these traditional uses of computer technology (Rafferty & Steyaert, 2009).
>
> In later chapters, we will describe electronic technologies that can run statistical tests, assist in interviewing respondents, help select a sample to use in data collection, and accomplish a host of other activities related directly to research fundamentals. Information technologies have also become an integral part of the literature review process through electronic database searches, which are available through libraries as well as directly on the Internet. Computers also help in report preparation as word processors, and graphic display programs have become essential in producing charts and figures to communicate the findings of research. In addition, such CMCTs as cell phones, iPods, PDAs, and cloud computing are rapidly changing the way we do research. All these technologies need to be understood for two reasons: first, these technologies are integral tools in the research process. Second, their capabilities and impact on social life force us to adapt the research process to conduct valid and reliable research.
>
> CMCTs also are rapidly entering use for human service practice tasks. For example, digital technologies and cloud computing can now be used to assess client states, provide measures of client improvements over time, access help in establishing AIDS and teen pregnancy prevention programs, and find agency assistance in conducting evaluations of programs (Card & Kuhn, 2006; Rafferty & Steyaert, 2009).
>
> With creativity, these service delivery applications can be harnessed to make applied research easier and more feasible. This service base also increases the possibilities for making use of research in practice. Our discussion of information technologies and computer applications illustrates a central theme of this book—namely, that there are important linkages between social research and human service practice, and that the imaginative application of digital technology is another way of forging this linkage.
>
> Good information about the uses of digital technologies in human service research can be found in the *Journal of Technology in Human Services* (http://wweb.uta.edu/faculty/schoech/cussn/jths/default.htm) and *Social Science Computer Review* (http://hcl.chass.ncsu.edu/sscore/sscore.htm). To promote this theme, many chapters in this book have a section titled "Information Technology in Research." The goal is to educate you regarding the many ways in which modern information technologies impact the field of social research today and to stimulate your thinking about ways of using this technology to link practice with research.

"Information Technology in Research." Each of these inserts describes a particular research use of computer or information technology relevant to the topic of that chapter. In addition, a feature titled "Exploring the Internet" appears in each chapter; through exercises, this feature shows you how to use the Internet for a variety of research purposes.

Each chapter ends with a section titled "Review and Critical Thinking," which provides the student with a variety of ways to review the material covered in the chapter. The book ends with two appendices. The first is a guide to using the library for research in the human services. Effective use of library resources is an essential step in most research projects. The second presents ways of generating and using tables of random numbers, which have many uses in research and are discussed in several chapters.

REVIEW AND CRITICAL THINKING

Main Points

- The human services are those professions with the goal of enhancing the relations between people and societal institutions to enable people to maximize their potential and alleviate distress.

- While the primary goal of the human services is to deliver services to clients, research has become a fundamental part of such service delivery. In fact, a major theme of this book is the important parallels and linkages between research and human service practice.

- A knowledge of research is necessary for both consumers of social research and those who produce it.

- Social research is a systematic examination of empirical data, collected firsthand, concerning the social or psychological forces operating in a situation.

- Social research seeks to achieve the goals of description, prediction, explanation, and evaluation.

- Social research also can involve basic research or applied research.

- The links between social research and human service practice can be identified in five focal areas: understanding human functioning in social environments, policy planning and development, assessment of client functioning, program evaluation, and practice effectiveness evaluation.

- The evidence-based practice approach to the human services emphasizes the use of the best evidence in deciding which policy and practice interventions to implement.

- Conducting accurate and unbiased research on members in the context of diversity and difference confronts social researchers with special problems.

- Research and practice follow similar, parallel paths in approaching a problem. Research, for example, follows a series of steps that have parallels to the steps in practice intervention.

- Many human service professions have established core competencies that all practitioners in the profession should be skilled at; some of these competencies have to do with social research and research-related skills and activities.

Important Terms for Review

applied research	evidence-based practice	predictive research	research design
basic research	explanatory research	pretest	social research
descriptive research	human services	pure research	
evaluation research	pilot study		

Critical Thinking

The term *critical thinking* refers to a mode of assessment or a reflective process that helps you assess information and decide on courses of action (Browne & Keeley, 2012; Paul, 1993). It is a careful and purposeful assessment that follows certain procedures or guidelines for gaining knowledge or making decisions. The logic of research that is presented in this book provides one set of procedures for critical thinking. The kind of analysis that is used in scientific work can be adapted for use in evaluating information in the realms of human service practice and policy as well as in your daily lives and the everyday world. Even with evidence-based practice, where scientific research serves as a key source of direction, scientific evidence is rarely perfect, complete, or unambiguous. Practitioners must still engage in inference, interpretation, and judgment to determine appropriate applications. In our everyday world we are confronted with much information—some of it contradictory and some of it incomplete. In all these cases, the critical thinking procedures provided by scientific reasoning provide some assistance in deciding how to proceed. They offer logical and organized procedures for sifting through this information and extracting some sense from it. Each Critical Thinking section in subsequent chapters will explore some ways in which the research procedures discussed in the chapter can serve as a guide to critical thinking.

Exploring the Internet

When using an Internet search engine, it is always a good idea to check out the "Help Page" for tips on refining your search. Also, once you locate one promising source, look for its own key terms. By substituting them in your search, you may locate additional sites. The class may wish to establish an online discussion list to share information on research topics as you discover them.

One specific website to explore is Social Work Search (http://www.socialworksearch.com). This site is sufficiently broad-based such that it can appeal to social workers as well as other human service professionals and has links to research and statistics topics. For additional materials specifically on evidence-based practice in social work, explore the website made available by the social work library at the University of Michigan: guides.lib.umich.edu/EBP-Research. A tutorial on evidence-based practice as used by health professionals can be found at the University of Minnesota library (http://hsl.lib.umn.edu/learn/ebp). Many other libraries will have such websites available.

For Further Reading

Brownson, R. C., Baker, E. A., Leet, T. L., Gillespie, K. N., & True, W. R. (2011). *Evidence-Based Public Health*, 2d ed. New York: Oxford University Press. This text provides a case for evidence-based public health and practical guidance on how to choose, implement, and evaluate evidence-based programs and policies in public health settings. Extensive formal training in public health sciences is not required to grasp the presentation.

Hayes, S. C., Barlow, D. H., & Nelson-Gray, R. O. (1999) *The Scientist–Practitioner: Research and Accountability in the Age of Managed Care*, 2nd ed. Boston: Allyn & Bacon. This is an excellent book on the linkage of research and practice. Although it focuses on psychology, it will be of interest to any professional attempting to establish a scientist–practitioner model.

Hoover, K. R., & Donovan, T. (2011). *The Elements of Social Scientific Thinking*, 10th ed. Belmont, Calif.: Wadsworth, Cengage Learning. This book is an initiation to social science research intended for those who use the results of research or who are just beginning as researchers. Through several editions, it has remained to the point and up to date.

Kemeny, J. G. (1959). *A Philosopher Looks at Science*. Princeton, N.J.: Van Nostrand. This book provides a discussion of the philosophical underpinnings of science and scientific research. To truly understand research, you need some knowledge of the basic logic of science, a field generally referred to as the "philosophy of science."

Kirk, S. A., & Reid, W. J. (2002). *Science and Social Work: A Critical Appraisal*. New York: Columbia University Press. The authors analyze major efforts to integrate social work research and practice, including scientifically based practice, computer-assisted social work practice, research-based practice (evidence-based practice), and research dissemination and utilization.

Lindsey, D., & Shlonsky, A. (Eds.), (2008). *Child Welfare Research: Advances for Practice and Policy*. New York: Oxford University Press. An excellent source on research methods applied to the field of child welfare, this book provides a sound discussion of evidence-based practice in child welfare. It should be of particular interest to social workers; it provides many illustrations of linkages between practice and research.

Roberts, A. R., & Yeager, K. R. (2006). *Foundations of Evidence-Based Social Work Practice*. New York: Oxford University Press. The authors provide a concise introduction to evidence-based social work practice, highlighting the central role of research in it. The book includes definitions of key evidence-based practice terminology and discusses the importance of evidence-based practice and critical thinking.

Rossman, G. B., & Rallis, S. F. (2011). *Learning in the Field: An Introduction to Qualitative Research*, 3rd ed. Thousand Oaks, Calif.: Sage. This text provides a comprehensive overview of qualitative research, discussing when it is preferred over quantitative research and how it is conducted.

Somekh, B., & Lewin, C. (Eds.), (2011). *Research Methods in the Social Sciences*, 2nd ed. Thousand Oaks, Calif.: Sage. This book provides a good overview of social science research and a balanced discussion of both theory and practical application in social research. The book provides insights into the nuances of particular approaches, but also demonstrates how methods complement one another.

Class Exercises for Competency Assessment

Use this case illustration to do Exercise 1.1.

> While making a routine night patrol through a partially developed construction area on the outskirts of town, a sheriff's deputy notices fresh tire tracks in the new-fallen snow that lead suspiciously toward a clump of trees and some bulldozed construction debris. There had been complaints of vandalism on the construction site, so the deputy investigates. As he drives closer, the spotlight reveals a large, older style SUV. However, the vehicle occupants are not the expected adolescent trouble-makers, but a homeless family seeking a protected spot to rest for the night. A frightened looking man and woman shield their eyes from the spotlight glare while three sleepy-eyed children peer out from under blankets in the back. The woman clutches an infant in her arms.
>
> The officer learns that the couple is from out of state. The man relates how they gave up their apartment back home and bought this large vehicle to transport them and their meager belongings to Texas where he'd been promised a job. But 300 miles from home, he got a call informing him that the company just shut down. Now there was no job and to make matters worse, the fuel pump on the truck was acting up and he didn't know how much farther the SUV could go without an expensive repair. They've been running the engine a little off and on for heat, but they only have a little food and no idea of where or how to get help in the morning.
>
> The officer radios dispatch, describes the situation and consults on what to do next.

1.1. **[Research & Practice] [Evidence-Based Evaluation]** We have emphasized the parallels between practice and research. With this in mind, do the following:

   a. Make a list of some problems in this referral that call for human service intervention. What additional information would you need to formulate an intervention plan?

b. Make a list of research problems or questions that are suggested in this incident. How is this list similar to or different from your list of intervention problems?

c. How might conducting research on the identified questions contribute to future effective practice?

1.2. [Research & Practice] Professional journals in the human services typically include a mixture of research articles, practice delivery and service delivery descriptions, and policy issue discussions. Select recent issues of a major journal in your profession, such as *Social Work, Child Welfare, Social Service Review* or *American Sociological Review*, and identify the articles that qualify as research articles. Two or three students should independently review the same journal issue so that findings can be compared. What features distinguish a research article from other types of articles?

1.3. [Research & Practice] This chapter discusses several goals of research. For each of the research articles located during Exercise 1.2, determine whether it is primarily descriptive, predictive, explanatory, or evaluative. Explain why you classified each article as you did. If you are uncertain as to how an article should be classified, indicate why, and state what additional information is needed to help you classify the study.

1.4. [Research & Practice] [Evidence-Based Evaluation] For each research study, state how it applies to human service practice in terms of the five focal areas discussed in the chapter.

Chapter 2

The Logic of Social Research

Sources of Knowledge
Tradition
Experience
Common Sense
Journalism
Science
Scientific Practice

Theories in Research and Practice
What Is a Theory?
The Functions of Theories

Concepts and Hypotheses
Defining Concepts
Developing Hypotheses
Concepts and Operational Definitions among Minority Populations

Perspectives on Science
Deduction versus Induction
Types of Explanations
Paradigms in Science

Cause-and-Effect Relationships

Review and Critical Thinking
Main Points
Important Terms for Review
Critical Thinking
Exploring the Internet
For Further Reading
Class Exercises for Competency Assessment

After dashing through the Looking-glass House to view its garden, Alice says,

> I should see the garden far better … if I could get to the top of that hill: and here's a path that leads straight to it—at least, no, it doesn't do *that* … but I suppose it will at last. But how curiously it twists! It's more like a corkscrew than a path! Well this turn goes to the hill, I suppose—no it doesn't! This goes straight back to the house! Well then, I'll try it the other way. (Carroll, 1946, pp. 21–22)

Understanding the world—especially human behavior—sometimes bears a striking resemblance to Alice's convoluted and frustrating journey in Wonderland. People do what we least expect, and without any apparent rhyme or reason: A prisoner on parole who appeared to be "making it on the outside" suddenly commits another offense and goes back to jail; a marriage of 25 years that seemed to be quite solid suddenly ends in divorce; a respected and successful business executive commits suicide. Human service providers, in particular, are familiar with experiences such as these, and the path to understanding often mirrors Alice's corkscrew.

Science, however, provides a method for mapping and understanding that corkscrew. In this chapter, we discuss the basic logic underlying scientific research, beginning with an assessment of how science differs from other ways of gaining knowledge. Then, we analyze the importance of theories and their role in scientific research, drawing a parallel with the use of theories in human service practice. Following this, we discuss the role of concepts and hypotheses, showing how hypotheses serve to link theory and research. Finally, we analyze the nature of causality, because research is, at its core, a search for cause-and-effect relationships among phenomena.

SOURCES OF KNOWLEDGE

Human service practice is based on knowledge of human behavior and the social environment. There are numerous ways of gaining such knowledge, but all sources of knowledge have their pitfalls. We argued in Chapter 1 that practice knowledge should be grounded in scientific research. This does not mean that science is infallible, but science does have advantages as a source of knowledge that makes it superior to other ways of gaining knowledge.

To see why this is the case, we contrast science with four other common sources of knowledge: tradition, experience, common sense, and journalism. We then discuss how science can improve professional practice.

Tradition

Traditional knowledge is knowledge based on custom, habit, and repetition. It is founded on a belief in the sanctity of ancient wisdom and the ways of our forebears. People familiar with the musical *Fiddler on the Roof* will recall how the delightful character Tevye, a dairyman in the village of Anatevka, sang the praises of tradition:

> Because of our traditions, we've kept
> our balance for many, many years. Here
> in Anatevka we have traditions for
> everything—how to eat, how to sleep,
> how to wear clothes …. You may ask,
> how did this tradition start? I'll tell you—
> I don't know! But it's a tradition. Because
> of our traditions, everyone knows who he
> is and what God expects him to do.
> Tradition. Without our traditions, our
> lives would be as shaky as—as a fiddler on
> the roof! (Stein, 1964, pp. 1, 6)

For Tevye and the villagers of Anatevka, where traditions come from is unimportant. Traditions provide guidance; they offer "truth"; they are the final word. Traditions tell us that something is correct because it has always been done that way.

Traditional knowledge is widespread in all societies. Many people, for example, believe that a two-parent family is preferable to a single-parent family because the former provides a more stable and effective socializing experience for children and reduces the likelihood of maladjustment. In some cases these beliefs are grounded in religious traditions, whereas in other cases they are accepted because "everybody knows" how important two parents are to a child's development. In fact, some human service providers accept these beliefs about the traditional two-parent family despite the existence of considerable research suggesting that the two-parent family may not always be essential for high-quality adoption or foster care. For example, one review of research into this issue concluded, "In the studies reviewed here, single-parent families were found to be as nurturing and viable as dual-parent families. In fact, single-parent adoption emerged as a good plan for children" (Groze 1991, p. 326).

Human service providers can be affected in other ways by traditional beliefs. For example, the works of a Sigmund Freud or an Erik Erikson might be accepted without question, and emphasis might be placed on remaining true to their words rather than on assessing the accuracy or utility of their ideas.

Tradition can be an important source of knowledge, especially in such areas as moral judgments or value decisions, but it can have some major disadvantages. First, tradition is extremely resistant to change, even for those cases in which change might be necessary because new information surfaces or new developments occur. Second, traditional knowledge easily confuses knowledge (an understanding of what *is*) with values (a preference for what *ought to be*). For many people, the traditional emphasis on the two-parent family actually is based on a value regarding the preferred family form rather than on a knowledge of the effect that such a family has on child development.

Experience

Experience as a source of knowledge refers to firsthand, personal observations of events. **Experiential knowledge** is based on the assumption that truth and understanding can be achieved through personal experience, and that witnessing events will lead to an accurate comprehension of those events.

Experience is a common source of knowledge for human service workers, who have numerous opportunities to make firsthand observations of emotionally disturbed children, people with physical disabilities, foster children, and other service populations. From these contacts, practitioners can develop an understanding—not necessarily an accurate one— of what motivates their clients and what social or psychological processes have influenced them.

For example, a person working in a spousal abuse shelter will have considerable contact with women whose husbands have physically and psychologically abused them. Because of this, the worker likely is sensitive to the harm that can come to women from their husbands. After seeing women who have been so abused, this worker may conclude that marital counseling with such spouses cannot work in a climate of violence and anger, and may even be dangerous. In fact, social worker Liane Davis (1984) found that shelter workers were much less likely to recommend marital counseling than were family court judges. Family court judges did not have the powerful experience of seeing women when the effects of their abuse were most visible; moreover, family court judges have a mandate to maintain the integrity of the family. For them, marital counseling seems to be both a feasible and an appropriate way to keep the family intact. So we see that the experiences of shelter workers and judges in different settings can lead them to perceive problems and assess solutions differently.

This experiential knowledge about family dynamics and abuse may be reinforced by traditional knowledge about the importance of family life. Armed with this knowledge, a practitioner might shape an intervention effort that focuses on individual counseling or on marital counseling.

Experiential knowledge, however, has some severe limitations that can lead to erroneous conclusions. First, human perceptions are notoriously unreliable. Perception is affected by many factors, including the cultural background and the mood of the observer, the conditions under which something is observed, and the nature of what is being observed. Even under the best conditions, some misperception is likely; thus, knowledge based on experience often is inaccurate.

Second, human knowledge and understanding do not result from direct perception but, rather, from *inferences* that are made from those perceptions. The conclusion that marital counseling doesn't work is an inference—that is, it is not directly observed. All that has been observed is that these women have been battered by their husbands. There is no observation of the effectiveness of any type of counseling. (We discuss making inferences from observations in more detail when we address the issue of causality later in this chapter.)

Third, the very people in positions to experience something directly frequently have vested interests in perceiving that thing in a certain way. Teachers, for example, observe that the students who do poorly are the ones who do not pay strict attention during class. However, teachers have a vested interest in showing that their teaching techniques are not the reason for poor performance among students. Therefore, teachers probably would be inclined to attribute students' failings to the students' lack of effort and inattentiveness rather than to their own inadequacies as educators.

A final limitation on experiential knowledge is that it is difficult to know if the people directly available to you are accurate representatives of all the people about whom you wish to draw conclusions. If they are not, then any conclusions drawn from your observations may be in error. To use our earlier example, are the battered women who contact a spousal abuse shelter representative of all battered women? If the women who contact a shelter are different in some way, and if these differences influence the effectiveness of counseling in the shelter, then you cannot generalize conclusions from their outcomes in counseling to the experiences of all battered women. Battered women who go to a shelter may be more affluent or less isolated and, therefore, might demonstrate different outcomes in counseling than less affluent or more isolated women would.

Common Sense

The accumulation of knowledge from tradition and experience often blends to form what people call **common sense**: practical judgments based on the experiences, wisdom, and prejudices of a people. People with common sense are presumed to be able to make sound decisions even though they lack specialized training and knowledge. Yet, is common sense an accurate source of knowledge? Consider the following contradictory examples. Common sense tells us that people with similar interests and inclinations will be likely to associate with one another. When we see a youngster who smokes marijuana associating with others who do the same, we may sagely comment, "Birds of a feather flock together." Then, however, we see an athletic woman become involved with a bookish, cerebral man, and we say, "Opposites attract."

In other words, common sense often explains everything—even when those explanations contradict one another. This is not to say that common sense is unimportant or always useless. Common sense can be valuable and accurate, which is not surprising, because people need sound information as a basis for interacting with others and functioning in society. However, common sense does not normally involve a rigorous and systematic attempt to distinguish reality from fiction. Rather, it tends to accept what "everyone knows" to be true and to reject contradictory information. Furthermore, common sense often is considered to be something that people either have or don't have, because it is not teachable. In fact, it often is contrasted with "book learning." This discourages people from critically assessing their commonsense knowledge and tempering it with knowledge acquired from other sources. For this reason, commonsense knowledge should be accepted and used cautiously. As a basis for human service practice, knowledge needs to be based on the rigorous and systematic methods used in scientific research. Common sense or a vague feeling of "helping" is not enough.

Journalism

The materials prepared by journalists for newspapers, magazines, television, websites, or other media are another important source of knowledge about the world for most people. With the explosion of news sources available on cable television and the Internet, people now have access to vast amounts of journalistic information. Though some journalism consists of opinion pieces based on the speculations and inferences of the journalist, much of it, like science, is grounded in observation: Reporters interview people or observe events and write their reports based on those observations. In addition, with modern technology, journalists often are in a position to provide a video and/or audio record of what happened at a scene.

So it may seem, at first glance, that science and journalism have much in common as sources of knowledge, and significant similarities between the two endeavors can be identified. Both use observation to seek out accurate knowledge about the world. In fact, some journalism can, at times, take on many of the characteristics of social science research. Some journalistic output, for example, can look a lot like the in-depth interviews and case studies we will discuss in Chapter 9. However, although scientific standards require that scientists use the systematic procedures discussed in this book, journalism can—and often does—fall far short of meeting these standards.

A key difference between science and journalism is that the observations of scientists are much more systematic in nature. This means that scientists utilize far more careful procedures than journalists to reduce the chances that their conclusions will be inaccurate. For example, a journalist interested in the experiences of prison inmates probably will interview a few inmates who are made available to him by prison authorities and then use these interviews to draw conclusions, at least implicitly, about the experiences of all prisoners. Social scientists would recognize that prisoners selected by the authorities are likely to differ from other prisoners in some important ways: They may have been selected because they committed less serious offenses or were model prisoners. Their experience of prison also is likely to be very different from that of a more serious offender or someone who has chronic confrontations with prison authorities. Recognizing this, social scientists would be very careful about how they selected inmates on whom to make observations, and usually would not accept a sample selected by prison authorities. The best sampling procedures, which will be discussed in Chapter 6, would be those that ensure that all types of prisoners have a chance to appear in the sample. This could be done, for example, by interviewing all the prisoners or, if that were not feasible, interviewing a randomly selected group of prisoners. If sampling procedures fall short of these standards, then social scientists have reduced confidence in the resulting conclusions. Journalists often do not use such rigorous sampling procedures.

A second key difference between science and journalism is that journalism is not concerned with theory building and verification as a way of developing an abstract explanation of people's behavior. Journalists are much more focused on, as the saying goes, "just the facts." Scientists, on the other hand, recognize that facts often don't speak for themselves—they need to be interpreted in the context of a theoretical understanding to fully comprehend their meaning.

Science

Winston Churchill, the prime minister of Britain during World War II, is reported to have said that democracy is an imperfect form of government, but that it is far superior to all other forms. Many scientists have a similar view of science: They realize it is imperfect and limited, but they also recognize that it is far superior to other sources of knowledge for gaining an understanding of the world. **Science** is a method of obtaining objective knowledge about the world through systematic observation. (The term *science* also sometimes is used to refer to the accumulated body of knowledge that results from scientific inquiry.) Science has five distinguishing characteristics that, taken together, set it apart from the other sources of knowledge.

First, science is *empirical*, which simply means that science is based on direct observation of the world. Science is not, as some people mistakenly believe, founded in theorizing, philosophizing, or speculating. At times, scientists do all these things; but eventually, they must observe the world to see whether their theories or speculations agree with the facts. Because of this, the topics that can be subjected to scientific scrutiny are limited; any issue that cannot be resolved through observation is not within the scope of science. For example, the questions of whether God exists or what values should underlie a human service profession are not scientific issues, because it is impossible to determine their truth (or lack thereof) through observation. These are matters of faith or preference, not of science.

Second, science is *systematic*, meaning that the procedures used by scientists are organized, methodical, public, and recognized by other scientists. One dimension of the systematic nature of science is that scientists report, in detail, all the procedures used in coming to a conclusion. This enables other scientists to assess whether the inferences and conclusions drawn are warranted given the observations made. A second dimension of the systematic nature of science is *replication*—that is, repeating studies numerous times to determine if the same results can be obtained. Scientists are very cautious about drawing hard-and-fast conclusions from a single observation or investigation. In fact, and quite at variance with experiential knowledge, scientists assume that a single direct observation is as likely to be incorrect as correct. Only repeated observations can reduce the chance of error and misinterpretation (Rosenthal, 1991).

Third, science is *the search for causes*. Scientists assume that there is order in the universe, that there are ascertainable reasons for the occurrence of all events, and that scientists can discover the orderly nature of the world. If we assumed there was no order, no pattern, then there would be no need to search for it. We could write off events as the result of chance or the intervention of some benevolent (or malevolent, or indifferent) otherworldly force that we can never understand.

Fourth, science is *provisional*, which means that scientific conclusions are always accepted as tentative, as subject to question and possible refutation. There are no ultimate, untouchable, irrevocable truths in science. There are no scientists whose work is held in such esteem that it cannot be criticized or rejected. As the philosopher Jacob Bronowski (1978, pp. 121–122) put it, "Science is not a finished enterprise.... The truth is [not] a thing that you could find ... the way you could find your hat or your umbrella." Science is a process of continuous movement toward a more accurate picture of the world, and scientists fully realize that we will never achieve the ultimate and final picture.

Finally, science strives for *objectivity*, which means that scientists try to avoid having their personal biases and values influence their scientific conclusions. This is a controversial and complicated characteristic of science, because many social scientists would argue that true objectivity is impossible for human beings to achieve. We will discuss this issue at a number of points in this book, but it is sufficient to say here that all scientists are concerned that their scientific conclusions are not solely (or merely) a product of their own personal biases and values. This doesn't mean that scientists should be devoid of values. Quite the contrary, they can be as passionate, concerned, and involved as any other group of citizens. However, they realize that their values and biases can—and probably will— lead to erroneous scientific conclusions. To address this problem, science incorporates mechanisms to reduce the likelihood of biased observations becoming an accepted part of the body of scientific knowledge. For example, publicizing all research procedures enables others to assess whether the research was conducted in a way that justifies the conclusions reached. Furthermore, such detailed reporting permits replication so that other researchers, with different values, can see if they come to the same conclusions regarding a set of observations.

Despite these checks, of course, values and biases will still be found in research. The very decision of what topics to investigate, for example, often is shaped by the researcher's values: One person studies family violence because a close friend was the victim of spousal abuse, and another studies factors contributing to job satisfaction because of a personal belief that work is central to identity. Values and biases also enter research through the interpretation of observations. For personal reasons, one researcher may desperately want to show that the criminal justice system rehabilitates (or does not rehabilitate). This may well influence how he or she goes about conducting research and interpreting the results. There are even a few cases (most commonly in biomedical research) of outright falsification of data to show a certain conclusion. The point is that values and biases commonly intrude on scientific research, but the overall scientific enterprise is organized to reduce their impact on the body of scientific knowledge.

The scientific method, then, with the characteristics just described, is viewed by scientists as preferable to other ways of gaining knowledge, because it is more likely to lead to accurate knowledge of the world. To return to our earlier example of single-parent families and adoption, science views all knowledge regarding the family as provisional and open to question, and there have been many scientific investigations of the role of the family in these matters. Child adjustment and development in two-parent and single-parent families have been compared in both adoptive and biological families as well as in stepfamilies.

The conclusion from these various studies is that the traditional, two-parent family does not seem to play the indispensable role that much commonsense knowledge would accord it—or at least that the role of parents in families is more complicated than was once thought. For example, the research shows that adoption by a single parent is not always detrimental when compared with two-parent adoptive settings; some adoptees with one parent do quite well (Groze & Rosenthal, 1991; Shireman & Johnson, 1986). A related finding is that nontraditional family structure (having one rather than two parents) probably is less critical to children's development than is family process (warm relationships and low conflict between parents and children). The negative consequences often associated with single-parent families may arise from the conflict that often accompanies divorce, because divorce is how many single-parent families are produced (Amato & Booth, 1997; Jekielek, 1998; Lansford et al., 2001). Also, single-parent families often experience certain negative factors: low income, inadequate parental guidance, and less access to community resources. Single-parent families that overcome these difficulties do as well as other family forms in raising children (McLanahan & Sandefur, 1994). So the commonsense or traditional view that the two-parent family is always superior to the single-parent setting is shown by research to be vastly oversimplified at best.

In this fashion, then, scientific knowledge overcomes many of the weaknesses of traditional, experiential, and commonsense knowledge. In particular, it enables us to accumulate accurate information despite the personal biases of individual researchers or practitioners. These positive attributes of science do not mean, however, that science is perfect. Scientists do make errors. But, as Jacob Bronowski (1978, p. 122) so aptly put it, "Science is essentially a self-correcting activity." If proper scientific procedures are followed, today's errors will be corrected by researchers in the future, whose errors in turn will be corrected by still more research.

Scientific Practice

With this more detailed understanding of science and its characteristics, we can return to the concept of evidence-based practice introduced in Chapter 1 and elaborate on what this approach says about the parallels between science and practice. Basically, this approach argues that effective human service practice should have characteristics that parallel those of science (Hayes, Barlow, and Nelson-Gray, 1999; Rosen, 1996). Human service practice would be enhanced if it was shaped by a consideration of each of the five characteristics of science just discussed. First, practice, like science, should be *empirical*, stressing problem assessment involving direct observation of client problems, actual counts of behaviors, and independent observations from multiple data sources. Such data are less subject to distortion and bias than self-reports, speculations, and philosophizing. Second, practice, like research, should be *systematic*. To the extent that practice procedures are well organized, clearly specified, and made public, they can be replicated and tested by others. In this manner, ineffective procedures can be eliminated, and promising ones can be refined and improved. One of the recurring criticisms of many human service interventions is that the intervention itself is not well specified. Consequently, research evaluating the intervention cannot clearly indicate what did (or did not) work. Practice models also involve *causality* in terms of specifying a clear link between cause and effect or explaining why a proposed intervention should work with the particular identified problem. Again, a criticism of human service projects in the past has been that many of them have consisted of a conglomeration of intervention efforts without a clearly articulated linkage between cause and effect.

Practice theory, like science, should be *provisional*. All practice models and techniques should be viewed as fair game for criticism and refutation. Through such a process of testing and challenging existing practices, healthy growth can occur in practice methodology.

Finally, human service professionals must deal with the problem of professional *objectivity*. The determination of the utility and effectiveness of practice procedures needs to be done under objective conditions. Just as the researcher must attempt to safeguard against the intrusion of values into the conduct of research, so practitioners must guard against the intrusion of values into practice. This issue of values and objectivity is particularly difficult for human service practitioners, who often approach problems with a strong set of values, both personal and professional. Personally, practitioners may have strong feelings about such matters as abortion, alcohol use, or domestic violence that may clash with those of the groups with which they work. Furthermore, some human service providers are conventional and middle class in their personal lives, which may influence what they see as successful social functioning. In addition to these personal values, human service practice itself is heavily imbued with professional values. In fact, as one human service educator put it, "Social work is among the most value based of all professions.... [It] is deeply rooted in a fundamental set of values that ultimately shapes the profession's mission and its practitioners' priorities" (Reamer, 2006, p. 3).

At times, these values may emphasize a conservatism or pressure to preserve the status quo; at other times, the values may reflect a commitment to support vulnerable or oppressed populations. In either event, it is challenging to satisfy the recommendation that human service providers not let their values intrude into the provision of services to clients. In fact, it probably is impossible to mount an effective change effort without some imposition of values, either implicit or explicit. Even more, some therapeutic approaches, such as those of Carl Rogers, Albert Ellis, and Hobart Mowrer, include as one of their goals the acceptance by the client of new—and more realistic—values.

So even though professional practice in the human services is clearly oriented toward the fulfillment of certain values, practicing in the profession requires that the worker establish checks on the intrusion of values into practice, much as the researcher does in the conduct of research. In later chapters, we will discuss research techniques that are less subject to biases in observation and measurement. Application of these principles in practice also can help restrict the unwanted intrusion of personal values into service delivery. Another way to control the influence of values is to do research on the role of values in practice and to design agency procedures that help provide services objectively. As Research in Practice 2.1 illustrates, the influence of values on the actual conduct of practice cannot be totally eliminated. However, by relying on a practice approach that is empirically based, employing procedures supported by research, and incorporating rigorous evaluation procedures, it is possible to sensitize professionals to the impact of their value positions and, thus, enhance the objectivity of service delivery.

THEORIES IN RESEARCH AND PRACTICE

Theory is a word that is misunderstood by many people. To the neophyte, theories often are associated with the abstract, the impractical, or the unreal. In actuality, nothing could be further from the truth. In both research and practice settings, theories play a critical role in our understanding of reality and our ability to cope with problems. In fact, people commonly use theories in their daily lives without recognizing that they do so.

What Is a Theory?

A **theory** is a set of interrelated, abstract propositions or statements that offers an explanation of

> **RESEARCH IN PRACTICE 2.1** **Practice Effectiveness: Providing Services to Gays and Lesbians**
>
> Human service practitioners often deal with clients or situations that involve value-laden controversies. One area where this clearly is the case is the issue of whether gays or lesbians should be permitted to have custody of their children or to adopt. Traditional—and, in some cases, religious—values lead some people to the conclusion that only intact, heterosexual, married couples provide a suitable environment for child rearing and that being raised by a gay or lesbian parent would be harmful to a child. The difficult problem for the human service provider is how to serve clients within the context of one's own personal and professional values.
>
> The movement toward evidence-based practice in the human services suggests that it is possible to use scientific research to assess whether personal or professional values are unreasonably influencing the services provided to clients. One of the primary features of evidence-based practice involves identifying general trends gleaned from a review of studies that are applicable to practice. The provision of child welfare services to gay and lesbian clients offers an excellent example of this feature. A human service professional charged with making recommendations about child custody and adoption would approach this situation by systematically searching the literature and asking the question: How well do gays and lesbians perform in the role of parent?
>
> Marcus Tye (2003) summarizes the theoretical and empirical evidence currently available to answer this question. Over the past quarter century, beginning with the work of Karen Lewis (1980), a considerable body of research has accumulated on the development and experiences of the children of lesbians and gay men (Stacey & Biblarz, 2001). For the most part, this research does not support the negative developmental outcomes for the children that would be predicted by much traditional and experiential knowledge or some people's personal values. Children raised by gay or lesbian parents do not differ in their sexual orientation or personal development from children raised by heterosexual parents (Goldberg, 2009; Gottman, 1990).
>
> By the 1990s the research focus had shifted from looking at the quality of family life after a parent had acknowledged his or her homosexuality toward the examination of gay men and lesbians who, often in the context of a committed homosexual relationship, were opting to have children via the processes of adoption, artificial insemination, or surrogate mothers. This research also has found no negative effects for adopted children raised in gay- or lesbian-headed families. These adoptive families exhibited a level of family functioning that, by many measures, was at least as high as that found in other types of families (Erich et al. 2005; Leung, Erich, & Kanenberg, 2005).
>
> So this evidence-based review suggests that children can be reared into healthy adults in families parented by homosexuals and sexual orientation should not preclude individuals from serving as adoptive or foster parents. Thus the general trends in the existing data help provide direction for shaping agency policy. Science cannot inform human service workers regarding what their personal values ought to be, but it can point out practice situations in which personal values seem to be unreasonably intruding on intervention decisions. Such research also safeguards against the danger that decisions based on personal values will masquerade as "in the client's best interest" by providing an empirical knowledge base for decision making.

some phenomenon (Skidmore, 1979). Three key elements in this definition are important to understanding theories. First, theories are made up of **propositions**, which are statements about the relationship between some elements in the theory. For example, a proposition from the differential association theory of crime is that a person becomes criminal because of an excess of definitions favorable to the violation of the law over definitions unfavorable to the violation of the law. Elements in this proposition include "criminal" and "definitions favorable to the violation of the law" (Sutherland, 1939). Behavior modification theory also contains numerous propositions, such as: Behavior change can occur through a reorganization of the environmental cues that reward and punish behavior (Sulzer-Azaroff & Mayer, 1991). The elements in this proposition include "behavior change," "environmental cues," and "reward and punish behavior."

A second important part of our definition of theory is that theories are *abstract* systems, meaning they link general and abstract propositions to particular, testable events or phenomena. In many cases, these abstract systems are *deductive* systems, a general set of propositions that can be used to deduce further, more concrete relationships between the elements of the theory. Differential association theory is again illustrative. As noted, this theory relates definitions favorable to the violation of the law with the greater likelihood of criminal behavior. This means that the theory is supposed to apply to *all* specific types of crimes, such as robbery, larceny, and auto theft. So it would be logical to deduce from the theory that greater exposure to definitions favorable to the violation of the law would be associated with higher incidences of robbery, larceny, and auto theft. Theories are abstract, because they have this deductive power: The broader and more abstract the propositions and their related concepts, the more numerous the specific relationships that can be deduced from them.

The third key aspect of theories is that they provide *explanations* for the phenomena they address. Indeed, the ultimate purpose of a theory is to explain *why* something occurred. In differential association theory, the phenomenon to be explained is criminal behavior, and the explanation is that criminality is learned through much the same process as noncriminal behavior is. The content of what is learned—namely, definitions favorable to violation of the law—makes the difference. Thus differential association provides an explanation for the development of criminal behavior.

In comprehending theories and the roles they play, it is helpful to realize that we all use theories in our everyday lives, although we may not call them *theories* or even be consciously aware of using them. Nonetheless, we base our decisions and behavior on our past experiences and what we have learned from others. From these experiences, we generalize that certain physical, psychological, and social processes are operative and will continue to be important in the future, with predictable consequences. This is our "commonsense theory" about how the world operates and forms the basis for our decisions. For example, most people have certain general notions—that is, personal theories—about what causes poverty. Some personal theories emphasize poverty as an individual problem: People are poor because of their individual characteristics, such as laziness, low intelligence, poor education, or lack of marketable skills. Others' theories of poverty emphasize structural features of the American economy dictating that, even in times of economic expansion, some people will be left impoverished through no fault of their own. Which of these theories people identify with most closely determines, in part, how they react to poor people and which public policy provisions toward poverty they support. Advocates of the individualistic theory might be hostile toward the poor and programs to aid them, because they believe the poor are undeserving people who suffer only from their own shortcomings. Supporters of the structural theory may view the poor as victims and tend to be more benevolent toward them.

Personal theories like these concerning poverty may be extreme and misleading, because they are based on casual observations, personal experience, or other information lacking the rigorous concern for accuracy of scientific investigations. Unlike commonsense theories, the theories in research and practice are precise, detailed, and explicit. It is important, however, to recognize that a theory is always tentative in nature—that is, any theory is best viewed as a *possible* explanation for the phenomenon under investigation. By conducting research, scientists gather evidence that either supports or fails to support a theoretical explanation or practice intervention. No theory stands or falls on the basis of one trial. Theories are tested over a long period of time by many investigations. Only with the accumulation of research outcomes can one begin to have confidence concerning the validity of a theory.

The Functions of Theories

We have all heard the refrain "It's only a theory" or "That's your theory." Such phrases often are used in the context of deflating an argument. Actually, these comments, though often intended in a disparaging sense, convey some truth regarding theories. In particular, they point out that theories are sometimes *untested* (but testable) assertions about reality and that theories are not the end product of scientific investigation but, rather, a part of the process of science. Theories have particular purposes in both research and practice settings. In fact, the same theories often are used in both research and practice, because both researchers and practitioners turn to them for similar reasons. We can identify three major functions of theories in research and practice.

Explanation of Phenomena. As we have seen, theories provide an explanation for phenomena. They say not only what will happen under certain conditions (which is what hypotheses also do, but more concretely) but also why it will happen. This provides a much more powerful understanding of human behavior. In differential association theory, for example, the phenomenon to be explained is criminal behavior, and the explanation is that criminal behavior is a product of learning appropriate behaviors from others who are important to us. Thus, differential association theory provides a broad, abstract explanation for the development of criminal behavior that links such behavior with general processes of conformity and group process. People learn to be criminals in the same way they learn to be doctors, nurses, or lawyers—namely, by learning through association with other people.

Guide for Research and Practice. Theories guide and direct research and practice. They focus attention on certain phenomena as relevant to the issues of concern. If we were to dispense with theories altogether, as some would suggest, then what would we study? What data would be collected? What intervention strategy would be adopted? Theories help us find answers to these questions.

Imagine that a counseling center wants to attack the problem of teenage alcohol consumption at a particular high school and the staff decides to study the problem. Where to begin? What variables are important? As a first step, it is essential to fall back on some theory related to these issues. We might, for example, use the theory of differential association, which posits that alcohol consumption results from attitudes and patterns of behavior that are learned in association with other people, particularly peers. To test this theory, we could determine whether alcohol consumption is more common when it is viewed as an acceptable form of behavior among peers. We are then in a position to collect data on attitudes toward alcohol and patterns of alcohol consumption in peer groups. If the theory is confirmed, then it supports the idea that effective intervention will need to focus on attitudes toward alcohol consumption in peer groups.

We could have selected a different theory regarding alcohol consumption. For example, some theories posit an inherited predisposition toward alcoholism. Other theories suggest that alcoholism results from a nutritional deficiency that is satiated by alcohol consumption. We do not presume to suggest which theory is more accurate—future research will settle that issue, one hopes. The same thing occurs in practice intervention. If a practitioner used crisis intervention theory to deal with the disruption caused by an alcoholic parent, then the theory would direct attention to such factors as family coping strengths and emotional adaptation. Community-organization practice theory, on the other hand, would focus on the community resources available to recovering alcoholics and community services for their families. The point is that the theories used by researchers and practitioners guide their approaches and focus their attention on particular phenomena.

Integration of Multiple Observations. Theories help integrate and explain the many observations made in diverse settings by researchers and practitioners. They tell us *why* something happened, and they enable us to link the outcomes of numerous studies and interventions made in a variety of settings. As long as the findings of these efforts remain individual and isolated, they are not particularly valuable to science. Recall that a single observation is viewed with considerable skepticism. Single research findings may be in error, may be passed over and forgotten, or their broader implications may be missed entirely. Theories enable us to organize these dispersed findings into a larger, explanatory scheme. For example, someone investigating problem pregnancies among teenagers might observe that the groups of teenagers among whom such pregnancies are common tend to view an out-of-wedlock parenthood in a positive fashion. A familiarity with differential association theory would suggest that the social learning processes important in teenage drinking also may be relevant in problem pregnancies among teenagers. If this is the case, practitioners working in one area may be able to borrow strategies for intervention from the other area. Thus, theories integrate the findings from independent research endeavors and provide implications for intervention strategies.

Theories, then, play an important part in both research and practice, but one point needs to be reiterated: The utility of theories must be based on their *demonstrated* effectiveness. Theories should never be allowed to become "sacred cows," the use of which is based on tradition or custom. Most authorities would agree with this conclusion: "The most important criterion to consider is the extent to which a given theory has been supported by empirical research" (Hepworth & Larsen, 1990, p. 18). In other words, has the intervention been shown to produce the desired results? In scientific research, this is called the **verification** of theories. Researchers approach the problem of verification by developing and testing hypotheses. This process of verification is diagrammed in Figure 2.1, which also shows a parallel process as it occurs in human service practice.

CONCEPTS AND HYPOTHESES

Defining Concepts

An important part of theories is **concepts**: mental constructs or images developed to symbolize ideas, persons, things, or events. Concepts are the elements of theories discussed earlier; they are the building blocks that are interrelated in propositions to form the explanatory statements of a theory (Alford, 1998). Some of the concepts in behavior modification theory, for example, are reinforcement, conditioning, learning, and behavior change.

Concepts are similar in function to the words we use during everyday communication. The word *automobile*, for example, is the agreed on symbol for a particular object that is used as a mode of transportation. The symbol or word is not the object itself, but, rather, something that stands for or represents that object. Scientific concepts, like words in everyday language, also are symbols that can refer to an extremely broad range of referents. They may refer to something fairly concrete, like gender, or to something highly abstract, like reinforcement or cohesion.

Despite the similarities between scientific concepts and ordinary words, some differences are critical to the scientific endeavor. In particular, concepts used in scientific research must be defined very carefully. We can get along quite well with the words

FIGURE 2.1 The Process of Theory Verification in Research Compared with Practice Intervention we use for everyday communication, having only a general idea of how these words are defined. In fact, it is doubtful whether most people could give a dictionary-perfect definition of even the most commonly used words. Such imprecision in the use of scientific concepts, however, is totally inadequate. Scientists, who are widely scattered both geographically and temporally, carry on research that tests various aspects of theories. For these disconnected research projects to produce information of maximum utility, all the bits of knowledge need to be integrated into an explanatory scheme—namely a theory. This accumulation of knowledge is severely hampered— in fact, it becomes practically impossible— if these isolated scientists use different definitions of the same concepts.

For example, many studies of the relationship between reinforcement and learning have been conducted. If the results of different studies are to be comparable, then the concepts of reinforcement and learning should be defined the same way. Learning, for instance, can be defined in *behavioral* terms (as the performance of a new behavior) or in *cognitive* terms (as the understanding of how a particular behavior might be performed). When defined in these two different ways, the concept refers to something quite different in the world, and the results from two investigations using the different definitions would not be directly comparable. Perhaps, for example, behavioral learning occurs under quite different conditions than cognitive learning does.

Scientific analysis involves two types of definitions of concepts, each functioning at a different level of analysis and each serving a different purpose. At the theoretical or abstract level, concepts are given **nominal definitions**: verbal definitions in which scientists agree that one set of words or symbols will be used to stand for another set of words or symbols. Nominal definitions are directly analogous to the dictionary definitions of ordinary words in which a phrase is designed to give meaning to the word or concept being defined (Cohen & Nagel, 1934). For example, a nominal definition of "poverty" might be a deficiency in resources to the extent that people are not able to maintain a lifestyle considered to be minimally acceptable in a particular society (Sullivan, 2012).

An important step in moving from the abstract level of theory to the concrete level of research is to give concepts **operational definitions**: definitions that indicate the precise procedures or operations to be followed in measuring a concept. For example, Mollie Orshansky developed one of the most widely used operational definitions of poverty for the Social Security Administration (Ruggles, 1990). Her measure, still used by the government as a basis for policy decisions, is based on what it costs to purchase a low-budget, nutritious diet for a family. If we use U.S. Department of Agriculture figures, the poverty line is determined by the cost of food, the size of the family, and other factors. This operational definition of poverty yields a series of income cutoffs below which families are defined as poor. This is a precise definition that lists the exact operations—in this case, mathematical operations—to follow in defining poverty. Anyone using this definition measures the same thing in the same way.

The process of moving from nominal to operational definitions can be complex, because concepts are very general and abstract and controversy often arises over exactly what they refer to. Some concepts that have been a part of the literature for decades have yet to be operationalized in a way that is fully satisfactory. For example, "alcoholism" has proved to be extremely difficult to operationalize, especially in terms of establishing where social drinking leaves off and alcoholism begins (Schuckit, 2006). Because of substantial individual and cultural differences, simple measures relying on the amount and frequency of consumption are inadequate. Researchers have been forced to operationalize alcoholism on the basis of such symptoms as family or work problems, morning drinking, poor eating, and recurrent blackouts. Whereas symptom-based measures of alcoholism avoid the errors inherent in consumption measures, substantial controversy remains concerning which symptoms are the best indicators, how many symptoms must be evident, and how serious they must be before the label of *alcoholic* may be meaningfully applied.

Even the concept of poverty, which may seem straightforward and easy to operationalize, has proven to be controversial. There is, of course, the issue of where to set the income cutoffs. Orshansky's cutoffs are based on the assumption that the average American family spends one third of its income on food; some critics have argued that this results in poverty thresholds that are too low. Furthermore, Orshansky's definition sets a fixed income level as the poverty level; thus, it is unaffected by changing levels of affluence within society as a whole. Some have argued for a relative definition of poverty that defines as poor those who earn one third or one half of the median family income (Bell, 1987). With such a definition, the poverty thresholds would rise automatically if the affluence of society as a whole increased. So it should be evident that operationalizing concepts can be difficult, complex, and sometimes, controversial. The process of moving from the nominal to the operational level is called *measurement*, and it is treated extensively in Chapters 5 and 13.

Developing Hypotheses

A common strategy in scientific investigations is to move from a general theory to a specific, researchable problem. A part of this strategy is to develop **hypotheses**, which are testable statements of presumed relationships between two or more concepts. Hypotheses state what we expect to find rather than what has already been determined to exist. A major purpose of developing hypotheses in research is to test the accuracy of a theory (see Figure 2.1). The concepts and propositions of which theories are composed usually are too broad and abstract to be directly tested. Concepts such as *reinforcement* and *learning*, for example, need to be specified empirically through operational definitions before they are amenable to testing. Once operationally defined, these concepts generally are referred to as **variables**, or things that are capable of taking on more than one value. If hypotheses are supported, then this supplies evidence for the accuracy of the theory on which they are based.

In the construction of hypotheses, the relationship between variables is stated in one of two possible directions: a positive relationship, or a negative (also called an inverse) relationship. In a *positive relationship*, the values of the variables change in the *same* direction, such as both increasing or both decreasing. For example, we might hypothesize that the acceptance of the use of alcohol among an adolescent's peers will lead to an increased likelihood that the adolescent will consume alcohol. In other words, as acceptance of the use of alcohol by one's peers increases, so does the adolescent's own use of alcohol. In a *negative relationship*, or an *inverse relationship*, the values of variables change in *opposite* directions. We might hypothesize, for example, that, among adolescents, reduced parental supervision will lead to an increase in the likelihood of substance abuse. In this case, as the value of one variable (parental supervision) declines, the value of the other (substance abuse) is predicted to increase.

Useful guidelines to keep in mind for developing hypotheses include the following:

1. *Hypotheses are linked to more abstract theories.* Although generating hypotheses without deriving them from theories is possible, hypotheses are always linked to theories because the theories provide explanations for why things happen.

2. *It is important that the independent and dependent variables in hypotheses be clearly specified.* The **independent variable** is the presumed active or causal variable—the one believed to be producing changes in the dependent variable. The **dependent variable** is the passive variable, or the one that is affected. In the previous examples, peer acceptance of alcohol and parental supervision are the independent variables, and alcohol use and substance abuse are the dependent variables.

3. *It is important that the precise nature and direction of the relationship between variables be specified in the hypothesis.* Students sometimes are tempted to state hypotheses like this: "Parental supervision will have an effect on teenage alcohol use."

However, although this statement says that there *is* a relationship, it doesn't say *what the nature or direction of the relationship is*. A proper hypothesis, as above, would state how changes in one variable will be associated with particular changes in the other: "As parental supervision decreases, teenage alcohol use increases."

4. *Hypotheses should be stated in such a way that they can be verified or refuted*. If this is not the case, then they are not hypotheses. Hypotheses, after all, are statements about which we can gather empirical evidence to determine whether they are correct or false. A common pitfall is to make statements that involve judgments or values rather than issues of empirical observation. For example, we might hypothesize that investigations should be increased to reduce the incidence of welfare fraud. On the surface, this statement might appear to be a hypothesis, because it relates to investigations and welfare fraud in a negative direction. As stated, however, it is not a testable hypothesis. The problem is the evaluative "should be." What should or should not be social policy has no place in hypotheses. However, the statement can be modified so that it qualifies as a testable hypothesis: "Increased levels of investigation tend to reduce the incidence of welfare fraud." The hypothesis now makes an empirical assertion that can be checked against fact.

5. *All the concepts and comparisons in hypotheses must be clearly stated*. For example, consider the following hypothesis: "Southern Baptists have superior moral standards." The concept of "moral standards" is so abstract and vague that it is impossible to know what it means. This would have to be clearly specified in terms of what is considered to be a moral standard. In addition, to say that someone's standards are superior requires a referent for comparison: superior to whom or what? It could mean higher than some other religious group, or it could mean higher than some chosen, absolute standard.

Developing hypotheses from theories is a *creative* process that depends, in part, on the insight of the investigator. Because hypotheses link theories to particular, concrete settings, the researcher's insight often is the trigger for making such connections. In addition, researchers, at times, combine two or more theories to develop hypotheses that neither theory alone is capable of generating.

Concepts and Operational Definitions among Minority Populations

When conducting research on minority populations, considerable opportunity for bias exists if concepts and operational definitions are not carefully developed. This has been a chronic problem with research on crime. For example, many people believe that nonwhites commit crimes at a higher rate than we would expect, given their numbers in the population. Although this is partly true, it greatly oversimplifies a complex reality, and it reflects how crime is typically operationalized. Official crime statistics from the Federal Bureau of Investigation (Federal Bureau of Investigation, 2012) are an important source of data on crime. The FBI operationalizes some crimes as "offenses cleared by arrest" and others as "offenses known to the police." In other words, an occurrence is not officially considered to be a crime until it is "known to the police" or "cleared by arrest." These official crime statistics show that nonwhites commit more crimes, proportionate to their numbers in the population, than whites do. However, this is a function, in part, of how the official statistics operationalize the concept of crime. We know that nonwhites are more likely to be arrested for a given offense, suggesting that it may be arrest that is more common among nonwhites rather than the actual commission of crimes. It has been proposed that nonwhites also are more likely to commit highly visible crimes, such as armed robbery or assault, that are more frequently reported to the police and result in an arrest. Some suggest that whites, on the other hand, commit more "hidden" crimes, such as embezzlement or fraud, that are less likely to come to the attention of the police. Research suggests that there may be no class difference in the amount of hidden crimes that are committed (Elliott & Huizinga, 1983). In addition, there are other ways to operationalize crime, such as through victimization studies (asking people if they have been a victim of a crime) and self-reports (having people anonymously report their own involvement in crime). Studies based on these operational definitions tend to show much smaller differences between white and nonwhite crime rates.

Another area in which poorly constructed operational definitions have produced misleading conclusions is that of intimate partner violence (Lockhart, 1991). Most studies have found rates of intimate partner violence to be considerably higher among African Americans than among whites. Typically, these studies have used one of the following as an operational definition for the occurrence of abusive violence: a homicide involving a domestic killing, a battered woman seeking care in an emergency room or social service setting, a wife-abuse claim handled by a domestic court, or a domestic dispute call to a police department. It is well known, however, that African Americans are overrepresented among people who come to the attention of police, emergency room personnel, or social service workers. Because they generally are overrepresented among these populations, they will appear to have higher rates of abuse than whites will when abuse is operationalized in this fashion. These problems can be reduced by selecting a sample of people from a community and having them answer questions about the amount of conflict and violence that occurs in their own families. This avoids the biased effect of looking only at certain locales. The National Family Violence Resurvey, for example, employed a sampling strategy that selected about 6,000 cases representing all racial and ethnic groups (Straus & Gelles 1988).

The Committee on the Status of Women in Sociology (1986) has indicated another area in which operational definitions have led to misleading results: studies of work and social contribution. Often, work is operationalized in terms of paid employment, but this excludes many other types of work from consideration, such as community service or home-based work. With this kind of operational definition, if an employee of a carpet-cleaning firm shampoos the carpets in a home for a fee, that counts as work, but if a woman does the same activity on her own time in her own home, that is not classified as work. Such an operationalization of work tends to underestimate the extent of productive activity engaged in by women, because women are less likely than men to be paid for their social contributions.

So in developing operational definitions, care must be taken to assess whether these definitions might lead to a distorted view of minorities. In some cases, this calls for careful consideration of what a concept is intended to mean. For example, is the focus of the research on paid employment, or is it on social contribution? In other cases, it calls for careful assessment of whether a definition will lead to an inaccurate, over- or underrepresentation of minorities.

PERSPECTIVES ON SCIENCE

Up to this point in these first two chapters, we have presented science as if it is a coherent, unified activity about which all scientists are in agreement. It isn't. Or, more accurately, we should say that some people believe it is a coherent and unified activity, whereas others are critical of that claim. Scientists vigorously debate a number of issues concerning the best ways to engage in scientific work. One such debate is whether science should be deductive or inductive in nature.

Deduction versus Induction

We mentioned earlier that theories often are deductive systems. This means that hypotheses can be logically derived from the propositions that make up a theory. So **deductive reasoning** involves deducing or inferring a conclusion from some premises or propositions. If the propositions—or the theory—are correct, then hypotheses logically derived from them also will be correct. In Figure 2.1, deduction involves moving from the level of theory to that of hypotheses or an intervention plan. Deductive reasoning is central to the scientific process.

Inductive reasoning, however, enables us to assess the validity of the hypotheses and the theory. **Inductive reasoning** involves inferring something about a whole group or class of objects from our knowledge of one or a few members of that group or class. We test one or a few hypotheses derived from a theory, and then we infer something about the validity of that theory as a whole. Thus, inductive reasoning carries us from the observations or interventions in Figure 2.1 to some assessment regarding the validity of the theory. The logic of scientific analysis involves an interplay between deduction, or deriving testable hypotheses, and induction, or assessing theories based on tests of hypotheses derived from the theories.

At times, inductive research is conducted without the benefit of previous deductive reasoning. This occurs in descriptive or exploratory research, where no theory exists from which to deduce hypotheses. In the absence of theory, we begin to make observations and then develop some theoretical propositions that would be plausible given those observations. For example, practitioners may observe that clients with problem pregnancies tend to come from families with low socioeconomic status. Based on the assumption that the parent–child bond is weaker in low socioeconomic families and, therefore, that such parents have less control over their children, the practitioners could inductively conclude that a weak parent–child bond leads to an increased risk of unwanted pregnancy. In other words, the observations are used to infer a proposition regarding the causes of unwanted pregnancies. In fact, as we will explore in more detail in Chapter 9, some researchers claim that such inductive approaches can be superior to deductive approaches, because the former can involve fewer hidden assumptions or preconceived notions on the part of the scientist. Some of these inductive approaches permit the data to shape the theory rather than having a preconceived theory impose meaning on the data. Inductive research of this sort can serve as a foundation for building a theory, and that theory, in turn, can serve as a source of testable hypotheses through deductive reasoning. Thus, induction and deduction are key links in the chain of scientific reasoning, and they parallel the reasoning process that is found in practice intervention.

Research in Practice 2.2 describes research projects that highlight many of the issues discussed in the previous two sections regarding the use of theories and hypotheses in research and the importance of inductive and deductive reasoning.

Types of Explanations

Beyond deciding whether to use deductive or inductive approaches, scientists also need to decide what type of explanations will be contained in the theory. Earlier in this chapter, we defined theories as involving explanations of some phenomena. An explanation is one way of gaining knowledge of something; it tells why something happens or specifies the conditions under which something occurs. Theories can focus on two different types of explanations (Miller, 1987; Nagel, 1961).

Nomothetic Explanations. **Nomothetic explanations** focus on a class of events and attempt to specify the conditions that seem common to all those events. We will use the social control theory of deviant behavior as an illustration. Social control theory argues, in part, that delinquent behaviors such as shoplifting are produced by weak attachments to parents. A nomothetic explanation, then, might attempt to prove that all juveniles who shoplift have weak attachments to their parents. The focus of the explanation is on understanding the entire category of youth who shoplift. These explanations do not focus on understanding all the causes of a phenomenon. In fact, control theory would recognize that a complex behavior such as shoplifting probably has many causes other than weak social bonds, and that other theories would be necessary to locate and identify those factors. For nomothetic explanations, knowledge results from an understanding of a particular cause in relation to a class of events.

Nomothetic explanations attempt to develop knowledge that can be generalized beyond a single study or set of circumstances. In a sense, a

RESEARCH IN PRACTICE 2.2 Practice Effectiveness: Social Theory and Burnout among Social Workers

A social worker: I began to despise everyone and could not conceal my contempt.

A psychiatric nurse: Sometimes you can't help but feel "Damn it, they want to be there, and they're fuckers, so let them stay there." You really put them down …

A social worker: I find myself caring less and possessing an extremely negative attitude.

[Maslach, 1979, p. 217]

These are hardly the caring, empathic reactions one would expect from human service workers, yet negative attitudes toward clients are expressed at some point by many social workers, nurses, psychologists, and others. The problem of burnout is of considerable concern to human service professionals, because it can impair their ability to deal with client problems. *Burnout* refers to a service worker's emotional disengagement from clients, dissatisfaction with his or her job, feelings of worthlessness, and physical and interpersonal problems (Arches, 1991). Commonsense approaches often focus on the personal abilities of human service workers to explain why they suffer burnout: They lack sufficient emotional strength or distance from clients, or they overidentify or overempathize with their clients. Rather than relying on such intuition, scientific researchers turn to theories for direction in identifying variables that might play a part.

When social work researcher W. David Harrison (1980) approached these issues, he turned to *role theory*, which views human behavior as resulting from conformity to expectations that are associated with particular roles. One of the tenets of role theory is that role expectations should be clear, unambiguous, and achievable. Furthermore, the various expectations associated with a role should not conflict with one another. Previous research suggested that situations in which role expectations are conflicting, incompatible, or unclear lead to personal stress and dissatisfaction. Role theory enabled Harrison to identify two different kinds of role difficulty: *Role conflict* refers to a situation in which conflicting and incompatible demands are placed on a person in a role, and *role ambiguity* refers to a lack of clarity in terms of what is expected of a person in a particular role. Harrison's research on child protective service workers showed that role difficulties, especially role ambiguity, produced job dissatisfaction and burnout among these social workers.

In contrast, Joan Arches (1991) turned to *theories of organizational structure and change*, reasoning that recent developments in social service organizations might have an impact on burnout. These theories suggest that increasing bureaucratization and centralization in organizations can reduce workers' feelings of autonomy, and, in turn, this can contribute to the job dissatisfaction that often is a part of burnout. Arches's research then provided evidence that this was the case, offering further verification for those organizational theories.

Burnout continues to be a topic of interest to social scientists and human service practitioners throughout the world. Peter Janssen and his colleagues at Utrecht University in the Netherlands reviewed the extensive body of research on burnout that has accumulated over the past few decades and designed a study of Dutch nurses (Janssen, Schaufeli, & Houkes, 1999). Their research examined work-related and individual determinants of burnout by using *conservation of resources theory* as a framework. This theory focuses on the impact of work-related demands and resources on different dimensions of burnout. They found that a scarcity of resources, in the form of excess job demands and work overload, increased emotional exhaustion (one dimension of burnout) but not depersonalization (another dimension of burnout).

Thus, the theoretical considerations of role theory, organizational theory, and conservation of resources theory do not point toward excessive empathy or emotional weakness as the culprits in burnout among human service workers. Rather, the organizational and role structures that surround them are important. These investigations illustrate the importance of grounding research in theory, because it is theory that suggests which variables might be important and how they might relate to one another. Theory also shows how hypotheses can be developed through deductive reasoning. Once confirmed, the hypotheses of these researchers provide support, through inductive reasoning, for the interpretations of these theories in regard to the causes of burnout in the human services. Based on this slow, methodical accumulation of knowledge, we should eventually establish a solid foundation from which to develop programs to alleviate the problem of burnout among human service workers.

nomothetic explanation is designed to produce the conclusion that weak attachment to parents in all cases increases the likelihood that shoplifting will result. This doesn't mean that every person who experiences weak attachment will shoplift; however, it does mean that those people have a higher probability of engaging in shoplifting. To put it another way, a randomly selected group of teens with weak parental attachments will have a higher rate of shoplifting than a randomly selected group with strong attachments. The explanation or knowledge that is gained is probabilistic in nature: It tells us something about the probability of events occurring. The knowledge gained is about the aggregate, or the whole group, rather than about specific individuals in the group.

Once you understand what nomothetic explanations consist of, you can begin to see their weaknesses. One weakness is that you cannot say for sure what will happen in any particular case or to any specific person. You cannot say whether Joe Smith, who has experienced weak parental attachment, will become a shoplifter. A second weakness is that you cannot make any claims of knowing the totality of causes that produced some event or phenomenon. So the knowledge, though valuable, is incomplete. There may be, for example, some key factors that must occur in combination with weak parental attachments to produce shoplifting.

Idiographic Explanations. Idiographic explanations focus on a single person, event, or situation and attempt to specify all the conditions that helped produce it. An idiographic explanation of shoplifting, for example, might focus on one juvenile who shoplifts and attempt to understand the multiple factors that contributed to bringing about the shoplifting behavior in that person. The focus of the explanation is on a particular, unique individual or situation. These explanations do not attempt to understand all instances of shoplifting; in fact, they recognize that other shoplifters may be propelled by a different combination of causes. For idiographic explanations, knowledge results from a thorough understanding of the particular.

Idiographic explanations see causality in terms of a complex pattern of factors that combine over a period of time to produce an outcome. To truly understand something, researchers need to comprehend that whole patterned sequence, the whole complex context in which something occurs. When the nomothetic approach isolates particular variables for study, knowledge is incomplete for two reasons: First, some factors or variables have not been included in the investigation. Second, the isolating approach cannot see how the combination of, or the interaction among, the various elements plays a critical role in producing an outcome. It may be, for example, that weak parental bonds produce shoplifting only when they combine or interact with a host of other factors. In fact, it may be that the particular combination of factors that produces shoplifting in one person is unique and does not occur in other cases. It also may be that each distinct case of shoplifting is produced by a unique combination of factors. In other words, the explanation or knowledge that we gain is idiosyncratic.

Nomothetic explanations are probabilistic in nature, but idiographic explanations are deterministic in that the event being studied, such as shoplifting, actually did occur in the case being studied. In addition, the idiographic explanation identifies the causes that determined that outcome.

As with nomothetic explanations, idiographic explanations have weaknesses. One major fault is their limited generalizability. With such explanations, it is difficult to determine whether knowledge can be extended beyond the particular case or situation being studied.

Combining Explanations. Because each type of explanation has its strengths and its limitations, you might have guessed that our conclusion is going to be that neither type is inherently better than the other. As we alluded to in the beginning of this chapter with the excerpt from *Through the Looking Glass*, numerous routes to gaining knowledge about the world exist, and each type of explanation provides us with a valuable, though incomplete, route. In later chapters, we will see that some research methodologies, such as surveys and experiments, tend to be used to develop nomothetic explanations and that other methodologies, such as field research, in-depth interviewing, and historical comparative research, often are used to develop idiographic explanations. The point is to understand the logic of each type of explanation and be aware that conclusions supported by research using both types of explanations are more complete than if the research only uses one type.

Paradigms in Science

Over the centuries, philosophers and scientists have debated the nature of reality and how people can know that reality (Couvalis, 1997; Miller, 1987). These have been controversial issues for scientists who study the physical world, but they are even more contentious among social scientists, who study human beings and their psychological and social reality. Part of the reason for this heightened contention is the belief that human beings are different from the natural world of physical objects and events. People emote, remember, speculate, love, and hate—they think about what is happening to them and have feelings about it. People refuse to behave the way a scientist hypothesizes that they might. People do the unexpected or the unpredictable. Atoms, molecules, and chemical compounds do not have these elusive properties, and this is one of the reasons why natural scientists often can make certain nonprobabilistic predictions about what will happen: Under a certain set of conditions, all water molecules, for example, will freeze when the temperature drops below zero degrees centigrade. Thus far, however, social scientists have been unable to make such statements about social reality.

Another reason that the issue of how we know the world has been controversial among social scientists is that the scientists who study social reality are people themselves, with personal values, goals, desires, and reactions to what they observe. These personal matters may interfere with their ability to comprehend the world accurately. Going a step further, the scientific endeavor is itself a social process, part of the social world that social scientists attempt to understand. After all, scientific work can advance one's career, help one make a living, and move one up (or down) in the stratification system. In doing their scientific work, scientists may be influenced by a variety of social and psychological factors that routinely influence other human beings in their social endeavors.

What does all this mean? For one thing, science is a much more complicated—and, in many respects, a much messier—enterprise than many people recognize. For another, a number of competing perspectives exist concerning the issues of how society works and what implications this has for how the scientific endeavor works. In fact, historian Thomas Kuhn (1970), in a groundbreaking study of scientific work over many centuries, concluded that scientific activity is shaped by **paradigms**, which are general ways of thinking about how the world works and how we gain knowledge about the world. Paradigms are fundamental orientations, perspectives, or world views that often are not questioned or subjected to empirical tests. People may not even be aware that their thinking about the world is shaped by an orientation or world view. In his study of the history of science, Kuhn discovered that, although paradigms change over time, scientific research at any given moment was shaped by the paradigm that was dominant at the time. Research that fell outside that paradigm was considered to be inappropriate, irrelevant, oddball, or just plain wrong. In a sense, the world of paradigms falls outside the scientific realm in that issues are not accepted or rejected on the basis of empirical evidence; instead, some things are considered true—and others false—because it is obvious that that is how things work. Evidence supporting the paradigm will be accepted and competing evidence either ignored or rejected.

At the risk of oversimplification, we can classify the paradigms in the social sciences into two general categories: *positivist approaches*, and a number of different approaches that we will call *nonpositivist approaches* (Alford, 1998; Benton, 1977; Smart, 1976). Keep in mind that these viewpoints are not necessarily mutually exclusive; people may adopt ideas from more than one of them at the same time. In addition, one could agree with some parts of a paradigm but disagree with other parts of the same paradigm. We address this issue early in the book because it is a debate that arises repeatedly as we discuss different research methodologies.

Positivist Approaches. Positivism (sometimes also called **logical empiricism**) argues that the world exists independently of people's perceptions of it and that science uses objective techniques to discover what exists in the world (Blaikie, 1993; Durkheim, 1938; Halfpenny, 1982). Astronomers, for example, use telescopes to discover stars and galaxies, which exist regardless of whether we are aware of them. So, too, scientists can study human beings in terms of observable behaviors that can be recorded using objective techniques. Recording people's gender, age, height, weight, or socioeconomic position are legitimate and objective measurement techniques—the equivalent of the physicist measuring the temperature, volume, or mass of some liquid or solid. For the positivist, quantifying these measurements—for example, assessing the average age of a group or looking at the percentage of a group that is male—is merely a precise way of describing and summarizing an objective reality. Such measurement provides a solid, objective foundation for understanding human social behavior. Limiting study to observable behaviors and using objective techniques, positivists argue, is most likely to produce systematic and repeatable research results that are open to refutation by other scientists.

The natural and social world is governed by natural and social rules and regularities that give it pattern, order, and predictability. The goal of research in the natural and social sciences is to discover laws about how the world works and to express those discovered regularities in the deductive theories and propositions that are discussed in this chapter. As scientists conduct research, they move progressively closer to the truth, which involves uncovering the laws and patterns that underlie objective reality. So, at least in its ideal form, science is an objective search for the truth in which human values are a hindrance whose impact should be limited if not eliminated. Values can only interfere with the objective search for truth. For example, Emile Durkheim, an early sociologist, was a strong believer that sociologists could study the social world in much the same way that physical scientists could study the physical world. Durkheim believed that there were "social facts" that social scientists could observe and then use those observations to discover the social laws that govern the social world. He believed that once we discover these social laws, we will be able to both explain and predict human social behavior.

Of the various paradigms that we will review, positivism clearly is the most widely held view among natural scientists and, to a lesser degree, among social scientists. Among social scientists, those who adopt the positivist stance often tend to use certain kinds of research methodologies. For example, they tend toward **quantitative research**, which involves measurement of phenomena using numbers and counts. They also tend to use deductive and nomothetic explanations, experimental designs, and survey research. It is important not to oversimplify the link between a paradigm and the preferred research methodology, however, because positivists at times use **qualitative research**, which involves data in the form of words, pictures, descriptions, or narratives rather than numbers and counts. They also use inductive or idiographic explanations and field observations when these are appropriate to a research question.

Despite the popularity and dominance of the positivist paradigm, it has been subject to considerable criticism over the years. Some of this criticism arises out of empirical studies by social scientists of exactly how science operates (Galison & Stump, 1996; Lynch & Bogen 1997; Shapin 1995). What many of these researchers find is that what scientists actually do looks quite different from what the positivist paradigm says science should look like. This has led some critics to conclude that the positivist model is an idealized conception of science rather than an accurate description of it. Based on these and other concerns, alternative paradigms have emerged.

Nonpositivist Approaches. One prominent nonpositivist approach to science is what is called the interpretive approach. **Interpretive approaches** (also called interactionist or *verstehen* approaches) posit that social reality has a subjective component that arises out of the creation and exchange of social meanings during the process of social interaction. Social science must have ways to understand this subjective reality (Holstein & Gubrium, 1994; Smith, 1989; Wilson, 1970). Interpretivists argue that the objective, quantitative approaches of positivism miss this very important part of the human experience: the subjective and personal meanings that people attach to themselves and what they do. Reality is seen as something emergent and in constant flux that arises out of the creation and exchange of social meanings during the process of social interaction. Rather than seeing reality as something apart from human perceptions, interpretive social science sees reality—or, at least, social reality—as created out of human perception and the interpretation of meaning. These kinds of ideas led many nineteenth-century and early twentieth-century theorists, such as Wilhelm Dilthey, Ernst Troeltsch, and Max Weber, to conclude that social life cannot be understood by the same method that is used to study the natural world (Barnes, 1948).

Weber, for example, argued that we need to look not only at what people do but also at what they think and feel about what is happening to them (Weber, 1957, orig. pub. 1925). This "meaning" or "feeling" or "interpretive" dimension cannot be adequately captured through objective, quantitative measurement techniques. Researchers need to gain what Weber called **verstehen**, or a subjective understanding. They need to view and experience the situation from the perspective of the people themselves, "to walk a mile in their shoes." They need to talk to the people at length and immerse themselves in their lives so they can experience the highs and lows, the joys and sorrows, the triumphs and tragedies as seen from the perspective of the people being studied. Researchers need to see how individuals experience and give meaning to what is happening to them. Interpretive research methods provide an understanding through empathy or fellow feeling, whereas positivist methods provide understanding through abstract explanation. Yet, the important point is that both methods provide an understanding of the world, and both are a part of the scientific enterprise.

Qualitative research methods attempt to gain access to that personal, subjective experience; for interpretivists, quantitative research by its very nature misses this important dimension of social reality. Positivists, for their part, do not necessarily deny the existence or importance of subjective experiences, but they do question whether the subjective interpretations of the *verstehen* method have scientific validity.

According to the interpretivist approach, regularity and pattern in social life does not result from objective social laws that exist apart from the human experience and are discovered by scientists. Instead, pattern and predictability arise out of mutually created systems of meaning that emerge from social interaction (Rabinow & Sullivan, 1987; Roscoe, 1995). Regularity and pattern are created and maintained by people; they are not imposed by external force. Proponents of interpretive approaches argue that qualitative research methods enable the researcher to approximate *verstehen*, an understanding of the subjective experiences of people. Of course, actual access to such experience is impossible; thoughts and feelings, by their very nature, are private. Even when someone says how he or she feels, the speaker has objectified that subjective experience into words and, thus, changed it. Researchers, however, can gain some insight into subjective experiences by immersing themselves in the lives and daily experiences of the people they study. By experiencing the same culture, the same values, the same hopes and fears, researchers are in a better position to take on the point of view of these people. Despite its focus on subjective experiences, however, such research is still empirical in the sense that it is grounded in observation. Qualitative researchers consider their qualitative observations and conclusions to be no less systematic or scientific than the more positivistic quantitative research techniques. Although positivists would argue that subjective meaning is difficult to quantify and study objectively, interpretive researchers would argue that it is, nonetheless, a key part of human social reality.

Another important difference between positivists and interpretivists has to do with the role of science: Positivists argue that scientists merely discover what exists in the world, but some interpretivists claim that scientists actually help create social reality through their scientific work (Knorr, 1981). As researchers make observations, gather data, and draw conclusions, their activities contribute to the construction of patterns of meaning. Scientific principles and laws about social behavior become another aspect of reality that can influence people's behavior. Even something as simple as computing the average age of a group creates a new reality: Instead of recognizing that some people in the group are 22 years old, others 34 years old, and still others 43 years old, we now say that the "average age of the group is 36.7 years." This summary statement gives the impression—and creates the reality—that the group members share something in common in terms of age and that we know something very precise about their ages. That sense of commonality or precision, however, comes from the numbers created by the scientist, not from reality. In addition, though the average appears to be very precise, it actually is less precise than listing all the ages of the group members.

The interpretive approach focuses more on inductive and idiographic theory construction than on deductive and nomothetic approaches, considering the theories to emerge out of people's experiences rather than viewing them as abstractions developed by scientists. Understanding and truth come from an empathic grasp of the social meanings of a setting rather than from statistical analysis and abstract generalization to large numbers of cases. Once again, however, the link between paradigms and research approaches is not mutually exclusive. At times, interpretive social scientists do deductive and nomothetic theory construction, and they have even been known to use quantitative methods when appropriate.

Other nonpositivist characterizations of science exist as well. For example, critical and feminist approaches to research argue that science is inevitably linked to inequitable distributions of power and resources. These approaches posit that groups can and do use science to enhance their position in society, and that patterns of dominance and subordination may exist between researchers and those on whom they conduct research. Other nonpositivist critiques will be addressed in later chapters. At this point, we simply want to raise the controversy regarding positivist and nonpositivist views of science to stress that science and scientific research are more complicated than you might have originally thought. The goal for the student should not be to attempt to resolve these disputes or choose among the paradigms. Instead, the goal should be to understand the dimensions of the debate, recognize how the paradigms are similar to or different from one another, and comprehend the implications of each paradigm for the research process. In addition, the paradigms are not completely exclusionary of one another. All the paradigms agree with much of what will be covered in this book. For example, all the paradigms base their search for knowledge on systematic observation, and all agree that scientific work should be open and public. Of course, they may not always agree on what makes observations systematic, but there is not total agreement within each paradigm about that issue, either.

Another reason why the student need not adopt a preferred paradigm is that many researchers do not choose a particular perspective to follow exclusively (Alford, 1998). Many researchers find that each of the approaches offers some insights into social life and the scientific process that the others ignore. They move back and forth among the paradigms, using the best that each has to offer in understanding a particular aspect of human social life.

CAUSE-AND-EFFECT RELATIONSHIPS

One of the more important yet difficult tasks in scientific research is the search for causes—that is, the reasons *why* particular forms of behavior occur.

Why do child abuse and spousal abuse occur? Why do some juveniles become delinquent, whereas others present no behavior problems? Why do some people exhibit symptoms of mental illness and others appear to be psychologically stable?

Discovering causal relationships is a difficult task, because causality cannot be directly observed. Rather, it must be inferred from the observation of other factors. Because of this, the philosopher John Kemeny has labeled causality "the mysterious force" (1959, p. 49). We cannot see it, feel it, or hear it, but we often assume that it is there—and many scientists search for causality with hopefulness and tenacity. This search is a controversial task, because some philosophers, notably Bertrand Russell (1953), have argued for excluding the notion of causality from scientific investigation altogether. These people opt for restricting ourselves to description and analysis of "associations" without the implication that a "mysterious force" called causality lurks behind the scenes and orchestrates the actions of people and things. This controversy is longstanding; we do not presume to resolve it here. Nonetheless, it is important to understand the criteria that need to be satisfied if one wants to infer that one event caused another.

By **causality**, we mean that some independent variable (X) is the factor, or one of several factors, whose change produces variation in a dependent variable (Y). As noted, causality can only be inferred. We can observe the relationships among things in the world, and from that we can infer or deduce that changes in one factor are causing changes in another. However, it is always an inference. To infer the existence of a causal relationship, one must demonstrate the following:

1. A statistical association between the independent and dependent variables must exist.
2. The independent variable must occur prior in time to the dependent variable.
3. The relationship between independent and dependent variables must not be spurious; that is, the relationship must not disappear when the effects of other variables are taken into account.

TABLE 2.1 Effectiveness of Reading Media Reports on Smoking Cessation

		Person Reads Report	
		Yes	No
Person Quits Smoking	Yes	200 (50%)	135 (27%)
	No	200 (50%)	365 (73%)
	Totals	400 (100%)	500 (100%)

We will consider each requirement of causal inference in the context of an issue that is much in the news today—the campaign to reduce cigarette smoking. Over the years, there have been reports in the media about the negative impact of cigarette smoking on people's health. Some argue that making these reports public as part of a health campaign can motivate people to quit smoking. Table 2.1 presents hypothetical data that seems to show a link between reading such reports about smoking and actually quitting smoking: 50 percent of those who read the reports quit smoking, compared to only 27 percent of those who do not read the reports. Finding such a statistical relationship satisfies the first criterion for establishing a causal relationship.

The second requirement, that the independent variable occurs prior in time to the dependent, often is not as easy to establish. A major factor in this is the nature of the study. Some research techniques, such as the experiment or participant observation, are inherently *longitudinal*, which means that the researcher is in a position to trace the development of behavior as it unfolds over time. In these cases, establishing the time sequence of events generally is simple. Questions of temporal order are more difficult to resolve when dealing with *cross-sectional* data, such as surveys, in which measurements of the independent and dependent variables occur at the same time. This is especially true if the question of temporal sequence is not addressed until after the data have been collected. It is sometimes possible to sort out the time sequence of variables in survey data by asking additional questions. If the researcher does not gather the necessary information at the time of the survey, however, then establishing the appropriate time order of the variables may be impossible—hence the emphasis on the importance of carefully considering issues of data analysis when originally developing a research design.

The data in our illustration may suffer from this problem. One interpretation is that reading reports is the independent variable that influences whether people quit smoking, the dependent variable. For this interpretation to be correct, the reports would have to have been publicized before the people quit smoking. If the respondents were not asked when they quit smoking, then it would be impossible to say whether they quit smoking before or after reading the reports. Obviously, if they quit smoking before reading the reports, then such health campaigns could not have caused their change in behavior. In our example, without knowing the temporal sequence, one could argue logically for either factor being the cause of the other. Obviously the health campaign could encourage people to quit smoking if they become frightened by learning the dire consequences of their habit. However, those who quit smoking also could be happy with and proud of their victory and might enjoy reading reports on what could have happened to them had they not quit smoking. In this second scenario, quitting smoking would be the independent variable that increases the likelihood that people will read reports about the health threat of smoking, the dependent variable.

The final criterion necessary for inferring causality is that the relationship between the independent and dependent variables not be *spurious*, or disappear when the effects of other variables are considered. The logic of causal and spurious relationships is compared in Figure 2.2. This often is the most difficult of the three criteria to satisfy. In fact, one is never *totally* sure that some other variable—one you have not even considered—might not confound an apparent causal relationship. All

Causal Relationship between X and Y

X ⟶ Y   X produces changes in Y

Spurious Relationship between X and Y When Controlling for Z

Z ⟨ X / Y   Z produces changes in both X and Y

FIGURE 2.2 Causal and Spurious Relationships

that can be accomplished is to rule out as many extraneous variables as we can to the point where it is unlikely a variable exists that could render a given relationship spurious or noncausal.

Considerable effort is expended during the design stage of research to control as many potentially troublesome extraneous variables as possible. Experiments, for example, are particularly good for avoiding spurious relationships because of the high degree of control that the experimental situation affords the researcher. Surveys, on the other hand, provide far less control, such that several variables capable of producing spuriousness typically have to be considered during data analysis. Several statistical techniques exist to control extraneous variables when the data are analyzed.

Returning to our example of smoking cessation, suppose we had solved the time sequence problem and, thus, had satisfied the first two requirements for establishing a causal relationship. We would now begin to consider variables that might render the relationship spurious. One variable that might do this is the level of education of the people studied. (The logic of this is outlined in Figure 2.3.) Considerable research links education with health behavior. Generally, people with higher levels of education engage in more health-promoting activities, such as quitting smoking or getting regular exercise. How do we determine whether the link between report reading and smoking cessation is spurious? We introduce the level of education as a control variable,

Causal Relationship

Read report ⟶ Quit smoking

Spurious Relationship

Level of education ⟶ Read report
Level of education ⟶ Quit smoking

FIGURE 2.3 Causal and Spurious Relationships between Reading a Report and Quitting Smoking

TABLE 2.2 Effectiveness of Reading Media Reports on Smoking Cessation, Controlling for Education

Less Than High School Education

		Person Reads Report		
		Yes	No	Totals
Person Quits Smoking	Yes	20 (20%)	75 (19%)	95 (19%)
	No	80 (80%)	325 (81%)	405 (81%)
	Totals	100 (100%)	400 (100%)	500

High School Education or More

		Person Reads Report		
		Yes	No	Totals
Person Quits Smoking	Yes	180 (60%)	60 (60%)	240 (60%)
	No	120 (40%)	40 (40%)	160 (40%)
	Totals	300 (100%)	100 (100%)	400

which is illustrated with our hypothetical data in Table 2.2, in which we have divided the respondents in Table 2.1 into those with at least a high school education and those with less than a high school education. First, we can see by examining the row totals in each table that education is related to health behavior: 60 percent of the better-educated group have quit smoking, compared to only 19 percent of the less-educated group. However, we are really interested in what happens to the link between report reading and smoking cessation, and Table 2.2 shows that the relationship largely disappears: Within each educational group, the same percentage of people quit smoking among those who read the report as among those who did not. So educational level, not whether one has read the report, influences a person's likelihood of quitting smoking. Furthermore, in our hypothetical example, educational level also influences whether one reads the report: 300 out of 400, or 75 percent, of those with a high school education read the report, compared with only 100 of 500, or 20 percent, of those with less than a high school education. So in our example, the link between reading the report and quitting smoking is spurious; it occurs only because each of those two variables is affected by the same third variable.

If we had found the link between report reading and smoking cessation to be nonspurious when we controlled for education, could we conclude that the relationship was causal? The answer is no. We could not come to that conclusion—at least not yet. All that we would know was that the relationship remained when *one* alternative explanation was ruled out. Any other variables that could render the relationship spurious also would have to be investigated—and the relationship still hold—before we could argue with any confidence that it was, in fact, causal. (More intricacies of this sort of analysis are addressed in Chapter 15.)

We said at the outset that establishing the existence of causal relationships is difficult. Statistical relationships are easy to find but, on further investigation, all too frequently turn out to be spurious. The appropriate time sequence also can be problematic, especially with survey data. All in all, establishing causal relationships is a difficult but an important and challenging task.

REVIEW AND CRITICAL THINKING

Main Points

- Science is one source of knowledge, along with tradition, experience, common sense, and journalism; but it is a superior source of objective and accurate knowledge about the world.
- The five key characteristics of science are that it is empirical, systematic, provisional, objective, and searches for the causes of events. These crucial characteristics also are central features of scientifically based practice.
- Theories are sets of interrelated, abstract propositions that explain phenomena. Theories perform three major functions: They provide explanations, they guide research and practice, and they integrate observations from research.
- Concepts are mental constructs that symbolize ideas, persons, things, or events, and form the basis for propositions and theories.
- Concepts are given both nominal definitions, which explain their meaning, and operational definitions, which indicate how they are measured. Care must be taken in developing operational definitions in research on minorities to ensure that such definitions do not lead to a distorted view of these populations.
- Hypotheses are statements that predict relationships between two or more variables and are tested through research.
- Theories are developed and elaborated by going back and forth between the abstract, conceptual level and the concrete, empirical level, using either deductive reasoning or inductive reasoning.
- Theories also differ in the types of explanations they seek, some nomothetic and others idiographic.
- Two paradigms, or ways of understanding how we know the world, are predominant in the social sciences: positivism, and nonpositivism. Each tends to be associated with particular research methodologies. The goal for the student in this debate should be to understand the dimensions of the debate, to recognize how the paradigms are similar to or different from one another, and to comprehend the implications of each paradigm for the research process.
- Causality means that some independent variable produces variation in a dependent variable.
- To demonstrate a causal relationship, one must establish a statistical association between two variables, show that the independent variable occurs first temporally, and demonstrate that the relationship is not spurious.

Important Terms for Review

causality
common sense
concepts
deductive reasoning
dependent variable
experiential knowledge
hypotheses
idiographic explanations
independent variable
inductive reasoning
interpretive approaches
logical empiricism
nominal definitions
nomothetic explanations
operational definitions
paradigms
positivism
propositions
qualitative research
quantitative research
science
theory
traditional knowledge
variables
verification
verstehen

Critical Thinking

This chapter covers some of the building blocks of the scientific method: theories, propositions, hypotheses, concepts, variables, and so on. In using these building blocks, scientists try to be very careful when describing and analyzing the world in order to avoid misunderstanding. You can utilize some of these same building blocks in trying to critically analyze information for policy or practice purposes or for your everyday life.

Consider the following when reading or hearing something.

1. What sources of knowledge serve as the basis for a claim or assertion? What are the strengths or weaknesses of those sources of knowledge?
2. Specify any theories, concepts, or hypotheses that are contained in the information. Keep in mind that, in practice, policy, or everyday realms, these elements may be implicit in what people say and you may have to figure out what they are.
3. Is there any evidence that theories have been verified? How much verification?
4. Are there claims to objectivity (positivism)? Is there any indication that subjectivity, values, or interests play a part in shaping the knowledge?
5. Are there any causal statements being made? Does the evidence presented satisfy the criteria that warrant a causal inference?

Exploring the Internet

One of the central themes of this book is how research can inform practice. For Internet resources on applying research to human service practice, we suggest you use a search engine and search for such phrases as "children's mental health" or "evaluation outcomes." A site we found from such a search was the home page of the Office of Alcoholism and Substance Abuse Services (OASAS) of New York state (http://www.oasas.ny.gov). In this chapter, we discussed the development of hypotheses and introduced the ideas of operational definition, dependent variable, and independent variable. As a way of applying these concepts to actual research, select several of the research studies reported at the OASAS site. For each study you find, identify one or more hypotheses that the study addressed. Determine if the review identifies how the dependent and independent variables were operationally defined. Finally, if the review describes how the independent and dependent variables are measured, state whether success in the program would be expected to show an inverse or direct relationship between the dependent and independent variables.

We covered some fairly core and controversial issues in social research in this chapter, especially in relation to the positivist and nonpositivist paradigms. Suppose that you work for a research organization and your boss wants you to create an online discussion of these paradigms. You need to locate people, organizations, or resources on the web that espouse one position or another on these issues. Use a search engine and enter one or more of the terms used to identify the paradigms or that have some relationship to the paradigms: "positivism," "logical positivism," "subjectivism," "relativism," "postmodernism," "feminism," and so on. From your search, discuss how many different social sciences address issues having to do with these paradigms. Do some social sciences address different issues than other social sciences? Do the same kind of analysis for the natural sciences. Also address whether fields that are nonscientific, such as the humanities, address these issues. Can you put together the online discussion your boss has requested?

For Further Reading

Bengtson, V. L., Acock, A. C., Allen, K. R., Dilworth-Anderson, P., & Klein, D. M. (2005) *Sourcebook of Family Theory and Research*. Thousand Oaks, Calif.: Sage. This reference work on theory and methods for family scholars demonstrates how the development of theory is crucial to the future of family research. The work focuses on the process of theory building and designing research.

Glaser, B. G., & Strauss, A. L. (1967). *The Discovery of Grounded Theory*. New York: Aldine. An excellent book about the virtues and procedures of developing theoretical propositions from data. This approach emphasizes qualitative research and induction.

Hoover, K. R., & Donovan, T. (2011). *The Elements of Social Scientific Thinking*. 10th ed. Belmont, Calif.: Wadsworth/Cengage Learning. A brief and readable initiation into social science thinking and research. It is intended for those who use the results of research and for those just getting into the field.

Merton, R. K. (1968). *Social Theory and Social Structure*. 2nd ed. New York: Free Press. A classic statement by a sociologist on the relationship between theory and research.

Shoemaker, P. J., Tankard, J. W. Jr., & Lasorsa, D. L. (2004). *How to Build Social Science Theories*. Thousand Oaks, Calif.: Sage. This book traces theories from their most rudimentary building blocks (terminology and definitions) through multivariable theoretical statements, models, the role of creativity in theory building, and how theories are used and evaluated. The book includes a discussion of concepts and their theoretical and operational definitions.

Turner, J. H., ed. (1989). *Theory Building in Sociology: Assessing Theoretical Accumulation*. Newbury Park, Calif.: Sage. In this collection of essays, one of the foremost U.S. theoreticians in sociology addresses a key assertion of the positivist approach: Does knowledge accumulate through the deductive approach of theory building and hypothesis testing?

Van de Ven, A. H. (2007). *Engaged Scholarship: A Guide for Organizational and Social Research*. Oxford: Oxford University Press. The author is a leading management researcher and writes from that perspective, but the issues he addresses are relevant to human service research as well. He especially addresses the issue of whether research findings and knowledge should be useful for science, practice, and policy. He also discusses how such research should be designed, carried out, and disseminated to achieve the twin goals of rigor and relevance.

Watts, D. J. (2011). *Everything Is Obvious* (*Once You Know the Answer)*. New York: Crown. This is an entertaining and insightful exploration of common sense as a source of knowledge—pointing to its weaknesses and failures as a foundation for thinking, reasoning, and planning.

Class Exercises for Competency Assessment

2.1. **[Critical Thinking]** Many commonsense beliefs relate to child development, such as "spare the rod and spoil the child," or the belief that age-graded schools enhance learning. Through class discussion, develop a list of such "known" principles of child development. For each such principle, decide whether it is based on traditional knowledge, experiential knowledge, or a combination of both. How might you conduct systematic observations to determine the worth of these statements as scientific knowledge?

2.2. A mental health worker assigned to a large residential facility for senior citizens receives a request from staff members to "do something" about a new resident, a 72-year-old woman. From the information provided, the woman has apparently been assigned to an eighth-floor room, but she refuses to take the elevator alone or if it is crowded. The woman becomes terrified of the enclosed space and uses the stairs unless she can ride the elevator with a staff member. The woman's husband died about six months ago, and she is now living alone for the first time.

   a. **[Critical Thinking] [Evidence-Based Evaluation]** Consider this case from the alternative theoretical positions of behavior modification versus traditional Freudian psychology. (You may substitute some other relevant theories of human behavior with which you are familiar.) What are some major theoretical concepts from each theory that apply to this case?

b. **[Research & Practice]** For the concepts you identified in part (a), use the illustrative case to develop operational definitions for each concept.

2.3. **[Evidence-Based Evaluation] [Research & Practice]** Using each theory from Exercise 2.2, construct a possible explanation for the woman's behavior. Now try to state your explanations in terms of testable hypotheses. Can you foresee any problems in assessing causality when testing these hypotheses? Compare the hypotheses you developed with those of other students in terms of the theory used, the concepts selected, and the variables identified. How are the concepts and variables that are derived from the same theory alike? How do they differ from those derived from the other theory?

2.4. **[Research & Practice]** We have made the point that the same theories can be useful to both practitioners and researchers. Using the hypotheses developed in Exercise 2.3, explain how they could be used either to help the worker change the woman's behavior or to conduct a study. How might the hypotheses need to be changed to be useful in both practice and research?

2.5. **[Critical Thinking] [Diversity]** A clinician in a treatment program for woman batterers notices that about 75 percent of the individuals who are mandated by the court to participate in group therapy also have a history of substance abuse problems, such as arrests for drunk driving. Furthermore, a large proportion of the clients had been drinking prior to committing the assault. Can the clinician conclude that substance abuse causes woman battering? Identify what conditions would need to be met to support this contention. Prepare a diagram involving a third variable that might show that the relation between substance abuse and woman battering is spurious.

Chapter 3

✴

Ethical Issues in Social Research

The Minority Experience: The Need for Ethical Standards

Ethical Issues

Informed Consent

Deception

The Right to Privacy: Anonymity and Confidentiality

Harm, Distress, and Benefit

Sponsored Research

Scientific Misconduct and Fraud

Scientific Advocacy

Protecting Vulnerable Clients

Withholding Treatment for Research Purposes

Codes of Ethics

Review and Critical Thinking

Main Points

Important Terms for Review

Critical Thinking

Exploring the Internet

For Further Reading

Class Exercises for Competency Assessment

People are the subjects of social research, and because people have rights and feelings, special considerations apply in social research that do not confront the chemist studying molecules or the physicist investigating gravity. Consider, for example, the area of substance-abuse control and treatment. In recent years, considerable controversy has arisen over the use of drug testing to deal with the problem. Some employers have instituted random drug testing of their employees as a condition of gaining employment or remaining employed. Some college athletes are randomly tested, as are prison inmates. In the context of social research, drug testing of a population would be a useful method for assessing the effectiveness of drug interdiction programs or substance-abuse counseling programs. To be most effective, such testing should be required of all people affected by a program. So if new security procedures to control the entry of drugs into a prison are established, their effectiveness can be measured by random testing of a sample of inmates. Likewise, if a drug education program is established in a college, random testing of a sample of students at that college could assess the program's effectiveness.

Would such involuntary drug testing of inmates or students, however, be proper? This question can be answered only by referring to some cultural, professional, or personal values that help us decide what is right and proper behavior. In the United States, three such values have been articulated in the Belmont Report (National Commission, 1978), a document that is considered to be a pillar of human research ethics. These principles are:

1. *Respect for persons:* We recognize the personal dignity and autonomy of individuals, and we should provide special protection of those persons with diminished autonomy.
2. *Beneficence:* We have an obligation to protect persons from harm by maximizing anticipated benefits and minimizing possible risks of harm.
3. *Justice:* The benefits and burdens of research should be distributed fairly.

Viewing drug testing in this context, some would argue that people's rights to autonomy and privacy preclude taking bodily fluids against their will to find out something about them. Is such an invasion of the privacy of college students proper or acceptable? What about prison inmates? Involuntary testing of a whole population also would seem to violate self-determination. The subjects have no choice about participating in the research. Because a person who tests positive for drugs might be subject to criminal prosecution or stigmatization, it raises the question of whether the research could bring harm to the person. Finally, who bears the cost of, and who benefits from, such research? Some would be quick to employ drug testing to evaluate a treatment program with prison inmates, but would be reluctant to subject participants in a middle-class community program to such scrutiny, even though the program may be implemented there once it is proven to be effective.

These are complicated issues. We do not presume that our statement of values is the final word or that the application of these values to particular cases is easy or straightforward. They do serve as an introduction, however, to the discussion of ethical issues in social research.

Ethics is the study of what is proper and improper behavior, of moral duty and obligation (Drewry, 2004). Moral principles can be grounded in philosophy, theology, or both. For social researchers, ethics involves the responsibilities that researchers bear toward those who participate in research, those who sponsor research, and those who are potential beneficiaries of research. It covers many specific issues. For example, is it ever permissible to harm people during the course of a research project? Should people who participate in a research project ever be deceived? Is it appropriate to suppress research findings that cast a sponsor's program in a negative light? Should researchers report to the police crimes they uncover while conducting a research project? The ethics of a given action depends on the standards used to assess the action, and those standards are grounded in human values. Because of this, ethical questions have few simple or final answers and no scientific tests that can show us whether actions are ethical. In fact, debate continues among scientists about ethical issues, because such issues involve matters of judgment and assessment.

Our purpose in this chapter is to identify the basic ethical issues in social research and suggest some strategies for making sure that ethical considerations are covered in the conduct and use of research. Furthering that goal, each of the remaining chapters in this book will include a short section titled "Eye on Ethics," in which a specific ethical issue related to that chapter is discussed.

THE MINORITY EXPERIENCE: THE NEED FOR ETHICAL STANDARDS

Ethical issues do not exist in a vacuum but, rather, within the context of a particular society and its historical development. Two events in the twentieth century—one abroad and the other in the United States—served as major catalysts for efforts to codify a set of ethical standards for research.

The first event occurred in Europe during World War II: the heinous series of medical experiments conducted by the Nazis on Jews and others in concentration camps (Beauchamp et al., 1982). Prior to this, there had been no codification of scientific ethics, and researchers had been left largely to their own devices in deciding how to conduct their studies. The revelation of the German atrocities by the Nuremberg trials of 1945 and 1946 shocked the sensibilities of the world and left an indelible imprint on research ethics. The cruelty of these experiments is almost inconceivable. Healthy people were intentionally infected with such serious diseases as spotted fever or malaria to observe the course of the disease with and without medication. Others were used as subjects to test the effects of various poisons. Some had parts of their bodies frozen to test new treatments. Still others were deliberately wounded to study new antibiotics and other treatments. Perhaps most evil of all were the excruciating decompression studies designed to test reactions to high-altitude flight (Katz, 1972). These gruesome experiments brought home exactly how far people would go in using research to further their own ends. They also brought home the vulnerability of minorities to exploitation in research, especially when the resources and authority of powerful groups support researchers with few ethical standards. Public outrage over these experiments led to heightened concern to establish codified standards for the ethical conduct of medical research on human subjects.

The second event that influenced the development of a codified set of ethical standards was an infamous study of syphilis conducted by the U.S. Public Health Service (PHS). This study began in 1932 with black males from Tuskegee, Alabama— 425 of them with syphilis and 200 of them without syphilis. All were poor and only semiliterate. None was told that he had syphilis. The intent was to observe the men over a span of years to learn how the disease progressed. When the study began, there was no cure for syphilis. Fifteen years later, penicillin was discovered to be an effective cure for this affliction, but the PHS continued the syphilis study for an additional 25 years, withholding treatment from all but a fortunate few who discovered its existence on their own and requested it. The justification for deceiving the men was that, because they were poor and semiliterate, they would in all likelihood not seek treatment even if they knew about it. Left untreated, syphilis can cause paralysis, insanity, blindness, and heart disease. Ultimately, it can even be fatal. Yet, these men were allowed to spread the disease to their wives and lovers. Many of the afflicted participants in the Tuskegee study suffered serious physical disorders or died as a result of not receiving treatment for the disease (Jones, 1992; Reverby, 2000).

Most Americans today—and especially those in the human services—would agree that the actions of the PHS were repugnant, racist, and unethical in the extreme. In fact, President Bill Clinton issued an apology on behalf of the nation for the Tuskegee Syphilis Study during a White House ceremony in 1997 (Eckenwiler, 1999). When the study began, however—and even when effective treatment for syphilis became available—the subordinate position of blacks and poor people in American society resulted in their receiving fewer political, economic, and even medical rights than whites and more affluent citizens received. It is unlikely that well-to-do whites would have been treated in the same arrogant fashion, and one would hope that no such debacle would be seriously contemplated today. Yet we should keep in mind that the PHS study continued into the 1970s—an era we like to consider as more enlightened regarding human rights—and ended only when it received public notoriety. This further documents the extent to which minorities (and others) can be at risk of dangerous and inhumane treatment from researchers who are not governed by clear and enforceable ethical standards.

The immoral treatment of some minorities in research during the twentieth century, especially the Nazi and PHS episodes, brought home the need to codify standards for ethical conduct so that researchers would have guidelines available and the research subjects would be afforded some protection. The first effort along these lines was the Nuremberg Code, developed in 1946 in direct response to the atrocities committed during World War II. The Nuremberg Code was limited to issues of ethics in medical research. In 1966, the PHS established ethical regulations for medical research that emphasized the following: (1) full disclosure of relevant information should be made to the participants; (2) the decision to participate must be completely voluntary; and (3) researchers must obtain documented, informed consent from participants (Gray, 1982; Reynolds, 1979). In 1974, the U.S. Department of Health, Education, and Welfare (DHEW, now the U.S. Department of Health and Human Services or DHHS) decreed that the PHS guidelines would apply to social science research. Furthermore, the DHEW recognized that codes of conduct alone would not ensure ethical research without some oversight procedures in place. To this end, the DHEW required research institutions, such as universities, to establish institutional review boards, or IRBs, that would review research proposals and ensure that the guidelines were followed. These regulations have been broadened to apply not only to those projects directly funded by that agency but also to any research carried on in organizations that obtain DHHS funding. Today, some research is conducted by researchers or agencies that are not a part of a university or other organization that has IRB services. For these researchers, there are unaffiliated IRBs that are not owned or operated by a university or other research organizations. There is also an accreditation process for these independent IRBs, which serves as a check on the quality of their services.

The DHHS regulations are codified at Title 45, Part 46, of the Code of Federal Regulations. Those basic regulations became final in 1981 and were subsequently revised in 1983 and again in 1991. The 1991 revision was especially important, because it involved the adoption of the Federal Policy for the Protection of Human Subjects that had been set forth in the Belmont Report. Those principles of respect, beneficence, and justice are now accepted as the three quintessential requirements for the ethical conduct of research involving human subjects. Although few would take issue with the basic ethical principles that had been expressed in the 1974 DHEW policy, the fact that those regulations initially originated in the context of medical research did cause concern for social scientists. A common feeling is that the risks to participants in most social science research are minimal and different from the risks to participants in medical research (Murray et al., 1980). In social science research, breach of confidentiality, not direct harm, is the most likely ethical problem. There was concern that the original regulations would obstruct important research, hinder response rates, and reduce the validity and generalizability of findings.

In response to these concerns, the DHHS, under a policy issued in 1981, exempted the following research methodologies from IRB review: evaluation of teaching procedures or courses, educational testing, survey or interview techniques, observation of public behavior, and documentary research (Huber 1981). The only exceptions are research dealing with "sensitive" behavior, such as drug and alcohol use, illegal behavior, or sexual conduct. In assessing social science research that is not exempt from IRB review, the IRBs have tended to subscribe to a risk–benefit doctrine (Smith, 1981). This means that questionable practices, such as deception or disguised observation, may be used if the purpose of the study is viewed as sufficiently important to justify them.

Although the DHHS regulations exempt much social science research from IRB review, many universities and other research institutions require that *all* research projects be reviewed to determine whether they are legitimately exempt. Furthermore, it has become increasingly common for private foundations to require IRB review as a prerequisite for funding (Ceci, Peters, and Plotkin, 1985). When planning research, an application to conduct the research should routinely be submitted to the appropriate IRB to determine whether the research is exempt and, if it is not, to gain permission to conduct the research. Table 3.1 lists the content that the DHHS expects to find on an IRB application form.

ETHICAL ISSUES IN SOCIAL RESEARCH

TABLE 3.1 Criteria for IRB Approval of Research

In order to approve research covered by this policy, the IRB shall determine that all of the following requirements are satisfied:

1. Risks to subjects are minimized:
   (i) by using procedures which are consistent with sound research design and which do not unnecessarily expose subjects to risk; and
   (ii) whenever appropriate, by using procedures already being performed on the subjects for diagnostic or treatment purposes.
2. Risks to subjects are reasonable in relation to anticipated benefits, if any, to subjects, and the importance of the knowledge that may reasonably be expected to result. In evaluating risks and benefits, the IRB should consider only those risks and benefits that may result from the research (as distinguished from risks and benefits of therapies subjects would receive even if not participating in the research). The IRB should not consider the possible long-range effects of applying knowledge gained in the research (for example, the possible effects of the research on public policy) as among those research risks that fall within the purview of its responsibility.
3. Selection of subjects is equitable. In making this assessment, the IRB should take into account the purposes of the research and the setting in which the research will be conducted. The IRB also should be particularly cognizant of the special problems of research involving vulnerable populations such as children, prisoners, pregnant women, mentally disabled persons, or economically or educationally disadvantaged persons.
4. Informed consent will be sought from each prospective subject or the subject's legally authorized representative, in accordance with and to the extent required by §46.116.
5. Informed consent will be appropriately documented, in accordance with, and to the extent required by §46.117.
6. When appropriate, the research plan makes adequate provision for monitoring the data collected to ensure the safety of subjects.
7. When appropriate, there are adequate provisions to protect the privacy of subjects and to maintain the confidentiality of data.

SOURCE: Adapted from Part 46.111, Protection of Human Subjects Code of Federal Regulations, Title 45, Public Welfare, DHHS National Institutes of Health Office for Protection from Research Risks, 2001.

As you read the rest of this chapter, you will see that many of the ethical issues discussed are addressed by the criteria listed for such applications. Even if a project is exempt from IRB review, researchers are not exempt from ethical concerns. Whether one's research will be reviewed or not, one still has the responsibility to consider the impact of the research on those who participate and on those who might benefit from it. As we will see, ethical guidelines do not eliminate the controversy that surrounds ethical issues, because guidelines need to be interpreted and applied to specific contexts. Much debate surrounds such interpretation and application.

The debate over the Nazi experiments is not over. Controversy persists in terms of whether the data from that research are valid and reliable and, if so, whether those data should be used today (Moe, 1984; Schafer, 1986). Some have argued that use of the data is justified if the data are scientifically valid and no other source of such data exists. If the data are used, it is argued, one should feel compelled to express horror and regret at the manner of collection. On the other side, some argue that our collective outrage at the treatment of minorities by the Nazis should be so great that use of the data is repulsive. In this view, refusing to use these data is a symbolic denunciation of such atrocities, and using the data might be interpreted as an acceptance of the methods that were used to collect them—or at least a willingness to let the importance of the Holocaust diminish with the passage of time. Between these two extremes, some researchers argue that the data should be used only if any overriding need demands it, and the objective of using the data overrides our symbolic rejection of the manner in which the data were collected.

Recent assessments suggest that the data from the Nazi experiments are seriously flawed—even fraudulent in some cases—and therefore should not be used, regardless of the ethical issues surrounding how the data were obtained (Berger, 1994). This controversy remains long-lasting and deeply rooted in ethical research issues.

ETHICAL ISSUES

Six basic ethical issues arise in social science research: informed consent, deception, privacy (including confidentiality and anonymity), physical or mental distress, problems in sponsored research, scientific misconduct or fraud, and scientific advocacy. The unique situation confronting the human service researcher raises two additional considerations: protecting vulnerable clients and withholding treatment for research purposes.

Informed Consent

Informed consent refers to telling potential research participants about all aspects of the research, which might reasonably influence the decision to participate. Very often, people are asked to sign a *consent form*, which describes the elements of the research that might influence a person's decision to participate (see Table 3.2). General agreement exists concerning the desirability of informed consent in behavioral science research, primarily because in the United States, cultural values place great emphasis on freedom and self-determination. Whether the issue is whom to marry, what career to pursue, or whether to participate in a research project, we value the right of individuals to assess information and weigh alternatives before making their own judgments. To deceive potential research participants is to deny them the ability to determine their own destinies.

Although consensus exists about the general principle of informed consent, the debate regarding exactly how far the obligations of researchers extend in this realm is still a hot issue. At one extreme,

---

TABLE 3.2 Basic Elements of an Informed Consent Form

The Following Information Shall Be Provided to Each Subject:

(1) A statement that the study involves research, an explanation of the purposes of the research and the expected duration of the subject's participation, a description of the procedures to be followed, and identification of any procedures that are experimental;

(2) A description of any reasonably foreseeable risks or discomforts to the subject;

(3) A description of any benefits to the subject or others, which may reasonably be expected from the research;

(4) A disclosure of appropriate alternative procedures or courses of treatment, if any, that might be advantageous to the subject;

(5) A statement describing the extent, if any, to which confidentiality of records identifying the subject will be maintained;

(6) For research involving more than minimal risk, an explanation as to whether any compensation or any medical treatments are available if injury occurs, and, if so, what they consist of, or where further information may be obtained;

(7) An explanation of whom to contact for answers to pertinent questions about the research and research subjects' rights and whom to contact in the event of a research-related injury to the subject; and

(8) A statement that participation is voluntary and refusal to participate will involve no penalty or loss of benefits to which the subject is otherwise entitled, and that the subject may discontinue participation at any time without penalty or loss of benefits to which the subject is otherwise entitled.

SOURCE: Part 46, Protection of Human Subjects. Code of Federal Regulations, Title 45, Public Welfare. DHHS National Institutes of Health Office for Protection from Research Risks, 2001.

researchers known as *ethical absolutists* argue that people should be fully informed of all aspects of the research in which they might play a part (Baumrind, 1985; Elms, 1982; Kimmel, 1988). Even when research is based on the public record, such as agency documents, or on observations of behavior in public, some absolutists argue that people about whom the observations have been made should be informed of the research. Otherwise, they do not have the full right to decide whether to participate.

Rigid adherence to the absolutist position, however, makes social research much more difficult to conduct. First, such adherence rules out many practices that some researchers consider important or essential. Many experiments, for example, rely on some degree of deception, at least to the extent of not telling participants the true research hypotheses. The reason for this is that people might respond differently if they knew about these hypotheses. All such studies would be unacceptable to the absolutists, however, and could not be conducted. Absolutists also would disallow disguised observation, during which people in public settings are not aware they are being observed. No longer could researchers engage in such effective strategies as infiltrating organizations—unless, of course, they told all employees what they were doing. The net result would be to make social science research highly conservative and limited. It would become the study of people who volunteer to be studied; and research shows that people who volunteer differ in many ways from people who do not volunteer. This would seriously reduce the generalizability of research findings.

Second, the absolutist approach would call for obtaining informed consent in all research projects, and research has shown that obtaining written consent can reduce people's willingness to participate in research. One study found that formally requesting informed consent prior to conducting an interview reduced the rate of cooperation by 7 percent in comparison to cases in which a formal request was not made (Singer, VonThurn, & Miller, 1995). Because any reduction in response rate will reduce the generalizability of the findings, as we will explain in Chapter 7, obtaining informed consent in survey research can have serious, negative consequences in terms of the validity of the research.

Written informed consent probably reduces people's willingness to participate because it appears to some respondents to contradict the researcher's assurance of confidentiality. One minute people are being told that their answers will remain confidential, and the next they are being asked to put their names on a consent form! Even though signing a consent form need not impede the maintenance of confidentiality, it is not surprising that respondents may not perceive it that way. Anything that undermines the belief of respondents in the confidentiality of their answers will reduce the response rates. Signing a consent form also may affect the quality of the data obtained, because those who do give consent may be less candid in their responses than they otherwise might have been.

Because of these problems with the absolutist approach to informed consent, many researchers take a less extreme position. They argue, first of all, that people should be informed of factors that might reasonably be expected to influence their decision to participate, such as any harm that might occur or how much time and effort will be involved. However, they also use a risk–benefit approach: Questionable research strategies, such as deception, are appropriate if they are essential to conduct the research, if they will bring no harm to participants, and if the outcome is sufficiently important to warrant the research. Lively debate continues over the use of questionable practices and their routine approval by IRBs (Baumrind, 1985).

A final issue regarding informed consent has to do with the possibility that a person might feel pressured to agree or might not understand precisely to what he or she is agreeing. After all, asking a person to participate in a study can involve social pressures not unlike those in other settings. We often feel pressured to help others when they ask for our assistance, and some people find it difficult to say no to a face-to-face request. In addition, scientific researchers represent figures of some authority and status, and people often are disinclined to refuse their requests. In other cases, people may be temporarily confused about what is being asked of them.

To resolve these problems, a study involving institutionalized elderly people used a two-step consent procedure (Ratzan, 1981). In the first step, people were told what their participation would involve, what risks were entailed, and that several days later, they would be asked whether they were willing to participate. This was meant to reduce any immediate pressures to agree and to enable people to talk with others and clarify any confusing issues. The second step, occurring a few days later, involved obtaining the actual consent. In that study, all those who were asked refused to participate. This probably resulted from the fact that a part of the study involved having a needle inserted in a vein continuously for eight days to take blood samples. However, some of the people might have agreed to participate had they been asked to sign a consent form during the first interview. Yet, it is questionable whether any consent obtained at that time would have been as informed and considered as it should have been. The goal of obtaining informed consent is not to pressure people into participating in the research but, rather, to gain participation that is truly informed.

Deception

Despite its status as a controversial strategy, deception is still fairly common in some areas of social science research such as social psychology (Korn, 1997). One reason for this is that some research would be difficult—or even impossible—to conduct without some level of deception. At a minimum, many experiments necessitate not telling the participants the true research hypotheses; this withholding of information is a form of deception. As another example, field research sometimes uses disguised observation, where people in public settings are observed but are unaware that the observation is occurring. Some argue that this involves an implicit deception of those being observed. Other types of field research can involve more explicit deception to gain the cooperation of those being observed.

Richard Leo (1996), in his field study of police interrogators, withheld or concealed information regarding his own views about crime, punishment, homosexuality, and other issues from the police that he observed. In fact, he dubbed what he did the "chameleon strategy": "I consciously reinvented my persona to fit the attributes, biases, and world-view of my subjects" (Leo,1995, p. 120). Before the detectives, he feigned opposition to abortion, support for the death penalty, and antipathy toward gays. He created this persona to gain their cooperation and encourage them to act openly and naturally in front of him. If the police interrogators had known his true views on these issues, Leo claims, they might have distrusted him and not acted openly in front of him. Because his observations produced ground-breaking sociological research on this topic, he felt that the deception was warranted, given that little harm came to the police officers.

Ethical absolutists would rule out all such deception on the grounds that it is unethical to deceive other human beings deliberately (Erikson. 1967). Leo, however, argues that the situation is more complicated: "Fieldwork is a morally ambiguous enterprise that is fraught with moral hazards, contingencies, and uncertainties" (Leo, 1996, p. 125). There are trade-offs and compromises to be taken into account. Furthermore, Leo makes the distinction between "acts of commission," in which the researcher intentionally falsifies information, and "acts of omission," in which information is withheld. Some would argue that Leo did the former when he "reinvented" his persona, but Leo claims that his research strategy involved only omission, and thus was ethically justifiable. In addition, he argued that his use of deception passed the test of the three major criteria that are applied: (1) The research is important; (2) no other way to conduct the research is available; and (3) no harm came to those who were studied.

When deception is used, it is a sound practice to conclude the period of observations with a *debriefing*, during which people are told the true purposes of the research and informed of any deceptions that were used. This should be done in a positive and supportive way so the participants feel they were joint partners in a worthwhile enterprise rather than dupes of the researchers. Usually, this can be achieved by explaining the reasons for the deception and the impossibility that anyone could have detected the deceptions before being informed of them. In some research, of course, debriefings are not possible, such as in disguised observations in field settings where the researcher never has a chance to contact the participants after the observations are made.

The Right to Privacy: Anonymity and Confidentiality

The right to privacy is one of the key values and ethical obligations mentioned at the beginning of this chapter. **Privacy** refers to the ability to control when and under what conditions others will have access to your beliefs, values, or behavior. Intrusions on our privacy have become endemic in modern society; with the growth of social research during the past century, the danger of even greater intrusion arises. Virtually any attempt to collect data from people raises the issue of privacy and confronts investigators with the dilemma of whether threats to privacy are warranted by the research. Two well-known research projects illustrate the complexity of this issue.

Two Case Studies. The sociologist Laud Humphreys (1970), in an effort to understand a particular type of sexual behavior, made observations of men having quick and impersonal sexual encounters with other men in public restrooms. To gather his data without arousing suspicion, Humphreys played the role of the "watch queen"—that is, someone who keeps watch and warns participants of approaching police or "straight" males who might disrupt the activities. None of the men who went to the restrooms to engage in sex was aware that a researcher was recording his behavior. Humphreys also noted the license plates on the cars of these men, and was able to find their home addresses through public motor-vehicle records. He then interviewed them in their homes but did not inform them of the real reason for the interviews or that he had observed them earlier in the restrooms.

Humphreys was heavily criticized for using deception, for not obtaining informed consent, and for violating the privacy of these men who were engaging in highly stigmatized actions that, were they to be made public, might disrupt their family lives or threaten their jobs. Many sociologists believe that research on such sensitive topics is not simply a matter of confidentiality—that is, of not letting people's identities become known. Rather, these sociologists believe such data should not even be collected at all, because the men obviously were trying to conceal their actions. Social science researchers, it is argued, should respect that privacy.

Humphreys defended his research on the grounds that the confidentiality of his subjects was maintained and the results of the study were of significant scientific value. In fact, no one else has devised another method to study such sexual behavior. Humphreys discovered that the men who engage in this type of sexual activity were not unusual or deviant in the rest of their lives and, for the most part, were normal, respectable citizens with a rather unusual sexual outlet. Humphreys believed that the greater understanding of what had been considered to be deviant sexual conduct justifies the threat to privacy that these men experienced. In addition, the public setting in which they performed their acts, he argued, reduced their claim of a right to privacy.

Another field study illustrates further difficulties in protecting people's privacy. When research describes an actual group or community of people, a common practice is to report results by giving fictitious names to the people and places to protect privacy. This procedure works fairly well as long as researchers do not become so detailed in their descriptions of places, events, and people that the protection afforded by fictitious names is undermined. A now infamous example of this was *Small Town in Mass Society*, by Arthur Vidich and Joseph Bensman. First published in 1958, this observational community study described the power relationships and local governmental operations in a small town the authors called Springdale (Whyte, 1958). The authors had assured all the people they interviewed that confidentiality would be maintained, and no identities were directly revealed. However, it was easy for the residents of the small community to recognize the people and events described in the highly detailed report. Because the study was critical of some residents of Springdale, these people understandably became outraged. Local newspapers vociferously attacked the researchers for betraying the community. The townspeople even held a Fourth of July parade that featured a full manure spreader carrying mired effigies of the authors. To avoid such breaches of confidentiality, one must balance enthusiasm for producing a highly detailed account against the ethical obligation to fully protect the identities of those observed.

Single-system research requires particular caution in this regard. As we will explain in Chapter 11, single-system research involves observing changes in the feelings or behavior of an individual over a period of time. Furthermore, the clients in these studies often suffer from some conditions, such as a mental disorder, that might lead to stigmatization should others find out about it. Therefore great care must be taken to ensure that people's identities are not unintentionally revealed in the process of describing the case. Researchers often must tread a fine line between providing sufficient case detail and minimizing the risk of identifying a client. Final reports should always be written with sensitivity to this issue.

As these two case studies show, the right to privacy often is a difficult ethical issue to resolve. Researchers have come up with three major ways to deal with the problem of protecting people's privacy: (1) Let subjects edit their data; (2) keep the data anonymous; and (3) keep the data confidential.

Editing the Data. One very effective way to protect privacy is to offer participants the opportunity, after the data has been collected, to destroy any data they wish to keep private. This has been done in studies of couples and family problems that use audio or video recordings of interactions between family members (Margolin, 2005). Even though the couples and families consent to the recording, investigators, sensitive to the issue of privacy, sometimes offer the opportunity for participants to review the recordings and edit out anything they wish. The assumption is that, despite agreeing to participate, family members might do something on the spur of the moment that they would prefer not be made public. Surprisingly, few family members exercise this option. This and other research suggests that people are generally more tolerant of invasions of privacy than researchers might expect. Nonetheless, it should always be the research subject's decision; the researcher should never assume that people will be tolerant of invasions or breaches of their privacy.

Anonymity. A second means of ensuring privacy is to accord the participants **anonymity**, which means that no one, including the researcher, can link any data to a particular respondent. This can be accomplished by not including any identifying names or numbers with the data collected. True anonymity means that even the researcher can never link data to a particular respondent. This method of protecting privacy is ideal, because the data are collected in such a way that it is impossible for anyone to determine which data come from which individual. In many research situations, however, it is not possible or feasible to collect data in this fashion, so researchers turn to confidentiality.

Confidentiality. A third way of protecting privacy is through **confidentiality**, which means ensuring that information about or data collected from those who participate in a study are not made public in a way that can be linked to an individual. Researchers, of course, commonly release their data to the public, but usually only in aggregate forms— that is, reporting on how a whole group responded rather than how specific individuals responded. In many studies, the data are not of a sensitive nature, and thus confidentiality would seem to be less important; but it is impossible to predict what bits of data all participants will want to be kept confidential. Because aggregate and anonymous reporting of results is all that is necessary in most research studies, confidentiality is routinely extended to encourage people's participation and honest responses.

It is worth pointing out that anonymity and confidentiality are quite distinct. With confidentiality, the researcher can link responses to particular respondents but does not release this information publicly; with anonymity, even the researchers cannot link responses to particular respondents. So if a researcher sends out mailed questionnaires that are returned with no names or other identifiers on them, then the respondents have true anonymity. If the same questionnaires are mailed back with a name or any other identifier on them, however, then only confidentiality is possible, because the researcher can link responses to respondents. Even if the identifiers are removed as soon as the questionnaire is received, it would still be ethical to make promises of confidentiality only, because the researcher could link responses to respondents at the point when the questionnaires are received. Obviously, it is unethical to tell respondents that they will have confidentiality when they will not, but it also is wrong to claim that responses will be anonymous when all that will actually be protected is confidentiality.

In some cases, confidentiality can be breached merely by a person's involvement in a research project becoming known. If it becomes known, for example, that an individual was part of a study of drug users, then knowledge that the individual is a drug user has become public even if none of the data collected from that individual has been made public. So one aspect of confidentiality is to ensure that the identities of those who are research subjects are kept hidden, especially when that research is sensitive.

Confidentiality also can be threatened when third parties, such as the people sponsoring the research or the courts, seek to identify research participants. Intrusion by a sponsor is relatively easy to avoid, however. When establishing a research agreement with a sponsoring agency or an organization, one should make clear in the agreement that identities will not be revealed under any circumstances. If the sponsor objects, then researchers should refuse to accept the agreement. We have more to say about sponsors and ethics later in this chapter.

Court and Legislative Challenges to Confidentiality. The courts as well as some laws and statutes pose a more complicated threat to confidentiality. Most communications that physicians, lawyers, and clergy have with their clients are protected from judicial subpoena. Social workers in their clinical capacity also are afforded such protection in many instances, although the degree of protection varies with agency settings and jurisdictions. Social researchers, however, do not have a legal protection of privileged communication with the people from whom they gather data (Kimmel, 1988; Reece & Siegal, 1986). In addition, physicians, most human service professionals, and, in some cases, researchers are required by many state laws to report to public agencies when they observe evidence for mistreatment of children or the elderly. Thus, courts or public agencies may subpoena research data that reveal participants' identities, and failure to comply with such a subpoena renders researchers open to charges of contempt of court. Actually, social science researchers have been treated somewhat inconsistently by the courts in civil cases. During a civil suit in California, for example, the court refused to force a researcher to reveal the identities of respondents in confidential interviews (Smith, 1981).

In criminal cases, however, the courts generally have held that the right of the public to be protected from criminal activity or the right of suspects to a fair trial supersedes any assurance of confidentiality in research. In one case, for example, the researcher had been making field observations in a restaurant when it was heavily damaged by a suspicious fire (Brajuha & Hallowell, 1986). Police wanted the researcher's field notes to determine whether any evidence of arson could be substantiated. One court squashed a subpoena for the field notes, but another upheld it. Eventually, a compromise was reached: The researcher's field notes were considered to be subject to a subpoena, but the researcher was allowed to remove any material that would have violated confidentiality. With rulings like this, the courts seem to recognize that the confidentiality a legitimate social science researcher establishes in a research relationship should be protected if possible while still protecting the rights of the public and criminal suspects.

In another case, a sociologist actually spent time in jail because he refused to give information in court that he believed violated his promise of confidentiality to his research subjects. Rik Scarce (2005) conducted research on activists in the animal liberation movement during the 1990s. A federal grand jury was investigating break-ins by such activists at university laboratories, and some of the activists in whom the grand jury was interested had been interviewed by Scarce as part of his research. Scarce refused to answer certain questions about these activists that were put to him by the grand jury, because he thought it would violate the confidentiality he had extended to the people he interviewed. He was jailed for four months on contempt-of-court charges. In his study of police interrogators described earlier in this chapter, Leo was compelled to testify in court under threat of contempt-of-court charges. As these cases illustrate, the courts generally have held that confidential communication between a researcher and a research participant is not protected in criminal cases; however, some courts also have recognized that the confidential relationship is an important and special one, and efforts should be made not to violate it. Because of cases like these, some researchers have called for federal legislation to give social science researchers protection—even if limited—from being compelled to violate their confidential relationships (Leo, 1995; Scarce, 2005).

Concern over a possible subpoena of their research data has led some researchers to adopt elaborate measures to protect that data. For example, it is common to establish computer files with the data identified only by numbers rather than by names. Often, it is unnecessary to retain name identification for research purposes once the data have been collected. In such cases, the names should be destroyed. If name identification is required—for example, because you want to interview the same people at a later time—the names should be stored in a separate computer file. This procedure reduces the possibility of unauthorized persons linking names with data.

One of the best means of securing confidentiality for sensitive research, such as that dealing with AIDS, substance abuse, or criminal behavior, is to use certificates of confidentiality, which were made available by the Public Health Service Act Amendments of 1974 (Beskow, Dame, & Costello, 2008; Bonnie & Wallace, 2003). Certificates of confidentiality are issued by the National Institutes of Health (NIH) and other Health and Human Service offices to protect identifiable research information from forced disclosure. They allow the investigator and others who have access to research records to refuse to disclose identifying information about research participants in any civil, criminal, administrative, legislative, or other proceeding, whether at the federal, state, or local level. By some interpretations, the certificates of confidentiality supersede even laws that require mandatory reporting of instances of mistreatment involving children and the elderly. Certificates generally are awarded only for research on sensitive topics, such as illegal drug use or sexual behavior, and regardless of whether the research project receives federal funding. While some believe that the certificates provide almost complete protection, some courts have insisted on at least partial disclosure of some information that the certificates were meant to protect. While courts take the certificates seriously, they also tend to view them as only one factor that influences how civil and criminal legal disputes should be resolved. At least some courts have taken the position that the constitutional rights of a plaintiff or defendant may supersede the legal protections offered by the certificates (Beskow, Dame, & Costello, 2008; National Cancer Institute, 1998).

So intrusion by courts is a real danger with research, especially regarding some topics, although it is not terribly common. Nonetheless, researchers have an obligation to inform potential subjects accurately about any possible threats to confidentiality that might arise, including what would likely happen should their data be subpoenaed by the courts. The lengths to which investigators will go to protect privacy indicate the importance of this ethical issue. The bottom line is that no one should be threatened with harm to themselves or their reputation as a result of participating in a scientific study.

Harm, Distress, and Benefit

Researchers should avoid exposing participants to physical or mental distress or danger. If the potential for such distress exists in a research investigation, then the participants should be fully informed, the potential research findings should be of sufficient importance to warrant the risk, and no possibility should exist of achieving the results without this risk. People should never be exposed to situations that might cause serious or lasting harm.

Research in the human services rarely involves physical danger, but there are research settings in which psychological distress may be an element. Some studies, for example, have asked people to view such things as pornographic pictures, victims of automobile accidents, and the emaciated inmates of Nazi concentration camps. Certainly, these stimuli can induce powerful reactions—in some cases, emotions that the participants had not expected to experience. A strong emotional reaction, especially an unexpected one, can be very distressful. In some studies, people have been given false feedback about themselves to observe how they respond. People have been told, for example, that they failed an examination or that tests show they have some negative personality characteristics. Any situation in which people might learn something about themselves of which they were previously unaware also can be distressing. Even the minor deceptions that are part of much research can be distressful to people who thought they could not be deceived so easily.

Another area in which social science research contains the potential for harm to those who are studied is in field research of people engaging in stigmatized, deviant, or illegal behavior. The potential harm comes if the researcher says or does anything that might lead the research subjects to be sanctioned for the deviant or illegal behaviors they displayed in front of the researcher (Klockars, 1979). This is a complex topic that will be explored in detail in Chapter 10, but the problem can arise because field research often involves an implicit or explicit agreement between the researcher and those being observed. In this agreement, the observed consent to letting the researcher join them and make observations on them; in return, they expect the researcher will support their illegal or deviant behavior—or at least not do anything to get them in trouble for it. For example, if police interrogations of suspects were likely to include some harsh or even illegal treatment of the suspects, police officers would be unlikely to let a researcher observe the interrogations unless they believed that researcher would support their actions or not report them to authorities or testify against them in court. In other words, the police would likely expect the researcher, in return for being permitted to observe them, to act like fellow officers and support them in their actions. In developing a relationship with the police, the researcher may give the impression that he or she understands this, or the police may just assume that the researcher understands. This actually creates a moral dilemma for the researcher, because either choice of the researcher is morally compromised. If the researcher supports the police and doesn't report the harsh treatment of the suspect, the suspect is harmed by the researcher's actions, but if the researcher supports the suspect and reports the actions, the police are harmed both by having their implicit agreement with the researcher violated and by being sanctioned for their behavior. This kind of ambiguous dilemma is inherent in some field research on deviant lifestyles and is part of what Leo meant by his comment that field work is "a morally ambiguous enterprise" (Leo, 1996, p. 125).

Assuming that the scientific benefits warrant the risk of distress and the participants are fully informed, it is then the researcher's obligation to alleviate the impact of whatever distress actually does occur. As with problems created by deception, alleviating problems related to harm or distress often is accomplished through a debriefing that assesses people's psychological and emotional reactions to the research.

For some social scientists, an ethical standard that rests only on avoiding harm is far too limited. They would argue that those on whom we conduct research also should gain some positive benefit from their participation. This stance has been put forth most clearly by feminist researchers (as discussed in Chapter 2) and collaborative researchers (Nyden et al., 1997; Reinharz, 1992). Viewing research as a two-way street, they argue that both the researcher and the research subject should gain something positive from the project. Researchers, of course, get data from the research enabling them to publish books and articles, which advances their careers; but what do the research subjects get? This raises the ethical issue of what the research community owes to research subjects. These subjects could be paid for their time and effort, or the research results could be translated into social policies or practices that benefit the community from which the research subjects come. Or, by participating in the research, the subjects might develop knowledge or skills that will enable them to make their own lives better. The point is that, from this perspective, researchers have an ethical obligation not only to not leave research participants worse off, but also to compensate them for their time and effort and, in some way, leave them better off for having participated in the research.

Research in Practice 3.1 explores some of the difficulties surrounding such issues as privacy, confidentiality, harm, and informed consent, especially when the research topic is sensitive.

Sponsored Research

Because much social research is conducted under the auspices of a third-party sponsor, certain ethical considerations arise from that relationship. When research is sponsored, some type of research agreement—essentially, a contract—is developed. Researchers and sponsors alike should exercise great care in drafting this agreement. The potential for ethical problems to arise later is reduced when the research agreement clearly specifies the rights and obligations of the parties involved.

Three areas are of particular concern in sponsored research (King, Henderson, & Stein, 1999).

First, it is common for sponsors to want to retain control over the release of the collected data. The precise conditions of release should be specified in the research agreement to avoid conflicts. One limitation that should not be tolerated, however, is the conditional publication of results—that is, agreeing to publish results only if they turn out a certain way (usually so when they support the preconceived notions of the sponsor). Such conditional publication violates the integrity of the research process and the autonomy of the researcher (Wolfgang, 1981). If the researcher agrees to some other type of limitation on release, however, it must be honored. To do otherwise would be a breach of the agreement and, therefore, unethical.

The second major concern in sponsored research is the nature of the research project itself. The precise purpose and procedures of the study should be specified in the agreement. Ethical questions arise if the researcher heavily modifies the study to cover matters not in the agreement. Often sponsors will allow researchers to use the data gathered for scientific purposes beyond the needs of the sponsor, but it is unethical to agree to do a study that a sponsor wants and then change it for personal reasons so it no longer meets the sponsor's expectations.

A third area of ethical concern in sponsored research relates to the issue of informed consent—namely, revealing the sponsor's identity to participants. Although controversy exists in this regard, some researchers take the stance that truly informed consent can be given only if a participant knows who is sponsoring the study and for what purpose the study is being conducted. Some people might object, for example, to providing data that would help a company better market a product, a political party to better present a candidate, or the government to propagandize its citizens. In fact, studies show that people are less likely to participate in research they know to be sponsored by commercial organizations, which suggests that information about sponsorship can influence the decision of whether to participate (Fox, Crask, & Kim, 1988). Each researcher, then, must carefully consider whether to make the sponsorship of a research

> **RESEARCH IN PRACTICE 3.1**   Practice Effectiveness: Sex Offenders as Participants
>
> Applied social researchers often find themselves doing socially sensitive research, research on people who arouse intense and sometimes negative emotions in others—murderers, rapists, prostitutes, or illegal drug users, to name only a few. Such research often involves evaluation research or program evaluations (discussed in Chapters 1 and 12) and can be very challenging, especially in terms of maintaining ethical standards.
>
> One example of such research is a program evaluation assessing two methods of treating people convicted of child molestation (Jenkins-Hall & Osborn 1994). The goal of the research was to provide observational evidence regarding which treatment approach is more effective. In conducting the research, the researchers had to consider the rights of the child-molester participants as well as the safety of staff. There were potential negative consequences for each group from participating in the research. The researchers identified three general areas of concern:
>
> 1. informed consent and voluntary participation;
> 2. confidentiality of data and privacy; and
> 3. protection against dangers that a participant may pose to himself or to others.
>
> Informed consent was considered to be so important by the researchers that they incorporated a multiphase consent process requiring participants to give consent at each stage of the process. All clients completed a general consent form that covered the basic requirements of the DHHS. Prior to a comprehensive psychological and social assessment that was a necessary part of the research, the clients completed an evaluation consent form that spelled out the assessment process. Additional consent forms were completed in conjunction with each subsequent treatment component. Given the complexity of the intervention, this multiphase consent process, though unusual, ensured that participants understood the program and were freely consenting to participation throughout the project.
>
> Confidentiality and privacy also were considered to be very important because of the negative consequences that might occur to the molesters if information about their participation in the program were ever released. One protection of privacy was the use of federal certificates of confidentiality. Additional steps also were taken: the project was located in a public office building suite and was not identified as a treatment site for sex offenders. Each participant was given a six-digit ID number that appeared on all documents. Names and other identifying information were removed from all correspondence, consents, and records from referral sources. Staff addressed participants by first name only, and information was never released without signed waivers of confidentiality that specified what information could be released and to whom. Because the program involved the delivery of treatment services, each participant was provided with a client advocate who was a volunteer clinician not affiliated with the project; this advocate's sole responsibility was to protect the rights of the client.
>
> In addressing the issue of harm or distress, the researchers considered not only harm to the participants, but also, given that the participants were convicted sex offenders, potential danger to the staff or members of the local community. Several measures were employed to reduce such risks. One concern for the project was quick detection if a participant were in danger of committing another sexual offense. Researchers argued that the project had an ethical and, perhaps, legal duty to protect potential victims. The project provided each participant with a 24-hour crisis call service as well as therapists to deal with minor crises, such as loss of employment or a breakup with a significant other. Over a two-year period, three cases required involuntary commitment of participants because of deterioration in their mental health status. In several cases where the participant was exhibiting negative signs, he was temporarily removed from the project and offered alternative treatment. If a participant who was at risk of relapse failed to follow the terms of a crisis intervention plan, the director of the project was notified and authorities were alerted. Failure to comply on the part of the participant would result in termination from the project.
>
> To assure the safety of the staff, the program employed a variety of procedures. Staff were directed to have unlisted personal phone numbers, never to reveal home addresses, never to be alone with clients in the suite, and never to enter a room that was lockable from the inside with a client. Each office and work area contained a "panic button" that sounded an alarm in the office and at the university police office. Entry to the project was strictly controlled so that client interaction with other office building occupants was minimal. Participants were routinely debriefed after treatment sessions to ensure that they would not leave the center in a distressed, agitated, or aroused state.

project explicit. At a minimum, to deceive people regarding the sponsorship of a study to gain their participation is certainly unethical.

Scientific Misconduct and Fraud

When a research project reaches the final stage—that is, the dissemination of results—the primary consideration regarding ethical conduct shifts from avoiding harm to the participants in research to making sure the consumers of the research are not adversely affected. Results of a study typically are communicated in the form of a report to a sponsoring organization, a publication in a professional journal, or possibly a news release to the media. The preeminent ethical obligation in this regard is not to disclose inaccurate, deceptive, or fraudulent results. To do so risks misleading scientists who depend on previous research to guide their own work. Ethical violations concerning disclosure of results undermine the very nature of the scientific process, which, as we saw in Chapter 2, depends upon building future knowledge on the foundation of existing knowledge. If we cannot depend on the accuracy of existing knowledge, then the scientific endeavor is threatened. In that case, the credibility of all research is damaged by such violations. Furthermore, deceptive or fraudulent disclosures of research results can cause human service practitioners to design useless—or even dangerous—interventions based on previous faulty studies.

Many ethical violations can occur in the process of reporting research (Gibelman & Gelman, 2001). **Fraud** is the deliberate falsification, misrepresentation, or plagiarizing of the data, findings, or ideas of others. These include such things as falsifying data, embellishing research reports, reporting research that has not been conducted, or manipulating data in a deceptive way. **Misconduct** is a broader concept that includes not only fraud, but also carelessness or bias in recording and reporting data, mishandling data, and incomplete reporting of results. Other questionable practices are irresponsible claims of authorship (listing coauthors who did not really make contributions to the research) and premature release of results to the public without peer review.

Estimates regarding the actual amount of scientific misconduct that occurs suggest the problem is relatively small. The Office of Research Integrity of the DHHS, which keeps track of such matters, reports that 100 to 200 new cases of alleged misconduct are brought to its attention each year, and many of these allegations prove to be unfounded (Office of Research Integrity, 2010). Of course, underreporting could hide a larger problem, but even if the number of cases is small, any misconduct in research can still damage the credibility of all research and place human service clients—and, by extension, human service providers—at risk.

The issue of who has the responsibility for detecting scientific misconduct is still very controversial (Gibelman & Gelman, 2001). For many years, governmental agencies that fund research pushed this responsibility onto the shoulders of universities and other institutions where research was actually conducted. By the late 1980s, however, both the NIH and the DHHS had established their own offices to watch for misconduct. Yet, most scientists still consider protection against misconduct to be primarily a responsibility of the scientific community, which uses two major mechanisms to detect fraud: *peer review* and *replication*. There are, however, limitations to each of these mechanisms, as illustrated by a case of fraud in medical research involving Dr. Robert Slutsky (Engler et al., 1987).

The prolific Dr. Slutsky had authored or coauthored 137 articles on cardiological and radiological research over a seven-year period. During an evaluation of his appointment as a researcher at a university, questions were raised about duplicate data in two of his papers. In the ensuing investigation, 12 articles were deemed fraudulent, and 48 were considered questionable. In some cases, articles described experiments that had never been conducted. How is it that these articles eluded the net of peer review by respected medical journals? There seemed to have been two problems: First, peer review of article submissions cannot detect plausible, internally consistent fabrications. Second, the sheer number of research articles submitted to publications for review requires a large number of qualified reviewers who understand both the methodology and the content of the article.

If peer review does not detect and deter fraud, then will replication solve the problem? It might. The effectiveness of replication, however, has been severely crippled by the modern research system, because research funds often are not appropriated for replication. Agencies prefer to fund research efforts that delve into new areas. Furthermore, when replication does occur, it tends to be reserved for projects that have produced unusual results. Fraudulent studies that enhance the prestige of researchers but do not run counter to accepted findings in a field are not likely to arouse enough attention to warrant replication (Engler et al., 1987).

Beyond peer review and replication, there are several ways of reducing the chances of fraud or, if it occurs, detecting it. One is to supervise novice researchers until they demonstrate good practices, ethical conduct, and technical competency. Second, organizations need to guard against overly prolific researchers. Senior researchers and coauthors should not simply allow their names to be associated with research reports without carefully examining the work. Third, journals can reduce fraud by requiring more complete data to be submitted to reviewers, even if all the data cannot be included in the published article. When fraud is detected, journals have a responsibility to make the fraud public so that others will not unsuspectingly base research or treatments on the fraudulent material.

Though not as unethical as purposeful deception, careless errors in research have the same effect of creating misinformation. Social researchers owe the scientific community carefully conducted research that is as free of error as possible. As with fraud, errors are discovered and corrected either through critical review of research and reanalysis of data or through replication. For example, a study from the 1980s claimed to document substantial negative economic consequences of divorce for women; this study was an important foundation for developing social policy. Partly because these findings were somewhat at variance with the results of other studies, a reanalysis of the data was undertaken (Peterson, 1996). This reanalysis showed that the original conclusions were partly the result of errors in the original analysis. The reanalysis showed that women do suffer economically after divorce, but not nearly as severely as the original analysis had suggested. Had the original research conclusions not been based on an inaccurate analysis, subsequent policy development might have been different.

Beyond the problems of fraud and carelessness, researchers also have an obligation to report their results thoroughly. Researchers must take care to ensure that what they report does not give a distorted picture of the overall results. In addition, researchers should point out any limitations that might qualify their findings. Researchers also must be concerned with how the findings are applied to human service practice and policy decisions. Research projects on the effectiveness of arrest as a deterrent to intimate partner violence (see Chapter 10 for a detailed discussion) are excellent examples. A study conducted in Minneapolis has been singled out as a primary catalyst for widespread adoption of pro-arrest policies. Critics have argued that propaganda generated by some of the participating agencies was a key factor in the study's impact on policy, an impact they say was unjustified by a single study. Subsequent replications in several cities failed to support the findings of the Minneapolis study and have underscored the call for caution in rushing to apply findings to practice (Sherman, 1992). This was not a case of publishing fraudulent results or misrepresenting data, but rather an issue of the researcher's role in applying the research findings.

Scientific Advocacy

Scientific knowledge rarely remains the exclusive domain of the scientific community but, typically, finds its way into public life in the form of inventions, technological developments, or social policy. This raises potential ethical dilemmas in terms of the role of researchers as advocates for particular uses of their research results. What responsibility, if any, do scientists have for overseeing the use to which their results are put? To what extent should scientists become advocates for applying knowledge in a particular way? Quite naturally disagreements arise on how to resolve these issues. This controversy is compounded in the case of human service researchers, because their research normally is initiated with some explicit, clinical application in mind. The classic approach to these issues derives from the exhortations of the sociologist Max Weber (1946, orig. pub. 1922) that science should be "value-free." Social scientists, according to Weber, should create knowledge, not apply it. Therefore, they have no special responsibility for the ultimate use to which that knowledge is put. Furthermore, according to Weber, they are under no obligation to advocate particular uses of scientific knowledge. Indeed, advocacy is frowned on as threatening objectivity, which is a central concern of science. So although remaining value-free is difficult, many argue that abandoning the effort would be disastrous, for it would prevent us from acquiring an accurate body of knowledge about human social behavior and might threaten the researcher's credibility as a disinterested expert (Gibbs, 1983; Gordon, 1988; Halfpenny, 1982).

Karl Marx (1964, orig. pub. 1848) originally developed the opposite stance in this controversy. Marx championed the cause of the poor and downtrodden; he believed that social researchers should bring strong moral commitments to their work and strive to change unfair or immoral conditions. Following Marx, some modern researchers believe that social research should be guided by personal and political values and directed toward alleviating social ills (Brunswick-Heinemann, 1981; Fay, 1987). Furthermore, scientists should advocate for uses of their research by others that would help accomplish these personal goals.

Sociologist Alvin Gouldner (1976) developed a compromise position on the value-free controversy. Gouldner pointed to the obvious—namely, that scientists have values just as other human beings do. Furthermore, he noted, those values can influence research in so many subtle ways that their effects can never be totally eliminated. So instead of denying or ignoring the existence or impact of these personal values, scientists need to be acutely aware of and up front about them in research reports. Being thus forewarned, consumers of their research are better able to assess whether the findings have been influenced by personal bias. In addition, Gouldner argued that social scientists have not only the right, but also the duty to promote the constructive use of scientific knowledge (Gouldner, 1976). Because someone will make decisions concerning the use of scientific knowledge, scientists themselves are best equipped to make those judgments. As Gouldner states, technical competence would seem to provide a person with some warrant for making value judgments. People who take this position view the value-free stance as a potentially dangerous dereliction of a responsibility that accrues to scientists by virtue of their expertise and role in developing new knowledge.

Clinician-researchers, in particular, may be attracted by this stance. Because their research is conducted, in part, to advance the practice goals of the profession, they would probably view ensuring that any clinical application of the results be faithful to the outcome of the research as one of their duties. Thus, human service researchers are more likely than many other behavioral scientists to take a strong stand in favor of advocacy.

Nothing is wrong with researchers openly pressing for the application of scientific knowledge in ways they deem to be desirable—so long as their advocacy is tempered with respect for objectivity. The danger of advocacy is that scientists can come to feel so strongly about the issues they promote that those feelings hamper the objective collection and analysis of data.

Protecting Vulnerable Clients

Human service clients, because they often are involuntary recipients of services, may find themselves vulnerable against pressures to cooperate in research projects conducted by the organizations that provide them with services. Such clients are likely to be sought out as research subjects, either because they often are viewed as being deviant in some way, and therefore interesting to study, or because they may be easier than other groups to locate and keep track of during a research project.

Welfare recipients, children in day care settings, patients in public mental hospitals, and participants in job-training programs, to name only a few, are likely candidates for participation in social research projects. In fact, it is common for operators of new or special programs to be required by their funding sources to research the effects of their programs as a condition for receiving those funds. Although such safeguards as codes of ethics and governmental regulations may serve as useful guides, special obligations fall on human service practitioners to safeguard their clients from unreasonable pressures to participate in research.

A crucial issue in this regard is the matter of voluntary and informed consent. Can clients actually give consent freely? This is one of the reasons that much research using prison inmates as subjects has been discontinued: It is debatable how free inmates really are to give consent. If participation in the research brings significant rewards in the form of separate living quarters or greater privacy, these rewards may be almost coercive in the Spartan, degrading, and often dangerous world of the prison inmate. Although participation in the research is, on the face of it, voluntary, inmates may not seriously weigh the disadvantages or dangers of the research when their participation is perceived as a means of avoiding assault or rape.

Similar ethical questions also arise with research on people who have significant psychopathologies. If the psychopathology involves defective comprehension or impaired insight, then the subjects may be unable to give truly informed consent. Research on such a population would have to be approached very carefully and could be justified only if it could not be done on a less vulnerable group. If the same research goals could be accomplished with a less vulnerable group, then that would be the route to follow. If it were decided to do research on a group with significant psychopathology, then informed consent should be approached in ways that protect potential participants from even covert coercion. For example, consent could be sought by some party other than the researchers (to avoid the force of authority), or it could be sought in the presence of a relative, friend, or other advocate for the individual (to provide the social support to allow a refusal). If the psychopathology completely impairs the ability to give consent, then most forms of research would be unethical unless it could be shown that either the patient or society would benefit significantly and the research could be done in no other way (Oeye, Bjelland, & Skorpen, 2007).

The problem of voluntary consent may be somewhat more subtle among other recipients of human services. Even if refusal to participate is not linked to termination of benefits, clients might not be sure of this, and thus might be disinclined to take the risk of finding out. In addition, the reading level of clients receiving public assistance often is less than that of the eighth grade; yet the reading level necessary to comprehend many welfare documents is above 13 years of education. Thus it may be that clients who are accustomed to being confused by welfare requirements might not aggressively seek to determine their right to refuse participation in a research project. We are not suggesting that research never be conducted on prisoners or recipients of public welfare. Rather, clinician–researchers need to exercise additional caution—and, in some cases, possibly forgo valuable research projects—in the interests of ensuring truly voluntary informed consent.

Research in Practice 3.2 discusses ethical issues involving harm, misconduct, and protecting vulnerable clients and what can be done to protect clients who might be negatively affected.

Withholding Treatment for Research Purposes

An issue of particular concern to human service providers is the research practice of withholding treatment from a control group to assess whether a given treatment is effective. The **control group** serves as a comparison group. If a group receiving the treatment shows more improvement than the control group over a certain span of time, we can feel justified in claiming that the treatment brought about the improvement. With no control group,

> **RESEARCH IN PRACTICE 3.2** *Program Evaluation: Vulnerable Clients at Risk*
>
> Science must maintain constant vigilance against research that harms people or is a product of fraud and misconduct. This is especially true in applied research where social or medical interventions may affect people's lives. Several recent cases of such ethical violation demonstrate this point. In 1996, the internationally respected researcher Dr. Francis Collins, famous for his work on the government's project to map all human genes, retracted five research papers because a junior colleague had fabricated data. The studies, which were on leukemia, had been published in leading scientific journals (Altman, 1996). Another case involved the cellular biologist Robert P. Liburdy, who published studies purporting to demonstrate a link between exposure to electromagnetic fields and cancer. Eventually, the Office of Research Integrity of the DHHS concluded that much of his data was fictitious, but not before several multimillion-dollar liability suits had been initiated against power companies (*Federal Register*, 1999).
>
> When such fraud occurs in the context of human service research, the consequences can be especially chilling. The case of Dr. Stephen Breuning came to light in the 1980s. He had published research alleging beneficial effects of certain drugs for the control of behavior in severely developmentally disabled individuals. Social interventions were implemented to help many developmentally disabled children based on the results of his research. Yet, Breuning's results were based, in part, on falsified data. Eventually, the case led to a criminal indictment, and Dr. Breuning was sentenced to 60 days in a halfway house and five years of probation. However, detecting, documenting, and acting on this fraud was a long battle (Garfield & Welljams-Dorof, 1990).
>
> A recent example of ethical violations in the protection of human subjects in applied research comes from the University of Oklahoma, where it was alleged that the principal researcher and an oversight official repeatedly violated federal regulations meant to protect human subjects in cancer research (Pound, 2000). These researchers reportedly were unqualified to conduct the research, the vaccine injected had not been properly tested, and the IRB had failed to monitor the tests. What makes this case especially significant for this illustration is not only the nature of the violations, but also the manner in which the ethical violations came to light. It was not a high-level scientist or an IRB that detected the ethical problems; rather, it was a registered nurse with a limited background in clinical research who had been recently hired at the project and was troubled by what she saw as violations of safety rules, suppression of information, and lying to patients and federal regulators. When her university superiors failed to address her concerns, she didn't give up; instead, she advocated for the patients by writing to federal health regulators. As a consequence, government regulators shut down all government-funded research at the Tulsa

however, we cannot say with confidence that the improvement shown by the treatment group was the result of the treatment. It could be that the improvement would have occurred even in the absence of the treatment. The control group, which is comparable to the treatment group in all ways except that it does not receive the treatment, makes it possible to rule out this possibility. Control groups thus are very important to the ability to state whether an independent variable causes change in a dependent variable (see Chapters 2 and 10). In fact, the evidence-based practice approaches discussed in Chapter 1 give the most credence to evidence resulting from research designs that use random assignment of people to treatment and control groups. These EBP approaches argue that such research designs provide the "best" evidence.

Presumably, research is being conducted on some treatment because that treatment is believed to be effective. Herein lies the ethical dilemma: Some service providers believe it is unethical to withhold a treatment that might help people. They believe that withholding treatment deprives people in the control group of the possibility of improvement. This is a serious problem that is not easy to resolve, but there are a number of issues to consider: First, we might ask whether it is ethical to use untested treatments. We pointed out in Chapter 1 that evidence-based approaches to human service professions explicitly caution against the use of treatments without proven campus and directed the university to address the problems. The case emphasizes the importance for all human service professionals, not just scientists, to understand the principles of research and research ethics. Although cases of ethical violation in social and medical research may be rare, detection and prevention of such conduct may well depend on the vigilance of the human service practitioner who encounters the subjects of research.

These cases highlight several disturbing issues in ethics, research, and human service practice. First, some of this research managed to pass through the filters of review panels and institutional procedures without question. How well can the institutionalized research system prevent fraudulent work? Second, when unethical practices are discovered, who bears the responsibility for alerting practitioners and the public to potentially harmful implications? In manufacturing, the government can require product recalls, but how do we protect the public from the implementation of fraudulent research? Third, how do we safeguard those who detect potential fraud? In many cases, the people most likely to discover such fraud are colleagues, assistants, students, and others close to the research. To the extent that these people perceive disclosure as risking unpleasant consequences for themselves, they will be reluctant to come forward. Finally, the slow, plodding nature of the bureaucratic process raises the question of what can be done to process cases efficiently while also protecting the rights of individuals accused of fraud.

A close study of the Breuning case suggests that the procedures of the scientific process do afford some protection against the widespread impact of fraudulent data on both science and practice. Based on the assumption that influential research will be widely cited in other research studies, an ingenious study used the *Science Citation Index* and the *Social Science Citation Index* to examine the number of citations made by other researchers to Breuning's 20 publications between 1980 and 1988 (Garfield & Welljams-Dorof, 1990). The 200 citations found suggested that his work was influential. However, when the researchers evaluated who had made the citations and the *context* of the citations to better understand the effects of the Breuning studies, things looked a bit different. For example, of the 200 citations, 40 percent were self-citations by Breuning or his coauthors. In addition, following the publication of a critical review of Breuning's work, citations to his work by others declined sharply. Finally, of 38 studies judged to be materially affected by Breuning's publications, 21 led to negative conclusions, disagreeing with his findings or criticizing his methods. The authors concluded that the pattern of citations suggests the process of scientific publication and critique is capable of purging science, to a degree, of fraudulent studies.

effectiveness. Providing services is expensive and time-consuming, and it also raises clients' expectations for improvement. Is it ethical to do this when no evidence documents that the treatment will be beneficial? For the most part, we would not think of marketing new medicines without a thorough test of their effects, both positive and negative. We should expect no less from the human services we offer.

Alternatives sometimes can be found to withholding treatment. One alternative would be to offer the control group a treatment that is known to be effective and then see whether the new treatment provides more or less improvement. In this way, all clients are receiving a treatment that is either known to be or suspected of being effective.

In the study of the effectiveness of suicide intervention programs, for example, one certainly would be reluctant to evaluate a new intervention by using a control group that received no intervention at all. One study of outpatient interventions targeting suicidal young adults used a randomized experiment in which subjects were assigned either to a new experimental treatment or to a control group that received a treatment that had been commonly used for these interventions. Although both groups showed improvement, the experimental treatment was more effective in retaining the highest-risk participants (Rudd, Rajab, & Orman, 1996).

Another alternative to withholding treatment would be to delay giving the treatment to the

Information Technology in Research — Ethical Challenges in Internet-Based Research

The Internet offers a vast new arena in which to conduct social science research. After all, the online interactions of people represent yet another setting in which human beings engage with one another, and these interactions often are readily accessible and convenient to researchers. However, not all people warmly welcome scientific scrutiny in this venue. Although it has great promise, use of the Internet as a vehicle for research raises new and complicated questions about the application of ethical principles, such as informed consent and privacy.

Eysenbach and Till (2001) use the term "Internet communities" to refer to the various ways people now communicate using the web. Included are discussion boards on websites, chat rooms, social networking sites, blogs, and newsgroups. All these venues could be settings in which social researchers gather data. Some of these communities address sensitive issues such as dealing with breast cancer or surviving childhood sexual abuse. In assessing what constitutes ethical research in such communities, most professional research organizations, such as the Association of Internet Researchers (Ess et al., 2002) and the American Sociological Association (1997), would agree that informed consent is required when the behavior is sensitive and occurs in a private setting. Conversely, it is ethical to collect data from people when their behavior is public and nonsensitive without gaining informed consent.

However, with research on Internet communities, the complexities only begin with such a straightforward statement because what is considered "public" on the Internet can be complicated and ambiguous. In fact, one ethicist (Sveningsson Elm, 2009) has argued that the terms "public" and "private," when referencing the Internet, represent not a dichotomy but a continuum. In other words, we have to ask how public or how private an Internet venue is. So some online environments seem clearly *public* (such as chat rooms or web pages) because anyone can access them. Social networking sites, on the other hand, might be called *semipublic* because they involve some registration or membership before one can use, or fully use, the site. Some Internet venues are available (sometimes after registration) only to members of a particular company or organization, such as parts of a company's website, and these might be called *semiprivate* websites. Finally, *private* online settings, such as private rooms within chat rooms, are open only to people who are invited.

Generally, researchers would agree that public Internet sites do not require informed consent while private sites do. The other two possibilities call for more judgment and assessment. In making these decisions, researchers might call on fellow researchers or ethicists to help them explore the issues, as well as seek guidance from IRBs. Considering the thoughts of ethicists such as Eysenbach and Till and Sveningsson Elm, we can suggest some considerations in deciding whether to conduct research online or whether informed consent is required:

- *Intrusiveness*—Will the research involve passive analysis of Internet postings versus active involvement of the researcher in the community by participating in communications?
- *Perceived privacy*—Do participants perceive their community as private, possibly because it is a closed group requiring registration or because group norms define what transpires there as private?
- *Vulnerability and harm*—Will the intrusion of the researcher or publication of results potentially upset or bring harm to individuals or the community as a whole?
- *Confidentiality and anonymity*—Can confidentiality or anonymity truly be protected given the potential of online search technology (if verbatim quotes are used in a research report, search engines may be able to locate the source of the quote)?

When a researcher does want to obtain informed consent in such online research, how does one go about doing so? One suggestion is to send a message to the mailing list describing the research and giving participants the opportunity to withdraw. A second option is to retrospectively ask persons whose postings will be used to give permission. In terms of privacy, Eysenbach and Till point out a special wrinkle that can thwart privacy. A researcher may judiciously separate identifiers from comments, but if the report includes verbatim quotes, then the original participant comments sometimes can be located on the Internet by anyone using a search engine.

Thus, research via the Internet is a new field where social scientists, IRBs, and funding agencies are confronting new challenges related to ethics and finding ways to address basic ethical issues in this rapidly changing medium.

control group and make the comparisons between those receiving treatment and the control group over this period of time. For example, in a study of two different approaches to controlling people's smoking, all participants in the study were told that, if they were randomly placed in the group that would not receive immediate treatment, not only would they receive treatment when the study was over, they would receive whichever treatment the study showed to be most effective (Coehlo, 1983). This resolves the ethical problem by ensuring that all participants will receive treatment at some point.

In cases without such alternatives, however, clinician–researchers must use the risk–benefit approach: Does the benefit to be gained from the research outweigh the risks of withholding treatment from the people in the control group? If we were studying people at high risk of suicide, we would be cautious about withholding treatment. In the treatment of nonassertiveness, on the other hand, we might decide that a delay of a few weeks in treatment would not be terribly detrimental and that whatever damage occurred could be undone once treatment was initiated. As with so many other ethical issues, this is ultimately a judgmental one over which clinician–researchers will continue to agonize.

CODES OF ETHICS

A point emphasized in this chapter is that ethical judgments are difficult and often controversial because they involve interpretation and assessment. Most professional organizations establish written codes of ethics to serve as guides for their members to follow. These codes by no means settle all debate, but they do stand as a foundation from which professionals can begin to formulate ethical decisions. These codes can be found at the websites and in publications of the major organizations of professionals who conduct research in the social sciences and human services. See, for example, the web pages of these organizations:

- American Sociological Association (http://www.asanet.org)
- National Association of Social Workers (http://www.naswdc.org)
- Association for Applied and Clinical Sociology (http://www.aacsnet.net)
- American Association for Public Opinion Research (http://www.aapor.org)

The codes of ethics of other social science and human service professions would be similar to these.

REVIEW AND CRITICAL THINKING

Main Points

- What is ethical in research and practice is based on human values and varies as those values change.
- The mistreatment of minorities in research has been a major impetus to the development of ethical standards for research in the United States and abroad.
- Social research typically is evaluated in terms of risks versus benefits, with some "questionable practices" allowed if the research promises sufficient benefits.
- Informed consent assures participants the ability to determine their own destiny, but may prevent the use of some research methods and force the study of only those persons who volunteer.
- Some level of deception is sometimes used in research, but whether or under what conditions deception is acceptable has been highly controversial.
- Research subjects have a right to privacy, and it can be protected by letting them edit data about themselves from a data set, keeping the

- data anonymous, or keeping the data confidential.
- Confidentiality and anonymity are not the same thing. Intrusion by third parties, such as courts of law, occasionally can be a threat to the guarantee of confidentiality.
- Exposing subjects to physical or mental distress should be kept to a minimum and should never be done without fully informed consent. Subjects should be thoroughly debriefed at the conclusion of the research.
- When conducting research for a sponsor, many ethical difficulties can be avoided by a detailed research agreement that covers and reveals topics such as the purpose and nature of the research, the rights of publication, and the sponsor of the research.
- Researchers have an obligation to report their results fully and honestly and avoid any kind of scientific misconduct or fraud. Replication is a major tool of science for correcting research errors and fraudulent reports.
- It is the researcher's own decision regarding the degree to which he or she will become an advocate; however, caution is required so that objectivity is not undermined.
- Because of their disadvantaged status, human service clients often are vulnerable to coercion to participate in research projects and, therefore, require special protection.
- Withholding treatment from control groups raises an ethical dilemma, but it often is justified when testing unproved approaches.
- Most professional organizations have established codes of ethics that provide useful guidelines for making ethical decisions.

Important Terms for Review

anonymity	control group	fraud (scientific)	misconduct (scientific)
confidentiality	ethics	informed consent	privacy

Critical Thinking

Along with human service practitioners and policy makers, people in their everyday lives grapple with some of the same issues that are described as research ethics issues in this chapter. Just as researchers operate in a context of moral principles and cultural values, all people have moral, philosophical, or theological beliefs that tell them what constitutes proper behavior. Everyone must apply these beliefs or standards to particular situations in deciding how to behave. You can learn some lessons from this chapter in terms of how to critically analyze ethical issues in practice and policy settings as well as in your everyday life:

1. In your everyday relationships with other people, how do things like informed consent, deception, confidentiality, privacy, and the other ethical issues discussed in this chapter come into play, especially as they relate to assessing information? Give an example of each from your everyday life or from practice or policy realms.
2. How do we regulate ethical behavior in our everyday lives?
3. What "codes of ethics" do we rely on in order to do this? How are these codes of ethics similar to or different from the codes of ethics of the professional organizations discussed in the chapter?

Exploring the Internet

Use the search engines on the Internet to locate the web pages of professional organizations other than those already mentioned in the text—research organizations, such as the American Psychological Association or the American Society of Criminology, or practitioner organizations, such as the American Medical Association or the American Nurses Association. Explore those sites for topics related to ethics. Also use the search engine to look for a variety of key words such as "ethics," "science," "research fraud," "IRB," or some combination of these.

A site that is especially informative about IRBs is http://www.irbforum.org, which is the IRB Forum, maintained by a university research institute and a hospital in Pennsylvania. It has links to wide-ranging resources on IRBs. An invaluable source for ethics information is the Office of Research Integrity (http://www.ori.hhs.gov), located in the Office of Public Health and Science in the DHHS. The mission of the ORI is to promote integrity in biomedical and behavioral research supported by the PHS. You can access the full text of the Belmont Report, the Nuremburg Code, and other major documents.

The NIH has an extremely useful website where ethics materials can be downloaded: The NIH guidebooks cover practically all the issues discussed in this chapter, including certificates of confidentiality. Universities often present their guidelines for research on their websites, so you can learn how their IRBs operate and how they protect human subjects. If you go to a university's web page, you may find a link such as "Guidelines for Researchers" or "Research Policies and Procedures," with issues related to the ethical conduct of research.

Another website is called Ethics in Science (http://www.chem.vt.edu/chem-ed/ethics). This site has links to many resources and other sites related to ethical issues in research. Many of the links relate to the physical and natural sciences. Some apply to the social sciences, however, and many ethical issues span disciplines. A highly recommended Canadian site that does a particularly nice job of explaining key ethics terms is the National Council on Ethics in Human Research (http://www.ncehr-cnerh.org). Another Canadian site especially useful for ethics information related to research on children and families is the Centre for Children and Families in the Justice System (http://www.lfcc.on.ca/ethical.html).

For Further Reading

Caplan, A. L., Ed. (1992). *When Medicine Went Mad*. Totowa, N.J.: Humana Press. This volume contains articles relating to the research conducted by the Nazis during World War II. Although it deals with an extreme situation, it does provide an illustration of what can happen when science "goes mad."

Corey, G., Corey, M. S., & Callanan, P. (2011). *Issues and Ethics in the Helping Professions*. 8th ed. Belmont, Calif.: Brooks/Cole Cengage Learning. A comprehensive review of ethical issues in the many realms of human service practice. Given the linkage between research and practice, the analysis of practice ethics is relevant to clinician–researchers in the human services.

Crossen, C. (1994). *Tainted Truth: The Manipulation of Fact in America*. New York: Simon & Schuster. An enlightening book by a journalist about the many frauds that can be perpetrated by scientists. The author shows how frauds can be artfully crafted, and how they can adversely affect us all.

Forbes Citro, C., Ilgen, D. R., & Bagle, C. (2003). *Protecting Participants and Facilitating Social and Behavioral Sciences Research*. Washington D.C.: The National Academies Press. This report examines three key issues related to human participation in social research: obtaining informed, voluntary consent from prospective participants; guaranteeing the confidentiality of information collected from participants; and using appropriate review procedures for "minimal-risk" research.

Lee, R. (1993). *Doing Research on Sensitive Topics.* Newbury Park, Calif.: Sage. Ethical issues become especially important and complicated when doing research on sensitive topics, and this author suggests ethical guidelines for navigating such treacherous waters.

Mertens, D. M., & Ginsberg, P. E., Eds. (2009). *The Handbook of Social Research Ethics.* Thousand Oaks, Calif.: Sage. The handbook provides a comprehensive understanding of the history, theory, philosophy, and implementation of applied social research ethics through a collection of writings by eminent, international scholars across the social and behavioral sciences and education. It also examines the ethical dilemmas that arise in the relationship between research practice and social justice issues.

Washington, H. A. (2006). *Medical Apartheid: The Dark History of Medical Experimentation on Black Americans from Colonial Times to the Present.* New York: Doubleday. The author provides a comprehensive history of medical experimentation on African Americans. The book details the way both slaves and freedmen were used in hospitals for experiments conducted without a hint of informed consent—a tradition that the author argues continues today within some black populations.

Zimbardo, P. G. (2007). *The Lucifer Effect: Understanding How Good People Turn Evil.* New York: Random House. The researcher who conducted the now famous Stanford prisoner experiment addresses the question: What makes good people do bad things? Although research ethics is not the primary subject, the author's discussion of his controversial study provides rich illustrations of research ethics.

Class Exercises for Competency Assessment

3.1. **[Ethics] [Critical Thinking] [Research & Practice]**
A criminal justice major needs to do a research project as a course requirement. The student is working part-time as an undercover store detective in a large discount department store, and he proposes to do observational research on the shoplifting behavior he encounters as a part of his job. In addition, he has access to store records on suspects who have been apprehended for shoplifting in the past. He also plans to interview a sample of shoppers about shoplifting without disclosing that he is a store detective. Discuss how the issues of informed consent, confidentiality, and disclosure of results apply to this case.

3.2. What recommendations could you make to the student in Exercise 3.1 to safeguard the ethical standards for research in this case? Consider each of the ethical issues discussed in this chapter. Do you think the study could be done ethically at all? Support your conclusion.

3.3. **[Ethics] [Critical Thinking] [Research & Practice]**
Suppose you are working in an alcoholism treatment unit, and a proposal is made to initiate a new treatment program that looks promising but is largely untested. Under what conditions do you think it would be acceptable to use a control group as a comparison group that does not receive any treatment? Under what conditions would it be ethically unacceptable? How might you avoid some of the ethical dilemmas that come from withholding treatment but still use some form of control group for comparison?

3.4. **[Ethics] [Critical Thinking] [Research & Practice]**
In addition to her faculty position, Professor Courtney Thompson receives a contract with a local clinic to take over running a therapy group for women survivors of intimate partner violence. The program has been in operation for several years. The agency protocol for the group requires the participants to complete an intake questionnaire and an exit questionnaire, both of which include a depression inventory and an anxiety scale. They also complete a follow-up telephone interview at three months after treatment. The information is used by the agency to compile its service statistics and evaluate the program. Dr. Thompson has access to the clinic data from previous years. What do

you see as ethical issues that she must address if she wants to use this data for the purpose of publishing research articles in professional journals?

3.5. **[Ethics] [Critical Thinking] [Research & Practice]** Although the routinely collected data are useful for her research, Dr. Thompson proposes adding an additional scale for measuring posttraumatic stress. Although valuable for her research, the additional scale is not required for the agency's purpose. Could Dr. Thompson use the additional scale? If so, what ethical issues would need to be addressed?

3.6. **[Ethics] [Research & Practice]** Invite a representative of the IRB at your college or university to address your class on the kinds of ethical issues that arise in research done by faculty or students. Explore with this person the safeguards that can be built into research designs to protect against such ethical problems.

Chapter 4

✳

Issues in Problem Formulation

Selecting a Research Problem
Personal Interest
Social Problems
Testing Theory
Prior Research
Program Evaluation and Policy Implementation
Human Service Practice
Minorities in Research: The Political Context of Problem Selection

Shaping and Refining the Problem
Conceptual Development
Review of the Literature
Units of Analysis
Reactivity
Qualitative versus Quantitative Research

Cross-Sectional versus Longitudinal Research

Feasibility of a Research Project
Time Constraints
Financial Considerations
Anticipating and Avoiding Problems

Review and Critical Thinking
Main Points
Important Terms for Review
Critical Thinking
Exploring the Internet
For Further Reading
Class Exercises for Competency Assessment

Suppose you were required, as many students in social research courses are, to design and conduct a research project. Our experience teaching research courses in the social sciences and human services is that some students respond to this assignment by drawing a total blank. Others, however, grasp eagerly onto a topic, such as "the cause of drug addiction," and rush off with total confidence that they are about to solve this enduring problem. In each case, the student is having difficulty adequately formulating a research problem. In the first case, the difficulty is in locating a problem to investigate, whereas in the second, the trouble lies in formulating a problem sufficiently specific that it is amenable to scientific research.

We assure you this problem is not unique to students. Every researcher must grapple with problem formulation. Because it is the initial step and provides the basis for the complete research project, problem formulation is of crucial importance. Many potentially serious difficulties can be avoided—or at least managed—by careful problem formulation. In this chapter, we present the major issues to be considered in problem formulation, beginning with how to select a problem on which to conduct research. Then we analyze how to refine the research question so it can be answered through research. Finally, we discuss factors relating to the feasibility of research.

SELECTING A RESEARCH PROBLEM

The first hurdle confronting a researcher is to select an appropriate topic for scientific investigation. Actually, this is not as difficult as it may first appear, because the social world around us is teeming with unanswered questions. Selecting a problem calls for some creativity and imagination, but researchers can turn to a number of places for inspiration.

Personal Interest

Research topics often are selected because a researcher has an interest in some aspect of human behavior, possibly owing to some personal experience. One social scientist, for example, conducted research on battered women and women's shelters in part because of her own earlier experience of being abused by her husband; another researcher, who had grown up in the only African-American family of a small rural town, did research on prejudice, discrimination, and the experience of minorities (Higgins & Johnson, 1988). Research sometimes focuses on behavior that is unique or bizarre, and thus compelling to some. Examples of such research abound, including studies of nudist colonies, pool hustlers, juvenile gangs, striptease dancers, burglars, homeless heroin addicts, and body piercers (Bourgois, Lettiere, & Quesada, 1997; Miller & Tewksbury, 2001; Polsky, 1967; Weinberg, 1968).

Researchers who select topics from their personal interests must be careful to demonstrate the scientific worth of their projects. Recall from Chapter 1 that the goals of scientific research are to describe, explain, predict, and evaluate. The purpose of research is to advance our knowledge, not just satisfy personal curiosity. For example, in her study of female strippers, psychologist Tania Israel (2002) was interested in learning how people adapt to a job that many consider to be deviant. Such a focus placed her research firmly in an established area of study and amplified its scientific contribution. A researcher who chooses a topic based on personal interest—especially if it deals with some unusual or bizarre aspect of human behavior—should be prepared for the possibility that others will fail to see the worth of that research. Even though Israel, as noted, established a legitimate scientific rationale for her study of strippers, she was subjected to considerable criticism by those who failed to appreciate its scientific value; critics derided her research as lacking in rigor, illegitimate, and embarrassing.

Social Problems

In selecting a topic, researchers often need look no farther than the daily newspaper, which is full of the many social problems that our society faces. Such problems as crime, delinquency, poverty, pollution, overpopulation, drug abuse, alcoholism, mental illness, sexual deviance, discrimination, and political oppression have all been popular sources of topics for social research. The Society for the Study of Social Problems—a professional organization to which many social scientists and human service providers belong—publishes the journal *Social Problems,* whose sole purpose is to communicate the results of scientific investigations into current social problems.

Each of these general categories of social problems encompasses a range of issues for study. Many studies, for example, focus on the sources of a problem. Others are concerned with the consequences these problems have for individuals or society. Still others deal with the outcomes of social programs and other intervention efforts intended to ameliorate these problems. People in the human services, who are routinely involved with many of these problems, can find opportunities for research that are directly related to their professional activities.

Testing Theory

Some researchers select problems on the basis of their use in testing and verifying a particular theory. We noted in Chapter 2 that theoretical concerns should be at issue to some degree in all research. Nearly all research has some implications for existing theory. Certain research topics, however, are selected specifically to test some aspect of a given theory. Many theories relevant to the human services have not been thoroughly tested. In some cases, this means we do not know how valid the theories are; in others, it means we do not know how wide the range of human behavior is to which the theory can be applied.

Prior Research

One of the most fruitful sources of research problems is prior research, because the findings of all research projects have limitations. Some questions are answered, but others always remain. In addition, new questions may be raised by the findings. It is, in fact, common for investigators to conclude research reports with a discussion of the weaknesses and limitations of the research, including suggestions for future research that follow from the findings that have been presented. Focusing on these unanswered questions, or expanding on previous research, is a good way to find research problems.

Prior research also can lead to new research problems if we have reason to question the findings of the original research. As emphasized in Chapter 2, it is imperative that we not complacently accept research findings, especially when conclusions are based on a single study, because opportunities exist for error or bias to influence results. If we have reason to suspect research findings, we have a ready-made problem on which to conduct research ourselves. One of our own students, in fact, found his topic in just this way when faced with the course assignment of conducting a research project. The student had read a research article suggesting a number of differences between the social settings in which marijuana is used and those in which alcohol is used. The student disagreed, partly because of his own experiences, believing instead that the social environments in which the two substances were used were, in fact, quite similar. He designed a study that allowed him to determine whether his hypotheses—or those presumably verified by the previous investigation—would better predict what he would observe. As it turned out, many of his hypotheses were supported by his findings.

Program Evaluation and Policy Implementation

Program evaluation focuses on assessing the effectiveness or efficiency of some policy, program, or practice. As noted in Chapter 1, program and practice effectiveness evaluations have become increasingly important activities for human service professionals. Today, agencies or organizations that fund the human services typically demand that evaluation research be conducted if funding is to be granted or continued. Such research, developed for practical reasons, can take many forms. A social agency, for example, may require some needs assessment research to gather information about its clients if it is to deliver services to them efficiently. Or, a practitioner may need to know which intervention strategy—group work, psychotherapy, behavior therapy, or some other— will be most effective with a particular problem. Prison officials need to know which criminal offenders are the riskiest to parole. Home health care workers need information about how to ensure that people will take medications as prescribed. In all these cases, the practical information required by an agency or practitioner determines the focus of the research effort. Research in Practice 4.1 presents examples

> **RESEARCH IN PRACTICE 4.1** **Policy Planning and Development: Current Policy Implementation as a Source of Research Problems**
>
> Anne holds a master's degree in public policy and is a researcher and policy analyst for the Office of the Inspector General (OIG) of the Department of Health and Human Services (HHS), a large federal agency that administers major health and social service programs across the United States. According to Anne, the IG regularly searches for any apparent problems with the implementation of HHS programs. "Research ideas come from a variety of places—legislators, service professionals, and even IG staff. When we see a major issue that is getting a good deal of public attention, we often respond by drafting a research proposal and asking for approval from the head of our office. We are nonpartisan, so our goal is to create unbiased reports on the effectiveness of our programs and offer sound recommendations for increasing efficiencies and improving services. Legislative staffers regularly meet with IG staff for further information related to the programs we investigate and use this information in making recommendations to legislators." So this illustrates current policy implementation—or problems with it—as a rich source of research problems.
>
> One of the major investigations Anne led in 2009 pertained to the Indian Health Service (IHS) which provides health services to 1.9 million Americans who are members of federally recognized tribes (American Indian or Alaskan Natives) through small health clinics offering routine care (Office of Inspector General, 2009). When required services are not available through these clinics, IHS and the tribes purchase services through Contract Health Services (CHS) which are delivered primarily through hospitals. When CHS are purchased through Medicare-participating hospitals, HHS sets reimbursement caps at Medicare rates. However, the IG found that, in some cases, CHS payments paid more than Medicare rates (either because they were overpayments or because services were delivered outside of Medicare-participating hospitals). This was expensive for the government as well as for the service recipients, who were required to pay some of this overage. The research was designed to show what levels of cost savings would be created by requiring all CHS units to accept Medicare caps for reimbursements and how to strictly monitor and enforce these rates.
>
> As Anne explains, "Working for an agency like the IG gives us a very rich set of data. We can access all medical claims for Medicare, Medicaid and other programs and performance data for any number of client groups." With access to this set of data, Anne and her coworkers examined all CHS payments and compared all medical expense claims to established Medicare rates for similar services. They found that 22 percent of hospital claims between January and March 2008 were above Medicare rates, and that preventing overpayments to Medicare-participating providers and also capping all CHS services to Medicare rates would have created a savings of $13 million during the three-month period being investigated.
>
> So, based on their research, they recommended that the Indian Health Service and tribes take action to prevent overpayments to Medicare-participating health care providers and that all CHS payments—including those of non-Medicare-participating providers—be capped at Medicare rates.
>
> (Based on personal interviews conducted in January 2012.)

of research ideas being generated by reviews of how well social policies are being implemented.

The ability to find problems in practice settings that could be the focus of program evaluation research is limited only by the creativity and imagination of the practitioner. This was brought home to us by two of our students during a recent social research course. They were doing a field placement in a community mental health clinic while taking our research course, so they decided to search for some problem at the clinic to serve as the focus of their research paper. These students noticed that one problem the clinic faced was the failure of clients to show up for appointments. In addition to creating difficulties in achieving effective intervention, this also resulted in an inefficient use of staff resources, because counselors were left idle because of missed appointments. The students designed a very simple investigation in which some clients were given a reminder phone call a day or so before their appointment and other clients were not contacted, as had been the previous practice. The researchers' concern was to establish whether the reminder call increased the rate at which people showed up for their appointments. After implementing this procedure for a while, the students concluded that the phone call did help, and would be a useful and efficient addition to the functioning of the agency.

Human Service Practice

The linkage between human service practice and evaluation research is obvious, but service delivery can serve as the catalyst for basic research as well. During the course of working in human service programs, practitioners confront social problems and human diversity daily as they interact with clients who are struggling with life problems. Often, human service workers encounter client behavior that is unusual or even dramatic, and it stimulates questions about human behavior and society. The protective service worker who faces child abuse and neglect may derive research questions about parent–child bonding or human development. Hospice staff may generate questions about the dying process and grieving. Although answers to these questions may have practice implications, research that addresses issues such as these also has important implications for social science theory.

It is not only the behavior or characteristics of clients that generate research questions in practice settings; the mode and process of human service practice itself may even be the topic of research. For example, the mechanisms by which some human service agencies differentially allocate services according to social class or race might be a research issue. In fact, study of the human service delivery system has generated many of the major theoretical advances in our understanding of human behavior and social environments. For instance, Glaser and Strauss (1965) based their classic studies concerning death and social worth on observations of hospital patient care. More recently, controversy has surfaced in the human services over what appears to be the intergenerational transmission of family violence, suggesting that experiencing or observing violence during childhood results in subsequent violent behavior as a parent or spouse. Not only does research into this issue have practical implications for intervention programs, it also is directly relevant to developing our understanding of learning, human development, the family, and society as well (Burgess & Youngblade, 1988).

Minorities in Research: The Political Context of Problem Selection

From the preceding discussion of how to select a research problem, one could get the impression that the problem selection process is largely a matter of personal preference. Guided by personal interest or experience, the prospective researcher identifies a worthy problem and then sallies forth in the pursuit of knowledge. Like most other types of human activity, however, problem selection cannot be explained solely in such individual terms. In fact, if we asked students in research courses why they chose the term paper topics they did, we might find that, in addition to personal interest, theoretical orientation, or practice interest, their choices were governed by factors such as these: "My instructor had a data set available on this problem." "I got financial aid to work as a research assistant." "I knew my prof was interested in this topic, so I hoped studying it might help me get a better grade." In other words, issues of political efficacy can influence problem selection as well.

In the world of professional research, the situation is not unlike that of the student. The stakes are much higher, however, and the consequences much greater. Although the number of possible research problems may be infinite, the resources that society can allocate to research them are not. Research is a major societal enterprise in which universities, governmental organizations, private research corporations, and independent researchers compete with each other for limited resources. At the same time, societal forces are working to make sure that the concerns of vested interest groups receive attention from the research community. Thus, problem selection is very much a political issue, and the problems that affect minorities and other groups with little clout may not receive the research attention they deserve.

Consider the example of spousal abuse. Men have been assaulting their wives since long before there was social research. Before the 1970s, however, one would have been hard pressed to find much research on the topic. Today, the social science and human service literature is replete with studies on spousal abuse, and the research endeavor in this area has expanded into a focus on intimate-partner violence. What explains the change? There is no single answer, but a major factor has been the rise of the women's movement. Before the 1960s, women as a group had considerably less political power than they have today, and the special problems of this minority often received little research attention. Woman battering is now an important issue to the women's movement, and this politically powerful group has been able to translate its concerns into public policy. Partly because of its pressure, the government has allocated money specifically for research on intimate-partner violence. In addition, with the changing roles of women in society, more women during the past three decades have chosen to pursue careers as researchers in the social sciences. One consequence of more women in research positions is that, given the role of personal interest in the selection of research topics, women are more likely to identify woman battering as a problem warranting research investigation. As the topic gained more prominence in the social science and human service fields, editors of journals became more receptive to publishing research articles on the topic. All these factors, over time, had a snowball effect. The availability of funds, the potential for publication, and the desire to contribute knowledge to an area of public concern attracted researchers seeking problems to study to this area.

So, one major factor influencing the allocation of research funds is the existence of a powerful, articulate, and effective interest group that can push for research on a particular problem (Lally, 1977; Varmus, 1999). Other factors include the following:

- Support for research by influentials at the national policy-making levels
- Definition of a condition as a social problem by national influentials
- Public awareness of and concern about the condition
- Severity, extent, and economic costs of the condition
- Amount of publicity about the condition
- Amount of support for research on the condition by the major funding agencies

On this last point, it is important to recognize that major agencies of the government, such as the Department of Health and Human Services (DHHS) and the National Science Foundation (NSF), dispense millions of dollars for research each year. Support from congressional leaders and key personnel in these major departments is essential for problem areas to be deemed worthy of financial backing for research. Typically, funding sources publish *requests for proposals* (RFPs), which outline the organization's funding priorities and requirements. Researchers are invited to submit proposals for competitive consideration. Proposals may be for millions of research dollars, and the competition for funding is as intense and high pressure as any major business deal.

Given that the political process plays a major role in determining which problems are sufficiently important to warrant research attention, it is not surprising that those people who lack access to social power in our society also are those whose interests are least likely to be served by the research conducted. One recent—and particularly disturbing—example of minority status influencing funding was with AIDS research. During the early years of the spread of AIDS in the United States, almost all people contracting the virus were men who had sex with other men. Today, this has changed: Currently, only 68 percent of new HIV infections involve male-to-male sexual contact or intravenous drug use, and 31 percent result from heterosexual contact (Centers for Disease Control and Prevention, 2011). In the earlier years, however, AIDS was associated in many people's minds with two groups of people—homosexuals and intravenous drug users—who were seen as marginal and highly stigmatized by many Americans, especially those in positions of power. In fact, people widely defined AIDS for a number of years as a "gay disease," and thus as something that most Americans need not worry about. The attitude of many was summed up by the comment of a person who was later to be a staff member at the White House: "Those poor homosexuals. They have declared war on nature, and nature is exacting an awful retribution" (Shilts, 1987, p. 311). As long as AIDS was defined as a disease of deviants, funds for research on its cause and prevention were slow in coming.

Other reasons for the delayed response to the AIDS crisis existed beyond the marginality and stigma the early victims suffered (Shilts, 1987). For instance, the Reagan administration, which entered office in 1981, expressed as policy the emphasis on smaller government and austerity in social and health programs. The first AIDS victims in the United States appeared in 1980. The competition for government funds during the early 1980s was fierce, and AIDS researchers typically lost the battle, partly because those suffering from AIDS had less clout in the policy-making process than other groups competing for dwindling funds.

In short, society's response to the minority status of those afflicted with AIDS, along with other political factors, contributed to a significant delay in attacking the problem. It wasn't until AIDS began to threaten the supply of blood available for transfusions and fear arose that AIDS was entering the heterosexual population that considerable research support was forthcoming.

The selection of research problems is thus a highly political process. Although powerful interest groups will always play a role in this process, researchers need to avoid the perceptual blinders that often hinder the ability of the powerful to see which problems are sufficiently important or serious to warrant attention. Human service professionals, whether they actually conduct research or not, can play an important role in the political issues surrounding problem selection. In the course of practice, human service providers deal directly with the poor, with those labeled as deviant, with minorities, and with the powerless. This puts these providers in a position to serve as advocates for inclusion on the societal research agenda of problems relevant to their clientele.

We have discussed numerous sources of research topics for practitioner–researchers. Although we have discussed them separately, more than one of these factors often influences a given choice of a research topic. Finding a research topic, however, is only the first step in problem formulation. The next step is to shape it into a problem that empirical research can solve.

SHAPING AND REFINING THE PROBLEM

As we mentioned, a frustrating trap in which novice researchers often become ensnarled is choosing a topic that is so broad and encompassing that, by itself, it offers little guidance in terms of how to proceed. Finding the "causes of juvenile delinquency" or the "weaknesses of the modern family" sounds intriguing, but these topics provide little direction concerning where to begin to look. The next step in the research process, then, is to begin translating a general topical interest into a precise, researchable problem by narrowing the scope of the problem to manageable proportions. A single investigation is unlikely to uncover the causes of juvenile delinquency, but it might provide some insight regarding the influence of particular variables on the emergence of particular delinquencies. Refining, narrowing, and focusing a research problem do not occur all at once, but rather form a continuous process involving a number of procedures.

Conceptual Development

In Chapter 2, we discussed the role of theories and hypotheses in the research process, pointing out that concepts are one of the central components of theories. In the refining of a research problem, one of the key steps is *conceptual development:* identifying and properly defining the concepts on which the study will focus. In exploratory studies, of course, we are entering areas where there is little conceptual development, and a major purpose of the research itself may be to identify and define concepts. In cases where theory and research already exist, however, some conceptual development occurs as a part of formulating a research problem. One part of this process, already discussed in Chapter 2, is to clearly define the meaning of concepts. Another part of the process is to narrow the focus of the concept so it encompasses a topic that is feasible to research in a single study. For example, practitioners in a youth home who had an interest in juvenile delinquency might ask themselves, "Are we interested in all forms of delinquent behavior or only in some types?" In reality, the concept of delinquency is an extremely broad category that includes all actions by juveniles that violate criminal or juvenile codes. We have no reason to assume that a single cause can explain all types of delinquency. The focus of the research therefore might be narrowed to include only certain behaviors, such as violence or truancy. The goal of this specification process, then, is to make clear exactly what the focus of the research effort is.

Once the key concepts are clearly defined, the next consideration is their measurability. Only concepts that are in some way measurable can be used in the research process. Eventually, of course, concepts will have to be operationalized, as discussed in Chapter 2, so any that cannot be readily measurable will have to be dropped. Measuring concepts sometimes can be difficult, as we note in more detail in Chapter 5. In fact, theories at times include concepts that are difficult to operationalize. However, if the concepts in a proposed study cannot be measured, then some modification in the project—and, possibly, in the theory—is necessary. This process of refining and developing concepts as a part of the research process illustrates a point made in Chapter 2 regarding the interplay between theory and research: Theories provide concepts and hypotheses for research, whereas research modifies theories through conceptual development. The Eye on Ethics section explores some of the ethical dimensions of selecting and conceptualizing research problems.

Review of the Literature

With concepts clarified and deemed measurable, we are ready to conduct a review of previous research that relates to our research problem. This review of the literature is a necessary and important part of the research process (Locke, Silverman, & Spirduso, 2010). We do it to familiarize ourselves with the current state of knowledge regarding the research problem and to learn how others have delineated similar problems. Unless we are planning a replication, it is unlikely that we will formulate our problem precisely like any one of these previous studies; rather, we are likely to pick up ideas from several that we can integrate to improve our own. Through reviewing the relevant literature, we can further narrow the focus of the research project and ensure that we do not unnecessarily duplicate what others have already done. Researchers undoubtedly will find that pitfalls can be avoided by learning from others' experiences. For example, suppose that one or more specific approaches to a topic have proven unproductive—that is, several studies have failed to find significant results or strong relationships. In this case, unless there is good reason to believe that these earlier studies contained methodological weaknesses, the same approach is likely to lead to failure once again. Future research is likely to be more productive if it focuses on studies that have achieved some positive results.

A thorough literature review calls for familiarity with basic library utilization skills (including how to locate books, professional journals, and public documents) as well as online search skills. To help with this important aspect of doing research, we have included Appendix A in this book, which deals with the basic information retrieval skills. This appendix shows how to find the books, journals, government documents, and other sources for finding reports of research. Even those with some experience using both the library and online searches likely will find some helpful new information in this appendix.

In a literature review, we conduct a systematic search of each research report for certain kinds of information. First, the reviewer pays attention to

> **EYE ON ETHICS** — **The Ethics of Selecting and Conceptualizing Research Problems**
>
> Social research has an impact on people's lives. Sometimes it brings them advantages, but other times the consequences are negative. Yet some groups have more social and economic resources, and these resources can mean that these groups are better equipped to sponsor research that may bring them benefits. Disadvantaged groups may find an inordinately small share of research resources being devoted to their concerns. In addition, more powerful groups are more likely to control the political and economic structures that enable them to influence how research problems are conceptualized. Should a problem such as poverty or drugs be conceptualized in an individualistic way (due to the weaknesses or failings of the poor or the addicted) or a systemic way (due to breakdowns in familial, political, or economic structures)? Answers to these questions will shape how research is done and how victims of poverty and drugs will be treated. As one psychologist put it: "The ethical implications come on board when we reframe the political as personal, and in so doing become complicit in agendas that maintain oppressive and neglectful social conditions" (O'Neill 2005, p. 19).
>
> One way of addressing this problem focuses on basic issues of defining and conceptualizing problems: Ask whose agenda is served by the research we conduct and the way in which we conduct it. This may help us decide whether we are complicit in maintaining social conditions that are viewed as negative by some groups.
>
> A second way to address this problem is for researchers to seek out research problems that are not on the agenda of more powerful groups (Bonacich, 1990). This is essentially what happened, over a period of years, with the topic of spouse abuse discussed earlier in the chapter.
>
> A third way to approach this problem is for researchers to listen to the voices of all the stakeholders in the research, irrespective of who is funding the research. A stakeholder is any person or group who stands to gain or lose from the research. The powerful stakeholders, of course—especially those who are funding the research—will have their voices heard. It is the less powerful stakeholders that the researcher needs to seek out and listen to. So, for example, if a state department of corrections funds a study on some aspect of prison life, then the corrections administrators will certainly have an influence on what is researched and how it is done. But other stakeholders to this research include the prisoners themselves and their families as well as the correctional officers who are in daily contact with them. What kind of research might benefit or work to the disadvantage of these groups? Social science and human service researchers who strive to make research more ethical would make efforts to ensure that the voices of the inmates and correctional officers are heard in the design and conduct of the research.

theoretical and conceptual issues: What concepts and theories are used, how well developed are they, and have they been subjected to empirical tests before? If the theories and concepts are well developed, they can serve as an important guide in designing the planned research and explaining the relationships between variables. If they are not well developed, one will have to rely more on personal insight and creativity. In this case researchers sometimes consider doing exploratory research, which may involve loosely structured interviews and less quantitative measuring devices, as a way of advancing conceptual and theoretical development.

The *research hypotheses,* including identification of the *independent* and *dependent variables,* represent a second component of a literature review. Are the hypotheses clearly stated and testable? Are they related to the variables and hypotheses being considered in the planned study? Existing research can provide some fairly specific direction in terms of already tested relationships between independent and dependent variables.

The *measurement* and the *operational definitions* used in previous research are a third focus of a literature review. As noted, successful operationalization of concepts often is difficult. Previous work in this area is invaluable in finding workable measures for concepts. Past measures may require modification to meet current needs, of course, but making these modifications probably is easier than developing completely new measures, which is a difficult and time-consuming process.

A literature review also informs us about a fourth important element of research—the most appropriate *research technique* for a particular research problem. Successful approaches by others should be noted and unsuccessful approaches avoided. It is of the utmost importance that the problem determines the research technique that is used, and not the other way around. Many data-gathering techniques exist, because no single method is always best. As we note in subsequent chapters, each technique has its own strengths and weaknesses, and each is suitable for answering some questions but not others.

The *sampling strategy* is a fifth element of a literature review. Previous research can be useful in determining the sampling strategy to use and avoiding sampling problems that others have encountered. For example, suppose the study we propose calls for the use of mailed questionnaires. An ever present problem with mailed questionnaires is making sure that a sufficient number of people complete and return them. It would be useful for us to know what other investigators have experienced with people like those we plan to survey. Not all groups respond to mailed questionnaires with the same degree of enthusiasm. If the group we are proposing to sample has exhibited notoriously low return rates during the previous studies, we have to plan accordingly: We would probably increase the number of questionnaires mailed, and we would certainly use all available means of obtaining the highest possible response rate. Or, if we anticipate very low return rates, we may want to search for another group to study—or even consider whether this particular project is feasible at all.

Statistical technique is a sixth element of a literature review. In Chapters 5, 14, and 15, we will discuss issues relating to appropriate use of statistics. In the literature review, we must be aware of whether the appropriate procedures were used, if any inappropriate procedures were used, and what constraints the concepts, variables, and hypotheses placed on the kind of statistics that would be appropriate.

Finally, a literature review notes the *findings and conclusions* of the studies that are examined. Which hypotheses were confirmed, and what guidelines for future research were presented? One aspect of the findings to watch for is the *effect size,* which refers to how big an effect an independent variable has on a dependent variable. Although we discuss this concept more fully in Chapter 15, we need to assess whether a dependent variable is affected in only a small but measurable way, or whether the impact is dramatic (Gibbs, 1991).

A thorough literature review involves evaluating and comparing many research reports, identifying where they used similar procedures and reached similar outcomes, and where there were discrepancies between studies. This can be a complicated process, especially when hundreds of studies may be involved. It sometimes is helpful to produce a summary table, such as Table 4.1, to make comparisons. Notice that the table cites each separate study in the left-hand column, along with a brief description of the intervention model used in the study. The next three columns give information about the research design, sampling procedures, and measurement devices. Then, a column contains a summary of the results of each study. The final column on the right addresses any limitations found in the research. A systematic literature review of this sort provides the most useful information from previous studies. One can see at a glance how many studies came to similar conclusions and how commonly certain measuring devices were used. The ability to compile and summarize succinctly the features of studies in this fashion is essential to formulating a research problem and refining it into a research question that can be empirically investigated.

Units of Analysis

An important element in the process of shaping and refining a research problem is the decision regarding the unit of analysis to be investigated. **Units of analysis** are the specific objects or elements whose characteristics we wish to describe or explain and about which we will collect data. Although there are many units of analysis, five that are commonly used in human service research are individuals, groups, organizations, programs, and social artifacts (see Table 4.2). Different units of analysis are used in studying documents; these are discussed in Chapter 8.

TABLE 4.1 A Summary Table of a Literature Review of Research on Rural Homelessness

Authors (area)	Methods	Measures	Sample	Results	Limitations
Mondello, Bradley, McLaughlin, & Shore (2009) (service use and costs)	Use of available data (human service agency records of actual costs of services)	Cost comparisons of housing and other services (before and after supportive housing) based on the actual costs recorded in agency files	Availability sample: All chronically homeless Maine residents with disabilities living in permanent supportive housing (163 agreed to participate)	Costs of services were greater for those individuals and families prior to supportive housing than after supportive housing placement (when factoring both housing and other services costs).	Limited to Maine residents (in rural areas). Limited to those with service records (including costs records) both before and after supportive housing placement.
First, Toomey, & Rife (1990) (demographics, coping behaviors)	Survey research (from in-person interviews)	Survey questions measure living arrangements, use of services, mental health and psychiatric assessments; Homeless Permanent Survey Instrument; Psychiatric Status Schedule	Snowball sample of 921 homeless adults in 21 rural counties in Ohio, located through homeless advocates, advisors and contact persons who were knowledgeable of each county	Minorities are greatly over-represented in rural homeless population. Roughly 40% were living in shelters, 14% outdoors or other substandard shelter, and 46% were staying with family and friends.	Conducted in 1990. Limited to Ohio residents.
Hilton & DeJong (coping behaviors, felt experiences)	Qualitative (semi-structured interviews)	Open-ended interview questions provide data on living arrangements, use of services, social relationships, self-perceptions of felt experience of homelessness	Snowball sample of 55 homeless adults in Michigan's Upper Peninsula	Four main types of coping patterns identified: shelter users, couch hoppers, campers (living outdoors), and mixed (multiple forms of coping). Implications for social relationships and felt experiences discussed.	Limited to Michigan's Upper Peninsula; representativeness of the sample unknown.

TABLE 4.2 Possible Units of Analysis in Research on Juvenile Delinquency

Unit of Analysis	Example	Appropriate Variables	Research Problem
Individuals	Adolescents arrested for larceny	Age, sex, prior arrests	Do males receive different penalties than females for similar offenses?
Groups	Delinquent gangs	Size, norms on drug usage	Are gangs involved in drug trafficking more violent than other gangs?
Organizations	Adolescent treatment agencies	Size, auspices, funding level	Do private agencies serve fewer minority and lower-class delinquents than public agencies?
Programs	Delinquency prevention programs	Theoretical model, type of host setting	What services are most frequently included in prevention programs?
Social artifacts	Transcripts of adjudication hearings	Number of references to victim injury	To what extent does the level of violence in the offense affect the kind of penalty imposed?

Much social research focuses on the *individual* as the unit of analysis. The typical survey, for example, obtains information from individuals about their attitudes or behavior. Whenever we define a population of inquiry with reference to some personal status, we are operating at the individual level of analysis. For example, unwed mothers, welfare recipients, mental patients, retarded children, and similar categories all identify individuals with reference to a status they occupy.

If we identify our unit of analysis as individuals, then it is important to recognize that the entire analysis will remain at that level. For the sake of describing large numbers of individuals, it is necessary to use summarizing statistics, such as averages. For example, we might, as part of a study of unwed mothers, note that their average age when giving birth was 16.8 years. Aggregating data in this fashion in no way changes the unit of analysis. We are still collecting our data about individuals.

Social scientists sometimes focus on social *groups* as their unit of analysis and collect data on some group characteristic or behavior. Some groups consist of individuals who share some social relationship with the other group members. For example, in families, peer groups, occupational groups, or juvenile gangs, the members have some sense of membership or belonging to the group. If we study families in terms of whether or not they are intact, then we are investigating the characteristics of a group—the family—and not the characteristics of individuals. Other groups of interest to social scientists are merely aggregates of individuals with no necessary sense of membership, such as census tracts, cities, states, or members of a particular social class. For example, we might study the relationship between poverty and delinquency by comparing the rates of delinquency in census tracts with low income and census tracts with high income. In this case, we have collected data regarding the characteristics of census tracts rather than data regarding individuals.

Social scientists also deal with *organizations* as the unit of analysis. Formal organizations are deliberately constructed groups that are organized to achieve specific goals. Examples of formal organizations include corporations, schools, prisons, unions, government bureaus, and human service agencies. For example, our experience may lead us to suspect that organizations providing substance abuse services can more effectively serve their clients if they have an open and democratic communication structure rather than a closed and rigidly stratified one. If we compare the success rates of organizations with different communication structures, then our study would use organizations, not individuals or groups, as the unit of analysis. Although individuals may experience success at overcoming substance abuse, only organizations can have a *success rate*.

Research in the human services also can focus on *programs* as the basic unit of analysis. The program may provide services for individuals, and it may exist as part of an organization. However, it is still a separate unit of analysis about which data can be collected. Like organizations, programs can have success rates or be assessed in terms of overall costs. For example, one research project investigated 25 programs that provided services for pregnant and parenting teenagers (Fernandez & Ruch-Ross, 1998). This research assessed each program according to its overall success rate: A successful program was one in which the clients were more likely to stay in school or stay employed and less likely to get pregnant than were clients in the other programs. Note that a program can have a success rate (in other words, a certain proportion of their clients succeeding) but an individual can only succeed or fail (rather than show a rate of success). The researchers compared the programs to determine the characteristics of successful and unsuccessful programs. Programs might cut across a number of different organizations, such as social service agencies, in which case the unit under observation is the effectiveness of the combination of services provided by these organizations.

Finally, the unit of analysis may be *social artifacts,* which are simply any material products that people produce. Examples are virtually endless: newspapers, buildings, movies, books, magazines, ipads, automobiles, songs, graffiti, and so on. Of all the units of analysis, social artifacts are the least frequent focus of human service research, but as reflections of people and the society that produces the artifacts, analysis of social artifacts is useful. Books and magazines, for example, can be used as artifacts in the assessment of sex-role stereotyping. Children's books have been attacked for allegedly reinforcing traditional gender roles through their presentations of men and women (Crabb & Bielewski, 1994). Any kind of legal or administrative statute also is an artifact worthy of study. One effort, for instance, used state juvenile codes as the independent variable in a study of whether legal statutes made a difference in how courts handled juvenile cases (Grichting, 1979).

Clearly specifying the unit of analysis in research is important to avoid a serious problem: an illegitimate shift in the analysis from one unit to another. Jumping from one level to another can result in erroneous conclusions being drawn. One way this can happen is called the **ecological fallacy:** inferring something about individuals based on data collected at higher units of analysis, such as groups. In other words, a mismatch occurs between the unit of analysis about which data are collected and about which conclusions are drawn. Suppose, for example, a study found that census tracts with high rates of teenage drug abuse also had a large percentage of single-parent families. We might be tempted to conclude that single-parent families are a factor promoting teenage drug abuse. Such a conclusion, however, represents an illegitimate shift in the unit of analysis. The data have been collected about census tracts, which are at the group level. The conclusion being drawn, however, is at the individual level—namely, that teenage drug abusers live in single-parent families. The data, however, do not show this. In fact, the data only show the association of two rates—substance abuse and single parenthood—in census tracts. (Perhaps two-parent families are a minority in a census tract, but a high proportion of children in these families abuse drugs.) It is, of course, possible that relationships found at the group level will hold at the individual level, but they may not. In our hypothetical study, some other characteristic of census tracts may lead to both high rates of drug abuse *and* single-parent families. The error comes in the automatic assumption that correlations at the group level necessarily reflect relationships at the individual level.

Fallacious reasoning can occur in the opposite direction as well; in this case, it is called the **reductionist fallacy:** inferring something about groups or other higher levels of analysis based on data collected from individuals. Suppose we collected data from individual teenagers about their drug use and family environments and found an association—namely, that teens from single-parent families are more likely to abuse drugs. Could we then conclude that communities with high rates of single-parent families would have high rates of teenage drug abuse? The answer, once again, is that we could not draw that conclusion about the group level (communities) with any certainty, because the data we have is about social process at the individual level (what happens in the lives of individual teens). It may well be that the social process that produces high rates of drug abuse in communities is different from the social process that leads individuals to use drugs. When data are collected at one level of analysis, it is always an empirical question as to whether conclusions can be drawn from that data about other levels of analysis. A clear awareness of the unit of analysis can help ensure that we do not make such illegitimate shifts.

A final point needs to be made about the unit of analysis in contrast to the source of data. The unit of analysis refers to the element *about which* data are collected and inferences made, but it is not necessarily the source *from which* data are collected. A common example is the U.S. Census, which reports data for *households*. We speak of household size and income, but households don't fill out questionnaires—people do. In this case, individuals, such as the heads of households, are the *source* of the data, but the household is the unit of analysis *about which* data are collected. When the unit of analysis is something other than the individual, attention must be paid to the source of that data, because this might introduce bias into the data analysis. For example, when the household is the unit of analysis, we often collect data from one member of the household. In single-parent families, headed primarily by women, we would be gathering data mostly from women. In two-parent families, we would be obtaining data from both men and women, because either could be the head of the household. In some cases, men might be the majority of those from whom we collect data. If men tend to answer some questions differently from women, then there could be a sex bias in the results even though our unit of analysis was not linked to sex. A difference that we attribute to single-parent as compared to two-parent families may result from the fact that the former involves mostly women answering questions while the latter involves mostly men.

Reactivity

The issue of reactivity is another consideration in refining a research problem. The term **reactivity** refers to the fact that people can react to being studied and may behave differently than when they don't think they are being studied. In other words, the data we collect from people who know they are the objects of study might be different from the data we collect from the same people if they do not know. So, a reactive research technique changes the very thing that is being studied. Suppose, for example, that you are a parent. A researcher enters your home and sets up videotaping equipment to observe your interactions with your children. Would you behave in the same way you would if the observer were not present? You might, but most people would feel strong pressures to be "on their toes" and present themselves as good parents. You might be more forgiving of your child, for instance, or give fewer negative sanctions.

Reactivity in research can take many forms, and it is a problem for virtually all sciences. It is especially acute in social research, however, because human beings are self-conscious and aware of what is happening to them. Refining a research problem and choosing a research design are done with an eye toward reducing as much as possible the extensiveness of reactivity. We consider this in assessing the various research strategies during later chapters.

Qualitative versus Quantitative Research

Another aspect of refining a research problem is to decide whether to use one of two broad strategies toward research: *qualitative research*, or *quantitative research*. **Qualitative research** involves data in the form of words, pictures, descriptions, or narratives. **Quantitative research** uses numbers, counts, and measures of things (Berg & Lune, 2012; Wakefield, 1995). In general, two factors come into play in deciding whether to conduct qualitative or quantitative research: the state of our knowledge on a particular research topic, and the individual researcher's position regarding the nature of human social behavior. Regarding the first factor, when knowledge is sketchy or there is little theoretical understanding of a phenomenon, it may be impossible to develop precise hypotheses or operational definitions. In such cases, researchers often turn to qualitative research, because

> **RESEARCH IN PRACTICE 4.2** **Behavior and Social Environments: Feminist Research Methods: Do Males and Females Have Different "Voices"?**
>
> Positivism assumes that "one size fits all"—that there is one way to know the world, and that the diversity of people in the world is irrelevant to how we gain knowledge. One of the areas in which the debates over the scientific paradigms discussed in Chapter 2 probably have been most intense is feminist research. Feminist researchers have argued that one size does *not* fit all—that the diversity in the world also produces diverse ways of gaining knowledge of the world. This has led some feminist researchers to explore the nonpositivist paradigms for a more complete and complex methodology to understand human behavior (Olsen, 1994; Reinharz, 1992; Schiebinger, 1999). One profound question that feminists have raised is whether ways of knowing are gendered: Are males and females socialized to perceive the world and acquire knowledge in fundamentally different ways? Furthermore, is positivism merely one of several ways of knowing rather than the only way of knowing?
>
> The basic argument is that, because of differences between the genders—either due to biology or socialization—there is a male model of knowledge development and a female one, and the two are, to an extent, alien to each other (DeVault, 1999; Nielson, 1989). In developing some of these ideas, Carol Gilligan (1982) used the term "voice" to mean modes of thinking about the world, and tried to describe the differences between male and female "voices." Women emphasize the importance of relationships and the danger of being separated from others. Women see connectedness between people and feel obliged to protect and nurture those to whom they feel connected. This leads to a concern about the needs of others, but the needs of self and others exist primarily in the context of relationships with other people. So women's voices focus on the individual who is embedded in a social network. This emphasis on connectedness and relationships means that problems and people are inextricably intertwined. Neither problems nor the people they affect can be fully understood if they are separated from one another.
>
> By contrast, men's voices speak of separation and autonomy. They emphasize independence and, to an extent, alienation—at least in the sense that people can be abstracted from their relationships, from their context, and even from their own uniqueness. For men, the separate individual has some meaning and importance and, possibly, even more value than a person who is encumbered by relationships and connections. This view treats these abstracted individuals the same, ignoring the unique needs or contexts of each person. To this extent, men's voices are abstract and formal. People and their problems can be separated.
>
> Proponents of the male–female distinction argue that these male and female voices are fundamentally contrasting ways of perceiving and developing knowledge about the world. The distinction suggests a paradigm that differs from the positivist one, with some affinities to a variety of nonpositivist paradigms. The male voice tends to be logical and objective and to avoid or downplay feelings while focusing on accomplishing practical goals. It tends to view the world in terms of separation: The researcher extracts data from the "subject" or "respondent" and, in the interests of objectivity, avoids any personal relationship (or connectedness) between them. All contact except that

it can be more exploratory in nature. The research can be descriptive, possibly resulting in the formulation of hypotheses rather than the verification of them. When enough previous research exists on a topic, however, it may be more feasible precisely to state concepts, variables, and hypotheses. It also may be possible to develop quantifiable operational definitions of what the researcher is interested in, which then allows research to take on a more quantitative nature.

The second consideration in choosing between quantitative and qualitative research stems from a more fundamental controversy over the nature of human social behavior. We saw in Chapter 2 that the choice between qualitative and quantitative research is related to whether one follows positivist or nonpositivist paradigms toward science. This complicated issue, which is discussed in more detail in Chapters 2 and 9, basically involves debate over whether we can meaningfully reduce the human experience to numbers and measures. Some social scientists argue that the human experience has a subjective dimension—that is, the personal meanings and feelings that people have about themselves and what they do. These meanings or feelings necessary to collect data is avoided. The male researcher prefers a more quantitative approach, with standardized measuring instruments and procedures, on the assumption that treating all people alike will produce the most valid and objective data. A number of procedures commonly used in positivist research can be seen as efforts to strip away the context from the individual: placing them in laboratory settings; using random assignment to conditions; using aggregate responses from large-scale surveys; and isolating variables for study. All these procedures assume that the context in which a person lives is merely interfering "noise," and that more meaningful information can be obtained without it. Through quantification, the male voice minimizes the uniqueness and subjectivity of experiences by providing summary responses of the aggregate; so the fact that Jane Doe got pregnant at age 13 under a certain set of unique and meaningful circumstances gets lost when we conclude that the average teenage pregnancy in a high school occurs at 14.7 years of age.

The female voice, on the other hand, stresses feeling, empathy, and the subjective side of life, and emphasizes connectedness: Researcher and respondent are tied together in a relationship that influences the data produced. Objectivity, in the positivist sense, is impossible, because the meaning and importance of data relate to specific individuals and their relationships with one another. The researcher and subject are partners in the relationship of producing research. Subjects are collaborators. The feminist researcher also disdains the notion of the objective, impartial researcher in favor of involvement with the topics of their research. In the feminist view of gaining truth, researcher and subject work together, although in different ways, to develop understanding; truth-seeking is a mutual, cooperative effort on their part. Research questions emphasize connectedness: keeping people in their social contexts, and studying the complexity of the whole. In short, qualitative approaches are preferred. People can be studied in their homes or where they work and play. Some research methods, such as the field methods we will discuss in Chapter 9, are better suited to emphasizing this connectedness. Feminist research also emphasizes in-depth interviews, where people have an opportunity to express the fullness and complexity of their lives in their own words.

Obviously, it is possible for men to speak with a "female" voice and for women to speak with a "male" voice. The point is that these are fundamentally different ways of knowing the world. Feminist researchers do not reject positivism; they recognize that it is different but not superior. In fact, some critics argue that researchers in the social sciences, whether male or female, generally have been trained in graduate schools with a male voice, because that is what has dominated over the years among graduate faculty. Yet, neither voice is inherently superior, and neither is complete or totally objective. Each is a valid way of gaining knowledge about the world, and each involves a perspective that has some limitations. The basic insight of feminist researchers is that all people, including researchers, are fundamentally gendered beings and—whether we admit it or not—this shapes how we perceive and think about the world, how we do research, and what research results are produced.

---

cannot be captured very well through numbers or measures. Instead, narrative descriptions of people going about their daily routines or lengthy and broad-ranging interviews with them better express those meanings and feelings. Such techniques are better able to capture the critical subjective meanings that are an essential element of understanding human behavior. Quantitative research, on the other hand, provides us with much more precise statements about human behavior.

The line between qualitative and quantitative approaches is not always completely clear, and the choice between the two can be difficult. Many research projects incorporate both approaches to gain the most benefit. Research in Practice 4.2 presents some additional elaboration on this issue.

Cross-Sectional versus Longitudinal Research

In addition to deciding on the unit of analysis to investigate, refining a research problem also requires a decision about the time dimension. Here, the basic issue is whether the researcher wants a single snapshot in time of some phenomenon or an ongoing series of photographs over time. The former is called **cross-sectional research**, and it focuses on a cross section of a population at one point in time. Many surveys, for example, are cross-sectional in nature.

Although researchers collect all the data in cross-sectional research at one time, we can use such studies to investigate the development of some phenomena over time. For example, to study the developmental problems of children of alcoholic parents, one could select groups of children of varying ages—say, one group at age 5, another group at age 10, and a third group at age 15. By observing differences in developmental problems among these groups, we may infer that a single youngster would experience changes as he or she grew up similar to the differences observed among these three groups. Yet one of the major weaknesses of such cross-sectional studies is that we have not actually observed the changes an individual goes through; rather we have observed three different groups of individuals at one point in time. Differences among these groups may reflect something other than the developmental changes that individuals experience. Because of this disadvantage, researchers sometimes resort to the other way of handling the time issue: longitudinal studies.

Longitudinal research involves gathering data over an extended period, such as months, years, or even, in a few cases, decades. One type of longitudinal approach is the **panel study,** in which the same people are studied at different times. This allows us to observe the actual changes these individuals go through over time. For example, a study of the social, psychological, and familial characteristics that influence whether drug addicts can successfully remain free of drugs followed the same 354 narcotics addicts for more than 24 years, collecting data on their family experiences, employment records, and a host of other factors (Bailey et al., 1994). Another longitudinal approach is the **trend study,** in which different people are observed at different times. Public opinion polling and research on political attitudes often are trend studies.

Both the nature of the research problem and practical considerations typically determine the decision about whether to use a longitudinal or a cross-sectional approach. Longitudinal studies, especially panel studies, have the advantage of providing the most accurate information regarding changes over time. A research question regarding such changes, then, probably would benefit from this approach. A disadvantage of panel studies is that they can be reactive: People's responses or behavior at one time may be influenced by the fact that they have been observed earlier. For example, a person who stated opposition to abortion in one survey may be inclined to respond the same way six months later so as not to appear inconsistent or vacillating, even if his or her attitudes had changed in the interim. Another disadvantage of panel studies is that people who participated early in a panel study may not want to—or may be unable to—participate later. People die, move away, grow uninterested, or become unavailable in other ways as panel studies progress. This loss of participants can adversely affect the validity of the research findings. The disadvantages of all longitudinal studies are that they can be difficult and expensive to conduct, especially if they span a very long period of time.

Cross-sectional research is cheaper and faster to conduct, and one need not worry about the loss of participants. However, cross-sectional research may not provide the most useful data for some research questions. Thus, the decision regarding the issue of the time dimension should be based on considerations of both the nature of the research problem and practical issues. There are times, of course, when practical feasibility plays a large part in the decision.

FEASIBILITY OF A RESEARCH PROJECT

By the time researchers have selected, shaped, and refined a research problem, the problem should be sufficiently clear that a consideration of practical issues involving the feasibility of the project is in order.

Practical considerations of what the research can reasonably accomplish given the time and resources available can force researchers to reduce— sometimes painfully—the scale of a project. A careful and honest appraisal of the time and money required to accomplish a project is useful in determining the feasibility of that project as envisioned, and it can reveal whether a change in goals is called for. In making a feasibility assessment, one should keep in mind a couple of axioms that apply to research projects: "Anything that can go wrong will" (Murphy's Law), and "Everything will take longer than possibly imagined."

The practical aspects of a project's feasibility center primarily on two related concerns: time and money (Kelly & McGrath, 1988).

Time Constraints

In developing a research project, one of the major considerations is whether there will be sufficient time to adequately complete what you hope to do. In later chapters, as we consider specific research techniques, we will see how different techniques vary in terms of how much time they take. Here we want to mention some of the major factors related to time considerations.

One factor concerns the population that is the focus of the research. If that population has characteristics that are fairly widespread, then a sufficient number of people will be readily available from which to collect data. For instance, if we were studying the differing attitudes of men and women toward work-release programs for prison inmates, we could select a sample of men and women from whatever city or state we happened to be in. If, however, our study focuses on people with special characteristics that are somewhat rare, problems may arise. In general, the smaller the number of people who have the characteristics needed for inclusion in a study, the more difficult and time-consuming it will be to contact a number sufficient to make scientifically valid conclusions. For example, a study of incestuous fathers—even in a large city—may encounter problems obtaining enough cases, because relatively few such people will be openly known.

A second problem relating to time constraints involves the proper development of measuring devices. Researchers should test all techniques used for gathering data before the actual study is conducted, and this can be very time-consuming in itself. A pretest, as we saw in Chapter 1, refers to the preliminary application of the data-gathering techniques to assess their adequacy. A pilot study is a small-scale "trial run" of all the procedures planned for use in the main study. In some studies we may need to conduct several pretests as we modify data-collection devices based on the results of earlier pretests. All in all, the refining of data-gathering procedures can consume a lot of time.

A third major factor related to time considerations is the amount of time required for actual data collection, which can range from a few hours for a questionnaire administered to a group of "captive" students to the years that are necessary in many longitudinal studies. Because the amount of time required for data collection is so variable, the issue of time requires close scrutiny when addressing the question of the feasibility of a particular research design.

A fourth consideration related to the time issue is the amount of time necessary to complete the analysis of the data. In general, the less structured the data, the more time will be required for its analysis. The field notes that serve as the data for some observational studies, for example, can be very time-consuming to analyze (see Chapter 9). Likewise, videotapes collected during an experiment or during single-subject research may need several viewings before they are adequately understood (see Chapters 10 and 11). Highly structured data in quantified form, however, also can be time-consuming to analyze (see Chapters 14 and 15). Although some quantitative data can be quickly entered into a computer file if it is in a form that can be optically scanned or submitted from a website, other data must be manually entered. Even optically scanned or web data, however, require considerable advance programming and preparation before the data can actually be submitted. Also, raw data often must be manipulated and transformed before they are ready for analysis, and this can be time-consuming as well. So, the time needed for data analysis requires careful consideration owing to wide variation in the amount of time that may be necessary.

The fifth area in which time becomes a factor is the writing of the report itself. The amount of time this consumes depends on the length and complexity of the report and the skills of the investigator. Each researcher is in the best position, based on past writing experiences, to assess the amount of time he or she requires. As a final reminder, it will likely take longer than you expect.

Financial Considerations

The financial expenditures associated with a research project are another constraint on feasibility. Good research is not always expensive. In many instances, students and human service practitioners can get by with only modest costs, because data are easy to obtain, analysis procedures are simple, and the labor is either voluntary or provided at no additional charge. Even small projects, however, are likely to require money for telephone calls, typing and duplicating questionnaires, computer equipment, Internet access, and other services that can quickly stress the tight resources of a small human service agency. At the other extreme, it is not unusual for the price tag of major research and demonstration projects in the human services to run into six figures or more. For example, between 1997 and 2003, the National Institute of Justice (2003) provided annual grants of about $1 million for the development and evaluation of educational programs to assist teenagers in developing skills to avoid drug use or other forms of delinquency and to avoid becoming victims of crime. Table 4.3 shows the budget for a hypothetical survey research project of modest scale and indicates some of the general expenditure categories to consider when assessing the feasibility of any project.

The salaries of those who conduct the study are potentially the most expensive item, especially for studies that require large interviewer staffs. Such expenses include not only the interviewers' wages, but also transportation costs and living expenses, which can be sizable. Interviewers may require hours of training before they can begin to collect data. If respondents are not available, callbacks may be necessary, which further increases the cost of each interview. To get the work done in a timely fashion and ensure reliability, investigators may need to hire people or contract with an organization to code the raw data into an analyzable format.

Computer expenses also can be formidable. A few decades ago, data analysis comprised the bulk of computer costs, but now computing services of one kind or another are used for questionnaire design, project management, data collection, literature

TABLE 4.3 An Illustrative Budget for Conducting Face-To-Face Interviews of 400 People

ELEMENTS OF THE INTERVIEW	COST	% OF TOTAL
Materials for Interview: print or electronic maps; interviewer manuals; printed questionnaires;	$500	2%
Interviewer Training Sessions: 2 days of training, wages for trainer and interviewers	$2,400	9.8%
Conduct Interview: Travel Costs: travel to and locate residence (inc. 60 callbacks for people not home); 1 hour per interview; $10 per completed interview	$4,000	16.3%
Conduct Interview: contact respondent; 1.5 hours per interview	$9,000	36.7%
Clerical and Data Entry Tasks: code or transcribe interviews; enter data into an electronic data file (1 hour per interview at $10 per hour)	$4,000	16.3%
Professional Supervision: coordinating and supervising all of the above tasks (160 hours at $60,000 total annual compensation)	$4,620	18.8%
TOTAL:	$24,520	100%

searches, and report preparation. A significant cost here is for the software packages and Internet access that actually perform these procedures, in addition to the cost of the computer itself and peripherals like printers, scanners, zip drives, and so on.

Another major cost consideration is expenditures for office supplies and equipment. Under this category are such items as paper, envelopes, postage, tape, printing, and the like. Paper products might seem to be inexpensive at first glance, but given the large samples that are used for some surveys, this cost can be substantial. For example, suppose we conduct a survey of approximately 500 people. Each person receives a large envelope containing a letter of introduction; a professionally printed, four-page questionnaire; and a postage-paid return envelope. In addition, all members of the sample receive a reminder letter urging them to respond, and about 250 nonrespondents receive a second questionnaire. The cost for printing, envelopes, and postage could easily exceed $2,000. Different kinds of studies present different cost issues. For example, studies based on direct observation of behavior may necessitate high-cost equipment, such as video cameras, recorders, and videotape. Unless these are already available, the project will require substantial outlays.

Providing incentives to ensure the cooperation of people in the study also may be a cost factor. This may range from giving stickers or balloons to schoolchildren for completing a questionnaire to paying respondents in recognition of the large time commitment required for a longitudinal study. A study evaluating the effectiveness of advocacy services to women leaving their abusive partners (Sullivan, 1991) illustrates participant incentive costs. Women were interviewed before the program and at 5, 10, and 20 weeks following the program. Not only was it difficult to maintain contact with this highly mobile population, completing a survey form was a low priority for these women, given the stress and disruption in their lives. To encourage the women to participate, the 46 participants were paid $10, $20, $30, and $40, respectively, for the four interviews, for a total cost of $4,600. Payment of subjects is more of an issue in experiments that require more time investment and greater commitment from participants than usually is required in most surveys or observational studies.

Dissemination of research findings also generates costs. Besides the additional printing and office supplies for preparing reports, this expense category may include travel to professional meetings to present papers. Program evaluation studies also may entail hosting workshops or conferences with sponsors and other interested parties to ensure that the findings are incorporated into the policy and intervention planning process.

Finally, some costs associated with a research project are difficult to specify. When research is conducted under the auspices of a university, a human service agency, or a research center, some organizational resources will partially or indirectly support the research. For example, money will be spent to heat and light the building where the research project is housed, but this cost is difficult to assess precisely. A major factor in awarding a research project to a particular organization may be the fact that the organization has an extensive research library, sophisticated computer facilities, or an extensive research laboratory. The organization maintains these facilities for general use, not just for a particular research project, so it is difficult to ascertain how much of the overall cost of supporting the facilities should be assigned to a given project. Consequently, the concept of "indirect cost," typically a percentage of the total grant request, is employed to cover these real but hard-to-specify costs. Each organization negotiates its rate with the granting agency on the basis of the facilities and equipment that the organization has for research. The amount charged to indirect costs varies from 15 percent to well in excess of 100 percent of the basic grant.

Anticipating and Avoiding Problems

Problems related to time and financial considerations arise during virtually all research projects, but their impact on the outcome of the research can be minimized if they are anticipated as much as possible, especially during the planning stage, when the details

INFORMATION TECHNOLOGY IN RESEARCH

Searching the Literature: Lessons from Evidence-Based Practice

Whether one is a researcher seeking to hone a research idea into a feasible project or a human service practitioner seeking the best means to help a client, efficient access to the literature is essential. In fact, literature access represents one of the linkages between practice and research, and developments along these lines in evidence-based practice serve the needs of researchers and practitioners alike.

Evidence-based practice means integrating individual human service expertise with the best available external evidence from systematic research. A major challenge for evidence-based practice is to provide a means whereby practitioners and researchers can find the evidence in a readily useable form. To meet this challenge, social scientists from around the world developed the Campbell Collaboration. It has three main review groups: social welfare, education, and criminology. Formally organized in 2000, it was inspired by a similar group that focused on research in the health field, the Cochrane Collaboration (Hannes & Claes, 2007). Although the Campbell Collaboration Library is designed for both practitioners and researchers, each may use it for different purposes. The attraction for practitioners is that the Library provides rapid access to the latest research to help answer questions such as "How well does the intervention I'm considering work with problems like those I'm confronting?" The researcher might want to know "How well defined is the knowledge about my topic? What measurement tools have been used? What recommendations for further research have previous studies identified?"

The Cochrane Collaboration (2003) points out that the major bibliographic databases cover less than half the world's literature for health care and are biased toward English language publications. A similar situation holds true for the human service fields. Although common online literature databases such as Sociological Abstracts or Social Work Abstracts enable the user to locate studies, the user must sort through all the studies and draw relevant conclusions. A central feature of the Campbell Collaborative is not simply that it provides access to studies, but that it includes a database of systematic reviews, which consists of full-text articles reviewing the research available on human service. Each review follows a highly structured and systematic format and covers particular content areas, such as the methodologies used on a particular area of research, the criteria for including studies in the review, and the conclusions from the research. The plan for conducting a systematic review is developed according to guidelines from the Campbell Collaboration, and the resulting review is itself peer-reviewed before it is included in the Campbell Library topics (http://www.campbellcollaboration.org/library.php). The Library can be searched by title, author, and keyword. Consequently, researchers and practitioners can have confidence in the quality and findings of each Campbell review.

---

of the project are easier to change. A number of steps can be taken to anticipate problems. First, learn as much as possible from the experiences of others through the studies consulted during the literature review. We mentioned earlier that finding problems other researchers encountered is one purpose of the literature review. Also, solicit personal advice from experienced researchers who might be available for consultation. A knowledgeable researcher may be able to identify potential trouble spots in the plans and suggest modifications to avoid them.

Second, obtain whatever permissions or consents may be needed early in the planning stages of the project. Depending on the people the researcher wishes to study, it may be necessary to obtain permission from them to collect data. For example, some studies are aimed at school-age children and seek to gather data while the children are in school. To protect students from undue harassment and themselves from parental complaints, school administrators frequently are cool to allowing researchers into their schools. It may take considerable time to persuade whatever authorities are involved to grant the permissions needed—if they are granted at all. It certainly is wise to obtain any needed permissions before expending effort on other phases of the project; that effort might be wasted if permissions cannot be obtained.

The final—and, perhaps, most important—suggestion for avoiding problems is to conduct a pilot study. As noted, a pilot study is a preliminary run-through, on a small scale, of all the procedures

Of course, having the empirical data available in readily useable form is still only one part of the equation. The other part is accessing the data, and the key to access is asking the right questions for the database search. In addition to the Campbell review, practitioners and researchers may also need to locate actual studies. Whether searching for a review or for individual research studies, evidence-based practice experts point out that a good question for a systematic search must be clear and describe exactly what is being sought—just as a good research hypothesis clearly specifies the independent and dependent variables (Sackett et al., 2000). A widely accepted evidence-based practice principle for framing search questions is the acronym "PICO," which stands for:

- P—People or patient population of interest. The demographic characteristics, the problem or condition, and the particular setting (such as community or institution) should be specified.

- I—Intervention. The intervention should be specified as clearly as possible, such as cognitive behavioral therapy, couples counseling, or bipolar support group.

- C—Comparisons which will be made. This category would be included if the reviewer wishes to specifically limit inclusion of studies to those using control groups, placebos, or alternate treatments in the research design.

- O—Outcomes. Here the reviewer specifies the kinds of outcomes such as behavior change, prevention, reduced cost, etc., that are of interest.

For example, an evidence-based literature search related to unintended pregnancy included the following key questions (identify the PICO elements in each of these questions):

1. How effective is counseling in a clinical setting at changing knowledge, skills, and attitudes about unintended pregnancies?
2. What is the association between behaviors that support fertility desires and the prevention of unintended conceptions?
3. What are the potential harms of contraception counseling?
4. What is the cost-effectiveness of counseling in the clinical setting to prevent unintended pregnancy? (Moos, Bartholomew, and Lohr, 2003, p. 116)

The questions provide the road map for navigating through the various databases appropriate to the practitioner's interest. In addition to helping identify search terms, the questions provide guidance for including and excluding studies from the plethora of articles one is likely to encounter. (See Appendix A for databases useful to the human services that are widely available online.)

---

planned for the main study. For surveys, contact and interview a small part of the sample—say, 20 people. Then, analyze the data as you would for the complete project. In experiments, the researcher should run a few groups through all procedures, looking for any unexpected reactions from participants. Observational researchers should visit the observation sites and make observations as planned for the larger study. The focus is, again, on problems that might force modifications in research plans. Deal with any problems that surface during the pilot study before the main project is launched.

Given all the pitfalls a project might encounter, it is quite possible that, at some point, the researcher may conclude the project is not feasible as planned. Before calling it quits, however, give careful consideration to possible modifications that would enhance the project's feasibility. If inadequate time or money is the problem, perhaps the project can be scaled down. It might be possible to reduce the sample size or the number of hypotheses tested to make the experiment manageable. If face-to-face interviews were originally planned, consider a mailed questionnaire or even a telephone survey as cost-cutting and time-reducing measures. If the problem is with procedures, such as may occur in an experiment, consider how they might be changed so the project can proceed. The point is that a project should not be abandoned until all efforts to make it feasible have been investigated.

REVIEW AND CRITICAL THINKING

Main Points

- Suitable topics for research come from a variety of sources, including personal interest, social problems, theory testing, prior research, program evaluation and policy implementation, and human service practice.
- Political factors also influence problem selection: Powerful interest groups encourage the expenditure of research resources on issues that are of interest to them and that may not serve the interests of less advantaged or minority groups.
- A general topic for research must be narrowed and focused into a precise, researchable problem.
- An important part of refining a research problem is conceptual development: identifying and defining the concepts on which the study will focus.
- Reviewing previous research related to the selected topic is a crucial step in problem development and preparing to conduct a research project. This review should produce information about theoretical and conceptual issues, research hypotheses and variables, measurement and operational definitions, research techniques, sampling strategies, statistical techniques, and findings and conclusions.
- The units of analysis must be clearly specified as individuals, groups, organizations, programs, or social artifacts.
- Continual awareness of the operative unit of analysis ensures avoidance of such errors as the ecological fallacy and the reductionist fallacy.
- Reactivity refers to the fact that people may behave differently when they are being watched than when they are not being watched, and the effects of reactivity must be considered when shaping a research problem.
- Qualitative research emphasizes the description of how people experience the world; it relies on data in the form of words, pictures, descriptions, and narratives. Quantitative research uses numbers, counts, and measures to assess statistical relationships between variables.
- Cross-sectional research is based on data collected at one point in time, which makes accurate conclusions about trends or behavioral changes difficult. Longitudinal studies are based on data collected over a period of time and are particularly useful for studying trends or behavioral changes.
- Once fully refined, the practical feasibility of a proposed research project requires realistic assessment.

Important Terms for Review

cross-sectional research
ecological fallacy
longitudinal research
panel study
qualitative research
quantitative research
reactivity
reductionist fallacy
trend study
units of analysis

Critical Thinking

Critical thinking calls for the careful assessment of the nature, extent, and various facets of a problem to be addressed. So human service practitioners, policymakers, and people in their everyday lives need to devote attention to formulating, shaping, and refining a problem. It doesn't have to be a scientific problem, which is the focus of this book; it could be a problem confronting an individual, a family, or an organization. Careful and systematic thinking about a problem can pay off in a much more clear view of the problem:

1. Why is this problem considered to be a problem at all? Are there some personal interest or political issues that lead some people to see it as a problem?
2. Are the nature and terms of the problem clear and precise? Could you engage in the equivalent of what researchers call "conceptual development" to produce a clearer and sharper focus on exactly what the nature of the problem is?
3. What have others said about this problem? Is there some equivalent to what researchers call a "review of the literature" that could uncover other ideas, perspectives, or data about the problem and its solution?
4. How do people's subjective perceptions shape how they formulate a problem? Do you tend to perceive the problem differently if you take a "quantitative" approach versus a "qualitative" approach?

Exploring the Internet

Search for websites that focus on issues such as poverty or drug abuse. An initial perusal of such sites can help identify important issues for developing the research problem such as the following: "How is the concept defined?" "Does there appear to be consensus on what the concept is?" "What controversies or issues are being debated about the topic?" You also may find organizations and resources, such as measurement tools, that may prove useful during later steps in the research process. Select a topic to research, and explore some of the websites that the search locates.

The Internet can be extremely useful in discovering prior research. Many websites consist of bibliographies or include them as a special section. One example is the National Criminal Justice Reference Service. Access this site (at http://www.ncjrs.gov) and select "Victims," which is listed under "Topics." This will lead to a diverse listing of sources on victims of crime. Select one of the victim categories, such as "Special Populations," and peruse some of the available sources. As another example, the Substance Abuse and Mental Health Services Administration (http://store.samhsa.gov/home) provides immediate access to a wealth of articles related to substance abuse. Try out this site by entering a combination of terms, such as "alcohol" and "violence."

For Further Reading

Berg, B. L., & Lune, H. (2012). *Qualitative Research Methods for the Social Sciences,* 8th ed. Boston: Pearson. Although this book focuses primarily on how to conduct good qualitative research, it also contains a good comparison of qualitative and quantitative research and assesses when each is the most appropriate design.

Bransford, J. D. & Stein, B. S. (1995). *The Ideal Problem Solver: A Guide for Improving Thinking, Learning, and Creativity,* 2nd ed. New York: Freeman. Sound thinking combined with creativity clearly are important to formulating research problems. This guide assists in improving thought processes, drawing logical deductions, enhancing creativity, and even improving communication skills.

Gross, R. (1993). *The Independent Scholar's Handbook.* Berkeley, Calif.: Ten Speed Press. This book contains many examples of how successful scholars developed personal hunches and notions into serious research inquiries. It also is filled with practical advice about such things as obtaining resources and communicating with other researchers who share similar research interests.

Higgins, P. C. & Johnson, J. M. (1988). *Personal Sociology.* New York: Praeger. This book includes many illustrations of how personal life events and experiences shaped the research interests of a variety of sociologists.

Hunt, M. (1985). *Profiles of Social Research: The Scientific Study of Human Interactions.* New York: Basic Books. As its title implies, this book presents a series of descriptions of major research projects. Follow these projects from inception to completion, and see successful social scientists at work.

Locke, L. F., Silverman, S. J., & Spirduso, W. (2010). *Reading and Understanding Research*, 3rd ed. Thousand Oaks, Calif.: Sage. This is an excellent and thorough overview of how to do a good literature review and extract the appropriate information from it in an organized fashion.

Menard, S. (2002). *Longitudinal Research*, 2nd ed. Newbury Park, Calif.: Sage. This book provides a readable overview of both longitudinal and cross-sectional research. It discusses when each is an appropriate design and some of the problems that arise in doing good longitudinal research.

Reinharz, S. (1992). *Feminist Methods in Social Research.* New York: Oxford University Press. This book is a massive compilation of examples for all types of research conducted by researchers identified as feminists. Anyone interested in conducting research from this perspective is well advised to consult this impressive work.

Class Exercises for Competency Assessment

In working through the exercises in this chapter, we suggest that you review Appendix A, which covers the basic issues involved when conducting research in a library. We also have found it helpful for students in our research classes to schedule a one- or two-hour workshop with the reference personnel to help familiarize themselves with the materials available in their library, especially the human service resource material.

4.1. **[Critical Thinking] [Research & Practice]** Following are several broad topic areas relevant to the human services. Select one that has the greatest personal appeal to you. Identify why this topic interests you. How do your selection and the reasons for it compare with those of other students?
   a. child abuse
   b. dementia
   c. emotionally disturbed children
   d. victims of crime
   e. violence in the family
   f. alcoholism and drug addiction
   g. discrimination against minorities
   h. homelessness
   i. community living for the developmentally disabled
   j. effects of unemployment
   k. recipient rights for mental health clients

4.2. **[Research & Practice]** Use your library's resources to locate several research studies published in the professional literature on the topic you selected. Your search efforts should include—but need not be limited to—the following: a popular search engine such as Google; a specialized social science service such as socINDEX, or Social Work Abstracts; government documents through the Federal Digital System, (http://www.gpo.gov/fdsys); and the library's public catalog or a service such as WorldCAT. Be prepared to discuss with the class how you located your studies.

4.3. **[Critical Thinking] [Research & Practice]** For each research study you locate, do the following:
   a. Indicate which factors seemed to influence the researcher's selection of topic in the study—that is, personal interest, social problems, theory testing, program evaluation and policy implementation, prior research, or practice experience.
   b. What was the unit of analysis for each study? Was it the same as or different from the source of the data? If different, indicate the source. Can you think of any reasons for selecting a different unit of analysis?

c. What specific problem did the study address? From the presentation of the study, what factors influenced the final, actual problem formulation? In particular, were there issues of cost, time, or feasibility that necessitated a modification of the problem from the initial proposal?

4.4. [Ethics] [Critical Thinking] [Research & Practice] Chapter 3 presented a discussion of ethical issues in research. Did a concern for ethics influence what specific research problem emerged from an interest in studying the general topic? If so, what ethical issues confronted the researchers in studying the problem?

4.5. [Diversity] [Research & Practice] We have made the point that problem selection in research is a social process in which power, interest groups, and other factors play significant roles. One practice issue that has received considerable attention in recent years is transracial adoption—the placement of minority children, especially Native-American children, in foster and adoptive homes with white families. A quick Internet search on the key words "transracial adoption" will generate sufficient information for this exercise.

a. Have one group of students imagine that they are members of an adoptive/foster parent association that has been asked to provide suggestions to the DHHS for research priorities. What research problems would this group want to have studied?

b. Have a second group of students imagine that they are tribal leaders representing the interests of Native Americans. What priorities would they have, and what questions might this group suggest? Contrast the problems suggested by each group.

Chapter 5

✦

The Process of Measurement

Ways of Measuring
   From Concepts to Indicators
   Techniques of Measuring
   Positivist and Nonpositivist Views of Measurement

Levels of Measurement
   Nominal Measures
   Ordinal Measures
   Interval Measures
   Ratio Measures
   Discrete versus Continuous Variables

Evaluating Measures
   Validity
   Reliability

   Measurement with Diverse Populations

Errors in Measurement
   Random Errors
   Systematic Errors
   Improving Validity and Reliability

Choosing a Measurement Device

Review and Critical Thinking
   Main Points
   Important Terms for Review
   Critical Thinking
   Exploring the Internet
   For Further Reading
   Class Exercises for Competency Assessment

A crisis counselor working with a mental health agency receives a call from the county jail. The deputy there is concerned about an inmate he describes as severely depressed. The counselor responds by asking a number of questions, attempting to make an initial assessment of the severity of the inmate's depression. Has the inmate been eating his meals? Is he sleeping too much or too little? Is his affect flat when he responds to questions? Has he made any remarks about committing suicide? Later, the counselor may interview the inmate directly, request psychological testing, or refer him to a psychiatrist for further evaluation. Such assessments are analogous to a process in research called *measurement*. Just as the clinician used a variety of observations by the deputy as indicators of the inmate's condition, researchers use various observations as indicators of the concepts of interest in a research project. **Measurement** refers to the process of describing abstract concepts in terms of specific indicators by assigning numbers or other symbols to these indicants in accordance with rules. At the very minimum, one must have some means of determining whether a variable is either present or absent, just as the counselor needs to know whether the inmate is eating or not. In many cases, however, measurement is more complex and involves assessing how much, or to what degree, a variable is present. An example of this is the counselor's question about how much the inmate is sleeping—"amount of sleep" being a variable that can take on many values.

Measurement is a part of the process of moving from the abstract or theoretical level to the concrete. Recall from Chapter 2 that scientific concepts have two types of definitions: *nominal* and *operational*. Before research can proceed, researchers must translate nominal definitions into operational ones. The operational definitions indicate the exact procedures, or operations, that the researchers will use to measure the concepts. Measurement is essentially the process of operationalizing concepts. Figure 5.1 illustrates the place of measurement in the research process.

In this chapter we discuss the general issues that relate to all measurement, beginning with some of the different ways in which we can make measurements. We then analyze how measurements that are made at different levels affect the mathematical operations that can be performed on them. Finally, we present ways of evaluating measures and determining the errors that can occur in the measurement process.

WAYS OF MEASURING

From Concepts to Indicators

Normally, we cannot observe directly the concepts and variables that are the focus of both research and practice. We cannot see such things as poverty, social class, mental retardation, and the like; we can only infer them from something else. Take something as seemingly obvious as child abuse. Can you directly observe child abuse? Not really. What you directly observe is a bruise on a child's back, an infant's broken leg, or a father slapping his daughter. And even the slap may not relate to child abuse, because parents sometimes slap their children without its being a case of child abuse. However, all these things—the bruise, the broken leg, the slap— may be used as *indicators* of child abuse. In research and in practice, an **indicator** is an observation that we assume is evidence of the attributes or properties of some phenomenon. What we observe are the indicators of a variable, not the actual properties of the variable itself. Emergency room personnel may assume that a child's broken leg is an indicator of child abuse even though they have not observed the actual abuse.

Child abuse represents a good illustration of the difficulties of moving from nominal to operational

FIGURE 5.1 The Measurement Process

definitions with variables involving social and psychological events. At the nominal level, we might define child abuse as an occurrence in which a parent or caretaker injures a child not by accident but in anger or with deliberate intent (Gelles, 1987; Korbin, 1987). What indicators, however, would we use to operationalize this definition? Some things would obviously seem to indicate child abuse, such as a cigarette burn on a child's buttock, but what about a bruise on the arm? Some subcultures in our own society view hitting children, even to the point of bruising, as an appropriate way to train or discipline them. Furthermore, some people would argue that a serious psychological disorder a child suffers is an indicator of child abuse, because it shows the parents did not provide the proper love and affection for stable development. In short, one of the problems in operationalizing child abuse, as with many other variables in human service research, is that its definition is culture-bound and involves subjective judgments. This illustrates the importance of good conceptual development and precise nominal definitions for research. It also shows how the theoretical and research levels can mutually influence one another: As we shape nominal definitions into operational ones, the difficulties that arise often lead to a reconceptualization, or a change, in the nominal definition at the theoretical level (see Figure 5.1).

The example of child abuse also illustrates another point about measurement—namely, that more than one indicator of a variable may exist. The term **item** is used to refer to a single indicator of a variable. Items can take numerous forms, such as an answer to a question or an observation of a behavior or characteristic. Asking a person her age or noting her sex, for example, would both produce items of measurement. In many cases, however, the process of operationalizing variables involves combining a number of items into a composite score called an **index** or a **scale**. (Although scales involve more rigor in their construction than indexes do, we can use the terms interchangeably at this point; Chapter 13 will present some distinctions between them.) Attitude scales, for example, commonly involve asking people a series of questions, or items, and then summarizing their responses into a single score that represents their attitude on an issue. A major reason for using scales or indexes rather than single items is that scales enable us to measure variables in a more precise and, usually, more accurate fashion. To illustrate the value of scales over items, consider your grade in this course. In all likelihood, your final grade will be an index, or a composite score, of your answers to many questions on many tests throughout the semester. Would you prefer that your final grade be determined by a one-item measure, such as a single multiple-choice or essay question? Probably not, because that item would not measure the full range of what you learned. Furthermore, an error on that item would indicate that you had not learned much in the course, even if the error were the result of ill health or personal problems on the day of the exam. For these reasons, then, researchers usually prefer multiple-item measures to single-item indicators.

We began this discussion by noting that because variables are abstract, we normally cannot observe them directly. Variables differ in their degree of abstraction, however, and this affects the ease with which we can accomplish measurement. In general, the more abstract the variable, the more difficult it is to measure. For example, a study of child abuse might include the variable "number of children in family," on the theoretical presumption that large families create more stress for parents and, therefore, are more likely to precipitate abusive attacks on children. This is a rather easy variable to measure, because the concepts of "children" and "family" have readily identifiable, empirical referents, and are relatively easy and unambiguous to observe and count. Suppose, however, that the child abuse study also included as a dependent variable "positiveness of child's self-concept." Because it can take many different forms, "self-concept" is a difficult notion to measure. Although we have narrowed it to the "positive–negative" dimension, it is still more difficult to measure than "number of children in family," because we could ask a whole variety of questions to explore how positively people feel about themselves. We also can measure self-concept by behaviors, on the theoretical presumption that people who feel positively about themselves behave differently from those who do not. The point is that highly abstract concepts usually have no single empirical indicator that is clearly and obviously preferable to others as a measure of the concept.

We have emphasized the point that measurement involves transition from the abstract and conceptual level to the concrete and observable level, and this is what most typically occurs in research. Exploratory studies, however, can involve measurement in the opposite direction: First, we observe empirical indicators and then formulate theoretical concepts that those indicators presumably represent. In Chapter 2, we called this *inductive reasoning*. In a sense, you might think of Sigmund Freud or Jean Piaget as having done this when they developed their theories of personality and cognitive development, respectively. Piaget, for example, observed the behavior of children for many years as he gradually developed his theory about the stages of cognitive development, including concepts like egocentrism, object permanence, and reversibility (Ginsburg & Opper, 1988). Piaget recognized that the behaviors he observed could be understood only if placed in a more abstract, theoretical context. In a sense, he measured something before he knew what it was he had measured. Once his theories began to develop, he then developed new concepts and hypotheses and formulated different measuring devices to test them deductively. The point is that whether one shifts from the abstract to the concrete, or vice versa, the logic is the same, involving the relationship between theoretical concepts and empirical indicators.

Techniques of Measuring

We will discuss specific techniques for measuring variables in other chapters in this book, but we find that discussing these techniques briefly at this point helps clarify the issues surrounding measurement. Measurement techniques in the social sciences and human services vary widely because the concepts we measure are so diverse. These techniques, however, mostly fall into one of three categories (see Figure 5.2).

1. *Verbal reports*. This is undoubtedly the most common measurement technique in social research. It involves people answering questions, being interviewed, or responding to verbal statements (see Chapters 7 and 9). For example, research on people's attitudes typically uses this technique by asking people how they feel about commercial products, political candidates, or social policies. In a study of school performance, to mention another example, we could measure how well students do in school by asking them what their grades are or how much they know about a particular subject.

2. *Observation*. Social researchers also measure concepts by making direct observations of some phenomena (see Chapter 9). We watch people at school or at work and make notes of what they say and do. We may even make an audio or video recording as a way of preserving the observations. In a study of school performance, we could measure how well students do in school by directly observing their behavior in the classroom and noting how often they answer questions posed by teachers, how often their answers are correct, and how they get along with teachers and students.

3. *Archival records*. Researchers also use a variety of available recorded information to measure variables (see Chapter 8). These records might take the form of statistical records, governmental or organizational documents, personal letters and diaries, newspapers and magazines, or movies and musical lyrics. All these archival records are the products of human social behavior and can serve as indicators of concepts in the social sciences. In the study of school performance, for example, a researcher could use school records to locate students' grades, performance on exams, attendance records, and disciplinary problems as measures of how well they are doing in school.

These are the major ways that social scientists measure concepts. Researchers must specify exactly what aspects of verbal reports, observations, or available data will serve as indicators of the concepts they

FIGURE 5.2 The Major Strategies Used by Social Scientists to Measure Variables

Verbal Reports: People answering questions, being interviewed, or responding to verbal statements

Measuring School Performance: Ask students to tell us what their grades are or how much they know about a particular subject

Observation: Directly watch people at school, work, or other setting and make note of what they say and do

Measuring School Performance: Directly observe their behavior in the classroom, noting how often they answer questions posed by teachers, how often their answers are correct, and how they get along with teachers and students

Archival Reports: Review available recorded information

Measuring School Performance: Use the school records to locate students' grades, performance on exams, attendance records, and disciplinary problems

---

want to measure. In addition, researchers use some key criteria to help them decide whether a particular indicator is a good measure of some concept. These criteria will be discussed later in this chapter.

Positivist and Nonpositivist Views of Measurement

Much of the foundation for measurement and operationalization in the social sciences derives from the work of statisticians, mathematicians, philosophers, and scientists in a field called *classical test theory* or *measurement theory* (Bohrnstedt, 1983; Stevens, 1951), which provides the logical foundation for issues discussed in this chapter and derives largely from the positivist view of science discussed in Chapter 2. The logic of measurement can be described by the following formula:

$$X = T + E$$

In this formula, X represents our observation or measurement of some phenomenon; it is our indicator. It might be the grade on an exam in a social research class, for example, or a response to a self-esteem scale (see Table 5.1). Also in this formula, T represents the true, actual phenomenon that we are

TABLE 5.1   Elements in the Process of Measurement

X	=	T	+	E
Observation	=	True Phenomenon	+	Error
Reading on a weight scale	=	Your actual weight	+	Clothing you are wearing; Heavy object in your pocket
Grade on an examination in social research class	=	Actual knowledge you acquired in social research class	+	Heat and humidity in test room; Distraction due to fight with partner
Score on a scale measuring self-esteem	=	Your actual level of self-esteem	+	Incorrectly marking a self-esteem scale; Questions on self-esteem scale that are difficult to understand

attempting to measure with X; it would be what a student actually learned in a social research class or what his or her true self-esteem is. The third symbol in the formula, E, represents any measurement error that occurs, or anything that influences X other than T. It might be the heat and humidity in the classroom on the day of the social research exam, which made it difficult to concentrate, or it could reflect the fact that a subject incorrectly marked a choice on the self-esteem scale, inadvertently circling a response that indicated higher or lower self-esteem than he or she actually possessed.

The formula is very simple—but also very profound and important: Our measurement of any phenomenon is a product of the characteristics or qualities of the phenomenon itself and any errors that occur in the measurement process. What we strive for is measurement with no error:

$$E = 0$$

and, therefore,

$$X = T$$

The ideal to strive for is a measurement of the phenomenon that is determined only by the true state of the phenomenon itself. Scientists recognize, however, that they normally cannot achieve this ideal state in its entirety. In reality, we attempt to reduce E as much as possible. Later in this chapter, we will complicate this measurement formula a bit, but for now, it can stand as a shorthand way of understanding the process of measurement.

Before going deeper into the process of measurement, it is important to consider the nonpositivists' critique of classical measurement theory. Many nonpositivists argue that we haven't examined a huge assumption in this at all, one that may render the entire topic somewhat problematic. The assumption is that the phenomenon being measured (T) exists objectively in the world and that our measurement device is merely discovering it and its properties. Some things do exist in the world independently of our perceptions and our judgments about them. The computer monitor on which these words are being written, for example, has a screen that is nine inches tall—we just measured it with a ruler. Our measurement of it was a discovery of its properties, and the measurement process did not create or change those properties. Now, however, think about a social science concept, such as self-esteem. We measure it by asking subjects to agree or disagree with a series of statements. We score a "strongly agree" response as "4" and a "strongly disagree" response as "1"; then, we sum up those responses to all the separate items in the scale and give a self-esteem score that ranges from 10 to 40. What, however, is the objective reality behind this measurement? If a subject receives a score of 32 on our measurement device, what does that 32 correspond to in his or her subjective world, or mind, or consciousness? The 32 is the X in our measurement formula, but what is the T that it corresponds to? Is the link between the measurement of a computer screen and its actual length as direct as the link between the score of 32 on the self-esteem measure and the actual subjective experience of self?

> **RESEARCH IN PRACTICE 5.1   Behavior and Social Environment: Controversies in Measuring Violence against Women**
>
> An extensive body of literature has accumulated regarding the topic of violence against women. In the process of building this knowledge base, considerable disagreement has arisen about which harmful behaviors to include in a definition of nonlethal violence and how best to go about measuring this violence. Consider the two following excerpts, the first from a qualitative study and the second from a summary of a national, randomized survey:
>
>> I was raped by my uncle when I was 12 and my husband has beat me for years. For my whole life, when I have gone to a doctor, to my priest, or to a friend to have my wounds patched up, or for a shoulder to cry on, they dwell on my bruises, my cuts, my broken bones. The abuse in my life has taken away my trust in people and in life.
>>
>> It's taken away the laughter in my life. I don't trust myself to be able to take care of my kids, to take care of myself, to do anything to make a difference in my own life or anyone else's. That's the hurt I would like to fix. I can live with the physical scars.
>>
>> It's these emotional scars that drive me near suicide sometimes.
>>
>> —A respondent interviewed by DeKeseredy and MacLeod (1997, p. 5)
>
> Women experience significantly more partner violence than men do: 25 percent of surveyed women, compared with 8 percent of surveyed men, said they were raped and/or physically assaulted by a current or former spouse, cohabiting partner, or date in their lifetime; 1.5 percent of surveyed women and 0.9 percent of surveyed men said they were raped and/or physically assaulted by such a perpetrator in the previous 12 months. According to survey estimates, approximately 1.5 million women and 834,700 men are raped and/or physically assaulted by an intimate partner annually in the United States.
>
>> —Tjaden and Thoennes (1998, p. 2)
>
> The gut-wrenching words of a violence survivor or the decimal precision of an executive summary: Which approach is the better measure of domestic violence? The qualitative study vividly portrays one person's experience, an experience with which many victims can identify. The survey lacks the rich description, but appears to capture the immensity of the problem in terms of numbers of victims. The two approaches have fueled a debate over what focus to use when we attempt to measure violence against women.
>
> Traditionally, many survey researchers have used operational definitions that include physical abuse indicators, such as beatings or kicks, or sexual assault features, such as forced penetration. For example, the Conflict Tactics Scale asks people to indicate how often a partner has "used a knife or gun on them" or "beat them up" (Straus et al., 1996). An argument in favor of such an approach is that it lends itself to readily quantifiable measures. One can count the number of times a victim was beaten, the number of visits to the emergency room, or the number of workdays lost because of injury. Standardized instruments such as the Conflict Tactics Scale permit researchers to make comparisons across studies and with different populations. So, in the case of the survey quoted above, the researchers can estimate the number of women who were raped or physically assaulted, and the results can be used in conjunction with those of other surveys to estimate the extent of the problem.

The nonpositivists argue that many social science concepts do not have such clear and objective referents in the world. Our concepts are based on an intuitive and theoretical understanding of what parts of the world are like. In other words, we are *constructing* the world, not just *discovering* it. We believe that something like self-esteem exists, but it is our construction of it that we measure with the self-esteem scale, not the thing itself (if the thing itself even exists). This does not make measurement theory useless, but it does suggest that the whole process is more complicated—and not nearly as objective—as the positivists suggest. Nonetheless, many nonpositivists agree that some social science measurement can follow the model of measurement theory. Some social phenomena, such as age and sex, do have some objective existence in the world. A person's age has something to do with how many times the earth has circled the sun since his or her birth, and sex has something to do with a person's physical genitalia. The social

However, is this really what is most important? The victim who is quoted in the qualitative study makes an eloquent plea to focus on the psychological hurt that she endures forever as a consequence of living with an abusive partner rather than counting the number of assaults or physical injuries that happened. In an article discussing definition and measurement issues, Walter DeKeseredy (2000) points out that many North American surveys have followed a narrow definition, based in part on the argument that grouping physical assault with psychological, spiritual, and economic abuse muddies the water and makes causal determination impossible. Another argument is that to include "soft" abuse, such as verbal aggression and psychological damage, trivializes what most people agree is seriously abusive. In contrast, many researchers, especially those using qualitative methods, contend that violence against women is much more than just physical blows; that it is multidimensional, and actions such as harming pets, threatening children, and verbal degradation also are essential elements. The qualitative data presented above can be part of a convincing argument that the psychological damage resulting from abuse is far from trivial.

In fact, when it comes to estimating the amount of violence, DeKeseredy argues that narrow definitions generate low incidence and prevalence rates and that these constitute a significant problem. He points out that policymakers react only to large numbers; thus, underestimating the amount of abuse may have important policy implications. Furthermore, narrow definitions create a ranking of abuse based on what is defined as crime rather than on women's true feelings. Finally, narrow definitions increase the problem of underreporting, because research participants will only disclose abuse that fits the narrow definition rather than include other experiences that hurt them deeply. Although it may be problematic to include a wide array of abusive experiences, DeKeseredy points out that qualitative research, such as that quoted above, emphasizes the need to incorporate into survey research the features of violence that women find so devastating. As the debate developed, qualitative research served as the catalyst for forcing the research community to broaden its definition of abuse. Several measurement tools, created partly in response to the work of qualitative researchers, now tap nonphysical and nonsexual abuse. These include Tolman's (1989) Psychological Maltreatment of Women Inventory and the psychologically/emotionally abusive and controlling behaviors data elements developed by the National Center for Injury Prevention and Control, Centers for Disease Control and Prevention (Saltzman et al., 1999).

This debate over how to measure domestic violence shows the benefits of using both qualitative and quantitative research approaches and considering both positivist and nonpositivist arguments about measurement. DeKeseredy, for example, makes a case for the use of multiple measures to further enhance measurement. He argues that using open-ended, supplemental questions in addition to such quantitative measures as the Conflict Tactics Scale increases the chance that silent or forgetful participants may reveal abuse not reported in the context of the structured, closed-ended instrument. In summary, we see that careful definition of terms, inclusion of both qualitative and quantitative research, improvement of measurement instruments, and use of multiple forms of measurement all advance our understanding of the dynamics of important social issues, such as violence against women.

---

significance of these characteristics is another matter, of course, but in many cases, the measurements of age and sex can follow classical measurement theory. Research in Practice 5.1 addresses some of these measurement issues in regard to the significant social issue of domestic violence.

A major problem in most measurement has to do with which indicators to use in a particular research project. This depends in part, of course, on theoretical concerns, but there are other matters to consider as well. One such matter has to do with whether a particular measure permits one to perform mathematical operations on it; we turn to this issue next.

LEVELS OF MEASUREMENT

We have seen just a few of the many ways of measuring phenomena, such as asking questions or noting observations. Measures differ from one another in terms of what is called their **level of measurement**, or the rules that define permissible mathematical operations that can be performed on a set of numbers produced by a measure. There are four levels of measurement: *nominal, ordinal, interval,* and *ratio*. If we keep in mind that variables can take on different values, then measurement basically involves assessing the value or category into which a particular entity falls. Measuring age, for example, is the process of placing each person into a particular age category.

Nominal Measures

Nominal measures classify observations into mutually exclusive and exhaustive categories. They represent nominal variables at the theoretical level. Variables such as sex, ethnicity, religion, or political party preference are examples. Thus, we might classify people according to their religious affiliation by placing them into one of five categories: Protestant, Catholic, Jewish, other, or no religious affiliation. These are mutually exclusive categories, because membership in one precludes membership in another. They are exhaustive categories because there is a category for every possible case (for this measure of religious affiliation, the "other religion" and "no religion" categories assure this). For purposes of data analysis, we might assign numbers to represent each of the categories. We could label Protestant as 1, Catholic as 2, Jewish as 3, other as 4, and no religious affiliation as 5. It is important to recognize, however, that the assignment of numbers is purely arbitrary; the numbers making up a nominal measure have none of the properties, such as ranking, ordering, and magnitude, that we usually associate with numbers. None of the usual arithmetic operations, such as adding, subtracting, multiplying, or dividing, can legitimately be performed on numbers in a nominal scale. The reason for this is that the numbers in a nominal scale are merely symbols or labels used to identify a category of the nominal variable. We could just as easily have labeled Protestant 2 as 1.

Ordinal Measures

When variables can be conceptualized as having an inherent order at the theoretical level, we have an

TABLE 5.2 Ordinal Ranking of Socioeconomic Status

Category	Ranks
Upper-upper	7
Lower-upper	6
Upper-middle	5
Middle	4
Lower-middle	3
Upper-lower	2
Lower-lower	1

ordinal variable and, when operationalized, an ordinal measure. **Ordinal measures** are of a higher level than nominal measures, because in addition to having mutually exclusive and exhaustive categories, the categories have a fixed order. Socioeconomic status, for example, constitutes an ordinal variable, and measures of socioeconomic status are ordinal scales. Table 5.2 illustrates how we might divide socioeconomic status into ordinal categories. With ordinal measurement, we can speak of a given category as ranking higher or lower than some other category; lower-upper class, for example, is higher than middle class but not as high as upper-upper class. It is important to recognize that ordinal measurement does not assume that the categories are equally spaced. For example, the distance between lower-upper class and upper-upper class is not necessarily the same as between lower-middle class and middle class, even though in both cases the classes are one rank apart. This lack of equal spacing means that the numbers assigned to ordinal categories do not have the numerical properties necessary for arithmetic operations. Like nominal scales, we cannot add, subtract, multiply, or divide ordinal scales. The only characteristic they have that nominal scales do not is the fixed order of the categories.

Interval Measures

The next highest level of measurement is interval. **Interval measures** share the characteristics of ordinal scales—mutually exclusive and exhaustive categories and an inherent order—but have equal spacing between the categories. Equal spacing comes about because some specific unit of measurement, such as a degree on a temperature scale, is a part of the measure. Each of these units has the same value, which results in the equal spacing. We have an interval scale if the difference between scores of, say, 30 and 40 is the same as the difference between scores of, say, 70 and 80. A 10-point difference is a 10-point difference regardless of where on the scale it occurs.

The common temperature scales, Fahrenheit and Celsius, are true interval scales. Both scales have degrees as units of measurement, and the equal spacing that is characteristic of interval scales. A difference of 10 degrees is always the same, no matter where it occurs on the scale. These temperature scales illustrate another characteristic of true interval scales: The point on the scale labeled zero is arbitrarily selected. Neither 0°C nor 0°F is absolute zero, the complete absence of heat. Because the zero point is arbitrary in true interval scales, we cannot make statements concerning ratios—that is, we cannot say a given score is twice or three times as high as some other score. For example, a temperature of 80°F is not twice as hot as a temperature of 40°F. Despite not having this ratio characteristic, interval scales have numbers with all the other arithmetic properties. If we have achieved interval-level measurement, then we can legitimately perform all the common arithmetic operations on the numbers.

Considerable controversy exists over which measures used in behavioral science research are true interval measures; only a few measures are clearly of interval level. For example, one that is relevant to the human services is intelligence as measured by IQ tests. The IQ tests have specific units of measurement—points on the IQ scale—and each point on the scale is mutually exclusive. Furthermore, the distance between IQs of 80 and 90 is equivalent to the distance between IQs of 110 and 120. An IQ scale has no absolute zero point, however, so we cannot say that a person with an IQ of 150 is twice as intelligent as a person with an IQ of 75. As with temperature scales, the IQ scale is, in part, an arbitrary construction that allows us to make some comparisons but not others.

Beyond a few measures such as intelligence, however, the debate ensues. Some researchers argue, for example, that we can treat attitude scales as interval scales (Kenny, 1986). The questions that make up attitude scales commonly involve choosing one of five responses: strongly agree, agree, uncertain, disagree, or strongly disagree. The argument is that people see the difference between "strongly agree" and "agree" as roughly equivalent to the distance between "disagree" and "strongly disagree." This perceived equidistance, some argue, makes it possible to treat these scales as interval measures. Other researchers argue that there is no logical or empirical reason to assume that such perceived equidistance exists, and therefore we should always consider attitude scales as ordinal rather than interval measures.

We do not presume to settle this debate here. Rather, we raise the issue because level of measurement influences which statistical procedures to use at the data analysis stage of research (see Chapters 14 and 15.) The results of research in which the researcher used an inappropriate statistical procedure for a given level of measurement should be viewed with caution.

Ratio Measures

The highest level of measurement is ratio. **Ratio measures** have all the characteristics of interval measures, but the zero point is absolute and meaningful rather than arbitrary. As the name implies, with ratio measures, we can make statements to the effect that some score is a given ratio of another score. For example, one ratio variable with which human service workers are likely to deal is income. With income, the dollar is the unit of measurement. Also, as many are all too well aware, there is such a thing as no income at all, so the zero point is absolute. Thus, it is perfectly legitimate to make statements such as this about income: An income of $20,000 is twice as much as $10,000, but only one third as much as $60,000. (We recognize, of course, that income is a ratio measure only as an indicator for the *amount* of money available to a person; if income is used as a measure of a person's *social status*, for example, then a difference between $110,000

TABLE 5.3 **The Characteristics of the Four Levels of Measurement**

Level of Measurement	Mutually Exclusive and Exhaustive	Possesses a Fixed Order	Equal Spacing between Ranks[a]	True Zero Point[a,b]
Nominal	y			
Ordinal	y	y		
Interval	y	y	y	
Ratio	y	y	y	y

y = possesses that characteristic
[a]Permits standard mathematical operations of addition, subtraction, multiplication, and division.
[b]Permits statements about proportions and ratios.

and $120,000 does not necessarily represent a shift in status equivalent to that between $10,000 and $20,000.) Given that ratio scales have all the characteristics of interval scales, we can, of course, perform all arithmetic operations on them.

We summarize the characteristics of the four levels of measurement in Table 5.3. Keep in mind that, even though researchers have no control over the nature of a variable, they do have some control over how they define a variable, at both the nominal and operational levels, and this affects the level of measurement. It sometimes is possible to change the level of measurement of a variable by redefining it at the nominal or the operational level. This is important, because researchers generally strive for the highest possible level of measurement: Higher levels of measurement generally enable us to measure variables more precisely and to use more powerful statistical procedures (see Chapters 14 and 15). It also is desirable to measure at the highest possible level because it gives the researcher the most options: The level of measurement can be reduced during the data analysis, but it cannot be increased. Thus, choosing a level of measurement that is too low introduces a permanent limitation into the data analysis.

The primary determinant for the level of measurement, however, is the nature of the variable we want to measure. The major concern is an accurate measure of a variable (a topic we will discuss at length in the next section). Religious affiliation, for example, is a nominal variable, because that is the nature of the theoretical concept of "religious affiliation." There is no way to treat religious affiliation as anything other than a merely nominal classification, but by changing the theoretical variable somewhat, we may open up higher levels of measurement. If, instead of religious *affiliation,* we were to measure *religiosity,* or the strength of religious beliefs, then we would have a variable that we could conceptualize and measure as ordinal and, perhaps, even as interval. On the basis of certain responses, we could easily rank people into ordered categories of greater or lesser religiosity. Thus, the theoretical nature of the variable plays a large part in determining the level of measurement. This illustrates, once again, the constant interplay between theoretical and research levels (see Figure 5.1). The decision regarding level of measurement at the research level might affect the conceptualization of variables at the theoretical level.

Finally, note that nominal variables are not inherently undesirable. The impression that variables capable of measurement at higher levels are always better than nominal variables is wrong. The first consideration is to select variables on theoretical grounds, not on the basis of their possible level of measurement. Thus, if a research study really is concerned with religious affiliation and not with religiosity, then the nominal measure is the correct one to use and not a measure of religiosity (even though it is ordinal or, possibly, interval). Also, researchers do strive for more accurate and powerful measurement. Other things being equal, a researcher who has two measures available, one ordinal and one ratio, generally prefers the ratio measure.

Discrete versus Continuous Variables

In addition to considering the level of measurement of a variable, researchers also distinguish between variables that are *discrete* or *continuous*. **Discrete variables** have a finite number of distinct and separate values. A perusal of a typical client fact sheet from a human service agency reveals many examples of discrete variables, such as sex, household size, number of days absent, or number of arrests. Household size is a discrete variable because households can be measured only in a discrete set of units, such as having one member, two members, and so on; no meaningful measurement values lie between these distinct and separate values. **Continuous variables**, at least theoretically, can take on an infinite number of values. Age is a continuous variable because we can measure age by an infinite array of values. We normally measure age in terms of years, but theoretically, we could measure it in terms of months, weeks, days, minutes, seconds, or even nanoseconds! There is no theoretical limit to how precise the measurement of age might be. For most social science purposes, the measurement of age in terms of years is quite satisfactory, but age is nonetheless a continuous variable.

Nominal variables are, by definition, discrete in that they consist of mutually exclusive or discrete categories. Ordinal variables also are discrete. The mutually exclusive categories of an ordinal variable may be ranked from low to high, but there cannot be a partial rank. For example, in a study of the military, rank might be ordered as 1 = private, 2 = corporal, and so on, but it would be nonsensical to speak of a rank of 1.3. In some cases, interval and ratio variables are discrete. For example, family size or number of arrests are whole numbers or discrete intervals. (We can summarize discrete interval and ratio data by saying, for example, that the average family size is 1.8 people, but this is a summary statistic, not a measurement of a particular household.) Many variables at the interval and ratio level are continuous, at least at the theoretical level. A researcher may settle for discrete indicators either because the study does not demand greater precision or because no tools exist that can measure the continuous variable with sufficient reliability. In some cases, researchers debate over whether a particular variable is discrete or continuous in nature. For example, we used social class as an illustration of an ordinal variable, suggesting that several distinct classes exist. Some argue that social class is inherently a continuous interval variable, and that we only treat it as ordinal because of the lack of instruments that would permit researchers to measure it reliably as a true continuous, interval variable (Borgatta & Bohrnstedt, 1981).

A variable, then, is continuous or discrete by its very nature, and the researcher cannot change that. It is possible to measure a continuous variable by specifying a number of discrete categories, as we typically do with age, but this does not change the nature of the variable itself. Whether variables are discrete or continuous may influence how we use them in data analysis. Knowing the level of measurement and whether variables are discrete or continuous has implications for selecting the best procedures for analyzing the data.

EVALUATING MEASURES

We have seen that there normally are a number of indicators, sometimes a large number and at different levels of measurement, that we can use to measure a variable, but how do we choose the best of these measures for a particular study? A number of factors come into play in making this decision, including matters of feasibility (discussed in Chapter 4). Here, we want to discuss two additional and very important considerations in this regard—that is, the validity and reliability of measures (Alwin, 2007).

Validity

Validity refers to the accuracy of a measure: Does it accurately measure the variable it is intended to measure? If we were developing a measure of self-concept, a major concern would be whether our measuring device measures the concept as it is theoretically defined. There must be a fairly clear and logical relationship between the way a variable is nominally defined and the way it is operationalized. For example, if we propose to measure self-concept on the basis of how stylishly people dress, then we probably would have an invalid measure. Many factors influence the way people dress at any given time. The slight possibility that one of these factors might have something to do with self-concept is not sufficient to make the suggested measure valid. The validity of measures is very difficult to demonstrate with any finality. Several approaches to the question of validity exist, however, and they can offer evidence regarding the validity of a measure.

Face validity involves assessing whether a logical relationship exists between the variable and the proposed measure. It essentially amounts to a rather commonsense comparison of what makes up the measure and the theoretical definition of the variable: Does it seem logical to use this measure to reflect that variable? We might measure child abuse in terms of the reports that physicians or emergency room personnel make concerning injuries suffered by children. This is not a perfect measure, because health personnel might be wrong. It does, however, seem logical that an injury reported by such people might reflect actual abuse.

No matter how carefully done, face validity clearly is subjective in nature. All we have is logic and common sense as arguments for the validity of a measure. This makes face validity the weakest demonstration of validity, and it usually should be considered as no more than a starting point. All measures must pass the test of face validity. If they do, then we should attempt one of the more stringent methods for assessing validity.

An extension of face validity is called **content validity** or **sampling validity**, which has to do with whether a measuring device covers the full range of meanings or forms that are included in a variable to measure. In other words, a valid measuring device provides an adequate, or representative, *sample* of all *content*, or *elements*, or *instances*, of the phenomenon being measured. For example, if one were measuring general self-esteem, it would be important to recognize that self-esteem can relate to many realms of people's lives, such as work, school, or the family. Self-esteem might get expressed or come into play in all those settings. A valid measure of self-esteem, then, would take that variability into account. If a measure of self-esteem consisted of a series of statements to which people expressed degrees of agreement, then a valid measure would include statements that relate to those many settings in which self-esteem might be expressed. If all the statements in the measuring device had to do, say, with school, then it would be a less valid measure of general self-esteem.

Content validity is a more extensive assessment of validity than is face validity, because it involves a detailed analysis of the breadth of the measured concept and its relationship to the measuring device. Content validity involves two distinct steps: (1) determining the full range or domain of the content of a variable; and (2) determining whether all those domains are represented among the items that constitute the measuring device. It is still a somewhat subjective assessment, however, in that someone has to judge what the full domain of the variable is and whether a particular aspect of a concept is adequately represented in the measuring device. There are no agreed-on criteria that determine whether a measure has content validity. Ultimately, it is a judgment, albeit a more carefully considered judgment than occurs with face validity.

One way to strengthen confidence in face or content validity is to gather the opinions of other investigators, especially those who are knowledgeable about the variables involved, regarding whether particular operational definitions are logical measures of the variables. This extension of face or content validity, which sometimes is referred to as **jury opinion**, is still subjective, of course. Because more people serve as a check on bias or misinterpretation, however, jury opinion is superior to individual tests of face or content validity.

Criterion validity establishes validity by showing a correlation between a measurement device and some other criterion or standard that we know or believe accurately measures the variable under consideration. Or we might correlate the results of the measuring device with some properties or characteristics of the variable that the measuring device is intended to measure. For example, a scale intended to measure risk of suicide, if it is to be considered valid, should correlate with the occurrence of self-destructive behavior. The key to criterion validity is to find a criterion variable against which to compare the results of the measuring device.

Criterion validity moves away from the subjective assessments of face validity and provides more objective evidence of validity. One type of criterion validity is **concurrent validity**, which compares the instrument under evaluation to some already existing criterion, such as the results of another measuring device. (Presumably, any other measuring devices in this assessment have already been tested for validity.) Lawrence Shulman (1978), for example, used a form of concurrent validity to test an instrument intended to measure the practice skills of human service practitioners. This instrument consisted of a questionnaire in which clients rated the skills of practitioners. Shulman reasoned that clients would view more skilled practitioners as more helpful, and that those practitioners would have more satisfied clients. Thus Shulman looked for correlations between how positively clients rated a practitioner's skills and the perceived helpfulness of practitioners or satisfaction of clients. These correlations offered evidence for the validity of the measure of practitioners' skills.

Numerous existing measures can help establish the concurrent validity of a newly developed measure. (Following are only some of the compilations of such measures available in the social sciences and the human services: Bloom, Fischer & Orme, 2009; Fischer & Corcoran, 2007; Fredman & Sherman, 1987; Magura & Moses, 1986; McDowell, 2006; Miller & Salkind, 2002; Robinson, Shaver, & Wrightsman, 1991; Schutte & Malouff, 1995; Touliatos et al., 2001.) More measures can be found in research articles in professional journals. In addition, the Consulting Psychologists Press and other organizations publish catalogs of measures they make available to assess a wide array of skills, behaviors, attitudes, and other variables. (This also suggests, as pointed out in Chapter 4, that a thorough review of the literature, undertaken before going through all the work of creating a new measure, may unearth an existing measure that meets one's needs and has already been demonstrated to have adequate validity and reliability.) Then it is a matter of applying both measures to the same sample and comparing the results. If a substantial correlation is found between the measures, we have reason to believe that our measure has concurrent validity. As a matter of convention, a correlation of $r = .50$ is considered to be the minimum required for establishing concurrent validity.

The inherent weakness of concurrent validity is the validity of the existing measure that is used for comparison. All we can conclude is that our measure is about as valid as the other one. If the measure we select for comparison is not valid, then the fact that ours correlates with it hardly makes our measure valid. For this reason, researchers should use only those measures that have been established as being valid by research for comparison purposes in concurrent validity.

A second form of criterion validity is **predictive validity**, in which an instrument predicts some future state of affairs. In this case, the criteria that are used to assess the instrument are certain future events. The Scholastic Assessment Test (SAT), for example, can be subjected to predictive validity by comparing performance on the test with how people perform in college. If people who score high on the SAT do better in college than those who score low, then the SAT is, presumably, a valid measure of scholastic ability. Some measures are created for the specific purpose of predicting a given behavior, and these measures are obvious candidates for assessment by predictive validity. For example, researchers have attempted to develop a measure that can predict which convicted criminals are likely to revert to high involvement with crime after being released from prison (Chaiken & Chaiken, 1984). Information about the number and types of crimes that people commit, the age at which they commit their first crime, and involvement with hard drugs serves as the basis for these predictions. Ultimately, a measure's ability to make accurate predictions about who actually experiences high involvement with crime after release validates that measure.

Because this may require numerous applications and many years, the scales can be assessed initially for validity on the basis of their ability to differentiate between high and low crime involvement among current criminals. We expect that if a measure can make this differentiation, it also can predict future involvement in crime. This variation on predictive validity is the *known groups* approach to validity. If we know that certain groups are likely to differ substantially on a given variable, then we can use a measure's ability to discriminate between these groups as an indicator of validity. Suppose, for example, we were working on a measure of prejudice. We might apply the measure to a group of ministers, whom we would expect to be low in prejudice, and to a group of people affiliated with the neo-Nazi group Aryan Nation, whom we would expect to be high in prejudice. If these groups differed significantly in how they responded to the measurement instrument, then we would have reason to believe that the measure is valid. If the measure failed to show a substantial difference, we would certainly doubt its validity.

Despite the apparent potential of the known groups approach, it does have its limitations. Frequently, no groups are known to differ on the variable that we are attempting to measure. In fact, the purpose of developing a measure often is to allow the identification of groups who do differ on some variable. Thus, we cannot always use the known groups technique. When we do, we also have to consider a further limitation—namely, that it cannot tell us whether a measure can make finer distinctions between less extreme groups than those used in the validation. Perhaps the measure of prejudice just described shows the members of Aryan Nation to be high in prejudice and the ministers to be low. With a broader sample, however, the measure may show that *only* the Aryan Nation members score high and that *everyone else,* not just ministers, scores low. Thus, the measure can distinguish between groups only in a very crude fashion.

Construct validity, the most complex of the types of validity we discuss here, involves relating an instrument to an overall theoretical framework to determine whether the instrument is correlated with all the concepts and propositions that comprise the theory (Cronbach & Meehl, 1955). In this case, instruments are assessed in terms of how they relate not to one criterion, but rather to the numerous criteria that can be derived from some theory. For example, if we develop a new measure of socioeconomic status, we can assess construct validity by showing that the new measure accurately predicts the many hypotheses that can be derived from a theory of occupational attainment. In the theory, numerous propositions would relate occupational attainment and socioeconomic status to a variety of other concepts. If we do not find some or all of the predicted relationships, then we may question the validity of the new measuring instrument. (Of course, it may be that the theory itself is flawed; this possibility must always be considered when assessing construct validity.)

Construct validity takes some very complex forms. One is the **multitrait–multimethod approach** (Campbell & Fiske, 1959). This is based on two ideas: First, two instruments that are valid measures of the same concept should correlate rather highly with each other even though they are different instruments. Second, two instruments, even if similar to each other, should not correlate highly if they measure different concepts. This approach to validity involves the simultaneous assessment of numerous instruments (multimethod) and numerous concepts (multitrait) through the computation of intercorrelations. Wolfe and colleagues (1987) used this technique to assess the validity of children's self-reports about negative emotions, such as aggressiveness and depression. The point is that assessing construct validity can become highly complex, but this complexity offers greater evidence for the validity of the measures.

The types of validity we have discussed so far—face, content, criterion, and construct—involve a progression in which each builds on the previous one. Each type requires more information than the prior ones but provides a better assessment of validity. Unfortunately, many studies limit their assessment to content validity, with its heavy reliance on

> ### Eye on Ethics — The Ethics of Measuring Shameful, Harmful, or Deviant Behavior
>
> How do you validly measure people's willingness to engage in shameful, even harmful behavior in an experiment and remain ethical? For many, Stanley Milgram's classic study on obedience to authority (Milgram, 1974) exemplifies exposing participants to unacceptable harm in the conduct of research. Milgram set up a teaching laboratory where participants were told that the study concerned the effects of punishment on learning. Each participant was led to believe that he had been assigned the role of teacher who would administer electrical shocks to a "learner" in order to enhance learning. There was an imposing-looking shock generator machine, complete with red warning danger labels and appearing to administer electrical shocks up to 450 volts in 15-volt increments. Milgram measured how far up the scale participants would go in administering shocks as the "learner" on the other side of the wall expressed more distress with the increase in voltage, finally falling silent as if severely injured. The disturbing result was that 65 percent of participants continued administering shocks all the way to the maximum 450 volts.
>
> Milgram's last studies were conducted about the time that the U.S. Department of Health, Education, and Welfare was establishing its ethical guidelines and mandating Institutional Review Boards (see Chapter 3). Given the furor over perceived risk of psychological harm raised by Milgram's work, it seemed unlikely that anyone would ever gain approval for similar studies from a modern IRB. But the question Milgram examined is still of vital interest today. The Holocaust and Abu Ghraib cause us to continue asking how people can engage in inhumane behavior.
>
> Recently, psychologist Jerry Burger sufficiently addressed ethical concerns that he was able to secure IRB approval and thus conduct a modern replication of Milgram's research. Burger resolved the ethical issues by modifying the dependent variable measurement through what he calls the "150 Volt Solution" (Burger, 2009, p.2). Previous studies showed that about 79 percent of participants who were willing to administer shocks of 150 volts continued on through the full range to 450 volts. Burger argued that little additional data was gained by subjecting participants to demands to administer higher and higher levels of shock. He argued that the 150-volt limit was a valid measure of people's willingness to engage in behavior that was very harmful to other people, but that it was ethical because it did not subject people to the great stress of thinking they were administering very large shocks. The researcher included other safeguards in order to gain IRB approval: a screening process for applicants, multiple reminders that they could withdraw their participation, immediate debriefing, and presence of a clinical psychologist who was instructed to end the session immediately at the sign of participant distress. So what did the study show? As with Milgram, most of Burger's participants complied with the authority figure's instructions and delivered the maximum shock.

the subjective judgments of individuals or juries. Although this sometimes is necessary, measures subjected only to content validity should be used with caution. The Eye on Ethics section discusses some ethical considerations that can arise in trying to develop valid measures of some behaviors.

Reliability

In addition to validity, measures also are evaluated in terms of their **reliability**, which refers to a measure's ability to yield consistent results each time it is applied. In other words, reliable measures only fluctuate because of variations in the variable being measured. An illustration of reliability can be found at any carnival, where there usually is a booth with a person guessing people's weights within a certain range of accuracy—say, plus or minus three pounds. The customer essentially bets that the carnie's ability to guess weights is sufficiently unreliable that his or her estimate will fall outside the prescribed range, and if so, the customer will win a prize. A weight scale, of course, is a reliable indicator of a person's weight because it records roughly the same weight each time the same person stands on it, and the carnie provides such a scale to assess his or her guess of the customer's weight. Despite the fact that carnies who operate such booths become quite good at guessing weights, they do occasionally guess wrong—influenced, perhaps, by aspects of the customer other than his or her actual weight, such as loose clothing that obscures a person's physique.

In general, a valid measure is reliable. So, if we were certain of the validity of a measure, then we would not need to concern ourselves with its reliability. Evidence of validity, however, is always less than perfect, and this is why we turn to other ways of evaluating measures, including reliability. Reliability gives us more evidence for validity, because a reliable measure may be valid. Fortunately, we can demonstrate reliability in a more straightforward manner than we can demonstrate validity. Many specific techniques exist for estimating the reliability of a measure, but all are based on one of two principles—namely, stability and equivalence. *Stability* is the idea that a reliable measure should not change from one application to the next, assuming that the concept being measured has not changed. *Equivalence* is the idea that all items that make up a measuring instrument should measure the same thing and, thus, be consistent with one another. The first technique for estimating reliability, test–retest reliability, uses the stability approach; the others discussed use the equivalence principle.

Test–Retest. The first and most generally applicable assessment of reliability is called *test–retest*. As the name implies, this technique involves applying a measure to a sample of people and then, somewhat later, applying the same measure to the same people again. After the retest, we have two scores on the same measure for each person, as illustrated in Table 5.4. We then correlate these two sets of scores with an appropriate statistical measure of association (see Chapter 15). Because the association in test–retest reliability involves scores obtained from two identical questionnaires, we fully expect a high degree of association. As a matter of convention, a correlation coefficient of .80 or better normally is necessary for a measure to be considered as reliable. In Table 5.4, the *r* means that the particular statistic used was the Pearson's correlation coefficient, and the value of .98 indicates that the measurement instrument is highly reliable according to the test–retest method.

TABLE 5.4 **Hypothetical Test–Retest Data**

Subjects	Initial Test	Retest
1	12	15
2	15	20
3	22	30
4	38	35
5	40	35
6	40	38
7	40	41
8	60	55
9	70	65
10	75	77

$r = .98$

Lawrence Shulman (1978), in addition to subjecting his measure of practice skills to the tests of validity mentioned earlier, also tested its reliability. He did so by sending versions of the questionnaire to a set of clients and then sending an identical questionnaire two weeks later to the same clients. This provided him with a test–retest assessment of reliability, and he obtained a correlation coefficient of .75. When a reliability coefficient is close to the conventional level, as in this case, the researcher must make a judgment about whether to assume the instrument is reliable (and the low coefficient is a result of factors other than the unreliability of the instrument) or to rework the instrument to obtain higher levels of association.

In actual practice, we cannot simply use the test–retest method as suggested, because exposing people to the same measure twice creates a problem known as *multiple-testing effects* (Campbell and Stanley 1963). Whenever we apply a measure to a group of people a second time, they may not react to it the same as they did the first time. They may, for example, recall their previous answers, and that could influence their second response. People might respond as they recall doing the first time to maintain consistency, or people might purposely change responses for the sake of variety. Either case can have a confounding effect on testing reliability. If people strive for consistency, then their efforts can

TABLE 5.5 Design for Test–Retest

	Initial Test	Retest
Experimental group	Yes	Yes
Control group	No	Yes

mask actual unreliability in the instrument. If they deliberately change responses, then a reliable measure can appear to be less reliable.

A solution to this dilemma is to divide the test group randomly into two groups: an experimental group to test twice, and a control group to test only once. Table 5.5 illustrates the design for such an experiment. Ideally, the measure will yield consistent results in all three testing sessions; if it does, then we have solid reason to believe the measure is reliable. On the contrary, substantial differences among the groups may indicate unreliability. If, for example, the experimental group shows consistency in both sets of responses to the measurement instrument but the control group differs, then the measure may be unreliable and the consistency of the experimental group might result from the multiple-testing effects. On the contrary, if the experimental group yields inconsistent results but the control group shows responses similar to those of the experimental group's initial test, this outcome also may be caused by multiple-testing effects and result from the experimental group's changing answers during the retest. Despite the inconsistency in the experimental group, the measure still might be reliable if we observe this outcome. Finally, we may see that the results of all three testing sessions appear to be inconsistent. Such an outcome would suggest that the measure is not reliable. If either of the outcomes that leave the reliability of the measure in doubt occurs, researchers should conduct a second test–retest experiment with the hope of obtaining clearer results. If the same result occurs, then we should redesign the instrument.

The test–retest method of assessing reliability has both advantages and disadvantages. Its major advantage is that we can use it with many measures, which is not true of alternative tests of reliability. Its disadvantage is that it is slow and cumbersome to use, with two required testing sessions and the desirability of a control group. In addition, as we have seen, the outcome may not be clear, leading to the necessity of repeating the whole procedure. Finally, we cannot use the test–retest method on measures of variables whose value might have changed during the interval between tests. For example, people's attitudes can change for reasons that have nothing to do with the testing, and a measure of attitudes might appear to be unreliable when it is not.

Multiple Forms. If our measuring device is a multiple-item scale, as often is the case, we can approach the question of reliability through the technique of multiple forms. When developing the scale, we create two separate but equivalent versions made up of different items, such as different questions. We then administer these two forms successively to the same people during a single testing session. We correlate the results from the forms, as in test–retest, using an appropriate statistical measure of association, with the same convention of $r = .80$ or better required for establishing reliability. If the correlation between the two forms is sufficiently high, we can assume that each scale is reliable.

Multiple forms have the advantages of requiring only one testing session and needing no control group. These may be significant advantages if using either multiple-testing sessions or a control group is impractical. In addition, we need not worry about changes in a variable over time, because both forms are administered at the same time.

The multiple-forms technique relies on the two forms appearing to the respondents as though they were only one, long measure so that the respondents do not realize they are really taking the same test twice. This necessity of deluding people points out one of the disadvantages of multiple forms: To maintain the equivalence of the forms, the items in the two forms probably will be quite similar—so similar, in fact, that people may realize they are responding essentially to the same items twice. If this occurs, it raises the specter of multiple-testing effects and casts doubt on the accuracy of the reliability test. Another disadvantage of multiple forms is the difficulty of developing two measures with different items that really are equivalent. If we obtain inconsistent results from the two forms, it may be caused by differences in the forms rather than by the unreliability of either one. In a way, it is questionable whether multiple forms really test reliability and not just our ability to create equivalent versions of the same measure.

Internal Consistency Approaches. Internal consistency approaches to reliability use a single scale that is administered to one group of people to develop an estimate of reliability. For example, in the *split-half approach* to reliability, the test group responds to the complete measuring instrument. We then randomly divide the responses to the instrument into halves, treating each half as though it were a separate scale. We correlate the two halves by using an appropriate measure of association. Once again, we need a coefficient of $r = .80$ or better to demonstrate reliability. In his study of practice skills mentioned earlier, Shulman (1978) used a split-half reliability test on his instrument in addition to the test–retest method. He divided each respondent's answers to his questions about practitioners' skills into two roughly equivalent sets, correlated the two sets of answers, and found a correlation (following a correction, to be mentioned shortly) of .79. This is an improvement over the reliability that he found with the test–retest method, and comes very close to the conventional level of .80.

One complication in using the split-half reliability test is that the correlation coefficient may understate the reliability of the measure because, other things being equal, a longer measuring scale is more reliable than a shorter one. Because the split-half approach divides the scale in two, each half is shorter than the whole scale, and thus will appear to be less reliable than the scale as a whole. To correct for this, we can adjust the correlation coefficient by applying the Spearman–Brown formula, which Shulman did:

$$r = \frac{2r_i}{1 + r_i}$$

Where:

r_i = uncorrected correlation coefficient

r = corrected correlation coefficient (reliability coefficient)

To illustrate the effect of the Spearman–Brown formula, suppose we have a 20-item scale with a correlation between the two halves of $r_i = .70$, which is smaller than the minimum needed to demonstrate reliability. The Spearman–Brown formula corrects as follows:

$$r = \frac{(2)(.70)}{1 + .70} + \frac{1.40}{1.70} = .82$$

It can be seen that the Spearman–Brown formula has a substantial effect, increasing the uncorrected coefficient from well below .80 to just over it. If we had obtained these results with an actual scale, we would conclude that its reliability was now adequate.

Using the split-half technique requires two preconditions that can limit its applicability. First, all the items in the scale must measure the same variable. If the scale in question is a jumble of items measuring several different variables, it is meaningless to divide it and compare the halves. Second, the scale must contain a sufficient number of items so that, when it is divided, the halves do not become too short to be considered as scales themselves. A suggested minimum is 8 to 10 items per half (Goode & Hatt, 1952). Because many measures are shorter than these minimums, however, it may not be possible to assess their reliability with the split-half technique.

A number of other approaches to internal consistency reliability sometimes are used to overcome the weaknesses of the split-half approach. After all, the split-half approach only uses one random separation of the scale into two halves. Randomly dividing the items of a scale into halves could result in many different arrangements of items, and each would yield a slightly different correlation between the halves. One common approach to this problem is to use Cronbach's alpha, which may be thought of as the average of all possible split-half correlations. Theoretically, the scale is divided into all possible configurations of two halves. Then, a correlation is computed for each possibility, and the average of those correlations is computed to derive alpha (Cronbach, 1951). This is not actually how Cronbach's alpha is calculated, but it does describe the logic of the procedure. Another approach to internal consistency reliability is to correlate each item in the scale with every other item and then use the average of these correlations as the measure of reliability. This also is done by correlating each item with the overall scale score. (Statistical packages such as SPSS contain procedures that will produce Cronbach's alpha as well as other reliability tests based on inter-item correlations.)

Internal consistency reliability tests have several advantages. They require only one testing session and no control group. They also give the clearest indication of reliability. For these reasons, researchers prefer to use these methods of assessing reliability whenever possible. The only disadvantage, as we noted, is that we cannot always use them. Shulman's approach teaches a lesson, however: Use more than one test, if possible, to assess both reliability and validity. These issues are sufficiently important that the expenditure of time is justified.

Measurement with Diverse Populations

Researchers often first assess the validity and reliability of measuring instruments by applying them to white, non-Hispanic respondents, because they find such people to be the most accessible. We should almost never assume, however, that such assessments can be generalized to culturally diverse populations (Mushquash & Bova, 2007; Tran & Williams, 1994). The development of such instruments typically does not consider the unique cultural characteristics and attitudes of minorities. For some minorities, such as Asians, Hispanics, and Aboriginals, language differences mean that an English-language interview would have some respondents answering in a second language. Researchers cannot assume that such a respondent will understand words and phrases as well as—or in the same way as—a person for whom English is his or her first language. In addition, some concepts in English do not have a precise equivalent in another language.

It is important, therefore, to refine measuring instruments to assure that they are valid and reliable measures among minorities. A study of mental health among Native Americans, for example, had to drop the word "blue" as a descriptor of depression, because that word had no equivalent meaning among the Native Americans (Manson, 1986). Researchers also had to add a category of "traditional healer" to a list of professionals to whom a Native American might turn for help. A study of Inuits found that cultural context often caused different interpretations of questions. Because Inuit culture emphasizes tolerance and endurance, Inuits are less likely than Anglo-Americans to give in to pain by not working. A positive response from an Inuit to a question like "Does sickness often keep you from doing your work?" is thus considered to be a much more potent indicator of distress than the same answer by an Anglo-American.

These illustrations should make it clear that measurement in social research must be culturally sensitive. When conducting research on a group with a culture different from that of the researchers, the researchers can take a number of steps to produce more valid and reliable measurement instruments (Marin & VanOss Marin, 1991; Tran & Williams, 1994):

1. Researchers can immerse themselves in the culture of the group under study, experiencing the daily activities of life and the cultural products as the natives do.

2. Researchers should use key informants, people who participate routinely in the culture of the group under study, to help develop and assess the measurement instruments.

3. When translating an instrument from English into another language, researchers should use the most effective translation methods, usually *double translation* (translating from English into the target language and then back into English by an independent person), to check for errors or inconsistencies.

4. After developing or translating measurement instruments for use with minority populations, researchers should test the instruments for

validity and reliability on the population they intend to study.

ERRORS IN MEASUREMENT

The range of precision in measurement is quite broad—from the cook who measures in terms of pinches, dashes, and smidgens to the physicist who measures in angstroms (0.003937 millionths of an inch). No matter whether a measurement is crude or precise, it is important to recognize that *all* measurement involves some component of error (Alwin, 2007). There is no such thing as an exact measurement. Some measurement devices in the social sciences are fairly precise. Others, however, contain substantial error components, because most of our measures deal with abstract and shifting phenomena, such as attitudes, values, or opinions, which are difficult to measure with a high degree of precision. The large error component in many of our measurements means that researchers must pay close attention to the different types and sources of error. In measurement, researchers confront two basic types of error: *random* and *systematic*. In fact, we can modify the formula from the measurement theory introduced earlier in this chapter with the recognition that the error term in that formula, E, is actually made up of two components:

$$E = R + S$$

where R refers to random error and S refers to systematic error. Now, our measurement formula looks like this:

$$X = T + R + S$$

Our measurement or observation of a phenomenon is a function of the true nature of that phenomenon along with any random and systematic error that occurs in the measurement process.

Random Errors

Random errors are those that are neither consistent nor patterned; the error is as likely to be in one direction as in another. Essentially, random errors are chance errors that, in the long run, tend to cancel themselves out. In fact, in measurement theory, mathematicians often assume that $R = 0$ in the long run. For example, a respondent may misread or mismark an item on a questionnaire; a counselor may misunderstand, and thus record incorrectly something said during an interview; a computer operator may enter incorrect data into a computerized data file. All these are random sources of error and can occur at virtually every point in a research project. Cognizant of the numerous sources of random error, researchers take steps to minimize them. Careful wording of questions, convenient response formats, and "cleaning" of computerized data all keep random error down. Despite researchers' best efforts, however, the final data may contain some component of random error.

Because of their unpatterned nature, random errors are assumed to tend to cancel each other out. For example, the careless computer operator mentioned earlier would be just as likely to enter a score that was lower than the actual one as to enter a score that was higher. The net effect is that random errors at least partly offset each other. The major problem with random error is that it weakens the precision with which a researcher can measure variables, thus reducing the ability to detect a relationship between variables when one is, in fact, present. For example, consider a hypothetical study concerning the relationship between empathy on the part of human service workers and client satisfaction with treatment. Assume that higher levels of client satisfaction actually are associated with higher levels of empathy. For such a study, measurements would be taken of the level of empathy that a worker expressed and of client satisfaction. Suppose we monitor five client interviews by each of five workers—a total sample of 25 cases—for level of worker empathy and client satisfaction. To the extent that random error is present in our measures, some interviews will be scored too high and some too low, even though the overall mean empathy and satisfaction scores can be expected to be quite close to the true averages. In terms of individual cases, however, random measurement will produce some empathy scores that are erroneously low for their associated satisfaction scores. Conversely, random error will produce some empathy scores that are high for their associated satisfaction scores. Thus, the random error tends to mask the true correlation between empathy and satisfaction. Despite the fact that worker empathy and client satisfaction really are correlated, too much of this type of random measurement error may result in the conclusion that the relationship between these variables does not exist.

Fortunately, researchers can combat random error with a variety of strategies. One is to increase the sample size. Instead of using five workers and five interviews per worker, the researcher might use 10 workers and 10 interviews per worker, for a total sample of 100. A second strategy is to increase the "dose," or "contrast," between levels of the independent variable. For example, researchers might select workers for the study according to their empathy skills to assure some cases with low expression of empathy and some with high expression. Finally, the researcher might increase the number of items on the measurement scales or, in other ways, more precisely refine the tools. Such strategies can reduce the impact of random error, but the same is not true for systematic error.

Systematic Errors

Systematic error is consistent and patterned. Unlike random errors, systematic errors may not cancel themselves out. If there is a consistent over- or understatement of the value of a given variable, then the errors will accumulate. For example, we know that systematic error occurs when measuring crime using official police reports; the Uniform Crime Reports (UCR) of the Federal Bureau of Investigation (FBI) count only crimes that are reported to the police. The Department of Justice supplements these statistics with the National Crime Victimization Survey (NCVS), which measures the number of people who claim to be the victims of crime. Comparisons of these two measures consistently reveal a substantial amount of hidden crime—that is, crimes reported by victims but never brought to the attention of the police. For example, NCVS data indicate that only 40 to 50 percent of all violent and property crimes are reported to the police (Truman, 2011). So there is a large systematic error when measuring the amount of crime the way the UCR does because of the underreporting of most crimes (see Research in Practice 8.2 for a more detailed discussion of this issue).

Systematic errors are more troublesome to researchers than random errors because they are more likely to lead to false conclusions. For example, official juvenile delinquency statistics consistently show higher rates of delinquency among children of families with lower socioeconomic status. Self-report studies of involvement with delinquency suggest, however, that the official data systematically overstate the relationship between delinquency and socioeconomic status (Binder, Geis, & Bruce, 1988). It is easy to see how the systematic error in delinquency data could lead to erroneous conclusions regarding possible causes of delinquency as well as to inappropriate prevention or treatment strategies.

In Research in Practice 5.2, we discuss how measurement issues that concern researchers—problems of reliability, validity, and error—have direct parallels in practice intervention.

Improving Validity and Reliability

When a measurement device does not achieve acceptable levels of validity and reliability—that is, when much error occurs—researchers often attempt to redesign the device so it is more valid and reliable. We will discuss how to develop valid and reliable measuring devices at length in other chapters when we discuss how to design good measurement tools. Here, however, we mention a few techniques as a preview of what happens when a measurement device does not yield adequate validity and reliability:

1. *More extensive conceptual development*. Often, validity and reliability are compromised because the researcher is not sufficiently clear and precise about the nature of the concepts being measured and their possible indicators.

> **RESEARCH IN PRACTICE 5.2** **Assessment Of Client Functioning: Both Research and Practice Require Valid and Reliable Measurement**
>
> In this chapter, we emphasize the point that practitioners as well as researchers engage in a process of measurement, although for different purposes. A mental health practitioner, after all, is confronted with the task of determining whether a client is depressed or anxious and how depressed or anxious they might be. We have discussed the evaluation of measurement primarily as it applies to research settings. Yet practitioners also need to concern themselves about measurement issues to ensure that instruments used in practice are valid and reliable.
>
> One practice measurement tool that is widely used and well known among human service students and professionals is The Diagnostic and Statistical Manual, or DSM, of the American Psychiatric Association. As its name implies, the DSM is a manual used by mental health professionals (doctors, nurses, and social workers, among others) to diagnose cases of psychiatric disorder. The DSM tells mental health practitioners which behaviors and words can be taken as indicators of a particular mental disorder. As with other measurement instruments, the DSM provides a way to discover the nature or extent of some abstract phenomenon (such as depression or anxiety) by identifying indicators of it (such as the behavioral symptoms that are presumed to be associated with depression). The DSM has been extensively revised since first being published many decades ago and is currently coming out in its fifth edition.
>
> In assessing the DSM over the decades as a practice assessment instrument, one major concern has been the validity and reliability of its measurement (First, 2004; Phillips et al., 2010). After all, if a social worker or psychiatric nurse uses the diagnostic criteria of the DSM to conclude that a particular patient is depressed, the hope is that the patient is actually depressed (as opposed to having another disorder or no disorder at all). In other words, the DSM leads to a correct diagnosis. To assess the DSM along these lines, many of the tests of validity and reliability discussed in this chapter have been applied. From these many research studies, we know that the reliability of psychiatric diagnoses using the DSM is variable (Kirk & Kutchins, 1992; Teitelbaum & Mullen, 2000; Wood, Lilienfeld, & Garb, 2000). In some cases, diagnoses vary little from one practitioner to another (i.e. the DSM shows high reliability, and possibly validity); in other settings, there is great variation (i.e. suggesting low reliability and validity). The reliability of psychiatric diagnoses is affected by the nature of the disorder, the characteristics of the patient, the skill of the practitioner, the circumstances that surround the assessments, and the kinds of efforts that are made to reach agreement. This fluctuation in reliability certainly suggests that some of the diagnoses made by mental health practitioners are unreliable and possibly invalid as well.
>
> The point is that measurement issues should concern practitioners as much as they do researchers. Problems of validity, reliability, and error can result in ineffective and possibly harmful practice interventions. By observing how researchers deal with such problems, practitioners can learn systematic ways of evaluating practice measurement instruments.
>
> In addition, researchers often use measures developed for practice to measure the independent or dependent variables in research. Research on mental illness, for example, sometimes uses the DSM as a measurement tool for assessing the extent and type of mental illness. Fischer and Corcoran (2007), for example, describe a host of practice measures useful in research. They also assess what reliability and validity information exists about each measure.

Rethinking the concepts often helps in revising the measuring instrument to make it more valid.

2. *Better training of those who will apply the measuring devices.* This is especially useful when a measuring device is based on someone's subjective assessment of an attitude or state. Researchers show the people applying the device how their judgments can be biased or produce error and how they can guard against it in their assessments.

3. *Interview the subjects of the research about the measurement devices.* Those under study may have some insight regarding why the verbal reports, observations, or archival reports are not producing accurate measures of their behavior.

Information Technology in Research — Computerized Data Collection: Enhancing Researcher–Practitioner Collaboration

Both practitioners and researchers need information, or data. Practitioners need it to assess the problems facing their clients, as well as to satisfy the demands of agencies and monitoring organizations for documentation of progress and intervention outcome. Researchers need data to find solutions for social problems. Despite this common need for information, a gap often exists between research and practice (Clark, 2002). Practitioners may see participating in research as an interference with practice and complain that the results of research are not helpful in guiding practice. Conversely, researchers may complain that practitioners are uncooperative and fail to provide the structured, controlled data collection valued for research.

The field of substance abuse provides an exciting example of collaboration between addiction treatment practitioners and researchers, a collaboration that helped to bridge that gap through the design and implementation of a computer-assisted method of data collection (Carise, Cornely, & Gurel, 2002). The project involved the Treatment Research Institute, an organization specializing in substance-abuse treatment research, and a treatment provider, Fresh Start, which operates recovery houses. The implementation of a computerized data-collection system known as the Drug Evaluation Network System (DENS) proved both valuable to practitioners in delivering services and an excellent source of data for research.

The DENS features the Addiction Severity Index (ASI), a well-accepted instrument for measurement, as its primary data source. The ASI has been a popular assessment tool in substance abuse for more than two decades. Designed as a semistructured, 200-item interview, the index addresses seven potential problem areas in substance-abusing patients: medical status, employment and support, drug use, alcohol use, legal status, family/social status, and psychiatric status (McLellan et al., 1992). In its original paper-and-pencil format, a skilled interviewer requires about an hour to gather information on recent (past 30 days) and lifetime problems in all the problem areas. Practitioners have used the ASI with psychiatrically ill, homeless, pregnant, and prisoner populations, but mostly with adults seeking treatment for substance abuse problems.

Because treatment personnel use the ASI as an intake or assessment instrument, incorporating it into the DENS software system makes the DENS potentially useful to the treatment staff. The ASI also is widely used in clinical and health service research projects, so the DENS is of value to researchers who need scientifically valid information. Research cooperation in adopting the DENS program is especially attractive to the practitioner for two reasons: First, the computer form can be completed in less time and with fewer errors, thanks to an automatic error-checking feature, than the paper-and-pencil version of the ASI. Second, the software generates an admissions narrative report for clinical staff that serves as the basis for mandatory third-party reports to state regulatory agencies and insurance providers. The software also provides program administrators with aggregate comparison reports of their patients in terms of all intake variables. In short, the DENS helps the practitioner cope with that most dreaded feature of the job—paperwork. In the long term, research results should prove helpful in guiding practice, but the real selling point for the practitioner is this immediate, time-saving benefit.

For the researcher's purposes, treatment program staff collect ASI data, which are then transferred electronically to the Treatment Research Institute's computer server so that the researchers have immediate access to it. In addition, it is possible to add new questions to the data-collection instrument so researchers can follow emerging trends as they happen. At the time of reporting on the project, 72 treatment programs in five major cities were participating in the program.

A major factor in the success of this collaborative effort between researchers and practitioners was the fact that both parties clearly stood to benefit. Besides greater efficiency and reduced paperwork, the collaboration helped practitioners modify service delivery of the program to meet client needs. For example, when the data showed a high percentage of female clients reporting a history of sexual abuse, Fresh Start added a female staff member to provide group sessions aimed at the needs of women survivors of sexual abuse. Such benefits for practice motivated the clinicians to provide the best-quality data that the researchers required for valid, reliable measurement.

They may, for example, comment that the wording of questions is ambiguous or that members of their subculture interpret some words differently than the researcher intended.

4. *Higher level of measurement.* This does not guarantee greater validity and reliability, but a higher level of measurement can produce a more reliable measuring device in some cases. So when the researcher has some options in terms of how to measure a variable, it is worth considering a higher level of measurement.

5. *Use more indicators of a variable.* This also does not guarantee enhanced reliability and validity, but a multiple-item measuring device can, in some cases, produce a more valid measure than a measuring device with fewer items can.

6. *Conduct an item-by-item assessment of multiple-item measures.* If the measuring device consists of a number of questions or items, perhaps only one or a few items are the problem: These are the invalid ones that are reducing the validity and reliability of the instrument, and deleting them may improve validity and reliability.

After revising a measuring device based on these ideas, researchers must, of course, subject the revised version to tests of validity and reliability.

CHOOSING A MEASUREMENT DEVICE

We have seen that we can use a number of indicators, sometimes a large number and at different levels of measurement, to measure a variable. How do we choose the best of these measures to use in a particular study? If we are developing a new measuring device, how do we decide whether it is good or not? It is a complicated and sometimes difficult decision for researchers, but a number of factors, discussed in this or earlier chapters, can serve as guidelines for making this decision:

1. Choose indicators that measure the variables in ways that are theoretically important in the research, as discussed in Chapter 2.

2. Choose indicators based on their proven validity and reliability.

3. If two measuring instruments are equivalent in all other ways except for level of measurement, choose the indicator at the higher level of measurement.

4. Choose indicators that produce the least amount of systematic and random error.

5. Choose indicators with matters of feasibility, as discussed in Chapter 4, in mind.

REVIEW AND CRITICAL THINKING

Main Points

- Measurement is the process of describing abstract concepts in terms of specific indicators by assigning numbers or other symbols to them.

- An indicator is an observation we assume to be evidence for the attributes or properties of some phenomenon. Social research measures most variables through verbal reports, observation, or archival records. Positivists and nonpositivists disagree about the nature of measurement.

- The four levels of measurement are nominal, ordinal, interval, and ratio.

- The nature of the variable itself and the way it is measured determines the level of measurement achieved with a given variable.

- Discrete variables have a limited number of distinct and separate values. Continuous variables theoretically have an infinite number of possible values.

- Validity refers to a measure's ability to measure accurately the variable it measures.

- Face validity, content or sampling validity, jury opinion, criterion validity, and construct validity are techniques for assessing the validity of measures.
- Reliability refers to a measure's ability to yield consistent results each time it is applied.
- Test–retest, multiple forms, and internal consistency, such as split-half, are techniques for assessing the reliability of measures.
- Measurement in social research must be culturally sensitive; researchers should never assume a measurement instrument that is valid and reliable for a majority group will be so for minorities.
- Random errors are neither consistent nor patterned and can reduce the precision with which variables are measured.
- Systematic errors are consistent and patterned and, unless noted, can potentially lead to erroneous conclusions.
- Researchers can take a number of steps to improve the validity and reliability of measurement devices.
- Measurement devices are chosen on the basis of theoretical considerations, their validity and reliability, their level of measurement, the amount of systematic and random errors, and feasibility.

Important Terms for Review

concurrent validity
construct validity
content validity
continuous variables
criterion validity
discrete variables
face validity
index
indicator
Interval measures
item
jury opinion
level of measurement
measurement
multitrait–multimethod approach
nominal measures
ordinal measures
predictive validity
random errors
ratio measures
reliability
sampling validity
scale
systematic error
Validity

Critical Thinking

Measurement is all about being careful and precise. It is about linking the abstract world of concepts and ideas to the concrete world of observations. Much can be learned from how scientists do these things and translated into tips for critically analyzing any information or situations that you might confront:

1. When something is being discussed, can you identify any explicit or implicit indicators (or operational definitions) that are being used? In other words, how do people know if that thing exists or how much of it exists?
2. Would any particular group's values or interests be promoted by particular operational definitions? Does this produce any bias?
3. Is there any effort to evaluate these operational definitions (that is, assessment of validity and reliability)?
4. Could error in measurement be affecting what is being said or observed?

Exploring the Internet

Many websites can help you find existing measurement tools, such as scales and indexes. An excellent example is the website of the Buros Institute of Mental Measurements (http://www.unl.edu/buros/index.html). The institute monitors the quality of commercially published tests and encourages improved test development by providing critical analysis of individual instruments. Buros publishes the Mental Measurements Yearbook, and its website lists thousands of instruments and provides access to critical reviews of the various scales.

Another site with information on specific scales and measurement tools is the WALMYR Publishing Company home page (http://www.walmyr.com).

Another approach to finding Internet resources on measurement is to use a search engine and search for such terms as "measurement group" or "social work measurement." The former term produced the website of The Measurement Group (http://www.themeasurementgroup.com), a private consulting firm that focuses on evaluation research and policy development, primarily in the health area. At this website, you will find much information about measurement with standardized tests and instruments, as well as links to numerous other websites, journals, and professional associations relevant to measurement issues.

One specific area you might find valuable to search through is psychometrics, which is the study of personality and mental states and attributes, often used for diagnostic and clinical (rather than research) purposes. Psychometrics, however, is a highly quantitative field, and thus, a good area in which to explore measurement issues. You might try the home page of the American Psychological Association (http://www.apa.org), using its search feature or clicking on "More Psychology Topics," and then the "Testing Issues" button.

For Further Reading

Blythe, B. J., & Tripodi, T. (1989). *Measurement in Direct Practice.* Newbury Park, Calif.: Sage. This book looks at measurement issues from the standpoint of day-to-day efforts to apply successful interventions to help clients. It should be particularly useful for those who are currently in or planning to enter direct practice.

Campbell, D. T., & Russo, M. J. (2001). *Social Measurement.* Thousand Oaks, Calif.: Sage. This book provides a user-friendly presentation of Campbell's essential work in social measurement. The book includes his arguments as to why qualitative approaches belong with quantitative ones as well as his debate with deconstructionists and social constructionists over measurement validity.

Geismar, L. L., & Camasso M. (1993). *The Family Functioning Scale: A Guide to Research and Practice.* New York: Springer. This book provides an excellent illustration of measurement in both research and practice as it explores development of a family functioning scale for use in both realms. It is a good example of both the parallels and linkages between research and practice.

Hersen, M., Ed. (2003). *Comprehensive Handbook of Psychological Assessment,* 1–4. New York: Wiley. These volumes provide essential information about developing and using the major types of psychological assessment instruments. These assessment instruments address the same kinds of measurement issues as instruments used in research.

Hindelang, M. J., Hirschi, T., & Weis, J. G. (1980). *Measuring Delinquency.* Beverly Hills, Calif.: Sage. A good description of the development of a measuring device related to a human service issue. The volume covers all the issues related to problems of measurement.

Kirk, J., & Miller, M. L. (1986). *Reliability and Validity in Qualitative Research.* Beverly Hills, Calif.: Sage. This work presents the measurement issues of reliability and validity as they apply to qualitative research, such as field research (see Chapter 9). Unfortunately, reliability and validity often are presented only in the context of quantitative research.

Martin, L. L., & Kettner, P. M. (2009). *Measuring the Performance of Human Service Programs,* 2nd ed. Thousand Oaks, Calif.: Sage. This short book explains in detail how to measure and assess human service programs, especially with outcome measures. It includes such measures as levels of functioning scales and client satisfaction.

Miller, D. C., & Salkind, N. J. (2002). *Handbook of Research Design and Social Measurement,* 6th ed. Thousand Oaks, Calif.: Sage. A good resource work for scales and indexes focusing on specific human service concerns.

Class Exercises for Competency Assessment

5.1. **[Diversity] [Research & Practice]** Here is an interesting way to illustrate measurement issues. Imagine that a new student at your college is blind. She is trying to be independent of others and asks some students to help her measure the distance to such places as the nearest drinking fountain, the restroom, and the student lounge. Select a destination at least 50 feet from the classroom and preferably around a corner or two. Have four or five students independently count the number of steps to the destination, and report back their step counts. Compare the counts. How does this exercise illustrate the definition of measurement presented in this chapter? Given the responses of the volunteers, would the blind student be able to find the destination? Was this a valid and reliable measurement procedure?

5.2. **[Diversity] [Research & Practice]** What modifications could you make in the rules of measurement presented in Exercise 5.1 that would improve the validity and reliability of the measure?

5.3. **[Diversity] [Research & Practice]** The following list contains variables that researchers and practitioners in the human services commonly encounter:
   a. race
   b. income
   c. health
   d. drug use
   e. school achievement
   f. number of arrests
   g. depression
   h. marital satisfaction
   i. employment status
   j. assertiveness
   k. parenting skill
   l. client satisfaction

   How could each variable be measured? Which level of measurement is applicable to each of these variables? Which of these variables are discrete, and which are continuous? Which of these variables could be measured at more than one level of measurement? Which level is best?

5.4. **[Research & Practice]** Understanding levels of measurement can be challenging, and it helps to examine some actual variables in research. The Information Technology in Research insert describes the Addiction Severity Index (ASI). This assessment tool is considered to be public domain and is readily available in print or accessible on the Internet by using a search engine. The class can divide up the instrument, examine the various items in the ASI, and classify the variables as nominal, ordinal, interval, or ratio.

5.5. **[Critical Thinking] [Research & Practice]** Working independently or in teams of two or three students, locate some studies that have used one of the variables from the list in Exercise 5.3. Describe how the variable was operationalized in each study. Do you see any weaknesses in using this operational definition given the nominal definition of the variable? What problems might there be in obtaining valid and reliable measures of these variables based on the studies that you have reviewed?

Chapter 6

✳

Sampling

The Purpose of Sampling

Sampling Terminology
Populations and Samples
Sampling Frames
Learning From Experience: Poor Sampling Frames

Probability Samples
Simple Random Sampling
Systematic Sampling
Stratified Sampling
Area Sampling
Estimating Sample Size

Nonprobability Samples
Availability Sampling

Snowball Sampling
Quota Sampling
Purposive Sampling
Dimensional Sampling

Sampling with Diverse Populations

A Note on Sampling in Practice

Review and Critical Thinking
Main Points
Important Terms for Review
Critical Thinking
Exploring the Internet
For Further Reading
Class Exercises for Competency Assessment

A number of correctional systems have established programs that use behavior modification techniques to shape inmate behavior by rewarding sought-after behavior and withholding privileges from those who are recalcitrant or hostile. Each inmate who is placed in such a program becomes, in a sense, a test of the hypotheses about behavior change derived from behavioral theory. What can we conclude, however, if one inmate's behavior changes in a way that supports these hypotheses? Will the program work with other inmates?

This is the issue at the core of this chapter. Can knowledge gained from one or a few cases be considered knowledge about a whole group of people? The answer depends on whether the inmate is *representative* of some larger group of which the inmate is a "sample." Does he or she represent all inmates? Only inmates in a particular prison? Just inmates who have committed certain offenses? Or is this inmate not representative of any larger group? These issues are at the center of the problem of *sampling,* or selecting a few cases out of some larger grouping for study. All of us have had experience with sampling. Cautiously tasting a spoonful of soup is a process of sampling to see how hot it is; taking a bite of a new brand of pizza to see if we like it is a process of sampling. All sampling involves attempting to make a judgment about a whole something—a bowl of soup, a brand of pizza, or an inmate population—based on an analysis of only a part of that whole. Scientific sampling, however, is considerably more careful and systematic than casual, everyday sampling. In this chapter, we discuss the fundamentals of sampling along with the benefits and disadvantages of various sampling techniques.

THE PURPOSE OF SAMPLING

When we first encounter the subject of sampling, a common question is this: Why bother? Why not just study the whole group? A major reason for studying samples rather than whole groups is that the whole group sometimes is so large that studying it is not feasible. For example, human service workers might want to learn about welfare recipients, the mentally ill, prison inmates, or some other large group of people. It would be difficult—and often impossible—to study all members of these groups. Sampling, however, allows us to study a workable number of cases from the large group to derive findings that are relevant to all members of the group.

A second reason for sampling is that, surprising as it may seem, we can get better information from carefully drawn samples than we can from an entire group. This is especially true when the group under study is extremely large. For example, the United States takes a census of all residents at the beginning of each decade. Despite the vast resources that the federal government puts into the census, substantial undercounts and other errors occur. In fact, after recent censuses, numerous cities filed lawsuits complaining of alleged undercounts. Between the decennial censuses, the U.S. Census Bureau conducts *sample* surveys to update population statistics and collect data on other matters. The quality of the data gathered in these sample surveys actually is superior to the data in the census itself. The reason is that, with only a few thousand people to contact, the task is more manageable, involving better-trained interviewers, greater control over the interviewers, and fewer hard-to-find respondents. In fact, the U.S. Census Bureau even conducts a sample survey after each census as a check on the accuracy of that census. Indeed, were it not a constitutional requirement, the complete census might well be dropped and replaced by sample surveys.

Much research, then, is based on samples of people. Samples make possible a glimpse of the behavior and attitudes of whole groups of people, and the validity and accuracy of research results depend heavily on how samples are drawn. An improperly drawn sample renders the collected data virtually useless. So, an important consideration regarding samples is how *representative* they are of the population from which we draw them. A **representative sample** is one that accurately reflects the distribution of relevant variables in the target population. In a sense, the sample should be considered a small reproduction of the population. Imagine, for example, that a researcher wants to study the success of unmarried teenage mothers in raising their children, with the goal of improving the provision of services to these adolescents. The research sample should reflect the relevant characteristics of unmarried teenage mothers in the community. Such characteristics might include age, years of education, and socioeconomic status. To be representative, the sample would have to contain the same proportion of unmarried teenage mothers at each age level, each educational level, and each socioeconomic status that exists in the community as a whole. In short, a representative sample should have all the same characteristics as the population.

The representative character of samples allows the conclusions that are based on them to be legitimately generalized to the populations from which they are drawn. As we will see later in this chapter, nonrepresentative samples are useful for some research purposes, but researchers must always assess the representativeness of their samples to make accurate conclusions. Before comparing the various techniques for drawing samples, we will define some of the major terms that are used in the field of sampling.

SAMPLING TERMINOLOGY

Populations and Samples

A sample is drawn from a **population**, which refers to all possible cases of what we are interested in studying. In the human services, the target population often consists of people who have some particular characteristic in common, such as all Americans, all eligible voters, all school-age children, and so on. A population need not, however, be composed of people. Recall from Chapter 4 that the unit of analysis can be something other than individuals, such as groups or programs. Then, the target population is all possible cases of our unit of analysis. A **sample** consists of one or more elements selected from a population. The manner in which we select elements for the sample has enormous implications for the scientific utility of the research based on that sample. To select a good sample, we need to clearly define the population from which to draw the sample. Failure to do so can make generalizing from the sample observations highly ambiguous and result in inaccurate conclusions.

The definition of a population should specify four things: (1) content, (2) units, (3) extent, and (4) time (Kish, 1965). Consider the sample that James Greenley and Richard Schoenherr (1981) used to study the effects of agency characteristics on the delivery of social services. First, the *content* of the population refers to the particular characteristic that the members of the population have in common. For Greenley and Schoenherr, the characteristic that was common to the members of their population was that they were health or social service agencies. Second, the *unit* indicates the unit of analysis, which in our illustration is organizations rather than individuals or groups. (Although Greenley and Schoenherr collected data from practitioners and clients in the organizations, their focus was on comparing the performance of agencies.) Third, the *extent* of the population refers to its spatial or geographic coverage. For practical reasons, Greenley and Schoenherr limited the extent of their population to health and social agencies serving one county in Wisconsin. It was not financially feasible for them to define the extent of their population as all agencies in Wisconsin—or in the United States. Finally, the *time* factor refers to the temporal period during which a unit must possess the appropriate characteristic to qualify for the sample. Greenley and Schoenherr conducted a cross-sectional study, and only agencies that were in operation at the time those authors collected their data qualified. A longitudinal study might include agencies that came into existence during the course of the study.

With these four factors clearly defined, a population normally is adequately delimited. Then, we can construct what is called a *sampling frame*.

Sampling Frames

A **sampling frame** is a listing of all the elements in a population. In many studies, we draw the actual sample from this listing. The adequacy of the sampling frame is crucial in determining the quality of the sample, and the degree to which the sampling frame includes *all* members of the population is of major importance. Although an endless number of possible sampling frames exist, a few illustrations will describe some of the intricacies of developing good sampling frames.

In human service research, some of the most adequate sampling frames consist of lists of members of organizations. For example, if we wanted to expand the study, mentioned at the beginning of this chapter, regarding the impact of behavior modification on inmates, we could draw a larger sample of inmates in that prison using a straightforward sampling frame consisting of all inmates currently listed as residents of that institution. Given the care with which correctional facilities maintain accurate records of inmates, this sampling frame undoubtedly would be complete and accurate. Other examples of sampling frames based on organizational affiliation would be the membership rosters of professional groups, such as the National Association of Social Workers (NASW), the American Psychological Association, or the American Society of Criminology. These lists are not quite as accurate as an inmate roster, because people who have very recently joined the organization might not appear on the official lists. Clerical errors also might lead to a few missing names. These errors, however, would have little effect on the adequacy of the sampling frame.

When using organizational lists as a sampling frame, we must exercise caution about what we define as the population and about whom we make generalizations. The population consists of the sampling frame, and we can make legitimate generalizations only about the sampling frame. Many social workers, for example, do not belong to the NASW. Thus, a sample taken from the NASW membership roster represents only NASW members and not all social workers. When using organizational lists as sampling frames, then, it is important to assess carefully who the list includes and who the list excludes. Sometimes, research focuses on a theoretical concept that is operationalized in terms of an organizational list that does not include all actual instances of what the concept intends. For example, a study of poverty could operationalize the concept "poor" as those receiving some form of public assistance. Yet, many people with little or no income do not receive public assistance. In this case, the sampling frame would not completely reflect the population that the theoretical concept intended.

Some research focuses on populations that are quite large, such as residents of a city or state. To develop sampling frames for household-based surveys of these populations, two types of listings could be considered: (1) telephone numbers; and (2) lists of addresses in a community, which is referred to as "address-based sampling." A listing of telephone numbers in a geographic area can be considered a sampling frame of households, although there are a number of problems with using such a listing today. Even today, some people do not have telephone service (about 4 to 5 percent of households) (U.S. Census Bureau, 2011). Those without telephones tend to be concentrated among the poor, those who live in rural areas, and transient groups, such as the young. For a research project in which these groups are important, sampling based on telephone numbers could be unrepresentative. Another problem is the growth in use of cell phones, with almost one-third of households today having cell-phone service only (see the Information Technology insert at the end of the chapter). Cell phones are not as clearly tied to a particular household or geographic area as are traditional landlines. So, a person may live in a different geographic area from where the cell phone is registered. This makes it difficult to know what phone numbers are to be included in a sampling frame when selecting a random sample of households for a particular community. If cell phones are left out, it threatens the representativeness of the sample, because cell phone–only people tend to be younger, less affluent, and more transient. Telephone books do not provide a very good listing of telephone numbers because of the many unlisted numbers and cell phones, which are not listed in phone books. Instead, if telephone numbers are to be used as a sampling frame, some random number selection technique, such as *random-digit dialing* (RDD), can ensure that every household with telephone service has a chance of appearing in the sample. Of course, RDD does nothing about non-coverage resulting from the lack of telephone service in some households or some of the problems created by cell phones.

An alternative to telephone numbers as a population listing for a particular geographic area would be a listing of all the addresses in the community—address-based sampling (Iannacchione, 2011; Link et al., 2008). One source of such household listings—called the "traditional listing method"—consists of lists developed by some private or nonprofit survey research organizations that have trained people walk through a community, physically locate every housing unit, and note its address. This is probably the most complete listing of households in a community, but it is also expensive to purchase or develop.

A second source of such address-based lists is provided by the U.S. Postal Service Computerized Delivery Sequence File, which is a listing of all residential addresses that are served by the USPS in an area. These listings can be purchased from sampling vendors who are approved by the USPS, but these also have problems of noncoverage: Households can request that their address not be sold by the post office, and many rural addresses don't show up on the listing. The sampling vendors who provide them sometimes make efforts to overcome some of these shortcomings, so the completeness of lists can vary from one vendor to another.

Another household listing sometimes used for sampling is a list of customers from a local electric utility. Although some households do not have telephone service, relatively few lack electricity, and the problem of noncoverage therefore is less significant. A major problem, however, comes from multiple-family dwellings, which often list utilities only in the name of the building's owner rather than by the names of all the individual residents. The young, the old, and the unmarried are more likely to inhabit these multiple-family dwellings. Unless we supplement the utility listings, samples will systematically under represent people in these groups. Visiting the dwellings and adding the residents to the list of utility subscribers can overcome this problem, but this is a time-consuming task.

Finally, city directories, criss-cross directories, and other directories exist that are quite useful as household listings. Available in most libraries, on CD, and online, these directories contain, among other things, an alphabetical listing of streets and addresses with residents' names. This listing is fairly accurate, but it does exclude new construction. Some of these directories also include information on gender, age, length of residence, wealth, and other important characteristics.

Learning From Experience: Poor Sampling Frames

Some disastrous mistakes have occurred in past investigations because of inadequate sampling frames. A classic example of this was the attempt *Literary Digest* magazine made to predict the outcome of the 1936 presidential race between Alfred Landon and Franklin Roosevelt. When predicting an election, the target population is all likely voters. *Literary Digest,* however, did not use a sampling frame that listed all likely voters. Rather, they drew their sample from lists of automobile owners and telephone directories. On the basis of their sample results, they predicted that Landon would win by a substantial margin, but, of course, Roosevelt won the election easily. Why the error in prediction? A major part of the problem was a flawed sampling frame (Cahalan, 1989; Squire, 1988). In 1936, with the Great Depression at its peak, a substantial proportion of eligible voters, especially poorer ones, did not own cars or have telephones. In short, the sample was drawn from an inadequate sampling frame and did not represent the target population. In addition, because the poor are more likely to vote Democratic, most of the eligible voters excluded from the sampling frame voted for the Democratic candidate, Roosevelt.

We can construct adequate sampling frames for many human service projects from existing listings, but we must exercise caution in using such lists because they may inadvertently exclude some people. In fact, human service research is especially vulnerable to this, because we often study populations that are difficult to enumerate. For example, undocumented aliens are, by definition, not listed anywhere. We know they make up a large segment of the population in such urban centers as Los Angeles, but a study of the poor in these areas that relied on a city directory or another such listing obviously would miss large numbers of such people. Early studies of gay men also fell prey to this problem (Bell & Weinberg, 1978; Hooker, 1957). In some of these studies, the sampling frame was homosexuals who were listed as patients by psychotherapists who participated in the research.

The studies concluded that homosexuality was associated with personality disturbance. Yet it does not take great insight to recognize that the sampling frames did not list many gay men—namely, those feeling no need to see therapists—and, thus, were strongly biased toward finding personality disorders among gays.

We must assess sampling frames carefully to ensure that they include all elements of the population of interest. The remainder of this chapter is a discussion of the different ways in which to select samples. First, we discuss probability samples, for which we are most likely to have a sampling frame from which to draw the sample. Researchers use probability samples in some types of human service research, such as needs assessment and evaluation research. Then we discuss nonprobability samples, which researchers use in assessing client functioning and evaluating the effectiveness of intervention strategies.

PROBABILITY SAMPLES

With luck, almost any sampling procedure could produce a representative sample, but that is little comfort to the researcher who wants to be as certain as possible that his or her sample is representative. Techniques that make use of probability theory can both greatly reduce the chances of getting a nonrepresentative sample, and, more importantly, permit the researcher to estimate precisely the likelihood that a sample differs from the true population by a given amount. In these samples, known as **probability samples**, each element in the population has some chance of inclusion in the sample, and the investigator can determine the chances or probability of each element's inclusion (Schaeffer, Mendenhall, Ott, & Gerow, 2012). In their simpler versions, probability sampling techniques ensure that each element has an *equal* chance of inclusion. In more elaborate versions, the researcher takes advantage of knowledge about the population to select elements with differing probabilities. The key point is that, whether the probabilities are equal or different, each element's probability of inclusion in a probability sample is nonzero and known. Furthermore, probability sampling enables us to calculate **sampling error**, which is an estimate of the extent to which the values of the sample differ from those of the population from which it was drawn.

Simple Random Sampling

The simplest technique for drawing probability samples is **simple random sampling** (SRS), in which each element in the population has an equal probability of inclusion in the sample. Simple random sampling treats the target population as a unitary whole. We might begin with a sampling frame containing a list of the entire population—or as complete a list as we can obtain. We would then number the elements in the sampling frame sequentially and select elements from the list using a procedure known to be random. If we computerized the sampling frame, we could accomplish random selection merely by programming the computer to select randomly a sample of whatever size we desired. (Appendix B describes how to generate random samples both with the computer and by hand, using a table of random numbers.)

Although simple random samples have the desirable feature of giving each element in the sampling frame an equal chance of appearing in the sample, SRS often is impractical. A major reason for this is cost. Imagine doing a research project that calls for a national sample of 2,000 households. Even if one could obtain such a sample using SRS, which is unlikely, it would be prohibitively expensive to send interviewers all over the country to obtain the data. Furthermore, alternatives to SRS might be more efficient in terms of providing a high degree of representativeness with a smaller sample. Normally, SRS is limited to fairly small-scale projects that deal with populations of modest size for which we can obtain adequate sampling frames. The importance of SRS lies not in its wide application. Rather, SRS is the basic sampling procedure on which statistical theory is based; and it is the standard against which other sampling procedures are measured.

Systematic Sampling

A variation on SRS is called **systematic sampling**, which involves taking every *k*th element listed in a sampling frame. Systematic sampling uses the table of random numbers to determine a random starting point in the sampling frame. From that random start, we select every *k*th element into the sample. The value of *k* is called the *sampling interval,* and it is determined by dividing the population size by the desired sample size. For example, if we wanted a sample of 100 from a population of 1,000, then the sampling interval would be 10. From the random starting point, we would select every 10th element from the sampling frame for the sample. If the starting point is in the middle of the list, then we proceed to the end, jump to the beginning, and end up at the middle again.

In actual practice, dividing the population by the sample size usually does not produce a whole number, so the decimal is rounded upward to the next-largest whole number. This provides a sampling interval that takes us completely through the sampling frame. If we round downward, then the sampling interval becomes slightly too narrow, and we reach the desired sample size before we exhaust the sampling frame, which would mean that those elements farthest from the starting point have no chance of selection.

We commonly use systematic sampling when we draw samples by hand rather than by computer. The only advantage of systematic sampling over SRS is in clerical efficiency. In SRS, the random numbers will select elements scattered throughout the sampling frame. It is time-consuming to search all over the sampling frame to identify the elements that correspond with the random numbers. In systematic sampling, we proceed in an orderly fashion through the sampling frame from the random starting point.

Unfortunately, systematic sampling can produce biased samples, although this is rare. The difficulty occurs when the sampling frame consists of a population list that has a cyclical or recurring pattern, called *periodicity*. If the sampling interval happens to be the same as that of the cycle in the list, then it is possible to draw a seriously biased sample. For example, suppose we were sampling households in a large apartment building. The apartments are listed in the sampling frame by floor and apartment number (2A, 2B, 2C, 2D, 2E, 2F, 3A, 3B, and so on). Furthermore, suppose that, on each floor, apartment F is a corner apartment with an extra bedroom and correspondingly higher rent than the other apartments on that floor. If we had a sampling interval of three and randomly chose to begin counting with apartment 2D, then every F apartment would appear in the sample, which would bias the sample in favor of the more expensive apartments, and thus in favor of the more affluent residents of the apartment building. So, when we use systematic sampling techniques, we need to assess the sampling frame carefully for any cyclical pattern that might confound the sample and, if necessary, rearrange the list to eliminate the pattern. Or, we could use SRS instead of systematic sampling.

Stratified Sampling

With SRS and systematic sampling methods, we treat the target population as a unitary whole when sampling from it. **Stratified sampling** changes this by dividing the population into smaller subgroups, called *strata,* before drawing the sample and then drawing separate random samples from each of the strata.

Reduction in Sampling Error. One of the major reasons for using a stratified sample is that stratifying reduces sampling error for a given sample size to a level lower than that of an SRS of the same size. This is so because of a very simple principle: The more homogeneous a population on the variables under study, the smaller the sample size needed to represent it accurately. Stratifying makes each subsample more homogeneous by eliminating the variation on the variable used for stratifying. Perhaps a gastronomic example will help illustrate this point. Imagine two large, commercial-size cans of nuts, one labeled "peanuts" and the other "mixed nuts." Because the can of peanuts is highly homogeneous, only a small handful from it gives a fairly accurate indication of the remainder of its contents. The can of mixed nuts, however, is quite heterogeneous, containing several kinds of nuts in different proportions. A small handful of nuts from the top of the can cannot be relied on to represent the contents of the entire can. If the mixed nuts were stratified by type into homogeneous piles, however, then a few nuts from each pile could constitute a representative sample of the entire can.

Although stratifying does reduce sampling error, it is important to recognize that the effects are modest. We expect approximately 10 to 20 percent (or less) reduction in comparison to an SRS of equal size (Henry, 1990; Sudman, 1976). Essentially, the decision to stratify depends on two issues: the difficulty of stratifying, and the cost of each additional element in the sample. It can be difficult to stratify a sample on a particular variable if it is hard to get access to data on that variable. For example, we would find it relatively easy to stratify a sample of university students according to class level, because universities typically include class status as part of a database of all registered students. In contrast, we would find it difficult to stratify that same sample on the basis of whether the students had been victims of sexual abuse during childhood, because these data are not readily available and getting them would require a major study in itself. So, stratification requires either that the sampling frame include information on the stratification variable or that the stratification variable is easily determined. Telephone surveys and stratification of respondents by gender illustrate the latter situation. Telephone interviewers can simply ask to speak to the man of the house to obtain the male stratum and request to speak to the woman of the house for the female stratum. If no one of the desired gender is available, then the interviewer drops that household and substitutes another. The process may require some extra phone calls, but the time and cost of doing this can pay for itself in the quality of the sample. As for the effect of cost issues on the decision of whether to stratify, if the cost of obtaining data on each case is high, as in an interview survey, then stratifying to minimize sample size probably is warranted. If each case is inexpensive, however, then stratifying to reduce cost may not be worth the effort unless it can be easily accomplished.

Proportionate Sampling. When we use stratification to reduce sampling error, we normally use *proportionate* stratified sampling, in which the size of the sample taken from each stratum is proportionate to the stratum's presence in the population. Consider a sample of the undergraduates at a college or university. Although the students differ on many characteristics, an obvious difference is their class standing. Any representative sample of the student body should reflect the relative proportions of the various classes as they exist at the college as a whole. If we drew an SRS, then the sample size would have to be quite large for the sample to reflect accurately the distribution of class levels. Small samples would have a greater likelihood of being disproportionate. If we stratify on class level, however, then we can easily make the sample match the actual class distribution, regardless of the sample size. Table 6.1 contains the hypothetical class distribution of a university student body. If a researcher wanted a sample of 200 students with these proportions of students accurately represented, stratifying could easily accomplish it. The researcher would begin by developing a sampling frame with the students grouped according to class level, and then draw a separate SRS from each of the four class strata in numbers proportionate to their presence in the population: 70 freshmen, 50 sophomores, 40 juniors, and 40 seniors.

In actual practice, it is normal to stratify on more than one variable. In the case of a student population, for example, the researcher might want to stratify on sex as well as class level. That would double the number of separate subsamples from four to eight: senior men, senior women, junior men, and so on. Even though stratifying on appropriate variables always improves a sample, researchers should use stratification judiciously. Stratifying on a few variables provides nearly as

TABLE 6.1 Hypothetical Proportionate Stratified Sample of University Students

	Proportion in University	Stratified Sample of 200	
Seniors	20%	Seniors	40
Juniors	20%	Juniors	40
Sophomores	25%	Sophomores	50
Freshmen	35%	Freshmen	70
	100%		200

much benefit as stratifying on many. Because the number of subsamples increases geometrically as the number of stratified variables and the number of categories increase, attempting to stratify on too many variables can excessively complicate sampling without offering substantially increased benefits in terms of a reduction in sampling error.

Disproportionate Sampling. In addition to reducing error, we use stratified samples to enable comparisons among various subgroups in a population when one or more of the subgroups is relatively uncommon. For example, suppose we were interested in comparing two-parent families receiving welfare with other families receiving welfare. If two-parent families make up only about 2 percent of families on the welfare rolls, then a large SRS of 500 welfare families would be expected to contain only 10 such families. This number is far too small to make meaningful statistical comparisons. Stratifying in this case allows us to draw a larger sample of two-parent families to provide enough cases for reliable comparisons to be made. This is called *disproportionate* stratified sampling, because we do not sample the strata proportionately to their presence in the population. This type of sample is different from most probability samples, where we achieve representativeness by giving every element in the population an equal chance of appearing in the sample. With a disproportionate stratified sample, each element of a stratum has an equal chance of appearing in the sample of that stratum, but the elements in some strata have a better chance of appearing in the overall sample than the elements of other strata do.

Selection of variables on which to stratify depends on the reason for stratifying. If we were stratifying to ensure sufficient numbers of cases for analysis in all groups of interest, as in the example of two-parent welfare families, then we would stratify on the variable that has a category with a small proportion of cases in it. This often is an independent variable and involves disproportionate stratified sampling. On the other hand, if the goal of stratifying is to reduce sampling error, as is the case in proportionate stratified sampling, then we might use variables other than the independent variable. Stratifying has an effect in reducing sampling error only when the stratification variables relate to the dependent variables under study. So we should select variables that we know or suspect of having an impact on the dependent variables. For example, a study concerning the impact of religiosity on delinquency might stratify on socioeconomic status, because studies have shown that this variable is related to delinquency involvement. Stratifying on a frivolous variable, such as eye color, would gain us nothing, because it is unlikely to relate to delinquency involvement. It is worth noting, however, that stratifying never hurts a sample. The worst that can happen is that the stratified sample will have about the same sampling error as an SRS of equivalent size, and that the stratifying efforts will have gone for naught.

Area Sampling

Area sampling (also called **cluster sampling** or **multistage sampling**) is a procedure in which we obtain the final units to include in the sample by first sampling among larger units, called *clusters,* that contain the smaller sampling units. A series of sampling stages are involved, working down in scale from larger clusters to smaller ones.

For example, imagine that we wanted to conduct a needs assessment survey that would determine the extent and distribution of preschool children with educational deficiencies in a large urban area. Simple random and systematic samples are out of the question, because no sampling frame listing all such children exists. We could, however, turn to area sampling, a technique that enables us to draw a probability sample without having a complete list of all elements in the population. The ultimate unit of analysis in this needs assessment would be households, because children live in households and we can create a sampling frame of households. We get there in the following way (see Figure 6.1). First, we take a simple random sample from among all census tracts in the urban area. (The U.S. Census Bureau divides urban areas into a number of census tracts, which are areas of approximately 4,000 people.) At the second stage, we list all the city blocks in each census tract in our sample, and then we select a simple random sample from among those city blocks. In the final stage, we list the households on each city block in our sample, and then we select a simple random sample of households on that list. With this procedure, we have an "area probability sample" of households in that urban area. (Public opinion polling agencies, such as Roper, typically use area sampling or a variant of it.) Finally, we interview each household in the sample regarding educational deficiencies among children in that household. If we were sampling an entire state or the whole country, then we would include even more stages of sampling, starting with even larger areas, but eventually working down to the household or individual level, whichever is our unit of analysis. Research in Practice 6.1 describes an important national research study that uses sophisticated area sampling procedures and whose results will have long-ranging policy implications.

A number of factors can complicate area sampling. For example, selected blocks within an area often contain vastly different numbers of people—from high-density inner-city areas to the lower-density suburbs. We must adjust the number of blocks and the number of households per block that are selected into the sample to take into account the differing population densities. Another complication involves the estimation of sampling error. Fairly straightforward formulas for estimating sampling error exist for the simpler sampling techniques. With area sampling, however, the many stages of sampling involved make error estimation exceedingly complex (Kish, 1965; Scheaffer, Mendenhall, Ott, & Gerow, 2012).

Error estimation is quite important for area samples. These samples are subject to greater error than other probability samples, because some error is introduced at each stage of sampling: The more stages involved, the more the sampling error accumulates. Other factors affecting sampling error are the size of the areas initially selected and their degree of homogeneity: The larger the initial areas and the greater their homogeneity, the greater the sampling error. This may seem odd, because with stratified sampling, greater homogeneity leads to less error. Remember, however, that with stratified sampling, we select a sample from *each stratum,* but with area sampling, we draw samples only from *a few areas.* If the few areas in a sample are homogeneous in comparison with the others, then they are less representative. Small, more numerous, heterogeneous clusters lead to more representative area samples. Despite the complexity, area sampling allows us to draw highly accurate probability samples from populations that, because of their size or geographical spread, we could not otherwise sample.

Estimating Sample Size

As we have seen, a key issue in selecting a sample is that it *represent* the population from which it was drawn. People sometimes assume that a larger sample is more representative than a smaller one, and thus that one should go for the largest sample possible. Actually, however, deciding on an appropriate sample size is far more complicated. Five factors influence the sample size: (1) research hypotheses, (2) precision, (3) population homogeneity, (4) sampling fraction, and (5) sampling technique.

Research Hypotheses. One concern in establishing the desired sample size is that we have a sufficient number of cases with which to examine our research hypotheses. Consider a hypothetical study with three variables containing three values each. For an adequate test of the hypotheses, we need a

Step 1:
Take a random sample of census tracts in an urban area (the shaded tracts are those sampled).

Step 2:
Identify city blocks in each census tract, and take a random sample from a list of those city blocks (the shaded blocks are those sampled).

Step 3:
Using a table of random numbers, select a sample of five households from each city block sampled in each census tract sampled (addresses with an asterisk are those sampled).

1. 100 2nd St.*
2. 110 2nd St.
3. 120 2nd St.
4. 130 2nd St.*
5. 140 2nd St.*
6. 401 Ave. D
7. 415 Ave. D
8. 425 Ave. D
9. 435 Ave. D*
10. 201 3rd St.
11. 205 3rd St.
12. 209 3rd St.
13. 213 3rd St.*
14. 217 3rd St.
15. 400 Ave. C
16. 410 Ave. C
17. 420 Ave. C
18. 430 Ave. C

FIGURE 6.1 Drawing an Area Probability Sample

> **RESEARCH IN PRACTICE 6.1**   Policy Planning and Development: An Area Sample Using Address-Based Sampling in a National Children's Health Study
>
> The National Children's Study (NCS) is a major investigation into the environmental factors that shape child health and development (Michael & O'Muircheartaigh, 2008; Montaquila et al., 2009). It is sponsored by a variety of agencies, including the Department of Health and Human Services and the Environmental Protection Agency. It is a complex and ambitious effort that enrolls children into the study before they are born and continues to observe them until they are 21 years of age (a longitudinal panel study, as described in Chapter 4). The results of the study will be used to make recommendations for social policies that will impact the health and well-being of children for decades to come.
>
> To provide the most valid information, the designers of the study must be very careful about the sampling techniques used to select people for the study. The NCS uses "address-based sampling" with the units to be sampled being the household or housing unit and the sampling frame being a listing of all residential addresses in a particular area.
>
> The NCS is an example of a "multistage area probability household sample," which simply means that areas are sampled at a number of different stages with known probabilities of each area being selected, and that the household is the unit to be sampled. The first, or largest, sampling stage is the whole United States, from which is selected a sample of Primary Sampling Units (PSUs). PSUs are usually counties (or clusters of counties where there is low population density). The second sampling stage is to select a sample of geographic areas within each PSU. The third sampling stage is to select a sample of "segments" within each geographic area, each segment being a contiguous block of 500 to 1,200 housing units or households. For the NCS, all households in this final stage (segment) are surveyed, except for some very densely populated segments where a sample of households was selected to be surveyed.
>
> At each stage in a multistage sample, a sampling frame or complete listing of all the elements in that stage is necessary. So the NCS needed a complete listing of all PSUs in the United States, all geographic areas in each PSU, all segments within each geographic area, and finally all households in each segment. The NCS uses what is called a "traditional listing" method of establishing this final sampling frame. With the traditional listing method, "listers" go through an area and locate all residences. This traditional listing method is considered to be the "gold standard": It produces a more complete and accurate sampling frame than any other method.
>
> A drawback of the "traditional listing" method is the expense: It is costly to hire "listers" and pay them to physically inspect the community. This has led the NCS to explore whether other sampling frame generation methods might be less expensive and equally accurate (English et al., 2009). For example, research has been done comparing the "traditional listing" method with the U.S. Postal Service Computerized Delivery Sequence File. Both sampling methods provide a fairly complete and accurate sampling frame, although the traditional listing method does a better job in some situations, such as in rural areas. In urban areas, the two methods were equivalent. The research also finds significant differences in coverage among sampling vendors who distribute the CDSF, with some providing a more complete list. The NCS found that the most complete sampling frame was provided by combining the listing developed using the traditional method with a list made available by the most effective sampling vendor.
>
> This illustration of the sampling practices used in the National Children's Study shows the complexity of sampling procedures—especially in large surveys such as this—and the care and effort that researchers devote to developing a complete sampling frame.

cross tabulation of these three variables, and this would require a 3 × 3 × 3 table, or a table with 27 cells. If our sample were small, then many cells would have few or no cases in them, and we could not test the hypotheses. Johann Galtung (1967) has suggested that 10 to 20 cases in each cell provides an adequate test of hypotheses. We might use disproportionate stratified sampling here to ensure an adequate number of cases in each cell. When that is not possible, Galtung suggests the following formula to determine sample size:

$$r^n \times 20 = \text{sample size}$$

where *r* refers to the number of values on each variable and *n* refers to the number of variables. Thus, for our hypothetical study,

$$r^n \times 20 = 3^3 \times 20 = 27 \times 20 = 540$$

So, we would need a sample size of 540 to feel reasonably assured that we had a sufficient number of cases in each cell. The formula works only if, as in our example, all variables have the same number of values. Furthermore, this technique does not guarantee an adequate number of cases in each cell. If some combination of variables is rare in the population, we may still find few cases in our sample.

Researchers often use statistical procedures in testing hypotheses, and most such procedures require some minimum number of cases to provide accurate results. What is the smallest legitimate sample size? This depends, of course, on the number of variables and on the values they can take. Generally, however, 30 cases is considered to be the bare minimum; and some researchers conservatively set 100 as the smallest legitimate sample size (Bailey, 1987; Champion, 1981). Anything smaller begins to raise questions about whether researchers can properly apply statistical procedures.

Precision. Another factor influencing sample size is the level of precision, or the amount of sampling error, that a researcher is willing to accept. Recall that sampling error refers to the difference between a sample value of some variable and the population value of the same variable. Suppose that the average age of all teenagers in a city is 15.4 years. If we draw a sample of 200 teenagers and calculate an average age of 15.1 years, then our sample statistic is close to the population value, but there is an error of 0.3 years. Remember, however, that the ultimate reason for collecting data from samples is to draw conclusions regarding the population from which we drew those samples. We have data from a sample, such as the average age of a group of teenagers, but *we do not have those same data for the population as a whole.* If we did, we would not need to study the sample, because we already would know what we want to know about the population.

If we do not know what the population value is, how can we assess the difference between our sample value and the population value? We do it in terms of the likelihood, or probability, that our sample value differs by a certain amount from the population value. (Probability theory is discussed in more detail in Chapter 15.) So, we establish a *confidence interval,* or a range in which we are fairly certain the population value lies. If we draw a sample with a mean age of 15.1 years and establish a confidence interval of ± (plus or minus) 1.2 years, then we are fairly certain that the mean age in the population is between 13.9 and 16.3 years of age. Probability theory also enables us to be precise about how certain we are. For example, we might be 95 percent certain, which is called the *confidence level.* (The computation of confidence intervals and confidence levels is beyond the intent of this book.) Technically, this means that if we draw a large number of random samples from our population and compute a mean age for each of those samples, then 95 percent of those sample means would have confidence intervals that include the population mean and 5 percent would not. What is the actual population mean? We don't know, because we have not collected data from the whole population. We have data from only one sample, but we can conclude that we are 95 percent sure that the population mean lies within the confidence interval of that sample.

Precision is directly related to sample size: Larger samples are more precise than smaller ones. Thus, probability theory enables us to calculate the sample size required to achieve a given level of precision. Table 6.2 does this for simple random samples taken from populations of various sizes. As an example of how to read the table, a sample size of 1,024 would give you a 95 percent chance to obtain a sampling error of 3 percent or less with a population of 25,000 elements and a relatively heterogeneous population (a 50/50 split identifies a heterogeneous population, and an 80/20 split is a homogeneous population). In other words, a 95 percent chance exists that the population value is within 3 percent of the sample estimate. Again, to be technical, it means that if we draw many random samples and determine a confidence interval of 3

TABLE 6.2 Calculating Sample Size Based on Confidence Level, Sampling Error, Population Heterogeneity, and Population Size

	95% Confidence Level				99% Confidence Level			
	Sampling Error +/− 3%		Sampling Error +/− 5%		Sampling Error +/− 3%		Sampling Error +/− 5%	
Population Size	50/50 Split	80/20 split	50/50 Split	80/20 split	50/50 Split	80/20 split	50/50 Split	80/20 split
1,000	517	407	278	198	649	542	400	299
2,500	749	537	334	224	1062	802	525	364
5,000	880	601	357	245	1347	955	586	422
10,000	965	640	370	240	1557	1056	623	408
25,000	1024	665	379	244	1717	1127	647	418
50,000	1045	674	382	245	1778	1153	655	422
100,000	1056	679	383	246	1810	1166	660	423
1,000,000	1066	683	384	246	1840	1179	664	425
10,000,000	1067	683	385	246	1843	1180	664	425
100,000,000	1068	683	385	246	1843	1180	664	425

"Split" has to do with the heterogeneity of the population. A "50/50 split" indicates a fairly heterogeneous population on some characteristic of interest (e.g. it is roughly half male and half female or half smokers and half nonsmokers). An "80/20 split" indicates a homogenous population (e.g. most are males or most are smokers).

percent for each, then 95 percent of those confidence intervals will include the population value. Table 6.2 shows that sample size must increase when, other things being equal, the researcher wants less sampling error—that is, more precision—or the population size is larger or the population is more heterogeneous.

In actuality, of course, we draw only one sample; probability theory tells us the chance we run of a single sample's having a given level of error. There is a chance—5 times out of 100—that the sample will have an error level greater than 3 percent. In fact, there is a chance, albeit a minuscule one, that the sample will have a large error level. This is a part of the nature of sampling: Because we are selecting a segment of a population, there is always a chance that the sample will be unrepresentative of that population. The goal of good sampling techniques is to reduce the likelihood of that error. (Furthermore, one goal of replication in science, as discussed in Chapter 2, is to protect against the possibility that a researcher has unknowingly based the findings of a single study on a sample that contains a large error.)

If the 95 percent confidence level is not satisfactory for our purposes, we can raise the odds to the 99 percent level by increasing the sample size. In this case, only 1 out of 100 samples is likely to have an error level greater than 3 percent. A sample size large enough for this confidence level, however, might be expensive and time-consuming. For this reason, professional pollsters normally are satisfied with a sample size that enables them to achieve an error level in the range of 2 to 4 percent. Likewise, most scientific researchers are forced to accept higher levels of error—often as much as 5 to 6 percent with a 95 percent confidence level. At the other end of the spectrum, exploratory studies can provide useful data even though they incorporate considerably more imprecision and sampling error. So, the issue of sample size and error is influenced, in part, by the goals of the research project.

Population Homogeneity. The third factor affecting sample size is the variability of the sampled population. As we have noted, a large sample is more essential for a heterogeneous population than for a homogeneous one. Unfortunately, researchers may know little about the homogeneity of their target population and can make accurate estimates of population variability only *after* they draw the sample, collect the data, and at least partially analyze that data. On the surface, this would appear to preclude estimating sample size in advance. In fact, however, probability theory allows sample size to be estimated by simply assuming maximum variability in the population. In Table 6.2, the assumption of "50/50 split" means that we assume maximum variability. Such estimates are, of course, conservative: This means that the sample size estimates are larger than needed for a given level of precision if the actual variability in the population is less than assumed.

Sampling Fraction. A fourth factor influencing sample size is the *sampling fraction*, or the number of elements in the sample relative to the number of elements in the population (or n/N, where n is the estimated sample size ignoring sampling fraction and N is the population size). With large populations, we can ignore the sampling fraction, because the sample constitutes only a tiny fraction of the population. In Table 6.2, for example, a population of 10,000 calls for a sample size of only 370 (5 percent sampling error and 50/50 split), which is less than 4 percent of the population. For such samples, the research hypotheses, sampling error, and population homogeneity are sufficient to determine the sample size. With smaller populations, however, a sample that meets these criteria may constitute a relatively large fraction of the whole population and, in fact, may be larger than it needs to be (Moser and Kalton 1972). This is so because a sample that constitutes a large fraction of a population contains less sampling error than if the sample were a small fraction. In such cases, the sample size can be adjusted by the following formula:

$$n' = \frac{n}{1 + \left(\frac{n}{N}\right)}$$

Where:

n' = adjusted sample size,
n = estimated sample size ignoring the sampling fraction
N = population size.

As a rule of thumb, this correction formula should be used if the sampling fraction is more than 5 percent. For example, suppose a community action agency is conducting a needs assessment survey for a Native American tribal organization with 3,000 members. On the basis of the research hypothesis, sampling error, and population variance on key variables, it is estimated that a sample size of 600 is needed. The sampling fraction, then, is $n/N = 600/3{,}000 = 0.2$, or 20 percent. Because this is well over 5 percent, we apply the correction:

$$n' = 600/[1 + (600/3{,}000)]$$
$$n' = 600/1.20$$
$$n' = 500$$

Thus, instead of a sample of 600, we need only 500 to achieve the same level of precision. At costs that often exceed $50 per interview, the savings from this adjustment often are significant.

Sampling Technique. The final factor influencing sample size is the sampling technique employed. The estimates discussed thus far are for simple random samples. More complex sampling procedures change the estimates of sample size. Area sampling, for example, tends to increase sampling error in comparison with SRS. We can obtain a rough estimate of sample sizes for area samples by simply increasing the suggested sizes in Table 6.2 by one half (Backstrom & Hursh-Cesar, 1981). This estimate is crude and, probably, conservative, but it is simple to obtain. Stratified sampling, on the other hand, tends to reduce sampling error and decrease the required sample size. Estimating sample sizes for stratified samples is relatively complex (Kish 1965; Scheaffer, Mendenhall, Ott, & Gerow, 2012).

In an assessment of the implications of scientific work for clinical application, the issue of precision in sampling comes to the fore. Practitioners need to exercise judgment regarding how scientifically sound the research is and whether it is sufficiently valid to introduce into practice. As we have emphasized, practitioners should view single studies with caution—irrespective of how low the sampling error is. As numerous studies begin to accumulate, we must then assess them in terms of how much error we can expect, given the sample size and the sampling technique. If the sampling errors appear to be quite low, a few replications might confirm that the findings from these samples reflect the state of the actual population. With large sampling errors, however, the probability increases that the samples do not represent the population. In such cases, confidence in the outcomes can result only if a number of studies arrive at the same conclusions. More studies mean the drawing of more samples, which in turn reduces the likelihood that *all* the samples contain large sampling errors.

NONPROBABILITY SAMPLES

Probability samples are not required—or even appropriate—for all studies. Some research situations call for **nonprobability samples**, in which the investigator does not know the probability of each population element's inclusion in the sample. Nonprobability samples have some important uses (O'Connell, 2000). First, they are especially useful when the goal of research is to see whether a relationship exists between independent and dependent variables, with no intent to generalize the results beyond the sample to a larger population. This sometimes is the case, for instance, in experimental research, where future research in other settings will establish generalizability (see Chapter 10).

A second situation where nonprobability samples are useful is in some qualitative research, where the goal is to understand the social process and meaning structure of a particular setting or group (Maxwell, 2012). In such qualitative research, the research goal often is only to develop an understanding of one particular setting or group of people; issues of generalizing to other settings are either irrelevant or an issue for future research projects. As we will see in Chapters 9 and 16, some qualitative researchers see probability samples as inappropriate for, or at best irrelevant to, theoretically sound qualitative research.

A third situation in which nonprobability samples are useful is when it is impossible to develop a sampling frame of a population. With no complete list of all elements in a population, researchers cannot ensure that every element has a chance to appear in the sample. These populations sometimes are called "hidden populations," because at least some of their elements are hidden and either difficult or impossible to locate. In fact, the members of hidden populations sometimes try to hide themselves from detection by researchers and others because they engage in illegal or stigmatized behavior, such as drug use or criminal activity. Rather than giving up on the study of such populations, however, researchers use nonprobability samples.

Although nonprobability samples can be useful, they do have some significant limitations. First, without the use of probability in the selection of elements for the sample, we can make no real claim of representativeness. There is simply no way of knowing precisely what population, if any, a nonprobability sample represents. This question of representativeness greatly limits the ability to generalize findings beyond the level of the sample cases.

A second limitation is that the degree of sampling error remains unknown—and unknowable. With no clear population represented by the sample, we have nothing with which to compare it. The lack of probability in the selection of cases means that the techniques employed for estimating sampling error with probability samples are not appropriate. It also means that the techniques for estimating sample size are not applicable to nonprobability samples. Of the five criteria used in considering sample size among probability samples, the only one that comes into play for nonprobability samples is the first—namely, that researchers select sufficient cases to allow the planned types of data analysis. Even population homogeneity and the sampling fraction do not come into play, because the researcher does not know the exact size or composition of the population.

A final limitation of nonprobability samples involves statistical tests of significance. These commonly used statistics, which we will discuss in Chapter 15, indicate to the researcher whether relationships found in sample data are sufficiently strong to generalize to the whole population. Some of these statistical tests, however, are based on various laws of probability and assume a random process for selecting sample elements. Because nonprobability samples violate some basic assumptions of these tests, researchers should use these statistical tests with caution on data derived from such samples.

Availability Sampling

Availability sampling (also called **convenience sampling** or **accidental sampling**) involves the researcher's taking whichever elements are readily available. These samples are especially popular—and appropriate—for research in which it is either difficult or impossible to develop a complete sampling frame. Sometimes it is too costly to do so; in other cases, it is impossible to identify all the elements of a population. Helen Mendes (1976), for example, used an availability sample in her study of single fathers. Because it was practically impossible to develop a sampling frame of all single fathers, she turned to teachers, physicians, social workers, and self-help groups for assistance. She asked these people to refer single fathers to her. The limitation on generalizability, however, seriously reduces the utility of findings based on availability samples. It is impossible for Mendes to argue, for example, that the single fathers she studied were representative of all single fathers. It may well be that only fathers with certain characteristics were likely to become a part of her sample.

Availability samples often are used in experimental or quasi-experimental research. This is because it often is difficult to get a representative sample of people to participate in an experiment—especially one that is lengthy and time-consuming. For example, Ronald Feldman and Timothy Caplinger (1977) were interested in factors that bring about behavior changes in young boys who exhibit highly visible antisocial behavior. Their research design was a field experiment calling for the children participating in the study to meet periodically in groups over an eight-month period. Groups met an average of 22.2 times for two to three hours each time. Most youngsters could be expected to refuse such a commitment of time and energy. Had the investigators attempted to draw a probability sample from the community, they probably would have had such a high refusal rate as to make the representativeness of their sample questionable. They would have expended considerable resources and still had, in effect, a nonprobability sample. So they resorted to an availability sample. To locate boys who had exhibited antisocial behavior, they sought referrals from numerous sources: mental health centers, juvenile courts, and the like. For a comparison group of boys who were not identified as antisocial, they sought volunteers from a large community center association. Given the purpose of experimentation, representative samples are less important. Experiments serve to determine *if* we can find cause-and-effect relationships; the issue of how generalizable those relationships are becomes important only after the relationships have been established.

Availability sampling probably is one of the more common forms of sampling used in human service research, both because it is less expensive than many other methods and because it often is impossible to develop an exhaustive sampling frame. For example, in the 20 issues of the journal *Social Work Research* published from 1994 through 1999, at least 52 of the 88 research articles could be classified as reporting some form of availability sample. You can readily grasp the problems of trying to develop a sampling frame in the following studies:

- Turning points in the lives of young inner-city men previously involved in violence, illegal drug marketing, and other crimes and now contributing to their community's well-being: The sample consisted of 20 young men, most of whom were referred by intervention programs, pastors, and community leaders.

- A study on methods for preventing HIV/AIDS transmission in drug-abusing, incarcerated women: The sample consisted of inmates at Rikers Island who were recruited with posted notices and staff referrals.

- A study on the effectiveness of a program to reduce stress, perceived stigma, anxiety, and depression for family members of people with AIDS: Participants were recruited from an AIDS service program.

- Depression and resilience in elderly people with hip fractures: The sample consisted of 272 patients over age 65 who were hospitalized following hip fractures.

An exhaustive sampling frame that would make possible the selection of a probability sample in each of these studies might be, respectively, as follows:

- All reformed/rehabilitated young adult offenders.
- All drug-abusing, incarcerated women.
- All family members of people infected with AIDS.
- All elderly people with hip fractures.

Clearly, such probability sampling is beyond the realm of most investigators. Availability samples, though less desirable, make it possible for scientific investigation to move forward in those cases when probability sampling is impossible or prohibitively expensive.

Snowball Sampling

When a snowball is rolled along in wet, sticky snow, it picks up more snow and gets larger. This is analogous to what happens with **snowball sampling**: We start with a few cases of the type we want to study, and we let them lead us to more cases, which in turn lead us to still more cases, and so on. Like the rolling snowball, the snowball sample builds up as we continue to add cases. Because snowball sampling depends on the sampled cases being knowledgeable of other relevant cases, the technique is especially useful for sampling subcultures where the members routinely interact with one another. Snowball sampling also is useful in the investigation of sensitive topics, such as child abuse or drug use, where the perpetrators or the victims might hesitate to identify themselves if approached by a stranger, such as a researcher, but might be open to an approach by someone who they know shares their experience or deviant status (Gelles, 1978).

Snowball sampling allows researchers to accomplish what Norman Denzin (1989) calls *interactive sampling*—that is, sampling people who interact with one another. Probability samples are all noninteractive samples, because knowing someone who is selected for the sample does not change the probability of selection. Interactive sampling often is theoretically relevant, because many social science theories stress the impact of associates on behavior. To study these associational influences, researchers often combine snowball sampling with a probability sample. For example, Albert Reiss and Lewis Rhodes (1967), in a study of associational influences on delinquency, drew a probability sample of 378 boys between the ages of 12 and 16. They then asked each member of this sample to indicate his two best friends. By correlating various characteristics of the juveniles and their friends, the researchers were able to study how friendship patterns affect delinquency.

This interactive element, however, also points to one of the drawbacks of snowball sampling: Although it taps people who are involved in social networks, it misses people who are isolated from such networks. Thus, a snowball sample of drug users is limited to those users who are part of some social network and ignores those who use drugs in an individual and isolated fashion. It is possible that drug users who are involved in a social network differ from isolated users in significant ways. Care must be taken in making generalizations from snowball samples to ensure that we generalize only to those people who are like those in our sample.

Quota Sampling

Quota sampling involves dividing a population into various categories and then setting quotas on the number of elements to select from each category. Once we reach the quota for each category, we put no more elements from that category into the sample. Quota sampling is like stratified sampling in that both divide a population into categories and then take samples from the categories; but quota sampling is a nonprobability technique that often depends on availability to determine precisely which elements will be in the sample. At one time, quota sampling was the method of choice among many professional pollsters. Problems deriving from efforts to predict the very close 1948 presidential election between Harry S. Truman and Thomas E. Dewey, however, caused pollsters to turn away from quota sampling and to embrace the newly developed probability sampling techniques. With its fall from grace among pollsters, quota sampling also declined in popularity among researchers. Presently, use of quota sampling is best restricted to those situations where its advantages clearly outweigh its considerable disadvantages. For example, researchers might use quota sampling to study crowd behavior, for which they cannot establish a sampling frame given the unstable nature of the phenomenon. A researcher who is studying reaction to disasters, such as a flood or a tornado, might use quota sampling where the need for immediate reaction is critical and takes precedence over sample representativeness.

Researchers normally establish quotas for several variables, including such common demographic characteristics as age, sex, race, socioeconomic status, and education. In addition, they commonly include one or more quotas directly related to the research topic. For example, a study of political behavior would probably include a quota on political party affiliation to ensure that the sample mirrored the population on the central variable in the study.

In quota sampling, interviewers do the actual selection of respondents. Armed with the preestablished quotas, interviewers begin interviewing people until they have their quotas on each variable filled. The fact that quota sampling uses interviewers to do the actual selection of cases is one of its major shortcomings. Despite the quotas, considerable bias can enter quota sampling because of interviewer behavior. Some people simply look more approachable than others, and interviewers naturally gravitate toward these people. Interviewers also are not stupid. They realize that certain areas of major cities are less-than-safe places to go around asking questions of strangers, and protecting their personal safety by avoiding these areas can introduce obvious bias into the resulting sample.

While there is a risk of bias with quota samples, the technique does have some major positive attributes—namely, it is cheaper and faster than probability sampling. At times, these advantages can be sufficient to make quota sampling a logical choice. For example, if we wanted a rapid assessment of people's reactions to some event that had just occurred, quota sampling would probably be the best approach.

Purposive Sampling

In the sampling procedures discussed thus far, one major concern has been to select a sample that is representative of—and will enable generalizations to—a larger population. Generalizability, however, is only one goal, albeit an important one, of scientific research. In some studies, the issue of *control* may take on considerable importance and dictate a slightly different sampling procedure. In some investigations, control takes the form of choosing a sample that specifically *excludes* certain types of people, because their presence might confuse the research findings. For example, if a researcher were conducting an exploratory study of a psychotherapeutic model of treatment, he or she might wish to choose people for the sample from among "ideal candidates" for psychotherapy. Because psychotherapy is based on talking about oneself and gaining insight into feelings, ideal candidates for psychotherapy are people with good verbal skills and the ability to explore and express their inner feelings. Because well-educated, middle-class people are more likely to have these characteristics, a researcher might choose them for the sample.

This is called **purposive sampling**, or **judgmental sampling**: The investigators use their judgment and prior knowledge to choose for the sample people who best serve the purposes of the study. This is not "stacking the deck" in the researcher's favor, however. Consider the illustration given earlier: The basic research question is whether this type of psychotherapy can work at all. If we select a random sample, we get a variation based on age, sex, education, socioeconomic status, and a host of other variables that are not of direct interest in this study, but that might influence receptiveness to psychotherapy. Certainly, in a truly random sample, the effects of this variation would wash out. The sample, however, would have to be so large that we could not do psychotherapy on that many people. So, rather than use some other sampling technique, we choose a group that is homogeneous in terms of the factors that are likely to influence receptiveness to psychotherapy. This enables us to see whether psychotherapy works better than some other form of therapy. If it does not work with this ideal group, then we can probably forget the idea. If it does work, then we can generalize *only to this group,* with further research among other groups still required to see how extensively we can generalize the results.

Research in Practice 6.2 illustrates some of the kinds of research problems we can approach with nonprobability samples and how a sampling strategy might actually involve a creative combination of some of the sampling types discussed here.

Dimensional Sampling

It often is expeditious—if not essential—to use small samples. Small samples can be very useful, but we must exercise considerable care in drawing the sample. (The smallest sample size, of course, is the single case, which we discuss in Chapter 11.) **Dimensional sampling** is a sampling technique for selecting small samples in a way that enhances their representativeness (Arnold, 1970). The two basic steps to dimensional sampling are these: First, specify all the important dimensions or variables. Second, choose a sample that includes at least one case that represents each possible combination of dimensions.

We can illustrate this with a study of the effectiveness of various institutional approaches in the control of juvenile delinquency (Street, Vinter, & Perrow, 1966). The population consisted of all institutions for delinquents. To draw a random sample of all those institutions, however, would have made a sample size that would tax the resources of most investigators. As an alternative, the researchers used a dimensional sample. The first step was to spell out the important conceptual dimensions. In terms of juvenile institutions, this investigation considered three dimensions, each containing two values, as illustrated in Table 6.3: organizational goals (custodial or rehabilitative), organizational control (public or private), and organizational size (large or small). In the second step, the researchers selected at least one case to represent each of the eight possibilities that resulted.

Dimensional sampling has a number of advantages that make it an attractive alternative in some situations. First, it is faster and less expensive than studying large samples. Second, it is valuable in exploratory studies with little theoretical development to support a large-scale study. Third, dimensional sampling provides more detailed knowledge of each case than we would likely gain from a large sample. With a large sample, data collection necessarily is more cursory and focused (which is justified if previous research has narrowed the focus of what variables are important).

Despite their limitations, nonprobability samples can be valuable tools in the conduct of human service research; however, we want to reiterate two points. First, some research uses both probability and nonprobability samples in a single research project, and we have given some illustrations of this. The point is that the two types of samples should not be considered as competitors for attention. Second, we should view findings based on nonprobability samples as being suggestive rather than conclusive, and we should seek opportunities to retest their hypotheses using probability samples.

Research in Practice 6.2 Behavior and Social Environments: Using Nonprobability Samples to Study Hidden Populations

One of the major advantages of nonprobability samples is that they enable us to gain access to "hidden populations"—that is, people who are difficult to locate or who, for one reason or another, prefer to hide their identity or behavior from the prying eyes of authorities, social science researchers, and others (O'Connell, 2000). Typically, we cannot construct sampling frames for such groups. Area or cluster sampling is not feasible either, so probability samples are out of the question. Thus, studies of illicit drug users typically use nonprobability samples, with sampling strategies involving variants on or combinations of such strategies as snowball, quota, and purposive sampling. Douglas Heckathorn (1997), for example, used a variant of snowball sampling, which he called **respondent-driven sampling**, in a study of intravenous drug users and AIDS. He began with a small group of drug users, called "seeds," who were known to the researchers; each seed was asked to contact three other drug users he or she knew. The seeds received a payment for their interviews and an additional payment when each of the people they contacted came in for an interview. Each recruit interviewed then became a seed and was sent out to contact others. The procedure, especially the incentives, proved to be successful in recruiting other drug users and protected the privacy of the users, because the researchers didn't learn anyone's name until he or she voluntarily came in for the interview.

One drawback of snowball samples is that they can produce "masking"—that is, when a respondent protects the privacy of others by *not* referring them to the researchers. Researchers must take care in making generalizations from snowball samples to ensure that we generalize only to those people who are like those in our sample. Actually, Heckathorn presents evidence to show that his respondent-driven sampling procedure substantially reduces the masking bias.

With all the incentives available in Heckathorn's study, consider that a subject might try to take advantage of the situation. Given the overlapping networks among drug users, it is highly likely that more than one recruiter might contact a single user, creating the possibility that one user could get interviewed twice by assuming a false identity at the second interview (and thus get two rewards). Heckathorn reduced the likelihood of this happening by recording visible identifying characteristics of each person interviewed: gender, age, height, ethnicity, scars, tattoos, and other characteristics that, in combination, identify a particular person. The concern here is less about money than about validity: If one person contributes multiple interviews, then the overall results become biased in the direction of that person.

Targeted sampling is a sampling strategy with similarities to both quota and purposive sampling; it involves strategies to ensure that people or groups with specified characteristics have an enhanced chance of appearing in the sample. In other words, researchers target specified groups for special efforts to bring them into the sample. We might identify the targeted groups for theoretical reasons, because they would be especially useful for gathering certain kinds of information. Or, we might identify them during the data-collection process if we find that some groups are not showing up in the sample. So, targeted sampling is interactive, with the results of data collection possibly changing the method of sampling.

TABLE 6.3 An Illustration of Institutional Dimensions for a Dimensional Sample

	Custodial Goals		Rehabilitative Goals	
	Public	Private	Public	Private
Large Size				
Small Size				

An example of targeted sampling is a study of injecting drug users conducted by John Watters and Patrick Biernacki (1989). They began by constructing an "ethnographic map" of the city in which they were conducting their research. This told them where drug users and drug activity tended to occur, in what amounts, and what were the characteristics of users in different locations. This information provided the basis for deciding where to start recruiting people for participation in their study. This ethnographic map also told them that snowball sampling alone probably wouldn't work, because the drug scene they found consisted of many nonoverlapping social networks. This meant that any network in which they could not find an initial informant probably would not show up in their sample.

Watters and Biernacki targeted neighborhoods in the city for sampling based partly on racial composition. They wanted to ensure adequate numbers of black and Latino drug users in their sample. To enhance Latino participation, for example, they sent two Latino males who were familiar with the drug scene into the community to inform people of the research, to encourage their participation, and eventually to drive people to the center where the data were collected. As data collection proceeded, Watters and Biernacki recognized that an insufficient number of female injecting drug users was showing up in the sample, so they revised the sampling techniques to enhance participation by women. One reason for the low participation by women, they learned, was that some of the female users were prostitutes, and going to the center to participate in the research meant they lost time working the streets to earn money. To help alleviate this, the researchers established a "ladies first" policy at the data-collection sites: If there was a wait, women received precedence over men. This and other strategies were an effort to target women and get adequate numbers in the sample.

Heckathorn, in his respondent-driven sampling, also used a form of targeted sampling to reduce bias problems that might arise because some groups of drug abusers are isolated from contact with others. He used "steering incentives" in the form of bonus payments for contacting drug users with special characteristics. For example, female users also were somewhat rare in his sample, so anyone contacting a female injector who then showed up for an interview received an extra $5.

So, even though nonprobability sampling techniques such as those presented here are not suitable for population studies in which the goal is to obtain precise estimates of population parameters, nonprobability approaches are extremely valuable for accessing hidden populations and increasing our understanding of these groups. With these techniques, researchers may not be able to compute sampling error as we could with random sampling, but we still can improve the representative quality of the sample with such techniques as targeted sampling, and thus enhance the value of the study results. Given the goals of the study and the reality of accessing the population, a researcher's best option often is a nonprobability sampling strategy. The Eye on Ethics section points to some ethical issues that can arise with these sampling procedures.

SAMPLING WITH DIVERSE POPULATIONS

The key to selecting scientifically valid samples is to ensure their representativeness so we can make valid generalizations. Accomplishing this is an especially difficult challenge when we are conducting research on populations that are diverse in terms of race, ethnicity, gender, or other characteristics. One problem is that some minorities have "rare event" status—that is, they constitute a relatively small percentage of some populations. African Americans and Hispanic Americans, for example, each constitute approximately 12 percent of the U.S. population, while Native Americans are about 3 percent (U.S. Census Bureau, 2011). This means that a representative sample of 1,500 Americans would, if it included the proper proportions of minorities, contain 180 African Americans, 180 Hispanics, and 45 Native Americans. These numbers are too small for many data analysis purposes.

> **EYE ON ETHICS** — **Ethical Issues with Respondent-Driven Sampling**
>
> It's like a pyramid scheme, man. Somebody turns me on to the gig, and they make money off me doin' it. Then I get money for doin' it, for givin' up an hour or two of my time. Then I turn some buddies or some blood kin or maybe even some complete fuckin' strangers onto this here shit, and I get paid for each of them that do it.... It's a survival thing, and most of us is gonna jump this pyramid and dig it down as far and deep as we can. And it ain't 'cause we bad people or liars or thieves or nothin' like that. But the fact is, we got habits to support, and we got families to feed.
> —Intravenous drug user on respondent-driven sampling as income source. (Scott, 2008, p. 45)
>
> Research in Practice 6.2 describes the use of respondent-driven sampling (RDS) to study hidden populations, such as intravenous drug users (IDUs). Despite the advantages of RDS, researchers have identified significant ethical challenges that must be addressed when using RDS. One concern is the double-payment strategy. First, volunteers for a study are paid a modest amount, about $20, to participate. Second, they receive three coupons, worth $10 dollars each. They receive a $10 payment for each participant they recruit who actually participates in the study. Because payment depends on successful recruitment, the participant has a high incentive to get others to actually participate.
>
> One researcher, who has actually conducted research on how drug users respond to this payment system, has been particularly critical (Scott, 2008). Among his concerns about such payments are:
>
> - IDUs are generally poor, so might even a small payment jeopardize voluntary consent?
> - Might not payment simply facilitate more drug use?
> - Might participants lie about or distort the description of the program in order to entice potential recruits?
> - Might recruiters resort to strong-arm tactics and threaten others into participating, just to get their money?
>
> Experts in RDS acknowledge these problems, but argue that safeguards can alleviate them. They emphasize that, because recruiters are limited to three coupons, it prevents them from becoming "professional" recruiters. Researchers require informed consent from each individual recruited by participants, and this can protect against coercion or misrepresentation. Another strategy for addressing the concerns is to expect researchers to include documentation of the procedures they use in their research projects to reduce the risk. For example, just as study reports document statistical analysis, they should also include RDS details such as motivation for recruitment, motivation for study participation, assessment of coercion or undue influence, amount of payment for each recruit, and amount of payment for study participation (Semaan et al., 2009).

The Native Americans especially are so few that any analysis that breaks the sample down into subgroups would result in meaninglessly small numbers in each subgroup. Furthermore, these small numbers mean that the error rate becomes much higher for minority groups than for nonminority groups, because small samples are less reliable and have more error (A.W. Smith, 1987). These small sample sizes also make it difficult to assess differences of opinion or behavior within a minority group; thus it is easy to conclude—falsely—that the group is homogeneous. As a consequence we know little about gender, social class, regional, or religious differences among members of particular minorities. The outcome, according to A. W. Smith (1987, p. 445), is "little more than a form of stereotyping, an *underestimation* of the variability of opinions among blacks. This leads to an *overestimation* of the contribution of race, per se, to black–white differences" in attitude and behavior. The Committee on the Status of Women in Sociology (1986) makes the same recommendations regarding gender: "Research should include sufficiently large subsamples of male and female subjects to allow meaningful analysis of subgroups."

Some minorities have rare event status in another way that can cause problems in sampling. Because of substantial residential segregation of minorities in the United States, minorities who live in largely white areas are relatively small in number, and researchers can easily miss them by chance, even in a well-chosen, representative sample. The result is a biased sample that includes minorities living in largely minority communities, but not minorities living elsewhere. Because minorities living in nonminority communities probably vary in terms of attitudes and behavior, such a biased sample gives a deceptively homogeneous picture of the minority.

So efforts must be made in sampling to ensure that those rare events have a chance at selection for the sample. In some cases, we can employ disproportionate sampling, in which some individuals or households have a greater probability of appearing in the sample than other individuals or households do. Another way to avoid some of these problems is to use both probability and nonprobability sampling techniques when studying minorities (Becerra & Zambrana, 1985). A dimensional sample of Hispanics, for example, might specify an entire series of dimensions to cover in the sample. Thus, a researcher might specify certain age cohorts of Hispanic women (20–30, 31–40, and 41 and older) to include in the sample, or some minimum number of single-parent and two-parent Hispanic families. This would ensure that sufficient people with certain characteristics are in the sample for valid data analysis. A study of mental health among Asian immigrants in the Seattle area used the snowball technique to ensure a complete sampling frame (Kuo & Tsai, 1986). Those researchers used local telephone directories and gathered names from ethnic and community organizations to develop part of the sampling frame. Then, given the dispersion of Asian Americans in the area, researchers added the snowball technique.

A NOTE ON SAMPLING IN PRACTICE

Human service practitioners do not routinely engage in sampling procedures like those used for research purposes, yet parallels exist between what occurs in practice and in research. We can apply some of the sampling principles in this chapter to providing client services. The needs and characteristics of a particular client typically guide the assessments and actions of practitioners, but to what extent are judgments about one client based on experiences with other clients? The issue here, of course, is that of *generalizability*. As human beings, we constantly dip into our own funds of experience to help us cope with situations that we confront. Practitioners use their past experience with clients—sometimes very effectively—to grapple with the problems of subsequent clients. The critical judgment to make in this regard is whether it is legitimate to generalize past outcomes to current situations.

Practice settings rarely involve dealing with probability samples. Irrespective of whether the clients are welfare recipients, elderly people receiving nursing home care, child abusers, or individuals with problem pregnancies, practitioners have no way of knowing whether *all* people with such characteristics had a chance to be in the "sample"—that is, to be one of their clients—or how great that chance was. For all practical purposes, then, practitioners deal with nonprobability samples and all the limitations they entail. In most cases, practitioners have an availability sample of people who happen to come to their attention because they are clients. This means practitioners need to show caution in making generalizations from their observations; but this is no reason for despair. Remember that many scientific investigations are based on availability samples. We simply need to recognize their limitations and use care in generalizing.

If the main concern is to generalize to other clients with similar problems, then a reasonable assumption is that the clients are representative of others with similar problems who seek the aid of a practitioner. Whatever propels people to see a particular practitioner is probably operative for many—if not all—of that practitioner's other clients. If the practitioner's research interest concerns all people experiencing a certain type of problem, then agency clients are not an appropriate sample. Agencies both intentionally and unintentionally screen their prospective clients; thus, many people who could use services are not included in a sample of agency clients. The well-known study by

INFORMATION TECHNOLOGY IN RESEARCH   Sampling in a Cell Phone World

The dramatic increase in cell phone usage requires that survey researchers adopt new sampling strategies to deal with this technology. According to a recent Centers for Disease Control study (Blumberg & Luke, 2011), three of every 10 American homes (29.7 percent) had wireless-only telephone service during the last half of 2010. In addition, nearly one of every six American homes (15.7 percent) received all or almost all calls on wireless telephones despite having a landline.

How researchers cope with the implications of cell phone usage demonstrates the importance of several topics that you have already learned about. Consider the unit of analysis. Traditional telephones (now called "landlines") linked a phone number to a particular geographic location, such as a house or office. This was a physical link; the phone was literally wired to that location and the appliance could be used only at that place. Because most homes had only one telephone line, telephone listings were a very useful sampling frame when the household was the unit of analysis.

Cell phone technology is different in that a cell phone is free-ranging; it isn't inherently connected to a particular location or individual. An individual may have the contract for cell phone service, but the phone itself can be carried and used by others in any location. Besides the uncertainty of the geographic tie to a physical location, each individual has a personal cell phone, so a phone number is more likely a link to an individual, not a household. So, cell phone numbers are not a very good sampling frame for households since they are not linked in any meaningful or complete way to a household.

Probability of selection is another complication caused by cell phone usage. Many households now have numerous phones, such as a landline and one or more cell phones. This has an impact on the probability of being selected for a sample. If telephone listings are used as sampling frames, then each phone represents one chance for being selected into a sample. A household with one landline only has one chance of being selected. A household with one landline and two cell

NOTE: Adults are aged 18 and over; children are under age 18.

FIGURE 6.2 Percentage of U.S. Adults and Children Living in Households with Wireless-only Telephone Service or No Telephone Service, 2003–2010.

SOURCE: Centers for Disease Control/National Center for Health Staistics, National Health Interview Survey.

phones has three chances to be selected for the sample. Recall from this chapter that some probability samples are based on the idea that each element in a sampling frame should have an equal chance of appearing in the sample. Cell phone technology has dramatically changed that because of the many households with multiple phones. This problem is further complicated by the unit of analysis issue discussed above. Some households are cell phone–only, where all adults share one cell phone— more like a traditional landline. In other cases, each adult in the household has his or her own cell phone, which means that a telephone number is linked to an individual, not a household. So one phone might be the only link to several people or a single individual might have several phone numbers.

One way to address coverage and the potential for multiple phones is to do what are called "dual-frame surveys" in which samples are taken from both landline and cell phone numbers. Because people who have both types of phones have a greater probability of appearing in the sample, people contacted by cell phone are asked if they also have a landline; if they do, then the interview on the cell phone is terminated and they will be interviewed only if contacted on their landline.

These sampling issues can be of critical importance in both practice and policy research because of the possibility that poor sampling will produce unrepresentative samples and thus misleading or inaccurate results. The majority of people in some key demographic groups are now living in wireless only homes: adults aged 25 to 29; adults living only with unrelated adult roommates, and adults renting their home are good examples (Blumberg & Luke, 2011). Particularly when the study population is young adults or low-income individuals, relying on the more convenient and less expensive landline telephone sampling frame can result in biased samples that produce substantial underestimations of, for example, the prevalence of binge drinking, smoking, and HIV testing. Clearly, policies related to these problems could be more poorly designed if based on such distorted samples.

Ability to analyze subgroups and to perform cross tabulations is also compromised by relying on landline only samples. Even when overall population estimates of variables might be accurate based on a landline sampling frame, searching for patterns among particular groups, such as the old versus the young or married versus single, may require including cell phones in the sampling frame in order to assure enough cases of each group.

Even though it may seem obvious that cell phones should be included in a sampling frame, doing so is not an easy task. Cell phone numbers are not included in the telephone directory. Random digit dialing is a solution, but it is not without problems. Cell phone numbers drawn by random digit dialing are more likely to be nonworking, so researchers need to include a lot more of them to get a working number. There is also a legal wrinkle. In the U.S. it is illegal to use autodialing equipment for calling cell phones. Manually dialing a long list of cell phone numbers to get some working numbers adds to the time and expense of the project.

Researchers distinguish between the sample drawn and the sample obtained. Even though the initial sample is representative, nonworking numbers, caller ID, and refusals can potentially distort the sample and introduce bias. When a phone number is linked to a location, researchers have ways of checking for bias potential. Unlike for landline numbers, there are no commercially available sources with subscriber information such as name, address, or any demographics that can be linked reliably to cell phone numbers in the sample. With landline-based numbers, it is often possible for the researcher to identify characteristics of respondents versus nonrespondents, such as address or type of dwelling and neighborhood, which offer clues to such variables as race, age, and social status. So lacking this capacity may discourage researchers from including cell phone numbers in the sample.

Because of these challenges to cell phone random digit dialing, researchers are trying new ways of securing representative samples. One promising approach is to use address–based sampling (ABS) to draw a telephone sample. About 60 percent of ABS addresses can be linked to a landline telephone. Researchers then contact selected members of the remaining 40 percent with a mailed request asking potential participants to provide a telephone number by return mail, Internet, or toll-free call. With this approach, cell phone users are linked to a location so many of the undesirable features of cell phone samples are reduced. This is one example of how survey sampling techniques are evolving to keep pace with the changing world of wireless communication technology.

Robert Scott (1975) on agencies that serve the blind is a classic example. Scott found that these agencies concentrate their efforts on young, trainable clientele, even though most blind people are elderly or have multiple handicaps. If workers in such an agency assumed that the agency clientele represented all blind people, they would have a distorted perspective on the actual blind population.

Ways of checking on such distortions exist, of course. For example, practitioners can compare notes with each other. Do they find the same kinds of problems among their clients? If so, that is support for an assumption that one set of clients is representative of all people with similar problems. Practitioners also might consider using (at least informally) other sampling techniques, such as adopting a snowball technique by asking clients to recommend someone they know who has a similar problem but is not receiving any services. Especially with people whose problems may be of a sensitive nature, this snowball approach is a mode of entry with a considerable likelihood of success. Another possibly effective sampling technique is purposive sampling. For example, in an agency dealing with unplanned pregnancies among teenagers, suppose all clients are members of ethnic minorities. It might appear that the clients' behavior, such as hostility toward practitioners, is caused either by the crisis of the pregnancy or by the animosity of a minority member toward the welfare bureaucracy. The problem is that the sample is homogeneous with respect to the two variables that are important: All clients have problem pregnancies, and all clients are members of an ethnic minority. To get around this problem, the researcher might begin to choose a purposive sample in which the problem pregnancies occur among nonminority teenagers, and thus be in a better position to determine the source of the hostility.

In some ways, dimensional sampling is the most feasible form for practitioners. In our previous illustration, for example, there are two variables—namely, race and pregnancy status—with two values each—namely, white versus nonwhite and pregnant versus not pregnant. Thus, the analysis contains four possible cells. If for some reason, such as past experience, the researcher believes that these two variables interrelate in important ways in determining such factors as client hostility or adjustment, then he or she could make sure that at least one client was in each of those four cells to make some preliminary judgments regarding the importance of these two factors.

REVIEW AND CRITICAL THINKING

Main Points

- A population consists of all possible cases of whatever a researcher is interested in studying.
- A sample is composed of one or more elements selected from a population.
- A sampling frame is a list of the population elements that are used to draw some types of probability samples.
- The representativeness of a sample is its most important characteristic and refers to the degree to which the sample reflects the population from which it was drawn.

- Sampling error is the difference between sample values and true population values.
- Probability sampling techniques are the best for obtaining representative samples.
- The key characteristic of probability sampling is that every element in the population has a known chance of selection into the sample.
- Simple random, systematic, stratified, and area samples are all types of probability samples.
- Nonprobability samples do not assure each population element a known chance of selection into the sample and, therefore, lack the

degree of representativeness of probability samples.
- Availability, snowball, quota, purposive, and dimensional samples are all types of nonprobability samples.
- Data based on properly drawn probability samples are reliable and generalizable within known limits of error to the sampled populations.
- In studies of racial and other minorities, researchers must take care to ensure that sampling procedures do not result in unrepresentative samples, especially given the "rare event" status of many minorities.
- Cell phones have created sampling challenges for researchers because it is now more difficult to use telephone numbers as a sampling frame.

Important Terms for Review

accidental sampling	multistage sampling	respondent-driven sampling	snowball sampling
area sampling	nonprobability samples	sample	stratified sampling
availability sampling	population	sampling error	systematic sampling
cluster sampling	probability samples	sampling frame	targeted sampling
convenience sampling	purposive sampling	simple random sampling	
dimensional sampling	quota sampling		
judgmental sampling	representative sample		

Critical Thinking

Human service practitioners and policy makers, of course, draw conclusions from observations they have made. The critical thinking question is whether those observations provide an adequate basis from which to deduce something. The observations made in scientific research differ from everyday observations because they are much more systematic in nature, and being systematic has to do, in part, with sampling, or how you select which people or elements to observe. With what you have learned about sampling in this chapter, you have some tools with which to assess whether observations made in practice settings or everyday life provide a sound basis for drawing conclusions:

1. What is the whole group (or population) about which you want to draw conclusions?
2. What groups or people serve as the source of information? How were they selected? Are there people or groups who had no chance to show up in this sample? Could this lead to misunderstanding or inaccuracy?
3. Could the people observed be considered a probability sample? A nonprobability sample? What problems does this create as far as drawing conclusions to the whole group or population?
4. Are there other ways the sample could have been selected that could have produced a more accurate, or at least a different, conclusion or understanding?

Exploring the Internet

To expand your knowledge about sampling and how researchers use sampling in research, we recommend that you explore Internet sites affiliated with some of the major survey research endeavors that produce social science research data. Following are several sites that include information about the sampling processes in their surveys. Once you have accessed the main site, look for highlighted text about sampling procedures.

The General Social Survey (GSS) site (http://www.norc.org/GSS+Website) has its own search capacity, which makes locating material of interest fairly easy. Entering the term "sampling" in the search engine will lead to a variety of pages dealing with sampling. From this website you can learn how the GSS sample actually is selected, how the procedure has changed over time, and what controversies have arisen concerning the sampling system modifications. Also, search for the term "primary sampling unit," and describe what it is and what role it plays in sampling procedures (see Research in Practice 6.1).

The Crime Victimization Survey is a major survey conducted by the Bureau of Justice Statistics (http://bjs.ojp.usdoj.gov). Google "Survey Methodology of Crime Victimization" or explore the BJS site to find the actual results of the most recent crime victimization surveys and to learn about the sampling procedures used in the study.

The U.S. Bureau of Labor Statistics and the U.S. Census Bureau cooperate in conducting the Current Population Survey (CPS), the primary source of labor force statistics on the United States. To learn more about how sampling is done for this key survey, visit the CPS website (http://www.census.gov/cps) and click on the tabs for "Methodology" or "Data."

For Further Reading

Daniel, J. (2012). *Sampling Essentials*. Thousand Oaks, Calif.: Sage. This concise book is a handy guide to basic issues related to sampling. It also includes some interesting examples of research projects and the sampling procedures they used.

Fink, A. (2002). *How To Sample in Surveys*, 2nd ed. Thousand Oaks, Calif.: Sage. This book is also an excellent overview of the issues in sampling, with attention focused on sampling in survey research rather than other kinds of research methodologies.

Kish, L. (1995). *Survey Sampling*. New York: Wiley–Interscience. Considered to be the mainstay regarding sampling issues in social research, this book assumes that the reader has an elementary understanding of statistics.

Maisel, R., & Persell, C. H. (1996). *How Sampling Works*. Thousand Oaks, Calif.: Pine Forge Press. This book provides an excellent and detailed overview of scientific sampling as well as software to assist students in learning through working problems.

Scheaffer, R. L., Mendenhall, W., Ott, R. L., & Gerow, K. G. (2012). *Elementary Survey Sampling*, 7th ed. Belmont, Calif.: Cengage, Brooks/Cole. As the name implies, this book is intended as an introductory text on the design and analysis of sample surveys. Limited to coverage of probability sampling techniques, it provides the information necessary to successfully complete a sample survey.

Stuart, A.(1987). *The Ideas of Sampling*, 3rd ed. New York: Oxford University Press. This book is another good review of sampling strategies that can be used in many human service settings.

Sudman. (1976). *Applied Sampling*. New York: Academic Press. This book, along with the Kish work, will tell you almost all you need to know about sampling.

Wainer, H. (1986). *Drawing Inferences from Self-Selected Surveys*. New York: Springer–Verlag. This book focuses on the issue of self-selection into samples, and the problems this can create in terms of making inferences from samples to populations.

Class Exercises for Competency Assessment

A student is doing an internship with the Metropolis Senior Citizens Service Center (MSCSC) where she has been asked to help conduct a needs assessment. The MSCSC is a publicly funded agency that is supposed to serve all residents of Metropolis who are 60 years of age or older. Spouses of such individuals also are eligible to receive services if they are at least 50 years old. As a part of the internship, the director wants the student to conduct interviews with all senior citizens in this city of 25,000 inhabitants. A quick check of U.S. census data shows that about 20 percent of the population is age 55 or older, so that means contacting about 5,000 people. The student, having taken a research methods course, knows that this would be time-consuming and inefficient—as well as unnecessary. She suggests that selecting a probability sample and conducting careful interviews with those selected will yield better information with less interviewing time. The director tells her to develop a plan to convince the agency board how she might accomplish this.

6.1. [Critical Thinking] [Policy Practice] What is the population for this project? Define the population as specifically as possible.

6.2. [Critical Thinking] [Policy Practice] Three sampling frames the intern might use are (a) the city or criss-cross directory, (b) the local telephone book, and (c) a Social Security Administration listing of recipients of benefits for the county. What might be the advantages and disadvantages of each? Can you think of any other sampling frames that could be useful for this project?

6.3. [Research & Practice] Could you use a random-digit dialing method to sample this population? Indicate the reasons for and against using such a technique.

6.4. [Policy Practice] [Research & Practice] A staff member at the agency suggests dispensing with the sampling and just posting a link to an online survey on the center's web page and running a series of public service announcements on the local television station and in the newspaper that ask senior citizens to go to the web page and complete the survey. What kind of sampling process is being suggested? What are its advantages and disadvantages?

6.5. [Critical Thinking] [Research & Practice] Elderly who reside in nursing homes make up a group of special interest to the center, although they represent only 1.5 percent of the eligible residents. Describe how sampling procedures could address the problem of including a representative group of nursing home elderly in the sample.

6.6. [Research & Practice] Use your local city or criss-cross directory to compile a simple random sample of 25 households using the street address portion of the directory.

6.7. [Ethics] [Critical Thinking] [Research & Practice] In the previous exercises, options included random-digit dialing, the city directory, the telephone book, Social Security recipients, and online respondents to public service announcements. Evaluate each of these options in terms of its potential for under representing minorities in the sample. Which method would be best?

Chapter 7

✴

Survey Research

Designing Questions
   Closed-Ended versus Open-Ended Questions
   Wording of Questions

Questionnaires
   Structure and Design
   Response Rate
   Checking for Bias Due to Nonresponse
   An Assessment of Questionnaires

Interviews
   The Structure of Interviews
   Contacting Respondents
   Conducting an Interview
   Diversity and the Interview Relationship

   An Assessment of Interviews

Telephone Surveys

Online Surveys

Focus Groups

Practice and Research Interviews Compared

Review and Critical Thinking
   Main Points
   Important Terms for Review
   Critical Thinking
   Exploring the Internet
   For Further Reading
   Class Exercises for Competency Assessment

The term **survey** both designates a specific way of collecting data and identifies a broad research strategy. Survey data collection involves gathering information from individuals, called *respondents*, by having them respond to questions. We use surveys to gather data as a part of many of the research methods discussed in other chapters, such as qualitative studies, quantitative studies, experiments, field research, and program evaluations. In fact, the survey probably is the most widely used means of gathering data in social science research. A literature search in the online database *Sociological Abstracts* (SocAbs) for the five-year period from 1998 to 2002 using the keyword search terms "social work" and "survey" identified more than 600 English language journal articles. Surveys have been used to study all five of the human service focal areas discussed in Chapter 1. This illustrates a major attraction of surveys—namely, flexibility.

As a broad research strategy, **survey research** involves asking questions of a sample of people, in a fairly short period of time, and then testing hypotheses or describing a situation based on their answers. As a general approach to knowledge building, the strength of surveys is their potential for generalizability. Surveys typically involve collecting data from large samples of people; therefore, they are ideal for obtaining data that are representative of populations too large to deal with by other methods. Consequently, many of the issues addressed in this chapter center around how researchers obtain quality data that are, in fact, representative.

All surveys involve presenting respondents with a series of questions to answer. These questions may tap matters of fact, attitudes, opinions, or future expectations. The questions may be simple, single-item measures or complex, multiple-item scales. Whatever the form, however, survey data basically are what people say to the investigator in response to a question. We collect data in survey research in two basic ways: with *questionnaires*, or with *interviews*. A **questionnaire** contains recorded questions that people respond to directly on the questionnaire form itself, without the aid of an interviewer. A questionnaire can be handed directly to a respondent; mailed or sent online to the members of a sample, who then fill it out on their own and send it back to the researcher; or presented via computer, with the respondent recording answers using the mouse and keypad. An **interview** involves an interviewer reading questions to a respondent and then recording his or her answers. Researchers can conduct interviews either in person or over the telephone.

Some survey research uses both questionnaire and interview techniques, with respondents filling in some answers themselves and being asked other questions by interviewers. Because both questionnaires and interviews involve asking people to respond to questions, a problem central to both is what type of question we should use. In this chapter, we discuss this issue first, and then analyze the elements of questionnaires and interviews separately. An important point to emphasize about surveys is that they only measure what people say about their thoughts, feelings, and behaviors. Surveys do not directly measure those thoughts, feelings, and behaviors. For example, if people tell us in a survey that they do not take drugs, we have not measured actual drug-taking behavior, only people's reports about that behavior. This is very important in terms of the conclusions that can be drawn: We can conclude that people report not taking drugs, but we cannot conclude that people do not take drugs. This latter is an inference we might draw from what people say. So surveys always involve data on what people say about what they do, not what they actually do.

DESIGNING QUESTIONS

Closed-Ended versus Open-Ended Questions

Two basic types of questions are used in questionnaires and interviews: *closed-ended* or *open-ended* (Sudman & Bradburn, 1982). **Closed-ended questions** provide respondents with a fixed set of alternatives from which to choose. The response formats of multiple-item scales, for example, are all closed-ended, as are multiple-choice test questions. **Open-ended questions** require that the respondents write their own responses, much as for an essay-type examination question.

The proper use of open- and closed-ended questions is important for the quality of data generated as well as for the ease of handling that data. Theoretical considerations play an important part in the decision about which type of question to use. In general, we use closed-ended questions when we can determine all the possible, theoretically relevant responses to a question in advance and the number of possible responses is limited. For example, the General Social Survey question for marital status reads, "Are you currently—married, widowed, divorced, separated, or have you never been married?" A known and limited number of answers is possible. (Today, researchers commonly offer people an alternative answer to this question—namely, "living together" or cohabitating. Although cohabitation is not legally a marital status, it helps to accurately reflect the living arrangements currently in use.) Another obvious closed-ended question is about gender. To leave such questions open-ended runs the risk that some respondent will either purposefully or inadvertently answer in a way that provides meaningless data. (Putting "sex" with a blank after it, for example, is an open invitation for some character to write "yes" rather than the information wanted.)

Open-ended questions, on the other hand, are appropriate for an exploratory study in which the lack of theoretical development suggests that we should place few restrictions on people's answers. In addition, when researchers cannot predict all the possible answers to a question in advance, or when too many possible answers exist to list them all, then closed-ended questions are not appropriate. Suppose we wanted to know the reasons why people moved to their current residence. So many possible reasons exist that such a question has to be open-ended. If we are interested in the county and state in which our respondents reside, we can generate a complete list of all the possibilities, and thus create a closed-ended question. This list would consume so much space on the questionnaire, however, that it would be excessively cumbersome, especially considering that respondents should be able to answer this question correctly in its open-ended form.

Some topics lend themselves to a combination of both formats. Religious affiliation is a question that usually is handled in this way. Although a great many religions exist, there are some to which only a few respondents will belong. Thus, we can list religions with large memberships in closed-ended fashion and add the category "other," where a person can write the name of a religion not on the list (see Question 4 in Table 7.1). We can efficiently handle any question with a similar pattern of responses—numerous possibilities, but only a few popular ones—in this way. The combined format maintains the convenience of closed-ended questions for most of the respondents but also allows those with less common responses to express them.

When we use the option of "other" in a closed-ended question, it is a good idea to request that respondents write in their response by indicating "Please specify." We can then code these answers into whatever response categories seem appropriate for data analysis. Researchers should offer the opportunity to specify an alternative; however, even if for purposes of data analysis, we will not use the written responses. This is done because respondents who hold uncommon views or memberships may be proud of them and desire to express them on the questionnaire. In addition, well-educated professionals tend to react against completely closed-ended questions as too simple, especially when the questions deal with complicated professional matters (Sudman, 1985). The opportunity to provide a written response to a question is more satisfying to such respondents, and given this opportunity, they will be more likely to complete the questionnaire.

Another factor in choosing between open- and closed-ended questions is the ease with which we can handle each at the data analysis stage. Open-ended questions sometimes are quite difficult to work with. One difficulty is that poor handwriting or the failure of respondents to provide clear answers can result in data that we cannot analyze (Rea & Parker, 2005). Commonly, some responses to open-ended questions just do not make sense, so we end up dropping them from analysis. In addition, open-ended questions are more complicated to analyze by computer, because we must first code a respondent's answers into a limited set of categories, and this coding not only is time-consuming, but also can introduce error (see Chapter 14).

Another related difficulty with open-ended questions is that some respondents may give more than one answer to a question. For example, in a study of substance abuse researchers might ask people why they use—or do not use—alcoholic beverages. As a response to this question, a researcher might receive the following answer: "I quit drinking because booze was too expensive and my wife

TABLE 7.1 Formatting Questions for a Questionnaire

Please indicate your response to the following questions by placing an X in the appropriate box.

1. Which of the following best describes where you live?
   - [X] In a large city (100,000 population or more)
   - [ ] In a suburb near a large city
   - [ ] In a middle-sized city or small town (under 100,000 population) but not a suburb of a large city
   - [ ] Open country (but not on a farm)
   - [ ] On a farm

2. Have you ever shoplifted an item with a value of $10 or more?
   - [ ] Yes
   - [ ] No

   If Yes: How many times have you taken such items?
   - [ ] Once
   - [ ] 2 to 5 times
   - [ ] 6 to 10 times
   - [ ] More than 10 times

   Filter Questions → *Contingency Question*

3. Do you belong to an organized religion?
   - [ ] Yes
   - [ ] No (If *No*, please skip to Section C, question 1)

4. Please indicate the religion to which you belong:
   - [ ] Protestant
   - [ ] Catholic
   - [ ] Jewish
   - [ ] Other (please specify): _____

---

was getting angry at me for getting drunk." How should this response be categorized? Should the person be counted as quitting because of the expense or because of the marital problems created by drinking? It may be, of course, that both factors were important in the decision to quit. Researchers usually handle data analysis problems like this in one of two ways: First, the researchers may accept all the individual's responses as data. This, however, creates difficulties in data analysis; some people give more reasons than others because they are talkative rather than because they actually have more reasons for their behavior. Second, the researchers may handle multiple responses by assuming that each respondent's *first* answer is the most important one and considering that answer to be the only response. This assumption, of course, is not always valid, but it does solve the dilemma systematically.

The decision about whether to use open- or closed-ended questions is complex, often requiring considerable experience with survey methods. It is an important issue that can have substantial effects on both the type and the quality of the data collected, as illustrated in a survey of attitudes about social problems confronting the United States. The Institute for Social Research at the University of Michigan asked a sample of people open- and closed-ended versions of essentially the same questions (Schuman & Presser, 1979). The two versions elicited quite different responses. For example, with the closed-ended version, 35 percent of the respondents indicated that crime and violence were important social problems, compared with only 15.7 percent in the open-ended version. With a number of other issues, people responding to the closed-ended questions were more likely to indicate that particular issues were problems. One reason that the type of question has such an effect on the data is that the list of alternatives in the closed-ended questions tends to serve as a "reminder" to the respondent of issues that might be problems. Without the stimulus of the list, some respondents might not even think of some of these issues. A second reason is that people tend to choose from the list provided in closed-ended questions rather than writing in their own answers, even when provided with an "other" category.

In some cases, researchers can gain the benefits of both open- and closed-ended questions by using an open-ended format in a pretest or pilot study and then, based on these results, designing closed-ended questions for the actual survey.

Wording of Questions

Because the questions that make up a survey are the basic data-gathering devices, researchers need to word them with great care. Especially with questionnaires that allow the respondent no opportunity to clarify questions, ambiguity can cause substantial trouble. We will review some of the major issues in developing good survey questions (Sudman & Bradburn, 1982). (In Chapter 13, we will discuss some problems of question construction having to do specifically with questions that are part of multiple-item scales.)

Researchers should subject the wording of questions, whenever possible, to empirical assessment to determine whether a particular wording might lead to unnoticed bias. Words, after all, have connotative meanings—that is, emotional or evaluative associations—that the researcher may not be aware of, but that may influence respondents' answers to questions. In a study of attitudes about social welfare policy in the United States, for example, researchers asked survey respondents whether they believed the government should spend more or less money on welfare (T. W. Smith, 1987). Respondents, however, were asked the question in three slightly different ways. One group was asked about whether we were spending too much or too little on "welfare," a second group about spending too much or too little on "assistance for the poor," and a third group about money for "caring for the poor." At first glance, all three questions seem to have much the same meaning, yet people's responses to them suggested something quite different. Basically, people responded much more negatively to the question with the word "welfare" in it, indicating much less willingness to spend more money on "welfare" compared with spending money to "assist the poor." For example, 64.7 percent of the respondents indicated that too little was being spent on "assistance to the poor," but only 19.3 percent said we were spending too little on "welfare." This is a dramatic difference in opinion, resulting from what might seem, at first glance, to be a minor difference in wording. Although the study did not investigate why these differing responses occurred, it seems plausible that the word "welfare" has connotative meanings for many people that involve images of laziness, waste, fraud, bureaucracy, or the poor as being disreputable. "Assisting the poor," on the other hand, is more likely associated with giving and Judeo-Christian charity. These connotations lead to quite different responses. In many cases, the only way to assess such differences is to compare people's responses with different versions of the same question during a pretest.

In general, researchers should state questions in the present tense. Specialized questions that focus on past experiences or future expectations, however, are an exception. In these situations, researchers should use the appropriate past or future tense. Of major importance is making sure that tenses are not carelessly mixed. Failure to maintain consistent tense of questions can lead to an understandable confusion on the part of respondents and, therefore, to more measurement error.

Researchers should keep questions simple and direct, expressing only one idea, and avoid complex statements that express more than one idea. Consider the following double-negative question that appeared in a Roper Organization poll conducted in 1992 about the Holocaust: "Does it seem possible or does it seem impossible to you that the Nazi extermination of the Jews never happened?" (Smith, 1995, p. 269). The results showed that 22 percent said "possible," 65 percent "impossible," and 12 percent "don't know." Could it be that more than one fifth of Americans had doubts about the Holocaust and more than one third questioned it or were uncertain that it had occurred? Considerable controversy erupted over the survey results. In a subsequent Gallup Poll, researchers asked respondents the same double-negative question with this follow-up question: "Just to clarify, in your opinion, did the Holocaust definitely happen, probably happen, probably *not* happen, or definitely *not* happen?" (Smith 1995, p. 277). Of those who said it was possible that the Holocaust never happened in response to the first question, 97 percent changed their position to say that it did happen with the second question.

Statements that seem crystal clear to a researcher may prove to be unclear to many respondents. One common error is to overestimate the reading ability of the average respondent. For example, a national study of adult literacy found that more than 20 percent of adults in the United States demonstrate skills in the lowest level of prose, document, and quantitative literacy proficiencies. At this level, many people cannot total an entry on a deposit slip, identify a piece of specific information in a brief news article, or respond to many of the questions on a survey form (Kirsch et al., 1993). Such limited literacy skills are common among some clients of the human services, especially when English is a second language. Accordingly, the researcher should avoid the use of technical terms on questionnaires. For example, it would not be advisable to include a statement such as "The current stratification system in the United States is too rigid." The word "stratification" is a technical term in the social sciences that many people outside the field do not understand in the same sense that social scientists do.

Another practice to avoid is referring to things that we cannot clearly define or that depend on the respondent's interpretation. For example, "Children who get into trouble typically have had a bad home life" is an undesirable statement, because it includes two sources of vagueness. The word "trouble" is unclear. What kind of trouble? Trouble with the law? Trouble at school? Trouble with parents? The other problem is the phrase "bad home life," because what constitutes a "bad home life" depends on the respondent's interpretation.

Finally, for the majority of questions designed for the general public, researchers should never use slang terminology. Slang tends to arise in the context of particular groups and subcultures. Slang terms may have a precise meaning within those groups, but such terms confuse people outside those groups. Occasionally, however, the target population for a survey is more specialized than the general population, and the use of their "in-group" jargon may be appropriate. It would demonstrate to the respondents that the researcher cared enough to "learn their language" and could increase rapport, resulting in better responses. Having decided to use slang, however, the burden is on the researcher to be certain that he or she uses it correctly.

Once a survey instrument is developed, it must be pretested to see if the questions are clearly and properly understood and are unbiased. We can handle pretesting by having people respond to the questionnaire or interview and then reviewing it with them to find any problems. The way a group responds to the questions themselves also can point out trouble. For example, if many respondents leave a particular answer blank, there may be a problem with that question. Once the instrument is pretested and modifications are made where required, the survey should be pretested again. Any change in the questionnaire requires more pretesting. Only when it is pretested with no changes being called for is the questionnaire ready to use in research.

TABLE 7.2 Common Errors in Writing Questions and Statements

Original Question	Problem	Solution
The city needs more housing for the elderly and property taxes should be raised to finance it.	**Two questions in one:** Some respondents might agree with the first part but disagree with the second.	Questions should be broken up into two separate statements, each expressing a single idea.
In order to build more stealth bombers, the government should raise taxes.	**False premise:** What if a person doesn't want more bombers built? How do they answer?	First ask their opinion on whether the bomber should be built; then, for those who respond "Yes," ask the question about taxes.
Are you generally satisfied with your job, or are there some things about it that you don't like?	**Overlapping alternatives:** A person might want to answer "Yes" to the first part (i.e., they are generally satisfied) but "No" to the second part (i.e., there are also some things they don't like).	Divide this into two questions: one measures their level of satisfaction while the other assesses whether there are things they don't like.
How satisfied are you with the number and fairness of the tests in this course?	**Double-barreled question:** It asks about both the "number" and the "fairness," and a person might feel differently about each.	Divide this into two questions.
What is your income?	**Vague and ambiguous words:** Does "income" refer to before-tax or after-tax income? To hourly, weekly, monthly, or yearly income?	Clarify: What was your total annual income, before taxes, for the year 2000?
Children who get into trouble typically have had a bad home life.	**Vague and ambiguous words:** The words *trouble* and *bad home life* are unclear. Is it trouble with the law, trouble at school, trouble with parents, or what? What constitutes a *bad home life* depends on the respondent's interpretation.	Clarify: Specify what you mean by the words: *trouble* means "having been arrested" and *bad home life* means "an alcoholic parent."

We present these and other problems that can arise in writing good survey questions in Table 7.2. One of the critical decisions in survey research—and it is a complex decision—is whether to collect data through questionnaires or interviews. We discuss both types of surveys with an eye on the criteria to use in assessing which is more appropriate for a particular research project.

QUESTIONNAIRES

Questionnaires are designed so they can be answered without assistance. Of course, if a researcher hands a questionnaire to the respondent, as we sometimes do, the respondent has the opportunity to ask the researcher to clarify anything that is ambiguous. A good questionnaire, however, should not require such assistance. In fact, researchers often mail questionnaires or send them online to respondents, who thus have no opportunity to ask questions. In other cases, researchers administer questionnaires to many people simultaneously in a classroom, auditorium, or agency setting. Such modes of administration make questionnaires quicker and less expensive than most interviews; however, they place the burden on researchers to design questionnaires that respondents can properly complete without assistance.

Structure and Design

Directions. One of the simplest—but also most important—tasks of questionnaire construction is the inclusion of precise directions for respondents. Good directions go a long way toward improving the quality of data that questionnaires generate. If we want respondents to click on a button or put an "X" in a box corresponding to their answer, then we tell them to do so. Questionnaires often contain questions requiring different kinds of answers as well, and at each place in the questionnaire where the format changes, we need to include additional directions.

Order of Questions. An element of questionnaire construction that requires careful consideration is the proper ordering of questions. Careless ordering can lead to undesirable consequences, such as a reduced response rate or biased responses to questions. Generally, questions that are asked early in the questionnaire should not bias answers to those questions that come later. For example, if we asked several factual questions regarding poverty and the conditions of the poor, and later we asked a question concerning which social problems people consider serious, more respondents will likely include poverty than otherwise would have done so. When a questionnaire contains both factual and opinion questions, we sometimes can avoid these potentially biasing effects by placing opinion questions first.

Ordering of questions also can increase a respondent's interest in answering a questionnaire—this is especially helpful for boosting response rates with mailed questionnaires. Researchers should ask questions dealing with particularly intriguing issues first. The idea is to interest the recipients enough to get them to start answering, because once they start, they are more likely to complete the entire questionnaire. If the questionnaire does not deal with any topics that are obviously more interesting than others, opinion questions should be placed first. People like to express their opinions, and for the reasons mentioned earlier, we should put opinion questions first anyway. A pitfall we definitely want to avoid is beginning a questionnaire with the standard demographic questions about age, sex, income, and the like. People are so accustomed to those questions that they may not want to answer them again—and may promptly file the questionnaire in the nearest wastebasket.

Question Formats. All efforts at careful wording and ordering of the questions will be for naught unless we present the questions in a manner that facilitates responding to them. The goal is to make responding to the questions as straightforward and convenient as possible and reduce the amount of data lost because of responses that we cannot interpret.

When presenting response alternatives for closed-ended questions, we obtain the best results by having respondents indicate their selection by placing an "X" in a box (❏) corresponding to that alternative, as illustrated in Question 1 of Table 7.1. This format is preferable to open blanks and check marks (✔), because it is easy for respondents to get sloppy and place check marks *between* alternatives, rendering their responses unclear and, therefore, useless as data. Boxes force respondents to give unambiguous responses. This may seem to be a minor point, but we can attest from our own experience in administering questionnaires that it makes an important difference.

Some questions on a questionnaire may apply to only some respondents and not others. These questions normally are handled by what are called *filter questions* and *contingency questions*. A **filter question** is one whose answer determines which question the respondent goes to next. In Table 7.1, Questions 2 and 3 are both filter questions. In Question 2, the part of the question asking about "how many items they have taken" is called a **contingency question**, because whether a person answers it depends on—is contingent on—his or her answer to the filter question. Notice the two ways in which the filter question is designed with a printed questionnaire. With Question 2, the person answering "Yes" is directed to the next question by the arrow, and the question is clearly set off by a box. Also in the box, the phrase "If Yes" is included to make sure the person realizes that this question is only for those who answered "Yes" to the previous question. With Question 3, the answer "No" is followed by a statement telling the person which question he or she should answer next. Either format is acceptable; the point is to provide clear directions for the respondent. (When questionnaires are designed by special computer programs to be answered on a computer screen or online, the computer program automatically moves the respondent to the appropriate contingency question once the person answers the filter question.) By sectioning the questionnaire on the basis of filter and contingency questions, we can guide the respondent through even the most complex questionnaire. The resulting path that an actual respondent follows through the questionnaire is referred to as the *skip pattern*. As is true of many aspects of questionnaire design, it is important to evaluate the skip pattern by pretesting the questionnaire to ensure that respondents complete all appropriate sections with a minimum of frustration.

In some cases, a number of questions or statements may all have identical response alternatives. An efficient way of organizing such questions is in the form of a **matrix question**, which lists the response alternatives only once; a box to check, or a number or letter to circle, follows each question or statement. Table 13.1 on page 345 is an example of a matrix question. Multiple-item indexes and scales often use this compact way of presenting a number of items.

Researchers should use matrix questions cautiously, however, because these questions contain a number of weaknesses. One is that, with a long list of items in a matrix question, it is easy for the respondent to lose track of which line is the response for which statement, and thus to indicate an answer on the line above or below where the answer should go. Researchers can alleviate this by following every third or fourth item with a blank line so that it is easier visually to keep track of the proper line on which to mark an answer. A second weakness of matrix questions is that they may produce *response set*. (We will discuss the problem of response set and techniques for alleviating it at length in Chapter 13.) A third weakness of matrix questions is that they may tempt the researcher, to be able to gain the efficiencies of the format, to force the response alternatives of some questions into that matrix format when another format would be more valid. Researchers should determine the response format of any question or statement by theoretical and conceptual considerations of what is the most valid way to measure a variable.

Response Rate

A major problem in many research endeavors is gaining people's cooperation so that they will provide whatever data are needed. In surveys, we measure cooperation by the **response rate**, or the proportion of a sample that completes and returns a questionnaire or agrees to an interview. With interviews, response rates often are very high—in the area of 90 percent—largely because people are reluctant to refuse a face-to-face request for cooperation. In fact, with interviews, the largest nonresponse factor is the inability of interviewers to locate respondents. With mailed or online questionnaires, however, this personal pressure is absent, and people feel freer to refuse. This can result in many *nonreturns*, or people who refuse to complete and return a questionnaire. Response rates for questionnaires (especially mailed ones) vary considerably, from an unacceptably low 20 percent to levels that rival those of interviews.

Why is a low response rate of such concern? The issue is the representativeness of a sample, as we discussed in Chapter 6. If we selected a representative sample and obtained a perfect 100 percent response, then we would have confidence in the representativeness of the sample data. As the response rate drops below 100 percent, however, the sample may become less representative. Those who refuse to cooperate may differ from those who do return the questionnaire in some systematic ways that can affect the results of the research. In other words, any response rate less than 100 percent may result in a biased sample. Of course, we rarely achieve a perfect response rate, but the closer the response rate is to that level, the more likely that

TABLE 7.3   Items to Include in the Cover Letter of a Questionnaire or the Introduction to an Interview

Item	Cover Letter	Interview Introduction
1. Sponsor of the research	yes	yes
2. Address/phone number of the researcher	yes	if required
3. How the respondent was selected	yes	yes
4. Who else was selected	yes	yes
5. The purpose of the research	yes	yes
6. Who will utilize or benefit from the research	yes	yes
7. An appeal for the person's cooperation	yes	yes
8. How long it will take the respondent to complete the survey	yes	yes
9. Payment	if given	if given
10. Anonymity/confidentiality	if given	if given
11. Deadline for return	yes	not applicable

the data are representative. Researchers can take a number of steps to improve response rates. Most apply only to questionnaires, but we also can use a few of them to increase the response rates in interviews.

A Cover Letter. A properly constructed cover letter can help increase the response rate. A **cover letter** accompanies a questionnaire and serves to introduce and explain it to the recipient. With mailed or online questionnaires, the cover letter may be the researcher's only medium for communicating with the recipient, so the researcher must carefully draft the letter to include information that recipients will want to know and to encourage them to complete the questionnaire (see Table 7.3).

Researchers should feature the name of the sponsor of the research project prominently in the cover letter. Recipients want to know who is seeking the information they are being asked to provide, and research clearly indicates that knowledge of the sponsoring organization influences the response rate (Goyder, 1985; Rea & Parker, 2005). Questionnaires sponsored by governmental agencies receive the highest response rates. University-sponsored research generates somewhat lower response rates. Commercially sponsored research produces the lowest rates of all. Apparently, if the research is at all associated with a governmental agency, stressing that in the cover letter may have a beneficial effect on the response rate. Researchers also can increase the response rates of particular groups if their research is sponsored or endorsed by an organization that people in the group believe has legitimacy. For example, we can increase response rates of professionals if the research is linked to relevant professional organizations, such as the National Association of Social Workers, the American Nurses Association, or the National Education Association (Sudman, 1985).

The address and telephone number of the researcher also should appear prominently on the cover letter. In fact, using letterhead stationery for the cover letter is a good idea. Especially if the sponsor of the research is not well known, some recipients may desire further information before they decide to participate. Although relatively few respondents will ask for more information, including the address and telephone number gives the cover letter a completely open and aboveboard appearance that may further the general cooperation of recipients.

In addition, the cover letter should inform the respondent of how people were selected to receive the questionnaire. It is not necessary to go into great detail on this matter, but people receiving an unanticipated questionnaire are naturally curious about how they were chosen to be part of a study. A brief statement, for example, that they were randomly selected or selected by computer (if this is the case) should suffice.

Recipients also want to know the purpose of the research. Again, without going into great detail, the cover letter should explain why the research is being conducted, why and by whom it is considered important, and the potential benefits that are anticipated from the study. Investigations have shown clearly that we can significantly increase the response rate if we emphasize the importance of the research to the respondent. We must word this part of the cover letter carefully, however, so it does not sensitize respondents in a way that affects their answers to our questions. We can minimize sensitizing effects by keeping the description of the purpose general—certainly, do not suggest any of the research hypotheses. Regarding the importance of the data and the anticipated benefits, the researcher should resist the temptation of hyperbole and, instead, make honest, straightforward statements. Respondents will see claims about "solving a significant social problem" or "alleviating the problems of the poor" as precisely what they are—exaggerated.

The preceding information provides a foundation for the single most important component of the cover letter—namely, a direct appeal for the recipient's cooperation. General statements about the importance of the research are no substitute for a personal appeal to the recipient as to why he or she should take time to complete the questionnaire. Respondents must believe that their responses are important to the outcome (as, of course, they are). A statement to the effect that "your views are important to us" is a good approach that stresses the importance of each individual respondent and emphasizes that the questionnaire will allow the expression of opinions, which people like.

The cover letter also should indicate that the respondent will remain anonymous or the data will be treated as confidential, whichever is the case. "Anonymous" means that *no one, including the researcher*, can link a particular respondent's name to his or her questionnaire. "Confidential" means that even though the researcher can match a respondent's name to his or her questionnaire, the researcher will treat the information collectively and will not link any individuals to their responses publicly.

With mailed questionnaires, two techniques assure anonymity (Sudman, 1985). The best is to keep the questionnaire itself completely anonymous, with no identifying numbers or symbols; instead, the respondent gets a separate postcard, including his or her name, to mail back at the same time he or she returns the completed questionnaire. This way, the researcher knows who has responded and need not send reminders; yet no one can link a particular respondent's name with a particular questionnaire. A second way to ensure anonymity is to attach a cover sheet to the questionnaire with an identifying number and assure the respondents that the researcher will remove and destroy the cover sheet once receipt of the questionnaire has been recorded. This second procedure provides less assurance to the respondent, because an unethical researcher might retain the link between questionnaires and their identification numbers. The first procedure, however, is more expensive because of the additional postcard mailing, so a researcher may prefer the second procedure for questionnaires that do not deal with highly sensitive issues that sometimes make respondents more concerned about anonymity. If the material is not highly sensitive, assurances of confidentiality are adequate to ensure a good return rate. No evidence indicates that assuring anonymity rather than confidentiality increases the response rate in nonsensitive surveys (Moser & Kalton, 1972).

Finally, the cover letter should include a deadline for returning the questionnaire—that is, a deadline calculated to take into account mailing time and a few days to complete the questionnaire. The rationale for a fairly tight deadline is that it encourages the recipients to complete the questionnaire soon after they receive it and not set it aside, where they can forget or misplace it.

Payment. Research consistently shows that we also can increase response rates by offering a payment or other incentives as part of the appeal for cooperation, and that these incentives need not be large to have a positive effect. Studies find that, depending on the respondents, an incentive of between $2 and $20 can add 10 percent to a response rate (Warriner et al., 1996; Woodruff, Conway, & Edwards, 2000). For the greatest effect, researchers should include such payments with the initial mailing instead of promising payment on return of the questionnaire. One study found that including the payment with the questionnaire boosted the return rate by 12 percent over promising payment on the questionnaire's return (Berry & Kanouse, 1987). Researchers have used other types of incentives as well, such as entering each respondent in a lottery or donating to charity for each questionnaire returned, but these have shown mixed results as far as increasing response rates.

Mailing procedures also affect response rates. It almost goes without saying that researchers should supply a stamped, self-addressed envelope for returning the questionnaire to make its return as convenient as possible for the respondent. The type of postage used also affects the response rate, with stamps bringing about a 4 percent higher return rate compared with bulk-printed postage (Yammarino, Skinner, & Childers, 1991). Presumably, the stamp makes the questionnaire appear more personal and less like unimportant junk mail. A regular stamped envelope also substantially increases the response rate in comparison with a business reply envelope (Armstrong & Luck, 1987).

Follow-Ups. The most important procedural matter affecting response rates is the use of follow-up letters or other contacts. A substantial percentage of those who do not respond to the initial mailing will respond to follow-up contacts. With two follow-ups, researchers can achieve 15 to 20 percent increases over the initial return (James & Bolstein, 1990; Woodruff, Conway, & Edwards, 2000). Such follow-ups are clearly essential; researchers can do them by telephone, if the budget permits, and speed is important. With aggressive follow-ups, the difference in response rates between mailed questionnaires and interviews declines substantially (Goyder, 1985).

In general, researchers use two-step follow-ups. Some send follow-up letters to nonrespondents that encourage return of the questionnaire once the response to the initial mailing drops off. This letter should include a restatement of the points in the cover letter, with an additional appeal for cooperation. When response to the first follow-up declines, the researcher then sends a second follow-up to the remaining nonrespondents and includes another copy of the questionnaire in case people have misplaced the original. After two follow-ups, we consider the remaining nonrespondents to be a pretty intransigent lot, because additional follow-ups generate relatively few further responses.

Length and Appearance. Two other factors that affect the rate of response to a mailed questionnaire are the length of the questionnaire and its appearance. As the length increases, the response rate declines. No hard-and-fast rule, however, governs the length of mailed questionnaires. Much depends on the intelligence and literacy of the respondents, the degree of interest in the topic of the questionnaire, and other such matters. It probably is a good idea, though, to keep the questionnaire to less than five pages, requiring no more than 30 minutes to fill it out. Researchers must take great care to remove any extraneous questions, or any questions that are not essential to the hypotheses under investigation (Epstein & Tripodi, 1977). Although keeping the questionnaire to less than five pages is a general guide, researchers should not strive to achieve this by cramming so much material onto each page that the respondent has difficulty using the instrument—because, as mentioned, the appearance of the questionnaire also is important in generating a high response rate. As discussed earlier, the use of boxed response choices and smooth transitions through contingency questions help make completing the questionnaire easier and more enjoyable for the respondent, which in turn increases the probability that he or she will return it.

Other Influences on Response Rate. Many other factors can work to change response rates. In telephone surveys, for example, the voice and manner of the interviewer can have an important effect (Oksenberg, Coleman, & Cannell, 1986). Interviewers with higher-pitched, louder voices, and clear, distinct pronunciation have lower refusal rates. The same is true for interviewers who sound competent and upbeat. Reminders of confidentiality, however, can negatively affect the response rate (Frey, 1986): If an interviewer reminds a respondent of the confidentiality of the information partway through the interview, the respondent is more likely to refuse to respond to some of the remaining questions compared with someone who does not receive such a reminder. The reminder may work to undo whatever rapport the interviewer has already built up with the respondent.

A survey following all the suggested procedures should yield an acceptably high response rate. Specialized populations may, of course, produce either higher or lower rates. Because so many variables are involved, we offer only rough guidelines for evaluating response rates with mailed questionnaires. The desired response rate is 100 percent, of course. Anything less than 50 percent is highly suspect as far as its representativeness is concerned. Unless some evidence of the representativeness can be presented, we should use great caution when generalizing from such a sample. In fact, it might be best to treat the resulting sample as a nonprobability sample from which we cannot make confident generalizations. In terms of what a researcher can expect, response rates in the 60 percent range are good; anything more than 70 percent is very good. Even with these response rates, however, we should use caution about generalizing and check for bias as a result of nonresponse. The bottom line, whether the response rate is high or low, is to report it honestly so those who are reading the research can judge its generalizability for themselves.

Checking for Bias Due to Nonresponse

Even if researchers obtain a relatively high rate of response, they should investigate possible bias due to nonresponse by determining the extent to which respondents differ from nonrespondents (Groves, 2004; Miller & Salkind, 2002; Rea & Parker, 2005). One common method is to compare the characteristics of the respondents with the characteristics of the population from which they were selected. If a database on the population exists, then we can simplify this job. For example, if researchers are studying a representative sample of welfare recipients in a community, the Department of Social Services is likely to have data regarding age, sex, marital status, level of education, and other characteristics for all welfare recipients in the community. The researchers can compare the respondents with this database on the characteristics for which data have already been collected. A second approach to assessing bias from nonresponse is to locate a subsample of nonrespondents and interview them. In this way, we can compare the responses to the questionnaire by a representative sample of nonrespondents with those of the respondents. This is the preferred method, because we can measure directly the direction and the extent of any bias that results from nonresponse. It is, however, the most costly and time-consuming approach.

Any check for bias from nonresponse, of course, informs us only about those characteristics on which we make comparisons. It does not prove that the respondents are representative of the whole sample on any other variables—including those that might be of considerable importance to the study. In short, we can gather some information regarding such bias, but in most cases, we cannot *prove* that bias from nonresponse does not exist.

The proper design of survey instruments is important to collecting valid data. Research in Practice 7.1 provides an illustration of a use to which survey research is commonly put by human service practice organizations today.

An Assessment of Questionnaires

Advantages. As a technique of survey research, questionnaires have a number of desirable features. First, they gather data far more inexpensively and quickly than interviews. Mailed questionnaires require only four to six weeks, whereas obtaining the same data by personal interviews would likely take a minimum of several months. Mailed questionnaires also save the expense of hiring interviewers, interviewer travel, and other costs.

Second, mailed questionnaires enable the researcher to collect data from a geographically dispersed sample. It costs no more to mail a

> **RESEARCH IN PRACTICE 7.1** **Behavior and Social Environments: Surveys as an Evidence-Based Foundation for Practice Delivery**
>
> Paul is a social worker with a master's degree. He is the youth development associate for a nonprofit organization (GLCYD) whose mission is to provide various supports to other nonprofits that deliver services to youth. The goal of GLCYD is to increase the effectiveness of these other nonprofits through technical support and action-oriented research. One way GLCYD does this is through survey research.
>
> Every two years Paul oversees the administration of the Profiles of Student Life survey to 8th-, 10th-, and 12th-grade students in 16 school districts within a two-county area. Created by the Search Institute, a professional research firm, Profiles of Student Life evaluates 40 study assets, attitudes, and behaviors deemed beneficial to academic performance and overall social life. The survey also assesses levels of drug and alcohol use and experiences with violence, sex, and other behaviors considered risky. The availability of research firms such as the Search Institute has made sophisticated survey research available to and affordable by even small human service agencies. These firms provide a whole range of services—from design of the survey instrument to analysis of the resulting data—that only the larger agencies would have in-house staff to conduct.
>
> While many of the students who take the survey as 8th graders will also take it as 10th and 12th graders, Paul is careful not to refer to this as a panel study (see Chapter 4). "Students who take the survey in 8th grade are not exactly the same group as those who take it two years later in 10th grade and again in 12th grade two years after that," he explained. "Still, the vast majority are the same students and I believe that comparing data year to year can give us a real sense of trends within the counties" he continued.
>
> The surveys are administered by teachers, guidance counselors, and social workers in each of the schools. Paul trains them to administer the survey, which includes 160 profile questionnaire items and an additional 30 items developed specifically for students in these counties. These additional questions are referred to as the "side bar" portion of the survey and include items pertaining to nutrition and exercise, prescription drug use, Internet use and safety, and future career plans.
>
> Completed surveys are sent to the Search Institute where results are tabulated and compiled in a report. As Paul explains, "My job is to then interpret results and decide what information people would like to know and what data I would want people to know." GLCYD's clients, which include school districts, nonprofits and other community organizations, often use survey results when writing grant proposals to fund practice interventions. One local nonprofit, for example, used the survey's results in a recent grant proposal to argue for additional resources to support after-school programs. Substance abuse treatment agencies have used the data to tailor services for youth as patterns in drug use—specifically types of drugs consumed—have shifted in recent years. A domestic violence shelter and services agency uses the data to understand trends in youth victimization and adjust services accordingly.
>
> According to Paul, one of the greatest outcomes of the survey project is positive publicity for young people. "Many people in the area see young people as dangerous. Others think they're all using drugs or alcohol. Our data help us 'kill the boogeyman.' We can portray an accurate snapshot of young people so the public understands that not everyone is drinking or doing drugs. In fact, it is a small minority of students who are doing these things, and an even smaller group who them regularly."
>
> Paul also explained that parents have used the data in setting limits for their adolescent children. "Parents like to be able to have numbers to show that the limits they set for their kids are not unreasonable. They feel better about this when they can show their kids that not everyone their age is going to all-night parties or doing any number of risky behaviors," he stated.
>
> (Based on personal interviews conducted in September 2011.)

questionnaire across the country than to mail a questionnaire across the city. Costs of interviewer travel, however, rise enormously as the distance increases, making interviews over wide geographic areas an expensive process.

Third, with questions of a personal or sensitive nature, mailed questionnaires may provide more accurate answers than interviews. People may be more likely to respond honestly to such questions when they are not face to face with a person they perceive as possibly making judgments about them. In practice, researchers may use a combination of questionnaires and interviews to address this problem. Written questions, or computer-assisted self-interviewing, has been proven to generate more accurate information (Newman et al., 2002). In addition, a self-administered questionnaire increased reporting of male-to-male sexual activity over standard interview procedures in the General Social Survey (Anderson & Stall, 2002).

Finally, mailed questionnaires eliminate the problem of interviewer bias, which occurs when an interviewer influences a person's response to a question by what he or she says, his or her tone of voice, or his or her demeanor. Because no interviewer is present when the respondent fills out the questionnaire, an interviewer cannot bias the answers to a questionnaire in any particular direction (Cannell & Kahn, 1968).

Disadvantages. Despite their many advantages, mailed questionnaires have important limitations that may make them less desirable for some research efforts (Moser & Kalton, 1972). First, mailed questionnaires require a minimal degree of literacy and facility in English, which some respondents may not possess. Substantial nonresponse is, of course, likely with such people. Nonresponse because of illiteracy, however, does not seriously bias the results of most general-population surveys. Self-administered questionnaires are more successful among people who are better educated, motivated to respond, and involved in issues and organizations. Often, however, some groups of interest to human service practitioners do not possess these characteristics. If the survey is aimed at a special population in which the researcher suspects lower than average literacy, personal interviews are a better choice.

Second, all the questions must be sufficiently easy to comprehend on the basis of printed instructions. Third, there is no opportunity to probe for more information or to evaluate the nonverbal behavior of the respondents. The answers they mark on the questionnaire are final. Fourth, the researcher has no assurance that the person who should answer the questionnaire is the one who actually does. Fifth, the researcher cannot consider responses to be independent, because the respondent can read through the entire questionnaire before completing it. Finally, all mailed questionnaires face the problem of nonresponse bias.

INTERVIEWS

During an interview, the investigator or an assistant reads the questions directly to the respondents and then records their answers. Interviews offer the investigator a degree of flexibility that is not available with questionnaires. One area of increased flexibility relates to the degree of structure built into an interview.

The Structure of Interviews

The element of *structure* in interviews refers to the degree of freedom that the interviewer has in conducting the interview and that respondents have in answering questions. We classify interviews in terms of three levels of structure: (1) *unstandardized*, (2) *nonschedule-standardized*, and (3) *schedule-standardized*.

The *unstandardized interview* has the least structure. All the interviewer typically has for guidance is a general topic area, as illustrated in Figure 7.1. By developing his or her own questions and probes as the interview progresses, the interviewer explores the topic with the respondent. The approach is called "unstandardized" because each interviewer asks different questions and obtains different information from each respondent. There is heavy reliance on the skills of the interviewer to ask good questions and keep the interview going; this can only be done if experienced interviewers are available. This unstructured approach makes unstandardized interviewing especially appropriate for exploratory research. In Figure 7.1, for example, only the general topic of coping behaviors of homeless people guides the interviewer. The example also illustrates the suitability of this style of interviewing for exploratory research, where the interviewer is directed to search for as many types of coping behaviors as can be found.

The Unstandardized Interview

Interviewer Instructions: Identify coping behaviors used by homeless respondents. Coping behaviors refer to all methods of securing food, shelter, and clothing, including: reliance on family and friends, social service use, and self-help (e.g., camping, hunting, foraging, earning money through work or other means). Look for all of these and possibly others.

The Nonscheduled-Standardized Interview

Interviewer Instructions: Your task is to identify coping behaviors among homeless respondents. We are interested in behaviors and strategies that allow them access to food, shelter, and clothing. We would like to focus on several types of coping behaviors (listed below), however, the initial question is broad and open-ended. This is designed to help you build a rapport with the interviewee and to help show your non-judgmental attitude toward the homeless and your understanding of the day-to-day struggles associated with meeting basic needs.

1. Many people have described multiple challenges they have faced in surviving day-to-day while homeless. What sorts of challenges do you face? (Possible probes: What is your most pressing challenge right now? What, if anything, has been helpful in helping you address this issue?)
2. Let's focus on shelter.
   a. Do you receive shelter assistance from any social service agencies (e.g., shelter programs, temporary housing vouchers (including hotel coupons), transitional housing program assistance)?
   b. Do you ever get shelter assistance from family members or friends (e.g., a place to live or at least sleep)?
   c. How else do you find a place to sleep? (Possible probes: Do you camp? Do you sleep outdoors? Do you sleep in cars? Do you ever sleep in abandoned buildings?)
3. Let's focus on food.
   a. Do you receive food assistance from any social service agencies (e.g., food stamps, meals at soup kitchens, food baskets, or other donated foods from food pantries)?
   b. Do you ever get food assistance from family members or friends (e.g., meals, a place to prepare and or store food)?
   c. How else do you get food? (Possible probes: Do you purchase food at stores? Where do you store food? How do you prepare it?)
4. Let's focus on clothing.
   a. Do you receive clothing assistance from any social service agencies (e.g., free clothing or shoes, discounted clothing)?
   b. Do you ever get clothing assistance from family members or friends (e.g., hand-me-downs, a place to store clothing)?
   c. How else do you get clothing? (Possible probes: Do you purchase clothing at stores? Where do you store clothing?)

The Schedule Standardized Interview

Interviewer explanation to the homeless respondent: We are interested in learning about the ways that homeless adults survive in rural areas. We want to understand how people access food, shelter, clothing, and other basic necessities while homeless. We are especially interested in learning about any help received from family, friends and use of social services. In addition, we are interested in other strategies for surviving while homeless, including: living outdoors, cooking without a stove, and staying warm when it is cold outside. We have a checklist here of some of the possible ways that people access shelter while homeless. Think about the last month you were homeless and put a check to show how often you have accessed shelter using the tactic listed on each row. If you have never accessed shelter in any one of these ways then put the check in the column where it says "never".

(Hand the interviewee the first card dealing with shelter while saying "If you don't understand anything listed on the card, let me know and we'll talk about it. When the respondent completes this card, hand him or her the second card, saying, "Here is list of ways that homeless adults might access food. Do the same thing with the list.")

Method	Never	Only Once	More Than Once	Many Times
Stayed with a family member				
Stayed with a friend				
Stayed in a shelter				
Slept outdoors (including in a tent)				
Slept in a car				
Slept in an abandoned building or another building without permission.				
Other shelter arrangements (please identify):				

FIGURE 7.1 Examples of Various Interviewer Structures

Nonschedule-standardized interviews add more structure, with a narrower topic and specific questions asked of all respondents. The interview, however, remains fairly conversational; the interviewer is free to probe, rephrase questions, or ask the questions in whatever order best fits that particular interview. Note in Figure 7.1 that specific questions are of the open-ended type, allowing the respondent full freedom of expression. As in the case of the unstandardized form, success with this type of interview requires an experienced interviewer.

The *schedule-standardized interview* is the most structured type. An **interview schedule** contains specific instructions for the interviewer, specific questions to be asked in a fixed order, and transition phrases for the interviewer to use. Sometimes, the schedule also contains acceptable rephrasings for questions and a selection of stock probes. Schedule-standardized interviews are fairly rigid, with neither interviewer nor respondent allowed to depart from the structure of the schedule. Although some questions may be open-ended, most are closed-ended. In fact, some schedule-standardized interviews are quite similar to a questionnaire, except that the interviewer asks the questions rather than having the respondent read them. In Figure 7.1, note the use of cards with response alternatives handed to the respondent. This is a popular way of supplying respondents with a complex set of closed-ended alternatives. Note also the precise directions for the interviewer as well as verbatim phrases to read to the respondent. Relatively untrained, part-time interviewers can conduct schedule-standardized interviews because the schedule contains nearly everything they need to say. This makes schedule-standardized interviews the preferred choice for studies with large sample sizes and many interviewers. The structure of these interviews also ensures that all respondents receive the same questions in the same order. This heightens reliability and makes schedule-standardized interviews popular for rigorous hypothesis testing. Research in Practice 7.2 explores some further advantages of having more or less structure in an interview.

Contacting Respondents

As with researchers who mail questionnaires, those who rely on interviewers face the problem of contacting respondents and eliciting their cooperation. Many interviews are conducted in the homes of the respondents; locating and traveling to respondents' homes are two of the more troublesome—and costly—aspects of interviewing. It has been estimated that as much as 40 percent of a typical interviewer's time is spent traveling (Sudman, 1965). Because so much time and cost are involved, and because researchers desire high response rates, they direct substantial efforts at minimizing the rate of refusal. The first contact of prospective respondents has a substantial impact on the refusal rate.

Two approaches to contacting respondents that might appear logical to the neophyte researcher have, in fact, the opposite effect of that desired. It might seem that *telephoning* to set up an appointment for the interview is a good idea. In reality, telephoning greatly increases the rate of refusal. In one experiment, for example, the part of the sample that was telephoned had nearly *triple* the rate of refusal of those who were contacted in person (Brunner & Carroll, 1967). Apparently, it is much easier to refuse over the relatively impersonal medium of the telephone than in a face-to-face encounter with an interviewer. *Sending people a letter* asking them to participate in an interview has much the same effect (Cartwright & Tucker, 1967). The letter seems to give people sufficient time before the interviewer arrives to develop reasons why they do not want to cooperate. Those first contacted in person, on the other hand, have only those excuses they can muster on the spur of the moment. Clearly, then, interviewers obtain the lowest refusal rates by contacting interviewees in person.

Additional factors also can affect the refusal rate (Gorden, 1987). For example, information regarding the research project should blanket the total survey population through the news media to demonstrate general community acceptance of the project. With a few differences, information provided to the media should contain essentially the same information as provided in a cover letter for a mailed questionnaire (see Table 7.3). Pictures of the interviewers and mention of any equipment they carry, such as laptop computers, or video or audio recording devices, should be included. This information assists people in identifying interviewers and reduces possible confusion of interviewers with salespeople or solicitors. In fact, it is a good idea to equip the interviewers with identification badges or something else that is easily recognizable so they are not mistaken for others who go door to door. When the interviewers go into the field, they should take along copies of the news coverage as well. Then if they encounter a respondent who has not seen the media coverage, they can show the clippings during the initial contact.

The timing of the initial contact also affects the refusal rate. It is preferable to contact interviewees at a time that is convenient for them to complete the interview without the need for a second call. Depending on the nature of the sample, predicting availability may be fairly easy or virtually impossible. For example, if interviewers can obtain the information that is required from any household member, almost any reasonable time of day will do. On the other hand, if the interviewer must contact specific individuals, timing becomes more critical. If we must interview the breadwinner in a household, for example, we probably should make the contacts at night or on weekends (unless knowledge of the person's occupation suggests a different time of greater availability). Whatever time the interviewer makes the initial contact, however, it still may not be convenient for the respondent, especially if the interview is lengthy. If the respondent is pressed for time, use the initial contact to establish rapport and set another time for the interview. Even though callbacks are costly, this is certainly preferable to the rushed interview that results in inferior data.

When the interviewer and potential respondent first meet, the interviewer should give an introduction that includes most or all of the information listed in Table 7.3: basic information about the survey, the approximate length of the interview, the research sponsor, and so on. After the introduction, the interviewer should be prepared to elaborate on any points the interviewee questions. To avoid biasing responses, however, the interviewer must exercise care when discussing the purpose of the survey.

Conducting an Interview

A large-scale survey with an adequate budget often turns to private research agencies to train interviewers and conduct interviews. Often, however, smaller research projects cannot afford this, and have to train and coordinate their own team of interviewers, possibly with the researchers themselves doing some of the interviewing. It is important, therefore, to know how to conduct an interview properly.

The Interview as a Social Relationship. The interview is a social relationship designed to exchange information between the respondent and the interviewer. The quantity and quality of information exchanged depend on how astute and creative the interviewer is at understanding and managing that relationship (Fowler & Mangione, 1990; Holstein & Gubrium, 2003). Human service workers generally are knowledgeable regarding the properties and processes of social interaction; in fact, much human service practice is founded on the establishment of social relationships with clients. A few elements of the research interview, however, are worth emphasizing because they have direct implications for conducting interviews.

A research interview is a secondary relationship in which the interviewer has a practical, utilitarian goal. It is easy, especially for an inexperienced interviewer, to be drawn into a more casual or personal interchange with the respondent. Especially with a friendly, outgoing respondent, the conversation might drift off to topics like sports, politics, or children. That, however, is not the purpose of the interview. The goal is not to make friends or to give the respondent a sympathetic ear, but rather to collect complete and unbiased data following the interview schedule.

We all recognize the powerful impact first impressions have on perceptions. This is especially true during interview situations, in which the

RESEARCH IN PRACTICE 7.2 Assessment of Client Functioning: Merging Quantitative and Qualitative Measures

That survey research is necessarily quantitative in nature probably is a common misconception. Virtually every edition of the evening news presents the results from one or more surveys, indicating that a certain percentage of respondents hold a given opinion or plan to vote for a particular candidate, or offers other information that is basically quantitative or reduced to numbers. However, survey research is not limited to quantitative analysis. In fact, as we note in the discussion of Figure 7.1, interviews run the gamut from totally quantitative in the highly structured type to fully qualitative in the least structured variety—as well as any combination in between. Some researchers combine both quantitative and qualitative measures in individual studies to obtain the benefits of each approach.

Two studies of homeless families headed by females illustrate such a merging of interview styles. Shirley Thrasher and Carol Mowbray (1995) interviewed 15 homeless families from three shelters, focusing primarily on the experiences of the mothers and their efforts to take care of their children. Elizabeth Timberlake (1994) based her study on interviews with 200 families who were not in shelters, and focused predominantly on the experiences of the homeless children. In both studies, the researchers used structured interview questions to provide quantitative demographic information about the homeless families, such as their race/ethnicity, length of homelessness, and employment status.

As important as this quantitative information might be, the researchers in both studies wanted to get at the more personal meaning of—and feelings about—being homeless. For this, they turned to the unstructured parts of the interviews (sometimes called ethnographic interviews) which were designed to get the subjects to tell their stories in their own words. The goal of both studies was to assess the needs of the homeless families either to develop new programs to assist them or modify existing programs to better fit their needs. The researchers felt that the best way to accomplish this goal was to get the story of being homeless in as pure a form as possible from the people who lived it, and without any distortion by the researchers' preconceived notions. The open-ended questions that Timberlake asked the homeless children illustrate this unstructured approach: "Tell me about not having a place to live." "What is it like?" "What do you do?" "How do you feel?" "How do you handle being homeless?" "Are there things that you do or say?" The questions that Thrasher and Mowbray asked the homeless mothers were similar. Both studies used probes as needed to elicit greater response and to clarify vague responses.

An example from Thrasher and Mowbray illustrates how responses to open-ended questions provide insight into what the respondent is experiencing. Those researchers found that a common experience of the women in the shelters was that, before coming to the shelter, they had bounced around among friends and relatives, experiencing a series of short-term and unstable living arrangements. The researchers present the following quote from 19-year-old "Nancy":

> I went from friend to friend before going back to my mother and her boyfriend. And all my friends they live with their parents, and so you know, I could only stay like a night, maybe two nights before I had to leave. So the only thing I could do was to come here to the shelter and so that's what I did. After all, there is only so many friends. I went to live once with my grandmother for a week who lives in a senior citizens' high rise. But

---

interviewer and the respondent are likely to be total strangers. The first impressions that affect a respondent are the physical and social characteristics of the interviewer. So we need to take considerable care to ensure that the first contact enhances the likelihood of the respondent's cooperation (Warwick & Lininger, 1975). Most research suggests that interviewers are more successful if they have social characteristics similar to those of their respondents. Thus such characteristics as socioeconomic status, age, sex, race, and ethnicity might influence the success of the interview—especially if the subject matter of the interview relates to one of these topics. In addition, the personal demeanor of the interviewer plays an important role; interviewers should be neat, clean, and businesslike, but friendly.

After exchanging initial pleasantries, the interviewer should begin the interview. The they don't allow anyone to stay there longer than a week as a visitor. So, I had to move on. I finally went to my social worker and told her I don't have any place to stay. She put me in a motel first because there was no opening in the shelter. Then I came here.

As this example illustrates, there is no substitute for hearing the plight of these people in their own words to help those who are not homeless gain some understanding of what it is like not to have a stable place to call home.

In part because of her much larger sample, Timberlake did not tape record her interviews and so made no verbatim transcripts. Instead, she took field notes that summarized the responses of the homeless children. This resulted in a different approach to analysis, because she did not have the long narratives that Thrasher and Mowbray had. Instead, she had a large number of summarized statements from her notes. She ended up doing a more quantitative analysis by categorizing the respondents' statements into more abstract categories. Timberlake found that the responses clustered around three themes: separation/loss, caretaking/nurturance, and security/protection. Within each theme were statements along two dimensions, which Timberlake refers to as "deprivation" and "restoration," respectively—the negative statements about what is bad about being homeless, and the positive statements about what the children still have and how they cope. So children's statements such as "we got no food" and "Daddy left us" were categorized as reflecting deprivation related to caretaking/ nurturance. "Mama stays with us" and "I still got my clothes" were seen to reflect restoration related to separation/loss. Timberlake tabulated the number of each kind of statement. It seems rather indicative of the devastation of homelessness on the children that Timberlake found approximately three times as many deprivation statements as she did restoration statements. It is important to note that these categories and themes were not used by the respondents themselves but were created by Timberlake in an effort to extract some abstract or theoretical meaning from the narratives.

Neither of these studies used an interview format that would be suitable for interviewing a large, randomly selected sample of homeless people with the purpose of estimating the demographic characteristics of the entire homeless population. Imagine trying to organize and summarize data from several thousand interviews like those conducted by Thrasher and Mowbray! To reasonably accomplish such a population estimate, a schedule-standardized interview format, producing quantitative data, is far more appropriate. If the goal of the research project is to gain an understanding of the personal experiences and reactions to being homeless, however, as in the two studies just discussed, then presenting results in the respondents' own words is more effective. However, if researchers wanted to design a schedule-standardized survey project to do a population description of the homeless, studies such as the two discussed here would be invaluable for determining what concepts to measure and for developing the quantitative indicators such a study would demand.

These two studies illustrate that both qualitative and quantitative approaches are essential to social research. Which approach is most appropriate in a given situation depends on the particular goals of the research; in some cases, a blend of both quantitative and qualitative approaches in the same project obtains the desired results.

respondent may be a bit apprehensive during the initial stages of an interview. In recognition of this, the interview should begin with fairly simple, nonthreatening questions. A schedule, if used, should begin with these kinds of questions. The demographic questions, which are reserved until the later stages of a mailed questionnaire, are good to begin an interview. The familiarity of respondents with this information makes these questions nonthreatening and a good means of reducing tension in the respondent.

Probes. If an interview schedule is used, then the interview progresses in accordance with it. As needed, the interviewer uses **probes**, or follow-up questions, intended to elicit clearer and more complete responses. In some cases, the interview schedule contains suggestions for probes. In less structured interviews, however, interviewers must develop and use their own probes. These probes can take the form of a pause in conversation that encourages the respondent to elaborate or an explicit request to clarify or elaborate on something. A major concern with any probe is that it should not bias the respondent's answer by suggesting the answer (Fowler & Mangione, 1990).

Recording Responses. A central task of interviewers, of course, is to record the responses of respondents. The four most common ways are classifying responses into predetermined categories, summarizing key points, taking verbatim notes (by hand writing or with a laptop computer), or making an audio or video recording of the interview.

Recording responses generally is easiest when we use an interview schedule. Because closed-ended questions are typical of such schedules, we can simply classify responses into the predetermined alternatives. This simplicity of recording is another factor making schedule-standardized interviews suitable for use with relatively untrained interviewers, because no special recording skills are required.

With nonschedule-standardized interviewing, the questions are likely to be open-ended and the responses longer. Often, all we need to record are the key points the respondent makes. The interviewer condenses and summarizes what the respondent says. This requires an experienced interviewer who is familiar with the research questions and can accurately identify what to record, and then do so without injecting his or her own interpretation, which would bias the summary.

Sometimes, we may want to record everything the respondent says verbatim to avoid the possible biasing effect of summarizing responses. If the anticipated responses are reasonably short, then competent interviewers can take verbatim notes. Special skills, such as shorthand, may be necessary. If the responses are lengthy, then verbatim note taking can cause difficulties, such as leading the interviewer to fail to monitor the respondent or to be unprepared to probe when necessary. It also can damage rapport by making it appear that the interviewer is ignoring the respondent. Making audio or video recordings of the interviews can eliminate problems such as this but also can increase the costs substantially, both for the equipment and for later transcription of the materials (Gorden, 1987). Such recordings, however, also provide the most accurate account of the interview.

The fear some researchers have that tape recorders increase the refusal rate appears to be unwarranted (Gorden, 1987). If the recorder is explained as a routine procedure that aids in capturing complete and accurate responses, few respondents object.

Controlling Interviewers. Once interviewers go into the field, the quality of the resulting data depends heavily on them. It is a naive researcher, indeed, who assumes that, without supervision, interviewers will all do their job properly, especially when part-time interviewers who have little commitment to the research project are used. Proper supervision begins during interviewer training by stressing the importance of contacting the right respondents and meticulously following established procedures.

Although sloppy, careless work is one concern, a more serious issue is **interviewer falsification**, or the intentional departure from the designed interviewer instructions, unreported by the interviewer, which can result in the contamination of data (American Association for Public Opinion Research Standards Committee, 2003). A dramatic illustration of this was discovered in a National Institutes of Health (NIH) survey of AIDS and other sexually transmitted diseases (Marshall, 2000). Eleven months into the study, a data-collection manager was troubled by the apparent overproductivity of one interviewer. A closer look revealed that, although the worker was submitting completed interviews, some were clearly falsified. For example, the address of one interview site turned out to be an abandoned house. The worker was dismissed, and others came under suspicion. It took months to root out what was referred to as an "epidemic of falsification" on this research project. A cessation of random quality checks was identified as a major contributing factor to the problem.

Falsified data is believed to be rare, but survey organizations take this problem seriously and follow established procedures to address it. Factors that contribute to falsification include pressure on interviewers to obtain very high response rates and the use of long, complicated questionnaires that may frustrate both interviewer and respondent. The problem can be prevented by careful recruitment, screening, and training of interviewers; by recognizing incentives for falsification created by work quotas and pay structures; and by monitoring and verifying interviewer work (Bushery et al., 1999).

Diversity and the Interview Relationship

Many respondents in surveys have different characteristics than those of the interviewers. Does it make a difference in terms of the quantity or quality of data collected? It appears that it does. In survey research, three elements interact to affect the quality of the data collected: (1) the characteristics of the interviewer, (2) the characteristics of the respondent, and (3) the content of the survey instrument. Researchers should carefully consider the interrelationships among these elements to ensure that the least amount of bias enters the data-collection process.

As we have emphasized, an interview is a social relationship in which the interviewer and the respondent have cultural and subcultural expectations for appropriate behavior. One set of expectations that comes into play is the social desirability of respondents' answers to questions. Substantial research documents a tendency for people to choose more desirable or socially acceptable answers to questions in surveys (DeMaio, 1984; Holstein & Gubrium, 2003), in part from the desire to appear sensible, reasonable, and pleasant to the interviewer. In all interpersonal contacts, including an interview relationship, people typically prefer to please rather than offend or alienate. For cases in which the interviewer and the respondent are from different racial, ethnic, or sexual groups, respondents tend to give answers that they perceive to be more desirable—or, at least, less offensive—to the interviewer; this is especially true when the questions are related to racial, ethnic, or sexual issues. A second set of expectations that comes into play and affects responses during interviews is the social distance between the interviewer and the respondent, or how much they differ from each other on important social dimensions, such as age or minority status. Generally, the less social distance between people, the more freely, openly, and honestly they will talk. Racial, sexual, and ethnic differences often indicate a degree of social distance.

The impact of cross-race interviewing has been studied extensively with African-American and white respondents (Anderson, Silver, & Abramson, 1988; Bachman & O'Malley, 1984; Dailey & Claus, 2001; Gibson & Abrams, 2003). African-American respondents, for example, express more warmth and closeness for whites when interviewed by a white person and are less likely to express dissatisfaction or resentment over discrimination or inequities against African Americans. White respondents tend to express more pro-black attitudes when the interviewer is African American. This race-of-interviewer effect can be quite large, and it occurs fairly consistently. Some research concludes that it plays a role mostly when the questions involve race or other sensitive topics, but recent research suggests that its effect is more pervasive, affecting people's responses to many questions on a survey, not just the racial or sensitive questions (Davis, 1997).

Issues with respect to differences between researchers and interviewees are not limited to African Americans and whites. Many recent studies have revealed that differences with respect to ethnicity, cultural identity, nation of origin, socioeconomic status, and age impact researchers' access to many types of populations and their abilities to gain participants' trust and discuss a variety of issues (Arean et al., 2003; Becerra & DeAnda, 1999; Clark, 2006; Hyman, 1954; Manderson, Bennett, & Andajani-Sutjahjo, 2006).

Innes (2009), for example, found that being a Plains Cree tribal member gave him unique access to Native American research subjects, helped him develop trust with other tribal members and also increased participants' interest in his research. Alternatively, some researchers have argued that being "outsiders" and acknowledging lack of cultural knowledge within an interview can elicit more detailed responses from questions, minimize respondents' fears of researchers, allow researchers to ask sensitive questions that insiders may be expected to avoid, and help maintain critical distance between the researcher and the subject matter (Tinker & Armstrong, 2008).

Many researchers have argued that gender dynamics are always present within research interviews (Gibson & Abrams, 2003; Pini, 2005). Pini explains that when analyzing interviews, it is critical to consider not only the genders of the interviewer and respondent, but also their age, topics being discussed, and physical settings. In her study of Australian cane growers, for example, she found that when young, female graduate students interviewed male farmers in very rural areas where there are often few women, the interviews tended to portray the men in ways that exaggerated their masculinity. Another study (Wilson et al., 2002) found that men were less likely to report sex with strangers when interviewed by women than when interviewed by men. The study also found that women were less likely to report oral sex to older interviewers.

Some researchers recommend routinely matching interviewer and respondent for race, ethnicity, or gender in interviews on racial or sensitive topics, and this generally is sound advice. Sometimes, however, a little more thought is called for. The problem is that we are not always sure in which direction bias might occur. If white respondents give different answers to white as opposed to black interviewers, which of their answers most accurately reflect their attitudes? For the most part, we aren't sure. We generally assume that same-race interviewers gather more accurate data (Fowler & Mangione, 1990). A more conservative assumption, however, is that the truth falls somewhere between the data that the two interviewers of different race collect.

When minorities speak a language different from that of the dominant group, conducting the interview in the dominant group's language can affect the quality of data collected (Marin & VanOss, 1991). For example, a study of Native-American children in Canada found that these children expressed a strong white bias in racial preferences when the study was conducted in English; however, this bias declined significantly when interviewers used the children's native Ojibwa language (Annis & Corenblum, 1986). This impact of language should not be surprising, considering that language is not just a mechanism for communication but also reflects cultural values, norms, and a way of life. So when interviewing groups in which a language other than English is widely used, it is appropriate to consider conducting the interviews in that other language.

An Assessment of Interviews

Advantages. Personal interviews have several advantages compared with other data-collection techniques. First, interviews can help *motivate* respondents to give more accurate and complete information. Respondents have little motivation to be accurate or complete when responding to a mailed questionnaire; they can hurry through it if they want to. The control that an interviewer affords, however, encourages better responses, which is especially important as the information sought becomes more complex.

Second, interviewing offers an opportunity to *explain* questions that respondents may not otherwise understand. Again, if the information being sought is complex, then this can be of great importance, and interviews virtually eliminate the literacy problem that may accompany mailed questionnaires. Even lack of facility in English can be handled with multilingual interviewers. (When we conducted a needs assessment survey in some rural parts of Michigan's Upper Peninsula several years ago, we employed one interviewer who was fluent in Finnish, because a number of people in the area spoke Finnish but little or no English.)

Third, the presence of an interviewer allows *control* over factors that are uncontrollable with mailed questionnaires. For example, the interviewer can ensure not only that the proper person responds to the questions, but also that he or she does so in sequence. Furthermore, the interviewer can arrange to conduct the interview so that the respondent does not consult with and is not influenced by other people before responding.

Fourth, interviewing is a more *flexible* form of data collection than questionnaires. The style of interviewing can be tailored to the needs of the study. A free, conversational style, with much probing, can be adopted in an exploratory study. In a more developed study, a highly structured approach can be used. This flexibility makes interviewing suitable for a far broader range of research situations compared with mailed questionnaires.

Finally, the interviewer can add *observational information* to the responses. What was the respondent's attitude toward the interview? Was he or she cooperative? Indifferent? Hostile? Did the respondent appear to fabricate answers? Did he or she react emotionally to some questions? This additional information helps us better evaluate the responses, especially when the subject matter is highly personal or controversial (Gorden, 1987).

Disadvantages. Some disadvantages associated with personal interviews may lead the researcher to choose another data-collection technique. The first disadvantage is cost. Researchers must hire, train, and equip interviewers and also pay for their travel. All these expenses are costly.

The second limitation is time. Traveling to respondents' homes requires a lot of time and limits each interviewer to only a few interviews each day. In addition, to contact particular individuals, an interviewer may require several time-consuming call-backs. Project start-up operations, such as developing questions, designing schedules, and training interviewers, also require considerable time.

A third limitation of interviews is the problem of interviewer bias. Especially in unstructured interviews, the interviewers may misinterpret or misrecord something because of their personal feelings about the topic. Furthermore, just as the interviewer's characteristics affect the respondent, so the characteristics of the respondent similarly affect the interviewer. Sex, age, race, social class, and a host of other factors may subtly shape the way in which the interviewer asks questions and interprets the respondent's answers.

A fourth limitation of interviews, especially less structured interviews, is the possibility of significant but unnoticed variation in wording either from one interview to the next or from one interviewer to the next. We know that variations in wording can produce variations in response, and the more freedom interviewers have in this regard, the more of a problem this is. Wording variation can affect both reliability and validity (see Chapter 5).

TELEPHONE SURVEYS

Face-to-face interviews tend to be a considerably more expensive means of gathering data than either mailed questionnaires or telephone surveys (Rea & Parker, 2005). As Tables 4.3 (p. 95) and 7.4 show, face-to-face interviews can be more than twice as expensive as phone or mail surveys. The tables show that face-to-face interviews incur substantially higher costs for locating residences, contacting respondents, conducting interviews, traveling, and training interviewers. Mail or telephone surveys require no travel time, fewer interviewers, and fewer supervisory personnel. Although telephone charges are higher in telephone surveys, these costs are far outweighed by other savings. The cost advantages of the less-expensive types of surveys make feasible much research that otherwise would be prohibitively expensive.

The speed with which a telephone survey can be completed also makes it preferable at times. If we want people's reactions to a particular event, for example, or repeated measures of public opinion, which can change rapidly, then the speed of telephone surveys makes them preferable in these circumstances.

Certain areas of the country and many major cities contain substantial numbers of non–English

TABLE 7.4 An Illustrative Budget for Conducting Mail and Telephone Surveys of 400 People (for comparison, a budget for a similar face-to-face interview is displayed in Table 4.3, p. 95)

A. Mail Survey:

ELEMENTS OF THE SURVEY	COST	PERCENTAGE OF TOTAL
Materials for Survey: cover letter, printed questionnaires; address list (sampling frame)	$100	2%
Interviewer Training Sessions:	$0	0%
Conduct Interview: Mailing Costs: envelopes (2 per survey); addressing envelopes; postage for 2 mailings (mail-out and return); postage for 2 follow-up mailings	$1,500	27%
Conduct Interview:	$0	0%
Clerical and Data Entry Tasks: scan data into an electronic data file (15 minutes per interview at $10 per hour)	$1,000	18%
Professional Supervision: coordinating and supervising all of the above tasks (100 hours at $60,000 total annual compensation)	$3,000	53%
TOTAL:	**$5,600**	**100%**

B. Telephone Survey:

ELEMENTS OF THE SURVEY	COST	PERCENTAGE OF TOTAL
Materials for Interview: sampling frame of phone numbers, RDD, interviewer manuals; software to conduct survey	$1,000	9%
Interviewer Training Sessions: 12-hour training session, wages for trainer and interviewers	$2,400	21%
Conduct Interview:	$0	0%
Conduct Interview: 50 minutes per completed questionnaire; telephone charges	$5,000	44%
Clerical and Data Entry Tasks:	$0	0%
Professional Supervision: coordinating and supervising all of the above tasks (100 hours at $60,000 total annual compensation)	$3,000	26%
TOTAL:	**$11,400**	**100%**

speaking people. These people are difficult to accommodate with mailed questionnaires and personal interviews unless we know ahead of time what language a respondent speaks. We can handle non–English speaking people fairly easily, however, with telephone surveys. All we need are a few multilingual interviewers. (Spanish speakers account for the vast majority of non–English speaking people in the United States.) If an interviewer contacts a non–English speaking respondent, then he or she can simply transfer that respondent to an interviewer who is conversant in the respondent's language. Although multilingual interviewers can be—and are—used in personal interviews, this process is far less efficient, probably involving at least one callback to arrange for an interviewer with the needed language facility. A final advantage of telephone interviews is that supervision is much easier. The problem of interviewer falsification is eliminated, because supervisors can monitor the interviews at any time. This makes it easy to ensure that specified procedures are followed and any problems that might arise are quickly discovered and corrected.

Despite these considerable advantages, telephone surveys have several limitations that may make the method unsuitable for many research purposes. First, telephone surveys must be quite short in duration. Normally, the maximum length is about 20 minutes, and most are even shorter. This is in sharp contrast to personal interviews, which can last for an hour or longer. The time limitation obviously restricts the volume of information that interviewers can obtain and the depth to which they can explore issues. Telephone surveys work best when the information desired is fairly simple and the questions are uncomplicated.

A second limitation stems from the fact that telephone communication is only voice to voice. Lack of visual contact eliminates several desirable characteristics of personal interviews. The interviewer cannot supplement responses with observational information, for example, and it is harder for an interviewer to probe effectively without seeing the respondent. Furthermore, a phone interview precludes the use of cards with response alternatives or other visual stimuli. The inability to present complex sets of response alternatives in this format can make it difficult to ask some questions that are important.

Finally, as we noted in Chapter 6, surveys based on samples drawn from listings of telephone numbers may have considerable noncoverage, because some people do not have telephones at all, others have unlisted numbers, and still others have cell phones, which may have unlisted numbers and are not linked to specific geographic locations, such as a household. In addition, some people today have both a cell phone (sometimes more than one) and a landline; this means that, even with random-digit dialing, people with multiple phones have a greater likelihood of being selected for a sample than those with only one phone (or no phone). Although modern telephone sampling techniques, such as random-digit dialing, eliminate some problems, sampling bias remains a potential problem when using telephone numbers as a sampling frame. Because some human service clients are heavily concentrated in the population groups that are more likely to be missed in a telephone sample, we should exercise special care when using a telephone survey. The Eye on Ethics section discusses some ethical considerations that arise when surveying people on their cell phones.

Computer-mediated communications technologies now assist survey research through **computer-assisted interviewing** (CAI), or using computer technology to assist in designing and conducting questionnaires and interviews. One important form this takes is **computer-assisted telephone interviewing** (CATI), where an interview is conducted over the telephone: In CATI, the interviewer reads questions from a computer monitor instead of a clipboard and records responses directly into the computer via the keyboard instead of a paper form. Superficially, CATI replaces the paper-and-pencil format of interviewing with a monitor-and-keyboard arrangement, but the differences are much more significant. Some of the special techniques possible with CATI include personalizing the wording of questions based on answers to previous questions and automatic branching for contingency questions. These features speed up the interview and improve accuracy. CATI software enters the data from respondents directly into a data file for analysis. CATI programs help prevent errors from entering the data during the collection phase. For example, with a question that requires numerical data, such as "How old are you?" the program can require that only numerical characters be entered. Range checks also catch errors. Assuming one is interviewing adults, the age range might be set to 18 to 99 years. Any response outside that range would result in an error message or a request to recheck the entry.

> **EYE ON ETHICS**   Ethical Use of Cell Phones in Survey Research
>
> New technologies create new challenges for researchers, sometimes in terms of conducting ethical research. In Chapter 6, we discussed the implications of cell phones for sampling in survey research. These new technologies also introduce some important ethical considerations to be addressed by researchers who contact survey respondents on the respondent's cell phone (Lavrakas et al., 2007). First, people sometimes answer their cell phones when they are engaging in actions that are made more difficult or dangerous by talking on the phone, such as driving a car or operating harmful machinery. In some localities, talking on a cell phone while driving is illegal. Since the survey researcher is initiating the call, he or she incurs some ethical responsibility for possibly increasing the difficulties of the respondents. One way to handle this would be to not contact people on cell phones; however, as we saw in Chapter 6, this would have significant ramifications for the representativeness of samples. So, another option is to ask, after a brief introduction, if respondents are in a safe and relaxed environment where they can adequately respond to the questions. The downside of this strategy, of course, is that it gives the respondent a readymade excuse to refuse to participate. But other things being equal, ethical considerations would take precedence over concerns about response rate.
>
> Another ethical concern is that calling a cell phone may incur a cost to the recipient if the cell phone contract requires a charge for each call received. This can be handled by offering to reimburse the recipient for the charge.
>
> A third ethical concern is that people often answer cell phones in public places, and this may impact on their ability to keep their responses private and confidential. Once again, this can be handled by asking respondents if they are in a location where they feel comfortable answering questions.
>
> Finally, federal regulations control the use of cell phones, and researchers need to be careful not to violate them. For example, some interpretations of these regulations suggest that you are prohibited from using "mechanical dialers" to call cell phones unless the person has given prior consent to being called. Many researchers do use such devices when doing Random Digit Dialing with large samples (see Chapter 6). This problem can be avoided by manually calling the cell phone numbers, but this increases time and cost. It also may have an impact on respondent cooperativeness because some cell phone owners believe that such mass phone contacts are completely prohibited.

ONLINE SURVEYS

The emergence of the Internet has led to the growth of surveys conducted online rather than in person, through the mail, or by telephone. "Internet surveys," or "web surveys," sometimes are sent as email or an email attachment or are made available at a website. Online surveys are similar to other surveys in many respects, in that the basic data still involves people's answers to questions. The differences, however, are sufficiently important that they need to be discussed.

Online surveys have many advantages. Among the major advantages are their speed, low cost, and ability to reach respondents anywhere in the world (Fricker & Schonlau, 2002; Schonlau et al., 2004). Most studies find that compared with mailed or telephone surveys, online surveys can be done much less expensively and the responses are returned much more quickly.

Another advantage of online surveys is the versatility and flexibility offered by the technology. The questionnaire text can be supplemented with a variety of visual and auditory elements, such as color, graphics, images (static and animated), and even sound (Couper, Tourangeau, & Kenyon, 2004). (This is discussed in Chapter 13 as a measurement issue.) The technology also can provide randomized ordering of questions for each respondent, error checking, and automatic skip patterns so that respondents can move easily through the interview. In addition, the data can be entered directly into a database once the respondent submits it.

The anonymity and impersonal nature of online interaction also may have advantages in research. For example, in this chapter we discuss the problem of interviewer effects; that is, how interviewer characteristics—such as race or gender—and behavior may influence people's responses to questions. When answering questions online, there is no interviewer to produce such effects (Duffy et al., 2005). Similarly, the absence of an interviewer reduces the impact of social desirability; that is, respondents' concerns about how their responses appear to other people. Researchers may even find computer surveys to be a more ethical approach in terms of minimizing the harm associated with revealing sensitive data, such as child maltreatment (Black & Ponirakis, 2000). It also provides a good way to contact and collect data from groups that are difficult to access in other ways, possibly because they are relatively rare in the population or because of their involvement in undesirable or deviant interests or activities (Duffy et al., 2005; Koch & Emrey, 2001). In fact, people seem to be more likely to admit their involvement in undesirable activities during online surveys compared with other types of surveys.

Online surveys also have their disadvantages, of course. Sampling and representativeness are especially problematic (Duffy et al., 2005; Kaplowitz, Hadlock, & Levine, 2004; Schonlau et al., 2004). One problem is that not everyone has access to or actually uses the Internet. A second problem is that, even among those with Internet access, not everyone chooses to respond to requests to fill out an online survey. Given these problems, some argue that online surveys should be considered to be convenience samples rather than probability samples, with all the limitations in statistical analysis and generalizability that this implies (see Chapter 6). The population of people who use the Internet tends to be skewed toward those who are affluent, well-educated, young, and male. So, unless the research has a clearly defined population, all of whose members have access to and actually use the Internet, questions about the representativeness of online respondents are difficult to resolve. Even with a clearly defined population and sampling frame, nonresponse can significantly distort results. For example, an online survey of the faculty members at a university probably would involve a population where all members have Internet access; however, it may be the younger faculty or those from particular academic disciplines who are most likely to respond. Thus, researchers need to scrutinize the issues of response rate and representativeness, just as they do with other types of surveys. For needs assessment surveys, however, and some kinds of qualitative research where probability samples are not critical, researchers may find online surveys quite useful.

Strategies are being developed to deal with these problems of sampling and representativeness. One approach uses the random selection of telephone numbers to identify a probability sample of people who are representative of a particular population. These people are then contacted and asked to participate. Those who agree are supplied with Internet equipment and an Internet service connection (or they can use their own equipment). This panel of study members can then be repeatedly contacted by email and directed to a website to complete a survey. (Knowledge Networks is one organization that does this: http://www.knowledgenetworks.com.)

Another difficulty with online surveys is formatting: Different computer systems can change formatting in unpredictable ways. A survey that looks fine on the designer's computer screen may become partially unintelligible when emailed to a respondent's computer. Or, a web browser may not support all the design features in some web page design software. Earlier in this chapter, we mentioned the importance of survey appearance in terms of achieving high response rates and gathering complete and valid responses. If respondents with various computers receive differently formatted surveys, this may influence their willingness to participate or their responses (and introduce error into the measurement).

FOCUS GROUPS

Research situations sometimes arise in which the standardization found in most surveys and interviews is not appropriate and researchers need more flexibility in the way they elicit responses to questions. One area in which this is likely to be true is exploratory research. Here researchers cannot formulate questions into precise hypotheses, and the knowledge of some phenomena is too sketchy to allow precise measurement of variables. This also is true in research on personal and subjective experiences that are unlikely to be adequately tapped by asking the same structured questions of everyone.

In such research situations, the **focus group**, or **group depth interview**, is a flexible strategy for gathering data (Krueger & Casey, 2008; Morgan, 1996). As the name implies, this is an interview with a whole group of people at the same time. Focus groups originally were used as a preliminary step in the research process to generate quantitative hypotheses and develop questionnaire items, and they are still used in this way. Survey researchers, for example, sometimes use focus groups as tools for developing questionnaires and interview schedules. Now, however, researchers also use focus groups in applied research as a strategy for collecting data in their own right, especially when the researchers are seeking people's subjective reactions and the many levels of meaning that are important to human behavior. Today, tens of millions of dollars are spent each year on focus groups in applied research, marketing research, and political campaigns. One example of this is a study of the barriers that women confront in obtaining medical care to detect and treat cervical cancer, a potentially fatal disease that is readily detected and treated if women obtain Pap smears on a regular basis and return for follow-up care when necessary. These researchers decided that a focus group "would allow free expression of thoughts and feelings about cancer and related issues" and would provide the most effective mechanism to probe women's motivations for not seeking appropriate medical care (Dignan et al., 1990, p. 370).

A focus group usually consists of at least one moderator and up to 10 respondents, and it lasts for up to three hours. The moderator follows an interview guide that outlines the main topics of inquiry and the order in which they will be covered, and he or she may have a variety of props, such as audiovisual cues, to prompt discussion and elicit reactions. Researchers select focus group members on the basis of their usefulness in providing the data called for in the research. Researchers chose the women for the study on cervical cancer, for example, because, among other things, all had had some previous experience with cancer. Normally, focus group membership is not based on probability samples, which Chapter 6 points out as the most likely to be representative samples. This, therefore, can throw the generalizability of focus group results into question. In exploratory research, however, such generalizability is not as critically important as it is in other research. In addition, most focus group research enhances its representativeness and generalizability by collecting data from more than one focus group. The cervical cancer study, for example, involved four separate focus groups of 10 to 12 women each, and some research projects use 20 or more focus groups.

The moderator's job in a focus group is to initiate discussion and facilitate the flow of responses. Following an outline of topics to cover, he or she asks questions, probes unclear areas, and pursues lines of inquiry that seem fruitful. A focus group, however, is not just 10 in-depth interviews. Rather, the moderator uses knowledge of group dynamics to elicit data that an interviewer might not have obtained during an in-depth interview. For example, a status structure emerges in all groups, including focus groups; some people become leaders and others followers. The moderator uses this group dynamic by encouraging the emergence of leaders and then using them to elicit responses, reactions, or information from other group members. Group members often respond to other group members differently than they respond to the researcher/moderator. People in a focus group make side comments to one another—something obviously not possible in a one-person interview—and the moderator makes note of these comments, possibly encouraging group members to elaborate. In fact, in a well-run focus group, the members may interact among themselves as much as they do with the group moderator. In a standard interview, the stimulus for response is the interviewer's questions; in contrast, focus group interviews provide a second stimulus for people's responses—namely, the group experience itself.

The moderator also directs the group discussion, usually from more general topics in the beginning to more specific issues toward the end (Krueger & Casey, 2008). For example, in the focus group study of cervical cancer, the moderators began with questions about general life concerns and the perceived value of health, and ended with specific questions about cancer, cancer screening, and Pap smears. The general questions provided a foundation and a context, without which the women might not have been as willing—or as able—to provide useful answers to the more specific questions. Group moderators take great care in developing these sequences of questions. The moderator also observes the characteristics of the participants in the group to ensure effective participation by all members. For example, the moderator constrains a "rambler" who talks a lot but doesn't say much, and encourages "shy ones" who tend to say little to express themselves. In short, moderating a focus group is a complex job that calls for both an understanding of group dynamics and skills in understanding and working with people.

During a focus group session, too much happens too fast to engage in any useful data analysis on the spot. The focus group produces the data, which are preserved on videotape or a tape recording for later analysis. During this analysis, the researcher makes field notes from the recordings and then prepares a report summarizing the findings and presenting conclusions and implications. Data from a focus group usually are presented in one of three forms (Krueger & Casey, 2008). In the *raw data format*, the researcher presents all the comments that group participants made about particular issues, thus providing the complete range of opinions the group expressed. The researcher offers little interpretation other than to clarify some nonverbal interaction or nuance of meaning that could be grasped only in context. The second format for presentation is the *descriptive approach*, in which the researchers summarize in narrative form the kinds of opinions expressed by the group, with some quotes from group members as illustrations. This calls for more summary on the part of the researcher, but it also enables him or her to cast the results in a way that best conveys the meaning communicated during the group session. The third format is the *interpretive model*, which expands on the descriptive approach by providing more interpretation. The researcher can provide his or her own interpretations of the group's mood, feelings, and reactions to the questions. This may include the moderator's impression of the group members' motivations and unexpressed desires. The raw data model is the quickest manner of reporting results, but the interpretive model provides the greatest depth of information from the group sessions. Of course, the interpretive approach, because it does involve interpretation, is more likely to exhibit some bias or error.

Focus groups have major advantages over more structured, single-person interviews: The focus groups are more flexible, cost less, and can provide quick results. In addition, focus groups use the interaction between people to stimulate ideas and to encourage group members to participate. In fact, when run properly, focus groups have high levels of participation and, thus, elicit reactions that interviewers might not have obtained in a one-on-one interview setting. Unfortunately, focus groups also have disadvantages: The results are less generalizable to a larger population, and the data are more difficult and subjective to analyze. Focus groups also are less likely than interviews to produce quantitative data; in fact, focus group data may more closely resemble the field notes that are produced in field research, which we will discuss in Chapter 9.

PRACTICE AND RESEARCH INTERVIEWS COMPARED

The interview is undoubtedly the most commonly employed technique in human service practice. Therefore, it is natural for students in the human services to wonder how research interviewing compares with practice interviewing. The fundamental difference is the *purpose* of the interview. Practitioners conduct interviews to help a particular client, whereas researchers conduct interviews to gain knowledge about a particular problem or population. The practitioner seeks to understand the client as an individual, and often uses the interview to effect change; the researcher uses the data collected

> **INFORMATION TECHNOLOGY IN RESEARCH** — **Survey Design and Data Collection**
>
> An ever-expanding array of online survey tools is now available to researchers. A quick web search with the term "online surveys" generates a substantial list of websites promising quick, easy survey design and delivery that any novice can use to gather data and report results. At the other end of the spectrum are sophisticated survey sites which are relied upon by universities, research centers, and major corporations for survey design, delivery, analysis, and reporting. Examples of organizations offering extensive survey tools include Qualtrics (**https://www.qualtrics.com**), Survey Methods (**https://www.surveymethods.com**), and QuestionPro (**http://www.questionpro.com**).
>
> Our experience has been primarily with Qualtrics, but many of the features described here are common to other providers as well. Modern web-based survey organizations go beyond simply permitting a researcher to post survey questions on a website; they provide tools and services that cover the entire research process, including survey instrument design, sample selection, question delivery, data gathering, data analysis, and report generation and dissemination. Because they can incorporate all the media of the Internet, in addition to questions in text form, they employ audio and video presentations to elicit responses. Participants may record answers by typing words, clicking radio buttons, or manipulating a slide image among other means.
>
> To aid researchers in survey design, a question library is available. During the design process, the researcher can select individual questions or blocks of questions with a mouse click. In addition to drawing on hundreds of standard questions, researchers can store their own questions as they develop them for use in future surveys and use a survey they have created as a template for future surveys. Many different question formats are available. Once the survey has been developed, it can be printed for completion by hand, but completion online is generally preferred to take advantage of the full range of web features.
>
> For example, the practice of using the concept of contingency questions, or "skip-logic," is especially applicable to web surveys. The web survey only displays those questions that are relevant to a respondent based upon previous answers. As respondents progress through the survey, they need not deal with irrelevant items or be depended upon to follow directions such as "If your answer to question 5 was X, then go to Section 7." Similarly, individual answer options that are irrelevant to certain respondents can be dropped from the display, which simplifies and speeds up completion by the respondent. Response choices and blocks of questions can also be randomized to help detect and avoid bias due to response order. If the researcher wishes to imbed an experiment in the survey (such as comparing the effect of a question worded in two different ways), a simple menu choice within the program results in respondents' randomly getting one question version or the other.
>
> An obvious advantage of online surveys is that the data are stored directly in a database without the need for manual data entry. However, these programs not only store data, they can generate instant statistical analyses, including graphs and charts, and enable the user to distribute the results via the web or in printed reports. The data can also be downloaded for analysis with statistical software programs such as SPSS. Survey quality control is also facilitated because the program can provide overall survey statistics, such as drop-out rates, average response time per question, completion percentages, and start times. These are only some of the features that make web-based surveys so appealing. More in-depth coverage of web survey methodology can be found at the Qualtrics website under "Qualtrics University."
>
> For those situations where respondents have access to the Internet, such as many business organization and educational settings, online services are ideal. However, the temptation to employ web-based research because of ease of use, power, rapid results, and visual appeal can generate misleading results if a significant part of the population being studied lacks Internet access.

on individuals to describe the characteristics of and variations in a population. To the practitioner, the individual client system is central. To the researcher, the respondent is merely the unit of analysis, and the characteristics and variability of the population are of primary concern.

The difference in purpose is the basis for the differences between practice and research interviewing. Whereas we select *respondents* to represent a population, we accept *clients* because they have individual needs that the agency serves. Research interviews typically are brief (often single encounters);

practice relationships are often intensive, long-term relationships. Clients (or clients' needs) often determine the topic and focus of a practice interview, whereas the nature of the research project predetermines the content of the research interview. The ideal research interview presents each respondent with exactly the same stimulus to obtain validly comparable responses. The ideal practice interview provides the client with a unique situation that maximizes the potential to help that individual.

An emphasis on the differences between the two forms of interviewing, however, should not obscure their similarities. Both require that the interviewer make clear the general purpose of the interview. Both require keen observational skills and disciplined use of self according to the purpose of the interview. This last point is crucial to answering another question about interviewing: Do practitioners make good research interviewers? The answer depends on the nature of the particular interview task and on the interviewer's capacity to perform that task. Interviewers who display warmth, patience, compassion, tolerance, and sincerity best serve some situations; other situations require reserved and controlled interviewers who bring an atmosphere of objective, detached sensitivity to the interview (Kadushin & Kadushin, 1997). Some researchers have found that verbal reinforcement—both positive comments to complete responses and negative feedback to inadequate responses—results in obtaining more complete information from respondents (Vinokur, Oksenberg, & Cannell, 1979). Although successful in terms of amount of information gained, such techniques might be foreign to the style of interviewing that a practitioner uses. Thus, for the structured, highly controlled interview, a practitioner who is used to improvising questions and demonstrating willingness to help may be a poor choice as an interviewer. In situations requiring in-depth, unstructured exploratory interviews, however, that same practitioner's skills might be ideal. Again, the purpose of the interview and the nature of the task determine the compatibility of human service skills with the research interview.

REVIEW AND CRITICAL THINKING

Main Points

- Surveys are of two general types: (1) questionnaires completed directly by respondents, and (2) interviews with the questions read and the responses recorded by an interviewer.
- Closed-ended questions provide a fixed set of response alternatives from which respondents choose.
- Open-ended questions provide no response alternatives, leaving respondents complete freedom of expression.
- Once developed, survey instruments should be pretested for clearly understood and unbiased questions; after changes are made in the instrument, it should be pretested again.
- Questionnaires must provide clear directions, both to indicate what respondents should do and to guide them through the questionnaire.
- Researchers should order questions so that early questions maximize the response rate but do not affect the responses to later questions.
- Obtaining a high response rate (the percentage of surveys actually completed) is very important for representativeness in survey research.
- The cover letter, use of payments and follow-up letters, and length and appearance of the questionnaire are all central in efforts to maximize the response rate with the mailed questionnaire.
- Interviews are classified by their degree of structure as unstandardized, nonschedule-standardized, or schedule-standardized.

- Probes elicit clearer and more complete responses during interviews.
- Telephone surveys offer significant savings in terms of time and cost compared with interviews or mailed questionnaires and, in many cases, are a suitable alternative.
- Online surveys are fast and inexpensive compared to other surveys and permit flexible formatting and design, but they raise serious questions regarding sampling and representativeness.
- Focus groups rely on group dynamics to generate data that would not be discovered using a standard questionnaire or interview format.
- Websites are now widely available that will conduct surveys from beginning to end—from designing the survey instrument to the analysis of the data and the preparation of a report.

Important Terms for Review

closed-ended questions
computer-assisted interviewing
computer-assisted telephone interviewing
contingency question
cover letter
filter question
focus group
group depth interview
interview
interview schedule
interviewer falsification
matrix question
open-ended questions
probes
questionnaire
response rate
survey
survey research

Critical Thinking

The research techniques discussed in this chapter involve observations of what people say about the thoughts, feelings, or behaviors of themselves or others. This kind of research technique has advantages, but it also has drawbacks. Practitioners and policymakers, as well as people in their everyday lives, need to be cautious when confronted with information or conclusions based on similar data.

Consider the following:

1. Are the topic and the conclusions best addressed by what people say about their thoughts or behavior (a survey) or by direct observation? Is it legitimate to conclude something about people's behavior from what they have said?

2. What questions were asked and how were they asked? Do they contain any of the flaws that could produce bias or misinterpretation? Is there anything in their design (wording, context, etc.) that might lead to misunderstanding, misinterpretation, or bias in the information that results?

3. What about reactivity? Could the manner in which the information was gathered have influenced what people said?

4. What about sampling? Could the manner in which the information was gathered, such as by telephone, by cell phone, or online, have influenced who the observations were made on?

Exploring the Internet

Most major survey research centers maintain websites, and some of them are extremely useful. At many sites, you can find a basic overview of survey research, a discussion of ethics in surveys, and information on how to plan a survey. Some even provide the opportunity to examine questions used in actual surveys. It also is possible to download and read entire questionnaires and survey instruments.

By reviewing these surveys, you can explore how the researchers structured the instrument and ordered the questions, and you will see skip patterns and other features that enhance the research instrument's quality. Not only will you become more familiar with major survey projects around the world, you can learn a great deal about how to design good survey questions.

Here is a list of some worthwhile sites:
- The Odum Institute for Research in Social Science (http://arc.irss.unc.edu/dvn)
- The General Social Survey (http://www.norc.org/GSS+website)
- Courses in Applied Social Surveys (in England) (http://www.s3ri.soton.ac.uk/cass)
- American Association for Public Opinion Research (http://www.aapor.org)
- Survey Research Methods Section of the American Statistical Association (http://www.amstat.org/sections/SRMS)

Use the search engine on the web browser available to you to look for other survey research centers, such as these:
- UK Data Archive (http://www.data-archive.ac.uk).
- Statistics Canada (http://www.statcan.gc.ca).
- National Center for Health Statistics (http://www.cdc.gov/nchs/surveys.htm).

For Further Reading

Dillman, D. A., Smyth, J. D., & Christian, L. M. (2009). *Internet, Mail, and Mixed-Mode Surveys: The Tailored Design Method*, 3rd ed. New York: Wiley. This is an excellent introduction to survey research, and it also provides the most up-to-date overview of how to conduct surveys through the mail and on the Internet.

Gorden, R. (1992). *Basic Interviewing Skills*. Itasca, Ill.: Peacock. This useful how-to book on interviewing covers everything from developing questions to motivating good responses to evaluating respondents' nonverbal behavior.

Gubrium, J. F., & Holstein, J. A. (2001). *Handbook of Interview Research: Context and Method*. Thousand Oaks, Calif.: Sage. This complete handbook covers many forms of interviewing, including survey, qualitative, in-depth, and therapy. The book addresses technical issues, distinctive respondents, and analytic strategies.

Kadushin, A., & Kadushin, G. (1997). *The Social Work Interview: A Guide for Human Service Professionals*, 4th ed. New York: Columbia University Press. This is the standard text for social work interviewing. It covers all aspects of the helping interview, and it presents a solid comparison for the survey interview.

Krueger, R. A., & Casey, M. A. (2008). *Focus Groups: A Practical Guide for Applied Research*, 4th ed. Thousand Oaks, Calif.: Sage. This book is the standard for learning how to conduct a focus group. The fourth edition compares market research, academic, nonprofit, and participatory approaches to focus group research, and describes how to plan focus group studies and do the analysis, including step-by-step procedures.

Salant, P., & Dillman, D. (1994). *Conducting Surveys: A Step-by-Step Guide to Getting the Information You Need*. New York: Wiley. As the title states, this is a very useful guide to all the steps in conducting sound survey research.

Schuman, H., & Presser, S. (1996). *Questions and Answers in Attitude Surveys: Experiments on Question Form, Wording, and Content*. Thousand Oaks, Calif.: Sage. This is a comprehensive handbook on the rules, problems, and pitfalls of designing survey questions. It goes far beyond what this chapter is able to cover on this important topic.

Sue, V. M., & Ritter, L. A. (2012). *Conducting Online Surveys*, 2nd ed. Los Angeles: Sage. This volume is a comprehensive guide to the creation, implementation, and analysis of email and web-based surveys. The authors specifically address issues unique to online survey research such as selecting software, designing web-based questionnaires, and sampling from online populations.

Class Exercises for Competency Assessment

An article in the student newspaper reported that the Dean of Students Office estimated that over 50 students who failed to complete the winter term last year showed evidence of alcohol-related problems. (For example, some had asked for excused absence for being in-patients of the hospital substance abuse unit, some had been jailed for alcohol-related offenses, and others were injured in alcohol-related auto crashes). Campus safety reported a number of complaints involving intoxicated students in campus residence facilities. In addition to basic concern for the welfare of the campus community, the university administration recognizes that students who do not return to school or who perform poorly cost the university significant resources. The student government proposes the idea of a student designed and operated survey project to gain an accurate understanding of the issues. They argue that students will be more responsive to a student-run survey. You're on the team to develop a research proposal that can be submitted to the Dean of Students Office and the Office of Institutional Research for review. Assuming the proposal is approved, you will have a budget of $3,000 to conduct your study.

The following exercises explore some of the tasks and decisions you face in undertaking such a survey:

7.1. **[Critical Thinking] [Policy Practice]** Would you use mailed questionnaires, telephone surveys, personal interviews or a web-based format? Defend your choices. What additional information would help you make these decisions?

7.2. **[Research & Practice]** If the team decides to send a mailed questionnaire to students, what could you suggest to improve the response rate?

7.3. **[Critical Thinking] [Policy Practice]** One of the topics to cover is how much alcohol students consume. Write a closed-ended question and an open-ended question to deal with this topic. In your opinion, which type of question would be best?

7.4. **[Critical Thinking] [Research & Practice]** What would be the advantages and disadvantages of each of these interviewing formats: nonstandardized, nonschedule-standardized, or a schedule-standardized format?

7.5. **[Critical Thinking] [Research & Practice]** You have the task of selecting the interviewers to conduct face-to-face interviews with the students, and you have the following options: Dean of Students Office work-study employees, volunteers from a campus fraternity & sorority, interviewers from a political polling organization who are mostly middle-aged women; or graduate students in a social science research course from a nearby university. Which group would you pick, and why? What would be the advantages and disadvantages associated with each of these groups?

7.6. **[Critical Thinking] [Diversity]** Approximately 20 percent of the enrolled students are African Americans, and another 15 percent are Hispanic. What differences will the racial composition of this population make in terms of the way you suggest doing the study?

7.7. **[Critical Thinking] [Research & Practice]** The team develops a rough outline of the interview schedule. It includes the following general sections:

- Demographic data—age, gender, class, major, gpa, family income level, marital status
- Drinking behavior—frequency, amount consumed, how often intoxicated
- Last drinking event—amount consumed, setting, activity, consequences
- Problems related to drinking—missed classes, bad grades, problems with friends and family, health, etc.

How would you recommend ordering these sections? Why?

7.8. **[Ethics] [Critical Thinking] [Research & Practice]** Given the sensitive nature of this study, what steps could the team take to address the ethical issues of such a survey?

Chapter 8

✹

Analysis of Available Data

Statistical Data
   Sources of Statistical Data
   Using Statistical Data

Content Analysis
   Coding Schemes
   Units of Analysis
   Manifest versus Latent Coding

Issues in Content Analysis
   Validity
   Reliability
   Level of Measurement
   Sampling

Assessment of Available Data Analysis
   Advantages
   Disadvantages
   Using Available Data in Research on Minorities

Review and Critical Thinking
   Main Points
   Important Terms for Review
   Critical Thinking
   Exploring the Internet
   For Further Reading
   Class Exercises for Competency Assessment

Normally, researchers prefer to organize and direct the collection of the data themselves. This enables them to tailor the nature and form of the data collected to their research hypotheses and to the state of knowledge in the field (see Chapter 4). In some cases, however, this is far too costly and time-consuming. In other cases, it is either impractical or unnecessary. Consider, for example, a study by Deborah Wingard (1987) on the characteristics of adopted children and their parents in California. Wingard could have gotten a list of the children and their parents from agencies and then conducted mailed questionnaires or interviews. As we saw in Chapter 7, however, questionnaires suffer from nonresponse problems, and interviews are expensive. Furthermore, as a routine part of service delivery, adoption agencies gather information about the characteristics of children and both their birth and adoptive parents. So, in this case, Wingard did not need to collect data herself, because the data needed to test the hypotheses already existed in a computerized agency information file.

Data of this type are called **available data**: observations collected by someone other than the investigator for purposes that differ from the investigator's but that, nonetheless, are available. A vast array of this type of data exists for scientific analysis. In some cases, such data take the form of *statistical data,* or quantified observations of some element of human behavior. For example, various branches of government collect large amounts of statistical data and provide quantified information about crime, health, birth rates, death rates, and so on. *Documents* are another form of available data and refer, in their broadest sense, to any form of nonquantitative communication. Documents include such items as books, magazines, letters, memoranda, diaries, web pages, and other communication media, such as radio, television, movies, and plays. Documents also can make up a part of the records maintained by various institutions, such as military records, police records, court records, and social agency records. Some such records, of course, include both statistical and nonstatistical data.

Available data are a rich source for human service research, and sometimes are used in conjunction with data collected from other sources, such as surveys. Furthermore, researchers often can treat available data as if they were data the researchers had collected themselves. Wingard, for example, could work with the agency data much as she could have with survey data she collected. Available data, however, does present researchers with some new problems, and these problems are also covered in this chapter.

STATISTICAL DATA

Human service professionals often complain about the mountains of paperwork associated with the procedures of trying to help people, but the facts and figures that these procedures generate can be a rich source of data for research. Sometimes this agency data can be deficient in some critical respects when used as research data. However, an important contribution that research-knowledgeable human service professionals can make to both practice and research is to help develop data-collection procedures in agencies that generate useful statistical data. To make such a contribution, however, human service professionals must have an understanding of how researchers use available statistical data and what qualities enhance the usefulness of available data for research.

Sources of Statistical Data

Statistical data are collected for many reasons, and much of these data are available to human service researchers. First, some statistical data are collected as part of many research projects. Many research organizations, such as the Institute for Social Research at the University of Michigan or the Institute for Research on Poverty at the University of Wisconsin, collect large amounts of useful data that others may reanalyze with different research questions in mind. In this way, data collected for one project may be reanalyzed by a number of different people in the years that follow. Table 8.1 lists just a few of these data sets and describes the kinds of data they contain. This reanalysis of data collected for some other research project is called **secondary analysis** (Riedel, 2000; Sieber, 1991). Today, a number of national and international organizations have developed **data archives**, which are essentially libraries that lend or sell data sets much as libraries or bookstores lend or sell books (National Institutes of Health, 2012; Norwegian Social Science Data Services, 2012). Among the better known are the Inter-University Consortium of Political and Social Research (ICPSR) at the University of Michigan, the Roper Center at the University of Connecticut, and Networked Social Science Tools and Resources (NESSTAR). These organizations increasingly use the advantages of the web to make it easy to publish, locate, and access statistical data.

Some private organizations also have created data archives in specialized areas. The Sociometrics Corporation, for example, offers numerous data sets from studies focusing on adolescent pregnancy issues. Many individual researchers also make data

ANALYSIS OF AVAILABLE DATA 197

TABLE 8.1 Illustrations of Available Statistical Data Sets

Sample Data Sets	Location	Types of Data Available
Boston Police Department Domestic Violence Research	The National Archive of Criminal Justice Data (NACJD); http://www.icpsr.umich.edu/icpsrweb/NACJD and search for "Boston Police Department"	Criminal justice data collections for research and instruction are available. NACJD provides access to over 550 criminal justice data collections free of charge.
KIDS COUNT	The Annie E. Casey Foundation, Baltimore MD; http://datacenter.kidscount.org	This data set focuses on variables relating to the status of children and youth in society: infant mortality, infant and child health, teen pregnancy rates, suicide, school dropouts, and so on.
National Study of Protective, Preventive and Reunification Services Delivered to Children and Their Families, 1994	National Data Archive on Child Abuse and Neglect; http://www.ndacan.cornell.edu/ndacan/Datasets_List.html	The primary activity of the archive is the acquisition, preservation, and dissemination of high-quality data sets relevant to the study of child abuse and neglect.
Current Population Survey (CPS) and Public Use Microdata Samples (PUMS)	U.S. Census Bureau; http://www.census.gov or www.icpsr.umich.edu	The CPS is a national sample of households with data on labor force participation, employment status, income, education, and other variables. The PUMS are a variety of data sets based on a sampling of households that were included in the decennial census.

sets available to those with legitimate secondary uses for the data. Some funders of research, such as the National Science Foundation (NSF), now require that the data collected in research they fund eventually be delivered to a public archive as a stipulation for receiving research funds. Data collected for research purposes and available for secondary analyses tend to be of fairly high quality, because professional researchers collected them. Nonetheless, such data still suffer from some of the problems to be discussed shortly.

A second source of statistical data is the federal, state, and local human service agencies that collect data for either administrative or client service purposes. Community mental health centers, Head Start programs, departments of social services, and health and educational institutions are repositories of vast amounts of available data. For instance, for each suspected case of child abuse or neglect referred to the Department of Human Services (DHS) in Michigan, practitioners complete the form shown in Figure 8.1. The upper half provides space for various specific bits of case information, and the lower half provides a convenient coding scheme to ease the entry of information. Some of these data are quantitative—such as age of the client, number of prior referrals, and number of days the client is in foster care—and these variables are amenable to statistical manipulation. Agencies collect such data for many reasons that may have nothing to do with their eventual research purposes. Sometimes agencies are simply required by law to collect such information, which is then stored in data banks and may be available to researchers. The authors of this text combined the data on these forms with data from other organizational records in a study to assess the impact of a school social work program on the referral of cases of child abuse and neglect. Unfortunately, data from human service agencies often are not efficiently catalogued and indexed and, therefore, often are difficult for investigators to locate and use. Nonetheless, such data have grown to voluminous proportions over the decades. Research in Practice 8.1 gives further illustrations of agency records serving as a source of research data.

FIGURE 8.1 An Example of a Client Information Form Used in a Human Service Agency

> **RESEARCH IN PRACTICE 8.1** **Program Evaluation: Evaluating Outpatient Substance Abuse Treatment Services Using an Agency Database System**
>
> Human service agencies today generate enormous amounts of data as a byproduct of everyday service delivery. Great Lakes Recovery Center (GLRC), which provides both inpatient and outpatient substance abuse treatment services, is typical of this. GLRC uses a client database system that allows the agency to track clients' involvement in services from initial referrals to service termination. Secretaries begin this at the time of initial referral by creating case files as they receive service referrals. Intake workers then add to these files as they collect pertinent client information during intake interviews. Case managers add case notes to these electronic files summarizing adjustment issues clients are facing during their recovery and referrals made for services both inside and outside GLRC. Addiction counselors use the system to make therapeutic case notes, summarizing clients' progress in treatment. Administrators use these records to document services provided to justify reimbursements from insurance companies and other third-party payers. Administrators can also use these data to assess overall program performance and evaluate worker productivity. The extensive data required to trace the delivery of such extensive services and to evaluate outcomes can often only be found in data generated by the program itself.
>
> This system also gives GLRC administrators ready access to important agency data that can be helpful in program and policy decisions, such as creating new services and adjusting services to better serve clients and the surrounding community. Each year GLRC administrators distribute data to program managers and staff and ask them to interpret data pertaining to their programs. Managers and staff from each program create annual reports in which they present descriptive statistics on clients served, while also identifying important programmatic and client issues that have emerged over the year. These reports also allow managers and staff to reflect on trends within their programs and suggest service changes based on pressing concerns. A recent report made by the adult services unit, for example, revealed a rising number of clients who were veterans, which resulted in the agency's administrators applying for funds to create services tailored for veterans who may be experiencing PTSD or traumatic brain injuries, in addition to addictions. Another report by the youth unit revealed a sharp rise in the numbers of younger clients who have been victims of physical and or sexual trauma, which resulted in increased referrals for trauma counseling.
>
> Each year substance abuse treatment agencies like GLRC that receive federal funding are asked to submit program data to the Substance Abuse and Mental Health Services Administration's (SAMHSA) National Survey of Substance Abuse Treatment Services (NSSAT). GLRC's client database allows administrators to provide reliable survey data with relative ease (without having to compile counts from hard files). SAMHSA uses NSSAT data to identify particularly strong practice models and unmet service needs, and to make funding adjustments accordingly.
>
> GLRC's use of this database system illustrates the strong connection between human service practice and research. Collectively, individual client files constitute not only a client database, but also a source of data that can be used to create more effective services locally and nationally.
>
> (Based on personal interviews conducted in December 2011.)

A third source of statistical data is the organizations and governmental agencies that collect data as a public service or to serve as the basis for social policy decisions. The Federal Bureau of Investigation (FBI) and the National Center for Health Statistics, for example, collect vast amounts of data, as do state and local governments. The U.S. Census Bureau also collects enormous amounts of data to use for establishing and changing the boundaries of political districts and for allocating government funds that are based on population size. Often, researchers can use data from these sources in conjunction with other types of data—from questionnaires, for example, or from agency records—to test hypotheses. One study of caseworker accuracy hypothesized that the political and economic characteristics of the local community might influence caseworker errors (Piliavin, Masters, & Corbett, 1977). Data were based on interviews, questionnaires, and other sources. In addition, data from the U.S. Census Bureau measured the political and economic characteristics of each community regarding the percentage of poor people in the county, how the county voted in the most recent gubernatorial election, and the percentage of poor families headed by women. Thus, researchers can combine data from multiple sources to measure variables and test hypotheses in a single study.

Data collected by private organizations are distributed less widely than government statistics and, for that reason, may be more difficult to locate. Professional associations, such as the American Medical Association, the American Bar Association, and the National Association of Social Workers (NASW), produce statistics relating to their membership and issues of concern to their members. Additionally, research institutes and commercial polling firms also produce statistical data.

Using Statistical Data

When we use available statistical data, remember that most such data were not collected for research purposes—or at least not for the specific research questions for which we now intend to use them. They were compiled to meet the needs of whatever agency, organization, or researcher originally collected them, and the form in which the data were collected limits the analysis. This leads to some special problems that call for caution.

Missing Data. For a variety of reasons, a data set may not include complete data for every person studied or may fail to collect data from the entire population or sample of interest. For example, a person may refuse to answer certain questions, which results in a gap in his or her data set. Or, researchers may not have collected data in a particular neighborhood, which was considered too dangerous for interviewers to enter. Such gaps in a data set are referred to as **missing data**, and they appear, to some degree, in practically all studies. The problem when using available data files is that we have no control over this failure to collect a complete set of data. Missing data result in incomplete coverage, which, if extensive, throws into question the representativeness of the data. Furthermore, because statistical procedures are based on the assumption of complete data, missing data can result in misleading statistical conclusions. As we dig back into data from the past, it is not uncommon to find data for whole periods missing. This can occur for many reasons—such as data destroyed by fires, lost data, changes in policy, and the like. Finding data that cover only a portion of a target population also is quite common. For example, a study of changes in work-family conflict over time was based on statistical available data from two national surveys of adults, one done in 1977 and the other in 1997 (Nomaguchi, 2009). However, the sample in the 1977 survey did not include people who worked fewer than 20 hours per week. Although such people were included in the 1997 survey, they had to be excluded from the analysis since they were missing from the 1977 survey. These missing cases meant that conclusions about work-family conflict could be drawn only about those who work longer hours, and such people also tend to have more skilled jobs and are thus higher in socioeconomic status. So, when working with data that suffer from noncoverage, we should assess the implications of noncoverage for the results of the research.

Inductive versus Deductive Analysis. In research investigations that collect data firsthand, we commonly use a deductive approach. That is, hypotheses are deduced from a theory, variables in the hypotheses are operationally defined, and data are collected based on these operational definitions. In short, research moves from the abstract to the concrete: The theory and hypotheses we are testing determine the kind of data that we collect (see Chapter 2). In the analysis of available data, however, such a deductive approach often is impossible, because the data necessary to measure the variables derived from a theory may not have been included when the original data were collected. For example, a theory regarding

```
theories and hypotheses            modified theories and hypotheses
           ↓                                    ↑
  operational definitions      revised operational definitions
           ↓                           ↑
              data available
```

FIGURE 8.2 The Measurement Process with Available Statistical Data

caseworker effectiveness with clients might include the variable of the intensity of the casework relationship. Although intensity of relationship is a crucial concept in interpersonal helping, it is, unfortunately, not the type of variable that is included in routine agency data-collection procedures. In circumstances like this, it is not possible to operationalize the variable in the way that is most appropriate to the theory. If this difficulty is encountered, a compromise often is made. As we showed in Chapter 5, the measurement process often calls for modifying nominal and operational definitions (refer back to Figure 5.1). So, we revise operational definitions and, in some cases, hypotheses so we can test them with the data available (see Figure 8.2). In the example of caseworker effectiveness, we might measure intensity of relationship by looking at the amount of time a worker spent with a given client over the course of treatment, frequency of contacts, or duration of contacts. Although none of these variables may be the best measure for "intensity of relationship," we can readily derive them from the worker time sheets that are mandatory in many agencies. We may use total contact time, frequency of contact, duration of contact, or some combination of these, even though they are not thoroughly accurate measures of the variable of interest.

In other words, we modify our research to fit the data. When this occurs, research takes on a somewhat inductive character. In inductive research, we move from the concrete to the abstract: Starting with the data collected, we develop hypotheses and theories to explain what we find. The situation we have described is actually somewhere in between induction and deduction. We have begun with theories and hypotheses, but we also have had to let the available data influence how we test the hypotheses. This is a frequent problem in the analysis of available statistical data.

Validity. Recall from Chapter 5 that *validity* refers to whether a measurement instrument actually measures what it is intended to measure. Many data in existing statistical files are valid indicators of certain characteristics that they describe directly, such as age, sex, and racial profiles of clients, along with the amounts of different kinds of services provided. Validity problems, however, frequently arise in three areas.

First, many elements of agency operation, such as achievement of goals, success of programs, or satisfaction of clients, may not be measured directly by any data that are normally collected by an agency. To study these, we would have to search for indirect measures among the agency data that might enable us to infer such things as goal achievement, success, or satisfaction. These situations create the same kinds of validity problems that confront researchers using other methods, except that when we use available data we cannot consider and resolve validity problems *before* we collect the data. Because someone else has already collected the data, these problems are entrenched.

A second area in which validity problems frequently arise is data analysis that becomes inductive—that is, when we change operational definitions so we can measure variables with the

> **RESEARCH IN PRACTICE 8.2** **Policy Planning and Development: Hazards in Estimating the Crime Problem from Available Data**
>
> Combating crime is a key objective for many human service programs, whether it is running a neighborhood watch to increase safety for the elderly, providing late-night basketball for inner-city youths, or offering treatment groups for offenders. Whenever an organization embarks on an effort to design and implement a program like one of these, the planning process commonly requires that program planners demonstrate the need for the program by documenting the seriousness of the crime problem in a community. It is unlikely that most human service organizations have either the resources or the capacity to gather crime data themselves, so available data are an appealing alternative. As we noted in this chapter, one of the advantages of conducting research with available data is that somebody else paid to collect that data. It is, however, important to make serious inquiries about exactly how the data were collected and the numbers produced.
>
> The human service agency that uses available crime data faces several possible pitfalls. The Federal Bureau of Investigation (FBI) produces one of the most widely used sources of crime data. The Uniform Crime Reports (UCR) is published annually and is available in libraries and online (http://www.fbi.gov). On the surface, it might seem that data produced by an agency of the federal government, with all its authority and resources, would be reliable—and within limits, they are. Those limitations, however, can cause problems if they are not understood.
>
> One of the most basic questions about crime is: How much crime exists? The UCR data cannot answer even this apparently simple question well. For an event to be recorded as a crime in the UCR, it must come to the attention of some police official. In a minority of cases, police chance across a crime taking place, so it gets officially recorded. Most often, however, police must rely on citizens who are victimized by crime to report it—and herein lies one of the problems with the UCR data. A large percentage of even serious crime never gets reported to the police. A recent estimate by the Bureau of Justice Statistics suggests that only 40 to 50 percent of all violent and property crimes are reported to the police and make their way into the UCR data (Truman, 2011). Clearly, this reporting gap causes the UCR data to significantly understate the true impact of criminal activity in the United States.
>
> You may be wondering how such an estimate of unreported crime can be made. Another measure of criminal activity is the National Crime Victimization Survey (NCVS). The NCVS is conducted every year on a representative sample of more than 100,000 citizens, inquiring if they have been victims of crimes. The disparity between the NCVS data and the UCR data provides an indicator of the amount of crime that goes unreported by the UCR, and thus gives a clearer picture of the actual criminal activity. Another possible pitfall awaiting users of the UCR data is that reporting to the FBI is voluntary on the part of local law enforcement agencies, and this leads to a number of possible misinterpretations of the data. For example, researchers cannot compare different regions or localities and conclude with any certainty which area has the higher or the lower crime rate. Any differences noted might

available data. The more the definitions are changed, the more the validity of the measures is called into question. Sometimes, the operational definitions may be changed so drastically that they no longer measure the theoretical concepts they were first intended to measure.

Finally, validity questions arise when the procedures that an agency or organization uses in gathering data change over the years. Changing modes of collecting data, such as dropping some questions or developing new definitions of something, are quite common in any agency or organization. These procedural changes, however, can affect the comparability of data collected at various times and the validity of using the same operational definitions. Crime statistics are a good example. Researchers commonly use data from the Uniform Crime Reports (UCR) compiled by the FBI as a measure for the volume of crimes in the United States, and Research in Practice 8.2 explores some of the problems that can arise when using this particular set of data.

be real, or they might merely be differences in the willingness of local officials to report to the FBI.

A related problem confronts anyone who is interested in longitudinal analysis. Over the long history of the UCR, the percentage of police agencies that report their numbers has steadily increased. This, of course, means that any comparison over time has a built-in problem. Even if crime has not increased over time, it will appear to have increased because of the higher rate of reporting in more recent years.

Yet another problem stems from the fact that during the first several decades of the UCR, crime rates were computed not from updated population estimates, but from the most recent census count. The census is conducted only once every 10 years, and this meant that, for years, the basis for computing crime rates stayed the same for a decade until the numbers from a new census became available. Of course, however, a population does not remain stagnant and then suddenly explode every 10 years. The population steadily increases from year to year, meaning that there are more people to commit crimes and to become crime victims. Using the same census number to compute crime rates meant that apparent increases in crime from year to year were inevitable. Then, when a new census number was used, there would appear to be a substantial drop in crime. Obviously, this "drop" was not the result of a real decline in criminal activity, but rather of the census number used to compute the crime rate catching up with the population increase. This is no longer a problem with the UCR data, because the UCR now uses yearly population estimates, which are quite accurate, in computing the crime rates. It does, however, typify the kind of traps that may await the unsuspecting researcher using other people's data.

Finally, when working with data collected over a long period of time, such as the UCR data, an important question is this: Have definitions or categorizations changed over time that would hamper meaningful comparisons? Again, the UCR is illustrative. According to Barlow (1996), during the history of the UCR, the FBI's classification system for counting crime has changed several times. In fact, in 1979, the FBI added an additional crime, arson, to those that make up the "crime index"—that is, the crimes that are tracked and used to compute the general crime rate. In addition to arson, the index crimes are homicide, aggravated assault, sexual assault, robbery, burglary, larceny, and auto theft. Naturally, when arson was added to the index, it appeared that crime had suddenly—and dramatically—increased when, of course, the change in measurement primarily caused the change in the numbers.

As illustrated by the UCR data, a researcher who uses available data must be careful not to fall into possible traps hidden in that data. Such risks do not mean we should avoid available data, but rather that we should use such data with caution. For example, the UCR data are not without value, because they reflect changes in people's willingness to report crime to the police. In some periods, the UCR data have shown a marked increase in the number of reported rapes, whereas the NCVS data have shown no such increase. This difference is evidence for an increased willingness of victims to report the crime to the police.

CONTENT ANALYSIS

Whenever activity is recorded in some document—whether a book, diary, case record, film, or tape recording—it is amenable to scientific analysis. Although the data discussed in the previous section were already quantified when they were made available for research, the documents we now discuss contain basically *qualitative* data that researchers must quantify. Consider the following research studies by various social scientists:

- A study of the lyrics in modern rap music shows that rap is a cultural form with messages of resistance and empowerment for minorities in the United States, and serves as subcultural social criticism that expresses distrust and anger at what minorities perceive as a racist and discriminatory dominant white culture (Martinez, 1997).

- A study of prime-time television programs explores what messages about alcohol use appear in this medium, especially as alcohol use affects adolescents (Mathios et al., 1998).

- A study of magazine advertisements determines whether the behavior displayed in advertisements is different for men and women, and assesses whether stereotypical portrayals of men and women have changed over the past two decades (Kang, 1997).
- A study of how emotions are expressed and interpreted in different settings reviews audiotapes of emergency 911 calls (Whalen & Zimmerman, 1998).

Content analysis refers to a method of transforming the symbolic content of a document, such as words or other images, from a qualitative, unsystematic form into a quantitative, systematic form (Franzosi, 2008; Neuendorf, 2002). In the above examples, the "documents" consist of music lyrics, television programs, magazine advertisements, and 911 audiotapes. Content analysis is a form of *coding,* a practice we discuss in Chapters 7 and 9 as a way of transforming data in some surveys and observational research. **Coding** refers to categorizing behaviors or elements into a limited number of categories. In surveys and observational research, we perform coding on data the investigator collects firsthand for particular research purposes. In content analysis, coding is performed on documents produced for purposes other than research, but then made available for research purposes. In both survey data coding and content analysis we develop categories and coding schemes to quantify verbal or symbolic content.

Coding Schemes

A major step in content analysis is to develop a coding scheme for analyzing the documents at hand. Coding schemes in content analysis, like coding schemes in observed behavior, are quite variable, and their exact form depends on the documents being studied and the hypotheses tested in the research project.

Existing Coding Schemes. In some cases, researchers can find existing coding schemes for content analysis. For example, Robert Bales (1950) developed a set of coding categories for the analysis of social interaction in groups, and this coding scheme has been widely used in research. Bales's coding scheme emerged from his analysis of social processes and interactional strategies common to all groups. In particular, he argued that all behavior in groups relates either to "task" issues (instrumental or goal-oriented behavior) or "social–emotional" issues (having to do with feelings, emotions, or morale). Within each of those categories, he identified three specific behavioral forms it could take. For task issues:

1. Gives or asks for suggestions or directions.
2. Gives or asks for opinions or evaluations.
3. Gives or asks for orientation (information, clarification).

For social–emotional issues:

1. Shows solidarity or antagonism.
2. Shows tension or tension release.
3. Agrees or disagrees.

Each behavior of a person can then be classified into one of these categories. Over the years, researchers have used this coding scheme to test hypotheses about how common certain kinds of strategies are, the conditions under which they occur, and how effective they are at producing certain outcomes.

Some human service researchers have developed a somewhat analogous coding scheme to analyze the content of a clinician's responses to patients in interviews (Duehn & Proctor, 1977). In a study of the impact of clinicians' responses on whether clients continued with treatment, researchers developed a coding system using three categories:

1. *Substantive congruent responses:* clinician responses that referred to the client's immediately preceding response or that contained some elements of that response.
2. *Nonsubstantive congruent responses:* clinician responses, such as "I see" or "Yes," that

indicate the clinician is aware of and paying attention to the client's verbalizations.

3. *Incongruent responses:* clinician responses that appear to be unrelated to what the client has said.

Others interested in similar aspects of the practitioner–client interview might use the same coding scheme.

In conducting content analysis, then, we find it beneficial to search for an existing coding scheme that applies to the research problem at hand. The use of an existing coding scheme results in considerable savings for the researcher in terms of time, energy, and money. It also serves to make the research project comparable with other studies that use the same coding system.

We can find coding schemes in the many journals that report research relevant to the human services, or in books, such as those by Holsti (1969), Krippendorff (2012), or Smith (2000) that are devoted to the study of content analysis.

Characteristics. Like categories in any measurement process, those used in content analysis should be exhaustive and mutually exclusive. Categories are *exhaustive* when a category is available for every relevant element in the documents. If there are only a few possibilities and they can be clearly defined, an exhaustive set of categories is not difficult to develop. If what we are trying to measure is rather open-ended, however, and has many possibilities, then developing an exhaustive set of categories is difficult. For example, researchers have analyzed presidential speeches in terms of the values expressed, but so many values exist that developing an exhaustive list is unlikely. One such list contained 14 value categories, which undoubtedly cover the most important or commonly mentioned values (Prothro, 1956). It is doubtful whether even that many categories are really exhaustive, however. If it is impossible to be exhaustive, then we use the most common or most important categories and make available a residual category ("other") for those items that do not fit any of the categories.

Coding categories should also be *mutually exclusive,* which means that each coded item can fall into one—and only one—category. This requirement forces researchers to provide precise definitions for each category so no ambiguity exists concerning which items it includes and which it does not. Failure to meet this requirement can totally befuddle the measurement process, because coders who are confused by overlapping categories will place items every which way. Lack of mutual exclusiveness likely will show up in low levels of reliability as the coders disagree on the placement of items into categories.

Units of Analysis

With the categories established, the next research decision concerns precisely what aspects of the documents to record. Generally, there are four units of analysis: a word, a theme, a major character, or a sentence or paragraph. (We discussed the units of analysis commonly found in research other than content analysis in Chapter 4.) An often convenient unit of analysis is a *single word,* because we can code the presence of certain words in documents easily and with a high degree of reliability. If a single word qualifies as a valid indicator of what we wish to measure, then it is a good choice for the unit of analysis. For example, as a part of their study of colonial families, Herman Lantz and his colleagues (1968) counted the frequency with which the word "power" was associated with men or women in colonial magazines. In this context, the single word was used as a measure of the perceived distribution of power between men and women during colonial times. When using single words as the unit of analysis, it often is helpful to make use of a *context unit,* which is the context in which the single word is found. The words surrounding the word being used as the unit of analysis modify it and further explain its meaning. We then take this contextual information into account when coding the unit of analysis. For example, in the study just mentioned, the investigators needed to know whether the word "power" referred to men or to women. The context surrounding the word supplied this crucial information. The amount of context needed to explain the use of a given word adequately is, of course, variable.

The *theme* as a unit of analysis refers to the major subject matter of a document or part of a document. An entire document can be characterized as having a primary theme. Novels, for example, can be described as mysteries, science fiction, historical, and so on. In a study of the images of women during World War II and their treatment by government propaganda agencies, one researcher analyzed themes relating to the role of women in the workforce found in fiction pieces published by two magazines that were popular during the war, *The Saturday Evening Post* and *True Story* (Honey, 1984). Themes, however, can be difficult to delineate. The overall theme may or may not be clear, or there may be multiple themes. Coder reliability is likely to be lower than when easily identifiable words are the unit of analysis.

A third unit of analysis in documents is the *main character*. The use of this unit of analysis is, of course, limited to documents that have a cast of characters, such as plays, novels, movies, or television programs. A study of children's television programs, for example, used the major dramatic character as the unit of analysis. That study, funded by the Ford Foundation and the Carnegie Foundation, found that only 16 percent of the major characters were women and that "females were portrayed as married, less active, and with lower self-esteem" (Corry, 1982).

The fourth unit of analysis is a *sentence* or *paragraph*. The study described earlier regarding congruency in clinician–client interaction used a similar unit of analysis: Each clinician's response, preceded and followed by a client comment, was considered the unit to code, as either congruent or incongruent. A paragraph or even a single sentence, however, often contains more than one idea, and this may make these larger units more difficult to classify while maintaining mutually exclusive categories and intercoder reliability. Indeed, reliability often is lower than with the word or main character units. Yet, the larger units often are more theoretically relevant in the human services. In clinician–client interaction, for example, it makes little conceptual sense to characterize an interchange as congruent on the basis of one word. Meaning in social interaction normally arises from a whole block of words or sentences. So, as we emphasized when discussing units of analysis in Chapter 4, the primary consideration in selecting a unit of analysis is theoretical—that is, which unit seems to be preferable given theoretical and conceptual considerations.

Manifest versus Latent Coding

In content analysis, researchers distinguish between *manifest coding* and *latent coding*. The term **manifest coding** refers to coding the more objective or surface content of a document or medium (Holsti, 1969). One example of manifest coding notes each time a particular word appears in a document. Another example occurs in a study of the portrayal of African Americans in children's picture books, which observed whether blacks, whites, or people of other racial groups appeared in the pictures (Pescosolido, Grauerholz, & Milkie, 1997). In some cases, it may be difficult to judge the race of a particular character—certainly more difficult than deciding whether a particular word appears in a document. This is still manifest coding, however, because there is a fairly direct link between the image in the document and the coding category.

Latent coding, on the other hand, inherently involves some inference in which the coder has to decide whether the representation in the document is an instance of some broader category of phenomena. Coders assess the representations in the document for what they say about a more abstract or implicit level of meaning. The study just mentioned also used latent coding to judge the nature of the black representations in the picture books and of the black–white interactions portrayed. So the coders made judgments about how central the black characters were in the pictures and about how intimate or egalitarian the black–white interactions were. "Centrality," "intimacy," and "egalitarianism" are qualities that a coder must infer on the basis of a judgment or assessment of the materials.

Another example that used both manifest and latent coding was the study of how alcohol use is portrayed in prime-time television shows (Mathios et al., 1998). The manifest coding involved recording incidents where alcohol use was a part of such shows, noting the type of alcohol used and the gender of the people involved; all of this was easily observed, with little need to make judgments or inferences. The latent coding involved judging the personality characteristics of those portrayed consuming alcohol. For example, the coders had to rate each such character on a four-point scale, ranging from "very powerful" to "very powerless" and from "very admirable" to "very despicable." To do this latent coding, the observers had to make some fairly sophisticated and subjective judgments about personality from the behaviors and overall portrayal of the characters on the television shows. As these two examples illustrate, manifest coding generally is more reliable than latent coding, but latent coding often is a more valid way to get at some fairly complex and theoretically important social processes and characteristics.

ISSUES IN CONTENT ANALYSIS

When developing coding categories for content analysis, researchers confront several issues. Remember that content analysis is a form of measurement—that is, measurement of aspects of a document's contents. As such, we encounter the familiar concerns regarding validity and reliability, along with problems of choosing a level of measurement and a sample (see Chapters 5 and 6).

Validity

In content analysis, *validity* refers to whether the categories we develop and the aspects of the content coded are meaningful indicators of what we intend to measure. Developing coding schemes that are valid indicators can be challenging. For example, Anne Fortune (1979) reported on an effort to study communication patterns between social workers and their clients in which recordings of interviews were content analyzed. The goal of the research was to discover which interview techniques bring about cognitive and affective changes in clients. Fortune particularly wanted to know how techniques varied when the clients were adults rather than children. First, she developed a typology of communication techniques based on William Reid's work regarding task-centered casework. Because there are many ways to execute a particular verbal technique in a therapeutic setting, it was impossible to base the content analysis on a single word or phrase. Instead, Fortune provided coders with a description of each technique and examples of the verbal forms that each technique might take. For example, the communication technique of "exploration" was described as "communication intended to elicit information, including questions and restatements or 'echoes' of client's communications." Examples of this technique provided to the coders included such phrases as "What class was that?" and "You said your son misbehaved...." The communication technique of "direction" was exemplified by "I think the first step would be to talk this over with your daughter" (Fortune, 1979, p. 391). By providing specific examples of how to code comments, she hoped the resulting coding would have greater validity than if the coders were left on their own.

Depending on the nature of the research and the documents to analyze, researchers might apply any of the methods for assessing validity discussed in Chapter 5. The logical approaches of content validity and jury opinion are the most generally used assessments of validity in content analysis, although researchers sometimes use criterion validity. For example, in a content analysis of suicide notes, one study attempted to identify aspects of the content of real suicide notes that would differentiate them from simulated ones written by people who had not actually attempted suicide (Jones & Bennell, 2007). The researchers compared the genuine notes with the simulated ones and found, among other things, that genuine notes used shorter sentences, gave more instructions to survivors about such things as financial matters, and expressed more positive affect than did the simulated notes. Using these criteria, people who did not know which notes were real and which were simulated were able to predict correctly the genuine notes with a high level of accuracy. The results suggest that the identified content of the notes were valid indicators of the authenticity of the notes.

Researchers must be able to argue convincingly that indicators are valid to attain acceptance of their scientific outcomes. Even though most content analyses do not go beyond content validity or jury opinion, it is important to remember that these are the weakest demonstrations of validity. Whenever possible, more rigorous tests should be attempted.

Reliability

Reliability refers to the ability of a measure to yield consistent results each time we use it. In content analysis, reliability relates to the ability of coders to apply the coding scheme consistently. The question is this: Can several workers code the documents according to the coding scheme and obtain consistent results? Reliability in content analysis depends on many factors, including the skill of the coders, the nature of the categories, the rules guiding the use of the categories, and the degree of clarity or ambiguity in the documents (Franzosi, 2008; Holsti, 1969). The clarity of the documents in any given study is largely fixed, so our discussion of control over reliability is limited to coders and categories used.

First, researchers can enhance reliability by thoroughly training coders and having them practice applying the coding scheme. Anyone who continually deviates from the others in his or her coding during this practice period should not be relied on as a coder. We must be cautious, however, about eliminating coders without assessing whether their deviation indicates poor performance or an ambiguous coding scheme.

Second, the nature of the categories to be applied to the document also is important for reliability. The simpler and more objective the categories, the higher the reliability. Vaguely defined categories or those requiring substantial interpretation decrease reliability, because they create greater opportunity for disagreement among the coders.

Measuring reliability in content analysis is much the same as measuring reliability when coding observed behavior (see Chapter 9). One simple method is to calculate the percentage of judgments on which coders agree out of the total number of judgments they must make:

$$\text{percent of agreement} = \frac{2 \times \text{number of agreements}}{\text{total number of observations recorded by both observers}}$$

This measure of intercoder reliability, however, does not take into account the extent to which intercoder agreement can occur by chance. Paula Allen-Meares (1984) presents other ways of measuring intercoder reliability. Accepted levels of reliability are 75 percent or better agreement between coders. Well-trained coders using well-constructed coding schemes should achieve better than 85 percent agreement.

A certain tension exists between validity and reliability in content analysis. The simplest coding schemes, such as those employing word frequency counts, produce the highest reliability, because they are easy to apply in a consistent manner. As noted, however, word frequency counts may not validly measure what we want to measure. We may have to sacrifice some degree of reliability for the sake of validity. Researchers often end up performing a balancing act between the dual requirements of validity and reliability.

Level of Measurement

Like other methods of collecting data, content analysis involves a decision about the level of measurement to use (see Chapter 5). The level of measurement achieved depends on the variable being measured and the process being used to measure it. The variable being measured puts an upper limit on the level of measurement that we can reach. For example, if we rate main characters in a book according to marital status, the highest level of measurement would be nominal, because marital status is a nominal variable. No amount of measurement finesse can change this once we have selected the key variables. Researchers do have some control over the level of measurement, however, depending on the process being used to measure the variables. The important factor is how we quantify the unit of analysis in the coding process. Coding systems in content analysis generally fall into one of four categories: (1) presence or absence of an element; (2) frequency of occurrence of an element; (3) amount of space or time devoted to an element; or (4) intensity of expression.

The simplest rating system is merely to indicate *the presence or the absence of an element* in a document. For example, we might rate interviews as to whether the clinician mentions certain subjects, such as sexual behavior or parent–child relationships. This simple system yields nominal data and conveys a minimum of content information. Several important questions remain unanswered. We do not know whether the clinician addressed the subject in a positive or a negative light, nor do we know how the client reacted. Also unknown is how much time was devoted to that subject and how frequently it was repeated. Consideration of these factors would make the study more informative.

Frequency counts are common methods of rating: We simply count how often an element appears. For example, Jack Levin and James Spates (1970) sought to compare the dominant values expressed in middle-class publications with those in the so-called underground press. The investigators rated the frequency with which statements of various values appeared in the two types of publications. On the basis of the frequency counts, the study concluded that the underground press emphasized values related to self-expression, whereas the middle-class publications stressed values related to various types of personal achievement. Frequency counts reveal more information about the document than a simple present-or-absent approach does, and they open the way for more sophisticated statistical analysis, because with the appropriate theoretical concepts, they can achieve an interval- or ratio-level of measurement.

Coding systems based on *the amount of space or time devoted to an element* have proved useful for analyzing the mass media. In newspapers or magazines, the normal approach is to measure column inches. The equivalent for films or television is time. For example, in a study about the contribution of social work writers to the development of professional knowledge, Merlin Taber and Iris Shapiro (1965) counted the number of column inches that selected social work journals devoted to a discussion of different types of knowledge, such as theoretical versus empirical knowledge. We could measure, over a period of years, the amount of space devoted to a topic, such as family violence or the problems of lesbian mothers, to assess the impact of popular trends or political events on professional concerns about various issues. The major attraction of space/time measures is their ease of use. We can measure the amount of space devoted to a given topic far more rapidly than we can measure word frequency counts or even whether key words are present or absent. Because each document takes only a short time to analyze, space/time measures allow a larger sample size and, possibly, lead to greater representativeness. Space/time measures also can yield interval- or ratio-level measurement with theoretical concepts that are amenable to such a level of measurement.

Unfortunately, space/time measures are still somewhat crude. Other than the volume of space devoted to the particular topic in question, they reveal nothing further about the content. For example, time measures applied to the network news could tell us which types of news are allotted the most coverage, but nothing about more subtle issues, such as whether the news coverage was biased. As Ole Holsti (1969, p. 121) notes, "A one-to-one relationship between the amount of space devoted to a subject and the manner in which it is treated cannot be assumed."

The most complex rating systems involve a *measure of intensity*—that is, the forcefulness of expression in the documents. Developing intensity measures is difficult, however. Intensity of expression often is quite subtle and dependent on many aspects of word usage, which makes it extremely difficult to specify clearly the conditions for coding content elements. Coders have to make many judgments before deciding how to categorize the content, and this leads to disagreements and low reliability.

Developing intensity measures that produce reliable results is quite similar to constructing measurement scales, as we discuss in Chapter 13. We could, for example, have coders rate documents along a scale (as in the semantic differential or the Likert scales). Newspaper editorials dealing with public assistance programs might be rated as (1) very unfavorable, (2) unfavorable, (3) neutral, (4) favorable, or (5) very favorable. The study mentioned earlier on portrayals of alcohol use on television used an intensity measure: Coders had to rate characters on a four-point scale from "very powerful" to "very powerless" and from "very admirable" to "very despicable" (Mathios et al., 1998). The options for intensity scales are nearly endless given the vast variety of intensity questions that can arise concerning the contents of documents. Despite their complexity, intensity measures are the most revealing about a document's contents.

Sampling

In document analysis, the number of documents often is too vast for all of them to be analyzed; in this case, we have to take a sample from a group of documents. For example, we might want to study the extent to which concern for child abuse has changed among human service providers between the 1950s and the 2000s. We could do this by studying the extent of coverage of the topic in human service journals during those years. Considering the number of journals and thousands of pages involved, sampling clearly is necessary to make such a project feasible.

As with other types of sampling, representativeness is a critical issue. To generalize the findings of our document analysis, the sampling procedure must be likely to yield a representative sample, which often is difficult to achieve with documents. One problem is that the elements of the population of documents may not be equal. In studying child abuse, for example, some journals are more likely than others to publish articles on that topic—*Child Welfare* or the *Journal of Interpersonal Violence,* for example. A more general journal, like *Social Service Review,* would include a much smaller proportion of child abuse articles. Likewise, a journal specializing in a different area, such as the *Journals of Gerontology,* probably would not publish any articles on child abuse. A random sample of all human service journals, then, might include only a few journals most likely to publish articles on this topic. In other words, this random sample would be dominated by journals having a small likelihood of publishing family violence articles, making it more difficult to measure changes in practitioner concern for family violence. We can solve this problem by choosing our sample from among those journals specializing in areas related to family violence. Or we can stratify the journals by type and then select a stratified random sample, taking disproportionately more journals that are likely to publish articles on family violence (see Chapter 6).

A second issue in sampling documents is the difficulty in defining the population of documents. For example, for a study on the changing image of the social work profession, James Billups and Maria Julia (1987) conducted a content analysis of advertisements for job vacancies in social work positions. Because such ads are published in many different places—including local, state, and national publications—defining that population of documents was difficult. To get around this problem, they limited themselves to advertisements in national publications on the grounds that these would most likely reflect national trends in the changing image of social work. At a national level, the most ads were placed in *Social Casework* in 1960 and 1970 and in the *NASW News* in 1980. To assess trends over time, Billups and Julia did not need to sample documents from each year. Instead, they took a random sample of 10 percent of the ads appearing in these journals in 1960, 1970, and 1980, which covered the period in which they were interested. The changing trends in practice that the researchers found during their content analysis research reflected what other research had discovered: The distinction between casework and group practice had become less important over time, and social workers, especially those with graduate degrees, were more likely to find supervisory or administrative positions.

Assuming that we can adequately define the population to sample, we can apply to documents the normal procedures of sampling discussed in Chapter 6. Of those, simple random sampling probably is most common and most generally applicable (Scott, 1990). As we have seen, however, researchers may require stratified sampling to avoid bias when sampling from a population of unequal elements. We should approach systematic sampling cautiously because it is easy to be trapped by periodicity in documents (see Chapter 6). *Periodicity* is the problem in which elements with certain characteristics occur at patterned intervals throughout the sampling frame. For example, both the size and the content of newspapers vary substantially with the days of the week. If the sampling interval were seven or a multiple of seven, then a systematic sample would include only papers published on the same day of the week and could be very biased, depending on the aspects of content under study.

Sampling documents often involves multistage sampling. As in all multistage sampling, we start with large units and work down through a series of sampling stages to smaller and smaller units. The sample of the underground press by Levin and Spates (1970) illustrates multistage sampling. In the first stage, the researchers selected a sample of publications from the membership of the Underground Press Syndicate by choosing the top five publications in terms of circulation. In the second stage, they randomly selected a single issue of each publication for every other month from September 1967 through August 1968. This produced six sample issues for each of the five publications, for a total of 30 issues. In the final stage, Levin and Spates selected for analysis every other nonfiction article appearing in the sample issues. The resulting sample contained 316 articles to represent the underground press.

ASSESSMENT OF AVAILABLE DATA ANALYSIS

Like other research techniques, the use of available data has both advantages and disadvantages. A consideration of these helps determine when such analysis is the most appropriate and points out some potential problems as well. The Eye on Ethics section also discusses some ethical issues directly related to using available data.

Advantages

Lower Costs. Document analysis is one of the least costly forms of research, and using available statistical data can help reduce the costs of a research project. The producers of the documents or statistics bear the major expense of data gathering rather than the researcher. The sheer volume of data that the U.S. Census Bureau, the NASW, or the many local and state social agencies collects is so massive that only the best-endowed research projects could possibly duplicate their efforts. Document analysis becomes expensive if the documents of interest are widely scattered and difficult to obtain or if very large samples are employed. Also, the more complex the coding process, the more expensive the study. Overall, however, available data offer an opportunity to conduct valuable research at reasonable cost.

Nonreactivity. Like hidden observation and unobtrusive measures, available data are nonreactive (see Chapters 4 and 9). Unlike surveys or experiments,

> ### Eye on Ethics — Information Technologies and Ethical Research
>
> Developments in information technologies have brought new twists to the conduct of ethical research. For example, we now have inexpensive and portable data storage devices in the form of memory sticks and laptop computers. We can also easily transmit large amounts of data electronically over the Internet. In addition, medical and social service records are now often stored electronically. So it is now relatively easy for researchers to access and transmit these data sets. In addition, propelled in part by the demands of government funders of medical and social services, data-collection instruments are increasingly uniform across agencies and even states. All of these developments make it possible for researchers to archive, or combine, these data sets to include cases from multiple organizations, states, and time periods, resulting in multiorganizational and longitudinal research that can overcome some of the weaknesses of more traditional secondary analysis of statistical data. Such data sets can also answer many more questions relevant to evidence-based social policy than can more limited data sets (Jonson-Reid & Drake, 2008).
>
> One of the advantages of such nonreactive, available data is that the researcher confronts fewer ethical dilemmas compared to gathering data directly from people. Ethical concerns do arise, however, especially in trying to maintain the privacy (confidentiality and anonymity) of these data. For example, the easy portability of these storage devices makes it tempting to bring data home or to another location that is not secure. There have been cases where data stored on a memory stick or laptop computer was lost or stolen. Some research falls under the purview of government agencies and legislation, such as the Family Educational Rights and Privacy Act (FERPA) or Health Insurance Portability and Accountability Act (HIPAA), and this can provide some guidance regarding how to handle these privacy concerns. The HIPAA Privacy Rule, for example, suggests procedures for protecting the privacy of people whose health data will be used in available-data research (Centers for Disease Control, 2003; Office for Civil Rights, 2009). One approach is to use a "de-identified" data set, which means that 18 specified identifiers have been removed from the data set (such as names and telephone numbers). Such a data set would presumably have no information that could identify a particular individual. Another approach is to use a "limited" data set, in which most of these identifiers have been removed but a few are retained (such as some geographic identifiers or birth dates). However, the identifiers that remain in a limited data set must be essential to the research and must not be used to re-identify the individual.
>
> With research that involves available data spanning many organizations or time periods, there must be a way to identify particular individuals so that their data from different organizations or time periods can be connected. One way to handle this is to de-identify the final, or "use," database and subject it to limited security because it poses no threat to privacy (Jonson-Reid & Drake, 2008). Then the working, or "core," data set would have identifiers and would be used when new cases need to be added to the file and linked with previous cases. This core data set would require higher levels of security. For example, research organization rules might prohibit saving the core data set on a memory stick or other easily transportable device. Or there might be a security code required to open or save the core data set.
>
> Various federal agencies provide guidelines for how to gather and share such available data while meeting ethical standards (Centers for Disease Control, 2005). Researchers review these guidelines carefully for insight while designing their research.

in which the participants are aware that they are being studied, producers of documents normally do not anticipate a researcher coming along at a later date to analyze those documents. The contents of the documents are, therefore, unaffected by the researcher's activities. This does not mean, of course, that those who produced the documents did not react to some elements that might have biased the documents. For example, police officers might be more likely to record an instance of physical or verbal assault in an arrest report when the suspect is nonwhite than when the suspect is white, thus generating data that make nonwhites appear to be more abusive and introducing bias into arrest records. In addition, people who compile documents may be reacting to how people other than researchers, such as a supervisor or a politician, may respond to their document. Likewise, the preparer's hope for a "place in history" can shape the preparation of a document. Despite all this, researchers are not a source of reactivity with available data.

Inaccessible Subjects. When properly cared for, documents can survive far longer than the people who produce them. Document analysis allows us to study the ways of society long ago and the behaviors of people long dead. The study of the colonial family by Lantz and colleagues (1968) and the study of suicide notes by Jones and Bennell (2007) dealt with the behavior of people quite inaccessible by research techniques other than document analysis.

Longitudinal Analysis. Many statistical data and documents are collected routinely over a period of years—or even centuries. This contrasts sharply with the typical one-shot, cross-sectional survey data. With such longitudinal data, we can accomplish trend analysis—that is, looking for changing patterns over time. For example, Reynolds Farley (1984) used a longitudinal analysis of available data in an evaluation of the progress of African Americans in the United States since the 1950s. Using census data from the 1950s, 1960s, and 1970s, Farley compared the position of African Americans relative to whites over three decades, and he found mixed results. The census data revealed that African Americans as a whole had made substantial gains in quality of employment, family earnings, and educational attainment. Other indicators, such as residential integration, unemployment rate, and school integration, were less encouraging, however, showing little or no improvement. This type of research obviously is valuable in putting today's conditions into historical perspective; just as obviously, researchers can conduct this type of longitudinal analysis of past trends only through the analysis of available data. (Existing statistical data often lend themselves to the kind of time-series analysis that we will describe in Chapter 10.)

Sample Size. Many types of documents are abundant. As mentioned when discussing sampling, a researcher is likely to confront far more documents than he or she can analyze rather than too few. This means that a researcher can employ large samples to increase confidence in the results. The low cost associated with document analysis also contributes to the researcher's ability to use substantial sample sizes without encountering prohibitive costs.

Disadvantages

Variable Quality. Because documents are produced for purposes other than research, their quality for research purposes is variable. Unless researchers know the limitations of the documents, as with crime statistics, they may have little idea of the conditions under which the data were collected or the attention to quality that went into them. Researchers should, of course, investigate the issue of quality when possible to discover any deficiencies in the data. When we cannot do this, we simply have to draw conclusions cautiously.

Incompleteness. Documents, especially those of a historical nature, frequently are incomplete. Gaps of weeks, months, or even years are not uncommon. In addition, data may be missing in available statistics. The effect of these gaps on a study often is impossible to know, except that such gaps reduce confidence in the findings. Incompleteness is simply a common characteristic plaguing available data that researchers have to work around if they can.

Lack of Comparability over Time. Even though documents are commonly used in longitudinal analysis, this can be problematic, because change over time may create statistical artifacts in the data and render comparisons useless. With crime statistics, for example, changes in how the FBI collects data make it misleading to compare crime statistics over long periods of time. Researchers need to be careful of similar kinds of changes in other data.

Bias. Because documents are produced for purposes other than research, there is no assurance that they are objective. Data from private sources, for example, may be intentionally slanted to present a particular viewpoint. A researcher who blindly accepts such data can walk into a trap. Nonstatistical documents may suffer from biased presentation as well. A good example is the corporate annual report to stockholders, filled with glowing praise for management, impressive color photographs, bright prospects for the future, and presenting anything negative either in the most favorable light or camouflaged in legalese.

Sampling Bias. Bias may creep into otherwise objective data during the sampling process. As we have noted, sampling documents often is difficult because of unequal population elements and hard-to-define populations. We also have commented that document sampling frequently is complex, requiring several stages. Errors or bad decisions made during the sampling process can result in a highly biased sample that will produce misleading results.

Using Available Data in Research on Minorities

When studying emotionally charged topics, such as racism or sexism, reactivity can be a serious problem, because people are inclined to disguise true feelings or motives that might result in disapproval. Even though they may feel prejudice that influences their behavior, people may deny such feelings toward minorities or women when a survey researcher asks about them. One of the major benefits of available data, however, is that they often are less reactive than other data used to study behavior. Therefore, available data may be the preferred research method—or a valued adjunct to other research methods—when studying such emotion-laden topics.

Consider, for example, some of the uses to which researchers have put available data in the study of racism and sexism. If we ask people whether they are racists or sexists or whether they treat women or minorities unfairly, most people deny it, especially in the contemporary environment that frowns upon such attitudes and practices. Yet, the records of agencies and organizations might contain evidence of sexism or racism despite the denial of those who run those organizations. Are whites or males found disproportionately in the more prestigious or better-paying positions in an organization? Do whites or males earn substantially higher salaries than women or minorities in the organization? Such organizational practices suggest sexism or racism in the organization. It often is less reactive and more valid to measure the consequences of organizational decisions than to ask people about such things directly.

Another way to detect the persistence of prejudices and stereotypes is to study the portrayal of people in various cultural products, such as books, magazines, or movies. Two or more decades ago, the images of males and females that were presented in school textbooks, for example, typically reinforced traditional stereotypes: Males were pictured far more often than females; males were pictured in many occupations and women in few; and female pronouns, such as *her,* were uncommon. Things have improved, especially when efforts are made to produce materials that are nonsexist in their presentation, but stereotyping persists. More recent studies of children's picture books, for example, find that, although they are portrayed more often than in the past, women are still shown less often than men are (only one third of the illustrations are of women); women are still shown in fewer occupations than men; women are still likely to be portrayed in traditional gender roles associated with household work; and women are still portrayed as less brave and adventurous, and more helpless (Crabb & Bielawski, 1994; Peterson & Lach, 1990; Purcell & Stewart, 1990). Even college textbooks are not immune to these influences. Studies of the pictorial content of texts for college-level psychology and sociology courses found that women appear less often than men and are depicted more

INFORMATION TECHNOLOGY IN RESEARCH — Access to Statistical Available Data

Modern computer technology, especially the Internet, has made research based on available statistical data much more extensive and efficient than ever was possible in the past. Basically, modern computer technology allows researchers to share data sets, but what is so revolutionary about this? Researchers have done that for decades, after all. What is new, however, is the ease of doing this: The Internet makes such sharing much quicker—and much more accessible to researchers with limited budgets. It also means that data sets can be much more thoroughly analyzed than in the past, because many more researchers can use each set of data.

To understand the process, go to a website called Data on the Net, which is maintained at the University of California, San Diego (http://3stages.org/idata). This site is basically a portal to other sites that list locations of data sets. It has a search function that allows you to search for data sets on particular topics, and you can browse through lists (sometimes long) of data sets that might be of interest to you or data archives that might contain data sets of interest. This website also lists many other online gateways to social science data sets and data archives. So the first step in searching for available statistical data is to explore, via the Internet, what might be available. Many of these sites provide you with the actual questions or measurement instruments that were used to collect the data. These measurement instruments, remember, are the operational definitions of the variables in the data set.

When searching for statistical data sets that you might use, determine whether you can have access to the complete raw data set, to only parts of the data set, or to only reports that have been prepared based on the analysis of the data set. For most research purposes, access to the complete raw data set is most desirable—if not essential. With such access you can conduct whatever kind of statistical analysis your research questions require, using as many of the variables in the data set as necessary. If you can gain access to only parts of the data, then you may not be able to test some hypotheses or conduct some statistical tests. Some data archives, for example, only give access to frequency distributions on separate variables. If this is the case, then you cannot conduct any statistical analysis involving the correlation or comparison of two or more variables. Such a limitation makes the data set useless for most social science and human service research, which almost always involves looking at two or more variables at the same time. If the only access that a data archive permits is to reports summarizing the analysis of the raw data, then it may be useful in the literature review part of a research project, but it would not be of use in additional hypothesis testing and data analysis.

When searching for statistical available data, you also need to determine whether the data are free or involve some cost. The data, after all, come from many different kinds of data archives: government bureaus, private foundations, university research organizations, as well as private, commercial research firms. Commercial research firms in particular may charge a fee for the purchase of a data set they own, but some of the other data archives also may charge for use (if only a nominal fee to cover their costs). Even if a cost is attached, however, it is often quite small, and certainly far less than what it would cost a researcher to gather the data anew.

A final determination in using these statistical data sets is what stipulations and limitations you must agree to before you can download the data. Most suppliers of data will require that you cite the source of the data in any reports that are prepared using them. Many also will require that the data be made public only as aggregate data, not as individual cases, to prevent the identity of any research participants from being made public. In addition, some data archives will require that you make no effort to determine the identities of people who were the subjects of the research. If such a stipulation is required, then you could not, for example, seek out the subjects for purposes of gathering additional data from them. Still other stipulations may be required before you can use the data, depending on the particular nature of that data, but the point is that you will be required to agree to these stipulations before you will be allowed to download the data. And once you agree, you are morally bound to follow them; to violate the stipulations would be considered an unethical research practice.

passively and negatively than men (Ferree & Hall, 1990; Peterson & Kroner, 1992). For example, the psychology texts portray women as the victims of mental disorders and as the clients in therapy while picturing men as the therapists. Thus, cultural products, like books or newspapers, can serve as available data to detect gender stereotyping that might be undetectable by other research methods.

REVIEW AND CRITICAL THINKING

Main Points

- Available data include both statistical data collected by others and documents, which include any form of communication.
- Content analysis quantifies and organizes the qualitative and unsystematic information contained in documents.
- Content analysis is essentially a form of measurement, making the issues of validity and reliability paramount. Available data also must be analyzed carefully in terms of level of measurement, which is determined by the nature of the variable being measured as well as by the process being used in measuring it from the available data used.
- Document analysis normally includes some form of sampling procedure, which must be performed carefully for the sake of representativeness.
- Document analysis offers the advantages of low cost, nonreactivity, ability to study otherwise inaccessible subjects, easy longitudinal analysis, and often large samples.
- Problems in using available data include the variable quality of the data, incomplete data, changes in data over time, possible bias in data, and possible sampling bias.
- The analysis of available data often is less reactive than other research methods, which can make it useful in the study of emotionally charged topics, such as racism and sexism, where people may be inclined to hide their true feelings and emotions.

Important Terms for Review

available data	content analysis	latent coding	missing data
coding	data archives	manifest coding	secondary analysis

Critical Thinking

While this chapter introduces some new research methods, some of the issues discussed, such as measurement and reactivity, are familiar ones that have been discussed in other chapters. This illustrates the variety of forms that these issues can take and their centrality to the conduct of research. It also shows how important these issues are to evaluating information that you may come upon in practice or policy settings or in your everyday life. When evaluating information and conclusions, consider the following:

1. Are the conclusions based on information that is nonreactive? In other words, might the people observed behave differently because the observer is present?

2. If the information is based on available data (e.g., records or documents), what kind of

measurement problems does this create? Is the data limited or distorted in some fashion? Is the sampling limited?

3. If the information is qualitative in nature, is it transformed into a quantitative form? If so, how does this affect or change the meaning of the information?

Exploring the Internet

We identified three major sources of statistical data in this chapter: research organizations; federal, state, and local human service organizations; and organizations that collect data as a public service or as a basis for policy decisions. You can find each of these three general types of data sources on the Internet. First, explore the site of the Interuniversity Consortium of Political and Social Research (ICPSR; http://www.icpsr.umich.edu/icpsrweb). Click on "Find and Analyze Data," and you will find links to help you discover what this data archive contains.

Another site to explore is that of the National Archive of Computerized Data on Aging (NACDA), which is funded by the National Institute on Aging (http://www.icpsr.umich.edu/icpsrweb/NACDA/index.jsp). The NACDA's mission is to advance research on aging by helping researchers profit from the underexploited potential of a broad range of data sets. By preserving and making available the largest library of electronic data on aging in the United States, the NACDA offers opportunities for secondary analysis on major issues of scientific and policy relevance.

For Further Reading

Larose, D. (2005). *Discovering Knowledge in Data: An Introduction to Data Mining*. Hoboken, N. J.: Wiley Interscience. This book introduces students to several statistical methods used for exploring and analyzing existing quantitative data sets.

Lee, R.M. (2000). *Unobtrusive Methods in Social Research*. Philadelphia: Open University Press. This book provides an excellent overview of the different types of unobtrusive or nonreactive measures as well as the advantages and problems in using them.

McCulloch, G.. (2004). *Documentary Research in Education, History, and the Social Sciences*. New York: RoutledgeFalmer. This book offers an overview of documentary research. The chapters explore a wide range of documentary source materials that are available for researchers in the social sciences: policy reports, autobiographies, diaries, committee papers, correspondence, school magazines, textbooks, log books, newspapers, local registers, and visual sources such as photographs and paintings.

Murnane, R. J., & Willett, J. B. (2010). *Methods Matter: Improving Causal Inference in Educational and Social Science Research*. New York: Oxford University Press. This book examines ways in which researchers can help policymakers and other decision-makers make more informed decisions when using existing data while critically examining data collection and other research methodologies used in creating data sets.

Riedel, M. (2000). *Research Strategies for Secondary Data: A Perspective for Criminology and Criminal Justice*. Thousand Oaks, Calif.: Sage. Although it focuses on the field of criminology, this useful guide to the many sources of data available for secondary analysis also reviews some of the methodological issues that are important to consider in doing such data analysis.

Smith, T. W., Marsden, P. V., Hout, M., & Kim, J. (2011). *General Social Surveys, 1972–2010: Cumulative Codebook*. Chicago: National Opinion Research Center; Storrs, Conn.: The Roper Center for Public Opinion Research, University of Connecticut, http://www3.norc.org/GSS+ Website. This book describes a body of available statistical data based on surveys conducted since the 1970s. It includes data on many topics of interest to people in the social sciences and human services.

West, M. D. (2001). *Applications of Computer Content Analysis*. Westport, Conn.: Ablex. This is a basic introduction to the procedures used in conducting content analysis research, with special emphasis on the role of computers.

Class Exercises for Competency Assessment

8.1. Agency records are a valuable source of available data. If you are in a field placement, an internship, or doing volunteer work in a human service agency, ask the agency to provide sample copies or blank forms of required and routine data collected on clients. Of course you should be certain to obtain the forms and reports in a way that will not infringe on client or service-user confidentiality.

a. [Critical Thinking] [Research & Practice] Compare the types of information gathered in the agency with which you are affiliated to those gathered by other students in other agencies. Can you think of some specific research questions you could explore with these data? Can you suggest some changes in agency data-gathering procedures that might produce more data for research with little additional effort?

b. [Ethics] [Evidence-Based Evaluation] What steps are required to obtain existing data on clients so as to meet ethical safeguards for confidentiality?

8.2. [Critical Thinking] [Research & Practice] A researcher is interested in studying the impact of changing economic conditions on the retention of minority students in college. The researcher's hypothesis is that an economic recession will have a greater negative effect on the retention and graduation of minority students than it will on nonminority students. Using your own institution as the site for the project, what sources of data, already available in some data bank in your institution, might you use in such a study? What problems do you envision with these data in terms of sampling, unit of analysis, and levels of measurement?

8.3. The negative portrayal of public welfare service users in the media is a concern of human service professionals. (1) Is the image of welfare recipients really negative? (2) Has there been a trend toward improvement? (3) Does the image portrayed improve or deteriorate in conjunction with changes in the national economy? These are questions that you might approach through a content analysis of the news media. Suppose you were to conduct such a content analysis research in your community:

a. [Research & Practice] Suggest what elements you think the population being studied contains.

b. [Research & Practice] Identify some sampling issues the research would confront.

c. [Critical Thinking] [Research & Practice] What different problems are involved in answering the second and third questions in the above paragraph in contrast to the first question about negative image?

d. [Research & Practice] Assuming the research is confined to daily newspapers, suggest some possibilities for the unit of analysis.

e. [Critical Thinking] [Research & Practice] How could operational definitions of "negative image" and "welfare recipient" be developed?

Chapter 9

✸

Field Research and Qualitative Methods

Characteristics of Qualitative Methods
  Contextual Approach
  Grounded Theory Methodology
Field Research
  Participant Observation
  Unobtrusive Observation
Steps in Field Research
  Problem Formulation
  Selecting a Field Setting
  Entering the Field
  Developing Rapport in the Field
  Becoming Invisible
  Attitude of the Researcher
  Observing and Recording in the Field
  Exiting the Field
Recording Observations in Field Research
  Qualitative Observation: Field Notes
  Quantitative Observation: Coding Sheets
Other Qualitative Methods
  In-Depth Interviewing

  Case Studies, Life Histories, and Narratives
  Focus Groups
Issues in Observational and Field Research
  Sampling
  Validity and Reliability
  Reactivity
  Observational and Field Research on Diverse Populations
Assessment of Field Techniques and Qualitative Methods
  Advantages
  Disadvantages
Observation in Human Service Practice
Review and Critical Thinking
  Main Points
  Important Terms for Review
  Critical Thinking
  Exploring the Internet
  For Further Reading
  Class Exercises for Competency Assessment

Observational techniques refer to the collection of data through direct visual or auditory experience of behavior. With observational techniques, which include video or audio recordings of behavior, the researcher actually sees or hears the behavior or words that are the data for the research. Observational techniques can be either quantitative or qualitative in nature. As we discussed in Chapter 2, qualitative research basically involves research in which the data come in the form of words, pictures, narratives, and descriptions rather than in numerical form. A second way that observational techniques differ from one another is whether the observations are done in a naturalistic setting or in a laboratory or contrived setting. A *naturalistic setting* is a "real-life" situation in which people behave as they routinely would if they weren't the subjects of scientific observation. In fact, in some cases, people in naturalistic settings may not even know they are under observation. Contrived settings are created by the researcher and would not have occurred were it not for the research project. This chapter focuses on observation done in naturalistic, or field, settings. (We will discuss observation in contrived settings, such as laboratory experiments, in Chapter 10.)

Field research involves observations made of people in their natural settings as they go about their everyday life. Surveys involve people's reports to the researcher about what they said, did, or felt. With surveys and available data, the researcher does not directly observe what will be the focus of the research. With field research, on the other hand, the researcher actually sees or hears the behaviors that are the data for the research. Field research is most closely associated, in many people's minds, with the work of anthropologists, who live among indigenous peoples for extended periods and write ethnographic reports that summarize people's way of life. Yet, researchers in other social sciences and the human services also find field research to be a useful way to gather data. This chapter focuses mostly on qualitative field research, but also explores methods of collecting quantitative data in the field and some other types of qualitative methods. It is helpful to begin with a quick overview of some of the characteristics that set qualitative research methods apart from quantitative research methods.

CHARACTERISTICS OF QUALITATIVE METHODS

Contextual Approach

Chapters 2 and 4 introduced the distinctions between positivist and nonpositivist approaches to science and between qualitative and quantitative research. Although qualitative research methods at times might be conducted by people who take a positivist approach and might involve collecting some quantitative data, qualitative research has been closely associated over the years with nonpositivist or interpretive paradigms. Proponents of such paradigms argue that qualitative and contextual approaches offer access to a valuable type of data—namely, a deeper and richer understanding of people's lives and behavior, including some knowledge of their subjective experiences (Benton, 1977; Gubrium & Holstein, 1997; Lincoln, Lynham, & Guba, 2011). Because these subjective experiences are so central to the debate between positivists and nonpositivists, and so important to qualitative research methods, let's explore what each approach has to say about these subjective experiences and their role in understanding human behavior.

Positivism argues that the world exists independently of people's perceptions of it and that scientists can use objective techniques to discover what exists in the world (Durkheim, 1938; Halfpenny, 1982). Astronomers, for example, use telescopes to discover stars and galaxies, which exist regardless of whether we are aware of them. So, too, researchers can study human beings in terms of behaviors that can be observed and recorded using some kind of objective technique. Recording people's gender, age, height, weight, or socioeconomic position are legitimate and objective measurement techniques—the equivalent of the physicist measuring the temperature, volume, or velocity of some liquid or solid. For the positivist, quantifying these measurements—that is, assessing the average age of a group or looking at the percentage of a group that is male—is simply a precise way of describing and summarizing an objective reality. Such measurement provides a solid and objective foundation for understanding human social behavior. Limiting study to observable behaviors and using objective techniques, positivists argue, is most likely to produce systematic and repeatable research results that are open to refutation by other scientists.

Subjectivism (also called the *interpretive*, or *verstehen, approach*) provides a more nonpositivist perspective on these issues. It argues that these "objective" measures miss an important part of the human experience—namely, the subjective and personal meanings that people attach to themselves, to what they do, and to the world around them (Wilson, 1970). Max Weber, an early proponent of this view, argued that we need to look not only at what people do, but also at what they think and feel about what is happening to them (Weber, 1957, orig. pub. 1925). Researchers cannot adequately capture this "meaning," or "feeling," or "interpretive" dimension through objective, quantitative measurement techniques; they need to gain what Weber called **verstehen,** or a subjective understanding. They need to view and experience the situation from the perspective of the people themselves. To use a colloquialism, the researchers need "to walk a mile in the shoes" of the people being studied. They need to talk to these people at length and immerse themselves in their subjects' lives so they can experience the highs and lows, the joys and sorrows, the triumphs and the tragedies from the perspective of the people they are studying. Researchers need to see how the individuals experience and give meaning to what is happening to them. Qualitative research methods are an attempt to gain access to that personal, subjective experience. These qualitative approaches stress the idea that knowledge, especially of the subjective dimension, best emerges when researchers understand the full context in which people behave. For interpretivists, quantitative research, by its very nature, misses this important dimension of social reality. Positivists, for their part, do not necessarily deny the existence or importance of subjective experiences, but they do question whether qualitative methods, with their emphasis on the subjective interpretations of the *verstehen* method, have any scientific validity.

Grounded Theory Methodology

Many qualitative methods are closely grounded in the data, in that they let meaning, concepts, and theories emerge from the raw data rather than being imposed by the researcher. In many research methodologies in the social sciences, the role of theories parallels the positivist approach and the deductive model that we discussed in Chapter 2. Theories are abstract explanations containing a variety of concepts and propositions. From these theories, the researcher derives testable hypotheses and operational definitions of concepts. Then he or she makes observations to determine whether the hypotheses are true. This deductive approach, however, is not always appropriate—or even useful: Some research projects are exploratory in nature, meaning that there is little existing theory, concepts, or propositions from which to shape hypotheses or develop operational definitions. Another reason such a deductive approach is not useful for some research projects is that it involves the scientists, through theory and measurement, imposing structure, categorization, and meaning onto reality rather than letting the structure and meaning emerge from reality.

So, proponents of more inductive approaches to theory development argue that deducing hypotheses from existing theories sometimes is limiting, especially during the early stages of theory development when the theory may not include some relevant variables (Charmaz, 2006). If the variables are not in the theory, they cannot be part of hypotheses, and thus may be ignored. In other words, strict adherence to deductive hypothesis construction might blind researchers to some key phenomena. One of the more widely used approaches to these issues is called **grounded theory,** which is a research methodology for developing theory by letting the theory emerge from, or be "grounded" in, the data. With this method, there is a continual interplay between data collection, data analysis, and theory development. In the positivist model, these three elements are sequenced: data collection, followed by data analysis, followed in turn by theory development. Using a grounded theory method, these three elements can occur simultaneously as one goes constantly back and forth among them. Thus, theory development occurs in the midst of data collection rather than following it.

In the absence of theory, researchers begin by making observations. Those who use grounded theory often do qualitative research by making direct observations or conducting interviews in field settings. Without the restrictions of a preexisting theory, they describe what happens, identify relevant variables, and search for explanations of what they observe. Beginning with these concrete observations, researchers develop more abstract concepts, propositions, and theoretical explanations that would be plausible, given those observations. Inductive research of this sort can serve as a foundation for building a theory, and the theory that emerges can later serve as a guide for additional research and, possibly, even as a source of testable hypotheses through deductive reasoning.

Proponents of qualitative methods argue that concepts and theories produced by such grounded approaches provide a more valid representation of some phenomena, because they emerge directly from the phenomena being studied. In fact, in positivist science, we can engage in theory development without engaging in any data collection or data analysis at all. This is impossible in grounded theory, because the theory emerges from the data or observations. Theory produced in this manner, however, also could be subject to further verification by deducing and testing hypotheses. In fact, a common misconception of grounded theory is that it is entirely inductive in nature. To the contrary, grounded theory does, at times, use existing theory to understand and explain data, and it does include procedures for verifying theories. Thus, some of the considerations of more positivist approaches are relevant to grounded theory: Grounded theory uses evidence to verify theories, rigorously follows precise procedures, makes efforts at replication, and as one of its goals, generalizes about social processes across a variety of social settings.

We will discuss grounded theory in more detail in Chapter 16, in the context of analyzing qualitative data. It is helpful, however, to review these ideas about the contextual and grounded nature of qualitative research to recognize the commonalities among the different types of qualitative methods that we will explore.

FIELD RESEARCH

Field research is one of the more common types of qualitative methods in the social sciences and human services. A number of different approaches to conducting field research exist. Although there is some overlap among them, each introduces some special techniques of data collection.

Participant Observation

One technique for doing field research is **participant observation,** a method in which the researcher observes people in their natural environment (the "field") and the researcher is a part of and participates in the activities of the people, group, or situation being studied (DeWalt & DeWalt, 2011; Lofland et al., 2006). Participant observation research is naturalistic and involves some participation by the investigator, although, as we will see, the degree of such participation varies. In some cases, the investigator may have belonged to the group before the start of the research and can use this position as a group member to collect data. For example, a social worker might be interested in staff adaptation to antidiscriminatory hiring legislation. If he or she is on the agency personnel committee, such a position might serve as the context for participant observation. As the agency hires new staff members, the social worker can observe the reactions of the other staff in dealing with the new regulations. In other cases, a researcher must first gain access to a group to be a participant observer. Anthropologist Sue Estroff (1981) did this to learn more about the daily lives and problems of former mental patients. For two years, she joined in the lives of a group of deinstitutionalized mental patients, experiencing the drudgery and degradation of their daily routine. She worked at low-paying jobs, such as slipping rings onto drapery rods, that were the lot of these former patients. She took the powerful antipsychotic drugs that were routinely administered to them and that had distinctive side effects, such as hand tremors and jiggling legs. She also experienced the extreme depression and despair that result when patients suddenly stop taking these potent drugs. From her position as a participant in their subculture, she could observe the con games that characterized the relationships between patients and mental health professionals.

Through this type of participant observation, practitioners have access to a view of client groups that they cannot gain during an interview or therapy session. It is a unique view, because the researcher sees from the perspective of the client, which is especially valuable to anyone who works with groups that are stigmatized or commonly misunderstood by both practitioners and laypeople. Though many practitioners may not have the opportunity to engage in such observations personally, such research efforts by behavioral scientists can be used to develop a better understanding of client groups. Human service professionals should seek opportunities to conduct this kind of research themselves to understand particular groups or subcultures. In fact, practitioners might consider periodically engaging in participant observation of their clients, if possible, to detect ways in which the practitioner perspective may limit understanding of client groups.

Proponents of participant observation argue that it is the only method that enables the researcher to approximate *verstehen,* an empathic understanding of the subjective experiences of people. Of course, actual access to such experience is impossible; thoughts and feelings, by their very nature, are private. Even when someone talks about how he or she feels, the person has objectified that subjective experience into words, and thus changed it. Participant observers, however, can gain some insight regarding those subjective experiences by immersing themselves in the lives and daily experiences of the people who they study. By experiencing the same culture, the same values, and the same hopes and fears, researchers are in a better position to take on the point of view of these people. Despite its focus on subjective experiences, however, participant observation is still empirical, in the sense that it is grounded in observation, and issues of reliability and validity also concern those who use this method. Researchers using participant observation consider it to be no less systematic or scientific than the more positivistic research techniques.

So one reason researchers select participant observation and qualitative methods is because they have determined that an interpretive approach best advances knowledge in a particular area. A second reason for choosing these research methods is because the research is exploratory in nature, and theoretical development does not enable researchers to spell out relevant concepts or to develop precise hypotheses. Participant observation permits the researcher to view human behavior as it occurs in the natural environment without the restrictions of preconceived notions or explanations. Through observation, the researcher can begin to formulate concepts, variables, and hypotheses that seem relevant to the topic and grounded in the actual behavior of people.

It is important to recognize that, in participant observation, knowledge is gained from two distinct but linked kinds of observations. One is based on *participation,* where the researcher learns about the social world of those she observes by personally experiencing that world. This is the *verstehen* method proposed by Weber, and it provides understanding through empathic experience. This empathic experience is an important source of knowledge that offers an intersubjective understanding of other people's lives. The second is produced by *observation,* noting and recording how others behave and what occurs in a social setting. Observation provides understanding through a deep appreciation of the full context within which people live their lives. It enables social scientists to make rich descriptions of everyday social life.

Examples of Participant Observation. Some examples of participant observation can flesh out this discussion. In the mid-1980s, anthropologist Philippe Bourgois (1995), recently married at the time and looking for an apartment he could afford, moved into "El Barrio," an East Harlem neighborhood in New York. Although fieldwork was not his intent in moving there, he eventually used his residence as a springboard for doing research on the underground economy, social marginalization, and how the poor families in that community managed to survive. He lived there for three and a half years and got to know many of the community members. He visited their homes often and attended parties and celebrations with them. He observed how people managed to get by when they could get either no jobs at all or only poorly paying ones. Most of El Barrio's residents were law-abiding, but a small, publicly visible portion were involved in the drug trade. Bourgois became friends with two dozen street dealers and their families. He spent many nights on the streets and in the crack houses with both dealers and addicts. He saw how the residents who had nothing to do with drugs coped with the vibrant and, sometimes, violent drug world that pervaded their community.

With participant observation, then, researchers can observe processes and grasp levels of meaning that other, more objective methods, such as surveys or available statistical data, cannot uncover. Researchers also can identify differences between what people say they do and their actual behavior.

Observer Roles. In many types of research, the relationship between the researcher and those participating in the research is fairly clear-cut. In surveys, for example, participants know who the researchers are and that, as respondents, they are providing data to those researchers. In observational research and, especially, participant observation, the researcher–participant relationship becomes more problematic in that it can take a number of different forms. Two critical issues arise: the extent to which the observer will change the setting under observation, and the extent to which people should be informed that they are being used for research purposes. The way in which a researcher resolves these issues determines the nature of the observer–participant relationship for a given research project.

A participant observer is part of the activities being studied and, therefore, is in a position to influence the direction of those activities. For example, Sue Estroff might have wanted to organize the deinstitutionalized mental patients she studied into a lobbying group demanding better living conditions and improved treatment from mental health professionals. If she had done this early in her participant observation, however, would it have interfered with her research goals? Would she have learned all the sources of despair and degradation that these people experienced? Would she have learned how such groups, without the benefit of an intervening anthropologist, adapt to their plight? The resolution of this issue concerning the extent of intervention, of course, rests partly on the research question. If Estroff were interested in how such groups adapt without outside aid, then she should limit her influence on the group, even though humanitarian values might push her toward involvement. However, if she wanted to assess effective strategies for improving the lot of these groups, intervention on her part would be called for by the research question. Human service providers, in particular, need to be sensitive to this issue, because an important part of their role as practitioners is intervention. Providers need to recognize that intervention may, at times, be counterproductive to research goals.

This problem of the degree of intervention often is a question of whether the researcher is, first and foremost, a participant or an observer (Gold, 1958). Which of these two aspects should he or she emphasize? Let's look at each side of the issue. Those who emphasize the importance of participation by the observer argue that the investigator plays two roles—namely, that of scientist and that of group member. To fully comprehend the activities of the group and the dynamics of the situation, the researcher must become fully involved in the group. Otherwise, group members may not confide in the researcher. In addition, the researcher who does not participate is hampered in achieving *verstehen,* an empathic understanding of the deep meanings and experiences that are important to the group. To become fully involved, the researcher must act like any other group member—and this means intervening during those situations in which other group members might do so.

On the other side of the issue, those who emphasize observation over participation argue that the more fully one becomes a group member, the less objective one becomes. The real danger is that researchers will "go native"—that is, become so immersed in the group that they completely take on the perspective of that group and no longer view the situation from a less-interested perspective (Shupe & Bromley, 1980). Any semblance of a scientific perspective or judgment will be lost. Most participant observers attempt to strike a balance between total immersion and loss of objectivity on the one hand, and total separation with its consequent loss of information on the other. After all, going native can assist in developing the empathic understanding that is one of the goals of field research. In a sense, the field researcher must be somewhere between a stranger and a friend; it requires some judgment to detect the point beyond which friendliness has more negative than positive consequences for the research.

Another critical issue in the researcher–participant relationship is both practical and ethical: To what extent should the people who are studied be informed of the investigator's research purposes (Calvey, 2008)? This is an especially troubling problem in participant observation, because in some cases, fully informing people undermines the researcher's ability to gather accurate data. For example, a study of staff treatment of patients in a mental hospital was conducted by having researchers admitted to the hospital as patients without informing the staff of their research purposes (Rosenhan, 1973). Undoubtedly, hospital staff would have behaved quite differently had they known they were under surveillance. Therefore, some researchers take the position that concealment sometimes is necessary to conduct scientific work, and that researchers must judge whether the scientific gain justifies the deception and any potential injury—social or psychological—that might result. Others, however, hold adamantly to the position that any research on human beings must include "informed consent"—that is, that the people involved must be fully informed about the purposes of the research, any possible dangers or consequences, and the credentials of the researchers. Anything less, they argue, is both unethical and immoral, because it tricks people into cooperation and may lead to undesirable consequences of which they are not aware. (We dealt with this complex ethical dilemma at greater length in Chapter 3.)

In a classic piece on observational research, Raymond Gold (1958) identified three distinct observer roles that can emerge depending on how the issues of observer influence and informed consent are resolved: complete participant, participant-as-observer, and observer-as-participant. The distinguishing feature of the *complete participant* role is that the researcher's status as observer is not revealed to those who are being studied. The observer enters a group under the guise of being just another member and, essentially, plays that role while conducting the study. The researcher must be able to sustain this pretense for long periods of time, because studies using the complete participant role usually are characterized by lengthy involvement with the group studied. The complete participant role has proved to be valuable in studying groups, such as drug users or dealers, that otherwise might be closed to research if the observer's true

Research in Practice 9.1 Behavior and Social Environments: The Complete Participant Role in a Prison

Field research can be difficult and complicated to conduct, and it can put the researcher in situations where it is difficult to know what the proper action is. In fact, sociologist Richard Leo (1996, p. 125) put it this way: "Fieldwork is a morally ambiguous enterprise that is fraught with moral hazards, contingencies and uncertainties." A participant observation research study by James Marquart (2001) conducted in prisons illustrates some of these issues. Marquart's research also illustrates many of the steps in conducting field research discussed in this chapter.

Marquart first came into contact with the world of prisons while working on a project to evaluate the training of prison guards. He met a prison warden who invited him to visit his prison; Marquart did this a number of times over a period of a year or two. During these visits, Marquart came to know many of the guards and inmates, who encouraged him to learn what prison life was "really" like by working as a full-time prison guard. Marquart's specific research goal was to evaluate the effectiveness of a practice in the prison called the "building tender system," in which the prison used particularly dominant and aggressive inmates to control other inmates by meting out punishments, which included beatings. He recognized that becoming a prison guard and taking the complete participant role would give him a perspective on this system that he could gain in no other way. So, with the support of the warden, he began work as a full-time prison guard, a job he kept for about a year and a half.

One major issue that a field researcher confronts is what to tell the people he is observing in the field. Marquart's research was not truly disguised observation, because the warden and some of the guards knew that he was a sociologist making field observations of prison life. To those who knew of his research role, he never lied or misrepresented himself, yet he wasn't completely honest with them either. Although one of his major interests was in evaluating the building tender system, he didn't tell the prison officials this, because he feared they would become defensive about a practice they had implemented and refuse him access. Instead, he stated his interests to be something more general, involving the study of guards and guard work. This is what Richard Leo calls an "act of omission" (withholding information) rather than an "act of commission" (intentionally giving false information). Leo and some other field researchers argue that acts of omission are morally acceptable in field research because they are often necessary to get the research done (see Chapter 3). Marquart's belief was that if he had not withheld certain information, he could not have done his research. Yet, he clearly recognized that intentional falsification was morally unacceptable.

identity were known. Research in Practice 9.1 provides an interesting illustration of the complete participant role being used to better understand life in prison.

The *participant-as-observer* role differs from the complete participant role in that the researcher reveals his or her status as an observer to those who are being studied. In this role, the observer enters a group and participates in their routines but is known to be doing so for research purposes. As in the case of the complete participant role, the participant-as-observer spends a considerable amount of time observing in the group being studied. Community research often uses the participant-as-observer role, probably because of the large size of these groups and the need for direct access to information that the complete participant might find difficult or too time consuming to obtain while maintaining a disguise. Whyte's (1955) classic study, "Street Corner Society," is a fine example of the use of the participant-as-observer role.

The *observer-as-participant* role is similar to the participant-as-observer role in that the observer's true status is known to those being studied, but it differs with regard to the length of time that the observer spends with the group. The participant-as-observer role assumes a lengthy period of observation. The observer-as-participant role, however, involves brief contact with the group being studied—possibly for as little as one day. This brief contact tends to preclude the deep,

Prison life is filled with fear, danger, paranoia, suspicion, and factionalism—for both inmates and guards. It is a challenging environment in which to attempt to gain the rapport that is so essential to good fieldwork. Both guards and inmates came up with all kinds of theories as to who Marquart was and why he was working in the prison: He was a government agent, a spy, or a close relative of the warden. Marquart did a number of things over a period of time to build rapport. He worked hard and took on difficult and dangerous assignments, such as breaking up inmate fights. He lifted weights, boxed, and jogged with inmates to gain their respect. He also got into some serious and dangerous physical altercations with inmates. All of this enabled him, gradually, to become "invisible"—that is, perceived by both guards and inmates as just another prison guard.

One of the more difficult and morally ambiguous aspects of field research involves the researcher's responsibilities to those whom he or she observes in the field. In Marquart's case, the prison guards—and even the prisoners—let him into their world and their lives. What obligations did he have to them for doing this? When the guards accepted him in the role of prison guard, they expected him to perform that role well, and one part of that role was to provide support for other guards. This meant assisting the guards in their various tasks, coming to the aide of a guard attacked by a prisoner, and even, possibly, not informing on a guard who beats a prisoner. As Marquart put it, "The ability to 'keep one's mouth shut' was a highly prized asset and I quickly internalized this important value" (2001, p. 40). A good guard was expected to keep his mouth shut. Leo, Marquart, and some other field researchers argue that Marquart took on an implicit moral obligation when he moved into the role of prison guard. Implicit in the guards' and prisoners' acceptance of him was that he be a good guard and carry out all aspects of that role.

Prison is a violent place. Marquart observed prisoners brutalizing other prisoners. He watched guards beat inmates senseless with clubs as the inmates pleaded for mercy. He was so disturbed by some incidents he observed that he almost quit, yet he remained and developed a coping strategy of indifference. He also kept his mouth shut, not telling authorities outside the prison of any illegal or brutal actions he had observed. He respected the moral obligation he had incurred by going into the field, but it was surely a complex and ambiguous moral obligation. Other researchers might dispute the acceptability of his choices. Surely, there must be a line that can be crossed that nullifies the moral obligation. What if a guard killed an inmate? Some would argue that some of the actions Marquart observed crossed that line.

---

insightful results that characterize studies using the two previous roles. The observer-as-participant role is likely to generate shallower, superficial results. In fact, the brief contact that characterizes this role may lead the observer to misunderstand aspects of the group being studied. Because of these problems, the observer-as-participant role has been less popular for conducting serious social research.

Unobtrusive Observation

Some research questions call for or require the investigator to refrain from participation in the group being investigated. This is the case when the intrusive impact of an outsider might change the behavior of group members in ways that are detrimental to the research question. In such cases, the relationship adopted by the investigator is what Gold (1958) labeled the *complete observer role*—that is, the observer has no direct contact with or no substantial influence on those who are being observed. One way of doing such nonparticipant observation is an observational technique called **unobtrusive observation,** or **nonreactive observation:** Those under study are not aware that they are being studied, and the investigator does not change their behavior by his or her presence (Lee, 2000; Webb et al., 1981). Unobtrusive observation can be done in naturalistic or contrived settings, and involves both quantitative and qualitative observations. Two forms that unobtrusive observation can take are hidden observation and disguised observation.

Hidden Observation. In some research projects, we can observe behavior from a vantage point that is obscured from the view of those under observation—through a one-way mirror, perhaps, or by videotaping with a hidden camera. For example, some studies of aggressive behavior among children use observations in naturalistic settings by videotaping, with the camera in a hidden location, children at play in school yards (Pepler & Craig, 1995). The camera can be set up in a classroom window, out of sight of the children, and zoom lenses make possible clear observation of children's behavior from long distances. As long as the children are not aware of the cameras and the fact that they are being observed, the research is truly nonreactive in nature. This naturalistic, hidden observation is important in the study of aggression among children because children behave more normally under these conditions; in a contrived setting or an interview, it probably is impossible to make the same honest, natural observations. In fact, one group of researchers of such behavior noted that "the use of knives on our school playground tapes was so covert that it often took several passes through the audiovisual tapes to discern their presence" (Pepler & Craig, 1995, p. 550). Because the children clearly attempted to hide the knives from others, they would have been extremely unlikely to display such aggressive behavior to researchers in surveys or a contrived setting. Naturalistic and hidden observations are key to making such discoveries.

A major problem with hidden observations is ensuring that the observations are, in fact, hidden and truly unobtrusive. The unobtrusive nature of the study of children's aggression just mentioned, for example, was compromised in two ways: First, the school principal, teachers, and other adults supervising the children at play knew about the observations. All people have a tendency to react differently when they are being observed—they put their best foot forward or behave in a fashion they think is acceptable to the observer. The adults supervising these children may well have done the same thing—watching the children more closely or reacting more quickly to behaviors that hinted of aggression. If these adults behaved differently with the children than they would have if the children were not being observed, this would compromise the unobtrusive nature of the observations. A second compromise occurred because the researchers also wanted an audiotape of the children's conversations to fully understand the nature of their aggressive behavior. So the children had wireless microphones clipped to their clothing while they played in the school yard, thus making them aware that they were being observed. The researchers decided that both of these compromises were essential and that they had only minor effects on the validity of the observations made. The adults, for example, did not know exactly which children on the playground were being observed at a given time, and after a short period of being aware of the microphone, the children seemed to ignore it and play naturally. Other research supports this idea that people often tend to forget they are being observed and behave normally, especially if the observation occurs over a long period. This research on aggression among children does, however, illustrate the ways in which what appears at first to be hidden observation is not actually completely unobtrusive.

Disguised Observation. With some types of behavior, we can conduct what we call *disguised observation*: Researchers observe people in a naturalistic setting, but without participating or revealing that they are observing them. Any setting in which one can be present and not participate without calling attention to oneself is a potential scene for disguised observation. The observer enters a group under the guise of being just another member and then plays that role while conducting the observations.

One setting, for example, that might lend itself to such disguised observation is a public establishment, such as a bar or a tavern. A group of investigators interested in alcohol-related aggressive behavior (Graham et al., 1980) conducted exactly this kind of disguised observation. They decided that they could best gather information through unobtrusive observation of the behavior of people as they consumed alcohol in various bars of Vancouver, British Columbia. Teams of observers spent from 40 to 56 hours per week making observations in drinking establishments. Each team consisted of a male–female pair who would enter an establishment, locate a table with a good view of the saloon, and order a drink. They made every effort not to influence the people in the bar in any way. We consider such research to be nonparticipant rather than participant, because the investigators made efforts to have no contact with or influence on the behavior of the patrons. At times, this was impossible—a patron would wander over to their table and engage them in a conversation. In those cases, they quickly terminated the observations and left the bar. In other ways, we might question the unobtrusive character of their observation: The female observer often was the only Anglo female in the bar, the observers sometimes were the only people in the bar who were not at least slightly inebriated, and there often were social class differences between the dress and behavior of the observers and those being observed. Nonetheless, their impact on the behavior of the clientele probably was minimal, so we can consider this to have been disguised, nonparticipant observation.

STEPS IN FIELD RESEARCH

The exact steps taken in conducting field research vary depending on whether it is participant observation, unobtrusive observation, or some variant. Here, we will describe the steps taken in participant observation, recognizing that some parts of what follows may be unnecessary in other types of field research.

Problem Formulation

The first step in field research is to engage in problem formulation, including a literature review and conceptual development. From this assessment, the researcher establishes the specific goals of the research and decides whether field research is the most appropriate research strategy. A part of problem formulation also includes learning as much as we can about the people, groups, and settings that will be the focus of observation by reviewing previous research on the groups as well as any historical and literary materials that might enlighten us about the group and its culture. The more we learn before going into the field, the more effective we will be at making observations there.

Selecting a Field Setting

The second step is to decide which specific group to study. Whether we are studying deinstitutionalized mental patients, cocaine dealers, or motorcycle gangs, we have to decide exactly which group we will join and observe. One way to decide this is by finding a group that is accessible. Sometimes, a field setting presents itself as a by-product of some research or other activities. Barrie Thorne's (1993) participant observation in elementary schools arose because she was asked to assess issues of gender equity in the schools. She designed her field observations to achieve that goal, but she also obtained permission to make additional observations for her own research purposes. Clifford Stott was interested in how violence escalates among fans of British soccer teams, so this focus determined the necessity of making field observations of fans before, during, and after soccer matches (Stott & Reicher, 1998). A soccer fan himself, Stott joined other fans of the team he supported at international soccer matches, and these matches and fans became the focus of his participant observation. Anthropologist Nancy Scheper-Hughes (1992) selected a particular shantytown in Brazil as her field setting because she had lived there years earlier, before becoming an anthropologist, as a Peace Corps volunteer. Her earlier exposure had resulted in continuing ties with some people who lived there and made this shantytown a relatively accessible field setting for her.

Entering the Field

The third step is challenging: gaining entry into the group to be studied. In the complete participant role, this step is less of a problem, because the people do not know they are being studied—though we must be sufficiently like those being studied to gain access. In the other participant roles, however, where they know that we are outsiders and researchers, we must find some way to convince the people to accept our involvement as researchers. Several methods increase the likelihood that people will cooperate (Feldman, Bell, & Berger, 2003; Jorgensen, 1989). One way is to win the support of those with more status or influence in the group and then use our relationship with them to gain access to others. It would be best, for example, to approach the directors of a mental health center and enlist their aid before contacting caseworkers and ward staff.

Another way to increase cooperation is to present our reasons for conducting the research in a way that seems plausible and makes sense in the subjects' frame of reference. Esoteric or abstract scientific goals are unlikely to appeal to an agency director or a struggling single parent on welfare. Instead, we should emphasize that our major concern is understanding their thoughts and behaviors as being legitimate, acceptable, and appropriate. Nothing closes doors faster than the hint that we intend to evaluate the group. The door of a welfare recipient may open if we say we are studying the difficulties confronting parents on welfare, but it will surely be slammed shut if we say we want to separate the good welfare recipients from the bad.

Cooperation also is enhanced if we have some means of legitimizing ourselves as researchers—perhaps through an affiliation with a university that supports the study or an agency with an interest in the research. In a study of a sexually transmitted disease (STD) clinic, for example, Joseph Sheley (1976) gained entrance because he was involved with a larger community study of STDs. Such legitimization can backfire, of course, if the group we hope to study is suspicious of or hostile toward the organization with which we are affiliated. Sheley, for example, was allowed into the clinic but found himself with a degree of "outsider" status because of his association with the community STD study.

Finally, we may need to use informants to gain entry into some groups. An *informant* is an insider who can introduce us to others in the group, ease our acceptance into the group, and help us interpret how the group views the world. Especially with informal subcultures, the informant technique is a valuable approach.

Sometimes it takes a bit of creativity—or even courage—to gain entry into some field settings. Sociologist Ruth Horowitz (1987) wanted to study Latino gangs in a particular city, but as a Jewish woman, she did not have easy entry into these groups. So, she sat on a bench in a park frequented by gang members until they approached her—an obvious outsider on their turf. Eventually, one of the leaders of the gang asked who she was. She told him that she wanted to write a book about Latino youth and then convinced him to introduce her to other members of the gang.

In some cases, the researcher may know members of the group being observed, and these personal contacts can ease the researcher's entry into the group. For example, in a study of violence among British soccer fans, the anthropologist doing the study selected a particular group of fans to join and observe because he had grown up and gone to school with some of them (Armstrong, 1993). These personal contacts made it easier for the researcher to gain their cooperation.

Developing Rapport in the Field

The fourth step in participant observation is to develop rapport and trust with the people who are being studied so they will serve as useful and accurate sources of information. This can be time-consuming, trying, and traumatic. It is a problem with which the human service professional can readily identify. The community organizer attempting to gain the trust of migrant workers, the substance-abuse worker dealing with a narcotics addict, and the child welfare worker running a group home for girls can all attest to the importance of establishing rapport. Although in many cases the human service worker can express a sincere desire to help as a means of establishing rapport, the researcher cannot always employ this approach, because the research goals may not include providing such help. During the initial stages of the research, people are likely to be distant if not outright distrustful. We are likely to make errors and social gaffes that offend the people we have joined. More than one participant observation effort has had to be curtailed because the investigator inadvertently alienated the people being studied.

Many elements are involved in developing rapport or trust with our informants (Feldman, Bell, & Berger, 2003; Spano, 2006). Rapport can emerge if the informants and group members view the investigator as a basically nice person who will do them no harm. It matters little if the informants know of or agree with the research goals—only that they develop a positive attitude toward the investigator. Trust and rapport also can emerge if the investigator shows through behavior that he or she agrees with— or, at least, has some sympathy for—the group's perspective. If we join our field contacts in some of their routine activities, such as drinking beer or playing cards, they are likely to view us as someone who accepts them and someone they can trust. Of course, the researcher must balance the need for acceptance against personal and professional standards of behavior. Another way to enhance trust and rapport is to reduce the social distance between the researcher and those who are being observed. In field studies of schoolchildren, this often can be achieved by avoiding positions of authority or by avoiding intervening with the children in ways that other adults, teachers, or school officials do. For example, field researchers observing children avoid intervening in fights or other behavioral problems unless some serious accident or injury might occur (Mandell, 1988; Thorne, 1993). Finally, researchers can enhance rapport if the relationship between investigator and group members is reciprocal—that is, both the observer and the group members have something the other needs and wants. We might, for example, gain scientific data from our informants, whereas they hope to gain some publicity and attendant public concern from the publication of our results.

Becoming Invisible

In field research, being "invisible" means that those who are present perceive the observer as a natural part of the setting, not as an outsider or as someone in any way unusual. Even in the participant-as-observer role, when the people know we are researchers, we can become invisible if the others begin to see us as "just one of them." This has something to do with rapport: As rapport develops, the observer comes to be seen as a natural part of the setting by the people being observed. Becoming invisible also is partly a matter of time: The longer a person is in the scene, the less that he or she is noticed as being unusual or as an outsider. Initially, the presence of the observer may change behavior, but this effect often dissipates as time passes. People also become invisible when they join in the routine activities in the setting, whether working side by side at some task, drinking beer or smoking marijuana with the others at the scene, or joining in on some illegal behavior. By doing these things, the group comes to see the observer as a routine part of their setting. Another way to become invisible is to develop friendships with those being observed. When this happens, the friendship role, in the eyes of those being observed, becomes more important than the researcher role. As the friendship role becomes more salient, people become more open and honest and less guarded in their interactions with the observer. The Eye on Ethics section explores more dimensions of ethical behavior in the field.

Attitude of the Researcher

In positivist research, the researcher's attitude is presumed to be one of objectivity and detachment. In field research, however, researcher–subject

Eye on Ethics: The Moral Complexity of Research Work in Field Settings

Field researchers sometimes find themselves observing people who are doing something illegal, disreputable, or stigmatizing, such as dealing drugs, performing a strip tease dance, or engaging in deviant sexual behavior. On occasion, the subjects of the observation have asked or expected the researcher to participate in, or in some fashion assist them, in their illegal or deviant behavior, at least to the point of not interfering or not bringing any harm or punishment to them. What ethical obligations does a researcher have in such situations?

One solution to such ethical dilemmas, of course, is to not initiate field research among groups for whom such issues are likely to arise (Calvey, 2008). However, this is an extraordinarily limiting strategy in that it places many forms of social behavior beyond the reach of field research. In addition, one does not always know ahead of time when such ethical dilemmas will be an issue. In choosing to study police detectives, for example, one might not predict that those detectives might brutalize someone they have arrested. Should one avoid all field research on police? Again, that would remove extraordinary amounts of social life from the view of social science research.

Another solution to the dilemma rests on the purported value of the research and weighs that against the harm that might be caused by the deviant behavior of those being observed. By refusing to participate or by interfering, the researcher would likely threaten the rapport with the observed to the point where the research project becomes untenable. The observed may no longer cooperate, or may become so restrained and inauthentic in their behaviors that few valid observations can be made. Or, even worse, they might reject the researcher outright. In either event, the argument goes, the researcher is justified in ignoring, or even in some cases supporting, the deviant behavior in order to protect the integrity of the research project. This assumes, of course, that the benefits of the research are considerable and the harm of the deviant behavior is not too substantial. Judgments about this must be considered carefully, possibly including consultations with others without a stake in the research project.

Carl Klockars (1979) suggests a third solution to the dilemma which is based on the idea that the people being observed have, by virtue of permitting the researcher into their lives and space, placed a confidence in the researcher:

> This confidence and the access which is granted based upon it is a complex set of understandings, some explicit and some tacit, some formal, some taken for granted. In any given field research relationship it is very difficult to describe the details of such understandings as roles evolve and the rules and responsibilities proceeding from them evolve with them. However, in all field research with deviant subjects that confidence begins with a promise by the researcher not to "blow the whistle" on his subjects ... (Klockars, 1979, p. 275)

Klockars argues that field researchers develop complex relationships with those they observe in the field, and those relationships involve a plethora of moral obligations. The field worker is placed into a particular field role by the agreements, either implicitly or explicitly, that are forged by researcher and subject. Police officers, for example, may cast the observer into the role of "fellow undercover cop," and they fully expect that the researcher will live up to that role, just as another officer would. A fellow cop would not blow the whistle on another cop who harasses or brutalizes suspects, and the police expect the fieldworker to live up to that role. In fact, Klockars argues, the police have let the fieldworker into their lives precisely because of the moral assumption that the researcher will live up to those role obligations. Even though nothing was explicitly said about it, such a belief is at the foundation of the relationship.

So what does a researcher do if the police harass or brutalize someone in his or her custody? For Klockars, the resolution of the ethical dilemma is clear: "It is the immediate, morally unquestionable, and compelling good end of keeping one's promise to one's subjects" (Klockars, 1979, pp. 275–276). The researcher ignores and goes along. A civilian who is trying to be a "decent human being" might not ignore the deviance. But Klockars' answer to that is: "Decent human beings do not; morally competent fieldworkers do" (Klockars, 1979, p. 276). Not everyone would agree with Klockars's conclusion, and certainly police could cross a line that could not be ignored by a field researcher. However, whether one agrees with Klockars or not, his analysis does suggest the complexity of the relationships forged in the field and their implications for conducting ethical research.

relationships are more extensive, complex, and personal. As Philippe Bourgois put it, "in order to collect 'accurate data,' ethnographers violate the canons of positivist research; we become intimately involved with the people we study" (1995, p. 13). Another anthropologist put it this way: "The ethnographer must be intellectually poised between familiarity and strangeness, while socially, he or she is poised between 'stranger' and 'friend'" (Powdermaker, 1966, p. 20). So, the researcher's role may be that of friend or stranger—or somewhere in between. This complexity and ambiguity means that each field observer needs to address the issue of what his or her attitude should be toward those who are being observed.

In most field settings, the researcher's attitude probably should be one of *openness* to a wide range of types of behavior and of *respect* for the dignity of the research subjects. As the examples in this chapter show, field researchers sometimes find themselves observing behavior that they find morally offensive or politically unpalatable. The researcher's goal, however, is not to judge, but rather to observe, record, and learn. Moral or political reactions can interfere with these goals and may threaten the rapport that is necessary to achieving good field research. In addition, ethical principles (see Chapter 3) dictate that the people who let us into their lives should not be harmed, and taking moral or political offense can be a form of attack. Researchers who cannot achieve this attitude of openness and respect toward particular groups might be best served by not doing field research on those groups.

The researcher's attitude also needs to be *reciprocal,* recognizing that the subjects make as significant a contribution to the production and interpretation of knowledge as the researcher does. A dangerous attitude is one that Barrie Thorne (1993) calls "studying down," in which the researcher assumes that it is the researchers who produce or "discover" knowledge, and that the subjects are less informed and less able to contribute to the production of knowledge. Thorne ran across this attitude in research on children; many researchers seemed to dismiss the possibility that the children being observed could teach the researchers something and the children could help produce knowledge and understanding. Thorne approached her field observations "with an assumption that kids are competent social actors who take an active role in shaping their daily experiences. I wanted to sustain an attitude of respectful discovery, to uncover and document kids' points of view and meanings" (1993, p. 12).

Finally, the researcher needs to *balance* his or her attitude in terms of identifying both the positive and negative aspects of the settings or cultures being observed. Philippe Bourgois, in his field research on inner-city street culture, points out that:

[T]he methodological logistics of participant observation require researchers to be physically present and personally involved. This encourages them to overlook negative dynamics because they need to be empathetically engaged with the people they study and must also have their permission to live with them. (1995, p. 14)

This can produce an unwitting self-censorship when the researcher fails to notice or report on some of the negative aspects of the behavior or lifestyle of the subjects. Bourgois found aspects of the street culture that he studied to be violent, dangerous, and abhorrent. Yet, a balanced attitude requires that the researcher's overall picture is neither unrealistically negative nor unrealistically positive.

Observing and Recording in the Field

The center of attention in field research, of course, is observing and recording what occurs. This cannot truly begin, however, until we have accomplished the other steps just described. Although field researchers keep track of what they observe while entering the field and gaining rapport, the best observations depend on those things having been achieved. What observations to record and how to record them are discussed later in this chapter.

Exiting the Field

In most field research, the period of observations in the field ends because the researcher has collected sufficient data (or run out of grant money). When this time comes, the researcher must leave the field in a way that brings no negative consequences to the people being observed. Because field research involves the researcher living in some degree of intimacy with those being studied, it is not uncommon for some level of personal relationship to develop. Acquaintances, friendships, and maybe even more intense relationships can emerge. The researcher needs to sever these relationships in such a way that people don't experience significant social or emotional loss. This may mean that, throughout the period of being in the field, the researcher remains somewhat socially or emotionally distant so that complicating personal relationships don't develop to the point where difficulty in exiting the field occurs. This is one way to avoid expectations of excessive intimacy or permanency in a relationship. Of course, there is a balance here, because some level of friendly involvement may be essential to developing rapport. From the very beginning, however, the researcher has an eye on the exit in terms of developing relationships with respondents.

RECORDING OBSERVATIONS IN FIELD RESEARCH

Field research is most closely associated with qualitative research, but observations made in the field can involve either qualitative or quantitative data or both. Accordingly, the manner in which field researchers record observations depends on whether the observations primarily are quantitative or qualitative in nature. Qualitative observation typically calls for less structured *field notes,* whereas quantitative observation typically uses more structured recording of data on *coding sheets.*

Qualitative Observation: Field Notes

Detailed, descriptive accounts of the observations made during a given period are called **field notes.** The precise nature of field notes varies greatly from one study to another, but all field notes should include six elements (Bogdan & Taylor, 1975; Lofland et al., 2006):

1. A *running description* makes up the bulk of the field notes. This is simply a record of the day's observations, with a primary concern of recording accurately the concrete events that were observed. The researcher should avoid analyzing persons or events while in the field, both because there is not the time and because it interferes with observation of the ongoing scene. Instead, he or she should concentrate on faithfully recording what occurs.

2. Field notes also include *accounts of previous episodes that were forgotten or went unnoticed* but that the investigator remembered while still in the field. When preparing the field notes from any observation session, it is likely that the researcher may forget or leave out certain events. Subsequent observations may bring the forgotten episodes back to mind. The researcher should record these events when remembered, with the proper notation concerning when they originally occurred.

3. *Analytical ideas and inferences* refer to spur-of-the-moment ideas concerning such things as data analysis, important variables, speculation regarding causal sequences, and the like. Researchers should record these "flashes of insight" regarding any aspect of the study when they occur. Reviewing these ideas after the completion of observations can greatly benefit the final data analysis and writing of the report. Although most data analysis is reserved until after the observation period, no researcher wants to forget whatever analytical ideas occurred while in the field.

4. *Personal impressions and feelings* should be noted, because the possibility that bias might color our observations is always present. Recording

personal impressions and feelings helps minimize this bias by giving a sense of the perspective from which the observer is viewing various persons, places, or events. Does the observer simply dislike a certain person in the setting? If so, the observer should honestly record such a feeling when it first occurs. This can prove to be beneficial when reviewing accounts relating to that person to see if the researcher's personal feelings influenced the description.

5. *Notes for further information* are notes that observers write to and for themselves: plans for future observations, specific things or persons to look for, and the like. It is risky to rely on memory for anything important relating to the study.

6. *Methodological notes* refer to any ideas that relate to techniques for conducting field research in this setting. As researchers, we should note any difficulties we have in collecting data, any biases that might be introduced by the data-collection techniques, or any changes in how we make and record observations. The purpose of this is to better prepare us to assess validity (to be discussed shortly) and to provide insight for future researchers who might make observations in similar settings.

How to Record. Field notes can take a number of different forms (Bernard, 2006; Lofland et al., 2006). For example, parts of field notes might consist of brief jottings where researchers make note of something that is happening or something that occurs to them. Many field researchers carry a notepad at all times, even when not in the field, to make a note of things as they occur or as they think of them. Other parts of field notes might contain a more detailed and complete written record of what is happening in some setting. In some cases, instead of writing field notes, researchers use laptop or notebook computers or audiotapes to make their recordings. In other cases, conversations or interviews conducted in the field might be tape-recorded or videotaped for later analysis. The choice of which format to use depends on which most accurately preserves the record without interfering with rapport.

Recording field notes is particularly problematic for participant observers whose status as an observer is disguised. Because such observers must constantly guard against having their true identity revealed, they must take notes surreptitiously. In some settings, a bit of ingenuity on the part of the researcher can handle this problem quite nicely. For example, in her study of people's behavior in bars, Sheri Cavan (1966) solved the note-taking problem by making frequent trips to the restroom and recording her observations there. Given the well-recognized effect of alcoholic beverages on the human body, her trips probably raised little suspicion among the other bar patrons.

In many participant observation settings, no amount of innovation will allow the researcher to record observations on the scene. In these situations, there is no alternative but to wait and record observations after leaving the observational setting. Relying on memory in this fashion is less than desirable, however, because memory is fallible. The observer should record observations as soon as possible to minimize the likelihood of forgetting important episodes.

What to Record. For someone who has never conducted participant observation research, collecting data through field notes can be particularly frustrating and confusing. What should the researcher watch for? What should he or she include in the field notes? These are difficult questions even for veteran observers. In addition, because participant observation research may be exploratory, researchers often are only partially aware of what might be relevant. It is possible, nevertheless, to organize our thoughts around some general categories of things to observe and record (Bogdan & Biklen, 1992; Lofland et al., 2006; Runcie, 1980):

1. *The setting:* Field notes should contain some description of the general physical and social setting being observed. Is it a bar, a restaurant, or

a ward of a mental institution? Are there any physical objects or barriers that might play a role during the social interaction in this setting? In some cases, it would be valuable to begin each day's field notes with a drawing or photograph of the physical layout being observed. Such things as time of day, weather, or the presence of others who are not the focus of your observations are useful information in some field research. In short, the field notes serve to remind us—when we review them weeks, months, or even years later—of the characteristics of the setting in which we observed behavior.

2. *The people:* Field notes should include a physical and social description of the main characters who are the focus of our observations. How many people are there? How are they dressed? What are their ages, genders, and socioeconomic characteristics (as well as we can observe from physical appearance)? Again, field notes should tell us, for each separate day of observation, who was present, who entered and left the setting during observation, and how the cast changed from one day to the next.

3. *Individual actions and activities:* The central observations in most studies are the behaviors of the people in the settings. How do they relate to one another? Who talks to whom, and in what fashion? What sequences of behavior occur? In addition, we may want to record the duration and the frequency of these interactions. Do repetitive cycles of behavior occur? Is there a particular sequencing of behavior?

4. *Group behavior:* In some cases, the behavior of groups is an important bit of information. How long does a group of people remain on the scene? How does one group relate to another? It might be useful, for example, to know what cliques have formed in a setting. What we record here describes the social structure of the setting, such as the statuses and roles that various people occupy and the relationships between them.

5. *Meanings and perspectives:* Field researchers are sensitive to the subjective meanings that people give to themselves and their behavior, which is one of the reasons for doing qualitative field research. So, field notes should contain observations about these meanings and what words or behaviors are evidence of those meanings. *Perspectives* refers to general ways of thinking that people exhibit, evidence of which should appear in the field notes.

Quantitative Observation: Coding Sheets

When it is possible to do quantitative observation in field research, such observation often involves a process of **coding,** or categorizing behaviors into a limited number of preordained categories. To do this, researchers specify, as clearly as possible, the behaviors to be observed or counted during data collection. When possible, use of coding sheets is desirable. A *coding sheet* is simply a form designed to facilitate the categorizing and counting of behaviors. For example, a typical coding sheet lists various behaviors with blanks following them for checking off the behaviors as they occur. If the duration of a behavior also is important, additional blanks record the timing.

The coding sheet for a particular research project is likely to be a unique, highly specific document that reflects the special concerns of that project. Nevertheless, a number of coding schemes have sufficient generality to use in a number of different settings. For example, Table 9.1 presents a coding scheme based on Robert Bales's theory about the interactional strategies that people use when they interact in groups, described in Chapter 8 (p. 204). Table 9.1 presents a coding scheme of some of Bales's interaction categories as they might be used to study interaction in a counseling group for intimate partner abusers. So the column on the left of Table 9.1 shows a few of the conceptual categories Bales uses to understand strategies used in social interaction. The middle column presents some concrete examples of what each category might look like in actual social interaction in order to assist the coders in categorizing behaviors. The

FIELD RESEARCH AND QUALITATIVE METHODS 237

TABLE 9.1 Coding Categories for Bales's (1950) Theory of Social Interaction Strategies in Groups (see p. 204), Illustrated with Interaction in a Counseling Group for Intimate Partner Abusers

Description of Interaction Categories	Example of Behavior	Symbol for Coding Sheet
Social-Emotional Behavior:		
Shows solidarity	Gives other group members "high five" in response to member comment	1-1
Shows antagonism	Shouts, slams notebook on table	1-2
Shows tension release	Laughs and nods agreement when member pokes fun at his own childish behavior toward his girlfriend.	1-3
Shows tension	Glares and refuses to talk when leader confronts him about denying responsibility	1-4
Task Behavior:		
Gives suggestion or direction	Tells other group member to try taking a "time out" when he starts getting agitated	2-5
Asks for suggestion or direction	Describes conflict; asks group members what he could have done differently	2-6
Gives opinion or evaluation	States that showing trust in partner is important	2-7
Asks for opinion or evaluation	Asks if how he handled situation when wife was late getting home was good	2-8

NOTE: First number of symbol indicates whether a Social-Emotional or Task Behavior; second number indicates type of Social-Emotional or Task Behavior.

right-hand column shows the symbols that would be entered on the actual coding sheet to show that a particular interaction strategy had been displayed. The actual coding sheet is displayed in Figure 9.1. Using the symbols from Table 9.1, each observer would indicate, for each member of the group, which interaction strategies were displayed during each five-minute interval of the 30-minute counseling sessions. The result is a running account of the kinds of interaction strategies used by members of the group.

The development of an efficacious coding scheme requires considerable care. The coding categories should derive from the theories and hypotheses being tested in the research. In the example in Table 9.1, the researchers' concern was with the nature and quality of social interaction in a group, and the categories that were derived from Bales's theory reflect that focus. In addition, coding categories should be highly specific and behavioral. Obviously, the degree to which we can achieve this is limited, because overspecificity soon becomes cumbersome and meaningless. For example, in the study by intimate partner abusers, a category of "speaks" would be too general, because it does not inform us about the nature of verbal contribution. At the other extreme, a category such as "raises eyebrows" is so specific that we cannot determine the meaning of the behavior. Thus, we walk a fine line between being too specific and being too general in providing a coding scheme that enables us to answer our research questions. It is important to

Time Intervals	:00 - :05	:06 - :10	:11 - :15	:16 - :20	:21 - :25	:26 - :30
Group Member ID #						
001	1-1	1-3	1-1; 1-4		1-1	1-1
002	1-3			2-5	2-7	2-7
003				1-4		
004	2-1	2-1; 1-4			1-4	

FIGURE 9.1 Coding Sheet Used to Record Data in Five-Minute Intervals during Thirty-Minute Counseling Sessions, Using Categories Described in Table 9.1

recognize that, although coding behavior with such schemes may appear to be quantifiable and objective, a considerable degree of subjective interpretation is involved. The coder must decide, for example, whether a given response is positive or negative and shows solidarity or antagonism; these judgments are necessarily subjective.

The use of coding schemes is not limited to situations in which a group is small, well-organized, or engaging in highly structured behavior. If it is possible to specify concepts and hypotheses precisely—in other words, if the research clearly is hypothesis testing rather than exploratory—then it may be possible to develop a precise coding scheme for data collection. In their disguised observation study of alcohol-related aggression, Kathryn Graham and colleagues (1980) were able to do this. Their basic hypothesis was that aggressive behavior among men when they drink resulted from situational factors as much as from psychological predispositions toward violence. They hypothesized that aversive stimuli in bars (their independent variable) serve as cues that allow or encourage aggressive behavior (the dependent variable). They coded the dependent variable using a dichotomous coding scheme: non-physical aggression (swearing or other forms of abusive language), and physical aggression. Within the physical category, behavior was coded as physical threats or challenges to fight but no actual contact; aggressive but noninjurious physical contact, such as grabbing and pushing; and actual physical violence, such as punching and kicking.

The independent variable—situational factors eliciting aggression—was, needless to say, more complex to code. First, the researchers spent some weeks in the field observing and developing precise definitions and coding schemes for the situational variables. Here are a few of the coding categories they developed:

Location
1 = downtown bar
2 = suburban bar

Time of day:
1 = 9 a.m. to noon
2 = noon to 3 p.m.
3 = 3 p.m. to 6 p.m. and so on

Noise level:
1 = very quiet
2 = medium quiet
3 = medium loud
4 = loud

Sexual bodily contact:
1 = none, very casual
2 = discreet necking
3 = heavy necking, touching
4 = flagrant fondling

Friendliness to strangers:
1 = open, lots of conversation with strangers
2 = closed, people talk only to members of their own group

Each two-person observation team spent between two and two and a half hours in an establishment. Most recording of observations was done after leaving the establishment so that note-taking would not attract attention.

This unobtrusive observation illustrates the manner in which field observers can use a precise, quantifiable coding scheme if the hypotheses to be tested are sufficiently developed. The investigators also found, however, that coding, although the major form of data collection, was not sufficient by itself. They needed to collect qualitative data as well, because while they were in the field, more variables of importance began to emerge. The researchers wanted to record descriptive accounts of aggressive incidents to ensure a complete record. This provides an illustration of a grounded theory approach, where data collection changes while still in process, because evaluation suggests that some new theoretical concepts are important.

Coding schemes can become highly complex, involving many categories of behavior, timing of behaviors, measures of intensity, and the like. We can only use more complex coding schemes, however, in situations where we can record accurately all that is necessary. The study described in Table 9.1 of a single, small, task-oriented group enabled the use of a complicated coding scheme. In the study by Graham and colleagues, this would have been considerably more difficult, because the group (the clientele of a bar) was large and shifting in composition, much was going on, and the actual recording of observations had to wait until after the observation period had concluded. This research setting necessitated a simpler coding scheme. Furthermore, investigations using complex coding schemes that require intense concentration on the part of the observer often require a number of observers, each of whom records for a short period and is then relieved by another observer. This reduces error caused by observer fatigue or fluctuations in concentration. In some investigations, group behavior is recorded on videotape to reduce error and allow researchers to view the group as often as needed to code behavior properly. In developing a coding scheme, in short, researchers must make sure the scheme does not become so complex as to become unusable, given the resources at hand.

Coding schemes are not appropriate forms of recording observations in all field research. In some cases, as with exploratory research, we cannot develop hypotheses with sufficient precision to operationalize concepts through coding schemes, because the research is intended to explore and discover rather than to explain and predict. In other cases, a nonpositivist approach suggests that the nature of some phenomena does not lend itself to quantification; in fact, proponents of the nonpositivist approaches argue that quantification can lead to distortion and misunderstanding of what is going on. In these cases, the hypotheses involve variables and relationships that require considerable interpretive effort on the part of the observer in the field and cannot easily be condensed to a few coding categories. In still other cases, the complexity and lack of structure in the group being observed render coding schemes useless. In all these situations, the investigator is likely to turn to field notes as a means of recording observations.

OTHER QUALITATIVE METHODS

In addition to field research, the social sciences and human services use a number of other important qualitative research methods—sometimes on their own, and sometimes as part of a field research study.

In-Depth Interviewing

Chapter 7 discussed the use of interviews in survey research, but those interviews generally are more structured and focused than the in-depth interviewing that often is used in qualitative research. **In-depth interviews,** or **ethnographic interviews,** are informal and unstructured interviews that explore a wide range of topics and that may last for a long time, even days or weeks. Often, they are more like a rambling conversation, with the interviewer relatively nondirective and the person being interviewed fairly unconstrained in what they talk about (Fontana & Frey, 1994; Patton, 2002). Actually, there is some overlap between participant observation and in-depth interviewing, because participant observation often gathers some data through informal interviews with people in the field.

These interview data are a third source of data collected in participant observation, in addition to gathering data through participation and observation. Yet in-depth interviewing and participant observation are distinct, because, in contrast to in-depth interviewing, true participant observation research also gathers data through participation and observation. In addition, interviews can be a mechanism for collecting qualitative data apart from field research. For example, Sean Gilmore and Alicia Crissman (1997) studied the link between gender and violence among teens who play video games. Their main data-gathering tools were unstructured interviews, which enabled the researchers to explore issues of gender identity in great breadth and depth. This topic had been the focus of little previous research, so the researchers had no existing knowledge base from which to derive meaningful concepts or to develop hypotheses. Instead, they wanted the concepts and hypotheses to emerge from the freewheeling and friendly conversations that were their unstructured interviews. These interviews were supplemented with some direct observation of the teens' conversations and behavior as they played the video games. As another example of in-depth interviews, Betty Dobratz and Stephanie Shanks-Miele (1997) conducted a study of the white separatist movement in the United States by conducting in-depth interviews with leaders and members of the movement. They also, however, supplemented the interview data with field observations, such as attending white separatist rallies, dinners, congresses, and cross burnings. Although their data primarily came from the interviews, the field observations provided additional important information and insights that the interviews could not provide.

The researcher approaches an in-depth interview with some general topics of interest and asks questions that probe into those areas. The whole process, however, is much more interactive and collaborative and much less directive than that of survey interviews (Holstein & Gubrium, 1995). It is more like a conversation. The researcher talks, rather than just asking questions, to keep the conversation going. The researcher may talk about himself or herself, his or her life, and even respond to questions the respondent asks—something not normally done in a survey interview. The researcher also permits the interview to take unexpected directions if these appear to be rewarding in terms of the research question or essential to maintaining the rapport and interest of the respondent. In fact, the relationship between interviewer and respondent often becomes one of equals conversing rather than one of an expert gathering data from a subject. Yet, the general topics that the researcher needs to cover impose a structure of sorts on the interview. This is especially apparent when more than one person is interviewed, because the researcher must make sure that he or she covers the same general topics with each person.

The goal of the in-depth interview is similar to that of participant observation—namely, to explore how the world appears to the respondent without imposing inappropriate structure on the views that they express by using preestablished categories or an overly restrictive direction on what subjects explore and how they express it. The respondent's perspective should unfold and be framed in ways that make sense to him or her; it should not be limited or constrained by the researcher's preconceived category systems or structures of meaning. The value of such in-depth interviewing is especially remarkable when studying behavior in very diverse cultures, as Research in Practice 9.2 illustrates.

Case Studies, Life Histories, and Narratives

Another qualitative research technique is variously called *narrative inquiry, life histories,* or *case studies* (Clandinin & Connelly, 2000; Yin, 2009). Although there are some differences among these approaches, they all involve a detailed descriptive account of part or all of a particular individual's life or, in some case studies, of an organization or an event. The goal is to gain understanding through depth and richness of detail. The description in case studies and life histories is detailed and sometimes is called a "thick" description—that is, a complete and literal accounting of the person or setting under study. Some quantitative data might be included, but the emphasis is on telling a story in prose or narrative. Researchers base case studies and life histories on direct observation, interviews, document analysis, organizational records, or some combination thereof—basically, any data that contributes to a description of the case under study.

Case studies and life histories share with participant observation a desire to understand how the social world looks from the perspective of the person being studied. Anthropologist Bourgois (1995), for example, used a life-history approach in his participant observation research in El Barrio: He tape-recorded long conversations with his informants to see how their current circumstances and behavior were part of the flow of their lives. One of the strengths of case studies and life histories is that they permit the people being studied to play a big part in framing and providing meaning for their lives, rather than having meaning and interpretation imposed by the observer. Case studies take a much longer time perspective, however, because they typically explore a good part—if not the whole—of a person's life. Case studies and life histories have proven to be useful methodologies in feminist research and in interpretivist and critical approaches (Lawless, 1991).

The primary goal of most case studies and life histories is an idiographic explanation that focuses on an in-depth understanding of a particular case. Such an understanding might enhance our comprehension of other cases and situations, but the primary focus is description, not generalization. The advantage of these methods is the rich and detailed descriptions they provide of people's lives, experiences, and circumstances. In addition, the ability of these methods to allow people to speak in their own voices makes them valuable sources of data. Because they are based on one person's life, however, case studies and life histories are criticized on the grounds that the results are not generalizable beyond that one case. The data from such studies also contain a considerable element of subjectivity because of their dependence on the accounts of one individual. These methods also suffer from the normal errors of people's memories as well as from selective recall on the part of the individual. In fact, the data produced in narratives sometimes are the result of collaboration between researcher and subject, where the final story is one that they both find acceptable. To overcome some of these problems, people producing case histories sometimes check for errors or misinterpretations with others who are knowledgeable of the people or events in the case history. Of course, errors in memory or selective recall may be valuable data in themselves, in that we may learn as much about people from how they remember or reconstruct their past as we may from their actual past. In fact, proponents of case studies and life histories argue that a person's own story is important to understand, irrespective of the objective facts.

Focus Groups

We discussed focus groups as a form of survey research in Chapter 7 because they involve interviewing people, but focus groups deserve mention here as a qualitative research method. Focus groups also are called *group depth interviews,* because they are like an in-depth interview with a number of people at the same time. The advantage of focus groups is that they are flexible forms of data collection that leave the participants free to frame their answers and construct meaning as they wish. Although some quantitative data are collected as a part of focus groups, people are free to talk as much as they wish, and their complete responses serve as data for the research.

RESEARCH IN PRACTICE 9.2   Policy Planning and Development: Field Research to Inform Policy on Homeless Children in Diverse Cultures

Hasan Reza is a master's level social worker who has conducted several qualitative research projects in his home country of Bangladesh examining various social welfare issues impacting vulnerable populations. He has used his research to make policy and program recommendations to domestic and international advocacy and service organizations. According to Hasan, "Most research on social welfare issues in Bangladesh has been conducted by professional researchers from other places. These tend to be highly qualified researchers, but the value of the research is limited because it is rarely grounded in actual fieldwork nor does it fully capture the complexity of factors that create and perpetuate social welfare issues in Bangladesh."

Over the past several years while receiving advanced training in research methods as a social work doctoral student at the University of Chicago, Hasan has remained committed to advancing understandings of social welfare issues in Bangladesh. As he explains, "My goal is to use the theoretical and methodological training I have received in developing a research agenda that will help draw attention to the issues I have seen in my country. Truly understanding poverty and homelessness in a country like Bangladesh is very hard to do from a western perspective because these issues have different meanings there. For example, in poor households women are supposed to serve their husband first before they eat. The best part of the meal is usually consumed by him. Then children are served. Whatever is left is consumed by the wife, and in many cases this is very little. It is difficult for an outsider to understand this without in-depth knowledge about such cultural practices. Without understanding household dynamics of food distribution it is difficult to end women's poverty."

His dissertation project has focused on what he calls "street kids" in three cities in Bangladesh. According to Hasan, these children typically leave their homes at a young age and come to areas of cities where they can earn enough money to survive by doing a variety of odd jobs. While typically homeless, Hasan explains, these children very often report being better off than they were at home where they also commonly experience absolute poverty, food insecurity, and multiple forms of abuse.

As Hasan explains, "The typical outside perspective on these street kids is that these kids leave home because the families are too poor to care for them and that if family poverty were alleviated these children could be reunited with their families. The real picture is much more complicated than that. These children often face tremendous abuse and neglect at home. Polygamy is common and this contributes to unstable family dynamics. Fathers often leave their families to find work in cities and marry new wives, sometimes abandoning the first wife and children. Early death is common for mothers because of poor health care, and in many situations second wives are forced to care for children of previous wives. Stepmothers and fathers often resent these children and in many cases this contributes to abuse and neglect. Understanding these family and cultural factors helps in showing that these children are not just leaving home because their families are too poor to care for them. They leave because home life is unbearable for many reasons."

Hasan conducted at least two to three episodes of in-depth interviews with each of 75 street kids from three locations of Dhaka, the capital of Bangladesh. All interviews were audio-recorded. They all focused on factors that led to the children leaving home, transition experiences, and their survival on the streets,

ISSUES IN OBSERVATIONAL AND FIELD RESEARCH

Sampling

In most field research, it is difficult—if not impossible—to use probability samples, because we can establish no adequate sampling frame. In addition, the research questions that field research sometimes addresses do not call for probability samples. So nonprobability samples are widely used in field research. Especially common are snowball sampling, targeted sampling, and purposive sampling. (In Chapter 6, we described a number of field studies that used one of these sampling strategies or some combination of them.) These samples make possible sampling procedures in situations where sampling frames do not exist, particularly the use of social networks in meeting basic needs. Hasan developed a visual aid, adapted from Antonucci (1986), to help these children map their social networks. He showed each of these children a chart with a series of concentric circles and cartoon pictures of Bengali children, men, and women. Inner circles, he explained, represented close contacts—those whom the children contacted regularly and relied heavily on to meet basic needs. Outer circles represented occasional contacts. Children were asked to give names to each of the cartoon characters who represented people in their social networks and explain why they were in each circle.

"What I found is that these kids create very strong social networks that allow them to survive and even thrive in many ways. Most say they are much happier on the streets than they were at home. There are very strong bonds between these street kids. Offering financial supports to one another is common. These kids often give one another money, make small loans, and purchase food for those who need it. They sleep near one another for protection. They share information about resources in the community and ways to earn money. They will also care for someone who is sick, even buying medicine for someone who needs it without expecting them to pay it back."

Hasan also explained that, despite sleeping outdoors, these children were better off in many ways than they were while they were housed. "These kids have learned to survive on about fifty cents a day. The median daily income in my sample was just over a dollar fifty per day. These kids earn much more than they need to survive and actually save some money for when they need it for something like medicine. They do odd jobs like running errands for merchants in the marketplace. Some pick up discarded fruits and vegetables from merchants at a public market and sell them someplace else. Others recycle bottles and cans—picking up discarded refuse and then selling them to businesses that need these materials. Few complain much about working, and the majority report liking the freedom of working and living independently."

When asked what he hopes to do with his research, Hasan reported that he would like to present it to international children's development organizations and domestic [Bengali] service agencies so they have a more complete view of these children. "Many times these organizations will focus on reuniting these kids with their families or getting them into school. These are well-intentioned goals, but they may not be what these kids want or need. Few want to return home. School isn't attractive either if it means they can't work. These children definitely need help, but services should build on their current coping strategies, not replace them. Agencies offering drop-in type services—food, medicine, entertainment, a safe place to sleep on occasion, or just a place to spend time during the day--might have real success in developing relationships with these kids and offering real help. Education is needed, yes, but schools should be structured so that kids can both work and go to school. Without that, they are very unlikely to attend."

Hasan's work is a very good example of the importance of understanding social context in designing social policies, programs, and interventions to address social problems. It highlights the potential contributions of qualitative research in discovering the complex social meanings that are found in diverse cultures and in using that knowledge to inform policy and practice.

(Based on personal interviews conducted in January 2012.)

and they also encourage the researcher, especially with targeted and purposive sampling, to avoid samples that are biased as a result of some group being inadvertently missed by a particular sampling procedure.

In addition to the more common sampling issue of selecting participants for a project, observational and field researchers face another challenge—it often is impossible to conduct around-the-clock observation over the full length of the study, which may involve a considerable period of time. Participant observers record things as they happen, and more quantitative observers mark coding schemes for as long as an interchange or a social setting persists. In some situations, however, continuous data collection is costly and unnecessary. In addition, as we discussed with other forms of sampling in Chapter 6, it often is not necessary to collect data from *all* elements of a population. In studies of child development, for example, we may not need to record all that occurs during an hour, a day, or a week. Instead, we can gather valid data through **time sampling,** or making observations only during certain selected periods of time (Irwin & Bushnell, 1980). For example, with an observational study of adolescents in a group home, the prime hours for observation are those when the residents are most likely to be at the home, such as weekdays from 3 p.m. until lights out at 11 p.m. (40 hours per week) and Saturdays and Sundays from 7 a.m. until 11 p.m. (32 hours per week). The researcher can construct a sampling frame consisting of a weekly list of these 72 one-hour time segments and then select a random sample of these elements. To be sure to include both weekdays and weekends, the researcher might specify eight hours during the week and four hours during the weekend. The resulting sample of 12 one-hour time segments would provide sufficient time coverage for observation while reducing biases that might occur if, say, the researcher made all observations on weekdays after 8 p.m., when many youths are tired at the end of the day.

Keep some guidelines in mind when conducting time sampling (Suen & Ary, 1986). The length of each time-sampling interval and the distance between intervals depend on the nature of the behaviors being observed: These behaviors should occur with sufficient frequency as to appear during the sampled time periods; very infrequent behaviors might call for continual observations. The more frequently a behavior occurs, the smaller the number of intervals we have to sample. Furthermore, the time interval should be long enough for the behavior to occur and for the observer to make whatever recordings are necessary.

Many of the considerations in time sampling are the same as those in sampling subjects or respondents as we discussed in Chapter 6. If our primary concern is to be assured of observing *some* occurrences of the behavior under study, it is advisable to use the equivalent of a purposive sample. For example, in studying domestic violence, we want to observe instances of family quarreling. Observing at mealtime is one way to increase the probability of witnessing the sought after events. However, if we want to estimate accurately the frequency of occurrence of a particular event or study the pattern of responses over a time period, we should use the equivalent of a probability sample. For example, to observe nursing home residents for frequency of contacts with nonresidents, we could divide the week into hourly segments and then use a random selection of hours as the basis for the observations.

Particularly when the observation process is highly complex and difficult to sustain for long periods of time, some form of time sampling can help to improve the quality of the data collected.

Validity and Reliability

We assess observational techniques, like other forms of data collection, in terms of how valid and reliable they are (Kirk & Miller, 1986). Observation rests on human sense organs and human perceptions—both of which are notoriously fallible. This is an especially difficult and insidious problem, because we often are totally unaware of the ways in which our senses and our perspective lead us to misperceive situations. Especially with observational methods, people say resolutely, "I was there. I saw it. I comprehend what was going on." Yet, as any trial lawyer will readily attest, eyewitnesses often are highly unreliable spectators to events, and considerable experimental evidence indicates that firsthand accounts of events often are partially inaccurate (Wells & Olson, 2003). Given these problems, we need to consider carefully the validity and reliability of observations.

Little question exists that observational techniques have greater face validity as measures of behavior and events than techniques relying on secondhand accounts. Surveys depend on someone else's perception and recollection, which many factors beyond the control of the researcher can shape and cloud. Observational techniques, on the other hand, provide firsthand accounts of occurrences under conditions that the investigator at least partially controls. Misperception may still occur, of course, but the researcher is in a position to recognize its impact and, possibly, control its magnitude. For these reasons, observation has greater face validity than many other data-collection techniques.

As we showed in Chapter 5, we sometimes can measure the validity of an instrument by correlating the results of the instrument with the results achieved by some other instrument already known to be a valid measure of the variable. Often, however, such direct measures of validity are not possible in qualitative field research; nevertheless, we can employ certain procedures in field research to enhance the validity of the observations:

1. *Be as thorough as possible in describing and interpreting situations.* This increases the likelihood that we will make important observations and produce a valid assessment of a situation. Observations that seem to be unimportant while in the field may later be recognized as important. Observations not recorded, of course, are lost forever as data. Obviously, observers cannot record everything that happens in a situation, but it is preferable to err on the side of being too complete rather than too skimpy.

2. *Carefully assess our own desires, values, and expectations to see if these might bias our observations.* People's expectations—or lack of them—drastically shape their perceptions. If we expect something to occur, we are much more likely to observe it—whether it actually occurs or not. If we expect welfare recipients to be lazy, we will be acutely aware of all those behaviors among welfare recipients that might be interpreted as laziness. Thus, validity of observations is reduced to the extent that our expectations—recognized or not—mold our perceptions. We should assiduously look for the *opposite* of what we expect to happen, and we should be careful and critical if what we expect to find seems to be happening. On the other side of the coin, a lack of expectations may lead us to miss something of importance in a setting.

3. *Have other observers visit the same group or setting to see if they come to the same conclusions.* If they do, this provides validation that our conclusions are a response to the actual setting rather than to our expectations or biases—especially if the other observers had different expectations or biases.

4. *Compare the conclusions reached through field observations with the conclusions reached through other research methodologies.* These other research methodologies can be observational research in other settings or surveys, available data, or experimental research (Weinstein, 1982). This is a variation on criterion validity (discussed in Chapter 5). If the various methodologies yield the same conclusions, we have greater confidence that the field observations have validity. Field research whose conclusions are at wide variance with the results of other research requires careful review, especially if none of these other checks on validity are available.

5. *Consider how the condition of the observer might influence observations and conclusions.* Hunger, fatigue, stress, or personal problems can lead to distorted perceptions and interpretations. Likewise, physical characteristics, such as the lighting in an establishment, may lead to invalid observations. (This is another good reason for keeping complete field notes—they allow us to assess, at a later time, field conditions affecting validity.) If a number of these conditions exist, we may decide to terminate observation and resume when conditions are more favorable.

6. *Look for behavior that is illegal, stigmatizing, or potentially embarrassing or that risks punishment.* If people engage in these kinds of behaviors, especially when they know they are being observed, they are probably acting naturally and not putting on a performance for the benefit of the observer. In his study of a sexually transmitted disease clinic, Joseph Sheley argued that the validity of his data was quite

strong, because "staff members dropped their professional masks and displayed quite unprofessional behavior and ideas in the company of the researcher" (1976, p. 116). Under such conditions, we can assume that people are reacting to environmental stimuli that normally guide their behavior rather than shaping a performance for the benefit of the investigator. If the people being observed do not have *anonymity*, then their behavior may not be a true reflection of how they behave normally. Especially when controversial, sensitive, or potentially embarrassing issues are investigated, validity declines substantially if anonymity has not been ensured. For this reason, hidden or disguised observation as well as observation in which the researcher takes the complete participant role are more valid than other types of observation.

7. *If possible, make a video or audio recording of the scene.* Although such recordings have their weaknesses as records of what occurred, they do provide another way to check and validate our observations and conclusions. Others can review such recordings as well, offering yet further checks on possible bias or misinterpretation.

Thus, researchers should follow as many of these guidelines as possible in designing field research; the more we incorporate, the more confidence we have in the validity of the results. Although many of the conditions influencing validity are beyond our control as investigators, it is important to honestly assess their impact on the research so we can make an accurate appraisal of the results.

As for reliability of observational research, an individual researcher who is studying a single group or setting through participant observation has no practical way to assess reliability (Kirk & Miller, 1986). With more structured observations, such as when using a coding scheme, we can readily assess reliability with tests of *intercoder reliability,* or the ability of observers to code behaviors consistently into the same categories of the coding scheme: Two or more observers code the same behavior, with the resulting codes then being correlated to determine the degree of agreement between them. For example, in their study of barroom aggression, Graham and colleagues (1980) correlated the coding results from the two observers who visited each bar. They achieved reliabilities ranging from $r = .57$ to $r = .99$. Many experts suggest that structured observation should achieve an intercoder reliability of $r = .75$ or better (Bailey, 1987).

Reactivity

Reactivity, or the degree to which the presence of the researcher influences what is being observed, is a major concern in any research (Lee, 2000). To take an extreme example, suppose a researcher enters a group for the purpose of studying it through participant observation. Suppose, in addition, that the researcher takes an active role in the group's proceedings by talking a great deal, offering suggestions, and so on. Clearly, an observer behaving in this fashion will exert considerable influence on what occurs in the group, making the observer's presence highly reactive. This affects the validity of the observations, because we do not know whether we have measured the group's *natural* activities or their *reactions* to the observer. We are never sure if events different from those actually observed might have taken place if the researcher had conducted the observation in a less reactive manner. Reactivity also relates to the generalizability of findings. If the observer's presence is reactive, it is difficult to generalize findings to similar groups that have not had an observer in attendance.

Researchers generally agree that participant observation generates the best results when reactivity is kept to a minimum. This is a major argument in favor of the complete observer role (unobtrusive observation) or the complete participant role in participant observation, where the observer's true status is concealed. It is logical to assume that observation affects a group less if they are unaware of the observer's role as an observer than if they are aware of it. Using the complete participant role does not, however, guarantee a lack of reactivity. Observers must play the role properly—that is, as passively as possible—without raising suspicion. Even when a researcher accomplishes the beginning of an observational study without undue reactivity, he or she must be careful that reactivity does not increase during the course of the project. Such a situation occurred in a study of a group that had predicted the end of the world (Festinger, Riecken, & Schachter, 1956). On numerous occasions, situations arose that forced the observers to become active participants to the point where subsequent group activity was influenced by their actions.

Observational and Field Research on Diverse Populations

Issues of validity and reliability take on added importance when the observations involve diverse groups with varying social and cultural patterns. In most cultures, for example, gender is an important determinant of behavior, which often means that men and women have distinctively different ways of interacting. In general, men tend to be louder, more aggressive, and more domineering in their interactions. This often produces a problem in field research that one anthropologist labeled the "big man bias"— namely, the tendency for the more powerful, more assertive, and louder individuals (who also are more likely to be males) to gain the attention of ethnographers and have their behavior and lives recorded (Ortner, 1984). A field researcher, however, cannot observe and record everything that occurs in the field. Selectivity is inevitable, and this can lead to bias when some important things are ignored. A field researcher who is overwhelmed with stimuli has a natural inclination to find ways to choose among them. In the remote village of some indigenous tribe, the ethnographer may choose to pay more attention to the village leaders, who also are likely to be elder males. Thus, the perspectives of younger tribal members and women are less represented in the ethnographic understanding of the village. To the extent that age and gender produce significant variations in perspectives in this village, the ethnographer's choices can produce a biased description of life in the village.

Historians have noted for some time the danger that history can become more an account of the lives of societal elites than of non-elites. The elites, after all, leave more of the historical record that historians use as data in writing histories: The elites write books and memoirs, pass legislation, make speeches, and come to the attention of historians in other ways as well. To the extent that elites also are mostly male, histories written primarily from these sources reflect the activities, interests, concerns, and perspectives of male elites.

Sociologist Barrie Thorne even detected a big man bias in field studies of preschool and elementary school children:

> Large, bonded groups of boys who are physically assertive, engage in "tough talk," and actively devalue girls anchor descriptions of "the boys' world" and themes of masculinity. Other kinds of boys may be mentioned, but not as the core of the gender story. (1993, p. 98)

In other words, it was not just a bias in favor of males but a bias in favor of a limited range of males. The voices of females and the less visible or less dominant males were silenced or marginalized. Visibility could come from being a part of the large group of boys, from their loud and aggressive behavior, from popularity, or from athletic prowess. Thorne also argues that ethnographers are biased toward noticing things that are consistent with the ethnographers' own stereotypes or hypotheses. Like everyone else, ethnographers carry with them cultural assumptions and stereotypes about masculinity—that males are tough, are competitive, and tend to form dominance hierarchies. Boys who conform to this stereotype in the classroom or school yard get noticed, whereas quiet boys who hang out with only a few other friends and, possibly, even with some girls are less visible.

Thorne summarizes the problem by stating that "socially constructed contours of visibility skew ethnographic reports" (1993, p. 97). In her own and other field research, Thorne found a much richer and more complex social field among children's play groups than gender stereotypes suggest, whether for boys or girls. She found boys who were quiet, shy, and cooperative and girls who were aggressive and hostile. Furthermore, given the diversity actually found, it is not clear whether the stereotype even portrays the experiences of the majority of boys and girls. When the ethnographer begins with the stereotype that the play worlds of boys and girls are different, then he or she tends to notice the differences in the field. It takes a special effort to notice instances that do not conform to the stereotype.

ASSESSMENT OF FIELD TECHNIQUES AND QUALITATIVE METHODS

As this chapter has shown, observational techniques differ from one another in terms of how qualitative and naturalistic they are. Not surprisingly, the advantages and disadvantages of observational techniques also differ depending on whether they are qualitative or quantitative and contrived or naturalistic. The first two advantages described next would apply to all forms of observational research. The remainder of the advantages and disadvantages apply particularly to the more qualitative, naturalistic, or unstructured types of observational research.

Advantages

1. Unlike surveys, which are limited to dealing with verbal statements, observational research can focus on both verbal and nonverbal behavior. This is an advantage because we can study *actual behavior* in addition to people's *statements* about how they behave. By dealing with behavior, observational research avoids a potential source of error—namely, the gap between what people say they do and what people actually do. The ability of observational techniques to consider both verbal and nonverbal behavior puts the researcher in a better position to link the verbal statements with behavior.

2. Much observational research is longitudinal in nature, and thus enables researchers to make statements concerning changes that occur over the time of the research. In addition, by following activities over time, observers have less trouble establishing the correct causal sequence than they do with surveys. (As noted in Chapter 2, establishing the causal order with survey data sometimes can be difficult.)

3. The advantage most often claimed for observational research is that it provides deeper and more insightful data than most other methods generate. Especially with participant observation, researchers immerse themselves in the daily activities of those being studied to a greater degree than with other techniques. This places them in a position to gain information that they would likely miss with techniques such as questionnaires or interviews. This is especially true for the complete participant or those who have become "invisible": As accepted members of the group, they see people behaving freely and naturally, unaware that they are being studied. Even such techniques as in-depth interviews and case studies can produce a deep, rich understanding of people's lives. The survey interviewer, on the other hand, may generate more socially acceptable responses and a carefully orchestrated presentation of self; but the participant observer and the in-depth interviewer can go beyond these public fronts and penetrate the behind-the-scenes regions of human behavior.

4. Observational research can study the behavior of groups that are closed to other forms of research. Many studies cited in this chapter involve groups that, for various reasons, are not

open to research by other methods. These people may have something to hide, or they may view a stranger's intrusion as somehow threatening to their cohesion and values. The ability of the complete participant to conceal his or her identity and conduct research where we cannot otherwise go is a major advantage of this observational technique. Even participant observers and in-depth interviewers, whose status as researchers is known, may, over time, gain access to groups through the development of trust and rapport; these same groups might reject the more brief and superficial entreaties of an interviewer.

5. A frequently overlooked—but nevertheless significant—advantage of observational research is that the most qualified person often is directly involved in collecting data, because the senior researcher often is one of the observers (Denzin, 1989). This is very different from surveys, for example, in which the project director rarely conducts interviews, leaving this task to part-time interviewers hired specifically for the job. Surveys place the most knowledgeable person farthest from the data-collection effort.

Disadvantages

Most of the disadvantages of observational research relate to the more qualitative, naturalistic, and unstructured types. With less structure, the quality of the results from an observational study depends heavily on the individual skills of the researcher, and this leads to several criticisms:

1. A nagging concern with participant observation research is the possible effect of observer bias on the results. Such research does not have the same structured tools of other methods to help reduce such bias. If researchers are not careful, personal attitudes and values can distort research findings, rendering them virtually useless for scientific purposes.

2. Closely related to the issue of observer bias is the problem of the observer going native, or overidentifying with those who are being studied. Because the observer frequently becomes a part of a group for a substantial period of time, this possibility is quite real.

3. The lack of structure also makes exact replication—an important part of scientific research—difficult if not impossible. Observational studies often are such individualized projects that the possibility for replication is slight. Any observer in a natural setting will be forced to record what occurs selectively because of the sheer volume of behaviors and events. There is little chance that a replication attempt would select precisely the same aspects of a given setting on which to focus.

4. The nature of the data gathered in some observational research makes them very difficult to quantify. Some participant observers generate field notes that are basically rambling descriptions; data in this form are difficult to code or categorize in summary form, which makes traditional hypothesis testing more difficult. As a result, many observational studies fail to get beyond a description of the setting. (Of course, some nonpositivist researchers consider this to be an advantage of qualitative research.)

5. Although unrelated to its lack of structure, some critics have called the ethics of participant observation into question, with the complete participant role generating the most controversy. Some social scientists see it as unethical to conceal one's identity for the purpose of conducting research, because it deprives people of the opportunity to give informed consent. Whether disguised observation is ethical remains an open controversy in the social sciences. (As noted in Chapter 3, disguised observation is considered to be a questionable practice that requires approval by an institutional review board.) As long as the research is not trivial and the identities of participants are not revealed, however, disguised observation probably will be allowed.

6. As mentioned earlier, participant observation affords the researcher little control over the variables in the setting. A great deal may be

happening that the researcher is not in a position to control or moderate. This often leads to situations in which the researcher is at a loss to select the important causal factors in a situation.

7. Because of the physical limitations on any researcher's observing capabilities, a participant observation study will almost certainly study a limited sample of people. Although we could, with a sufficient number of observers, study a large sample, we rarely do. Observation more commonly is limited to a small group, such as a family or a gang, or to one setting, such as a bar or a restaurant. The explanatory power that comes from a large sample size therefore is not available.

OBSERVATION IN HUMAN SERVICE PRACTICE

Observation is the foundation of human service practice, and our analysis of scientific observation in this chapter has some important implications for observation in practice settings. Even though the goals of practice and research are somewhat different, we can carry over into practice some of the observational techniques that researchers have developed. Here are a few of the lessons to be learned:

1. The type of observation we engage in affects the kind of information that we can gather. Structured observation in a therapeutic setting offers practitioners considerable control over what occurs as well as comparability of information from one setting to the next. Yet, it is a somewhat artificial setting (from the client's perspective), and it may not capture the dynamics of real-life situations that the client experiences. For this, participant observation is more valuable.

2. Reactivity is a serious concern in any observation, whether done by a researcher or by a practitioner. Human service workers must be sensitive to the extent to which their presence affects—possibly profoundly—the behavior of others. Clients may put their best foot (or their worst foot!) forward when a caseworker is present. The effect may be subtle; even the client may not be aware of the change. A concern about reactivity may dictate the use of observational techniques that reduce the extent of the problem. We may choose unobtrusive observation or the disguised observer role to reduce the extent of reactivity.

3. Good observational techniques rest on sound methods of recording information. This means that the practitioner should spell out, as clearly as possible and before the recording begins, the kinds of behaviors that will be observed. The more specificity, the better: "Aggression" is too general; one should plan to look for "hitting, kicking, or verbal insults." Thus, a precise and specific coding scheme is an important tool in both research and practice observation. This leaves fewer decisions to make during observation, when the observer is likely to be rushed and concerned about other matters.

4. Observation has different purposes in research and in practice: In research, observation focuses on hypothesis testing and knowledge accumulation, whereas in practice, observation is a tool for change or amelioration of undesirable conditions. As stressed in Chapter 1, however, practice observations, if done properly, can add to our body of scientific knowledge.

5. Both research and practice observations should be done systematically, with certain explicit and publicly agreed-on rules so that others will know precisely how the observations were made and could repeat them if desired. At times, departure from a previously established, systematic plan of observation may be called for in practice. As a practitioner–client relationship develops or circumstances change, the intuition of the practitioner may call for such departures to maintain progress toward the goals of practice. Rarely, however, are such departures justified in research. In fact, they are practically always detrimental to the research process, because observations made using different procedures are not comparable.

Information Technology in Research — Handheld Computers in Field Research

Small, portable computers are rapidly becoming important tools for collecting observational data in field settings. These computers, variously called handheld computers or personal digital assistants (PDAs), are the size of a cell phone and have a small screen on which the data collection form is displayed. The operator records data using a stylus or small pen to make selections on the form displayed on the screen. Each mark on the screen is recorded as data by the software in the handheld computer. In some cases, the handheld computer also is a cell phone, in which case the data can be periodically and automatically submitted to a central data bank. For many uses in field settings, this format is replacing the more traditional use of paper-and-pencil data collection forms.

For example, one study involving disguised observation required researchers in the field to measure the propensity of beverage servers to serve alcohol illegally to underage or intoxicated patrons at community events, such as art fairs or music festivals (Fletcher et al., 2003). Some of the data collected were quantitative in nature, such as whether a person was intoxicated or whether a server provided alcohol to an under-aged buyer, and some data were more qualitative, involving written comments by the observers. Handheld computers enabled observers in the field to record data unobtrusively. Another project involved PDAs both as part of the intervention and the research data collection. (Dekker-van Weering, Vollenbroek-Hutten, & Hermens, 2012). The participants were patients suffering from lower back pain. One element of the treatment involved sending the participants personalized messages about increasing activity or suggestions for managing pain. The participants provided data via the same PDA. At regular intervals a visual image of a 10-point "thermometer" scale automatically popped up on the phone screen. Participants could indicate their pain level on the scale and the data were uploaded to the research center database.

Projects such as these illustrate that these handheld computers could be useful in field research or single-system research when the data are self-reports about such things as a person's mood, their level of pain, their reaction to life events, and so on.

These handheld computers seem to produce results that are as valid and reliable as those produced by paper-and-pencil data collection. In addition, handheld computers have shown themselves to have many advantages over the paper-and-pencil format. First, they are much quicker at placing the data in a central data bank in a way that is ready for data analysis. Second, handheld computers have many advantages in terms of managing the data-collection process. For example, they can automatically record the time and date on which data are collected, can automatically prompt (through sound or vibration) a subject to record data at a particular time, and can automatically follow the skip or branching patterns required by a particular questionnaire (see Chapter 7). In addition, they can present the items of a scale or questionnaire in a random order to avoid some of the tendencies toward response bias (see Chapter 13). Also, the automatic and periodic submission of data to a central data bank reduces the amount of missing or late data. They may also be more effective for gathering sensitive data and can effectively record "paradata" or data about the data collection process itself (McClamroch, 2011).

One of the disadvantages of using handheld computers is that it takes longer to program them than it does to prepare paper-and-pencil forms; they also require more training of observers for their use. Given the substantial advantages compared with such disadvantages, however, handheld computers are likely to become even more common as data-collection tools in observational field research, especially when paper-and-pencil formats are too cumbersome or obtrusive to use.

REVIEW AND CRITICAL THINKING

Main Points

- Observational techniques involve data collection through direct visual or auditory experience of behavior. In qualitative research, the data come in the form of words, pictures, narratives, and descriptions rather than in numerical form. Field research is one type of

- qualitative research. Two important characteristics of qualitative research are that it is contextual in nature and that it uses a grounded theory approach.
- One type of field research is participant observation, which is similar to the anthropologist's ethnographic research. Many field researchers base their work on the nonpositivist approach and often use the method of *verstehen*. Knowledge in participant observation is gained through both participation (empathic understanding) and observation (deep appreciation of context).
- A major decision for the participant observer is whether to reveal his or her status as an observer to those being studied. Also important is the extent to which the researcher's role will stress participation or observation.
- Unobtrusive observation, including both hidden observation and disguised observation, is designed to minimize reactivity.
- Steps involved in conducting field research include problem formulation, selecting a field setting, entering the field, developing rapport with people in the field, becoming invisible, observing and recording, and exiting the field.
- When variables cannot be easily quantified or when using the *verstehen* strategy, observers collect data in field research in the form of field notes, which are detailed, descriptive accounts of the observations made during a given period. When researchers can measure variables quantitatively in field research, they use coding schemes to measure and record observations. Coding sheets contain the categories of the coding scheme and facilitate the recording process.
- Another form of qualitative research is in-depth interviewing, an informal and unstructured interview that can explore a wide range of topics and may last for a long time, even days or weeks. It is quite different from the interviews done in survey research. Qualitative research also takes the form of narratives, life stories, or case studies, all of which involve a detailed descriptive account of part or all of a particular individual's life or, with some case studies, of an organization or an event. The goal is to gain understanding through the depth and richness of detail achieved with this method in comparison to quantitative methods. Focus groups also are a form of qualitative research.
- Time sampling in observational research reduces the volume of observations that researchers have to make. Validity and reliability in observational research mean that the observations correctly and accurately reflect reality.
- Some observational techniques, especially unobtrusive observation, minimize reactivity and, thus, are good for studying sensitive topics, such as racism and sexism.
- Observational techniques are relevant to both research and practice settings.

Important Terms for Review

coding	grounded theory	participant observation	verstehen
ethnographic interviews	in-depth interviews	reactivity	
field notes	nonreactive observation	time sampling	
field research	observational techniques	unobtrusive observation	

Critical Thinking

One of the strengths of qualitative research is its sensitivity to the perspectives of those being studied. It uses procedures that enable researchers to understand meaning and experience as it is constructed and intended by the people themselves. It avoids, as much as possible, the researcher imposing structure or meaning on people's lives from the outside. These are important lessons that can be utilized effectively in human service contexts or in our everyday lives.

When you are confronted with information about people or their way of life, consider the following:

1. Describe the context within which the information exists or emerges. Does the context influence the apparent meaning of the information?
2. To what extent is the information purely descriptive or is there an effort to place it in a more abstract framework that gives it some meaning?
3. Who provides the meaning framework? Does it flow from the words and actions of the people themselves? Or are there other "authorities" who, in some fashion, tell you what it means?
4. In the information available, are there any efforts to deal with problems relating to sampling, reactivity, validity, or reliability in observations?

Exploring the Internet

As you look online, pay attention to the number of different fields in the social sciences and human services that show an interest in qualitative research. A good way to begin is by searching under such terms as "qualitative methods," "participant observation," or "field research," although the last will produce many sites relating to the natural sciences because they also conduct something called "field" research. This, however, offers an important learning exercise: Can you identify the ways that the research or science discussed at the natural science websites is similar to or different from what we as social scientists do? For example, do the natural scientists appear concerned with the positivist versus nonpositivist debate?

One of the better launching points for an Internet exploration of observational methods is a site maintained by the School of Social and Systemic Studies at Nova Southeastern University (http://www.nova.edu/ssss/QR/web.html). One resource available through this site is *The Qualitative Report,* an online journal devoted to qualitative and critical inquiry. This site includes an extensive collection of links to qualitative research sites. Two additional qualitative research sites on the Internet are ESDS Qualidata at the University of Essex in England (http://www.esds.ac.uk/qualidata/about/introduction.asp) and *Forum: Qualitative Social Research* (FQS), an online journal devoted to qualitative research (http://www.qualitative-research.net/index.php/fqs/index).

Another website with an emphasis on qualitative observational research is maintained by the Centre for Applied Research in Education (CARE) at the University of East Anglia in the United Kingdom (http://www.uea.ac.uk/edu/research/care). The website includes descriptions of projects with which CARE is involved. You can review the descriptions for examples of how qualitative methods are used in applied research projects in such fields as education and health care. Another comprehensive site is Qual Page: Resources for Qualitative Research (http://www.qualitativeresearch.uga.edu/QualPage) at the University of Georgia.

For Further Reading

Anderson, E. (1990). *Streetwise: Race, Class, and Change in an Urban Community*. Chicago: University of Chicago Press. This is an excellent example of participant observation research in a community setting. In this case, changes in community life are described as the racial and social class composition of a neighborhood changes.

Berg, B. L., & Lune, H. (2012). *Qualitative Research Methods for the Social Sciences*, 8th ed. Boston: Allyn & Bacon. Berg provides more detail on the qualitative research methods discussed in this chapter, as well as some others that we have not included.

Corbin, J. & Strauss, A. (2008). *Basics of Qualitative Research: Techniques and Procedures for Developing Grounded Theory*, 3rd ed. Newbury Park, Calif.: Sage. This is a good overview of how to do qualitative research.

Denzin, N. K., & Lincoln, Y. S., Eds. (2011). *The SAGE Handbook of Qualitative Research*, 4th ed. Thousand Oaks, Calif.: Sage. This book of readings provides a comprehensive overview of all aspects of qualitative research, including the historical development of the field. It is one of the most complete and authoritative statements about this form of research.

Ferrell, J., & Hamm, M. S., Eds. (1998). *Ethnography at the Edge: Crime, Deviance, and Field Research*. Boston: Northeastern University Press. This remarkable book takes the pioneering—and not necessarily popular—stance that *verstehen* in field research requires that researchers gain experiential immersion in the criminal and deviant activities of those being studied. It is a realistic view of what happens in field research and raises many key methodological and ethical issues.

George, A. L., & Bennett, A. (2005). *Case Studies and Theory Development in the Social Sciences*. Cambridge, Mass.: MIT Press. This text presents a comprehensive analysis of research methods using case studies and examines the place of case studies in social science methodology. It argues that case studies, statistical methods, and formal models are complementary rather than competitive.

Hobbs, D., & Wright, R. (2006). The *SAGE Handbook of Fieldwork*. Thousand Oaks, Calif.: Sage. The authors present a major overview of this method in all its variety, introducing the reader to the strengths, weaknesses, and "real-world" applications of fieldwork techniques. Each chapter is based on a substantive field of empirical enquiry and written by an expert in the field.

Marshall, C., & Rossman, G. B. (2011). *Designing Qualitative Research*, 5th ed. Newbury Park, Calif.: Altamira Press. The authors of this book provide a good introduction to qualitative research methods in applied research and policy analysis. Although it emphasizes educational research, the book includes vignettes from other social science and human service areas.

Padgett, D. K. (2008). *Qualitative Methods in Social Work Research*, 2nd ed. Thousand Oaks, Calif.: Sage. This book provides a thorough coverage of qualitative methods applied specifically to social work–related topics. It covers six major approaches: ethnography, grounded theory, case study, narrative, phenomenological, and participatory action research.

Silverman, D. (2012). *Interpreting Qualitative Data*, 4th ed. Newbury Park, Calif.: Sage. This book discusses the theoretical issues involved in collecting and analyzing data from qualitative research and describes some of the particular data-collection techniques.

Class Exercises for Competency Assessment

9.1. A teacher asks a school counselor to assist her in controlling the behavior of four boys in her fifth-grade class. The teacher complains that the boys "horse around" a great deal. They don't work on their assignments; they throw paper wads, disrupt other children, get out of their seats, and make "smart remarks" instead of answering questions. The counselor suggests setting up a behavioral intervention but first wants to observe the class.

a. **[Critical Thinking][Research & Practice]** How might the counselor operationally define "horsing around" so it can be measured?

b. **[Critical Thinking][Research & Practice]** One idea is to observe at random intervals throughout the week. Another is to observe for one full morning. What do you think would be the advantages and disadvantages of each approach? Can you think of a better method of time sampling for this situation?

c. **[Research & Practice]** Develop a coding sheet that the counselor could use to record the frequency of the problems mentioned by the teacher.

d. **[Critical Thinking] [Research & Practice]** Beside the occurrence of these specific behaviors, what else should the counselor attempt to observe?

e. **[Ethics][Critical Thinking][Research & Practice]** What ethical issues need to be addressed in conducting and reporting on this type of observation? For example, is it necessary to have the students' permission? What about the parents'? What steps should the counselor take to ensure confidentiality of the data collected as a result of the observation?

9.2. Select one of the following locations for an observational study and spend about an hour there in actual observation: a veterinarian's waiting room, a beauty shop, a shoeshine stand, an adult bookstore, a fast-food restaurant, a bus stop, a hospital emergency room, or a garage sale.

a. **[Critical Thinking][Research & Practice]** For the location selected, what general categories of data will you look for?

b. **[Ethics][Research & Practice]** How will you gain entry to the setting? Whose permission will you need, and how will you obtain it?

c. **[Critical Thinking][Research & Practice]** Are any particular time periods preferable for making observations at the setting you have selected?

d. **[Critical Thinking][Research & Practice]** Which observational approach will you use—nonparticipant or one of the participant forms?

e. **[Critical Thinking][Research & Practice]** For the observational setting you selected, is it more appropriate to collect data in the form of field notes or to develop a coding scheme? Why?

Chapter 10

✳

Experimental Research

The Logic of Experimentation
   Causation and Control
   Matching and Randomization
   Internal Validity

Experimental Designs
   Preexperimental Designs
   True Experimental Designs
   Quasi-Experimental Designs
   Modes of Data Collection in Experiments

External Validity
   Reactive Effects of Testing
   Unrepresentative Samples
   Reactive Settings
   Multiple-Treatment Interference

   Enhancing the External Validity of Experiments
   Lack of Minority Participation and Analysis

Assessment of Experiments
   Advantages
   Disadvantages

Review and Critical Thinking
   Main Points
   Important Terms for Review
   Critical Thinking
   Exploring the Internet
   For Further Reading
   Class Exercises for Competency Assessment

When people think of "science" and "research," the word "experiments" often is the first word that comes to mind. All these terms conjure up images of laboratories, white coats, and electronic gear. This points toward a considerable misunderstanding about the nature of experimentation. In fact, we all engage in casual experimenting in the course of our everyday lives. For example, when a mechanical device malfunctions, we probe and test its various components in an effort to discover the elements responsible for the malfunction. In essence, we are experimenting to find the component (or variable) that caused the malfunction.

Human service practitioners also often engage in casual experimentation. For example, when working with clients having particular problems, human service workers often try new intervention strategies to see if they will prove beneficial. For instance, if behavior modification or role rehearsal does not bring about the desired effect, the human service worker might try a cognitive learning strategy. These are illustrations of casual rather than systematic experiments, but they point toward the essence of an **experiment**: It is a controlled method of observation in which the value of one or more independent variables is changed to assess the causal effect on one or more dependent variables.

The word "experimentation" as used in research, then, concerns a logic of analysis rather than a particular location, such as a laboratory, in which observations are made. In fact, experiments can be conducted in many settings. **Laboratory experiments** are conducted in artificial settings that are constructed in such a way that selected elements of the natural environment are simulated and features of the investigation are controlled. **Field experiments**, on the other hand, are conducted in natural settings as people go about their everyday affairs.

The logic of scientific experiments can be illustrated by a more careful look at two elements of the impromptu or casual experimenting that occurs in everyday human service practice. First, many casual experiments fail. In other words, manipulating the variables involved may not produce the desired result. No matter which approach to a client is used, for example, improvement in functioning may not be forthcoming. In part, failures in casual experiments stem from the fact that they are *casual*, and thus not carefully planned. For example, the wrong variables may have been selected for manipulation so that no matter how those variables were changed, the desired result could not be obtained. In scientific experimentation, on the other hand, criteria exist to increase the likelihood of success by ensuring that the experiment is soundly planned and that crucial procedures are carried out. It is not that following formalized procedures guarantees success—it does not. Failure in the sense of not achieving the desired results is an unpleasant—but fully expected—outcome of experimenting. Actually, it may be best not to conceive of failure to achieve predicted results as a failure per se. Not achieving predicted results—assuming the results are not caused by poor research techniques—serves to rule out one possible explanation.

The second feature of casual experimenting is a tendency to jump to conclusions that later prove to be incorrect. An effort to improve the performance of a client, for example, may produce temporary changes that later disappear. What went wrong? Maybe the practitioner's change in intervention strategy was not the real source of the change in the client's behavior, and something else actually caused the temporary changes. For example, perhaps the client found a job or his or her mother-in-law recovered from surgery, which led to a temporary improvement in performance. Or it may be that *any change* from one intervention strategy to another will result in short-term improvements that quickly dissipate. The point is that many things influence people's behavior, and casual experimentation is not organized to sort out these influences. Scientific experimentation is designed to do this, and thus to reduce the likelihood of reaching false conclusions.

The focus of this chapter is experimental research, but the techniques discussed here can be applied to practice settings. The impromptu experimenting attributed to human service practice certainly has its place. The approach of evidence-based practice, however, stresses the idea that knowledge based on experimentally designed research and practice is the most desirable foundation for practice decisions. A thorough grasp of the principles of experimentation can enhance the practitioner's knowledge-building and decision-making efforts.

THE LOGIC OF EXPERIMENTATION

Causation and Control

The strength of experiments as a research technique is that they are designed to enable us to make inferences about causality. The element that makes this possible is *control*: In experiments, the investigator has considerable control over determining who participates in a study, what happens to them, and under what conditions it happens. To appreciate the importance of this, let us look at some of the key terms in experimental research.

At the core of experimental research is the fact that the investigator exposes the people in an experiment, commonly referred to as *experimental subjects*, to some condition or variable, called the *experimental stimulus*. The **experimental stimulus**, or **experimental treatment**, is an independent variable that is directly manipulated by the experimenter to assess its effect on behavior. (Recall from Chapter 2 that independent variables are those variables in a study that are hypothesized to produce change in another variable. The variable affected by the independent variable is called the dependent variable, because its value is dependent on the value of the independent variable.) An **experimental group** is a group of subjects exposed to the experimental stimulus. **Experimental condition** describes the group of people who receive the experimental stimulus.

We can illustrate the logic underlying experimentation by means of a series of symbols. The following symbols are commonly used to describe experimental designs:

O = Observation or measurement of the dependent variable
X = Exposure of people to the experimental stimulus or independent variable
R = Random assignment to conditions

In addition, the symbols constituting a particular experimental design are presented in time sequence, with those to the left occurring earlier in the sequence than those farther to the right. With this in mind, we can describe a very elementary experiment in the following way:

O X O

In this experiment, the researcher first measures the dependent variable (the pretest), then exposes the subjects to the independent variable, and then remeasures the dependent variable (the posttest) to see if there has been a change. One major yardstick for assessing whether the independent variable in an experiment has had an effect is a comparison of the pretest scores or measures with those of the posttest. (Note that this is a slightly different use of the term "pretest" from that in Chapters 1 and 7. In those contexts, the purpose of the pretest was to assess the adequacy of a data-collection instrument before the actual data collection. In this context, the pretest involves the actual data collection, but before the introduction of the experimental stimulus.)

Suppose, for example, that we were interested in the ability of developmentally disabled children to remain attentive and perform well in classroom settings. We might hypothesize that behavior modification techniques, in the form of reinforcement with praise, would improve the children's performance. To test this hypothesis, we first measure the children's performance so we have a baseline against which to assess change. Then we expose the children to rewards for performance—the independent variable. For a specified period, we give the children praise each time they show certain specified improvements in performance. Finally, we again measure their performance—the dependent variable—to see if it has changed since the first measurement.

This illustration shows one of the major ways that experiments offer researchers control over what happens: The researcher manipulates the experimental stimulus. In this illustration, the researcher uses praise as reinforcement. The researcher specifies how and under what conditions the reinforcement is delivered, including how much praise is delivered for a given response. The researcher might use one standard level of reinforcement or multiple levels of reinforcement to assess the impact of such variation. The key point here is that the researcher controls the "when" and the "how much" of the experimental stimulus.

The purpose of an experiment, again, is to determine what effects the independent variables produce on the dependent variables. Variation in the dependent variable produced by the independent variable is known as **experimental variability** and is the focus of interest in experiments. Variation in the dependent variable, however, can occur for many reasons other than the impact of the independent variable. For example, measurement error may affect the dependent variable (see Chapter 5), or the people in the experiment may have peculiar characteristics that influence the dependent variable separately from any effect of the experimental stimulus.

It also is possible that chance factors can affect the dependent variable. Variation in the dependent variable from any source other than the experimental stimulus is called **extraneous variability**, and it makes inferences about change in the dependent variable difficult. Every experiment contains some extraneous variability, because chance factors other than the experimental stimulus always exist and influence the dependent variable. Researchers need some way of discovering how much variation is experimental and how much is extraneous; experiments can be designed to provide this information through the use of *control variables* and *control groups*.

Control variables are variables whose value is held constant in all conditions of the experiment. By not allowing these variables to change from one condition to another, any effects they may produce on the dependent variable should be eliminated. In the study of developmentally disabled children, for example, we might have some reason to believe that, in addition to the presumed impact of the experimental stimulus, the environment in which learning occurs—factors such as the lighting and heating—could affect how well the children perform. To control this, we would conduct all the observations in the same setting with no changes in lighting or heating. With such controls, we have greater confidence that changes in the dependent variable are caused by changes in the independent variable and not by the variables that are controlled.

A **control group** is a group of research subjects who are provided the same experiences as those in the experimental condition with a single exception: The control group receives no exposure to the experimental stimulus. **Control condition** refers to the state of being in a group that receives no experimental stimuli. When we include the control group in the elementary experimental design just described, we end up with the following design:

Experimental group: O   X   O
Control group: O   O

The control group is important in experiments because it provides the baseline from which to measure the effects of the independent variable. For example, in the study of developmentally disabled children, the experimental condition involves receiving reinforcement in terms of praise. It might be possible, however, that the children's performance would increase even in the absence of praise, possibly because of the attention they received just by being a part of an experiment. To test for this, it would be desirable to have a control group that receives the same attention as the children in the experimental group but is not rewarded with praise. Because both experimental and control groups experience the same conditions with the exception of the independent variable, we can more safely conclude that any differences in the posttest value of the dependent variable between the experimental and control groups result from the effect of the independent variable. So, another yardstick in addition to the pretest/posttest comparison for assessing whether an independent variable has an effect is the posttest/posttest comparison between experimental and control groups.

It is important to keep the ideas of a control variable and a control group distinct, because they serve quite different functions. Researchers use a control variable in an attempt to minimize the impact of a single, known source of extraneous variability on the dependent variable. They use a control group, on the other hand, to assess the impact of extraneous variability from any source—including variables that are unknown to the researcher—on the dependent variable.

Matching and Randomization

When making comparisons between the experimental and control groups to determine the effect of the independent variable, it is of crucial importance that the two groups be composed of people who are as much alike as possible. If they are not, then any comparison could be meaningless as far as the effects of the independent variable are concerned. For example, imagine that a teacher decides to experiment with a new teaching technique. As luck would have it, she has two classes on the same subject, one meeting in the morning and one in the afternoon. She uses the new teaching technique in the afternoon (the experimental group) and her conventional teaching methods in the morning section (the control group). At the end of the term, she notes that the afternoon class did substantially better on tests than the morning class. Can she conclude that the new technique is more effective than her old methods? Not with any great certainty. The students in the two classes may have differed from one another in systematic ways, and it may have been these differences between students, rather than the variation in teaching technique, that caused the differences in performance. It may be, for example, that students involved in extracurricular activities took morning classes so that their afternoons were free for those activities. Furthermore, the students involved in extracurricular affairs may have had less time to study or were less academically inclined. Thus, given the kind of students who tended to take morning classes, we would expect the afternoon class to perform better even if there had been no variation in teaching technique.

Two methods avoid the problem that this teacher encountered and ensure that the experimental and control groups are equivalent: *matching* and *random assignment*. The first has a certain intuitive appeal, but on closer inspection, it proves to be the less desirable of the two. As the name implies, **matching** involves matching individuals in the experimental group with similar subjects for a control group. People are matched on the basis of variables that we presume might have an effect on the dependent variable separate from that of the independent variable. By matching, we make the experimental and control groups equivalent on these variables so they could not account for any differences between the two groups on the dependent variable. For example, the teacher described earlier might use an IQ test as a matching tool.

A high-IQ student in the morning class would be matched with a high-IQ student in the afternoon class. Any students without equivalent matches on IQ in the other class would simply not be used in the data analysis. Other variables in addition to IQ, however, could affect the outcome. Race, sex, socioeconomic status, study habits, reading ability, and math proficiency—the list goes on and on. Though matching on IQ would not be too great a problem, the difficulty of matching would increase geometrically with the addition of more variables. For example, the teacher might need to find a match for an African-American female of middle-class background with good study habits and a ninth-grade reading ability who also is in the 95th percentile of math proficiency.

This illustrates one of the problems with matching: So many variables might be needed for matching that it becomes impractical to consider more than a few at a time. A second problem is that the researcher needs to know in advance which factors might affect the dependent variable so these can be included in the matching process. Often, however, such information is not available. On the positive side, matching is better than no attempt at all to control, and it sometimes may be the only type of control available. In our illustration, the teacher may have no control over which students get assigned to which class. Consequently, the best she can do is select subgroup members in one class who have counterparts in the other class in terms of a few key variables.

The second approach to ensuring equivalent groups is random assignment. As the name implies, **random assignment** uses chance to reduce the variation between experimental and control groups. This can be done in a number of ways. For example, each person in the experiment can be given a random number, and then the numbers arranged in order and every other person on the list placed in the experimental condition. Or the names of all the people in the experiment can be listed alphabetically and given a number, and then a computer randomly assigns each number to either the experimental group or the control group. (See Appendix B for details on generating and using random numbers.) The point is to make sure that each person has an equal chance of being placed into either the experimental group or the control group. In the long run, this technique offers the greatest probability that the experimental and control groups will have no systematic differences between them, thus allowing differences on the outcome measures to be confidently attributed to the effect of the independent variable. Chance rather than *a priori* knowledge of other variables is the foundation of random assignment.

The problem with relying on chance is that, even though in the long run and over many applications randomization generates equivalent groups, this approach can still yield nonequivalent groups on occasion, especially when the study sample is small. Table 10.1 illustrates the extreme difference between groups that can occur by chance when using randomization. In these hypothetical data, eight subjects have been identified by sex and height. The subjects are ranked according to their true position on the dependent variable before the experiment, with scores ranging from 2 to 18. The mean score for the entire group is 10. Thus, when divided into an experimental and a control group, the ideal situation (the row labeled "Ideal groups") is for each group to have the same mean score of 10—or at least very close to it—on the dependent variable. Probability theory tells us that, with random assignment, it is most likely that the experimental and control group means will be close to the overall mean. It is possible, however, to obtain groups with very different means, because, by chance, any combination of subjects in the two groups is possible. Table 10.1 shows one possible arrangement of subjects into one group with a mean score of 5 and another group with a mean score of 15 (labeled "Worst random").

To reduce the likelihood of such occurrences, researchers often use a combination of matching and randomization known as *blocking*. In **blocking**, the subjects are first matched on one or more key variables to form blocks of similar subjects. Members of each block then are randomly assigned to the experimental and control conditions. Blocking works by reducing the extreme range of groups that are possible. For blocking to be effective, however, the variable on which cases are blocked must be associated with the dependent variable. Notice in Table 10.1 that males have low scores and females have high scores. The variable of sex and the dependent variable are clearly associated, but no such association exists between height and the dependent variable. When blocking on the basis of sex, two males are randomly assigned to each group and two females to each group. The most extreme difference between groups that is possible in our hypothetical illustration with sex as the blocking variable would be group means of 8 and 12 (labeled "Worst block on sex"). This is a considerable improvement over the extremes of 5 and 15 that are possible with randomization alone. Notice, however, that when the groups are blocked on the basis of height (labeled "Worst block on height"), there is no improvement; the worst possible group difference is still 5 and 15, as it was under randomization. This demonstrates that blocking on an appropriate variable can help reduce differences between groups. Choosing a variable for blocking that is unrelated to the dependent variable does not make matters any worse than random assignment, but neither does it improve the chances of achieving equivalent groups. Whether or not blocking is worthwhile basically comes down to the anticipated improvement in group equivalence versus the cost and complexity of carrying out the blocking procedure. Research in Practice 10.1 describes a field experiment that combined randomization and matching with other procedures to ensure equivalence between experimental and control groups.

Internal Validity

The central issue in experimentation is that it allows us to make statements about causal relationships between phenomena. This is the reason for control variables, control groups, randomization, and matching. In what has come to be considered the definitive work on experiments and experimental designs, Donald Campbell and Julian Stanley (1963) discussed the importance of *internal validity* in experiments. Recall from Chapter 5 that the

TABLE 10.1 Randomization and Blocking Illustration

Subject	Sex	Height	True Dependent Variable Score
A	Male	Short	2
B	Male	Tall	4
C	Male	Tall	6
D	Male	Short	8
E	Female	Tall	12
F	Female	Short	14
G	Female	Short	16
H	Female	Tall	18
Total N = 8			Mean = 10

	Possible Groupings			
	Group 1	Group 1 mean	Group 2	Group 2 mean
Ideal groups	BCFG	10	ADEH	10
Worst random	ABCD	5	EFGH	15
Worst block on sex	ABEF	8	CDGH	12
Worst block on height	ABCD	5	EFGH	15

validity of a measure refers to whether it accurately measures what it is intended to measure. Likewise, **internal validity** in experiments refers to whether the independent variable actually produces the effect that it appears to have had on the dependent variable; it is concerned with ruling out extraneous sources of variability to the point where we have confidence that changes in the dependent variable are caused by the independent variable.

In the preceding discussion, we presented the basic logic involved in designing experiments that have internal validity. The problem is much more complex, however, because internal validity can be threatened in many ways. We now turn to the seven most serious threats to internal validity, as identified by Campbell and Stanley.

History. The threat of *history* concerns events other than the experimental stimulus that occur during the course of an experiment and that could affect the dependent variable. History is more of a problem for field experiments than it is for experiments conducted within the confines of a laboratory, because field experiments typically last longer, allowing more time for events that affect the outcome to occur. For example, the homicide rate in the United States declined dramatically between 1980 and 2000—by almost one half—and many commentators attributed this decline to policy changes in the criminal justice system, such as more police officers, better policing, and longer prison sentences for convicted felons. Yet, during the same time period, dramatic improvements occurred in emergency care, including the spread of 911 emergency systems, the development of rapid response emergency teams, and more effective trauma units in hospitals. These developments may well have produced some of the declines in homicide: By 2000, people had a better chance of surviving an assault with a knife or a gun that, before 1980 with less effective emergency interventions, would have resulted in death (Harris et al.,

2002). The effects of these historical events make it difficult to ascertain what effect the changes in criminal justice policies actually had on homicide rates.

Maturation. *Maturation* refers to changes occurring within experimental subjects as a result of the passage of time. Such things as growing older, hungrier, wiser, more experienced, or more tired are examples of maturational changes. If any of these changes are related to the dependent variable, their effects can confuse the effect of the independent variable. For example, many believe that people pass through a natural series of stages when grieving over the loss of a loved one: shock, then intense grief and a sense of loss, followed by recovery (Kamerman, 1988). In other words, time brings its own changes, or maturation, to the grieving individual. If we want to assess the effectiveness of some therapeutic intervention in helping people cope with the death of a loved one, then any improvements people show over time might result from maturation or the natural progression of the grief process rather than from the therapeutic intervention.

Testing. The threat of *testing* may occur whenever subjects are exposed to a measurement device more than once. Because many experiments use paper-and-pencil measures as well as "before" and "after" measurements, testing effects often are of concern. For example, people who are taking achievement or intelligence tests for a second time tend to score better than they did the first time (Frankfort-Nachmias & Nachmias, 2008), even when researchers use alternative forms of the same test. Similar changes occur on personality tests. These built-in shifts in paper-and-pencil measures can lead to changes in the dependent variable that result from testing rather than from the impact of the independent variable.

Instrumentation. The threat of *instrumentation* refers to the fact that the way in which variables are measured may change in systematic ways during the course of an experiment, resulting in observations being measured differently at the end of an experiment than they were at the beginning. In observing and recording verbal behavior, for example, observers may become more adept at recording and do so more quickly. This means that they could record more behaviors at the end of an experiment than at the beginning. If the observers do learn and become more skillful, then changes in the dependent variable may be the result of instrumentation effects rather than the impact of the independent variable.

Statistical Regression. The threat of *statistical regression* arises any time subjects are placed in experimental or control groups on the basis of extremely high or low scores on a measure in comparison to the average score for the whole group. When remeasured, those extreme groups will tend, on the whole, to have less extreme scores. In other words, they will *regress toward the overall group average*. For example, suppose the bottom 10 percent of scorers on a standard achievement test are singled out to participate in a special remedial course. On completing the course, they are measured with the achievement test again and show improvement. Could we conclude that the remedial course was responsible for the higher scores? We would certainly be hesitant to make this inference because of the effects of testing and maturation. In addition, however, there would be a regression effect. Some of those people scoring in the bottom 10 percent undoubtedly did so for reasons other than their actual level of ability—for example, because they didn't get enough sleep the night before, were ill, or were upset over a quarrel. (How many times do students score lower on an exam than they normally do because of such factors?) When these people take the exam a second time, the conditions mentioned will have changed, and they likely will perform better—even without the special remedial course. Recognize that many—and possibly most—people in the lowest 10 percent are performing at their normal level. In any such group based on a

> **RESEARCH IN PRACTICE 10.1** **Program Evaluation: Matching and Randomization in a Community-Level Alcohol Prevention Experiment**
>
> The evidence–based practice (EBP) approach promotes the idea that knowledge derived from controlled experiments provides the best evidence about which human service practices and policies work. The Center for Substance Abuse Treatment (CSAT) is part of the Substance Abuse and Mental Health Services Administration (SAMHSA). SAMHSA promotes EBP through the National Registry of Evidence-Based Programs and Practices (NREPP), which is a searchable database of interventions for the prevention and treatment of mental and substance use disorders (http://www.nrepp.samhsa.gov). Developed to help people, agencies, and organizations implement programs and practices in their communities, the service is one more way that researchers and practitioners are becoming more closely linked.
>
> NREPP includes an easy to use interface for locating relevant research. For example, we located the experiment discussed below by simply selecting "Substance Abuse Prevention" as an "Area of Interest" in the "Advanced Search Mode". The search yielded 96 studies, including Communities Mobilizing for Change on Alcohol (CMCA) (Wagenaar, Murray, & Toomey, 2000). The CMCA program is a community organizing program designed to reduce teens' access to alcohol.
>
> To evaluate the program, the research team used school district criteria to insure a sample of comparable participants and to minimize influence from other factors besides the independent variable such as impact of other community programs and interaction between intervention and control communities. Because communities and not individual students were the target of this study, the researchers applied randomization at the community level. Twenty-four eligible school districts were identified, and 15 agreed to participate. After all baseline data were collected, the 15 participating districts were matched on population size and presence of a college. From within matched sets, seven communities were randomly selected to receive the community organizing intervention, and the remaining eight were assigned to the control group.
>
> The intervention itself consisted of a community organizer working with local public officials, enforcement agencies, alcohol merchants and merchant associations, the media, schools, and other community institutions to change community policies to reduce youth access to alcohol. The target of the intervention was the entire community rather than individual young people. The organizing effort resulted in institutional policy changes such as alcohol merchant

single test administration, however, a certain number of people probably will score lower than their normal level. If the whole group repeats the exam—even without any intervening experimental manipulation—they can be expected to perform better; thus, the average score of the group will improve.

Selection. *Selection* is a threat to internal validity when the kinds of people who are selected for one experimental condition differ from those who are selected for other conditions. The threat of selection derives from improperly constituted experimental and control groups. Recall the importance of random assignment or matching to equalize these groups. As noted, improper composition of these groups can make findings based on comparisons between them meaningless.

Experimental Attrition. The threat of *experimental attrition* occurs when there is a differential dropout of subjects from the experimental and control groups. Especially in experiments that extend over long periods of time, some people fail to complete the experiment. People die, move away, become incapacitated, or simply quit. If there is a notable difference in attrition rates between the experimental and control groups, those groups may not be equivalent at the end of the experiment, even though they were at the beginning. An example of the attrition threat can be found in a study concerning the effects of sex composition on the patterns of interaction in consciousness-raising counseling groups (Carlock & Martin, 1977). One group was all women, and the other was both men and women. The women were randomly assigned to one group or the other. Originally, the all-policies and practices, increases in media coverage of alcohol issues, and changes in practices of law enforcement agencies.

Several outcome measures were employed, including surveys of high school students, surveys of youth age 18 to 20, and surveys of alcohol retailers. It is well known that self-reported survey data of sensitive information is subject to bias and underreporting, so even though that data was supportive of the program, this field experiment was made stronger by the fact that the researchers also used direct observation and archival data to measure program impact. Alcohol purchase attempts were conducted at bars, restaurants, liquor stores, and convenience stores. Archival data consisted of drunk driving (DUI) arrest data and traffic crash data for a six-year baseline prior to the program and three years of intervention. The researchers hypothesized the CMCA intervention would reduce DUI and disorderly conduct arrests and traffic crashes, particularly among 18- to 20-year-olds, since alcohol consumption was reduced among this age group.

The researchers reported that the CMCA organizing process was successful in changing institutional policies to reduce youth access to alcohol and decreased alcohol consumption among 18- to 20-year-olds (Wagenaar et al., 2000). The archival data on arrests and vehicle crashes suggest that this intervention also reduced alcohol-related problems among youth. Reductions were observed in all arrest and traffic crash indicators for both age groups.

For the practitioner responsible for helping a community to reduce alcohol-related problems, this study is encouraging. Although anyone seeking to design an intervention program might locate this study simply by conducting an independent literature search, the fact that an organization such as SAMHSA provides the National Registry of Evidence-Based Programs and Practices accomplishes several things:

- Locating research studies is quick and efficient.
- The search process locates groups of studies that meet the searcher's criteria.
- The user can be confident in the quality and rigor of the search results because not only the studies themselves but the review process and the selection criteria are carefully constructed and reviewed by experts in the field.

female group contained nine members, and the male-and-female group had 16 members. Before the experiment was completed, however, two female members of the male-and-female group dropped out. When the interactional patterns in the groups were compared, substantial differences were found. The authors concluded that these differences resulted from the differing sex compositions of the groups, but, as they noted, confidence in their findings was weakened because of the dropouts from the male-and-female group. With such small groups to begin with, the loss of two members from one group can substantially affect the results.

With this lengthy list of threats to the internal validity of experiments, can we ever be confident that changes in the dependent variable are the result of the independent variable and not some extraneous variability? In fact, such confidence can be established—and threats to internal validity controlled—through the use of good experimental designs.

EXPERIMENTAL DESIGNS

There are three categories of experimental designs. **Preexperimental designs** lack both the random assignment to conditions and the control groups that are such a central part of good experimental designs. Although they sometimes are still useful, they illustrate some inherent weaknesses in terms of establishing internal validity. The better designs are called *true experimental designs* and *quasi-experimental designs*. **True experimental designs** are more complex and use randomization and other techniques to control the threats to internal validity. **Quasi-experimental designs** are special designs that are used to approximate experimental control in nonexperimental settings.

Preexperimental Designs

On the surface, Design P1 in Table 10.2 might appear to be adequate. The subjects are pretested, exposed to the experimental condition, and then tested again. Any differences between the pretest and posttest measures should be the result of the experimental stimulus. As it stands, however, this design has serious weaknesses. With the exceptions of selection and experimental attrition, which are irrelevant because of the lack of a control group, Design P1 is subject to the other five threats to internal validity. If a historical event related to the dependent variable intervenes between the pretest and the posttest, its effects could be confused with those of the independent variable. Maturational changes in the subjects also could produce differences between pretest and posttest scores. If paper-and-pencil measures are used, then a shift in scores from the pretest to the posttest could occur because of testing effects. Regardless of the measurement process, instrumentation changes could produce variation in the pretest and posttest scores. Finally, if the subjects were selected because they possessed some extreme characteristic, differences between pretest and posttest scores could be the result of regression toward the mean. In all these cases, variation on the dependent variable produced by one or more of the validity threats could easily be mistaken for variation produced by the independent variable.

The other preexperimental design—the Static Group Comparison, or Design P2 in Table 10.2—involves comparing one group that experiences the experimental stimulus with another group that does not. In considering this design, it is important to recognize that the comparison group that appears to be a control group is not a control group in the true sense. The major threat to validity in this

TABLE 10.2   Preexperimental Designs

P1 The One Group Pretest–Posttest Design:

	pretest	treatment	posttest
Experimental Group:	O	X	O

P2 The Static Group Comparison:

	pretest	treatment	posttest
Experimental Group:		X	O
Control Group:			O

design is selection. Note that no random assignment, which would make the comparison groups comparable, is indicated. In Design P2, the group compared with the experimental group is normally an intact group picked up only for the purpose of comparison. There is no assurance of comparability between it and the experimental group. For example, we might wish to test the impact of a local assistance program by comparing a city that has the program to one that does not. Any conclusions we might reach about the effects of the program could be inaccurate because of other differences between the two cities.

Despite their weaknesses, preexperimental designs are used when resources do not permit the development of true experimental designs. Human service practitioners especially are likely to be faced with this dilemma. Conclusions based on such designs should be regarded with the utmost caution, however, and the results viewed as suggestive at best. These designs should be avoided if at all possible. If they are used, however, then efforts should be made to further test the validity of the findings using one of the true experimental designs.

True Experimental Designs

The Classic Experimental Design. Diagrams of true experimental designs are presented in Table 10.3. Probably the most common true experimental design is Design T1 in Table 10.3—the Pretest–Posttest Control Group Design with Randomization, which is identical to the design on

TABLE 10.3   True Experimental Designs

T1 The Pretest-Posttest Control Group Design with Randomization—the "classic" experimental design:

	pretest	treatment	posttest
Experimental Group: R	O	X	O
Control Group: R	O		O

T2 The Solomon Four-Group Design:

	pretest	treatment	posttest
Experimental Group 1: R	O	X	O
Control Group 1: R	O		O
Experimental Group 2: R		X	O
Control Group 2: R			O

T3 The Posttest-Only Control Group Design:

	pretest	treatment	posttest
Experimental Group: R		X	O
Control Group: R			O

T4 The Multiple Experimental Group with One Control Group Design:

	pretest	treatment	posttest
Experimental Group 1: R	O	X_1	O
Experimental Group 2: R	O	X_2	O
Experimental Group 3: R	O	X_3	O
Control Group: R	O		O

T5 The Factorial Design:

	pretest	treatment	posttest
Experimental Group 1: R	O	X_1Y_1	O
Experimental Group 2: R	O	X_1Y_2	O
Experimental Group 3: R	O	X_2Y_1	O
Control Group: R	O	X_2Y_2	O

page 259 except for randomization. This design is used so often that it frequently is referred to by its popular name: the *classic* experimental design. In all true experimental designs, the proper test of hypotheses is the comparison of posttests between experimental and control groups. This design uses a true control group, including random assignment to equalize the comparison groups, which eliminates all the threats to internal validity except for certain patterns of attrition. Because of this, we can have considerable confidence that any differences between experimental and control groups on the dependent variable result from the effect of the independent variable.

Let's take a closer look at how the classic design avoids the various threats to validity. History is removed as a rival explanation for differences between the groups on the posttest, because both groups experience the same events except for the experimental stimulus. Because the same amount of time passes for both groups, maturational effects should be equal and, therefore, not account for posttest differences. Similarly, because both groups are pretested, any testing influences on the posttest should be the same for the two groups. Instrumentation effects also are readily controlled with this design, because any unreliability in the measurement process that could cause a shift in scores from pretest to posttest should be the same for both comparison groups.

In situations where regression can occur, the classic experimental design controls it through random assignment of subjects with extreme characteristics. Thus, whatever regression does take place should be the same for both groups. Regression toward the mean, therefore, should not account for any differences between the groups on the posttest. Randomization also controls the validity threat of selection by assuring that the comparison groups are equivalent. Furthermore, the pretest results can be used as a check on precisely how similar the two groups actually are. Because the two groups are similar, attrition rates should be about the same for each group. In a lengthy experiment with a large sample, we would fully expect about the same number of subjects in each group to move away, die, or become incapacitated during the experiment. These can be assumed to be more or less random events. Attrition because of these reasons, therefore, is unlikely to create a validity problem. Attrition because of voluntary quitting, however, is another matter. The experimental stimulus may affect the rate of attrition. That is, subjects might find something about the experimental condition either more or less likable than the subjects find the control condition, so the dropout rate could differ. If this occurs, it raises the possibility that the groups are no longer equivalent at the time of the posttest. Unfortunately, there really is no effective way of dealing with this problem. About all that researchers can do is to watch for its occurrence and, if attrition bias appears to be a problem, interpret the results cautiously.

The Solomon Design. A second true experimental design—the Solomon Four-Group Design (Design T2 in Table 10.3)—is more sophisticated than Design T1 in that it uses four different comparison groups. In comparing Designs T1 and T2, we see that the first two groups of the Solomon Design constitute Design T1, indicating that it is capable of controlling the same threats to internal validity as that design does. The major advantage of the Solomon Design is that it can tell us whether changes in the dependent variable result from some *interaction effect* between the pretest and the exposure to the experimental stimulus. Experimental Group 2 is exposed to the experimental stimulus without being pretested. If the posttest of Experimental Group 1 differs from the posttest of Experimental Group 2, this may be the result of an interaction effect of receiving both the pretest and the experimental stimulus—something that we would not find out with the classic design.

Suppose, for example, that we wanted to assess the effect on prejudice toward racial minorities (the dependent variable) of receiving positive information about a racial group (the independent variable). We pretest groups by asking them questions regarding their prejudice toward particular groups. Then, we expose them to the experimental stimulus: newspaper articles reporting on civic deeds and rescue efforts by members of those racial groups. Lower levels of prejudice in Experimental Group 1 than in Control Group 1 might be caused by the independent variable. It also could be, however, that filling out a pretest questionnaire on prejudice sensitized people in the first group to these issues and, thus, that they reacted more strongly to the experimental stimulus than they would have without such pretesting. If this is the case, Experimental Group 2 should show less change than Experimental Group 1. If the independent variable has an effect that is separate from its interaction with the pretest, Experimental Group 2 should show more change than Control Group 1. If Control Group 1 and Experimental Group 2 show no change but Experimental Group 1 does show a change, the change is produced only by the interaction of pretesting and treatment.

Thus, the Solomon Design enables us to make a more complex assessment of the causes of changes in the dependent variable. In addition, the combined effects of maturation and history can be controlled (as with Design T1) and measured. By comparing the posttest of Control Group 2 with the pretests of Experimental Group 1 and Control Group 1, these effects can be assessed. Usually, however, our concern with history and maturation effects is only in controlling their effects, not in measuring them.

Despite the superiority of the Solomon Design, it often is passed over for Design T1 because the Solomon Design requires twice as many groups, thus substantially increasing the time and cost of conducting the experiment. Not surprisingly, many researchers decide that the advantages are not worth the added cost and complexity. If a researcher desires the strongest design, however, then Design T2 is the one to choose.

The Posttest-Only Control Group Design. Sometimes, pretesting is either impractical or undesirable. For example, pretesting might sensitize subjects to the independent variable. In these cases, we can still use a true experimental design—the Posttest-Only Control Group Design (see Design T3 in Table 10.3). Despite the absence of pretests, Design T3 is an adequate true experimental design that controls threats to validity as well as the designs with pretests do. The Posttest-Only Control Group uses random assignment to conditions, which distinguishes it from the preexperimental Design P2. The only potential question of validity raised in conjunction with Design T3 is selection: The absence of pretests means that random assignment is the only assurance that the comparison groups are equivalent. Campbell and

Stanley (1963), however, argued convincingly that pretests are not essential, and that randomization reliably produces equivalent groups. Furthermore, they argued that the lack of popularity of Design T3 stems more from the tradition of pretesting in experimentation than from any major contribution to validity from using pretesting.

The Multiple Experimental Group with One Control Group Design. The preceding experimental designs are adequate for testing hypotheses when the independent variable is either present (experimental group) or absent (control group). Yet, many hypotheses involve independent variables that vary in terms of the *degree* or *amount* of something that is present. For example, *how much* treatment of a client (intensity level) is needed to produce some desired behavioral change? In a study of abusive parents, the independent variable was exposure to positive parenting sessions (Burch & Mohr, 1980). Rather than just assess the effect of the presence or absence of such sessions, however, the researchers exposed some groups to *more* sessions than others. In cases such as this, the Multiple Experimental Group with One Control Group Design (see Design T4 in Table 10.3) can be used. This is an extension of Design T1 with multiple experimental groups and one control group. The symbols X_1, X_2, and X_3 refer to differing amounts or intensities of a single independent variable or treatment. Comparing the posttests of the experimental groups enables us to determine the impact of the differing amounts of the independent variable.

The Factorial Design. The experimental designs considered thus far can assess the impact of only a single independent variable at a time on the dependent variable. We know, however, that variables can *interact* with one another, and the combined effects of two or more variables may be quite different from the effects of each variable operating separately. For example, one experimental study investigated the impact of both social class and race on stereotypes of women (Landrine, 1985). People in that study were asked to describe society's stereotype of four different women: a middle-class black, a middle-class white, a lower-class black, and a lower-class white. Landrine found that social class and gender did affect stereotyping: Lower-class people received more negative stereotyping than middle-class people, and blacks were viewed less favorably than whites. Landrine did not, however, find an interaction effect. In other words, various class/race combinations did not produce more changes in stereotyping than the effects of class and race did separately.

The experimental design used in the Landrine study is called a Factorial Design (see Design T5 in Table 10.3). Design T5 illustrates the simplest factorial design, in which two independent variables (X and Y, or race and social class) each have only two values (X_1 or X_2 and Y_1 or Y_2). In factorial designs, each possible combination of the two independent variables constitutes one of the experimental conditions. Technically, there may not be a control group, as in the example above, when there can be no "absence" of the factors involved. After all, one cannot be without race or without social class. If the variables involve the presence or absence of something, however, then a condition that looks like a control group appears in the factorial design. Factorial designs involve enough groups so all possible combinations of the independent variables can be investigated. Assessment of interaction is accomplished by the comparison of Experimental Group 1—which is exposed to both independent variables—with Experimental Groups 2 and 3. We can see whether the combined effects of the independent variables differ from their separate effects.

Factorial designs can be expanded beyond this simple example. More than two variables can be investigated, and each variable can have more than two values. As the complexity increases, however, the number of groups required increases rapidly and can become unmanageable. For example, with three independent variables, each with three values, we would need a $3 \times 3 \times 3$ factorial design, or 27 different groups. Sometimes, however, field experiments designed to assess the impact of social programs involve such complex designs.

Research in Practice 10.2   Program Evaluation: Field Experiments on Police Handling of Domestic Violence Cases

The police telephone operator answered the call from a weeping woman: "Police."

Voice: I want a … a battered woman.
Operator: What, ma'am?
Voice: I am a battered woman.
Operator: Do you want the police to come, ma'am?
Voice: (sob) Yes.
Operator: Is he in the house now?
Voice: Yes—he's in the house now and I'm scared.

—Sherman (1992, p. 80)

This interchange between a victim of wife battering and the police was recorded in the course of a landmark experiment on law enforcement intervention in domestic violence conducted in Minneapolis. At first glance, the dialogue appears to stand as eloquent testimony to ethical and logistical barriers that prohibit using true experiments in the real world of human service. No matter how valuable the potential research findings, it is unthinkable to tell a victim, "Sorry, you're in the control group. We can't help you." And how could the researcher get the police officer on the scene to administer treatment A and not treatment B or C on a truly random basis?

On the other hand, the urgency of human need demands that researchers find the best ways of responding to such critical social problems. The most powerful rationale for using experiments in this way is that they deliver a more convincing case for causal relationships between variables than other research methods because of the control that researchers have over the variables—independent, dependent, and extraneous—in experimental research. If an intervention does prevent future assaults, a randomized experiment is the best way to find that out. Lawrence Sherman (1992) presents a fascinating account of the Minneapolis study and five replications in Omaha; Charlotte, N.C.; Milwaukee; Metro-Dade, Miami; and Colorado Springs. His presentation documents how researchers can overcome the barriers to experimentation in field settings and the lessons learned from the experience. Here, we will highlight three of these studies on responding to domestic assault and focus on how they dealt with three potential barriers to experimentation—namely, the ethics of withholding treatment, randomization, and ensuring that treatments actually are delivered as assigned.

The first of these studies was an investigation by criminologist Lawrence Sherman and sociologist Richard Berk (1984). These researchers randomly assigned 314 misdemeanor domestic assault cases to three types of police intervention: advising the couple (including informal mediation); separating the couple by ordering the offender to leave the house for eight hours; and arresting the offender so that he or she stayed in jail overnight. The independent variable was the mode of police intervention, and the dependent variable was whether the perpetrator was involved in another domestic violence incident during the six months following police intervention.

For ethical and practical reasons, the study was restricted to misdemeanor assaults—that is, milder cases lacking severe injury or a life-threatening situation. With such misdemeanor offenses, police *could* make an arrest or could advise or separate, but neither of these responses was *required*. Under normal conditions, police use their own judgment as to which intervention is called for. When participating in the Sherman–Berk study, however, police officers responding to a call first determined if the case fit the study criteria and, if so, applied one of the three intervention techniques. The ethical concerns raised by withholding treatment and random assignment to treatments thus were addressed by responding to all calls, providing one of three standard treatments to each case, and restricting the study to only misdemeanor cases.

Random assignment to experimental conditions was achieved by requiring each police officer to use a pad consisting of color-coded forms corresponding to the three different treatments: arrest, separation, and mediation. The forms were randomly ordered in the pad, and the officers were instructed to select their intervention according to whatever color form came up when they intervened in a case that met the study guidelines. In this study, the officers doing the intervening were responsible for making sure that the randomization was done properly. For the study to work as planned, the officers had to follow the instructions faithfully. In addition, the forms were numbered sequentially so the researchers could monitor how well the officers followed the assigned interventions. The researchers tried riding patrol with some of the officers to check, but this proved to be impractical because of the sporadic occurrence of assault complaints. Another approach was to have officers complete a brief form after each call that described what happened. Despite these efforts, the study was criticized on the grounds that the treatments might not have been delivered as assigned.

Sherman and Berk concluded that arrest was the most effective of the three options for dealing with a spousal abuser: Those arrested were significantly less likely to be involved in a repeat episode of domestic violence during the following six months. Encouraged by these findings, many communities developed more aggressive arrest policies toward domestic assault. Researchers and policymakers, however, cautioned against placing too much faith in the results of a single study. One criticism was that the study had a small sample size. In addition, a few officers had submitted a disproportionately large number of cases. This may have been because these officers patrolled a more violent section of town and, because of experience, were particularly effective at making arrest an effective deterrent. The officers who did not arrest many offenders may have been more effective at mediation or separation. If so, then the study was really about variations in the skills of police officers rather than about variations in the effectiveness of different treatments. This points toward the importance of assessing *internal validity*: Is it variation in the independent variable that produces changes in the dependent variable, or is it something else that produces these changes?

Yet another criticism of Sherman and Berk's study was inadequate control over which treatments actually were delivered and the possibility that surveillance effects from the multiple follow-up interviews distorted the impact of the treatment. Finally, if the sample was biased for any of the foregoing reasons, the results would not be generalizable to other settings (Hirschel, Hutchison, & Dean, 1992).

A follow-up study in Omaha differed from the Minneapolis project in several key respects (Dunford, Huizinga, & Elliott, 1989). First, in addition to evaluating the three treatments—arrest, mediation, or separation—the research included a unique facet. If the assailant was not present when the officers arrived but the case otherwise met the study criteria, the suspect was randomly assigned to either receive or not receive a warrant for his or her arrest.

To improve generalizability, the researchers wanted to be sure that the project covered all areas of the community, including sections populated by minorities. A competing goal was to maintain control by using those officers who were most likely to encounter assault cases rather than by training and monitoring the entire police force. A review of the 911 dispatch log revealed that about 60 percent of domestic assault calls occurred during the "C" shift (4 p.m. to midnight). Focusing the project only on this shift kept the project more manageable. As in Minneapolis, the Omaha study was restricted to cases involving probable cause of misdemeanor-level assault.

One criticism of the Minneapolis study had been the reliance on police officers to carry out randomization. The Omaha project addressed this criticism by having random assignment to treatment performed by the Information Unit of the Omaha police force. Upon establishing control at the scene, responding officers determined if the case met the project eligibility requirements, such as being a misdemeanor offense. After information such as time, date, and victim, and suspect characteristics had been reported to the Information Unit, the operator assigned an intervention treatment based on a computer-generated randomization procedure. In this way, randomization was centralized, and data about the case and the assigned treatment were immediately stored in the computer file.

For results to be valid, it was crucial that officers actually deliver the assigned treatment. This problem was controlled by three forms of monitoring. First, officers reported dispositions on a Domestic Violence Report form and forwarded it to the project. Second, victims were asked to describe what treatment was delivered. Finally, official records of the police, prosecuting attorneys, and courts were compared with the other forms of monitoring data. Analysis of these various case-monitoring systems indicated that 92 percent of the treatments were delivered as assigned.

Another replication of the original Minneapolis study, this time in Charlotte, N.C., also had unique features (Hirschel, Hutchison, & Dean, 1992): It included only cases involving female victims and male offenders in which both parties were at least 18 years old. The study covered the entire patrol division in around-the-clock, citywide sampling. The interventions also differed somewhat from the other studies. In

(Continued)

> **RESEARCH IN PRACTICE 10.2 Program Evaluation: Field Experiments on Police Handling of Domestic Violence Cases** (*Continued*)
>
> addition to arrest, the police could issue citations requiring a court appearance by both victim and offender, or they could advise and separate (a combination of the mediation and separation treatments in the other studies). An additional explicit criterion addressed the concern of victim and officer safety: Cases were excluded if the victim insisted on arrest, if the assailant threatened or assaulted the police, or if the officers believed that the offender posed an imminent danger to the victim. After restoring order at the scene, all victims were provided information regarding community resources, including the Victim Assistance Program and the battered women's shelter.
>
> Choosing the best way to operationalize key variables is an important lesson from these studies. A related issue was whether to rely on official arrest records or interview reports of victims (Maxwell, Garner, & Fagan, 2001). If repeat incidents of domestic assault are measured by rearrest of the perpetrator, repeat incidents appear to be rather small in number. If the occurrence of repeat events is measured by victims' reports to interviewers, however, repeat incidents appear to be common, which is another example of the issue of validity discussed in Chapter 5—namely,
>
> how accurately does a measurement tool measure some theoretical concept?
>
> The original Minneapolis study, based on 314 cases, concluded that arrest significantly reduced future assaults, and the policy implication appeared to be clear-cut: Implement an aggressive, pro-arrest policy to reduce spousal assault. Based on a total sample of thousands in the six cities included in the various replications, the general conclusions now are less clear-cut and more cautious and complicated (Maxwell, Garner, & Fagan, 2001; Sherman, 1992):
>
> - Arrest does, in general, reduce future episodes of domestic violence, but the effect is modest.
> - Arrest increases domestic violence among people who have nothing to lose, especially the unemployed.
> - A small but chronic portion of all violent couples produces the majority of domestic violence incidents.
>
> The research underscores the point that social problems and societal responses are complex and unlikely to yield singular solutions.

We have covered the major types of true experimental designs in this section. Often, however, circumstances require researchers to use a variant of one of these designs. Research in Practice 10.2 illustrates such a variation that, nonetheless, retains randomization. The designs presented here also form the basis for many other more complex designs that are capable of handling such problems in experimenting as multiple independent variables and order effects.

Quasi-Experimental Designs

Many times it is impossible, whether for practical or other reasons, to meet the conditions necessary to develop true experimental designs. The most common problems include an inability to assign people randomly to conditions and the difficulty of creating a true control group with which to compare the experimental groups. Although these can be problematic for experiments in any context, they are especially acute in field experiments and practice settings. Rather than rule out experimentation in such settings, however, the researcher may be able to use a *quasi-experimental design* that approaches the level of control of true experimental designs in situations where the requirements of the latter cannot be met. Quasi-experimental designs afford considerable control, but they fall short of the true experimental designs and, therefore, should be used only when conditions do not allow the use of a true experimental design (Achen, 1986). As we will see in Chapter 11, quasi-experimental designs also form the basis of single-system designs used in clinical practice.

The Time-Series Design. One of the simplest—and most useful—of the quasi-experimental designs is the Time-Series Design (see Design Q1 in Table 10.4), which involves a series of repeated measures, followed by the introduction of the experimental condition, and then another series of measures. The number of pretest and posttest measurements can vary, but it is unwise to use fewer than three of each. Time-series designs can be analyzed by graphing the repeated measures and inspecting the pattern that is produced. We can conclude whether the independent variable produced an effect by observing when, over the whole series of observations, changes in the dependent variable occur.

Figure 10.1 illustrates some possible outcomes of a time-series experiment. Of major interest is what occurs between O_4 and O_5, because these are the measures that immediately precede and follow the experimental stimulus. The other measures are important, however, because they provide a basis for assessing the change that occurs between O_4 and O_5. As Figure 10.1 shows, some outcomes suggest that the stimulus has had an effect, whereas others do not. In cases A, B, and C, stimulus X appears to produce an effect. In each case, the differences between measures O_4 and O_5 are greater than the differences between any other adjacent measures. Cases E and F illustrate outcomes where we can infer that changes result from something other than the stimulus, because the differences between measures O_4 and O_5 are not substantially different from those between some other adjacent measures. The results of a time-series design are not always clear-cut, as illustrated by case D. The sharp change between measures O_5 and O_6 could be a delayed effect of X, or it could be an effect of something else. More careful analysis would be required to reach a firm conclusion in that case.

In field studies involving a time-series analysis, the experimental stimulus often is not something the researcher manipulates; rather, it is something that occurs independently of the research. Thus, any natural event presumed to cause changes in people's behavior can serve as an experimental stimulus. In a study of how the criminal justice system handles violence against women, for example, the experimental stimulus was the passage of the Violence Against Women Act of 1994 (Cho & Wilke, 2005). The VAWA was intended to provide better social service interventions for women who experience intimate partner violence, and to improve the law enforcement response in such cases. The dependent variables included such measures of the impact of the VAWA as the incidence of domestic violence, rates of perpetrator arrest, and rates of reporting incidents to the police. The data was provided by the National Crime Victimization Survey of the Bureau of Justice Statistics (see p. 202). These measurements were done for each three-month period from 1992 to 2003. The researchers found a significant decrease in the rate of intimate partner violence and an increase in the arrest of perpetrators. The patterns shown in the time-series design gave them the confidence to conclude that the passage of the VAWA was at least partly responsible for these changes.

The time-series design fares quite well when evaluated on its ability to control threats to internal validity. With the exception of history, the other threats are controlled by the presence of the series of premeasures. Maturation, testing, instrumentation, statistical regression, and experimental attrition produce gradual changes that operate between all measures. As such, they cannot account for any sharp change occurring between measures O_4 and O_5. Because this design does not use a control group, selection is not a factor. Thus, history is the only potential threat to internal validity. It is always possible that some extraneous event could intervene between measures O_4 and O_5 and produce a change that could be confused with an effect of X. In many cases, there may not be an event that could plausibly produce the noted effect, and we could be quite sure it was caused by X. Nevertheless, the inability of the time-series design to control the threat of history is considered a weakness.

The Different Group Time-Series Design. The time-series design requires that we be able to measure the same group repeatedly over an extended period. Because this requires considerable cooperation from the subjects, there may be cases when the time-series design cannot be used. A design that avoids this problem, yet maintains the other

274 CHAPTER 10

TABLE 10.4 **Quasi-Experimental Designs**

Q1 The Time-Series Designs:

	pretests	treatment	posttests
Experimental Group:	$O_1 O_2 O_3 O_4$	X	$O_5 O_6 O_7 O_8$

Q2 The Different Group Time-Series Design:

	pretests	treatment	posttests
R	O_1		
R	O_2		
R	O_3		
R	O_4		
R		X	
R			O_5
R			O_6
R			O_7
R			O_8

Q3 The Multiple Time-Series Design:

	pretests	treatment	posttests
Experimental Group:	$O_1 O_2 O_3 O_4$	X	$O_5 O_6 O_7 O_8$
Control Group:	$O_1 O_2 O_3 O_4$		$O_5 O_6 O_7 O_8$

FIGURE 10.1 Possible Outcomes in a Time Series Quasi-Experimental Design

characteristics of the time-series design, is the Different Group Time-Series Design (see Design Q2 in Table 10.4). Rather than make repeated measures on one group, this design substitutes several randomly selected groups, each of which is measured only once but at different times. Design Q2 produces the same type of data as the regular time-series design and can be analyzed using the same graphing procedure. In terms of internal validity, Design Q2 controls the same threats as the time-series design. Random sampling is relied on to equate the several comparison groups. Design Q2 also has the same weakness as the time-series design: Historical events can intervene between measures O_4 and O_5, possibly confusing the results.

Because of the many random samples that this design requires, it is limited to situations in which the cost of those samples is low. For example, if it is possible to draw the samples and collect data by telephone, then the design is ideal. This is essentially the approach that commercial pollsters use to measure public opinion by conducting weekly or monthly telephone surveys of different random samples. Although pollsters do not conduct experiments, their repeated measures allow the assessment of the impact of events on public opinion. The event in question becomes the X in the design, and the levels of opinion are compared before and after X occurred. For example, the terrorist attacks on New York and Washington in 2001 and the Iraq War in 2003 each caused the popularity of President George W. Bush to climb considerably.

His popularity ratings dropped again a short time after each event, but because of the many before and after measurements, we have considerable confidence that it was the terrorist attacks and the war that temporarily increased the president's popularity.

The Multiple Time-Series Design. As noted, both of the preceding designs suffer from the validity threat of history. The addition of a control group to that time-series design controls this last remaining threat. The Multiple Time-Series Design (see Design Q3 in Table 10.4) illustrates this. Design Q3 controls all the threats to internal validity, including history. Events other than X should affect both groups equally, so history is not a rival explanation for differences between the groups after the experimental group has been exposed to X. A design that uses a control group without random assignment might be thought of as being suspect on the threat of selection. This is less of a problem than with preexperimental designs, however, because the series of before measures affords ample opportunity to see how similar the comparison groups are.

Data from Design Q3 are plotted and analyzed the same way as for the two preceding designs. This time, however, the two lines on the graph represent the experimental group and the control group. The patterns of the two groups are compared to see what effect X produced. Figure 10.2 illustrates this by assessing the impact of "stand your ground" laws on justifiable homicide rates. "Stand your ground" laws basically relax the

Justifiable Homicide and Stand Your Ground Laws

[Graph showing Homicide Rate per 100,000 from 2000 to 2010, with a dashed vertical line indicating "Stand Your Ground Laws Effective in 2006". Two lines represent Law States (solid) and Control States (dashed).]

FIGURE 10.2 Example of Multiple Time-Series Data: Justifiable Homicide Rates for States With "Stand Your Ground" Laws (Law States) and States Without Such Laws (Control States), 2000–2010.

SOURCE: Federal Bureau of Investigation, *Uniform Crime Reports*, various years.

conditions under which a person can legally use lethal force when under a perceived threat. Under such laws, a person is no longer required to try to get away from the threat before using lethal force. Figure 10.2 compares states that passed such laws in 2006 with states that did not have such laws during that period. The data in the figure suggest that rates of justifiable homicide increase when jurisdictions have such laws: In states where these laws became effective in 2006, the rates began to increase right after the laws came into effect and had not increased for some years before that. The control group (states without such laws) shows steady justifiable homicide rates through the whole period under study. The control group protects against the validity threat of history, because any events (other than the "stand your ground" laws) that might have affected justifiable homicide rates should have done so in the states without such laws as well.

Quasi-experimental designs have considerable potential for human service research, much of which involves repeated contact with the same clients. Records of clients' situations and progress are routinely kept, so the repeated measures that time-series designs require may be easy to obtain. Various treatments or programs used with clients constitute the experimental condition. Plotting the data as suggested for time-series analysis would reveal whatever impacts those procedures produced. (We will discuss some of these topics and the intricacies of such designs in more detail in Chapter 11.)

Modes of Data Collection in Experiments

A good grasp of experiments in research makes one thing clear: Experiments are defined by a logical and orderly way of collecting data rather than by the form those data take. The research methods discussed in Chapters 7 to 9 are defined by the type of data collected: Surveys collect data in the form of verbal reports, available data uses archival records, and field research uses direct observation. Experiments, on the other hand, can collect data through all three of those sources—surveys, available data, and direct observation. Regardless of the kind of data collected, what makes a research design an experiment is the presence of an experimental group, a control group, random assignment to conditions, and the other factors described in this chapter.

Some experiments, then, measure variables by getting people's responses to survey questions. The study discussed earlier concerning the impact of social class and race on gender stereotypes was of this sort: People were asked to state what society's stereotypes about different types of people were (Landrine, 1985). The Minneapolis study of domestic violence and its replications described in Research in Practice 10.2 relied partially on interviews with victims to measure variables, and also used available data in the form of arrest data (Sherman, 1992).

Direct observation also is a way of collecting data in experiments, as illustrated by a quasi-experimental field study assessing child care program quality (Ridley, McWilliam, & Oates, 2000). In this case, the researchers compared the quality of care delivered by two different licensing levels of child care centers in North Carolina. A key outcome variable was "engagement," which was defined as the amount of time children spent interacting with the environment in a developmentally and contextually appropriate manner. Observers used a systematic process to code group engagement. They simply counted the number of children who were visible in one pass and then made a second pass, counting the number of children who were nonengaged (e.g., wandering aimlessly, crying, or fighting). The percentage of engaged children was then computed and used as the dependent variable.

Technological advances in recording devices, such as video recorders and computers, have enhanced the capacity of researchers to collect data by observation. The Information Technology in Research section of this chapter explores some of the tools available to aid researchers in gathering high-quality observational data for use in experiments.

In designing an experiment, then, a researcher also has to consider the issues involved in the particular kind of data collection being used. If data will be collected for an experiment through a survey, for example, all the issues of question design, nonresponse, and others discussed in Chapter 7 must be addressed. This chapter focuses on the logic behind experiments and leaves the issues related to the various forms of data collection to their respective chapters.

EXTERNAL VALIDITY

In experiments, researchers make something happen that would not have occurred naturally. In laboratory experiments, for example, they construct a social setting that they believe simulates what occurs in the everyday world. In addition to its artificiality, the setting typically is simpler than what occurs naturally, because researchers try to limit the number of social or psychological forces operating so they can observe more clearly the influence of the independent variables on the dependent variable. Even field experiments, which are considerably more natural than those in the laboratory, involve a manipulation of an independent variable by the researcher—that is, a change in the scene that would not have occurred without the researcher's intervention.

This "unnaturalness" raises a validity problem that differs from internal validity as discussed earlier in this chapter. **External validity** concerns the extent to which causal inferences made in an experiment can be generalized to other times, settings, or groups of people (Shadish, Cook, & Campbell, 2002). The basic issue is whether an experiment is so simple, so contrived, or in some other way so different from the everyday world that what we learn from it does not apply to the natural world. This problem is a part of the difficulty in generalizing findings from samples to populations (discussed in Chapter 6). With experiments, however, some special problems arise that are not found with sampling in other types of research methods. Indeed, resolving the problem of external validity can be difficult, and is less straightforward than is the case with internal validity. Campbell and Stanley (1963, p. 17) succinctly state the problem:

> Whereas the problems of internal validity are solvable within the limits of the logic of probability statistics, the problems of external validity are not logically solvable in any neat, conclusive way. Generalization always turns out to involve extrapolation into a realm not represented in one's sample.

We will review four major threats to external validity as well as ways that these threats can be reduced.

Reactive Effects of Testing

In any design using pretesting, the possibility exists that experiencing the pretest can alter the subjects' reactions to the independent variable. For example, items on a paper-and-pencil pretest measure might make subjects more or less responsive to the independent variable than they would have been without exposure to those items. The problem this raises for generalizability is not difficult to understand: The populations to which we wish to generalize findings are composed of people who have not been pretested. Therefore, if the subjects are affected by the pretest, our findings may not accurately generalize to the unpretested population.

Whether reactive effects of testing are a threat to generalizability depends on the variables that are involved in the experiment and the nature of the measurement process used. Paper-and-pencil measures may be quite reactive; unobtrusive observation is likely not to be reactive. When a researcher plans an experiment, it is important to consider whether the reactive effects of testing are likely to be a problem. If so, then it is desirable to choose a research design that does not call for pretesting, such as Design T3, or one that includes groups that are not pretested, such as the Solomon Design. With the latter, it is possible to measure the extent of any pretesting effects.

Unrepresentative Samples

As emphasized in Chapter 6, the representativeness of the people who are studied in any form of research is crucial to the issue of generalizability. Unfortunately, it often is difficult to experiment on truly representative samples of any known population. Often, experimental subjects are volunteers, people who are enticed in some way to participate, or people who happen to be available to the researcher. The implications of this for generalizing experimental findings are quite serious. For example, repeated studies over the decades have demonstrated that people who volunteer to participate in experiments often differ in systematic ways from the people in the population from which they are drawn. The exact nature of the differences varies from one study to another: In some cases, volunteers are better educated, from a higher social class, female (or, in other cases, male), have a greater need for social approval, or have a higher achievement motivation (Boynton, 2003; Rosnow, 1993; Zelenski, Rusting, & Larsen, 2003). Some studies show no such differences. Clearly, if these differences exist in a particular study, they could be related to any number of the variables that are likely to be used in human service research. Generalizing findings from such volunteer subjects could be quite hazardous. The best-designed experiments make an effort to measure such differences by comparing the characteristics of the volunteers with those of the population from which they were taken, if such comparative data exist.

Although the use of coerced subjects may reduce the differences between experimental subjects and the general population from which they are drawn, this has problems of its own as far as generalization is concerned. Coerced subjects are likely to have little interest in the experiment and may be resentful about the coercion that was used (Cox & Sipprelle, 1971). This effect has been found even where the nature of the coercion was quite mild, such as gaining extra credit in a college class for agreeing to participate in an experiment. One can reasonably assume that these effects are amplified where the level of coercion is greater, such as court-ordered participation in a treatment program under threat of incarceration. In fact, a study of a drug treatment program involving court-ordered clients found this anticipated pattern (Peyrot, 1985): The coerced clients were resentful, uncooperative, and unwilling to commit to the therapeutic objectives of the program.

The threat to external validity created by unrepresentative samples is of great importance to human service workers because we conduct most of our research efforts to evaluate the effectiveness of treatment approaches on volunteers or coerced subjects. Volunteers may make programs look good because they are interested in the treatment and motivated to change in the direction promoted by the treatment. Not surprisingly, however, apparently effective treatment approaches on volunteers often fail when applied to nonvolunteer groups. Alternatively, because of their lack of interest and resentment, coerced subjects tend to make treatments appear to be ineffective when these treatments might be effective on persons who are not coerced.

Reactive Settings

In addition to reactivity produced by testing, the experimental setting itself may lead people to behave in ways that are different from their behavior in the everyday world. One reason for this is that experimental settings contain **demand characteristics**: subtle, unprogrammed cues that communicate to subjects something about how they should behave. For example, people in experiments tend to be highly cooperative and responsive to the experimenter. In fact, the psychologist Martin Orne (1962) deliberately tried to create boring and repetitive tasks for subjects so that they would rebel and refuse to do them. One task was to perform a series of additions of random numbers. Each page required 200 additions, and each person was given 2,000 pages. After giving instructions, the experimenter told them to continue working until he returned;

hours later, the subjects were still working—it was Orne who gave up and ended the experiment! On the basis of this and other research, it has become evident that experimental settings can exercise an influence on subjects powerful enough to damage the generalizability of experimental findings. This has been labeled as the problem of the *good subject*—that is, the subject in an experiment who will do whatever the investigator asks, even to the point of confirming the experimenter's hypotheses if they are communicated to the subject (Aronson, Brewer, & Carlsmith, 1985).

Subjects' reactions are not the only way that experimental settings can be reactive. Experimenters themselves can introduce distortion into the results that reduce generalizability. Experimenters, of course, usually have expectations concerning the results of the experiment, wanting it to come out one way or another. These **experimenter's expectations** can be communicated to subjects in such a subtle fashion that neither the experimenter nor the subjects are aware that the communication has taken place (Rosenthal, 1967). A classic illustration of how subtle this can be is recounted by Graham (1977) and involves a horse, not humans. The horse was called Clever Hans because of his seeming ability to solve fairly complex arithmetic problems. Hans and his trainer toured Europe during the early 1900s, amazing audiences and becoming quite famous. Hans would stand on stage pounding out the answers to problems with his hoofs. Amazingly, Hans was hardly ever wrong. Hans would perform his feats even when his trainer was not present. Could the horse really do arithmetic? After very careful observation, it was discovered that Hans was picking up the subtle cues given off by those who asked him questions. As Hans approached the correct number of hoof beats, questioners would move or shift just enough to cue the horse that it was time to stop.

The same phenomenon has been thoroughly investigated in the physician–patient relationship (Kline, 1988). When giving a patient a treatment that is known to be effective, a physician exudes confidence, and the patient picks up on this and expects to get better. The patient's hopeful mood then increases the likelihood that he or she will actually improve. When a physician, however, is giving a patient a placebo—that is, an inert substance the physician doesn't expect to work—his or her manner communicates doubt: The patient senses, without being aware of it, what the physician's expectations are and then helps create that reality. People in experiments often do the same thing. Subjects react to subtle cues given off unconsciously by an experimenter that tell them to behave in a way that the researcher wants. (The Eye on Ethics section discusses some ethical issues relating to reactivity in experiments.)

Reactive experimental settings can threaten external validity because changes in the dependent variable might be caused by demand characteristics or experimenter expectancies rather than by the independent variable. One procedure for reducing reactivity in experimental settings is to conduct the experiment in such a way that subjects are *blind*—that is, unaware of the experimental hypotheses—so this knowledge will not influence their behavior. In fact, subjects commonly are given a false rationale for what they are to do in an attempt to reduce their reactions that might interfere with the generalizability of the findings. As an ethical matter, however, subjects should be informed of the experiment's true purpose during the postexperimental debriefing session.

The surest way of controlling reactivity because of the experimenter is to run what is called a *double-blind experiment*. In a **double-blind experiment**, neither the subjects nor the experimenter knows which people are in the experimental condition and which are in the control condition. This makes it impossible for the experimenter to communicate to subjects how they ought to behave, because, for any given subject, the experimenter does not know which responses confirm the experimental hypotheses. Though simple in theory, maintaining a double-blind procedure in practice can be difficult. Another layer of personnel must be added to accomplish the assignment of subjects, sealed instructions issued to the experimenter, and the results tracked. Furthermore, all information

> ### EYE ON ETHICS — Deception and Informed Consent in Experiments
>
> Two of the most common ethical issues that arise in experimental research are deception and informed consent. Deception can occur when experimental subjects are not told about some key aspects of the experiment or are actually misled about them. Most commonly, subjects might not be told about the true purposes of the research, or they might actually be told something that is not true. For example, subjects might be misled by being given some tasks or a questionnaire that are really unrelated to the experiment.
>
> The reason this deception is necessary is that if subjects know the true purposes or the actual research hypotheses, they might behave differently. For example, they might try to help the researcher by behaving in a way that helps confirm the hypotheses. The subjects' behavior would then be a form of reactivity that throws into question the validity of the findings.
>
> Researchers justify these deceptive practices in a number of ways. They argue that the research findings are important and the research goals could not be achieved without the deception. They also argue that the deception in most cases is rather minor in nature.
>
> To alleviate some of the ethical concerns, researchers often have the subjects read and sign a consent form that informs them, among other things, that they may be deceived as to the true purpose of the experiment and may be asked to do some things to further that deception. Yet another way to deal with the problem of deception is to conduct a debriefing, a session following the experiment when subjects are told the complete nature of the study, including any deceptions used, and their reactions are assessed. Especially when deception is used, a debriefing is an ethical obligation of the researcher to ensure that people are in no way harmed by their participation. During debriefing, the researcher assesses whether the subject has had any kind of negative reaction to the deception or any other element of the experiment. It sometimes happens that things people read or do during an experiment produce feelings of anger, depression, or despair. The researcher's obligation is to assess these reactions and alleviate them, with professional assistance if necessary.
>
> Ethical absolutists would argue that no deception can be justified. They would question whether subjects can truly give informed consent if they are misled about some aspects of the research. Most social scientists, however, would argue that mild levels of deception, if done carefully, are necessary and ethically acceptable.

relating to these activities must be kept from those who are actually running the experimental groups. It is easy for this structure to break down so the double-blind feature is lost; however, for true protection against such reactivity, double-blind experiments need to be used. Unfortunately, the nature of the treatment sometimes interferes with use of the double-blind approach. Because of the different activities involved, it may be obvious which condition is experimental and which is control, thus clearly preventing the use of a double-blind experiment.

Multiple-Treatment Interference

In an experiment with more than one independent variable, the particular combination and ordering of experimental treatments may produce change in the dependent variable. If this same combination and this same ordering do not occur outside the experimental setting, however, the findings from the experiment cannot be generalized. Suppose, for example, that an experiment calls for subjects to experience four independent variables in succession. Furthermore, suppose that the last variable in the series appears to produce an interesting effect. Could the effect of that fourth variable be safely generalized on the basis of the experimental findings? The answer is no. The subjects in the experiment have experienced the three other independent variables first, which might in itself have affected the way that they reacted to the last variable. If people outside the experimental setting do not experience all the variables in sequence, then generalization concerning the fourth variable is risky. The problem of multiple-treatment interference is similar to reactive effects of testing in that the subjects in the experiment experience something that the people in the population at large do not.

The threat of multiple-treatment interference can be effectively eliminated through the use of complex designs in which the different experimental groups experience the independent variables in every possible sequence. If a given variable produces a consistent effect regardless of the ordering of the variables, then multiple-treatment interference is not a threat to the generalizability of the findings. An alternative is to isolate the variable of interest in a multiple-treatment experiment and then conduct a follow-up experiment with that variable as the only treatment. If the follow-up experiment produces an effect similar to that found when it was part of a series of treatments, multiple-treatment interference can be ruled out.

In designing experiments, especially those to be conducted in laboratory settings, problems of external validity need to be considered. Properly designed experiments can offer researchers substantial confidence in generalizing from an experimental sample to other settings or groups. Efforts to enhance external validity may, however, affect our ability to achieve internal validity, which brings us to the importance of replication for external validity.

Enhancing the External Validity of Experiments

Although both internal and external validity are important to experimental research, a tension exists between the two. On the one hand, internal validity is enhanced through greater control. Consequently, the researcher seeking internal validity is attracted to the laboratory experiment and precise testing. Yet, we have just seen that the reactive effect of testing is a threat to external validity. Seeking control, the researcher may use a homogeneous sample to avoid the confounding effects of other variables. In the effort to achieve internal validity, the researcher might, for example, use a sample of 18-year-old white males. Although the effects of race, sex, and age are now controlled, the threat to external validity from unrepresentative samples increases. We have suggested the use of complex designs to reduce the threat to external validity of multiple-treatment interference. Complex designs, however, are more difficult to implement in a way that retains the integrity of the research design. Thus there appears to be a dilemma between seeking internal validity on the one hand and external validity on the other.

Another way to approach the problem of external validity is, when possible, to conduct field experiments rather than laboratory experiments. Although issues of external validity do arise in field experiments, field experiments on the whole have greater external validity because they are conducted in the real world. This means that the results are more clearly generalizable to some settings in the real world, at least to settings that are similar to the one in which the field study was conducted.

The basic solution to this dilemma, however, is not to seek an answer to both internal validity and external validity in a single study. Ultimately, external validity is established through replication (Shadish, Cook, & Campbell, 2002). Confidence in generalizing from experimental findings increases as other researchers test and support the same hypotheses in a variety of settings with a variety of designs. Often, this takes the form of initial testing in the laboratory under ideal conditions to see if the hypothesis is supported at all. Then the same hypothesis can be tested under the less-than-ideal conditions of the field. Through replication, the dual objectives of internal and external validity can be achieved.

Lack of Minority Participation and Analysis

Depending on the setting in which an experiment is conducted, women and minorities may find themselves underrepresented in laboratory or field experiments—a problem that can affect both external and internal validity. Researchers often choose people who are easily accessible to them as subjects for experiments. For basic research in psychology and sociology, for example, students in introductory psychology or sociology classes often are selected as research subjects. The sex ratio of college students is fairly even: 46 percent male, and 54 percent female. African Americans constitute about 11 percent of all college students but account for 13 percent of the total U.S. population (U.S. Census Bureau, 2011). Thus experiments using a representative sample of college students will tend to underrepresent African Americans, Hispanics, and some other minorities. In addition, this underrepresentation is more severe at some colleges than at others: Some major research universities, even today, have only 1 percent or 2 percent black enrollment. So whenever experimental subjects are selected from a setting, care must be taken to ensure representation of minorities in a sample if the minorities are to be included in the generalizations made from the data. Otherwise, it should be mentioned that no special procedures were used in the sampling to enhance minority involvement.

A related problem is what one sociologist calls *gender insensitivity*: "ignoring gender as an important social variable" (Eichler, 1988, p. 66). In experiments, this can happen when no mention is made of the sex ratio of the subjects in the experiment, or when data are not analyzed separately for each gender. Eichler reports one issue of a psychology journal in which the only article to mention the sex of the subjects was one that used rhesus monkeys; none of those using human subjects did so, despite the fact that practically all those articles focused on variables, such as perception, verbal ability, and learning, on which people's gender might well have an influence.

A final problem relating to minority participation in experiments is failure to consider the gender or minority status of all participants in the experiment. In addition to the researcher and the subject, this might include interviewers, confederates of the experimenter, and any others who interact with the subjects during data collection. We know, for example, that people of the same gender interact differently with people of the opposite gender. Thus, a male interviewer responds differently when asking questions of a female subject than when interviewing a male subject. In the former case, he might be friendlier, more attentive, or more engaging without even realizing it, and this can influence the subject's response to questions.

These threats to external validity can be reduced by reporting the sex or minority status of the various people who are involved in experiments and analyzing the data with sex or minority status as an experimental or control variable. There are, of course, reasons for a homogeneous sample in an experiment—namely, to reduce extraneous variation when trying to establish a causal relationship between independent and dependent variables. If the results are to be generalized to all racial and ethnic groups and both sexes, however, then experiments need to be replicated using subjects from these groups.

ASSESSMENT OF EXPERIMENTS

Advantages

Inference of Causality. The major advantage of experimental research is that it places us in the most advantageous position from which to infer causal relationships between variables. (Recall from Chapter 2 that causality can never be directly observed. Rather, we infer that one thing caused another by observing changes in the two things under the appropriate conditions.) A well-designed and well-controlled experiment puts us in the strongest position to make that causal inference, because it enables us to control the effect of other variables, which raises our confidence that the independent variable is, indeed, bringing about changes in the dependent variable. Experiments also permit us to establish the time sequence necessary for inferring causality. We can measure the dependent variable to see if it has changed *since* the experimental manipulation. With other research methods, such as the survey, it often is not possible to directly observe whether the changes in one variable preceded or followed changes in another variable.

Control. Experimenters are not limited by the variables and events that happen to occur naturally in a particular situation. Rather they can decide what variables to study, what values those variables will take, and what combination of variables to include. In other words, researchers can create precisely what their hypotheses suggest are important. This is in sharp contrast to other research methods, such as the use of available data (see Chapter 8) or observational techniques (see Chapter 9), in which hypotheses need to be reshaped to fit the existing data or observations.

The Study of Change. Many experimental designs are longitudinal, which means they are conducted over a period of time, with measurements taken at more than one time. This makes it possible to study changes over time. Many other research methods, such as surveys, tend to be cross-sectional—they are like snapshots taken at a given point in time. In cross-sectional studies, we can ask people how things have changed over time, but we cannot *directly observe* that change.

Costs. In some cases, experiments—especially those conducted in laboratory settings—can be considerably cheaper than other research methods. Because of the element of control, the sample size can be smaller, and this saves money. Costly travel expenses and interviewer salaries found in some surveys also are eliminated. Some field experiments, however, can be expensive, because they may require interviewing—possibly more than once—to assess changes in dependent variables.

Disadvantages

Inflexibility. Experimental designs generally require that the treatment (or the independent variable) be well developed, and that the same treatment be applied to all cases in the experimental group. If the nature of the independent variable changes as the experiment progresses, this is extraneous variation, which makes it difficult to say what changed the dependent variable. Because of this inflexibility, experimental designs are not suitable during the early stages of research when treatments may not be well developed. This requirement for consistently measuring the independent variable is especially true of large-scale, longitudinal experiments, which are best suited for clearly designed treatments (Rossi, Lipsey, & Freeman, 2004).

Randomization Requirement. Human service organizations may be unwilling to accept random assignment to treatment and control conditions, despite the value of this technique for controlling extraneous effects. This is especially so when the design calls for a control group to receive no treatment at all. Organizations may have ethical concerns about randomization, or they may want to be sure that they "get something" for participating in a study, and thus are reluctant to serve as the control condition. In addition, with field experiments it sometimes is impossible to find or create a control group that is truly comparable to the experimental groups; thus the true experimental designs are ruled out. Despite the fact that randomization was achieved, both Research in Practice illustrations in this chapter emphasize the considerable difficulty in carrying out randomization.

Artificiality. The laboratory setting in which some experiments are conducted is an artificial environment created by the investigator, which raises questions of external validity. We often do not know what the relationship is between this artificial setting and the real world in which people live. We cannot be sure that people behave in the same fashion on the street or in the classroom as they do in the laboratory. Even field experiments of human service interventions are, to an extent, vulnerable to this criticism, especially when they create conditions that never exist naturally. For

Information Technology in Research — Computer Applications in Experimental Research

In defining "experiments," we stated that the essence of experimentation is a *controlled method of observation* in which the value of one or more independent variables is changed to assess its causal effect on one or more dependent variables. Researchers endeavor to eliminate variation resulting from any variables other than the independent variable. In this effort to reduce extraneous variation, computer technology can be helpful.

One strategy to reduce extraneous variation and produce higher-quality data is to have research participants themselves record data on some type of electronic device. Such research results in more accurate and timely data and is preferred by research participants over paper and pencil data collection methods (Haller et al., 2009; Lane et al., 2006). The computer also may incorporate a signaling function that alerts participants when it is time to record data (Tejani, Dresselhaus, & Weinger, 2010; Fahrenberg, 1996). For example, one research team employed handheld computer devices to study whether smokers found it more rewarding to smoke when they chose to rather than when told to by researchers. Participants completed short, 11-question surveys using Palm m505 handheld computer devices to evaluate their moods after smoking cigarettes at times of their choosing on three separate days. Participants later took the same survey after smoking cigarettes at times chosen by the researchers. The handheld computers signaled when participants should smoke. Results showed that participants reported it less rewarding (as measured by poorer moods, less reductions in cravings, and less improvement in overall feelings) when they smoked at prescribed times than when they smoked when they chose to (Catley & Grobe, 2008).

Gravlee et al. (2006) argue that handheld computers are also useful in field research for recording systematic observations of social and physical environments. They describe their use of handheld computers in completing Healthy Environments Partnership's Neighborhood Observational Checklists, a 140-item survey assessing community resources. Handheld computer devices, they argue, are preferable to paper and pencil formats because they are easy to use, allow for multiple users, create customized surveys based on variable sizes (e.g., the software cycles through series of street-level questions based on the number of streets in an area), improve data quality, and make exporting data much easier.

The number of available tools for data collection is expanding. One example is Palm-tungsten E2, which is popular because data can be easily downloaded from the handheld device to Access-Microsoft or Stata tables on a laptop or desktop computer. Another device, HanDBase professional is popular because of the ease with which filter and contingency questions (see Chapter 7) can be created as well as items that require pull-down menus. Surveys with response buttons, checkboxes, pop-up lists, and automatic date and number entries can also be created relatively easily with HanDBase (Haller et al., 2009).

---

example, the recipients of social services who are the subjects of research may be treated better by the research team than they would be during their everyday contacts with human service agencies. Under the watchful eye of a research team, much greater care may be taken in the form of monitoring and supervision to ensure that the treatment being delivered is true to the theoretical model than might be taken when the same intervention is delivered as a routine part of an agency's service.

Experimenter Effects. As discussed, artificiality of experimental settings in comparison to the real world exists, and there is another side to this coin: The experimental setting itself is a real world—that is, a social occasion in which social norms, roles, and values exist and shape people's behavior. Social processes arising within the experimental setting—and not a part of the experimental variables—may shape the research outcome. Thus, changes in the dependent variable may result from the demand characteristics of experiments, such as repeated measurement, or from the impact of experimenter expectations, which are factors that obviously do not influence people in the everyday world.

Generalizability. The logistics involved in managing an experiment often necessitate that experimenters use small samples. Furthermore, the goal of holding measurement error to a minimum often compels researchers to make these samples as homogeneous as possible. Despite the advantages of random sampling, experimenters frequently must settle for availability samples to obtain subjects who will participate in the study. The net result is that experiments often are conducted on small, homogeneous, availability samples, and it may be difficult to know to whom such results can be generalized. It often is assumed that representative sampling is not as essential in experiments as in other types of research because of the randomization and control procedures that are used. Although these help, we must still be cautious regarding the population to which we make such generalizations.

Timeliness of Results. Although experiments may produce the strongest evidence of causation, they often are time-consuming to conduct. The urgency of policy decisions may preclude using experimentation simply because it takes too long to generate funding for the project, design the research, and carry it out. If the results do not come in quickly enough, they may not be considered in the debate over a rapidly developing policy (Rossi, Lipsey, & Freeman, 2004).

REVIEW AND CRITICAL THINKING

Main Points

- Experiments are a controlled method of observation in which the value of one or more independent variables is changed to assess the causal effect on one or more dependent variables.

- Because of the control that experiments afford, they are the surest method of discovering causal relationships among variables.

- Major elements of control in experiments include control variables, control groups, matching, and randomization.

- Internal validity refers to whether the independent variable does, in fact, produce the effect that it appears to produce on the dependent variable.

- Numerous conditions may threaten the internal validity of experiments, but using true experimental designs can control all of them.

- Quasi-experimental designs are useful for bringing much of the control of an experiment to nonexperimental situations.

- External validity is the degree to which experimental results can be generalized beyond the experimental setting.

- Threats to external validity generally are not controllable through design, but are more difficult and less straightforward to control than are threats to internal validity.

- Double-blind experiments, in which neither the subjects nor the experimenters know which groups are in the experimental or control condition, are used to control both experimental demand characteristics and experimenter bias.

- To avoid race, ethnicity, or gender insensitivity, the minority composition of experimental groups should be reported, consideration should be given to analyzing the data by controlling for minority impact, and the minority status of all experimental participants should be considered.

- An understanding of experimental procedures can contribute to practice effectiveness as well as research endeavors.

Important Terms for Review

blocking	experimental condition	extraneous variability	quasi-experimental designs
control condition	experimental group	field experiments	random assignment
control group	experimental stimulus	internal validity	true experimental designs
control variables	experimental treatment	laboratory experiments	
demand characteristics	experimental variability	matching	
double-blind experiment	experimenter's expectations	preexperimental designs	
experiment	external validity		

Critical Thinking

Some people in the field of human service research argue that experiments are the preferred or model research design because they are the best at providing a solid logical foundation from which to infer causality. This also makes experimental designs a laudable model to serve as a guide for critical thinking in the practice and policy realms. People constantly ask questions about causality: Why do people commit crimes? Why did I lose my job? Why did she treat me that way? When confronted with information, especially when it involves some causal judgment, ask yourself the following questions:

1. Can the observations or information available be organized into an experimental design? Can you identify independent and dependent variables?

2. Is there anything like random assignment or a control group involved? If not, how does this compromise your confidence in the conclusions that can be drawn?

3. Does the information look anything like a quasi-experiment, such as a time-series design?

4. Is there anything that threatens the internal validity or the external validity of the information available? What factors other than the independent variable might be producing changes in the dependent variable?

5. What about replication? Is there information available from other sources (other "experiments") that could increase your confidence in the causal inferences?

Exploring the Internet

If you've been taking advantage of Internet resources that apply to the previous chapters, then you've no doubt discovered the value of using key chapter terms with various Internet search engines. For example, putting such terms as "random assignment" or "randomized control group" into Google or another search engine locates a number of websites that relate to experimental design in social science. The National Institutes of Health's web page (http://www.nih.gov) serves as a portal to information about experimental research on human volunteers. Its web page uses the term "clinical trials," but focuses mostly on experimental research. Use this web page to find illustrations of the different experimental designs discussed in this chapter. You can begin by looking for research on depression. Click on "Health Information," then look under "D" for Drug Abuse. Once you have explored drug abuse, look for research on other conditions or click on "ClinicalTrials.gov."

For Further Reading

Campbell, D. T., & Russo, M. J. (1999). *Social Experimentation*. Thousand Oaks, Calif.: Sage. Donald Campbell was one of the giants in the field of social experimentation. This book presents his views on how social experiments can be used for the betterment of society.

Fairweather, G. W., & Davidson, W. S. (1986). *An Introduction to Community Experimentation: Theory, Methods, and Practice*. New York: McGraw-Hill. An interesting book ideally suited to those involved in community action programs. It outlines the reasons for experimentation and supplies the designs to evaluate the effectiveness of various intervention programs.

Field, A., & Hole, G. J. (2003). *How to Design and Report Experiments*. Thousand Oaks, Calif.: Sage. This textbook provides a good overview to experimental design and statistical analysis.

Gabor, P. A., & Grinnell, R. M. Jr. (1994). *Evaluation and Quality Improvement in the Human Services*. Boston: Allyn & Bacon. Although this book covers many other research issues, it is especially good at showing the importance of experimental designs in program evaluations. It describes the use of many different kinds of designs used in human service settings.

Gottman, J. M. (1981). *Time-Series Analysis: A Comprehensive Introduction for Social Scientists*. New York: Cambridge University Press. "Comprehensive" is certainly the operative word in describing this book, because it details the mathematical analysis of time-series designs. The author also argues persuasively against the common "eyeballing" approach to time-series analysis.

Kirk, R. E. (1995). *Experimental Design: Procedures for the Behavioral Sciences*, 3rd ed. Belmont, Calif.: Cengage Learning Brooks/Cole. This is a thorough overview of how to design both simple and complicated experiments. It goes well beyond the review in this chapter.

Solomon, P., Cavanaugh, M., & Draine, J. (2009). *Designing, Developing, and Implementing Randomized Control Trials*. New York: Oxford University Press. This "pocket guide" deals specifically with designing and implementing randomized control trials (RCTs), a form of experimental research, in community-based settings. It provides researchers and social service practitioners insight into each step of an RCT.

Class Exercises for Competency Assessment

A senior citizens' service organization is concerned about the large number of purse snatchings and other attacks on elderly people in the community and decides to apply for a Department of Justice grant intended to assist local communities in fighting crime. A requirement for receiving such a grant is that the proposal include a plan for evaluating the program established with grant monies to assess effectiveness.

The center staff's first idea is to hire local teenagers to work out of the center as escorts to those people who request the service. Second, they plan to use the teenagers as a crime watch in those areas where attacks have been fairly frequent. Initially, the center will not be able to serve everyone, and the crime watch staff will only be able to cover some of the neighborhoods the senior center serves.

The senior center staff believes that this program will serve two objectives. First, it will reduce the threat of crime to the elderly. Second, putting young people into positions where they can work with and help the elderly will increase feelings of understanding between the generations.

You have been asked to help the center develop a research design with the purpose of assessing how well the program attains its objectives.

10.1. **[Critical Thinking] [Policy Practice]** What would be the independent and dependent variables for such a project? Give some examples of possible indicators for these variables. Which two experimental designs would be most appropriate to the research question? Which would be the most feasible?

10.2. **[Policy Practice]** One decision is whether to use the presence or absence of the program as the independent variable or to test different combinations of the independent variables. List some possible combinations of intervention efforts that could be used in a factorial design.

10.3. **[Ethics] [Diversity] [Research & Practice]** A major issue in experimental research is how to assign participants to experimental and control conditions.
   a. Consider just the escort service. How could participants be assigned to treatment and control conditions? Would random assignment be ethical? Indicate why or why not.
   b. Now consider the crime watch component, which serves anyone who happens to be in the patrolled area. Assume the senior center serves about a 50-block area of the city. Suggest some ways of developing experimental and control conditions.
   c. What control variables might be useful in this study? How would these control variables assist you in making causal inferences?

10.4. **[Critical Thinking] [Research & Practice]** How would you collect data to evaluate the effectiveness of the program in meeting its goals of reducing crime and increasing intergenerational understanding? Consider the alternatives of personal interviews, mailed questionnaires, observations, and existing data.

Now there's trouble in River City. It seems a local, very influential politician has gotten wind of the project. His mother lives in the program impact area, and under no circumstances will he support an evaluation where his mother may wind up as a control subject who will not be provided services. Without his support, there will be no grant.

10.5. **[Critical Thinking] [Research & Practice]** How could you design a quasi-experimental study that would not involve designating certain people or areas as experimental and control? What deficiencies would this design have in comparison to a true experiment?

10.6. **[Critical Thinking] [Research & Practice]** What are the major threats to internal and external validity in this research project? How have the designs considered in the preceding exercises helped reduce these threats?

Chapter 11

✴

Single-System Designs

The Clinical Research Model

The Clinical Research Process
  Identify Problems
  Establish Goals
  Select a Single-System Design
  Establish and Measure the Baseline
  Introduce Treatment
  Assess Treatment Effects

Types of Single–System Designs
  Single-Treatment Designs
  Specialized Designs

Generalizability of Single–System Designs

Assessment of the Clinical Research Model
  Advantages
  Disadvantages

Review and Critical Thinking
  Main Points
  Important Terms for Review
  Critical Thinking
  Exploring the Internet
  For Further Reading
  Class Exercises for Competency Assessment

The model of evidence-based practice begins with converting the need for information into answerable questions and then systematically seeking, through print and electronic sources, to track down the best evidence for guiding practice decisions. Using the available scientific knowledge base as a guide, however, is only one part of evidence-based practice. Human service professionals also are called upon to evaluate their own effectiveness and seek ways to improve future practice efforts (Sackett et al., 2000). Practitioners generally work with one client at a time. Even if the client system is a family or a group or a community, the practitioner does not have randomized control groups, placebo treatments, or other features that make clinical trials such a highly valued form of evidence for advancing practice. So beyond providing some interesting anecdotal evidence, how can the practitioner–client encounter serve as part of the research process? Seeking to answer this question has led many human service professionals to revise the conception of their roles as clinician–researchers.

The purpose of this chapter is to present a fundamental tool of this role and a central mechanism through which valid research can be conducted in clinical settings: the *single-system design*. **Single-system designs** are quasi-experimental research designs that involve assessing change in a dependent variable on a single research case or subject. In psychology, the term *single case* appears to be replacing "single subject" as the designation of choice (Levin, 1992). We have adopted a term that is more common to social work—single system—to signify the fact that the unit of analysis for this research may not necessarily be an individual person but also a couple, family, group, organization, or other human aggregate. Our own students have designed single-system projects in which the unit of analysis was an individual child with poor study behavior, a pair of squabbling siblings, a nursing home group with poor interaction among participants, and a medication-dispensing program in a mental health setting. In the latter case, the program was the system, and the dependent variable was the proportion of clients who received their weekly dosage of medication on time. So although the most common application is to focus on the behavior of an individual client, the design is flexible and lends itself to the study of a wide range of practice issues.

The distinguishing feature of the single-system design is that the dependent variable is repeatedly measured, most commonly during a baseline phase and again during one or more intervention phases, when the independent variable is manipulated. Experimental effects are inferred by comparisons of the subject's responses across baseline and intervention phases. We begin by discussing how and why a *clinical research model* has emerged in the human services. Then we analyze the clinical research process, showing how research can be merged with clinical practice. Next, building on the discussion of experimental designs in Chapter 10, we present the various kinds of single-system designs that are available to clinician–researchers. Finally, we analyze the advantages and disadvantages of single-system designs.

THE CLINICAL RESEARCH MODEL

A fundamental force behind the development of single-system designs is the human service practitioner's professional concern about knowing how a client is responding to intervention. This basic desire has been intensified by the pressure for more accountability in the human services. Funding sources, insurance providers, and regulatory organizations demand documentation that services are being delivered according to standards, and they want to see evidence that clients do, in fact, improve. Unfortunately, traditional research designs have significant limitations for meeting these needs in the practice community (Barlow, Nock, & Hersen, 2009; Gingerich, 1990). A major source of new knowledge for many practitioners has been group experiments. However, group experiments often are impractical—or even impossible—to conduct in practice settings. It may be too time consuming and costly to assemble clients with similar problems and randomly assign some to treatment groups and others to control groups. A second problem with group experiments in terms of practice implications is that the results often are an average of the whole group's response, obscuring individual reactions. The effects on individuals, of course, are of most interest to clinicians. For example, knowing that a given treatment was effective on 70 percent of an experimental group may be interesting, but it helps relatively little in predicting the reaction of a particular client in a practitioner's office.

Another problem in some traditional group experimentation is failure of the research design to capture the process by which change was induced. Thus, traditional research sometimes has been referred to as "black box" research, because subjects receive some treatment and are then compared with other subjects who did not receive the treatment. With only a pretest and posttest measure, experimenters may not have information on the process of how the change occurred, only on whether it occurred at all. It is as if the subjects passed through a mysterious black box and came out either improved or not improved. A fourth complaint about traditional group experiments has been that reliance upon statistical procedures for data analysis often requires a high degree of statistical expertise as well as access to data-analysis technology; this situation may necessitate that practitioners relinquish control of the study to outside methodologists. Such a reliance on direction from outside of practice may have contributed to the view that these studies are not relevant to practice.

Finally, the use of control groups from which treatment is withheld is a source of ethical concern to human service professionals. Thus, although group experiments are appropriate for some purposes, the deficiencies that are inherent in the method have led both practitioners and researchers to seek alternative approaches for evaluating individual change and refining intervention techniques. Single-system designs, as we shall see, effectively avoid the unattractive features of group experiments.

A second source of clinical knowledge prior to single-system designs was case histories. A case history, of course, is a report from a clinician about a client who has undergone treatment. Although many of these reports are intriguing, they often do not provide a sound basis for the accumulation of knowledge. First, they exhibit to only a limited degree the characteristics that distinguish science from other sources of knowledge (see Chapter 2). For example, vague treatments often are reported to have produced vague improvements. Because of this, other practitioners would have grave difficulty replicating the procedures if they wished. The ability to replicate is, of course, a fundamental characteristic of the scientific method—especially when one is working with a single case at a time. In addition, case histories often are prepared only on successes; information about failures, which may be of equal importance, is not communicated to other practitioners. Another problem with case histories is failure to report valid and reliable data to support conclusions; exaggerated claims of success become common in the absence of hard data (Barlow, Nock, & Hersen, 2009). Finally, with no controls, these studies fail to consider the possible impact of extraneous variables on the client.

So it was against this backdrop of unsatisfactory research techniques for clinical settings that the clinical research model emerged. The **clinical research model,** or the **empirical practice model,** became an effort to merge research and practice, and it includes much more than single-system designs. It involves a stance toward practice that is defined by the following characteristics:

1. Maximum use is made of research findings for understanding human service practice issues.

2. Data are collected systematically to monitor the intervention.

3. Interventions are evaluated empirically to determine their degree of effectiveness.

4. Problems, interventions, and outcomes are specified in terms that are concrete, observable, and measurable.

5. Research ways of thinking and research methods are employed in defining clients' problems, formulating questions for practice, collecting assessment data, evaluating effectiveness of interventions, and using evidence.

6. Research and practice are viewed as parts of the same problem-solving process.

7. Research is accepted as a tool to be used in practice.

The systematic evaluation of practice through the use of single-system designs is a core component of this model of practice. Through the mechanism of single-system designs, research and practice merge into one enterprise. This approach, however, does not reject traditional large-group research, which is still necessary for testing total programs and for confirming the generalizability of intervention effectiveness.

THE CLINICAL RESEARCH PROCESS

At the outset we wish to make clear that the clinical research model is not a radically new approach to intervention. In fact, many parallels exist between this model and traditional practice, and many practitioners are likely to do much of what the model calls for anyway. The model does, however, inject greater specificity, objectivity, and empiricism into the clinical process. By following the model, the clinician–researcher is in a position to know precisely what treatment was applied and how much effect was produced—and to have supporting data for proof. The model links research and practice by putting the practitioner in the enviable position not only of bringing about change, but also having valid evidence as to why that change occurred. What follows in this section is an outline of the clinical research process divided into six stages, which are summarized in Figure 11.1.

Identify Problems

Like all practice approaches, the clinical research model begins with an assessment of the client's problem. Typically, the problem involves some aspect of the client's functioning: behaviors, perceptions, attitudes, or feelings. During the initial stage, the practitioner strives to obtain as clear and specific an understanding of the problem as possible through commonly used assessment strategies, such as interviewing or paper-and-pencil assessment tools.

Establish Goals

After the problem is identified, the next step is to determine treatment goals. At this point, we encounter the first real difference between the clinical research model and traditional practice. The clinical research model requires, first, that goals be more specific and precisely defined than often is done in conventional practice and, second, that they be measurable in some way (Kazdin, 2010). Although these requirements of specificity and measurability are more rigorous under the clinical research model than in traditional practice, they are best seen as an extension of normal practice procedures rather than as something strangely different. As to the requirement for measurability of outcomes, some practitioners argue that some beneficial outcomes of intervention are so subtle that they are essentially unmeasurable. Countering this attitude in the field of social work is "The First Rule of EPM" (Empirical Practice Model): "There is and can be no such thing as effectiveness until there is measurable positive change in the client's problem" (Nugent, Sieppert, & Hudson, 2001, p. 3). The self-delusion is believing that a real but unmeasurable change has occurred when it actually has not. Effectiveness requires desired, positive change in the level of the client's problem.

One common difficulty in establishing goals is that goals are often long term, making it impractical for the clinician–researcher to monitor progress all the way to achievement of the final goal. In these cases, it may be necessary to identify proximate, intermediate goals whose achievement is evidence of progress toward the final goal. For example, the final goal for an underachiever might be improved academic performance—a long-term goal. Proximate goals that would demonstrate progress might include improved note taking, longer study hours,

Identify problems
↓
Establish goals
↓
Select a single-system design
↓
Establish and measure the baseline
↓
Introduce treatment
↓
Assess treatment effects

FIGURE 11.1 Steps in the Clinical Research Process

and more regular class attendance. Achievement of these proximate goals would be expected to relate to achievement of the final goal. Which measurable, intermediate goals can serve as valid indicators of long-term goals depends, of course, on a theoretical understanding of the long-term changes that are being sought through intervention.

Select a Single-System Design

Once a problem and a corresponding goal for intervention have been identified, the next phase of the clinical research process is to select an appropriate single-system design. Whereas the general principle of single-system research consists of comparing a series of preintervention and postintervention measurements, many variations on this basic scheme exist. Later in the chapter, we will present several common designs and discuss their strengths and limitations. At this point, however, we simply note that we can choose from many design options. We also point out that early in the process, the practitioner should be thinking about the design choices that will best suit the goals and constraints of the particular clinical case. For example, if his or her primary objective is to provide treatment and simply monitor the client's progress, then a simple design is adequate. For a general behavior deficit, however, where the proposed intervention involves working on increasing the desired behavior in different realms of the client's life, such as at home, in school, and when visiting with friends, more complicated designs take advantage of such an intervention strategy both to monitor client behavior and to maximize validity for research goals.

The point is that single-system designs are flexible and adaptive to many practice situations. Taking advantage of this flexibility requires the practitioner to have a clear notion of the problem to be addressed, an understanding of how the proposed intervention is supposed to effect change, and an awareness of strengths and limitations of single-system designs. Once a particular design is chosen, the practitioner can address the next step in the clinical research process—namely, establishing and measuring a baseline.

Establish and Measure the Baseline

Single-system designs are based on the quasi-experimental time-series designs discussed in Chapter 10, but they are modified to make them more appropriate for use with a single subject. As such, single-system designs call for repeated measures of the client's condition so that trends and changes can be noted. Typically, the frequency, intensity, or duration of some behavior of the client is measured, such as how many cigarettes are smoked, severity of pain, or how long a depression lasts.

Thus, the fourth step in the clinical research process is to establish a **baseline**: a series of measurements of the client's condition prior to treatment that form the basis with which to compare the client's condition after implementing treatment. By comparing measurements after treatment with those from the baseline period, the clinician can trace the effect that the treatment is having. Typically, three measurements are needed, as an absolute minimum, to establish a baseline (Barlow & Hersen, 1973). More measurements are better, especially if the variable's condition is unstable. It is important to note that all single-system designs rule out the simple procedure of using only two measurements—one pretest and one posttest—because this results in a preexperimental design that is extremely weak on internal validity (see Design P1 in Chapter 10).

Figure 11.2 illustrates how baseline measurement can serve as a basis for assessing treatment effects. The hypothetical data show a high level of undesirable client behavior before treatment. After treatment is instigated, however, this level drops sharply. Results are not always as clear and dramatic as these, of course, so making interpretations can be more difficult. (We will deal with the issue of assessing treatment effects in more detail later.)

Two major issues in establishing the baseline are (1) what to measure and (2) how to measure it. Typically, the clinical problem itself suggests the appropriate trait to measure. In general, what we seek to change through treatment is what we need to measure. For example, a child whose problem is disruptive behavior in school could be

FIGURE 11.2 Hypothetical Baseline Followed by Successful Treatment

monitored as to the frequency of disruptions that he or she causes each day. On the other hand, treatment philosophy might suggest monitoring the frequency of *appropriate* behavior as a means not only of measuring behavior, but also of setting the stage for change. (As emphasized in Chapter 5, measurement and operational definitions should be deduced from theoretical concepts, whether or not those concepts emerge from research or practice theories.)

Client problems without specific behavioral outcomes or manifestations are more difficult to measure (Bloom, Fischer, & Orme, 2009). Depression, for example, can be displayed in many different behavioral forms, and in such cases, it is preferable to use several measures. Also, where such an indirect link exists between a concept and behavioral manifestations, multiple indicators help reduce the effects of error in those measures. For depression, we might establish a separate baseline for a behavioral indicator (say, the percentage of the day spent alone), a paper-and-pencil measure of depression, and a self-report from the client for his or her subjective assessment. If the treatment produced positive gains on all measures, then we would have greater evidence for the treatment's effectiveness than if we relied on only one indicator.

Having decided which aspects of the client's condition to measure, we next confront the issue of how to measure them. Basically, the clinician–researcher has four choices: observation, existing records, paper-and-pencil measures, and client self-reports. Of these, observation is of the most general utility and also the most valid and reliable (Weiss & Frohman, 1985).

Unfortunately, many client problems are not directly observable, so there is a limit to the applicability of observation. When it is used, however, there are three important considerations. (These issues regarding observation were discussed in greater detail in Chapter 9.) First, the observations should be unobtrusive. If they are not, the client may behave differently because of the presence of the observers. This could result in faulty baseline data, which could obscure treatment effects. Second, multiple observers should be used where possible to assess the extent of observer reliability. In some cases, videotapes might be substituted for multiple observers, but in natural settings, their use is likely to be difficult. Third, if possible, observers should not be aware of when the treatment actually begins. If they are, their expectations for improvement might affect their objectivity. For example, borderline behaviors that were counted as disruptive during the baseline phase might be ignored during the treatment phase, thus tending to overstate the apparent effectiveness of the treatment to reduce disruptive behavior.

A second measurement approach is existing records. Some client problems relate to matters on which people other than the clinician or client routinely gather data. For example, existing records, such as grades and school attendance, often are used in assessing a child's school performance. Where existing records are appropriate, they are often a good choice. They also are unobtrusive because they are collected regardless of whether the client is under treatment. Furthermore, because persons other than the clinician–researcher collected them, time and cost factors are likely to be favorable. (We reviewed problems associated with using existing records for research purposes in Chapter 8.)

A third common measurement approach is paper-and-pencil measures, which are often useful when the client's problem does not lend itself to direct observation. If the decision is made to use a paper-and-pencil measure, it is advisable to use an existing one, if available, rather than devise a new one. In addition to the practical benefits from avoiding the time and trouble of developing a new measure, existing measures usually have established levels of validity and reliability. Furthermore, their use contributes to the accumulation of knowledge, because the standardized measuring devices make for greater comparability across studies. Fortunately, a large number of measures, covering a wide array of client problems, are available. The following are only some of the compilations of such measures: Fischer and Corcoran (2007); Fredman and Sherman (1987); Groth-Marnat (2009); Magura and Moses (1986); Miller and Salkind (2002); Spies, Carlson, and Geisinger (2010); and Zalaquett and Wood (1997). Other sources are available on the Internet, including Health & Psychosocial Instruments (HaPI) from Ovid Technologies (http://www.ovid.com).

Paper-and-pencil measures have some characteristics, however, that make them less than ideal for use in single-system designs. First, they are obtrusive, because clients obviously know they are being measured, which can create many problems. For example, completing a questionnaire concerning family relationships might make parents aware that they have been paying less attention to their children than they should, and this awareness could change their behavior. (Recall from Chapter 10 that this is the "testing" threat to internal validity in experiments. Although such change may be desirable, the problem, from a research standpoint, is that it is not possible to determine if the treatment or the measurement process caused the change.)

The second problem with paper-and-pencil measures is that of *demand characteristics* (also discussed in Chapter 10). Clients may deliberately change responses in the direction indicating improvement because of a desire to fulfill the expectations of the clinician. Furthermore, frequent exposure to the measure makes the client familiar with it and raises the specter of multiple-testing effects (see Chapter 10). These same issues appear to apply to computerized administration as well. A study comparing paper-and-pencil testing versus computerized testing found no difference in social desirability effects between the two modes of testing (Fox & Schwartz, 2002). Finally, some paper-and-pencil measures are projective tests, such as the Rorschach Inkblot Test, the Thematic Apperception Test, sentence completion tests, and figure drawings. All these tests rely heavily on the examiner's interpretation of client responses. After reviewing the evidence, Barlow, Nock, and Hersen (2009) strongly advise against the use of such measures because they do not have sufficient validity and reliability to provide a sound basis for single-system experiments.

The last measurement alternative is self-reports by clients who monitor their own behavior or feelings. Although clients' perceptions of their conditions are important, many problems are associated with overreliance on self-reports. First, evidence shows that self-reports do not correlate well with objective indicators. For example, studies of assertiveness among female college students have made use of subjects' own reports of how assertive they are, as well as trained observers' assessments of how assertively the subjects actually behave. Generally, researchers find that self-reports do not correlate with the observers' assessments (Frisch & Higgins, 1986).

Second, self-monitoring is reactive, because it sensitizes the client to some aspect of his or her behavior (Hayes, Barlow, & Nelson-Gray, 1999). Research has shown that the mere process of monitoring can change one's behavior. In one study, for example, objective baselines were gathered on how many cigarettes were consumed by a group of smokers (McFall, 1970). Half the subjects were then asked to monitor and record the extent of their smoking; the other half were asked to keep track of the times when they didn't smoke. Both groups showed a change from their baseline levels, but in the opposite direction. Those who were monitoring their smoking smoked more, and those who were monitoring their nonsmoking smoked less!

Because of the multitude of problems associated with self-report data, such measurements should be used with caution. Preferably, they should be used as an adjunct to other measures that are less subject to false reports.

Thus, it is evident that some of the measurement options available to clinician–researchers are better than others, so the most objective, valid, and reliable measure available in a given research context should be selected. As noted, direct observation usually is best if the client's problem lends itself to such observation. Otherwise, a more indirect measure is necessary, although these do have limitations. By using multiple measures, however, the weaknesses of the indirect measures can be reduced and the quality of the single-system experiment improved (Gottman, 1985).

Introduce Treatment

Once the baseline is established, the next stage in the clinical research process is to begin treatment. It is important to the clinical research model that only a *single*, coherent treatment be applied (Barlow, Nock, & Hersen, 2009), because each application of the model is essentially an experiment, with the treatment being the independent variable in that experiment. If more than one treatment is used and the client exhibits a change in behavior compared to the baseline, then we do not know which treatment produced the change and cannot learn anything that might be valuable with similar clients in the future. To assess the effects of the independent variable, we must be able to specify precisely what the treatment consisted of and be consistent in its application during the treatment phase.

The demand for a single, specific treatment is one aspect of the clinical research model that has led to its cold reception in some human service circles, particularly among nonbehaviorists (Nelsen, 1981). Nonbehavioral treatments often lack the specificity that allows practitioners to trace a particular treatment over the period of the treatment phase. In addition, nonbehavioral treatments can be complex, and may even mix a number of treatment modes, making it difficult to identify the precise factors that presumably resulted in change. This is less a criticism of the clinical research model, however, than a challenge to those using nonbehavioral treatments: "[Nonbehaviorists] must work hard at choosing interventions that may be effective and at defining their interventions precisely, preferably by addressing both what they do and how they do it" (Nelsen, 1981, p. 35).

Resistance to the discipline imposed by the clinical research model appears to be greatest among those who are least familiar with it. After some initial frustration with the specificity and single treatment required by the model, practitioners learning to apply the model generally come to accept it (Johnson, 1981). They appreciate that the model increases rationality in the selection of treatments, forces explicit consideration of the assumptions on which treatment is based, and requires specific practice skills rather than reliance solely on intuition or ingenuity. The greatest satisfaction, however, comes from the fact that the model provides solid evidence regarding whether the client benefited from treatment. Although it is rewarding to feel that one has been of assistance, it is even more rewarding to have objective evidence to support those feelings.

During the treatment phase, the measurement of the client's condition, started during the baseline phase, continues to track what changes—if any—the treatment is producing in the client's condition. It is crucial that the conditions under which measurements are made during the treatment phase remain consistent with those under which the baseline measurements were obtained. Any change in such things as observers, settings, examiners, or instructions could confound apparent treatment effects. Remember that a single-system design is an experiment, and only one variable—the treatment—should be allowed to change from one phase to another.

Assess Treatment Effects

When is a treatment judged to be effective? This seemingly simple question, which is addressed in the last stage of the clinical research process, has a surprisingly complex answer. Assessing the effectiveness of a treatment depends, first, on the pattern produced during the baseline measurements: The ease and clarity with which baseline measures can be compared with treatment measures depends, in part, on the *stability* of the baseline measures.

Figure 11.3 illustrates four possible baseline patterns: (1) stable, (2) rising (client worsening), (3) descending (client improving), and (4) unstable. In this discussion of baseline stability, we will assume that lower measurement scores represent improvement, as in the case of reducing the incidence of some problem behavior. If, however, the goal of treatment is to increase some aspect of client functioning, as it often is, then higher measurement scores indicate improvement. A stable baseline is the ideal, because then, posttreatment comparisons readily reveal treatment effects. If the treatment is helpful, we see a pronounced downward move in measurement levels. A treatment producing negative effects yields an upward move in measurement levels. Little change from baseline levels reveals an ineffective treatment. The value of a stable baseline is that it allows all three possible treatment outcomes to be readily noted.

FIGURE 11.3 Types of Baseline Patterns

Unfortunately, client conditions often are not stable but, instead, worsen, improve, or vary considerably. Assessing treatment effects with baselines like these is more difficult and often puts limits on what we can infer. A baseline with a rising trend (client worsening) is not too problematic, because an effective treatment will produce a reversal of the baseline trend. Such a change provides strong evidence that the treatment was effective. With ineffective or harmful treatments, however, it is difficult to tell if this is just a continuation of the baseline trend (ineffective treatment) or if the continued deterioration is the result of some harmful treatment. A baseline with a descending trend (client improving) has the opposite effect. If the treatment proves to be harmful, then the trend reverses, and the negative effect becomes readily apparent. If the client continues to improve during treatment, however, then it is unclear whether the treatment produced that improvement (effective treatment) or whether it was just a continuation of the baseline trend (ineffective treatment).

The unstable baseline is the most troublesome. With the client's condition changing from one measurement to another, it becomes difficult to identify changes that result from treatment. A couple of strategies do exist, however, for dealing with an unstable baseline (Barlow, Nock, & Hersen, 2009). One extends the period of baseline measurements with the hope that a stable pattern will emerge—with, of course, no guarantee of stabilization. In addition, we may find practical as well as ethical constraints on how long treatment can be postponed while awaiting baseline stability. A second strategy is the application of statistical techniques that can reveal trends and differences between pretreatment and posttreatment measures that are too subtle to be noted by visual inspection (Achen, 1986; Gottman, 1981). These statistics have limited effectiveness, however, if the pattern is extremely unstable.

The use of statistics to assess treatment effects also raises a problem beyond that of baseline stability—namely, how much change is necessary before we can say a treatment is effective. From a research perspective, any change from pretest to posttest measures is evidence that the treatment was effective in the sense of bringing about change in the dependent variable. In clinical settings, however, change can take the form of improvement or deterioration in a client's status. Practitioners seek improvement, of course, so treatment effectiveness in single-system designs normally is defined as an improvement in performance after treatment. Yet, assessing whether improvement has occurred is complex, because effectiveness can be based on three different criteria: therapeutic, experimental, or statistical.

A treatment is *therapeutically effective* when it leads clients to fully achieve the goals that have been set for them: The disruptive student is no longer disruptive, the underachiever is now achieving, or the teenage mother can care for her infant independently. When treatment produces these kinds of improvements, its effectiveness is obvious. Visual inspection of the measurements taken during the treatment phase clearly reveals the improvement when compared with the baseline measurements.

A treatment is *experimentally effective* when it produces a pronounced improvement in the client's condition, even though the ultimate goals have not been reached. For example, a claustrophobic person may have come to the point where he or she can use an elevator when alone but remains unable to use an elevator that is crowded. As with therapeutic effectiveness, the change in the client's condition from the baseline to the treatment phase is sufficiently dramatic that visual inspection normally reveals it.

Figure 11.4 displays two data plots from single-system designs conducted in a school classroom. In the first case, the teacher monitored disruptive classroom behavior. The second case represents a child in kindergarten who had difficulty adjusting to school; the problem was monitored by counting the number of requests she made during school to go home. These cases illustrate two criteria for establishing experimental effectiveness (Kazdin, 2010). The first case has nonoverlapping data. All the measurements taken during the treatment phase are higher or lower (whichever direction represents improvement) than those taken during the baseline phase. Stated another way, performance during treatment does not overlap with that of the baseline period. This is a fairly severe guideline—and one that, if met, is a strong demonstration of experimental effectiveness. The criterion achieved by the second case is somewhat less rigorous: All the measurements taken during the treatment phase are higher or lower than the *average* level of the baseline. This guideline is preferable if the baseline is not especially stable, but it is important to

FIGURE 11.4 Establishing Experimental Effectiveness in Single-System Research emphasize that these are only guidelines, not rigid rules. Quite possibly, a given single-system experiment could evidence clear experimental effectiveness and achieve neither of these guidelines. Following them, however, does make visual inspection more systematic and less a matter of judgment on the part of the clinician–researcher.

Statistical effectiveness is achieved when the treatment produces statistically significant improvement in the client's condition. In other words, the difference between baseline and treatment levels is sufficiently large that it is not likely to be caused by chance variation. (We will discuss the concept of statistical significance in detail in Chapter 15.) In addition to the magnitude of the difference between baseline and intervention, the number of observations in each phase also determines statistical significance—that is, more is better. So, assuming a relatively large number of observations in each phase—say, 20 or more—statistics may be sufficiently sensitive to detect smaller changes than visual inspection can. With many observations in each phase, statistical effectiveness sometimes requires the least improvement in the client to detect change.

This raises the issue of the difference between statistical significance and therapeutic or experimental significance. A treatment judged to be effective because it produced a statistically significant improvement in the client might be a near failure according to the other criteria. The reason for this is that, in some cases having to do with the peculiarities of statistical analysis, small differences between two measurements can produce a statistically significant result. For example, reducing a juvenile firestarter's behavior from seven episodes a week to five might be a statistically significant reduction, but we would not likely consider this to be a success from a therapeutic or experimental perspective. Because statistical significance may be only remotely related to treatment success, statistical analysis is most useful in cases with an unstable baseline, where visual analysis is difficult.

So the question of treatment effectiveness depends, in part, on the particular criterion of effectiveness that is applied. With the varying criteria, it is important to be aware of their differences and be precise when discussing what we mean by effectiveness. Furthermore, it is important to recognize that the effect of a treatment may be relatively permanent or may decrease after the treatment is withdrawn. To test for this, the posttreatment measurements become, in effect, a new baseline. Deviation from this baseline as time passes suggests a limit to how long the treatment is effective.

Before discussing various types of single-system research designs, Research in Practice 11.1 explores how single-system research can contribute to evidence-based practice.

TYPES OF SINGLE-SYSTEM DESIGNS

Although numerous types of single-system designs exist, all involve repeated measurements during the baseline and treatment phases and a comparison across phases as evidence of treatment effects. The designs differ in the number of phases involved, the number of treatments applied, and the number of baselines employed. Perhaps the most important differences, however, are in the internal validity of the designs. Some are more capable of providing evidence for the effect of a treatment when such an effect actually exists. Ideally, of course, clinician–researchers should select the most valid design that fits their particular case (see the discussions of validity in Chapters 5 and 10).

Single-Treatment Designs

The Basic *AB* Design. It has become customary to present single-system designs by using the first letters of the alphabet to symbolize various phases of the design. The letter *A* signifies a phase in which the client is not receiving treatment. This is the baseline period in all designs, but in some of the more complex designs, it also can refer to a period of treatment withdrawal. The letter *B* indicates a treatment phase during which some specific intervention is in progress. Subsequent letters of the

Research in Practice 11.1 Practice Effectiveness: Evidence-Based Practice through Single-System Designs

The evidence-based practice literature emphasizes randomized controlled trials (RCTs) as the "gold standard" for demonstrating program effectiveness (Nezu & Nezu, 2008). However, some human service practice problems do not lend themselves to evaluation by this method. Consider the case of children who are visually impaired and have additional disabilities. Visual impairment is a low-incidence condition and the additional disabilities they have can be highly varied (Ferrell, 2000). Such heterogeneity of disabilities and the geographic dispersion of cases make achieving the sample size necessary for an RCT improbable.

One viable option for practitioners with visually impaired clients would be to rely on single-system designs as a means of building a knowledge base for practice. Amy Parker and her colleagues (2008) demonstrated the feasibility of this approach by conducting a literature review similar to what one might find in a Campbell Collaboration review (see the Information Technology in Research box in Chapter 4), but focusing specifically on single-system design studies on visually impaired children with additional disabilities. They located 30 studies that matched their search criteria. They began with three research questions:

1. What studies used single-system research in communication instruction for children with visual impairments, including deaf and blind?
2. What practices and interventions were found to be effective?
3. Are there patterns of replication among the identified studies?

In Research in Practice 12.1, we present a guide, based on the elements of experimental designs, for evaluating the worthiness of evidence from research. Because the research considered here is single-system design and not RCTs, that study assessment guide and others developed by such organizations as the Campbell or Cochrane collaborations cannot be employed to rate the quality of these studies. The researchers turned to an assessment scheme developed specifically for rating single-system designs from the field of special education (Horner et al., 2005). This guide includes some features that one would use for any effectiveness evaluation, such as:

- Is there sufficient detail in the description of the participants and the setting to permit replication?
- Is the dependent variable operationally well defined?
- Is the independent variable (the program) described sufficiently for replication?
- Is the independent variable manipulated by and under the control of the experimenter?

Other assessment considerations are unique to a single-system design, such as:

- Is the dependent variable measured repeatedly over time?
- Does the design provide at least three demonstrations of experimental effect at three different points in time? For example, is there a change from baseline to treatment, treatment back to a second baseline, and again with another treatment?
- Does the particular design control well the threats to internal validity and does the pattern of results demonstrate experimental control?

In order for a practice to have been demonstrated effective, experimental control must be demonstrated across a range of studies, researchers, and participants. The guide developers proposed that a practice could be deemed "evidence based" when it meets three criteria:

1. A minimum of five single-system studies meeting the evaluation criteria had been published in peer-reviewed journals.
2. The studies were conducted by at least three different investigators at three different geographic locations.
3. The five or more studies include a combined total of at least 20 participants.

By employing criteria tailored to the unique features of single-system designs, the authors were able to make a convincing case that visually impaired students with multiple disabilities can develop communication skills and to identify promising interventions. They demonstrated that single-system designs can serve as a bridge for bringing scientifically based practices to special populations for which traditional experimentation is not feasible.

alphabet (*C*, *D*, and so on) symbolize the application of treatments different from *B*.

The *AB design* is the simplest of the single-system designs and forms the basis for the others. It consists of one baseline phase followed by one treatment phase. Treatment effectiveness is determined by comparing the client's condition during treatment with that of the baseline. The basic *AB* design is less than ideal, because its validity is threatened by history: Events other than the intervention could be responsible for the change in the client. Despite its limitations, however, the *AB* design provides better evidence of treatment effects than nonexperimental case histories do. The *AB* design also has the advantage of applying to most clinical situations, especially cases where more rigorous designs might be precluded.

Reversal and Withdrawal Designs. The *AB* design can be strengthened substantially by moving to a *reversal design* or *withdrawal design*, so called because, after one treatment phase, the treatment is interrupted for a period of time. Some sources distinguish between a withdrawal design (in which the treatment stops entirely after the first intervention phase) and a reversal design (in which the treatment is transferred to a different behavior). For example, a juvenile in a residential facility may participate in a token economy study on completing math homework. After a baseline period, he receives tokens each day for an intervention period based on the number of math problems he completes. In a withdrawal design, giving tokens is terminated (withdrawn) for another baseline. If a reversal design is used, tokens might be made contingent on a different behavior (reversed), such as pages of English read, while the number of math problems completed continues to be monitored for the study. We use the term *reversal design* to apply to both approaches in this discussion. There are basically two versions of the reversal design: *ABA* and *ABAB*. They differ only in that the *ABA* design ends in a no-treatment phase, whereas the *ABAB* design ends with the treatment being reintroduced (see Figure 11.5).

The value of reversal designs stems from their ability to demonstrate more conclusively that the treatment (not some extraneous factor) is producing change in the client's condition. If the client's condition deteriorates when the treatment is withdrawn, we have evidence that the treatment is the controlling factor. Even more evidence is provided with the *ABAB* design if the reintroduction of the treatment coincides with renewed improvement of the client. Although it is possible for a set of extraneous factors to produce the first client improvement, it is less likely that the same set of factors would recur at precisely the right time to produce the client improvement after reintroduction of the treatment. As Figure 11.5 illustrates, especially with the *ABAB* design, we have great confidence in the efficacy of a treatment that produces similar real-life results. In certain circumstances, the design can be expanded to include even more phases.

Despite their strengths in terms of internal validity, reversal designs often find their use restricted because of practical considerations. First, treatments that produce permanent changes in clients—often the goal of intervention—are not reversible. For example, if the treatment involves the clients' learning of something, they obviously cannot "unlearn" it at the command of the clinician–researcher. In such cases, reversal designs simply are not applicable. Second, it might be unwise or unethical to attempt to return clients to their pretreatment states; an obvious example would be a case where the suicidal tendencies of a client were alleviated. It is up to the clinician–researcher to decide on a case-by-case basis whether a reversal design is ethically justified.

Multiple-Baseline Designs. The *multiple-baseline design* involves establishing baselines for more than one aspect of a client's condition. Multiple baselines can be established for multiple behaviors, for one behavior in different settings, or for multiple clients who suffer from the same problem. For example, a practitioner working with several alcoholics might establish separate baselines for each, thus applying the multiple-baseline design across individuals. Although it is recommended that a minimum of three baselines be used, clinician–researchers should

The ABA Design

[Graph showing Client's condition vs Measurements 1-15, divided into Baseline (1-5), Treatment (6-10), and Withdrawal (11-15) phases]

The ABAB Design

[Graph showing Client's condition vs Measurements 1-20, divided into Baseline (1-5), Treatment (6-10), Withdrawal (11-15), and Treatment (16-20) phases]

FIGURE 11.5 Hypothetical Examples of Reversal Designs

not be deterred from using only two if conditions do not permit more. The more baselines, however, the stronger the design becomes in terms of internal validity (Barlow, Nock, & Hersen, 2009).

The multiple-baseline design is essentially a stacked set of AB designs, with the same treatment introduced sequentially into each of the baseline conditions:

First client: A_1B
Second client: A_1A_2B
Third client: $A_1A_2A_3B$

In the illustration, the initial baseline measurement (A_1) is made on each client, and then the treatment is introduced to the first client only. A second baseline measurement is taken from the remaining two clients, and then the treatment is introduced to the second client. A third baseline measurement is taken from the third client, who then also receives the treatment. Figure 11.6 illustrates the multiple-baseline design with a successful outcome. In each of the three conditions, the introduction of the treatment is followed by improvement.

The multiple-baseline design is fairly strong on internal validity. The efficacy of the treatment is assessed across three or more behaviors, settings, or individuals. Furthermore, sequential introduction of treatments makes it highly unlikely that extraneous factors could account for apparent treatment effects across the several baseline conditions.

FIGURE 11.6 Hypothetical Example of Multiple-Baseline Design

Thus, the multiple-baseline design generally is superior to the *AB* design, but the *AB* design with replication also overcomes some of the threats to internal validity, such as history (Harris & Jenson, 1985). The multiple-baseline design is not as strong on internal validity as reversal designs are, but where reversal designs are inappropriate, the multiple-baseline design is a good alternative.

Multiple-baseline designs can provide strong evidence for the validity of single-system outcomes, as Research in Practice 11.2 illustrates. They do have weaknesses, however. The seepage of treatment effects from one setting to another is a major limitation of the multiple-baseline design. The behaviors, settings, or individuals traced by the several baselines must be relatively independent, or else the treatment effects in one condition can produce changes in other, as-yet-untreated conditions. For example, it would be unwise to attempt a multiple-baseline design with members of the same family. Because of their routine interaction, treatment applied to one family member could affect the others. If the baseline conditions are highly interrelated, the treatment will show effects after the initial introduction, not only in the condition where it is applied, but also in one or more of the other conditions. If interrelatedness is sufficiently severe, the power of the multiple-baseline design can be destroyed, rendering it little more than an *AB* design with multiple indicators.

The multiple-baseline design also can reveal *contravariation*: positive changes in one area but negative changes in another (Jayaratne & Levy, 1979). For example, a multiple-drug abuser might respond to treatment by reducing the intake of one substance but increasing the intake of another. If we traced only one drug, perhaps the most dangerous, then the contravariation would remain undetected. A multiple-baseline design covering all the abuser's drugs, however, would readily reveal such an occurrence.

Specialized Designs

The designs we have just discussed comprise the simplest—and most generally useful—single-system designs, and they have in common the use of only a single treatment (although applied more than once in the *ABAB* design). Some situations, however, call for variations of these simpler designs to handle special problems. So many complex and specialized designs exist that we can touch on only a few of them here.

Multiple-Treatment Designs. In some settings, the practitioner may need to apply several treatments before finding an effective one. By an extension of the reversal designs, *multiple treatments* can be accommodated. A fairly simple extension is the *ABA-C-A* design. It should be apparent that the *ABA* segment comprises a basic reversal design. To that is added a second treatment phase with treatment C instead of treatment B, and then another return-to-baseline phase. This design can be extended to include as many treatments as a given case requires. One important limitation of this design is that, if both treatments show some effect, it is not possible to determine which is the most effective (Barlow, Nock, & Hersen, 2009). The culprit is history, because extraneous variables occurring during the *B* phase cannot be assumed to be the same as those occurring during the *C* phase.

Special designs also can be used when treatments are not applied individually but, rather, in combination to assess the relative effects of the components of the treatment package. The *ABAB-BC-B-BC* design, a complex extension of the reversal designs, accomplishes this. The first part, *ABAB*, is one of the basic reversal designs and provides a strong demonstration of effects of component B. The *BC-B-BC* segment indicates the effects of component C beyond those of component B alone. This design can, of course, be further extended to indicate additional treatments. Because both of these design extensions are based on reversal designs, however, they cannot be used with treatments that are irreversible or unethical to reverse.

Changing-Criterion Designs. Another specialized design with considerable utility is the *changing-criterion design* (Barlow, Nock, & Hersen, 2009). With this design, the goal, or criterion, of success changes over time as the client is led to attainment of the final treatment goal in stages—that is, by achieving a series of subgoals.

> **RESEARCH IN PRACTICE 11.2** Practice Effectiveness: A Multiple-Baseline Evaluation of Treating Panic Disorder

"It just happened ... I was walking and all of a sudden my heart started to beat fast and I started to sweat ... I didn't know what was going on ... I just felt weird ... that something bad was happening to me but I didn't know what."
—Quoted in Ollendick (1995, p. 517)

These are the words of a 14-year-old adolescent describing her first panic attack, a condition that is characterized by periods of intense fear or discomfort in which certain somatic and cognitive symptoms develop abruptly. Imagine the concern that such experiences raise for a person, wondering what caused it and when it might happen again, as well as suffering the embarrassment of behaving in such a bizarre manner.

One research project set out to evaluate the effectiveness of cognitive behavioral treatments on panic disorders in adolescents. The researcher chose the multiple-baseline design because it is superior to the AB design in reducing the threat of history while still providing a detailed record of individual process through treatment (Ollendick, 1995). The particular research design was a multiple-baseline across subjects. Four adolescents who were being seen at an outpatient clinic specializing in anxiety disorders of children and adolescents participated in the study. The subjects were evaluated on several screening instruments, and each met full criteria for panic disorder with agoraphobia. They reported that "they sometimes felt really scared, for no reason at all, that out of the blue they felt really scared and that they didn't know why," and that there were places that they didn't want to go because they were afraid they "would get scared all of a sudden and couldn't get help or get away."(Ollendick, 1995, p. 519). The researchers hypothesized that the cognitive behavioral treatments found to be effective among adults in treating such conditions also would prove effective with adolescents.

Multiple measures were used to assess the effectiveness of treatment. One indicator was the frequency of panic attacks. The adolescents were asked to monitor the date, duration, location, circumstance, and symptoms experienced. This provided a weekly measure for the frequency of panic attacks. Another indicator was self-efficacy in coping with three potential agoraphobic situations that were included in one of the screening tests used during assessment. Subjects were asked to rate from 1 to 5 how sure they were that they could cope with situations (1 = not at all sure, 5 = definitely sure). The third indicator was the adolescents' rating of the extent to which they had actually avoided agoraphobic situations, such as going to school, being in an auditorium, or going to restaurants. All indicators were modeled on measures found in the existing literature (Clum, 1990; Rapee, Craske, & Barlow, 1990).

Baseline measures were obtained for one week for subject 1, for two weeks for subject 2, three weeks for subject 3, and four weeks for subject 4. Following baseline, a treatment regimen began that included providing information on the nature of panic attacks and training in progressive muscle relaxation and proper breathing techniques. The adolescents were taught to use positive self-statements and cognitive coping strategies. Later sessions involved *in vivo* exposure to the situations that had aroused panic symptoms. The actual length of treatment varied from one subject to another, based on the termination criterion of two consecutive weeks with an absence of attacks. Brief maintenance sessions were held at two weeks and at one month following treatment, with a systematic follow-up at six months posttreatment.

Each way of assessing the effectiveness of the intervention (frequency of attacks, agoraphobic avoidance, and self-efficacy) was a dependent variable, and each produced a set of data plots that looked like Figure 11.6. If there were three subjects in the design, then Condition 1, 2, and 3 in Figure 11.6 would represent Subject 1, 2, and 3. The resulting data plots provided positive evidence that the treatment was effective in eliminating panic attacks. The project illustrates several points about using single-system designs in support of practice:

- Ollendick relied on the empirical literature to identify promising intervention methods. The literature helped him devise measurement strategies consistent with previous research and likely to be reliable and valid.

- Flexibility of the single-system design permitted this researcher to avoid interference with treatment and permitted documentation of the progress of each case while demonstrating that the intervention was the most likely cause of change.

- By using standardized tests before and after treatment and at the six-month follow-up, the researcher obtained independent, supporting evidence that corroborated the multiple-baseline data. Alone, such pretest/posttest data are weak, but using them in combination with the multiple-baseline strategy strengthened the project as a whole.

For example, a smoker can be brought to the final goal of abstinence through phased withdrawal. Figure 11.7 illustrates what a successful application of such treatment with a changing-criterion design might look like. Following the baseline measurement of cigarettes smoked per day, treatment begins. For example, assume the treatment consists of reinforcement. During the first treatment phase, the client is reinforced for achieving the first subgoal—say, a reduction of eight cigarettes per day. In the second treatment phase, reinforcement is received for achieving a reduction of an additional eight cigarettes—the second subgoal. The third treatment phase requires another reduction to receive the reinforcement. The process continues until the client progresses through the subgoals and achieves the final goal of no longer smoking.

The changing-criterion design is related to the multiple-baseline design. In the multiple-baseline design, intervention is independently implemented in relatively distinct areas of the subject's environment. In the changing-criterion design, each time a subgoal is achieved and a new, more stringent subgoal established, the preceding level essentially becomes a new baseline from which further improvement is measured. Like the multiple-baseline design, the changing-criterion design provides greater evidence for treatment effectiveness than the simple *AB* design. Each time the treatment leads to achievement of another subgoal, further evidence of its effectiveness is obtained. The only major limitation associated with the changing-criterion design is that it can be applied only to client problems that can be meaningfully broken up into subgoals.

FIGURE 11.7 Hypothetical Example of the Changing-Criterion Design Applied to Phased Withdrawal of Smoking

GENERALIZABILITY OF SINGLE-SYSTEM DESIGNS

To build a knowledge base for clinical practice, researchers must have findings that can be generalized to a wide variety of situations and cases. Of course, *one* successful single-system experiment has little generalizability beyond that particular case. Despite success and hard evidence to prove that the treatment produced change, there is no assurance that the same treatment would be effective with other clients, in different settings, or when used by another practitioner. This lack of generalizability, however, does not detract from the value of single-system experiments, because generalizability can be achieved through replication. It requires many replications before we develop a knowledge base concerning which clients can be helped by which treatment, which settings it will work in, and what the clinician must do to apply it successfully. This is a process of slow accretion, because each replication provides a little more knowledge concerning the extent of generalizability of treatment effectiveness. (Generalizability also relates to some special ethical considerations in single-system research; these are discussed in the Eye on Ethics section.)

It is valuable in this context to make a distinction between *direct replication* and *systematic replication*. **Direct replication** involves the repeated application of the same treatment by the same clinician to clients who are suffering from the same basic problem. In direct replication, only the individual clients vary; all other conditions remain constant. Direct replication serves two important functions: First, it increases confidence in the reliability of the findings. For example, a clinician with a series of successes in treating claustrophobics will have far greater confidence in the effectiveness of the treatment than he or she did after success with the first case. Second, direct replication builds generalizability across clients. As the treatment repeatedly proves effective with additional clients, we discover that the initial success was not a fluke. Direct replication is the beginning of establishing the generalizability of a treatment. It cannot, however, answer questions concerning generalizability across settings, practitioners, or other client problems.

Systematic replication is the attempt to extend a treatment to different settings, practitioners, or client disorders by varying one of these conditions or any combination of them. It normally is conducted after there is evidence from direct replication that the treatment may work. For example, the clinician mentioned earlier with the successful history of intervention with claustrophobics might begin systematic replication by applying the treatment to agoraphobics. If this is successful, it indicates that the treatment is generalizable to a different client disorder from that with which success originally was obtained. Additional replications that vary settings and clinicians would, of course, be required to establish generalizability across these conditions.

A study of using biofeedback to treat depression (Earnest, 1999) provides an example of a successful systematic replication involving different clients. The investigator presented examples of earlier case studies that demonstrated the effectiveness of electroencephalographic (EEG) biofeedback training for treating depression in adults. In this case, the intervention method was successfully extended to an adolescent client. Systematic replication with different clients and different therapists also was illustrated by a study on verbal self-guidance (Martini & Polatajko, 1998). Those authors reported that this intervention had been useful in helping children with developmental coordination disorder. They successfully replicated the intervention using a different therapist and four different children, thus adding further evidence indicating the potential of this intervention for effective treatment. When the same treatment proves effective in a replication with so many differences from a previous situation, it suggests that the treatment may have broad generalizability. Many more successful replications, of course, are needed before the parameters of effectiveness for this or any other treatment can be firmly established.

When single-system experiments and their replications are conducted, two practices are crucial. First, substantial information about client

> ### Eye on Ethics — Protecting Human Subjects and Single-System Designs
>
> The linkages between practice and research emphasized throughout this text are especially strong in the case of single-system designs. As desirable as the fusion between practice and research may be, however, blurring boundaries between the two can cause confusion in the area of ethical responsibilities and raise questions concerning the protection of human subjects in practice. For example, how do such principles as informed consent (discussed in Chapter 3) apply to conducting single-system evaluations of practice? If systematic evaluation is an integral part of service delivery, does the practitioner need to obtain approval from an institutional review board (IRB) before implementing an *AB* design as a means of documenting client progress, or is such routine evaluation exempt from review? Every practitioner who seeks to employ systematic evaluation must address questions like these.
>
> Although research and practice evaluation may involve many of the same procedures, such as measurement via direct observation or the use of standardized scales, several writers argue that it is important in terms of ethical conduct to distinguish between research and evaluation. Judith Nelsen (1994) makes a primary distinction between practice models in which objective monitoring of target problems is routine, such as behavioral and task centered models, and other models in which clients do not expect to participate in objective measurement, such as psychosocial or family treatment. She argues that where routine, systematic monitoring is part of the normal service delivery, the evaluation is an integral part of practice and, therefore, is part of practice rather than part of research. Issues of research ethics arise in cases where practitioners want to do monitoring that their practice model does not ordinarily require. For example, which clients get selected for special monitoring? To what extent does the client have the right to refuse additional monitoring or observation? Do issues of gender or racial bias influence which cases get selected for special monitoring? Nelsen suggests that such concerns may require informed consent in these cases and, possibly, even formal IRB review.
>
> Grigsby and Roof (1993) directly address the issue of IRB involvement. Like Nelsen, they distinguish between practice evaluation and research. They argue that the principle of generalizability is the distinction between evaluation (to determine whether the client's condition has improved over time and conducted for the benefit of client and practitioner) and research (to pursue knowledge for its own sake or to generalize knowledge). They argue that evaluation of practice using single-system designs is not research as technically defined in federal regulations; however, the matter is not entirely clear-cut. If evaluation data, originally collected as part of practice evaluation, are subsequently used to make generalizations and printed in any publications to report those generalizations, then IRB review would be required. Grigsby and Roof recommend that clinicians and researchers who use evaluation designs be encouraged to inform potential subjects from the outset that their records may be used for research purposes, and that they be given the opportunity to consent or object to the use of their individual records. The basic principle that triggers the need for IRB involvement is the intent of the practitioner–researcher to contribute to generalizable knowledge beyond the particular case by publishing the results of the evaluation.

characteristics and backgrounds should be collected to serve as *control variables* in assessing the complex effects that treatment can have on dependent variables. The necessity for this arises from the fact that replications often show treatment is not consistently effective or ineffective. The background information may be useful in sorting out the reasons for these mixed results. A simple example would be a treatment that was effective with men but either ineffective or less effective with women.

A second essential practice is that treatments be kept uniform from case to case so the results of replications are truly comparable. In addition, reports must be clear and include all information relevant to future replication efforts. At the outset we noted that one source of dissatisfaction with traditional case histories is the tendency for such reports to be too vague to allow replication. The full potential of single-system experiments will not be realized if reports include inadequate information for sound replication.

Information Technology in Research

Computer-Aided Single-System Data Analysis

In the discussion of data analysis for single-system designs, the point was made that visual analysis often is preferred. You can use common spreadsheet software, such as Microsoft Excel, to do this. A convenient approach is to design an analysis template—that is, a reusable form that contains no data. Once the template is created and saved, you need only enter new data for each case rather than recreate the entire spreadsheet. Here are the basic steps for setting up a template, but you can embellish and expand on this model to meet your own research needs. Enter some hypothetical data during the design process to make sure the spreadsheet works properly. Once you have tested the spreadsheet, clear these data before saving the final version.

For illustration purposes, assume that a practitioner has collected data on a child's temper tantrum behavior for a baseline of 12 days and a treatment period involving the use of "time out" for another 12 days (see Figure 11.8). The practitioner wants to document whether tantrum activity has declined. The example in Figure 11.8 has room for 28 total observations—more than enough for most practice situations. The *Observation* column is the numbers 1 through *N* (in this case, 1 through 28, representing 28 possible observations). Enter the dependent variable values for the baseline phase in the *Baseline* column and the intervention phase data in the *Treatment* column. Use the *Comparison* column to enter one of three standards for comparing baseline to intervention: the baseline mean, the baseline maximum, or the baseline minimum.

A common practice for visual analysis is to see if all intervention data points are better than some baseline standard, such as the baseline mean, maximum, or minimum. In this illustration, the purpose of intervention is to decrease the number of tantrums, so the research question is: Are all treatment observations below the baseline mean? This value is calculated in cell C35 of the illustration. A more stringent standard for visual analysis would be this: Are all the treatment observations better than the best of baseline? In this case, "better" would be below the baseline minimum, which is calculated in cell C37. (If the goal were to increase the behavior, then the value to use would be the maximum from cell C36.) By using the "Copy" and "Paste Special" functions, the selected value is entered into the comparison column. All the necessary data are now in place to generate a graph.

Three series of data points are printed on the graph:

- Baseline data
- Treatment data
- Comparison (either baseline mean, maximum, or minimum)

Once you have tested the template, you can reuse it with other clients by simply clearing the contents from the *Baseline*, *Treatment*, and *Comparison* columns and entering new data.

ASSESSMENT OF THE CLINICAL RESEARCH MODEL

Advantages

Promotes Better Service for Clients. The requisites of the clinical research model—careful assessment of treatment goals, use of specific treatments, and continuous monitoring of client progress—promote more effective treatment for clients and encourage the use of scientifically tested intervention strategies. The model encourages the application of specific practice skills in a systematic and rational fashion rather than a reliance on personal idiosyncrasy, intuition, or vague and shifting treatment efforts. Furthermore, the model promotes consideration of the assumptions underlying various treatment approaches, such as why a given treatment should produce positive results with a particular case. The net result is an increased likelihood that a successful intervention will be selected and that the client will be helped.

FIGURE 11.8 Graphing Single-System Design Data with Spreadsheet Software

Promotes Research Activity. The merger of practice and research in the clinical research model allows practitioners to conduct research when they otherwise might not do so. For obvious and practical reasons, the opportunities for most human service practitioners to be involved in traditional group research are limited. The clinical research model, however, makes each client a possible subject for a single-system experiment. In addition, single-system research is more practical for the typical clinician, because it is research on a small scale, involving minimal cost and avoiding the complexities of group research. Furthermore, involvement in single-system research can enhance the status of the practitioner, because the results often can be published. On a broader scale, increased research activity can promote the image of the human services as scientifically based professions.

Results Are of Both Immediate and Future Value. The clinical research model provides hard evidence for a client's progress, which is of immediate value to the practitioner. Tracking progress aids in the selection and application of effective treatments. After successful treatment, the data provide a clear demonstration that the client has been helped. In this age of increasing accountability, vague feelings of having helped clients—or even client testimonials—are no longer adequate. To document that intervention does work, critics increasingly demand scientifically based evidence, and single-system experiments hold the promise of providing that evidence.

Disadvantages

Impracticality. Under current practice conditions, application of the clinical research model often may be impractical. Some of the most rigorous of the single-system designs, such as the reversal designs, are especially difficult to apply, because irreversible treatments and ethical considerations may preclude their use. Furthermore, some designs contain many phase segments that may require too much time to complete. Beyond these problems is the fact that some client disorders call for immediate attention, precluding the baseline measurements so crucial to single-system designs.

Limited Generalizability of Results. As noted, results from one single-system experiment have virtually no generalizability beyond that particular case, and they provide less powerful tests of therapeutic effects than traditional group experiments do. Generalizability is obtained only through successful replication across clients, settings, disorders, and practitioners. This is a slow process, and the potential of single-system research to increase the knowledge base of the profession will not be realized quickly.

REVIEW AND CRITICAL THINKING

Main Points

- Single-system designs are quasi-experimental designs that are used to trace changes induced by treatments to individual clients in a clinical setting.
- Interest in single-system designs developed out of dissatisfaction with group experiments and case histories as sources of knowledge useful in clinical settings.
- The clinical research model using single-system designs is not a radical departure from traditional clinical practice, but rather an effort to increase the specificity and objectivity of practice and enhance opportunities for replication and knowledge accumulation.
- Although we have many specific single-system designs from which to choose, all involve a series of pretreatment measures (the baseline) and a series of posttreatment measures that are then compared with the baseline.
- Measurements typically consist of observations, available records, paper-and-pencil measures, or self-reports; observations usually are the most desirable and self-reports the least desirable.
- Effectiveness may be judged against three different standards—therapeutic, experimental, or statistical—with therapeutic effectiveness demanding the greatest client improvement and statistical effectiveness the least.
- The simple *AB* design is highly flexible, but not strong on internal validity.
- Reversal designs, such as *ABA* or *ABAB*, are strong on internal validity but often impractical to apply.
- Multiple-baseline designs are quite strong on internal validity and are reasonably flexible, making them a good choice when a reversal design cannot be used.

- In addition to these basic designs, many specialized designs can accommodate such things as changing treatments, combined treatments, or phased achievement of the treatment goal.
- Positive results from one single-system experiment are not generalizable, but generalizability can be built up over time through replication.
- Computer software can simplify and speed both the visual and statistical analyses of data from single-system research.

Important Terms for Review

baseline	direct replication	empirical practice model	single-system designs
clinical research model			systematic replication

Critical Thinking

Single-system designs permit the practitioner to more systematically assess the nature of problems presented by clients and to monitor and evaluate the outcome of an intervention with a particular client. The chapter distinguishes between therapeutic, experimental, and statistical significance, and also discusses some of the threats to validity posed by single-system designs.

1. When considering an actual case that you encounter in a human service setting, can you specify what therapeutic effectiveness is in observable, measurable terms?
2. What factors other than the intervention itself might account for improvement or deterioration in the target of intervention?
3. Assuming that you are working or training in a human service setting, consider a client with whom you are working. What behaviors or other measurable indicators could you monitor for a single-system design?

Exploring the Internet

Single-system design is a relatively narrow, specialized topic, so locating related resources on the Internet is more challenging than seeking material on more general subjects. Using such terms as "single case experiments" with standard search engines may locate some useful sites, but the search process can be frustrating. As an alternative, you can turn to some specialized tools for assistance. Single-system designs have long been used in the field of psychology, so a promising starting point is the American Psychological Association's home page (http://www.apa.org) and its section on the databases that can be accessed there. One of the resources it offers is APAPsycNET, a search engine that focuses on psychology-related topics.

An interesting way to explore how single-system designs have been applied to various human service practice evaluation studies is to use the web page of the *Journal of Applied Behavior Analysis* (http://seab.envmed.rochester.edu/jaba). You can select articles of interest and review an abstract of each. If you have a practice situation in mind for evaluation, these abstracts can provide guidance for planning and conducting a single-system design.

For Further Reading

Bloom, M., Ed. (1993). *Single-System Designs in the Social Services: Issues and Options for the 1990s*. New York: Haworth. A compilation of thought-provoking articles by leading human service professionals on the application of single-system designs to practice.

Bloom, M., Fischer, J., & Orme, J. (2009). *Evaluating Practice: Guidelines for the Accountable Professional*, 6th ed. Boston: Pearson. A thorough textbook on all aspects of single-system design for social work and other human services. Includes software for analysis.

Franklin, R. D., Allison, D. B., & Gorman, B. S. (1996). *Design and Analysis of Single-Case Research*. Mahwah, N.J.: Lawrence Erlbaum Associates. A complete source for in-depth information on single-case design, especially visual and statistical analysis issues.

Gast, D. L. (2010). *Single Subject Research Methodology in Behavioral Sciences*. New York: Taylor and Francis. This source provides an overview of single-subject research and includes detailed information on philosophical, ethical, and statistical and visual analysis of data. Although directed at the field of education, it is applicable to all human services.

Haynes, S. N., & O'Brien, W. H. (1999). *Principles and Practice of Behavioral Assessment*. New York: Kluwer Academic/Plenum Publishers. Psychological assessment is the primary focus of this book, which also includes substantial information related to using the single-case approach to assessment.

Morgan, D. L., & Morgan, R. K. (2009). *Single-Case Research Methods for the Behavioral and Health Sciences*. Thousand Oaks, Calif.: Sage. This guide to single-case design introduces readers to the history, epistemology, and strategies of single-case research design. It offers concrete information on how to observe, measure, and interpret change in relevant outcome variables, and how to design strategies that promote causal inferences.

Richards, S. B., Taylor, R. L., Ramasamy, R., & Richards, R. Y. (1999). *Single-Subject Research: Applications in Educational and Clinical Settings*. San Diego: Singular Publishing Group. For the reader seeking a basic, clear, concise coverage of single-system design, this is an excellent source. Very readable and well illustrated.

Class Exercises for Competency Assessment

11.1. A foster parent complains to the foster care worker that the 14-year-old placed in her home chronically oversleeps in the morning and is late for school. She wakes him every morning at about 7, leaving him two hours to get ready for school and be there on time.
   a. [Research & Practice] Establish the problems that the foster care worker might tackle with this adolescent and the goals to be accomplished. As you do this, keep in mind the importance of specificity and measurability.
   b. [Research & Practice] Identify some alternative ways of measuring a baseline for assessing change in this case.
   c. [Critical Thinking] What would be the advantages and disadvantages of having the foster parent versus the foster son do the data collecting? Can you identify any outside sources of data?

11.2. [Research & Practice] [Critical Thinking] Select a behavior from one of the following, devise a means of measuring it, and collect baseline data for a week, using yourself or someone else as the client. Report your results to the class.
   a. Cigarette smoking
   b. Speeding while driving
   c. Snacking
   d. Feeling depressed
   e. Praising your child
   f. Completing homework

11.3. A counselor in a spousal abuse shelter has been working with women in the shelter on their assertiveness in dealing with men. She would like to do a single-system design with a woman client to evaluate the effectiveness of the assertiveness training. She intends to have the staff collect data, using a coded observation form, on the client's level of assertiveness in a variety of situations.
   a. [Research & Practice] [Critical Thinking] What would be the advantages and disadvantages of the following designs for this research?
      1) *AB*
      2) *ABA*
      3) *ABAB*
   b. [Ethics] What steps would need to be taken to conduct this study in an ethical manner? Are there any special problems that are unique to each design type (*AB*, *ABA*, or *ABAB*)?

Chapter 12

Evaluation Research

What Is Evaluation Research?
  Why Evaluate?
  Evaluation Research and Basic Research
  The Politics of Evaluation Research
  Types of Evaluation Research

Formative Evaluation Research

Summative Evaluation Research
  Evaluability Assessment and the Logic Model
  Specification of Variables
  Measuring Variables
  Evaluation of Minorities in Evaluation Research
  Designs for Evaluation Research

  Nonpositivist Approaches to Evaluation
  Cost–Benefit Analysis
  Cost-Effective Analysis

Improving Utilization of Evaluation Research

Review and Critical Thinking
  Main Points
  Important Terms for Review
  Critical Thinking
  Exploring the Internet
  For Further Reading
  Class Exercises for Competency Assessment

A major theme of this book is the benefits accorded to the human service field by linking human service practice with scientific research to form a single endeavor seeking common goals. (We labeled this "evidence-based practice" and "scientific practice" in Chapter 1 and the "clinical research model" in Chapter 11.) In this chapter, we encounter a new element of this linkage in the form of *evaluation research,* which points toward a reason for conducting research rather than a new research methodology. **Evaluation research** refers to the use of scientific research methods to plan intervention programs, to monitor the implementation of new programs and the operation of existing ones, and to determine how effectively programs or clinical practices achieve their goals.

Although evaluation research has been around for many years, it has risen to considerable prominence over the past few decades for a number of reasons. One reason is the advances in theory and policy in the human services, such as evidence-based practice, that call as a matter of principle for greater scientific assessment of practice and policy. A second reason is that the amount of public and private funds being channeled into social programs has grown. These changes have led those providing the funds to seek more valid and reliable evidence regarding whether programs achieve their goals, how efficiently they do so, and whether they produce any unintended consequences. Evaluation research is a mechanism for gathering evidence about these issues, and it has become an integral part of most modern social programs.

WHAT IS EVALUATION RESEARCH?

Evaluation research offers a means of supplying valid and reliable evidence about the operation of social programs or clinical practices—how they are planned, how well they operate, and how effectively they achieve their goals. For example, a medical care facility may need to know if a need exists for a day care program for the elderly in a given community. Corrections officials may want to know the size at which a probation officer's caseload becomes too large to provide effective services. Hospital administrators may need to assess the impact on patient care of a 15 percent reduction in nursing staff. In these situations, and in others like them, evaluation research uses many of the research techniques that we have discussed in other chapters to provide evidence about the workings of programs and practices in the human services. A typical evaluation effort might involve some combination of interviews, questionnaires, observation, available data, and an experimental design. In fact, we have already discussed evaluation research in many places in this book without calling it by this name.

Why Evaluate?

Evaluation research is conducted for three specific reasons, and each of these reasons can relate to providing support for the evidence-based practice approach in the human services (Rossi, Lipsey, & Freeman, 2004). First, evaluation research may be conducted *to test hypotheses* or *to evaluate practice approaches*. These often amount to the same thing, however, because practice strategies often are based on hypotheses derived from social and psychological theories. Such evaluation not only provides information about a particular practice intervention but also adds to the fund of social scientific evidence about practice, which may be useful in the design of new intervention strategies.

A second reason for conducting evaluation research, which can also support evidence-based practice, is *impact assessment*—that is, to see what effects, if any, a program is producing. Typically, impact assessment identifies program goals and measures how well the program achieves those goals. The results provide the evidence to be used in making policy decisions regarding whether to expand, change, or curtail a program.

Third, evaluation research can be conducted for *administrative purposes,* such as to fulfill an evaluation requirement demanded by a funding source, to improve the service to clients, or to increase the efficiency of program delivery. Evaluations for administrative reasons tend to focus on assessing the daily operations of a program rather than on its overall impact, with the goal of finding the most efficient means to run a program or agency. These administrative evaluations can, nonetheless, provide data, or evidence, to support practice and policy.

Evaluation Research and Basic Research

Evaluation research is another form of applied research (see Chapter 1) that involves a special application of the general techniques of basic research. Because of this, there are similarities between the two, but there also are some important differences (DeMartini, 1982; Weiss, 1998). First, the results of evaluation research have immediate practical use in assessing operating programs. Basic research, on the other hand, is oriented toward more general information gathering and hypothesis testing.

Second, in contrast to evaluation research, in which the needs of the decision makers sponsoring the study are paramount in shaping the form and content of the research, the basic researcher has more control over which issues to investigate (Rossi, Lipsey, & Freeman, 2004). Some evaluations may allow latitude to expand beyond the issues of direct interest to the decision makers, but control over the content of the research is shared with them. This can become a source of conflict between researchers and sponsors.

A third difference is that evaluation, by its very nature, has a judgmental quality that often is not a part of basic research. The evaluation may deem a program to be a success or a failure based on how well it achieved its purposes; this judgmental quality also can be a source of tension between an evaluator and the sponsors of the evaluation. Understandably, the sponsors are concerned that a negative evaluation could have dire consequences for the existence of the program—and for their own livelihoods and careers.

The fourth difference between basic and evaluation research relates to the issues that are given priority in the research process. In basic research, quite naturally, the requisites for producing a scientifically sound study are given strong weight. Evaluation research, on the other hand, takes place in the context of an ongoing, operating program, and the demands of that program may conflict with the demands of sound scientific practices. When this happens, the program administrators may give higher priority to the program than to the evaluation. The scientific demands of an evaluation, for example, might call for the random assignment of nurses from a home health care agency to each new client of the agency. The agency administrator, however, may prefer to assign nurses on the basis of his or her assessment of their competencies and fit with the client. The agency head may be able to override the evaluators' requests and force them to modify their scientific procedures.

The differences in approach that sometimes are found between practitioners and researchers can, on occasion, aggravate these conflicts. Practitioners tend to emphasize the importance of providing services to people and the role of empathy and concern in the intervention process. Researchers, on the other hand, may give more weight to the understanding provided by rigorous scientific analysis and objectivity. Although these differences should not be overdrawn—researchers do have empathy, and practitioners do recognize the value of scientific analysis—there can be a difference in emphasis between practitioners and researchers, and this can be another source of tension. In fact, one of the beneficial outcomes of developing linkages between practice and research is that the process encourages people to develop ways of combining the two approaches so that advantages accrue to both.

A final difference between basic and evaluation research relates to making the results of the research public. One of the canons of science is that research results should be made public for others to see and criticize, and thus reduce the likelihood that errors or personal bias might find their way into the research (see Chapter 2). While evaluation results are often made public by being presented at professional meetings and published in professional journals and books, they are as likely to only be made available to the human service organization or administrator who sponsored the research. One consequence of this lack of public dissemination is that it thwarts the accumulation of information so necessary for scientific progress. A second consequence of no public dissemination centers on ethics oversight requirements. For Institutional Review Board (IRB) oversight purposes, federal regulations define research as "a systematic investigation, including research development, testing and evaluation, designed to develop or contribute to generalizable knowledge" (U.S. Department of Health and Human Services 2005). Because the primary purpose of evaluation is often simply to serve as a management tool for monitoring and improving the program, and not to develop or contribute to *generalizable* knowledge, it may be exempt from

IRB review. However, clearly not all evaluation research is exempt; this applies especially to any evaluations whose findings will be presented at a conference or submitted for journal publication. Furthermore, universities often will not grant approval retroactively, so it is advisable to err on the side of caution if there is any chance that the results of a study warrant wider dissemination. Of course, even in those cases where IRB approval is not required, evaluators should still follow the basic principles of research ethics presented in Chapter 3.

Despite the differences between evaluation and basic research, there are important similarities. First, both may choose, from the entire array of data-gathering techniques, those that best fit their needs. In fact, as noted, evaluation projects often involve a synthesis of data that are gathered in a variety of ways. Second, both forms of research can focus on determining cause-and-effect relationships. In basic research, researchers seek cause-and-effect relationships between variables of their own choosing, whereas in evaluation research, investigation focuses on variables that are a part of the program being assessed.

The differences between evaluation and basic research are of a practical nature, deriving mainly from the context in which evaluation research is conducted. Although these differences are important—and the potential conflicts alluded to are quite real—the actual process of inquiry is much the same in both types of research. In fact, evaluation research illustrates the dynamic and flexible quality of basic social research methods in that the core methods and techniques can be expanded and changed to confront new problems and issues. Evaluation research is a novel and challenging application of methods that have been used in many other contexts. As such, the distinction between basic and evaluation research is one of degree rather than of kind.

The Politics of Evaluation Research

Decades ago, many evaluation researchers took a fairly straightforward, positivist view of their activities. By this we mean that they viewed the social programs they were evaluating as interventions attacking clearly identifiable problems in the world. The researchers viewed these problems as obvious social ills that needed rectifying, assumed that almost everyone agreed on what the betterment of those social ills would entail, and saw their own methods as objective and scientific tools to assist in achieving that social betterment. The arguments of nonpositivist paradigms (discussed in Chapter 2), however, have led many evaluation researchers to recognize that reality is not as simple as the straightforward positivist view would suggest (Greene, 1994; Patton, 1987). In particular, these approaches have led to recognition that evaluation research and the programs they evaluate are inherently political in nature. Politics has to do with power—who has it, who exercises it, and who controls its resources. Social interventions have to do with controlling and distributing resources.

Let's illustrate these issues with an example—namely, programs to reduce teenage pregnancies. The problem of teen pregnancy can be approached in a number of different ways, such as encouraging sexual abstinence, making available safe and reliable contraceptives, or providing abortion services to those who become pregnant. Which of these approaches a particular social program takes is determined by the values of those who fund and control that program, and thus have the power to see their values prevail. These people shape what the program is like, which services it provides, and how it provides them. In so doing, policy makers and program managers have great influence on shaping people's definitions of both the problem of teenage pregnancy and the acceptable solutions to that problem. Thus, social programs are the product of political decisions that involve the establishment of priorities and the allocation of resources.

In recent decades, evaluation researchers have come to recognize the importance in social programs of **stakeholders**: all the people who have an interest in whether, or how well, a social program operates. Evaluation researchers also recognize that any program has a large variety of stakeholders, including its funders, administrators, personnel, and clients or beneficiaries. In most cases, these stakeholders have varied and competing interests. The teenagers receiving services from a pregnancy prevention program, for example, may benefit from different kinds of interventions than the bureaucrats who run the program or the policy makers who fund it.

Typically, however, evaluations are sponsored by only one or a few stakeholders, such as the governmental agency that funds the evaluation or the managers who run the program. These sponsors may want to see the evaluation come out a certain way, and they may pay for an evaluation that addresses some questions but not others. If the sponsors want to promote sexual abstinence, for instance, they may include measures in the evaluation that assess how well abstinence works, but they may not ask the teens if they would use contraceptives or abortion referral services if those were available. Thus, it is possible that an evaluation can be directed toward some conclusions and away from others, because only some stakeholders in the program are funding—and, in part, directing—the evaluation.

The new approach recognizes that social ills and their betterment are not objective conditions about which a social consensus exists. Rather, social ills and social betterment are political issues based on differing social definitions of reality, about which people disagree and come into conflict. In designing and conducting evaluation research, then, researchers must recognize these competing viewpoints and interests and consider the possibility that some research methodologies may be biased in the direction of certain conclusions and the interests of certain stakeholders.

Types of Evaluation Research

The term *evaluation research* is somewhat misleading in that there is not a separate set of research techniques that are distinctly applied for this single purpose. Rather, the phrase applies to a diverse collection of strategies that can be used for a broad range of evaluative purposes. One way that evaluation research methods may be classified is in terms of the unit of analysis. (For example, the single-system designs covered in Chapter 11 may be considered evaluation methods where the unit of analysis is a single system or an individual. Because of the unique features involved in doing such individual studies, we have chosen to devote a separate chapter to them.) This chapter considers evaluations that focus on programs or organizations as the unit of analysis.

Another useful way to conceptualize the diversity of evaluation research is in terms of the goals of the study. Evaluation research can achieve two basic goals: **Formative evaluation research** focuses on providing information to guide the planning, development, and implementation of a specific program. It is concerned primarily with ensuring a smooth-running, well-integrated program rather than with the ultimate worth or impact of the program. **Summative evaluation research** is concerned with the program's effects. Here, the purpose centers on assessing the effectiveness and efficiency of programs and the extent to which the outcomes of the project are generalizable to other settings and populations. Formative evaluation research has received less attention in the evaluation literature than summative evaluation. The two forms are closely linked, however, and may be likened to a foundation and a building. The formative component of evaluation may not be especially glamorous or attract much attention, but unless it is carefully prepared and well done, the summative study is difficult to carry out for high-quality results.

FORMATIVE EVALUATION RESEARCH

Formative research poses the questions that arise in the planning, implementation, and operation of social programs. To initiate a program, certain basic information is essential. First, it is necessary to gather data on the target population and their characteristics. The nature of their problems, the number of potential program users, their location in the community, and other demographic information are essential to planning a good program. Second, it is important to be aware of existing services that the program under development might duplicate, or on which it may rely for referrals or auxiliary services. Third, program planners need to know about specific intervention strategies that might apply to the problems they uncover. Fourth, program operators must be able to specify the staff skills required to deliver the program. Fifth, planners must determine if the program, as conceptualized, is feasible to offer and monitor.

To answer these questions, formative research might take the form of a **needs assessment**: collecting data to determine how many people in a community need particular services and assessing what level of services or personnel already exists to fill a need (McKillip, 1987). In needs assessments, researchers commonly use a sampling strategy and then survey members of the target population. Thus, survey research methods form the backbone of such needs assessments. We also can rely on direct observation or existing data to gain a profile of the population and identify its needs. Essentially, any techniques used for descriptive research may be employed to answer this question. We might learn about existing and related services through interviewing potential clients and representatives of existing agencies. Knowledge of possible intervention strategies and program components often results from a thorough literature search, a fundamental step in any research project. (Appendix A, on strategies of information retrieval in the library and online, is directly applicable to such a task.)

Formative evaluations also sometimes use *focus groups* (a group interview technique discussed at length in Chapter 7). Focus groups are especially useful when the formative evaluation is exploratory in nature or when planners want to learn about people's personal and subjective meanings and experiences. Focus groups are a useful strategy for drawing out such information.

Formative evaluation research also can take the form of a *pretest* or *trial run*, which tests all the procedures to be used in a program before the full program is implemented. An example can be found in a program to provide financial aid to newly released offenders (Rossi, Berk, & Lenihan, 1980). Those researchers began with a very modest project, involving six released inmates who received six weekly payments of $60, and 20 controls who received no payment. Relying on a review of the literature and existing statistics on the problems of released offenders, this modest project helped prepare for a large-scale program in several ways. It helped determine that it was logistically possible to make the payments and to interview and keep track of ex-inmates in the community. Had this pilot project shown that these operational elements could not be accomplished effectively, then it would have been foolish to continue with a larger project, even though the researchers were convinced of the overall value of the program.

Because the questions that formative research addresses often are modest in scope, the staff of the agency administering the program frequently conducts the research itself. Such research, however, also may be done on a national scale in conjunction with large programs. Programs such as Temporary Assistance for Needy Families (TANF), food stamps, and vocational rehabilitation involve large sums of money; and initiation of such programs involves estimating the number of potential recipients, which can vary considerably depending on which definition of poverty is applied. Before initiating such programs, formative research based on needs assessment is essential. Although formative evaluation cannot ensure success, it can help reduce instances of unnecessary intervention and increase the potential for success among those programs that are initiated.

Besides serving as a tool for planning an intervention program, formative research also may monitor the implementation of new programs and the ongoing operation of existing ones. Several basic issues in program monitoring are counterparts to program planning. First, is the target population actually being served? It is not uncommon to discover that people do not use programs in spite of obvious need. Even major social welfare programs have been plagued by this problem, which is referred to as the "take-up rate."

Studies have found that less than 50 percent of eligible recipients participated in the food stamps program. Inadequate information about food stamps and personal attitudes toward the use of food stamps had the greatest impact on the decision to participate (Coe & Hill, 1998). Another study (Kalra, Fieldhouse, & Alam, 2001) reported on the reasons for nonparticipation and avoidance of the New Deal for Young People (NDYP), a public policy program that tries to reduce unemployment among those in the 18–25 age group. Negative experiences at previous youth training programs and the perception that NDYP could not offer desirable jobs were identified as major barriers to involvement. As a means to assess the extent of such problems, a census of program users can compare their characteristics with those of the population for whom the services were intended. Any discrepancy suggests that some members of the target population are not receiving the services intended for them. Unless such issues are addressed during the formative evaluation stage, a full-scale program may be destined for failure.

Next, are the services that are supposed to be delivered actually being delivered, and is the quality of the service adequate? Experience with program effectiveness evaluations has shown that a key issue is program fidelity during intervention—that is, operating the program exactly as it was designed to run. Without implementation data, an evaluator might conclude that a program model is ineffective when the real culprit is inadequate implementation that did not permit a valid test of the program (Lynch et al., 1998). Service delivery may be assessed in a variety of ways, including questionnaires and direct observation. As in single-system designs, time samples may be used to determine if behaviors associated with service delivery are occurring as planned. Quality-control techniques not unlike those used in industry can monitor the delivery of services in many settings. State departments of social services routinely monitor major financial assistance services, such as TANF. Typically, the process involves selecting a random sample of recipients and examining the most recent action on their files to determine if the action resulted in a correct payment, an overpayment, or an underpayment. States are expected to keep their error rate within certain specific limits. Other settings use follow-up questionnaires to determine if the expected services were delivered.

Finally, agencies commonly use a time-reporting system to make sure that staff members are spending the expected amount of time on specified aspects of the program. When formative evaluation studies use such time-reporting data, they do not address the question of whether the program is actually doing any good; rather, they address the narrower issue of the extent to which the services actually being delivered are true to the intended plan.

SUMMATIVE EVALUATION RESEARCH

Summative evaluation research involves assessing the impact of a program, and good summative evaluations usually investigate other matters concerning the program's operation as well. The results of summative evaluations are intended for policy-making decisions—whether to continue, expand, or cancel a program, and whether to generalize the findings of a particular project to other settings and populations. Summative evaluations typically are large-scale projects involving considerable time, personnel, and resources. For this reason, as well as to avoid the biasing effect of personal interest, outside consultants, rather than agency staff, often conduct these evaluations.

Although the steps in the research process are much the same for all types of research, including evaluation research, some special planning is called for to take into consideration the unique problems of evaluation research.

Evaluability Assessment and the Logic Model

During the planning of evaluation research, an **evaluability assessment** often is conducted to enable investigators to decide whether a program has the necessary elements to be evaluated (Kellogg Foundation, 2004; Smith, 1989). A good framework for doing this is through the development of a **logic model**, which is basically a visual or verbal description of how you think a program should or does work. It provides a framework for deciding whether a program can be evaluated and how to go about evaluating it. Figure 12.1 presents an outline of such a logic model, with illustrations from a program to detect and reduce elder abuse (Navarro et al., 2010).

The logic model begins by identifying the problems that the program is intended to address, including determining the purpose of the evaluation—from the standpoint of the eventual users of the results. This identifies which aspects of the program to assess for impact. The logic model identifies the potential program elements for assessment, such as: program resources or inputs, program activities or interventions, and program goals (outputs, outcomes, and impacts). The resources/inputs and the activities/interventions are the independent variables that are presumed to have some impact on the dependent variables (goals). The resources might include the funding dollars available to the program as well as the training or expertise of agency staff. The interventions might include counseling or educational services that are provided to clients.

Evaluation requires that a program have clearly specified outcomes and goals, because they are the major criteria of the program's success. They are the dependent variables that the input variables are supposed to affect. Goals can take a number of different forms. For example, *outputs* refer to the things a program does, such as provide certain numbers and types of counseling or educational services. *Outcomes* refer to the changes in client knowledge, attitudes, or behaviors that the program is presumed to produce. *Impacts* refer to longer-term changes in larger social systems, such as communities or society as a whole, because of the program. So, a program evaluation could focus on one or more or these goals (outputs, outcomes, impacts). Unfortunately, the goals of many programs are either so vague or so global—for example, "improve family functioning"—as to be unusable for evaluation purposes. It may be necessary for an evaluator to become actively involved with the staff in developing a set of clear goals before a program can be evaluated.

So, an important part of an evaluability assessment is to study and gather information about the program design. What are the inputs and the expected results or goals? In addition, a program evaluation should attempt to determine the linkage between the inputs and the outcomes. Essentially, this linkage is the theory on which the program is based. It involves answering the following question: "Why, given these program inputs, should certain outcomes be expected?" This linkage specifies any assumed causal linkages between independent and

FIGURE 12.1 An Outline of the Logic Model in Program Evaluation dependent variables. Any program is likely to have a variety of inputs, activities, and goals. A good evaluability assessment would link specific inputs and activities with specific goals. So, there might be a set of hypotheses stating, for example, that Input A and Activity C are presumed to bring about specified changes such as Output B and Outcome F. Using the elder abuse example, we might hypothesize that increased education on issues of aging and elder abuse for direct caseworkers (the input or intervention) will produce more reports of elder abuse by the caseworkers (the outcome) because the caseworkers with this education will be more knowledgeable of the indicators of abuse. This theoretical linkage may be explicitly recognized as the basis of the program, or it may be implicit in, but derivable from, the program's rationale or operation. The purpose of identifying this rationale is that it is important in understanding the success or failure of the program. Notice that although the long-term impact of the program might be a reduction in elder abuse, the logic model predicts that the immediate effect of the program will be an *increase* in reports of such abuse. Without a well-specified model, such a finding could be confusing or interpreted as program failure.

The logic model also helps identify program deficiencies. For example, some programs may identify certain outcomes as goals but not direct any effort toward realizing them. (Quite obviously, if evaluated against these goals, the program probably would turn out to be a failure.) If we do not specify the linkage, then the reason for failure may be unclear, and in the case of a success, we would be at a loss to explain why. Knowledge of the linkage reveals the source of the problem as the failure to direct input resources toward those particular goals. During this step, it is important to monitor the program as implemented, because gaps sometimes develop between the stated program and the program as operated.

The final stage of an evaluability assessment is to review the program model to identify those aspects that are sufficiently unambiguous in terms of inputs, goals, and linkages to make evaluation feasible. The result of the assessment may be that the whole program can be evaluated, none of the program can be evaluated, or most commonly, only certain parts of the program are amenable to evaluation.

Specification of Variables

As in any research, an important part of evaluation research is the specification of variables and how they will be measured. In some evaluations, the variables of interest take the form of independent and dependent variables. The inputs to a social program, for example, might constitute the independent variables. In some cases, the independent variable takes the form of a dichotomous variable, such as participation or nonparticipation in a program. In other cases, the independent variable is the degree or duration of participation in a program, such as the frequency of contact with a counselor, the level of financial aid received, or the length of time that a service is provided. Commonly, the dependent variables in evaluation research are the goals of a program—precisely what it is supposed to accomplish. Of course, some evaluation research, especially the formative type, does not involve independent and dependent variables. Whatever form the variables take, however, a central issue in evaluation research is that the variables be clearly and properly specified, because numerous problems can arise along these lines. This is especially true when measuring the goals of a program.

A frequent problem is that the goals, as articulated by program administrators, do not easily lend themselves to evaluation. They may be vague, overly broad, or so long term that evaluation is not feasible. For example, a goal of Head Start preschool education is to develop capable and functioning adults who can rise out of poverty. Although the success of Head Start in achieving this goal may be its ultimate test, it would be necessary to wait 20 to 30 years before evaluating the program. Although this goal is a laudable and essential part of the program, funding agencies are understandably reluctant to expend funds for that length of time with no evaluation. Thus, such programs normally include what are called *proximate goals,* or goals that can be realized in the short run and are related to achievement of the long-term goals (Weiss, 1998). In the case of Head Start, academic achievement is a reasonable proximate goal, because performance in school is associated with social and occupational success in adulthood.

For other programs, of course, it is both possible and desirable to assess the long-term impact—for example, a 30-year follow-up of the Cambridge-Somerville Youth Study, a five-year experiment in delinquency prevention begun in Boston in 1939 (McCord, 1978). This field experiment focused on 506 boys, half of whom received counseling and other assistance, while the other half served as a control group. The experimental condition consisted of counseling sessions every two weeks, tutoring, medical and psychiatric assistance, summer camps, and organized youth activities. Thirty years later, researchers located 95 percent of the participants in the experiment. Many of the comparisons showed no differences between the two groups, but the differences that were found suggested that the experimental variables had the *opposite* effect from what was expected! The experimental group committed more crimes as adults, had higher rates of alcoholism, poorer mental and physical health, and less occupational success. The only positive result for the program appeared to be the participants' own subjective evaluations. Two-thirds of the experimental group thought that the program had been helpful to them, even though their objective situation was worse than that of those in the control group. The program may have produced harmful effects because it raised participants' expectations to an unrealistically high level. When those expectations were not realized, participants suffered frustration and added stress, which resulted in a greater tendency toward criminality and alcoholism and deleterious effects on their mental and physical health. Despite the need for early program evaluations, long-term evaluation—accomplished so well in this study—is still essential in assessing many programs.

Vague or overly broad goals must be clarified or reduced in scope so that they are amenable to evaluation. In this regard, it is helpful if program administrators consult with evaluators to develop program goals. During discussions with program administrators, it is important that evaluators not simply accept as all-inclusive the goals the administrators articulate. In fact, one of the major reasons for finding that a program does not have the intended result is that the program goals are too limited (Chen & Rossi, 1980). Too often, administrators state program goals from the standpoint of what they desire, which results in goals that are unattainable given the program inputs. When evaluated against these goals, the program naturally appears to be a failure. Evaluators should cast a wide net in seeking program effects, including not only those suggested by administrators but also others that could be logically expected given the nature of the program. The model developed during the evaluability assessment and the theoretical basis of the program are productive places to look for possible program effects to include in the evaluation. This approach promises a better chance of finding nonzero program effects and supplying information on what the program does—and does not—do.

Another problem in specifying the goals and variables for evaluation is that different stakeholders may have different conceptions of what the program should accomplish. All sides may be clear about what the goals should be, but disagree with one another on them. This points, again, toward the political dimensions of evaluation research and the possibility that those who control the resources (usually the program funders or administrators) will impose their version of what the program goals should be. The evaluation researcher needs to ensure that other significant stakeholders have input into the process of defining and clarifying the goals.

Measuring Variables

The goals specified for an evaluation program tend to be abstract statements of desired outcomes. Before an actual evaluation can proceed, measurable criteria or operational definitions must specify exactly what observations will be made to determine goal achievement. Evaluators thus distinguish between *goals,* which are the desired end states for a program, and *objectives,* the measurable criteria for success. For example, a goal of a substance-abuse prevention program might be to reduce experimentation with alcohol and cigarettes among junior high school students. An objective of the program might be that 85 percent of program participants be able to correctly list at least five health hazards associated with alcohol use. Some goals can be readily measured because they have clearly quantifiable outcomes. For example, standard achievement tests readily measure the academic effects of compensatory education programs, but measuring such effects of Head Start as improved self-esteem, better adjustment to the classroom environment, or enhanced parent–child relationships requires more inventiveness on the part of the evaluator.

When measures for program effects are considered, alternative indicators of the same program effect may exist. For example, in measuring the effects of a family planning program, we might use as a measure (1) the proportion of participants adopting contraceptive practices, (2) the average number of children desired, (3) the average number of children born, or (4) the attitudes toward large families. All these indicators logically relate to the effects of a family planning program.

Multiple indicators—though sometimes prohibited by budget—are more useful than single ones, because they are more sensitive, and therefore more likely to show an effect if the program produced one (Weiss, 1998). If multiple indicators are impractical, then a decision must be made as to which of the alternatives is best. In the case of the four alternatives for the family planning program, the clearest indicator of program success is a low birthrate among participants. Because we have to wait many years before such an evaluation can be completed, however, this indicator might be impractical for some purposes. The two indicators dealing with attitudes are not the best choices, because attitudes can change, and sometimes only a weak relationship exists between attitudes and behavior. Indeed, attitudinal measures should be avoided whenever a behavioral alternative is available. Of the four possible measures, then, the proportion of participants who adopt contraception probably is the best single indicator for the effectiveness of the family planning program. It is not perfect as a measure, however, because contraceptives must be used conscientiously to be effective, but it is adequate for the short run.

As we have noted, it is preferable to use existing measures where possible. This avoids the work involved in creating new measures, pretesting them, and establishing their validity and reliability. Furthermore, existing measures contribute to the accumulation of knowledge, because they make evaluations of different programs more comparable. The preference for existing measures, however, extends only to the point where good existing measures for the variables of interest can be found. If existing measures are only tangentially related to what we seek to measure, it is far better to develop new measures. Good measurement is crucial to meaningful evaluation; shortcuts that compromise quality cannot be tolerated.

Assuming that some new measures must be created, it is important to keep in mind the dual criteria for assessing them: *validity* and *reliability*. Measures used in evaluation research must meet the same standards of validity and reliability as those used in basic research, and the methods for assessing those characteristics (considered in Chapter 5) apply here as well.

Evaluation of Minorities in Evaluation Research

One area in which evaluation research has played an important role is in assessing the operation and impact of policies and programs affecting minorities. When the women's movement hit full stride in the 1970s, women began rapidly to enter what generally had been considered exclusively male occupations. Before long, studies were assessing the relative performances of men and women working the same jobs. As more of this research was amassed, serious questions were raised concerning the quality and fairness of the evaluations, particularly toward the women in traditionally male occupations.

Take the case of evaluating male and female police officers. Numerous research evaluations have been conducted over the decades on how gender influences the performance of police officers (Doerner & Hunter, 2006; Harrington, 2000). Not surprisingly, given the varying methodologies of the various studies, the results have been somewhat inconsistent. Generally, however, the studies have concluded that female police officers are neither better nor worse than their male counterparts, but the studies also find that female police officers are different. That is, women are better than male officers at some policing activities, but not as good as the male officers at others. If these differences are real, then such information can be quite valuable in allocating police personnel to maximize the strengths and minimize the weaknesses of both male and female officers, but what if the differences are merely artifacts of a faulty study design? Because assignments in police departments have implications for career advancement, we had better be sure that the findings of such evaluations are, indeed, valid before proceeding to use them as a basis for allocating personnel—or for any other reason.

A key issue in program evaluations of police-officer performance, then, is the validity of the measures used to compare male and female performance, and reviews of these studies (Harrington, 2000; Morash & Greene, 1986) point to a number of weaknesses in some studies: a tendency to choose variables based on male stereotypes of what is important in police work, such as marksmanship or frequency of arrests; a failure to evaluate performance on a representative sample of police tasks; an overemphasis on the violent and dangerous aspects of police work; and a failure to consider the differences between men's and women's experiences in the workplace, such as greater camaraderie among male officers. As these weaknesses suggest, even though attitudes toward women in police work have become considerably more positive over the decades, gender can still be a confounding factor that makes it difficult and complicated to design evaluations of police officer performance that produce both accurate and fair results.

So conducting occupational performance evaluations that take into account gender, race, sexual orientation, or other minority status is difficult and fraught with possibilities for invalid conclusions. The fact that such evaluations continue and their results are acted upon means that those who conduct evaluations must be cognizant of the potential pitfalls and ready to guard against biased results through the use of sound study designs. The Eye on Ethics section also addresses some ethical issues related to program evaluation, which may be especially salient when doing research on minorities.

Designs for Evaluation Research

Summative evaluation research often is concerned with cause-and-effect relationships. For example, the program being evaluated is presumed to bring about changes in such factors as client behavior, so a research design developed for such an evaluation needs to be based on an awareness of this cause-and-effect dimension. In Chapter 10, we noted that true experimental designs involving randomization are the better choice for establishing cause-and-effect relationships, because they best control the threats to validity that can lead to false causal inferences. The ideal approach to determining the effects of a program, therefore, is the randomized experiment. Any of the true experimental designs discussed in Chapter 10 is appropriate for evaluation purposes. Quasi-experimental designs are quite common, however, because these often are far more feasible and expedient than true experimental designs.

Randomized Experimental Designs. As we have noted, the requirements of a true experiment are two randomized equivalent groups, one that experiences the experimental condition and a control group that does not. In summative evaluation research, the experimental condition requires some level of participation in the program under consideration. The crucial feature of the true experiment is that members of the comparison groups are

> ### EYE ON ETHICS — The Ethics of International Research with Abandoned Children
>
> The plight of the poor and the powerless has been a consistent thread running through the development of research ethics. This theme has taken a new twist as research has become a global enterprise in the twenty-first century. Just as third-world countries have attracted corporations seeking cheap labor and lax regulation, the people of these poor countries can also be at risk of exploitation as research subjects. One ethical issue in particular stands out: Who benefits from the research and who bears the risk? It would be unethical if the developed world gets most of the benefits of research and the developing world bears much of its burdens.
>
> The Bucharest Early Intervention Project (BEIP) was a program evaluation study of the benefits of foster care over institutionalized care (Millum & Emanuel, 2007). It consisted of a randomized trial comparing institutional and foster care for abandoned children currently in institutions. There are thousands of institutionalized children in Romania, and at the time of the study, basic foster care was nonexistent. The children in the study are very young, abandoned, and lacking guardians to look out for their best interests. The study was funded from the United States, but no American children were participants. Given these conditions, the question arises: Are these children being exploited for research purposes?
>
> Millum and Emanuel defended the study as ethical because participants living in institutional care were experiencing conditions normal to Romania. Clearly, the researchers did not cause the poverty and abandonment, and institutional care was all that was available. The research results were expected to be integrated into the child welfare system of Romania for the benefit of its citizens, not for the benefit of developed nations. Thus, the population from which the participants were drawn would be the direct beneficiaries of the study results. In fact, the study found significantly improved cognitive development for children transferred to foster care before two years of age compared with institutionalized children; it provided strong support for the worth of developing a foster care system.

randomly assigned. This is the surest and most reliable way of producing equivalent groups.

Virtually all randomized experiments in evaluation are field experiments, taking place in the setting where the actual program is administered. Because of this, evaluators may encounter a number of impediments to conducting a randomized experiment. The first centers around the control group and the randomization procedure used to obtain it. To create a control group, it is necessary to deny some members of the target population access to the program under evaluation, and that denial must be made on a random basis. Evaluators may encounter substantial resistance to such denials. For example, the enabling legislation of some programs mandates that all persons who meet the eligibility requirements have a legal right to participate in the program. If this is the case, random denial of service must be ruled out.

In other programs, resistance to random denial of services may spring from the program administrators and staff. Practitioners are accustomed to providing services on the basis of need, and they may be disinclined to use a table of random numbers instead. To them, it seems cold, insensitive, and even immoral to withhold available services from people who need them, especially if intuition leads the practitioner to believe that the provision of services would have beneficial effects. In advocating a randomized experiment, evaluators sometimes find themselves in a no-win situation: If they discover that the program produces harmful effects, then they are blamed for subjecting the experimental group to the harmful program. If the program produces positive results, however, then they are blamed for withholding this valuable service from the control group. Imagine the ethical implications of a randomized experiment for evaluating something like a suicide prevention program, in which life-and-death issues are at stake.

Along these lines, it is important to keep in mind that intuition regarding the impact of programs often is faulty. In fact, the literature on evaluation research strongly suggests that practitioners' assumptions of positive program effects often are wrong. Leonard Gibbs (1991) documented this point with a diverse list of well-intentioned intervention efforts from the annals of medicine and human service—efforts that appeared to be reasonable in their time but later proved ineffective. Included were bloodletting, mercuric chloride as a drug, oxygen therapy for premature infants, neuroleptic medication for tardive dyskinesia, a juvenile awareness program known as "Scared Straight," encounter groups, and aggressive relocation of the aged. In the last illustration, a study on providing a full range of human services to the elderly who were mentally impaired reported that the death rate for clients receiving the intensive services was 25 percent, in contrast to only 18 percent for the controls. Although not statistically significant, the results should make us pause before we assume that good intentions assure a positive outcome. Because services that our intuition may suggest are effective often turn out not to be, the arguments against withholding services in a randomized experimental design are severely weakened, and as demonstrated in Research in Practice 10.2, studies involving true control groups are clearly feasible.

A second impediment to conducting randomized experiments in evaluation research is that they may be more time consuming and expensive than other designs. Experimental evaluations of programs typically are longitudinal: Sufficient time must pass for programs to have an effect. With many social programs, such as compensatory education or job training, the minimum length of the experiment might be at least one year. Furthermore, a listing of the target population, which is required for randomization, may be difficult or expensive to obtain. These practical considerations mean that randomized experiments are limited to those cases where the money and time are available for an elaborate, rigorous evaluation.

Before succumbing to the pressure to settle for a weaker design, however, consider the lesson of the Salk polio vaccine trials. Two experimental methods were used. One was a nonrandomized trial wherein one million volunteer second-graders were given the vaccine and unvaccinated first- and third-graders served as the control group. The other study was an experiment involving 800,000 volunteers randomly assigned to receive either the vaccine or a placebo without the doctors, parents, or children knowing which group they were in. Although the first study involved a larger sample and may have seemed easier to conduct without complicated randomization, its design proved inadequate for estimating the effect of the vaccine. It seems that polio was more prevalent in the middle classes because better hygiene prevented building up the natural immunity that lower-class children developed. Second-graders who volunteered tended to be middle class, and thus different from second-graders who did not volunteer and from the first- and third-graders in the control group. Citing this case in his argument for randomized experiments, Lawrence Sherman (1992, p. 59) concluded, "Only the randomized, fully controlled Salk vaccine experiment provided the clear estimate of the vaccine's benefits which was needed to adopt a national policy of vaccination."

Randomized experiments clearly are the best designs from which to assess causality. The evidence-based approach to human service practice that we have stressed in this book establishes the randomized, controlled experiment as producing the "best" evidence for guiding practice. Reports in such journals as *Evaluation Quarterly* document the widespread use of these designs. With some inventiveness on the part of evaluators, much of the resistance to randomized experiments can be overcome. Indeed, there is a growing consensus about the desirability of randomized experiments and an expanding literature documenting their use (Orr, 1998), which should work to reduce the barriers to future randomized experiments in evaluation.

One common situation in particular contributes to the possibility of a randomized experiment. When the target population is larger than the program's capacity to serve it—in short, when the demand for services exceeds the supply—services must be denied to some people. Many programs initially are instituted on a small scale, so excess demand often occurs. Because some members of the target population will not be served anyway, the determination of who will be served might as well be random unless there is some other clear-cut and defensible criterion, such as severity of need. In fact, a reasonable argument can be made that random allocation of services is the fairest method when resources are inadequate to serve everyone and no other criteria seem applicable.

If an evaluator is successful in obtaining approval for a randomized experiment, the random assignment process must be carefully monitored to ensure proper implementation. Lack of such monitoring can destroy the experimental design. For example, an employment and training program with which one of the authors of this book once consulted had agreed to a randomized study. When a large group of eager youths appeared at the agency on the first day, however, the staff was overwhelmed and simply threw the program open to all of them, totally destroying the randomization procedure. When such events go undiscovered, the comparison groups are not equalized, and the eventual results are misleading. A two-step procedure is desirable in which client information is gathered by personnel different from those who do the random assignment. In this way, those personnel handling the assignment do so without knowledge of client identities or characteristics. Insulating the assignment process in this way reduces the opportunity for deviations from randomness to creep in and eases the monitoring task (Cook, Cook, & Mark, 1977).

Alternatives to Randomized Experiments. The barriers to randomized experiments may be sufficiently formidable to require an alternative design. It is important to remember that anything other than a randomized experiment produces results in which confidence is reduced, because such alternative designs are weaker on internal validity (see Chapter 10). Properly conducted, however, these designs allow evaluation with a reasonable degree of certitude.

One alternative to the randomized experiment is to use a *quasi-experimental design*. When a program is meant to affect behavior about which data are routinely collected, a time-series design may be appropriate. For example, we described a time-series design in Chapter 10 (see Figure 10.2), which looked at whether changes in the laws for justifiable homicide changed the rate of justifiable homicide. The study looked at states that established so-called "stand your ground" laws in 2006, comparing rates of justifiable homicide before and after that date with states that did not have such laws. The comparison showed that states with such laws experienced a considerable rise in justifiable homicide after their passage, whereas states without such laws experienced no such increase. This is a multiple-time-series design that has a control group and thus protects against the validity threat of history. A time-series design without a control group would be subject to the validity threat of history.

A second alternative to randomized experiments is *matching*. If randomization is not feasible, it may be possible to match persons in the experimental group with persons having similar characteristics in a control group. Matching can be unreliable, however, because we can use relatively few variables, which leaves uncontrolled variables that might confound the results.

An example of an evaluation in which a form of matching was used was a study of the effectiveness of a short-term group care program for children in Connecticut (DeSena, 2005). The new program was sequentially introduced into communities in the state until, after a time, it was operating in all communities. For the evaluation, the experimental group consisted of a sample of children in the new program, whereas the control group consisted of a sample of children receiving traditional foster care in communities in which the program had not yet been implemented at the time of the evaluation. Because the program was implemented in whole communities at a time, it was not possible to randomly assign children to experimental and control groups. To increase the probability that the two groups were comparable, each child selected for the control group was matched on age, gender, and ethnicity with a child in the new program. This provided some assurance that the two groups were comparable (at least on the characteristics used for the matching).

> **RESEARCH IN PRACTICE 12.1** **Program Evaluation: Evidence-Based Evaluation: The Effectiveness of Programs to Reduce Recidivism**
>
> In Chapter 10, we discussed experiments as a research design, and in many ways, experimental designs are the most desirable of all research designs because they provide us with the most confidence in making causal statements. Because of this, some proponents of evidence-based practice take the elements of the experimental design as the standard against which to assess the worth of evidence. Because of this, evaluation research often tries to use one of the experimental designs. To provide a more in-depth understanding of what it means to assess evidence, we will present a guide, based on the elements of experimental designs, for evaluating the worthiness of evidence from research.
>
> We will illustrate how such guides can work by looking at a study designed to assess policies related to the most effective way to release inmates from prison. Policy makers, hoping to reduce recidivism, have promoted programs that provide financial assistance to former prisoners to help them make a successful transition to civilian life. Such programs typically provide a payment, like unemployment insurance, to provide financial support while the ex-inmate gets settled outside prison and searches for a job. Because many crimes are economically motivated, it seems reasonable to hypothesize that such financial assistance would reduce the likelihood that a newly released inmate would turn to crime.
>
> To test this hypothesis, the Baltimore Living Insurance for Ex-Prisoners (or Baltimore LIFE) Project was developed (Lenihan, 1977; Rossi, Berk, & Lenihan, 1980). In this field experiment, high-risk inmates scheduled for release by the Maryland Department of Corrections were given various financial and job-related supports to see if they had an impact on their recidivism. In the table below, we list some of the criteria that the evidence-based practice approach would apply to assess the evidence in this study and then point out how the study meets each criterion.
>
> | Criterion | Study |
> | --- | --- |
> | Independent variable (treatment) clearly defined | Two independent variables: 1) receive financial assistance ($60 per week for 13 weeks after release); and 2) receive job placement services. NOTE: One experimental group received both, one received only financial assistance, and one received only job placement services |
> | Random selection to sample | No sampling—all high-risk inmates being released were included |
> | Control group | Yes—one group received neither independent variable |
> | Random assignment to control group | Yes—also random assignment to the three treatment groups |

A third alternative to the randomized experiment (really another form of matching) is the use of *cohort groups*. Cohorts are groups of people who move through an organization or a treatment program at about the same time. For example, the following are cohorts: students in the same grade at a school; people receiving public assistance at the same time from a particular agency; and people in a drug rehabilitation program at the same time. Cohorts are valuable alternatives to randomized experiments, because we may be able to assume that each cohort in an organization or a program is similar to the cohort preceding it in terms of the characteristics that might affect a treatment outcome. In other words, each group should be alike in age, sex, socioeconomic status, and other characteristics that may be important. There can be very significant differences, however, and cohorts should always be assessed to detect any possible systematic variation.

An elaborate cohort study evaluating curriculum revision and televised instruction was conducted in El Salvador from 1969 to 1973 (Mayo, Hornick, & McAnany, 1976). Seventh-grade classes in 1969, 1970, and 1971 made up three separate cohorts of

Criterion	Study
Validity/reliability checks	Since the variables were well-defined behaviors, face validity was sufficient
Dependent variable (outcome) clearly defined	Yes—two dependent variables: 1) did they get a job; and 2) did they avoid future criminal activity

Some evidence-based approaches use a longer list of criteria, but this is adequate to illustrate the point that the characteristics of a controlled, randomized experiment can be used as a guide for assessing how good the evidence is in a particular study. Sometimes the list is used as a checklist, indicating how many of the criteria are met in a particular study. Other approaches assign a numerical value to each criterion (depending on how important it is considered to be), and summing these produces a numerical score for each study that can be compared to other studies. In either case, this approach provides an organized way to assess how much confidence we have in the evidence provided by a study: The more criteria met or the higher the score achieved, the more confidence we have in the evidence.

What did the recidivism study find? The men who received financial aid had an 8 percent lower rate of arrest for charges of theft. Arrests for other types of crime were not significantly different. Also, those who did not receive financial aid were arrested earlier, were more likely to be convicted, and were more likely to be returned to prison. Job placement services had no apparent impact on recidivism or occupational success.

The Baltimore LIFE Project also served as a model for a legislatively mandated program in California (Berk et al., 1985). It was designed much like the Baltimore LIFE Project except that the inmates actually applied for unemployment benefits once released from prison, and were eligible if they had worked sufficient hours per week in prison. Because of this, however, the random assignment of inmates to experimental and control groups for evaluation purposes was not done; thus, the best research design for assessing program impacts—the randomized experiment—was not used. Instead, investigators used a regression discontinuity design, in which the experimental group consisted of those inmates who had worked enough to be eligible for unemployment benefits and the control group contained those who had not. This did not affect the operation of the program, but it did make evaluation of it less certain. This would lead evidence-based practitioners and policy makers to give this later study a lower score in terms of the value of its evidence. Nonetheless, a conservative evaluation of its effects concluded that the program saved California $2,000 for each inmate involved. In other words, the costs of the program were far outweighed by the money saved, because some inmates in the program did not commit further crimes and the state saved the cost of incarcerating them.

students. Within the cohorts, some classes received a new curriculum, some the new curriculum with televised instruction, and some the old curriculum. The cohorts from 1969 and 1970 were followed for three years, and the cohort from 1971 was followed for two years. Comparisons among the groups produced mixed results. The new curriculum was consistently superior to the old one, and televised instruction was superior during its first year. The superiority of televised instruction wore off, however, as the students became accustomed to it.

The major weakness of cohorts is, again, the threat to validity from history. Because the measurements are taken at widely spaced times, extraneous variables may intercede and affect the results. The El Salvador example is instructive on this point. It would be unlikely that a similar cohort study could have been reliably conducted 10 years later, as the country became unstable because of guerrilla warfare. Comparing a cohort from a period of peace with one from a period of near civil war has obvious problems.

A fourth alternative to the randomized experiment is the *regression discontinuity design:* People are selected to receive a treatment based on their score on a test, their eligibility for a program, or some other criterion. The study of recidivism in California discussed in Research in Practice 12.1 was a regression discontinuity design in which prison inmates were eligible for the experimental group if they had worked sufficient hours in prison to be eligible for unemployment benefits when released. Inmates who had worked fewer hours were put in the control group. This design often is implemented for evaluation research field experiments, and it can be useful. Regression discontinuity designs suffer, however, from some of the threats to internal validity, particularly selection and, in some cases, statistical regression. Incidentally, the summative evaluation described in Research in Practice 12.1 was an outgrowth of the formative evaluation project described earlier in this chapter about the provision of financial aid to newly released prisoners.

The last major alternative to randomized experiments is the use of *statistical controls*, which are procedures that allow the effects of one or more variables to be removed or held constant so the effects of other variables can be observed. These procedures allow comparisons to be made between groups that differ from one another on some characteristics thought to be important. The effects of the variables on which the groups differ are removed through statistical manipulation so they cannot obscure the results. Statistical controls, however, even in their most elaborate application, can only approximate the level of control achievable in randomized experiments. As with matching, only variables that the researcher already knows to be potentially important can be statistically controlled, so there is always the possibility of leaving important extraneous variables uncontrolled. Furthermore, statistical controls tend to underadjust for differences between groups because of the error component in the measurement of the control variables (Berk & Rossi, 1990). The error allows at least some of the effects of the control variables to remain even after the statistical controls have been applied. Because of these limitations, statistical control alone may not be appropriate, but it is well suited as an adjunct to the physical control obtained through design. For example, in a matched design, we might find out after the fact that an important variable was left unmatched. Assuming that the necessary data were collected, we could make up for this error by applying statistical control to that variable.

The use of both design control and statistical control probably is the best overall approach for evaluation. This is because statistical control can even be useful in randomized experiments.

Nonpositivist Approaches to Evaluation

Nonpositivist approaches make quite different assumptions from positivist approaches about what is going on in a summative evaluation. First, nonpositivists assume that there are multiple stakeholders in—and, thus, multiple perspectives on—social interventions (Greene, 1994). A given research methodology may assess the program in terms of the interests of some, but not other, stakeholders. In fact, some critics of positivist approaches to evaluation argue that, because such evaluations typically are funded and supported by the sponsors and managers of the program, the evaluations tend to address issues of concern to those stakeholders— such as the economic efficiency of the program, numbers of people served, or other issues that can be measured in quantitative (often monetary) ways. These approaches tend to focus on the importance of assessing program outcomes, efficiency, and accountability, and, in fact, are the issues most readily addressed through the randomized experimental designs that positivists consider to be the ideal evaluation methodology. For evaluators who address different issues or the interests of other stakeholders, the randomized experimental design with control groups may be less important— or, possibly, even irrelevant—as a research design (Cook, 1985).

A second assumption of nonpositivist evaluators, especially those using an interpretive approach, is that interpretation and social meaning are at the core of social interventions (Denzin, 1989; Smith, 1989; Weiss, 1998). In this view, social reality doesn't just exist "out there," but rather is created by people as they interact and exchange meanings.

An interpretivist program evaluation focuses attention on how all the stakeholders— the sponsors and managers, as well as the recipients of services— experience a social intervention. From some perspectives, such as the perspective of those receiving the services, economic efficiency and other quantitative matters may not be the key elements of the program at all. The point is that nonpositivist evaluators refuse to define issues and solutions solely from the perspective of the more powerful and dominant stakeholders. These concerns lead nonpositivist evaluators to research methodologies that are more useful for discovering the interpretations and perspectives of the various parties to the program: participant observation, in-depth interviewing, case studies, and other, more qualitative, approaches. In these approaches, control groups, random assignment, and random samples are less important than discovering meaning in the social contexts in which people live and allowing participants to frame their own issues and define problems using their own meaningful categories.

A third assumption of nonpositivist evaluators, especially those using a critical approach, is that social interventions typically reflect and reinforce inequitable distributions of power and resources in society. A central goal of the critical program evaluator is to reveal the mechanisms whereby inequities are reinforced and increased and to show how social programs promote the agenda of the powerful, while doing relatively little for the less powerful. Critical evaluators might use either quantitative or qualitative approaches, but their approach is more participatory in nature: Less powerful stakeholders participate in designing and carrying out the evaluation, thus increasing the likelihood that the research designed will discover facts and relationships beneficial to them. They are consulted about the research all along the way, and one of the research goals is the empowerment of these groups. A part of this empowerment involves the evaluation serving as a catalyst for social change.

Research in Practice 12.2 provides an illustration of a program evaluation that uses a nonpositivist approach. Of course, the distinction between positivist and nonpositivist research does not rigidly follow the separation between quantitative and qualitative research, although there is a relationship. This also is true in the field of evaluation research. Although positivists and nonpositivists do have the methodological inclinations that we describe, the key distinctions between them have to do with assumptions rather than with particular research methodologies. Looking at both the positivist and nonpositivist perspectives achieves a much broader view of what evaluation research can accomplish and what issues and values can be attended to in such research.

Cost–Benefit Analysis

One particular type of evaluation research, *cost–benefit analysis,* involves some unique issues and premises, and thus warrants special attention. In an era of increasing accountability for social programs, this approach often serves as a foundation for social policy decisions, so it is important that it be used properly, with its strengths and limitations being well understood (Hummel-Rossi & Ashdown, 2002).

On the surface, **cost–benefit analysis** appears seductively simple: Add up the costs of a program, subtract them from the dollar value of the benefits, and get the result—either a net gain (benefits exceed costs), or a net loss (costs exceed benefits). Such an approach is appealing to many policy makers because it seems to clarify complex issues and programs through quantification. Policy makers would logically support and, perhaps, expand programs showing a net gain and curtail those showing a net loss. If only it were that simple! As we shall see, quantifying benefits and costs can be extremely difficult and often involves a number of unproved assumptions and estimates.

Cost–benefit analysis can be applied to a program during its planning stages, called *ex ante analysis,* or after the program has been in operation, called *ex post analysis* (Rossi, Lipsey, & Freeman, 2004). The major difference is that an *ex ante* analysis requires more estimates and assumptions than an *ex post* analysis, because no hard data exist regarding either costs or benefits. An *ex post* study has records of actual cost outlays, and can determine benefits empirically through normal evaluation

> **RESEARCH IN PRACTICE 12.2 Program Evaluation: A Nonpositivist Evaluation of a Juvenile Gang Intervention Program**

Research in Practice 12.1 presented a program evaluation that was positivist in nature, using quantitative measures of variables and focusing a lot of attention on the economic efficiency of the program. Little consideration, however, was given to treating the released inmates as stakeholders in the program; their views were not solicited. A more nonpositivist approach was used in an evaluation of a juvenile gang intervention program in a rural community (Stum & Chu, 1999). The program evaluated in this study was a school partnership program that followed the philosophy of community policing. The basic idea was to build positive police–citizen partnerships based on trust and mutual respect, accomplished, in part, through daily visits to schools by the police to interact with and get to know the youths. Because there had been little prior research on such programs, especially as they operate in rural communities, the researchers decided that a more nonpositivist, exploratory, qualitative approach was appropriate.

The researchers decided that focus groups (see Chapter 7) and content analysis (see Chapter 8) would be the best methodologies. Earlier in this chapter, we discussed using focus groups as a part of formative evaluations, but this research provides an illustration of the use of focus groups in summative evaluations. The research focused on gang members and at-risk youth, and it explored their perceptions of themselves, their peers, their communities, and the gang prevention and intervention programs operating in their schools. (As discussed in Chapter 9, these qualitative approaches better enable us to understand the subjective experiences of the people being studied, and better avoid the possibility that a researcher will impose his or her own meanings in a way that misses or distorts what is really going on.)

Recall that focus groups, also called group depth interviews, involve a moderator asking questions of a group and recording people's responses. The questions asked guide the discussion, but the moderator is free to ask additional questions and even to digress into new topics that seem fruitful based on the discussion. In addition, group interaction can stimulate responses that might not have occurred with other methodologies. Overall, focus groups are exploratory and encourage people to respond in their own words and by creating their own meanings. This is based on the assumptions made by nonpositivist program evaluators: The thoughts and perspectives of all stakeholders in a program should be assessed, and powerless or disadvantaged groups should have an opportunity to be heard.

In this study, data collection occurred in three separate focus groups in which each participant was involved. One addressed the school partnership policing program by asking youth about their contacts or relationships with the police. A second focus group addressed the youths' perceptions of themselves, their activities, and the crimes that they committed, as well as their perceptions of police, probation officers, judges, and others in positions of authority. The third group had to do with how the youths felt about their peers and their communities.

All focus group discussions were tape-recorded, and a research assistant prepared notes based on his or her observation of the group discussion so that the tapes and notes could be compared as a way of assessing reliability and validity. Then the tapes and notes were reviewed repeatedly to identify major themes in the data. If researchers disagreed about themes, they went back to the raw data (tapes and notes) to identify what led to the identification of a particular theme.

One of the conclusions the study arrived at was that, based on the opinions expressed by the youths in the focus groups, the school partnership program had serious weaknesses and might not be an effective intervention program for teens at risk. Most of the youth reported that they didn't know—or, at best, hardly knew—the police officers with whom they were supposed to be developing positive relationships. In addition, they expressed concerns that contact with police authorities might bring them difficulties—the police could identify them as potential troublemakers because of their involvement in a program for at-risk teens. With no prior research on these programs, this exploratory, qualitative methodology is more likely to discover attitudes like these.

research procedures. The use of estimates in *ex ante* analyses means that results are far more tentative, however, and accounts for why *ex ante* analyses conducted by different parties sometimes come to widely divergent conclusions: They use different estimates and assumptions. Sorting out whose estimates are most valid has produced some lively debates among policy makers. *Ex post* analyses require fewer estimates, however, and therefore are more reliable.

Estimating Costs. The easy part of cost–benefit analysis—although by no means simple—is determining the **direct costs** of a program. The program has either a record of actual expenditures (in *ex post* analysis) or a proposed budget for the program (in *ex ante* analysis). A budget proposal, however, is based on assumptions that may not be accurate. For example, the budget for a supplemental unemployment compensation program must assume a certain unemployment rate. If the actual rate changes, the cost of the program can skyrocket or fall dramatically.

Considerably more difficult to estimate than direct program costs are what economists call *opportunity costs*. **Opportunity costs** are the value of forgone opportunities. Suppose, for example, you are fortunate enough to win a $1,000 prize in a contest. You can invest the money or spend it on anything you like—a new computer, for instance. The direct cost of the computer is the $1,000 you spent on it, but there are opportunity costs. The opportunity costs are what you forgo by buying the computer. You lose the return you could have earned by investing the money or the value of other items you might have purchased, such as new clothes or the down payment on an automobile.

So it is with the funding of social programs. Agencies have limited resources. If they decide to fund a certain program, the cost of the program includes the opportunity costs of not funding alternative programs. Normally, the estimated value of the benefits of competing programs is used as the basis for computing the opportunity costs of the program being analyzed. Computing the benefits lost by not initiating a program is complex, which makes it difficult to calculate the opportunity costs of the funded program. Such estimates need to be made, however, to provide an accurate picture of the total costs of a program.

Estimating and Monetizing Benefits. The really difficult—and often unreliable—part of cost–benefit analysis comes in determining program benefits and *monetizing,* or attaching a dollar value, to them. This process may be either fairly straightforward or mystical, depending on the program. In general, if a program's benefits are related to some economic activity, they are easier to monetize—for example, the value of subsidized day care. The market price of private day care plus the added income of the parent who otherwise could not work constitute the major dollar benefits from the program, but what about program benefits less related to economic activity? How can we place a dollar value on such program benefits as improved mental health, improved self-esteem, reduced domestic violence, or other noneconomic outcomes? Cost–benefit analysis attempts, through complex procedures, to place a dollar value on practically anything. Doing so, however, requires many, often controversial, assumptions and value judgments. Thus, cost–benefit analysis is of the greatest utility when the relationship between program benefits and a certain dollar value is fairly clear.

Another complicating factor in cost–benefit analysis is that benefits and costs do not accrue at the same time. Costs are incurred immediately upon the program's implementation, whereas benefits may not accrue until some later date, possibly far in the future. In some programs, such as education or job training, at least some of the benefits are long term indeed. This temporal gap is a problem, because the value of both costs and benefits changes with time. A dollar today does not have the same purchasing power that it did 10 years ago. To make meaningful comparisons over time, we must adjust costs and benefits so that comparisons are made in constant dollars.

This adjustment involves the calculation of what is called the *discount rate*. The discount rate is the amount that future costs and benefits are reduced to make them comparable to the current value of money. Actual calculation of the discount rate involves some accounting procedures. There also are several competing approaches to its calculation (Rossi, Lipsey, & Freeman, 2004). As many disheartened investors will attest, predicting the future value of money is a risky business. Furthermore, the discount rate that is used has a marked effect on the outcome of the analysis. For all these reasons, it is common to run several analyses with differing discount rates to see how the program fares under different sets of assumptions.

Whose Costs, Whose Benefits? An important consideration in cost–benefit analysis is that costs and benefits are calculated from particular perspectives. Three different perspectives may be used: program participants, the funding source, or society as a whole. A comprehensive cost–benefit analysis would include all three.

Take the example of early childhood intervention programs, which are efforts by governmental or other agencies outside the family to support and improve the quality of life for youngsters from the prenatal period into the school years. These programs focus on providing health, education, and social service interventions. The theory behind such programs is that they will provide broad benefits to society because the children they support generally will be healthier, do better in school, and be less likely to create problems of crime or welfare dependence as adults. In Table 12.1, we have listed some of the potential costs and benefits of such early intervention programs, along with an indication of which perspective might see each as a cost or a benefit.

Let's look at some elements in the table. For the mothers (participants) who can work at paying jobs because of the services provided by the programs, their costs are the loss of welfare payments they would receive if they did not work. Their benefits are the income received by working (together with less tangible benefits, such as enhanced social status, job satisfaction, and freedom from child care responsibilities). Participants also benefit from any reductions in criminal activity that the mother or child experiences because of participation in the program.

TABLE 12.1 Perspectives on the Costs and Benefits of an Early Childhood Intervention Program

Benefits and Costs:	Perspective		
	Society	Participants	Funding Source
Costs of home visits to children	−	+	−
Reduction in emergency room visits by child	+	+	0
Increase in taxes paid by mother because of her increased employment income	+	−	+
Decrease in cost of government welfare payments to mother	0	−	+
Decrease in mother's arrest and jail costs	+	+	0
Decrease in child's arrest costs as an adolescent	+	+	0
Decrease in child's arrest cost as an adult	+	+	0
Income from mother's increased employment	0	+	0
Decrease in welfare payments to mother	0	−	+
Decrease in losses to crime victims	+	0	0

Key: + = an expected benefit from a given perspective
− = an expected cost from a given perspective
0 = neither a cost nor a benefit

SOURCE: Adapted from Karoly, L. A. et al. (1998). *Investing in Our Children: What We Know and Don't Know about the Costs and Benefits of Early Childhood Interventions.* Santa Monica, CA: Rand.

From the perspective of the funding sources—in this case, the federal government—the costs and benefits are quite different. The costs are the direct costs of running the program (e.g., costs of home visits) together with the opportunity costs of not using the money for something else. The benefits are the reduced costs of other public assistance programs and an increase in tax revenues because of the incomes of working mothers.

The societal perspective is the broadest and, frequently, the most difficult to calculate. (If the funding source is the government, we should not assume that the government's perspective coincides with the societal perspective. The government represents only those who control a particular government agency.) The costs to society of the early intervention program are the increased taxes or federal borrowing necessary to fund the program, plus the opportunity costs. Benefits are the increased productivity of the mothers, who are now more free to make economic, social, and cultural contributions to society (although we need to remember that performing as a parent or homemaker also is an essential contribution). Other less direct benefits might accrue if working and the additional income that it provides have positive effects on family relationships, the children's well-being, future aspirations, and the like. Of course, society as a whole benefits when costs associated with crime are reduced.

Early intervention programs involve more elements—and more costs and benefits—than we listed in Table 12.1, but that table helps clarify the idea that program costs and benefits need to be assessed from a variety of perspectives. People also might disagree over whether a particular element in the table is a cost or a benefit from a particular perspective, which only reinforces the point that cost–benefit analysis is difficult, complicated, and often, contentious. Incidentally, most cost–benefit analyses of these early childhood intervention programs conclude that, if run well, the programs do provide substantially more benefits than costs (Karoly et al., 1998).

Cost-Effective Analysis

Because it is difficult to monetize benefits, interest has developed in an alternative approach that does not require benefits to be ascribed a dollar value. **Cost-effective analysis** compares program costs measured in dollars with program effects measured in whatever units are appropriate, such as achievement test scores, skill performance level, coping abilities, or whatever effect the program is supposed to produce. Such analysis is most useful for choosing among competing programs rather than for evaluating a single program. For example, cost-effective analysis often is used in evaluating HIV prevention programs (Holtgrave, 1998). The challenge to comparing prevention programs is having a meaningful standard of comparison. One approach is to employ cost–benefit analysis by comparing programs based on the benefit of money saved in medical care by preventing an infection. Such cost–benefit analysis, however, is insufficient for policy makers, because medical care dollars saved hardly represent the positive impact of a prevention program.

Evaluators have developed an alternative, nonmonetary measure, called the $QALY$, for cost-effective analysis. The term $QALY$ refers to "quality-adjusted life years," or the number of years of additional life that result because infection did not occur, as well as the quality of that life (perfect health versus some diminished level of capacity). We will not get into the complexity of measuring QALYs except to make the point that a variety of prevention programs can be directly compared in terms of money spent for each additional QALY achieved. Based on experience with the standard of program costs per QALY saved, policy makers consider a ratio of $40,000 per QALY to be cost-effective.

Such cost-effective analyses of many competing programs make it possible to select the most efficient approach. Interpreting a single cost-effective analysis, however, is less clear-cut than a cost–benefit analysis, because the costs and benefits are not expressed in the same units. For this reason, cost-effective analysis is not an interchangeable substitute for cost–benefit analysis, because they answer different questions.

Like all forms of analysis, cost–benefit analysis is only as good as the data, the estimates, and the assumptions on which it is based. All these complex components should be explicitly discussed in the report and the users should be encouraged to evaluate their soundness. The real risk associated with cost–benefit analysis comes when bottom-line results are accepted blindly and become the overriding factor in decision making. At its current level of development, cost–benefit analysis is useful, but it must be cautiously interpreted as only one of many factors in the decision-making process concerning social programs.

IMPROVING UTILIZATION OF EVALUATION RESEARCH

At the beginning of this chapter, we described the purposes of evaluation research as improving service to clients, aiding in the policy-making process, and testing social science theories and practice approaches. In all these areas, the assumption is made that the research results will be used to produce some change in the status quo. In actuality, this often is not the case, because there are many barriers to use of the results of evaluation research (MacGregor, 2011).

One barrier is the fault of evaluators. Because of poor design or execution, the evaluation may not produce clear-cut results. It is difficult to overcome resistance to change unless the reasons for change are strong and the direction that change should take is clear. All too often, the basic conclusion of an evaluation is this: "The program as currently operated is not achieving its intended goals." What is one to do with such a conclusion? It offers no indication of why the program is failing or suggestions for improving it. To avoid results like this, evaluation should be broadly conceived so that the findings indicate not only what the program does not do but also what it does do and why.

A second barrier to the use of evaluation research results is poor communication on the part of evaluators (Miller, 1987). Researchers are used to communicating with other researchers who share a common technical language and background. When communicating with one another, they assume those commonalities and write their reports accordingly. If this is done in an evaluation report, the results may be quite unclear to the practitioners, program administrators, and policy makers who are going to use those results. Evaluation reports should be written so they are clear and understandable to the audience who will use them, and evaluators should work through the report with sponsors, explaining it thoroughly and answering all questions.

A third barrier to the use of evaluation research is the failure of the researchers to press for adoption of their research findings. Such an advocacy role is foreign to many researchers, who may feel that their job terminates once the data have been analyzed. Implementation of modifications to a program often is complex, however, and program staff are faced with competing interests. Without active participation by the researcher, adoption of recommendations may not take place at all.

A fourth barrier is the ever-present resistance to change. People become accustomed to established procedures, and vested interests are difficult to overcome. In human service evaluations, it is fairly common for program administrators to ignore results that contradict prevailing attitudes and feelings towards services or that disrupt existing administrative structures. Often this results in administrators and staff creating new rationales for continuing a program and rationalizing negative results. For example, a 2005 study of school districts' responses to evaluations of Drug Abuse Resistance Education (D.A.R.E.) programs found that these programs had little or no long-term impact on knowledge, attitudes, or use of drugs and alcohol (Birkeland, Murphy-Graham, & Weiss, 2005). Yet, many school districts continued to offer them. Staff at several of these programs explained that while the program did not lead to empirically verified improvements in drug-and alcohol-related behaviors and attitudes, it did create more positive relationships between law enforcement agents who administer the program and students. Some believed it was unreasonable to expect the program to have long-term impacts on students' behavior while emphasizing many intangible benefits it creates within the school. Others stated that the program was successful regardless of what formal evaluations showed, citing several specific cases where the program was linked to improvements in particular students.

One change suggested to improve research utilization is increased dissemination of results (Weiss, 1998). Earlier, we expressed concern over the fact that evaluation reports often are not widely circulated. Broader dissemination may bring a report to the attention of someone who is willing to use the results.

Evaluation research reports are published in a number of ways. Sometimes, they are published in social science or human service research journals, such as *Evaluation Review, Journal of Applied Behavioral Science,* or *Journal of Applied Social Science*. Over the past few decades, more outlets for the publication of evaluation research have developed. Evaluation research reports also are published in government documents and reports, especially when the study concerns a government program; these can be accessed like other government documents (see Appendix A).

Some evaluation reports are not published, however, and this can make them more difficult—but

---

INFORMATION TECHNOLOGY IN RESEARCH — **Online Interviews and Focus Groups in Evaluation Research**

In some cases, evaluation research collects data through interviews or focus groups, and some research organizations are now equipped to do this online, with the participants being in dispersed geographic locations (Anderson & Kanuka, 2003; Matthews & Cramer, 2008). All the participants need is a high-speed Internet connection, a current web browser, and a web camera and microphone; all the other necessary equipment and software are available from the research organization. Online surveys and focus groups can be based on text (not unlike a chat room) or can use audio or video input (not unlike a conference telephone call), depending on the technology available. The use of web cams is an especially valuable development because it makes it possible to conduct remote interviews without losing all the nonverbal and contextual information that would be available in face-to-face interviews. To use a term introduced in Chapter 9, this visual information provided by the web cam makes possible a more thick description of a phenomenon. In the case of focus groups, participants can view materials made available to all members of the focus group and hear the running conversation. Also, streaming video and other dynamic features can be made available to the participants. All the interaction is recorded and analyzed using the techniques of data analysis for surveys and focus groups discussed in Chapter 7. It is also possible to use sound recording software to make digital voice files of interviews and voice recognition software to create print transcripts. Equipment such as web cams and microphones are sufficiently inexpensive today that it is affordable by many agencies or organizations that conduct evaluation research. In fact, one incentive to induce participation is to allow the respondents to keep the equipment at the termination of the research.

One of the main advantages of conducting such research online is to include people who are dispersed geographically at a reasonable expense and without asking them to travel great distances. If people can participate from their home or office, the response rate should be higher, because participants need to exert less effort to participate. Suppose, for example, that you wanted to conduct focus group interviews involving the directors of domestic violence programs from all parts of your state. It might be possible to get all those people together in one location, maybe at a state-wide conference for such program directors. In lieu of that, a researcher could conduct an online focus group that was relatively inexpensive and where most such directors participated. Online research might also be appealing to some members of hidden populations, such as some members of the GLBT community who may not wish their identity to become known.

The disadvantage of such online research is that the quality of the data may be different as compared to that from face-to-face interviews. Text-based focus groups especially may produce data of less depth, for example, because people's responses tend to be briefer when they type rather than speak, and there are fewer nonverbal cues that communicate important information. Even online surveys and focus groups using audio and/or video input may be different, because the quality of the equipment makes for poorer communication than when face-to-face.

not impossible—to find. Unpublished results may be presented at meetings of applied research organizations, such as the Association for Applied and Clinical Sociology, the NTL Institute for Applied Behavioral Science, and the National Association of Social Workers. In some cases, unpublished research reports can be obtained from the researchers themselves or from the organizations or agencies for which the research was done. Unpublished reports can be difficult to locate, because they often are not included in the databases that can be accessed online or through libraries to search for published research reports (see Appendix A). Some may be found through an Internet search or by participating in networks of professionals doing research in the same area.

Another change that increases the use of the evaluation results is to involve the potential users in the evaluation research itself. Users can help design the research or serve as interviewers. This results in better communication between evaluators and users: The users perceive the evaluation as being more relevant and credible, and they are more committed to the evaluation (Dawson & D'Amico, 1985).

What is really needed to improve research utilization is for policy makers and program administrators to develop an increased willingness to put evaluation results to use. In fact, resistance to research utilization does appear to be declining, and there may be a growing awareness that common sense and conventional wisdom are inadequate bases for designing and operating effective social programs (Rossi, Lipsey, & Freeman, 2004). Years of experience with ineffective programs have made this conclusion evident. Such changing perspectives are encouraging for the future of evaluation research and its increased utilization.

REVIEW AND CRITICAL THINKING

Main Points

- Evaluation research is the use of scientific research methods to plan intervention programs, to monitor the implementation of new programs and the operation of existing ones, and to determine how effectively programs or clinical practices achieve their goals.

- Formative evaluation focuses on the planning, development, and implementation of intervention programs.

- Summative evaluation assesses the effectiveness and efficiency of programs and the extent to which program effects may be generalized to other settings and populations.

- Prior to beginning evaluation, an evaluability assessment is conducted to gain knowledge about the program as operated and identify those aspects of it that can be evaluated.

- Proximate goals are evaluable, short-run goals logically related to the achievement of long-term goals that are impractical to evaluate.

- Despite frequent difficulties associated with their use, randomized experiments constitute the strongest, most desirable designs for assessing program impact.

- Cost–benefit analysis, through the use of complex assumptions and estimates, compares the costs of a program with the dollar value of its benefits.

- Cost–benefit analysis and cost-effective analysis are not interchangeable. Cost–benefit analysis is useful for evaluating a single program, whereas cost-effective analysis is useful for choosing the most efficient program from among competing approaches.

- It is important that bottom-line results from either cost–benefit or cost-effective analyses not be accepted blindly, but rather that the data, estimates, and assumptions on which the results are based be considered carefully.

Important Terms for Review

cost–benefit analysis
cost-effective analysis
direct costs
evaluability assessment
evaluation research
formative evaluation research
logic model
needs assessment
opportunity costs
stakeholders
summative evaluation research

Critical Thinking

This chapter emphasizes the importance of evaluating social policies and programs through systematic observation. If a program or practice has been around for some time, well-intentioned people may just assume that it works; or they may use some kind of casual or anecdotal evidence to support their assertion. Or people may have a vested interest in believing that some social practice has positive effects. But this can lead people to miss or ignore information that doesn't support their belief. To avoid these problems, consider the following in assessing social programs or practices:

1. What are the goals, both stated and unstated, of the program or practice?

2. Can you identify what might be called independent and dependent variables? How are these variables measured? Are they valid measures? Are there other ways to measure variables? Would these other measures change the conclusions?

3. If a systematic evaluation was done, what kind of research design was used? A randomized experimental design? If not, what procedures were used to enhance confidence in the conclusions?

Exploring the Internet

The Internet is an excellent vehicle for locating evaluation research projects in any human service field. For instance, if the field of substance abuse interests you, then we suggest that you go to the National Clearinghouse for Alcohol and Drug Information (NCADI) prevention database (http://www.health.org). The NCADI offers substance abuse information via searchable databases. Click on "Research," and then you can access each database by clicking on its button and using the search mode attached. You can research these databases for bibliographic abstracts pertaining to such subjects as alcohol, tobacco, marijuana, cocaine, and other drugs.

The National Criminal Justice Reference Service (https://www.ncjrs.gov) provides access not only to bibliographic references, but also to the full-text versions of a wide range of evaluation projects in criminal justice. By searching this site, you can review projects and learn about the actual methodology used to evaluate them. One of the pages associated with this site is devoted to evaluation grants (https://www.ncjrs.gov/fedgrant.html). Here, you can review grant application instructions.

We pointed out that evaluation research differs from basic research in the role of the decision makers in program evaluation. We suggest that you review the specifications for one of the program evaluation projects with an eye toward how the sponsoring organization's needs affect the design of the research project. The Bureau of Justice Assistance also maintains a website with many resources and links related to evaluating criminal justice programs (https://www.ojp.usdoj.gov/BJA).

One professional organization that many people in the field of evaluation research belong to is the American Evaluation Association, or AEA (http://www.eval.org). This international professional association of evaluators is devoted to the application and exploration of program evaluation, personnel evaluation, technology, and many other forms of evaluation. The AEA maintains a current listing of Internet sites of interest to program evaluators, so whether you are interested in health, education, or any other human service area, this site will help you locate additional resources.

For Further Reading

Boruch, R. (1996). *Randomized Experiments for Planning and Evaluation.* Thousand Oaks, Calif.: Sage. This author stresses the point made in this chapter that good program evaluations should be based on randomized experimental designs. The book is packed with useful examples of how to do this, often in situations where it might seem to be impossible.

Campbell, D. T., & Russo, M. J. (1999). *Social Experimentation.* Thousand Oaks, Calif.: Sage. Donald Campbell was one of the giants in the fields of experimentation and evaluation research. This book presents his approaches to how social experiments should be designed and how they can improve society.

Fitzpatrick, J. L., Sanders, J. R., & Worthen, B. R. (2010). *Program Evaluation: Alternative Approaches and Practical Guidelines,* 4th ed. Englewood Cliffs, N.J.: Prentice Hall. This text provides an overview of a wide variety of approaches to evaluation and extensive practical guidelines for carrying out evaluation studies.

Ginsberg, L. H. (2001). *Social Work Evaluation: Principles and Methods.* Boston: Allyn & Bacon. In addition to traditional methods of outcome evaluation, this source includes chapters on licensure, accreditation, internal program evaluation, and user satisfaction that make the book relevant to the human service practitioner.

Gupta, K., with Sleezer, C. M., & Russ-Eft, D. F. (2007). *A Practical Guide to Needs Assessment,* 2nd ed. New York: Wiley/Pfeiffer. This book provides an overview of needs assessment, step-by-step details for several models of needs assessment, and illustrations of various data-collection tools. It is especially useful for staff training program assessment.

Nas, T. F. (1996). *Cost–Benefit Analysis: Theory and Application.* Thousand Oaks, Calif.: Sage. The author shows, in much more detail than could be included in this chapter, how to conduct good cost–benefit analyses. The book covers all the relevant issues.

Patton, M. Q. (2002). *Qualitative Research and Evaluation Methods,* 3rd ed. Thousand Oaks, Calif.: Sage. This book considers both theoretical and practical issues in conducting program evaluations. It also emphasizes the use of qualitative research and stresses the perspective that good program evaluations must be designed to be useful to program managers and policy makers.

Shadish, W. R., Jr., Cook, T. D., & Leviton, L. C. (1993). *Foundations of Program Evaluation.* Newbury Park, Calif.: Sage. This volume looks at the origins of program evaluation and the accumulated experiences of veteran program evaluators to provide an insightful discussion regarding both the development of the field and key issues that are relevant today.

Class Exercises for Competency Assessment

It is commonly known that many elderly people have strong emotional attachments to their pets. Generally, however, the necessity of moving into a nursing home or a medical care facility entails severing that relationship. Recently, experts in gerontology have confirmed the important role that animals can play in making residents feel at home in residential facilities. Consequently, some facilities have begun experimenting with pet therapy, a program in which volunteers bring pets to the nursing home on a regular basis so that interested residents may pet and play with the animals.

Assume you are a human service worker with a nursing home and have been approached by some residents or staff about starting such a program. You are aware that some local foundation money may be available to support the project and some local organizations—the Humane Society, an area kennel club, a cat fanciers' group—probably could be enlisted to provide both the animals and volunteers to help with the project. You also know that to get the money, you have to convince the administration that the program is worth the trouble and show the foundation that you have a well-designed program that will be effective in meeting its goals.

12.1. **[Evidence-Based Evaluation] [Research & Practice]** To make a formal proposal for funding, you must first do some formative evaluation research to determine if the program is needed and, if so, feasible. What are some initial research questions to ask in this regard?

12.2. **[Evidence-Based Evaluation] [Research & Practice]** What kinds of data will you need, and how might you collect them?

12.3. **[Critical Thinking] [Diversity]** State some specific goals that such a program might be expected to achieve.

Assume that you have done some formative evaluation work and the facility administrator has given the go-ahead to apply for a grant for the project. The board was somewhat skeptical about the idea, however, so the compromise that resulted specifies that the program be tried for six months, at the end of which time a thorough evaluation must be done to determine the effects of the program and the relative costs and benefits.

12.4. **[Critical Thinking] [Research & Practice]** What are some possible effects that the program might have? Remember to look for both positive and negative impacts. How would you suggest measuring these potential effects?

12.5. **[Evidence-Based Evaluation] [Research & Practice]** For a cost–benefit analysis, make a list of both costs and benefits. For each list, make a column with headings for three different accounting perspectives—society, the nursing home residents, and the funding source. For each cost and each benefit you identify, place a plus (+) sign in the column if that party stands to benefit, a zero (0) if the impact is neutral, or a minus (−) if that party stands to have a net cost. (See Table 12.1 for an example.)

12.6. **[Critical Thinking] [Research & Practice]** Given the kinds of benefits that might result from such a program, which ones are applicable to cost accounting? Which ones are not readily translatable into dollars? All things considered, is a cost–benefit analysis appropriate for this project?

12.7. **[Critical Thinking] [Research & Practice]** The program as planned will be available to any resident in the facility who wants to participate. Thus, it is not possible to assign residents randomly to receive or not receive the program. Given this condition, what are some alternate ways of providing experimental control for the project? What potential validity problems do your suggestions pose?

Chapter 13

Scaling

Advantages of Scaling
Improved Validity
Improved Reliability
Increased Level of Measurement
Increased Efficiency in Data Handling

Developing Scales
Sources of Scale Items
Characteristics of Scale Items

Scaling Formats
Likert Scales
Thurstone Scales
Semantic Differential Scales
Guttman Scales

Multidimensional Scales

Avoiding Response Bias
Sources of Response Bias
Reducing Response Bias

Scaling in the Human Services

Review and Critical Thinking
Main Points
Important Terms for Review
Critical Thinking
Exploring the Internet
For Further Reading
Class Exercises for Competency Assessment

We discussed measurement in research at some length in Chapter 5 and explained that some measurement is fairly straightforward and involves the use of only a single *item,* or indicator, of a variable. We can, for example, measure a person's age with one question that asks how old the person is. Likewise, variables such as marital status or number of children in a family normally are measured with a single item. These variables refer to phenomena that are fairly unambiguous and for which a single indicator provides a valid and reliable measure.

Many other variables, however, are much more difficult and complex to measure. In some cases, we may have more than one indicator of a variable. In other cases, the variable may involve a number of dimensions and call for multiple indicators. In still other cases, we may be concerned with the *degree* to which a variable is present. In cases where a single-item measuring instrument is inadequate, we use a **scale**: a number of items that combine to form a composite score on a variable. To measure people's attitudes toward having children, for example, we could ask how much they agree with a series of questions; together, those questions make up the scale that would indicate their overall attitude toward having children.

ADVANTAGES OF SCALING

When the concept to be measured is complex, multiple-item scales offer substantial advantages for the researcher—advantages that often outweigh the difficulty of the scale's construction. Scales have four major advantages over single-item measures: improved validity, improved reliability, increased level of measurement, and increased efficiency in data handling.

Improved Validity

When measuring abstract or complex variables, generally a multiple-item measure is more valid than a single-item measure. Consider the variable of self-esteem: It is typically measured by asking people to respond to multiple statements (items) rather than just one or a few because no single question or statement could possibly measure something as complex, multifaceted, and subject to change as a person's self-esteem. There are many multiple-item scales that measure self-esteem, and Table 13.1 presents five examples of the kinds of statements found in such scales. What single question could we ask that might encompass all the feelings that we have about ourselves? Clearly, self-esteem involves many aspects of a person's life situation—family, occupation, financial and social status, to name only a few. Multiple-item scales provide more valid measures of such complex phenomena.

Improved Reliability

In general (as shown in Chapter 5), the more items a measure contains, the more reliable it is, because the statements making up a scale actually are just a sample of the entire universe of statements that could have been used. A single-item measure is a sample of one, and less likely to be *representative* of the universe of statements than more than one item is. Multiple-item scales are larger samples from this universe, and more likely to be representative, and therefore more reliable than single-item measures.

Increased Level of Measurement

Single-item measures are likely to produce data that are nominal or, at best, *partially ordered data,* a term that refers to data with a few ordered categories but with many cases tied for each category. Although superior to nominal data, partially ordered data are

TABLE 13.1   Examples of Items (Statements) that Might Appear on a Self-Esteem Scale

	Strongly Agree	Agree	Disagree	Strongly Disagree
(1) On the whole, I feel good about myself.	SA[4]	A[3]	D[2]	SD[1]
(2) I more often feel bad about myself than good.	SA[1]	A[2]	D[3]	SD[4]
(3) I have a number of good qualities.	SA[4]	A[3]	D[2]	SD[1]
(4) I feel that I am not a very good student.	SA[1]	A[2]	D[3]	SD[4]
(5) When I am working at my job, I feel that I'm a person of worth.	SA[4]	A[3]	D[2]	SD[1]

less desirable than fully ordered data, in which nearly every case has its own rank (see Chapter 14). Multiple-item scales can produce fully ordered and, possibly, interval-level data. A higher level of measurement means better measurement in terms of precision and increased flexibility in data analysis.

Increased Efficiency in Data Handling

Because the items in a scale are all related (in that they all measure the same variable), we can summarize the responses to these items into a single number or score for each respondent. This achieves the quantification goal of measurement, and means all the separate responses to each of the items do not have to be analyzed individually. Each score summarizes a great deal of information about each respondent and facilitates analysis of the data.

DEVELOPING SCALES

Once a researcher decides to use a scale as a measuring device, he or she needs to find or develop an appropriate scale. In most cases, scales consist of questions to which people respond or statements to which they indicate their level of agreement. (In Chapter 7, we presented guidelines for writing questions to be used in questionnaires or interviews, and those same general rules apply to the development or selection of scale items. Readers should review those guidelines now and consider them in the context of scale construction.)

In many cases, it is possible to use a complete scale already developed by someone else if that scale is a valid and reliable measure of the variables under investigation. A scale also can be made up of statements—or even whole sections—taken from previously developed scales. A major advantage of existing items or scales is that their validity and reliability usually have already been established. A few of the many compilations of measurement scales are listed in the *For Further Reading* section of this chapter. In addition, scales are reported and described in the many research journals dedicated to the behavioral sciences.

If no existing scale will do the job, a new scale should be developed (DeVellis, 2012). A certain logic is common to the development of scales, and it generally involves the following steps:

1. Develop or locate many potential scale items, far more than will appear in the final scale.
2. Eliminate items that are redundant, ambiguous, or, for some other reason, inappropriate for the scale.
3. Pretest the remaining items for validity, reliability, or other measurement checks to be described shortly.
4. Eliminate items that do not pass the tests of Step 3.
5. Repeat Steps 3 and 4 as often as necessary to reduce the scale to the number of items required.

Sources of Scale Items

One of the most accessible sources of scale items is a researcher's own imagination. Once the researcher has developed and refined a concept, he or she has a pretty good idea of what is to be measured, and then can generate a range of statements to satisfy the criteria to be discussed. At this early stage in scale construction, we need not be too concerned with honing and polishing the statements to perfection, because much pretesting remains before an actual respondent ever sees any statement.

A second source of scale items is a group of people, sometimes called *judges,* who are considered especially knowledgeable in a particular area. If we are seeking items for a delinquency scale, for instance, it is reasonable to discuss the issue with juvenile probation officers and others who have daily contact with delinquents.

Two social psychologists used this approach to find items for a scale to measure people's tendency to manipulate others for their own personal gain (Christie & Geis, 1970). They turned to the writings of Niccolò Machiavelli, a sixteenth-century advisor to the prince of Florence in Italy. In his classic book *The Prince,* Machiavelli propounded what is essentially a con artist's view of the world and politics: According to Machiavelli, people are to be manipulated, in a cool and unemotional fashion, for one's own benefit. Lying, cheating, and underhandedness are justified to advance one's own personal position. In the writings of this Florentine four centuries ago, these social psychologists found such statements as "It is safer to be feared than to be loved" and "Humility not only is of no service but is actually harmful." They constructed a scale made up of Machiavelli's statements, somewhat revised, and asked people whether they agreed with each statement. Now known as the Machiavellianism Scale, it has been used widely in scientific research. One is tempted to wonder whether Signore Machiavelli, were he able to peer through the mists of time, would consider this scale a sufficiently cunning and beguiling use of his prose. In any event, this illustrates a particularly creative use of judges in the development of scales.

A third source of scale items is the people who are the focus of the research project. Claudia Coulton (1979), for example, was interested in person–environment fit among consumers of hospital social services. In developing her scale, she obtained a large number of verbatim statements from hospital patients and then began to form them into a scale. In a similar manner, if we were interested in attitudes among teenagers toward unwanted pregnancies, an excellent beginning would be to discuss the topic with teenagers themselves and gather as many statements from them as possible regarding the issue. When items are garnered from people in this fashion, however, only rarely are their statements usable without editing. Many statements would ultimately be rejected, and most would have to be considerably rewritten. Still, such people are likely to provide a range of statements with meaning from the perspective of the group under investigation.

Characteristics of Scale Items

Once the researcher has amassed a large number of scale items, he or she must select the best ones for the final scale. Good scale items have several characteristics, including validity, range of variation, and unidimensionality.

Validity. A primary concern in item selection is the validity of the statements (see Chapter 5). Each statement considered for inclusion should be assessed for content validity. For example, if we are creating a self-report delinquency scale, then we assess each statement by how it relates to measuring delinquent activity. Statements concerning participation in delinquent acts are reasonable as valid measures of how delinquent that person is. On the other hand, an item relating to how well the respondent gets along with his or her siblings probably is not a valid indicator of delinquency.

Range of Variation. Variables that are measured with multiple-item scales normally consist of a number of possible values or positions that a person can take. If we want to measure attitudes toward growing old, for example, people's positions on that variable could be extremely positive, extremely negative, or anywhere in between. When selecting items for measurement scales, we should ensure that the items cover the actual range of possible variation on the variable being measured. Failure to do so results in a poor scale. When selecting items on the basis of variability, the researcher needs to exercise care to avoid defining the range either too narrowly or too broadly. Failure to include a sufficiently wide range of items results in responses that pile up at one or both ends of the scale's range. If many respondents tie with either the lowest or the highest possible score, then the range in the scale is inadequate. This piling-up effect reduces the precision of the measurement, because we are unable to differentiate among the respondents with tied scores.

Going to extremes with items to define the range is not desirable either. If we include items that are too extreme, then they apply to few—if any—respondents. In the case of a delinquency scale, for example, an item pertaining to engaging in cannibalism would be such an extreme item as to warrant exclusion: The act is so rare in our culture that it is unlikely any juvenile has done it; thus it contributes nothing of benefit to the scale. The goal is to select items with enough variation to cover the actual range of alternatives that people are likely to choose, but without including items so extreme that they do not apply to anyone.

Unidimensionality. In the construction of a multiple-item scale, the goal is to measure one specific variable. We do not want the results confounded by items on the scale that actually measure a different (although possibly related) variable. The items of a **unidimensional scale** measure only one variable. If a scale actually measures more than one variable, it is called a *multidimensional scale*. In creating our delinquency scale, we might be tempted to include an item about school performance on the grounds that delinquents seem to perform poorly in school. Although an empirical relationship may exist between delinquency and school performance, these are separate variables, and they should be treated and measured as such.

In assessing the unidimensionality of scales, we distinguish between *different variables* and *different aspects of the same variable*. A single variable may have more than one aspect, and we need to be careful to recognize these aspects so they can be measured appropriately. Delinquency, for example, contains at least two aspects: namely, severity and frequency. In terms of severity, it is reasonable to distinguish between an adolescent who commits petty theft and one who commits aggravated assault. In terms of frequency, an adolescent who regularly commits petty theft might be properly considered to be delinquent—or even more delinquent than one adolescent with a single case of assault.

The different aspects of a variable need to be distinguished and analyzed carefully, because one may correlate with an independent or a dependent variable, whereas another may not. This, again, suggests the complexity of some variables. In a study of person–environment fit, for example, Claudia Coulton (1979) distinguished between the many aspects that might be parts of this variable. "Person–environment fit" refers to the extent to which an individual's needs can be satisfied and his or her aspirations fulfilled in the context of the demands and opportunities available in a particular environment. Coulton distinguished between "fit" in relation to one's economic activities, "fit" in terms of the amount and relevance of available information, "fit" in terms of one's family relations, and the like. In this case, the person–environment fit scale is unidimensional in that it measures one underlying variable; but it also contains a number of distinct aspects that are a part of that variable.

To gain systematic evidence for the unidimensionality of a scale, the researcher can intercorrelate each item in the scale with every other item in the scale, usually during a pretest. If some items do not correlate with the others, it is possible that they do not measure the same variable, or they are separate aspects of the variable and vary independently of one another. If we suspect these items measure a different variable we should eliminate them from the scale. If we find a few items that have nearly perfect correlations, we only need to use one of them in the scale. Two items to which people respond identically are simply redundant; using both adds nothing to the measurement abilities of the scale. Occasionally, however, highly correlated items should be included to detect response inconsistency or random answering. That exception notwithstanding, the final scale should be composed of statements that correlate fairly highly—but not perfectly—with one another.

Knowledge of the characteristics and sources of scale items provides an important and necessary foundation for the development of scales. By themselves, however, these offer only a general guide to scale development. The more complex intricacies of developing scales are best grasped by looking at specific types of scales and illustrations of how they were developed. Moreover, some types of scales have unique requirements not adequately covered by our previous discussion. We turn, then, to a discussion of the most important types of scales used in human service research.

SCALING FORMATS

Scaling can utilize a number of formats, and each format calls for some unique design elements.

Likert Scales

Rensis Likert (1932) developed one of the most popular approaches to scaling. A **Likert scale** consists of a series of statements, with each statement followed by a number of ordered response alternatives. An illustration of a Likert scale is presented in Table 13.1, with response alternatives ranging from "strongly agree" at one end of the scale to "strongly disagree" at the other end. Other Likert scales might have different response alternatives (such as "very satisfied" to "very dissatisfied," or "excellent" to "poor") depending on the statement that is used to measure a variable. Five is the most common number of alternatives, because it offers respondents a sufficient range of choices without requiring unnecessarily minute distinctions in attitudes. Sometimes, however, more or fewer than five alternatives are used. Notice in Table 13.1 the numbers ranging from 1 to 4 in brackets next to each response alternative. These numbers are included here for purposes of illustration only. They would not be printed on a scale for actual use, because their presence might influence the respondents' answers. These numbers are used when scoring the scale. The numbers associated with each response are totaled to provide the overall score for each respondent. If our self-esteem scale contained 10 items, then individual scores can range from a low of 10 (if the alternative with the bracketed "1" after it were chosen each time) to a high of 40 (if the alternative with the bracketed "4" after it were chosen every time). The Likert scale is one example of a **summated rating scale**, in which a person's score is determined by summing the number of questions answered in a particular way. Summated rating scales can take a number of different forms, although the Likert format is the most common.

Note that (as discussed in Chapter 5) each item in a Likert scale is an ordinal measure because the response alternatives have a fixed order, but not necessarily equal spacing between the alternatives. Because the total score of a Likert scale is the sum of individual, ordinal items, many researchers contend that a Likert scale is ordinal in nature. Technically, one should refrain from using such statistics as the mean and standard deviation with ordinal-level data. However, it is common, especially with well-established Likert scales, to see published studies in which scores are treated as if they were interval level. Whether this application of interval procedures is appropriate is a debated topic among researchers and cannot be resolved here.

As with all scales, constructing a Likert scale requires considerable time and effort. The researcher begins by developing a series of statements relating to the variable being measured. The general criteria for such statements, as outlined previously, should be carefully considered during this stage. No matter how diligent we are in following those guidelines, however, some of the statements turn out to be inadequate for a variety of reasons. Because we anticipate having to drop some unacceptable items, we should initially write substantially more statements than we plan to include in the final scale. A common rule of thumb is to start with three times the number of statements desired for the final scale.

A final criterion in deciding which items ultimately to use in a Likert scale is whether the scale items *discriminate* among people. In other words, we want the responses to an item to range over the four or five alternatives rather than bunch up on one or two choices. Imagine a scale with an item that reads, "People convicted of shoplifting should have their hands amputated." If such an item were submitted to a group of college students in the United States, it is likely that most would respond with "strongly disagree," and maybe a few with "disagree." It is highly unlikely that any would agree. So of what use is this item to us? We cannot *compare* people—that is, assess who is more likely to agree or disagree—because they all disagree. And we cannot correlate responses to this item with the social or psychological characteristics of the

> **RESEARCH IN PRACTICE 13.1** **Program Evaluation: Developing a Scale to Measure Intimate Justice**
>
> Quantifying intimate partner violence has been a challenge for researchers and human service practitioners alike. Instruments such as the Conflict Tactics Scale frame the problem in terms of conflict resolution and ask respondents to estimate the frequency of behaviors such as hits, slaps, and shoves. But experts and those on the receiving end of violence argue that counting events does not capture the emotional pain and underlying meaning of violence for the victim. Family therapist Brian Jory and colleagues made an effort to fill this gap by developing the Intimate Justice Scale (Jory, 2004). The IJS measures ethical dynamics of couple relationships that are evident in patterns of action and attitude expressed over the course of the relationship. How this scale was developed illustrates many features of good scale development presented in this chapter.
>
> The scale is based on a human service practice theory, in this case what Jory calls "intimate justice theory," which is about the ethical dynamics of close relationships. Intimate justice requires that a relationship be based on:
>
> 1. *Equality.* Treating others with respect, making oneself accountable to others, and supporting the freedom of others to make choices.
> 2. *Fairness.* Avoiding deception, reciprocity in work and stress of daily living, and accommodation to others and their limitations.
> 3. *Care.* Empathy for the needs of others, nurturing the strengths of others, and attachment based on responsibility, not exploitation.
>
> Intimate justice concerns how partners use power in relationships—either for beneficent or exploitive motives. Some scale items ask respondents about the ethical beliefs of their partners, regardless of whether the belief is acted upon. For example, one item asks respondents to agree or disagree with "My partner believes he or she has the right to force me to do things." The scale developers argue that believing in force is an effective weapon of domination even if physical force is not used. Other items ask about the impact of a partner's actions regardless of a partner's intentions. For example: "Sometimes my partner physically hurts me." Such items emphasize that unwanted or aggressive physical contact hurts, whether the act was intentional or not.
>
> The development of items for the Intimate Justice Scale was a multistage process.
>
> 1. Thirty abusive men and their female partners were interviewed individually for about two hours each. The interviews elicited ideas from victims about intimate justice with questions such as: "Do you think that your partner feels accountable to

students, because there is little or no variation in responses to the item.

We want, then, to eliminate nondiscriminating items from consideration for our scale. *Nondiscriminating items* are those that are responded to in a similar fashion by both people who score high and those who score low on the overall scale. Nondiscriminating items in a scale can be detected on the basis of results from a pretest in which people respond to all the preliminary items of the scale.

TABLE 13.2 Calculation of Discriminatory Power Score for One Item in a Scale

Quartile	N	1	2	3	4	5	Weighted Total	Weighted Mean	DP Score
Upper	10	0	1	2	4	3	39	3.90	
Lower	10	2	8	0	0	0	18	1.80	2.10
								2.10	

Response Value column headers span 1–5.

you, and in what ways?" Men were asked: "What if something strange happened and you were suddenly forced to switch places with your partner? Knowing how you treat her, would you still want to be in this relationship?" Analysis of these interviews generated 48 questions. These questions were then presented to members of a therapy group of 8 to 10 women who provided feedback on the items.

2. The questions were then presented to 54 marriage and family therapists, all of whom had considerable practice experience with intimate partner violence clients. The therapists rated each item on its perceived predictive value for physical violence and its value as an indicator of psychological abuse. The therapists recommended modifications to existing items and suggested additional items. As a result, 36 original items were retained, and four new ones were added.

3. Next, with the help of cooperating therapists, the 40 items were administered, along with the Conflict Tactics Scale and the Dyadic Adjustment Scale, to a sample of women who were involved in heterosexual relationships of at least one year's duration and who were receiving mental health treatment for any presenting problem, including but not limited to intimate partner violence. A statistical technique called factor analysis was used to select unidimensional items. Jory and his colleagues then eliminated redundant items and settled on 15 items that appeared relevant to a wide array of potential clients.

4. Finally, the researchers assessed the IJS for internal-consistency reliability and for validity (see Chapter 5). For example, the IJS results were shown to correlate positively with the Conflict Tactics Scale (which measures violence) and negatively with the Dyadic Adjustment Scale (which measures marital happiness). The developers also showed that the IJS differentiated between women who had experienced no violence, minor violence, and severe violence, according to the Conflict Tactics Scale.

The net result of all this scale development is a brief, quickly scored, 15-item instrument that can be used as a screening tool for human service practitioners or by researchers to measure an important but covert aspect of domestic violence—intimate partner justice.

One way to identify nondiscriminating items is to compute a **discriminatory power score** (or DP score) for each item. The DP score essentially tells us the degree to which each item differentiates between respondents with high scores and respondents with low scores on the overall scale. Although this approach is used less in actual practice today, because of the availability of other, more complex procedures that depend on computer support, it is a straightforward technique that illustrates well the principles of item selection.

The first step in obtaining DP scores is to calculate the total scores of each respondent and then rank those scores from the highest to the lowest. Next, we identify the upper and lower quartiles of the distribution of total scores. The *upper quartile* (Q_3) is the cutoff point in a distribution above which the highest 25 percent of the scores are located, and the *lower quartile* (Q_1) is the cutoff point below which the lowest 25 percent of the scores are located. With the quartiles based on total scores identified, we compare the pattern of responses to each scale item for respondents whose scores fall above the upper quartile with the pattern for respondents whose scores fall below the lower quartile. Table 13.2 illustrates the computation of DP scores for one item in a scale to which 40 people responded. Ten respondents are above the upper quartile, and 10 are below the lower quartile. We see that those with high scores tended to agree with this item, because most had scores of 4 or 5. Those with low scores tended to disagree, because they are totally concentrated in the 1 and 2 score range. The next step is to compute a weighted total on this item for the two groups, multiplying each score by the number of respondents with that score.

For example, for those above the upper quartile, the weighted total is:

$$(1 \times 0) + (2 \times 1) + (3 \times 2) + (4 \times 4) + (5 \times 3)$$
$$= 0 + 2 + 6 + 16 + 15 = 39$$

Next, we compute the weighted mean (average) by dividing the weighted total by the number of cases in the quartile. For the upper quartile, we have 39 ÷ 10= 3.9. We then obtain the DP score for this item by subtracting the mean of those below the lower quartile from the mean of those above the upper quartile. In this example, we have 3.9-1.8 = 2.1. This process is repeated for every item in the preliminary scale so that each item has a calculated DP score. (Statistical and spreadsheet software can be readily programmed to accomplish this task.)

Once we have DP scores for all the preliminary items, the final selection can begin. The best items are those with the *highest* DP scores, because this shows that people in the upper and lower quartiles responded to the items very differently. As a rule of thumb, as many items as possible should have DP scores of 1.00 or higher; and few—if any—should drop below 0.50. Applying this rule to the item in Table 13.2, we would conclude that it is a very good item and include it in the final scale.

Occasionally, researchers encounter DP scores with negative signs. Under no circumstances should an item with a negative DP score be included, because this means that those with high scores on the overall scale scored lower on this item than those with low scores did. If the size of the negative DP score is small, then it probably is an ambiguous statement that is being variously interpreted by respondents. If the negative DP score is large, however, then it is possible that the item was accidentally scored incorrectly—that is, a negative item was scored as if it were positive, or vice versa.

Many computer software packages have procedures for item analysis that rely on principles other than DP scores but accomplish largely the same task. For example, the statistical package SPSS includes the procedure Reliability Analysis, which performs an item analysis on the components of additive scales by computing coefficients of reliability. These coefficients show how each item correlates with every other item and with the overall scale. In addition, SPSS provides the reliability coefficient Cronbach's alpha (see Chapter 5) for the proposed scale. Using procedures such as these, the researcher can exclude from the scale those items that detract from or contribute little to the overall reliability of the instrument.

The Likert scale is one of the most popular multiple-item scales because of the many advantages it possesses. First, it offers respondents a range of choices rather than the limited yes/no alternatives of other scales. This makes Likert scales valuable if the theoretical assessment of a variable is such that it ranges along a continuum rather than being either present or absent. Second, data produced by Likert scales are considered to be ordinal level, which enables us to use more powerful statistical procedures than we can do with nominal-level data. Third, Likert scales are fairly straightforward to construct.

Although its advantages make the Likert scale one of the most widely used attitude scales, the Likert scale has the same disadvantages as many other scales. In particular, we must be careful in interpreting a single score based on a Likert scale, because it is a summary of so much information (separate responses to a number of items). Whenever we summarize data, we lose some information. (A grade in a college course is a summary measure of a student's performance, and, in calculating it, the instructor loses information regarding high—or low—scores on individual exams.) The summary score might hide information about patterns of variation in responses or about possible multidimensionality of the scale.

Research in Practice 13.1 discusses the development of a Likert scale for research in human service practice settings.

Thurstone Scales

L. L. Thurstone and E. J. Chave (1929) developed another approach to scaling. **Thurstone scales** are constructed such that they use *equal-appearing intervals*—that is, it is assumed that the distance between any two adjacent points on the scale is the same. This provides data of interval-level quality and enables us to use all the powerful statistical procedures that require interval-level data (see Chapter 5).

Construction of a Thurstone scale begins in much the same way as construction of a Likert scale—namely, with the selection of many statements that relate to the variable being measured. Once a sufficient number of statements is at hand, the next step is to provide a value between 1 and 11 for each statement. Figure 13.1 illustrates the Thurstone scale pattern ranging from 1 (the most favorable statement regarding an object, event, or issue) to 11 (the most unfavorable). Scale items, however, may be arranged positively (high scores represent a favorable attitude) or negatively (high scores indicate an unfavorable attitude). Point 6 on the scale is called "neutral" and is used for statements that are neither favorable nor unfavorable. For example, the statement "teenage girls who get pregnant are immoral" would be considered very unfavorable toward teenage pregnancies.

The task of rating each statement as to how favorable or unfavorable it is with regard to the measured variable is, again, assigned to judges. With each of the preliminary statements printed on a separate card, the judges rate the items by placing them in piles corresponding to points on the 11-point scale. The judges place in each pile statements they assess to be roughly equivalent in terms of their favorableness. All the judges will not agree on the exact rating of statements, of course, so the scale value of a particular Thurstone item is determined by using the median of the judges' ratings. The scale values derived by this process are displayed in the first column of Table 13.3.

Once the scale values are computed for all the preliminary items, the next step is to determine the items that are the least ambiguous, and therefore best for inclusion in the final scale. If the judges differed widely in their ratings on an item, something likely is unclear about the statement itself, leading to varying interpretations. So the degree of agreement among judges about the rating of an item is one indicator of ambiguity.

Scales should include the items with the most agreement among judges, and there should be a roughly equal number of items for each of the 11 scale values, ranging from unfavorable to favorable, moving upward in half-point increments. This requires a minimum of 21 items, although some argue that if reliability of .90 or better is desired, then as many as 50 statements may be needed (Seiler & Hough, 1970). Regardless of the number actually used, the last step in construction of a Thurstone scale is to order the items randomly for presentation to respondents.

Table 13.3 presents the first 13 statements contained in the original 45-item scale developed by Thurstone and Chave (1929), with the scale value of each item indicated in parentheses. This particular scale is designed so that items with high scale values are "unfavorable," and items with low scale values are "favorable" toward the church. The scale values would not, of course, be included on a working version of the scale, and are presented here for purposes of illustration. Note that respondents are required only to check the statements with which they agree, which makes the Thurstone format particularly easy for respondents.

Scoring a Thurstone scale is different from the simple summation procedure used with Likert scales. Because respondents agree to differing numbers of statements with different values, the simple sum of the item values is worthless. Rather, a respondent's score is either the mean or median of the scale values of the items that the person agrees with. For example, if a person agreed with

FIGURE 13.1 Equal-Appearing Intervals as Used in Thurstone Scale Construction

TABLE 13.3 Attitude toward Church Scale

Check (✓) every statement below that expresses your sentiment toward the church. Interpret the statements in accordance with your own experience with churches.

(8.3)*	1. I think the teaching of the church is altogether too superficial to have much social significance.
(1.7)	2. I feel the church services give me inspiration and help me to live up to my best during the following week.
(2.6)	3. I think the church keeps business and politics up to a higher standard than they would otherwise tend to maintain.
(2.3)	4. I find the services of the church both restful and inspiring.
(4.0)	5. When I go to church, I enjoy a fine ritual service with good music.
(4.5)	6. I believe in what the church teaches but with mental reservations.
(5.7)	7. I do not receive any benefit from attending church services, but I think it helps some people.
(5.4)	8. I believe in religion, but I seldom go to church.
(4.7)	9. I am careless about religion and church relationships, but I would not like to see my attitude become general.
(10.5)	10. I regard the church as a static, crystallized institution, and as such it is unwholesome and detrimental to society and the individual.
(1.5)	11. I believe church membership is almost essential to living life at its best.
(3.1)	12. I do not understand the dogmas or creeds of the church, but I find that the church helps me to be more honest and creditable.
(8.2)	13. The paternal and benevolent attitude of the church is quite distasteful to me.

*Scale value

SOURCE: Thurstone, L. L. & Chave, E. J. (1929). *The Measurement of Attitude*. Chicago: University of Chicago Press. Produced by permission of the University of Chicago Press.

statements 2, 4, 8, and 12 in Table 13.3, that person's Thurstone scale score would be 3.13. Another person choosing 1, 7, 10, and 13 would have a score of 8.18. This scoring procedure distributes respondents along the original 11-point scale.

Thurstone and Likert scaling techniques are essentially interchangeable methods of measuring attitudes. A major advantage of the Thurstone technique is that it provides interval-level data. If the interval-data properties are not needed, the Likert technique probably is preferable because of its higher reliability with fewer items and its reputed greater ease of construction. A second advantage of Thurstone scales is that people can respond to the items more quickly than with a Likert scale, because they need only indicate whether they agree with an item and need not ponder how much they agree or disagree. Because reliability calls for Thurstone scales to be longer, this advantage may be minimal, and, if the longer scale leads people to be overly quick or careless in responding to statements, can even become a disadvantage. Another major disadvantage of Thurstone scales is that they are costly and difficult to construct; however, modern data-processing techniques have substantially reduced the construction time (Seiler & Hough, 1970).

Semantic Differential Scales

Another scaling format that has proved to be quite popular is the *semantic differential* (SD) developed by Osgood, Suci, and Tannenbaum (1957). The **semantic differential** format presents the respondent with a stimulus, such as a person or event, to be rated on a scale between a series of polar

TABLE 13.4 An Example of the Format of a Semantic Differential Scale

Directions: Look at Picture 1 and circle the number at the point between each of the following adjective pairs that best represents your impression of the person in the picture.

Pleasant	1	2	3	4	5	6	7	Unpleasant
Warm	1	2	3	4	5	6	7	Cold
Unselfish	1	2	3	4	5	6	7	Selfish
Calm	1	2	3	4	5	6	7	Aggressive
Genuine	1	2	3	4	5	6	7	False

opposite adjectives. Normally, the scale has seven points, but it can have more or fewer if theoretical or methodological considerations call for it.

To illustrate a semantic differential scale, suppose a researcher were investigating how gender affected people's perceptions of police officers. A sample of people could be shown pictures of police officers—in some cases a male officer and in other cases a female officer. Their perceptions of the officers might be measured with a scale including items such as in Table 13.4. They would be told to choose the point between each adjective pair that best represents their assessment of the officer. The adjective pairs are selected based on some theory about which characteristics of officers might be relevant. So on the first line, circling the "6" means that you view the person as quite unpleasant; circling the "1" is an assessment of quite pleasant. In this example, all the positive adjectives are on the left and all the negative adjectives on the right. Sometimes, however, the positive responses to some adjectives are put on the right to discourage uninterested respondents from placing all their responses in the same column. If we found respondents who had done so, we would probably discard their data, because they obviously had not marked the scale seriously.

Based on their research with the SD, Osgood and colleagues have suggested that, depending on the sets of adjectives used, three different dimensions of a concept can be measured: evaluation, potency, and activity. Semantic differentials can be designed to measure any one—or all three—of these dimensions. The measure illustrated in Table 13.4 contains adjectives relating to all these dimensions.

One major problem in constructing an SD is the selection of relevant adjectives for rating a given concept. For example, the adjective pair "alive–dead" is not relevant to an SD rating self-concept. If the researcher is uncertain about the relevance of a set of adjectives, it is possible to supply the adjectives to a group of subjects and have the subjects rank-order them according to their relevance to the concept being rated. The researcher would then use the pairs of adjectives ranked highest by the subjects (Mitsos, 1961).

A second problem with SDs is determining which of the three dimensions a given pair of adjectives is measuring. Generally, intuition is not reliable for making this determination (Heise, 1970). Accurate identification of the dimension measured by a given adjective pair can be accomplished through the use of a rather complex statistical procedure called *factor analysis,* which correlates each variable with every other variable. Its use in SD construction is to indicate which of the three dimensions correlates most highly with a given set of adjectives, and hence which dimension is being tapped by those adjectives.

Many SDs are set up like the one in Table 13.4, with only the ends of the scale labeled with the adjectives. Some scales, however, employ such adverbs as "extremely," "quite," and "slightly" at appropriate points between the adjectives. One study found that the use of adverbs improved the quality of responses to SD scales (Wells & Smith, 1960). In light of these findings, it appears advisable to include adverbs when constructing SDs.

Scoring an SD can be done in a variety of ways, depending on the researcher's needs. One way is to treat the response to each adjective pair separately. This procedure is not common, however, because usually we want a summary score for each respondent. To accomplish this, responses on the adjective pairs that constitute each dimension can be summed to provide an overall score on each of the dimensions measured—another variant of the summated ratings scale.

Semantic differentials have several advantages in comparison with both the Likert and Thurstone formats. Unlike the other scaling techniques that require 20 or more items for adequate reliability, SDs require only four to eight adjective pairs for each dimension to reach reliabilities of .80 or better. Approximately 10 adjective pairs often are used to ensure adequate validity. This brevity means many concepts can be rated by respondents in a reasonable amount of time. In addition, because an SD is fairly easy to respond to, people can be expected to make at least 25 judgments in 15 minutes (Heise, 1970; Miller & Salkind 2002). Another advantage is that SDs are much easier and less time-consuming to construct than either a Likert or a Thurstone scale. Adjective pairs are easier to develop than unambiguous and unbiased statements about an issue. In addition, adjective pairs from prior studies are more readily adaptable to other studies because of the general and nonspecific nature of the adjectives. This is particularly important if a measuring scale is needed quickly. For example, if we wanted people's reactions to some unanticipated event, time would be of the essence. We would have to get their reactions while the event was still fresh in their minds. Only an SD-type scale could be readied in time.

About the only disadvantage of an SD is that, as with Likert scales, SDs generate ordinal data. If interval data are desired, a Thurstone scale is preferable.

Guttman Scales

Researchers make efforts to create scales that are unidimensional—that is, scales that measure a single variable or a single aspect of a variable. With a **Guttman scale**, the procedures used in the construction of the scale help ensure that the resulting scale will truly be unidimensional (Guttman, 1944).

Researchers using Guttman scaling achieve unidimensionality by developing the items in such a way that a perfect Guttman scale has only one pattern of response that will yield any given score on the scale. For example, if an individual's score is 5, then we expect that he or she agreed with the first five items on the scale. This contrasts with other scaling techniques that allow obtaining the same score by agreeing or disagreeing with any number of items and having completely different response patterns. Guttman scaling is able to do this because the items in the scale have an inherently progressive order, usually relating to the intensity of the variable being measured. The least intense items are referred to as "easy," because more people are likely to agree with them. The most intense items are referred to as "hard," because fewer people are expected to agree with them. If a person agrees with a certain item, then we also would expect him or her to agree with all the less-intense items; conversely, if a person disagrees with a particular item, we also would expect that person to disagree with all the more-intense items.

Table 13.5 illustrates a Guttman scale designed to measure attitudes toward gun control. The items are arranged with the "easiest" first and the "hardest" last. Often, only two response categories, either "agree" and "disagree," or "yes" and "no," are provided. Some Guttman scales, however, make use of the Likert-type response categories, as does the scale in Table 13.5. Because these categories are collapsed to a dichotomy at a later point in working with the scale, little is gained by their inclusion other than allowing the respondents greater freedom of expression.

The fact that the items in a Guttman scale are progressive and cumulative leads to the basic means of assessing whether a set of items constitutes a Guttman scale. This criterion is called *reproducibility*, or the ability of the total score of all respondents to reproduce the pattern of the responses to the scale items of each individual. For example, all persons with scores of 2 will have agreed with the two

TABLE 13.5 A Guttman Scale Measuring Attitudes toward Handgun Control

Do Not Favor or No Opinion	Strongly Favor or Somewhat Favor	Here are some proposals that have been made for controlling handgun violence. Would you please tell us how you feel about each of these proposals?
0	1	1. Institute a waiting period before a handgun can be purchased, to allow for a criminal record check.
0	1	2. Require all persons to obtain a police permit before being allowed to purchase a handgun.
0	1	3. Require a license for all persons carrying a handgun outside their homes or place of business (except for law enforcement agents).
0	1	4. Require a mandatory fine for all persons carrying a handgun outside their homes or places of business without a license.
0	1	5. Require a mandatory jail term for all persons carrying a handgun outside their homes or places of business without a license.
0	1	6. Ban the future manufacture and sale of nonsporting-type handguns.
0	1	7. Ban the future manufacture and sale of all handguns.
0	1	8. Use public funds to buy back and destroy existing handguns on a voluntary basis.
0	1	9. Use public funds to buy back and destroy existing handguns on a mandatory basis.

NOTE: The response alternatives in this study were "strongly favor," "somewhat favor," "do not favor," "no opinion," and "no response." They were collapsed into two categories for Guttman analysis: 1 = strongly favor or somewhat favor; 0 = do not favor or no opinion.

Guttman Scale Pattern

% Favoring	Item	0	1	2	3	4	5	6	7	8	9
87%	1. Waiting period	no	yes	yes	yes	yes	yes	yes	yes	yes	yes
61	2. Permit to purchase	no	no	yes	yes	yes	yes	yes	yes	yes	yes
72	3. License to carry	no	no	no	yes	yes	yes	yes	yes	yes	yes
66	4. Mandatory fine for no license	no	no	no	no	yes	yes	yes	yes	yes	yes
52	5. Mandatory jail term for no license	no	no	no	no	no	yes	yes	yes	yes	yes
40	6. Ban nonsporting manufacture/sale	no	no	no	no	no	no	yes	yes	yes	yes
23	7. Ban all handgun manufacture/sale	no	no	no	no	no	no	no	yes	yes	yes
19	8. Voluntary buy-back	no	no	no	no	no	no	no	no	yes	yes
17	9. Mandatory buy-back	no	no	no	no	no	no	no	no	no	yes
N = 1442	Coefficient of Reproducibility: .915										

SOURCE: Reprinted from *Journal of Criminal Justice*, Vol. 13, Raymond H. C. Teske Jr. & Michael H. Hazlett, "A Scale for the Measurement of Attitudes Toward Handgun Control," pp. 373-379. Copyright 1985, with permission from Elsevier.

"easiest" items and disagreed with the rest; persons with scores of 3 will have agreed with the three "easiest" items and disagreed with the rest, and so on. In a perfect Guttman scale, each respondent's score reproduces one of these patterns, as illustrated in Table 13.5. There is always one more perfect response pattern—namely, zero agreements—in a Guttman scale than there are items in the scale;

therefore, the nine-item scale in Table 13.5 would have 10 possible response patterns. In actual practice, perfect Guttman scales are virtually nonexistent; usually, some respondents do deviate from the expected pattern. Nevertheless, Guttman scales with high levels of reproducibility have been developed.

Constructing a Guttman scale is difficult and risky (to a certain extent), because we do not know whether the scale we have devised has sufficient reproducibility to qualify as a Guttman scale until after we apply it to a sample of respondents. As with the other scaling techniques, to create and select items for inclusion in the scale is a basic first step. In Guttman scaling, this task is further complicated by the need for those items eventually selected to have the characteristic of progression.

The procedure for selecting items for a Guttman scale is known as the *scale discrimination technique* (Edwards & Kilpatrick, 1948). As with both Likert and Thurstone scaling techniques, we begin by writing a large number of statements that relate to the variable to be measured. These statements are then rated by a group of judges along the 11-point Thurstone equal-appearing interval scale. Scale values and interquartile ranges (upper quartile minus lower quartile or $Q_3 - Q_1$) of the judges' ratings are obtained for each item. Half of the items with the lowest interquartile ranges are kept, and the remainder discarded. The items on which judges were in the greatest agreement are given a Likert-type response format and presented to a pretest group. The pretest results are used to calculate DP scores as described earlier for Likert scaling. Items for inclusion in the final Guttman scale are selected so that they cover the full Thurstone scale range and have the highest DP scores. Despite the effort involved in this approach, all it accomplishes is to increase the likelihood that the selected items will have sufficient reproducibility to constitute a Guttman scale; it does not guarantee reproducibility.

The only way to determine if we have succeeded in developing a true Guttman scale is to administer it to another pretest group and see if it has adequate reproducibility (Dotson & Summers, 1970). Table 13.6 illustrates the most common way of assessing the reproducibility of items. For the sake of simplicity, the illustrated scale contains only four items and data from only 20 subjects. As can be seen from the table, subjects are arrayed according to their total score for the four statements, from the highest (4) to the lowest (0). Subjects' responses to each statement are indicated by an X under either "1" or "0," corresponding to an "agree" or a "disagree" response, respectively. The statements are arranged from left to right from "hardest" (most disagreements) to "easiest" (most agreements). The lines drawn across each of the statement columns are called *cutting points* and indicate where the pattern of responses tends to shift from agree to disagree. The position of the cutting points must be determined carefully, because these points form the basis from which error responses are counted. Any "1" (agree) responses below the cutting points and any "0" (disagree) responses above the cutting points constitute error responses. Cutting points are drawn at positions that minimize the number of error responses. Inspection of the cutting points in Table 13.6 reveals that locating them in any other position does not reduce the number of error responses.

With the cutting points established, tabulation of error responses is straightforward. In the example under Statement 1 are three "1" responses below the cutting point with no "0" responses above it. Note that in the row marked "Error," these responses are tabulated as 3 and 0, respectively. The same counting procedure was followed for the other statements. As Table 13.6 illustrates, the error responses for individual statements are summed to indicate the total number of error responses. Tabulating error responses for a longer scale by hand is exceedingly tedious, but computer software, such as the SAS package, can assess the reproducibility of even a long scale quite rapidly.

The total number of errors is used in the following simple formula to calculate the coefficient of reproducibility (R_c):

$$R_c = 1 - \frac{\text{number of errors}}{(\text{number of items}) \times (\text{number of subjects})}$$

Inserting the values from Table 13.6. we have

TABLE 13.6   Example of Error Computation for a Guttman Scale

	Statements								
	1		2		3		4		
Subjects	1	0	1	0	1	0	1	0	Scores
1	x		x		x		x		4
2	x			x	x		x		3
3	x			x	x		x		3
4		x	x		x		x		3
5		x	x		x		x		3
6		x	x		x		x		3
7		x	x		x		x		3
8		x	x		x		x		3
9		x		x	x		x		2
10	x			x		x	x		2
11		x		x	x		x		2
12		x		x	x		x		2
13	x			x		x	x		2
14		x	x			x	x		2
15	x			x		x		x	1
16		x		x		x	x		1
17		x		x	x			x	1
18		x	x			x		x	1
19		x		x		x	x		1
20		x		x		x		x	0
Frequency	6	14	8	12	12	8	16	4	
Error	3	0	2	2	1	1	2	0	e = 11

$$R_c = 1 - \frac{11}{(4)(20)} = 1 - .14 = .86$$

Guttman (1950) suggested that a coefficient of reproducibility of .90 is the minimum acceptable for a scale to qualify as a Guttman scale. According to this criterion, our example does not qualify. Scales with reproducibility coefficients of somewhat less than .90, however, have given satisfactory results. In general, the more items in a Guttman scale, the more difficult it is to achieve a high level of reproducibility. For a very short scale, .90 would be the minimum acceptable coefficient of reproducibility; with a longer scale, the minimum reproducibility level can be adjusted downward slightly.

Suppose we develop a scale of 11 items, submit it to a pretest group, determine the reproducibility coefficient, and find it to be too low. The game is not over because of this initial failure. It is perfectly legitimate to rearrange the order of the items or drop items to achieve the necessary reproducibility. We might, for example, drop three or four of the items containing the most error responses, leaving a

> **EYE ON ETHICS**   **Revictimizing Victims through Research**
>
> Experiencing physical abuse or sexual assault at the hands of a parent or spouse is traumatic in its own right; so what happens when researchers interview the survivors of such horrific acts? The Conflict Tactics Scale asks research participants to acknowledge if they have ever been kicked, bitten, or hit with a fist; threatened with a knife or gun; burned or scalded on purpose; or caused to pass out (Straus et al., 1996). Does requiring participants to respond to such scales in a research context result in more distress for a victim? Furthermore, some argue that the victim of violence may not be able to sufficiently predict the degree of impact that the research will have, thus making it difficult to truly give informed consent.
>
> A team of researchers sought to directly address these ethical issues (Griffin et al., 2003). They examined participant reactions to different trauma assessment procedures in domestic violence, rape, and physical assault samples. Scales included in the interview process included the Clinician-Administered PTSD Scale for the acute physical/sexual assault sample and the Conflict Tactics Scale for the domestic violence sample. Following completion of the research interview about victimization experience, participants evaluated their distress levels. Results indicated that participation was very well tolerated by the vast majority of the trauma survivors. Only 5 percent indicated that they would not be willing to go through such an experience again. Participants generally found that the assessment experience was not distressing and was, in fact, viewed as an interesting and valuable experience. The researchers concluded that trauma survivors are not too fragile to participate in trauma research, even in the acute aftermath of a traumatic experience.

seven- or eight-item scale with adequate reproducibility to qualify as a Guttman scale.

It is important to note that a given Guttman scale may be group specific. This means that if we achieve adequate reproducibility with a given set of items with one sample of respondents, nothing guarantees the same items will scale when applied to another sample. Only after-the-fact analysis of each sample will reveal if the Guttman scale properties hold for subsequent applications of a scale.

The data generated by Guttman scaling are ordinal level. Given the relatively few items characteristic of these scales and the common "agree–disagree" format, there are few possible scores for respondents to achieve. This means that large numbers of respondents will have tied scores on the scale, so many statisticians believe it is better to consider these numbers as ranks (ordinal) rather than interval- or ratio level data. Guttman scales are unique, however, for the characteristics of unidimensionality and reproducibility. If these attributes are desired, they are apt to more than outweigh the presence of all the tied scores.

Given the extreme complexity of creating Guttman scales, most human service workers seldom have occasion to develop one. A substantial number of such scales, however, are already in existence, making an understanding of their operating characteristics worthwhile. This is especially true because of the need to check the reproducibility level of a scale each time it is applied to a new sample.

The Eye on Ethics section explores some ethical issues that researchers can confront when using multiple-item scales to measure painful or traumatic experiences.

Multidimensional Scales

All the scaling techniques presented so far were developed a number of years ago. More recent activity has centered on what is called the **multidimensional scale** for measuring variables composed of more than a single dimension. These scaling techniques are too complex for full presentation here, but we can discuss the basic logic that underlies them.

One purpose of the preceding scaling techniques is to locate respondents' scores along some sort of continuum to determine that various groups or people exhibit more or less of the

FIGURE 13.2 Hypothetical Two-Dimensional Space of Client Motivation

variable being measured. With these unidimensional techniques, the straight line of a single scale is sufficient to indicate the location of all people on a given variable. When we come to variables of more than one dimension, however, this single line is no longer adequate. Instead, we must think of locating responses somewhere in either two-, three-, or N-dimensional space. A common analogy exists between multidimensional scaling and cartography or mapmaking: Just as the cartographer locates various places along the dimensions of latitude and longitude, multidimensional scaling locates people along the various dimensions of a variable. For example, if we conceive of people's motivation as being composed of the two dimensions of "discomfort" and "hope," then Figure 13.2 illustrates how multidimensional scaling might locate these people with regard to these dimensions (Kogan, 1975). It might be possible to use multidimensional scaling of client motivation to predict the chances of success with clients undergoing various forms of treatment.

Multidimensional scaling can, of course, deal with variables composed of many more than two dimensions.

AVOIDING RESPONSE BIAS

As we saw in Chapter 5, a key issue in measurement is whether people's answers to questions are accurate reflections of their actual feelings, beliefs, or behaviors. In other words, our measure of some phenomenon should be determined by the nature of the phenomenon itself and not by systematic or random errors (review the measurement formula on p. 122). One source of such error in responses to questions or statements is called **response bias**: the tendency for answers to questions to be influenced by something other than true feelings, beliefs, and behaviors. Response bias can result in a patterned overestimation or underestimation of variables (Bradburn, 1983).

Sources of Response Bias

One source of response bias is called **response set**: Some people tend to be either yea-sayers or nay-sayers, tending either to agree or disagree with statements regardless of their content. This sometimes is called the *acquiescence response set,* because it more often takes the form of people being predisposed to agree with statements. To illustrate this, look again at the self-esteem scale in Table 13.1. If the scale were constructed so that "strongly agree" always indicated high self-esteem, then people who tend to agree with statements would score higher on self-esteem than they actually should, because they tend to agree with statements irrespective of content. This would throw into question the validity of the scale, because it would produce systematic error (discussed in Chapter 5).

Another source of response bias is **response pattern anxiety**: Some people become anxious if they have to repeat the same response all the time, and they change their responses to avoid doing so. If this occurs, their reactions to statements do not reflect their actual attitudes, but rather their reaction to certain response patterns, and the validity of the scale is reduced. (Students sometimes experience this when taking a multiple-choice exam. If several consecutive questions all have the same letter answer, they become concerned and may doubt answers that they were fairly sure of just because the pattern of responses differs from the more random pattern they expect.)

Another source of response bias is the **social desirability effect**: people's tendency to give socially acceptable, popular answers to present themselves in a good light. For example, the Conflict Tactics Scale is an instrument for measuring modes of conflict resolution and violence between intimate partners (Straus et al., 1996). It does so by asking (among other questions) whether people have ever used a gun or a knife in resolving a dispute with an intimate partner. Because it is socially unacceptable for most people to admit using a knife or gun on a partner, this may affect how people respond to the Conflict Tactics Scale. People may deny using a knife or gun, even if they have done so, to avoid appearing socially unacceptable to an interviewer.

Reducing Response Bias

Researchers use a number of strategies in an attempt to reduce response bias. Response set and response pattern anxiety can be avoided by designing statements so positive statements are not always an expression of the same attitude. Likert scales are routinely designed like this. In the items in Table 13.1, choosing "strongly agree" on items 1, 3, and 5 is an expression of high self-esteem; choosing "strongly agree" on items 2 and 4, on the other hand, is an expression of low self-esteem. If "strongly agree" were an expression of high self-esteem for all items, some respondents would have to choose the same alternative on every item to express their opinion. Mixing the response pattern of items is taken into account when scoring Likert scales. The alternatives that indicate an expression of the same opinion or feeling are given the same numerical score. In our example, for instance, all high-esteem alternatives (whether they are "strongly agree" or "strongly disagree") are given a score of 4. Then, each person's responses to all items can be summed for a total scale score.

Another technique for avoiding response bias is to present sensitive issues in a neutral and non-judgmental context. In the Conflict Tactics Scale, Murray Straus and his colleagues (1996) presented questions about violent acts in the context of disagreements and conflicts, which presumably would appear more socially acceptable to people than abuse and violence.

A third way to reduce response bias has to do with the ordering of questions: Questions can be asked in a hierarchical order, beginning with the less sensitive issues and gradually moving to the more sensitive issues. The Conflict Tactics Scale begins with a few items that reflect positive ways of resolving conflict ("I explained my side of a disagreement to my partner") before moving to questions about psychological and physical abuse. Questions about the use of violence do not appear until well into the instrument. The rationale for this design was that people feel less reticent about divulging acts of violence if they have been given the chance to show that such acts were "the last straw" after attempting other means of conflict resolution.

A fourth strategy for reducing response bias is to use an interspersed pattern for the items, where socially acceptable items are interspersed with the less acceptable items. So, in the Conflict Tactics Scale, positive items, such as "I said I was sure we could work out a problem," are followed by such items as "My partner needed to see a doctor because of a fight with me." The reason for this pattern is that a straight hierarchical ordering may open the door to a form of response set: A respondent may blindly answer "never" to every item once items begin referring to violent acts. Interspersing sensitive items with positive ones encourages participants to think more carefully about each item. Thus, the Conflict Tactics Scale actually uses a combination of hierarchical and interspersed ordering of sensitive items. For any given scale, whether a hierarchical pattern or an interspersed ordering produces the least bias is an empirical question to be settled through research on the scale itself.

A fifth technique that helps reduce response bias is called *funneling*. A researcher might ask respondents first about conflict in their city, then about conflict in their local community and among neighbors, and finally about conflict in their own family. As another example of this, Moser and Kalton (1972) suggested phrasing questions so respondents can answer in the third person. For example, "Many men have hit their wives at one time or another. I wonder if you know under what circumstances it happens?" This can be followed with a direct question asking if the respondent has done it.

SCALING IN THE HUMAN SERVICES

Scaling is arguably the best example of a strong linkage between practice and research. Scales developed for research purposes may prove extremely useful in practice, and scales developed for human service practice may be equally useful for research. Practitioners use scales for several purposes. First, scales strengthen the general intake process by providing a systematic means of detecting areas for intervention. For example, the Multi-Problem Screening Inventory (MPSI) scale is a multidimensional self-report measure that helps practitioners assess the magnitude of client problems across a wide array of personal and social functioning areas (Hudson & McMurtry, 1997).

Second, human service practitioners use scales to assess specific problems for intervention. Research in Practice 13.2 describes several scales that are particularly useful for this purpose.

Third, the practitioner uses scales to document the progress of intervention. Although simply administering a scale before and after treatment makes for a weak research design, it still provides more rigorous evidence of improvement than the casual observation that is common in many practice situations. For the practitioner seeking to document case outcomes with stronger evidence, standardized scales may supplement repeated measures in a single-system design. This strategy was illustrated by a report on the treatment of panic disorder. During baseline, treatment, and follow-up, social workers used the client's daily rating of anxiety level for the single-system *AB* design. In addition, the client also completed a standardized instrument, the Clinical Anxiety Scale, before and after treatment. Both the daily rating and the scale scores indicated client improvement (Alfonso & Dziegielewski, 2001).

Finally, human service organizations rely on scaling as part of their overall program quality and effectiveness-monitoring process. One team of researchers described the use of a comprehensive set of scales both to assess individual clients and to help guide program evaluation in the field of substance-abuse treatment (Joe et al., 2002). Such use of scales both to inform the practitioner about individual client progress and to provide data for program evaluation is a key element in the evidence-based practice approach that we introduced in Chapter 1. Because the documentation of practice effectiveness is measured using scales that are recognized to be valid and reliable, it can be used in evaluation research as a valuable source of evidence for guiding future practice decisions.

Properly employed, scales can be of immense benefit to practice, but a danger also exists that the

Research in Practice 13.2   Assessment of Client Functioning: Rapid Assessment Instruments

One of the most common applications of scaling in the human services is problem assessment. Protective service workers use scales to systematically assess the risk of child abuse (Children's Research Center, 1999). At the other end of the age spectrum, gerontology practitioners use instruments such as the NEECHAN Confusion Scale for rapid and unobtrusive assessment of acute confusion in hospitalized older patients (Neelon et al., 1996) and the FEAR scale to assess generalized anxiety in elderly primary care patients (Krasucki et al., 1999).

Both the confusion scale and the anxiety measure are illustrations of an increasingly popular category of scale known as *rapid assessment instruments,* or RAIs, which are distinguished from other measures by several main features. RAIs are short, easy to administer, easy to complete, and written in clear, easy-to-understand language with uncomplicated directions to minimize disruption of the intervention process. Scoring normally takes only a few minutes, without the need for special equipment. RAIs have been developed to cover a wide array of settings and common targets of human service intervention, and have been applied in family service agencies (Toseland & Reid, 1985) and in agencies serving children and youth (Edlesen, 1985; Nelson-Gardell, 1997). Ogles, Lambert, & Masters (1996) identified instruments for depression, anxiety, and phobias. A number of instruments have been developed in the area of substance abuse, such as the Hudson Index of Alcohol Involvement (Rapp et al., 1999). Probably the best current reference for practitioners seeking measurement instruments to aid in practice evaluation is Fischer & Corcoran (2007).

A good illustration of an RAI is the Michigan Alcoholism Screening Test (MAST), a 25-item questionnaire designed to provide a rapid and effective screening for lifetime alcohol-related problems and alcoholism. The MAST can be completed in less than 10 minutes, and scored in less than five minutes. It can be used in either paper-and-pencil or interview format or online, and it has been productive in a variety of settings with varied populations.

Practitioners may wonder whether it is worth the resources to go beyond a basic interview and use an RAI such as the MAST, or to go a step farther and employ a more comprehensive scale. One agency undertook a systematic comparison of the relative benefits of each approach by comparing results obtained with the MAST to those from a screening interview and to information gathered via the Alcohol Use Inventory (AUI), a complex, 147-item, multiscale instrument (Skinner, 1981). The researcher administered the three forms of measurement to a sample of 327 individuals with alcohol problems to assess the relative benefits and liabilities of each approach. In addition, several other instruments were used to assess further the validity of the three procedures, including the Lifetime Drinking History, a detailed, structured interview procedure that yields quantitative indexes of drinking patterns. Other measures included several scales to test for understanding of scale items and measures of the tendency to present oneself in a favorable light.

The study found that asking individuals a few simple questions during the intake process was effective in obtaining useful data about alcohol usage. However, although the intake interview permitted detection of a potential problem, the MAST procedure was superior, because it produced reliable information on the severity and nature of the alcohol problem. Furthermore, this additional information was gained with only a slight increase in time and money required for the assessment process. In contrast, the AUI procedure required considerably more time to complete the 147-item, multiscale instrument, and also required considerable time and skill to score and interpret the results. For the added cost, it did provide detailed information about styles of use, patterns of symptoms, and perceived benefits of use.

The researcher concluded that human service professionals who are in a position to detect alcohol-related problems would definitely benefit from including a procedure such as the MAST in their client-screening routine. The added reliability and validity over and above what can be gained in a brief screening are obtained for very little additional cost. On the other hand, the added precision and fine distinctions that are possible through use of the AUI cannot be justified for referring agencies. The AUI is better suited for specialized treatment facilities that can set up efficient procedures for scoring and analysis and make use of the added information in treatment planning for alcoholics. Therefore, the selection of measurement tools and the decision to incorporate scales into practice should be based on the demonstrated capacity of the measurement tools weighed against the added costs in terms of time, money, and skill required for their use.

Information Technology in Research: Measurement Issues in Online Research

As more research moves online, we are beginning to understand how this new technological modality impacts on measurement issues and the use of scales to measure variables. Although these technologies are still quite new, we are beginning to see the broad outlines of how research might be affected.

One effect is that the web makes it possible to include a broad range of visual effects in a measurement device, such as a survey or a measurement scale (Couper, Tourangeau, & Kenyon, 2004). In the past, when measurement devices consisted mostly of the printed page, measurement issues focused mostly on the words that made up the questions and statements to which people respond. Chapter 5 discussed these issues at length. On the web, however, one can use a wide variety of typefaces, colors, images (both static and animated), sound, and streaming video as a part of what people respond to when we measure variables. For example, the presentation of color photographs and other images to respondents as stimuli to measure people's attitudes or emotions may offer one of the more striking departures from the past, when the stimuli for such measurement were simply words and sentences printed in black and white. Of course, it may turn out that such images, at least in some cases, are disadvantageous to measurement, because they tend to be more ambiguous and subject to more varying interpretations than words and sentences. Not much research has been conducted on this question, but the research that does exist suggests that photographic images do influence people's interpretation of the text of a question, and sometimes in inconsistent ways. All of this, of course, has to do with the assessment of validity and reliability of any measuring device, which are discussed in Chapter 5 and in this chapter. Any measurement done on the web, using whatever stylistic features, must be subject to validity and reliability checks.

Another effect of the web on research is that subjects may respond to standard measurement formats differently online than in printed modes (Duffy et al., 2005; Fricker et al., 2005). With measurement scales, for example, there is some evidence that people filling out scales online are more likely to choose midpoints in the scale, or the "don't know" option, than are those responding to printed measurement devices. Still other research shows that people responding online tend to choose the more extreme response alternatives. And yet other research suggests that people are more likely to respond to individual items in an online survey than are people in telephone surveys. While some of the results of this research are contradictory at this point, it does tell us that we cannot just switch from print to online measurement and assume we are measuring the same thing in both modalities. Again, tests of validity and reliability need to be conducted.

---

uninformed use of scales, or the use of poorly constructed scales, will provide false or misleading information. False data are, in some ways, worse than no data at all, because people believe they have gained some understanding when, in fact, they have not. Social policy or practice techniques based on such erroneous data actually may exacerbate problems rather than alleviate them. For these reasons, we need to be exceedingly cautious about using scales developed without the extensive pretesting and analysis outlined in this chapter. Some people are under the mistaken impression that one can gather usable data from statements that have been constructed with no pretesting or analysis. It is tempting to believe that a couple of intelligent people can sit down and write unbiased, valid, and reliable statements to measure variables. It is also a dangerously erroneous belief. Great care is always called for in constructing scales. These concerns illustrate the profound responsibility of social researchers and practitioners to take all the steps necessary to ensure that their findings are valid. Any investigator—including a human service practitioner—who casually develops scales without rigorous safeguards, and then distributes results based on those scales is, many would argue, engaging in unethical behavior.

The temptation to simply make up a scale rather than seek out a valid and reliable instrument may be especially strong in areas where an understanding of the concepts seems obvious to the practitioner. Terms like "helpful," "supportive," and "sensitive" are commonplace in the human services, so it seems at first glance that a practitioner could quickly make up a good measurement scale by asking a few questions such as "On a scale of 1 to 5, how helpful was the therapist?" What concepts do these terms really represent, however, and how well do the items measure them? What it takes to answer these questions well can be glimpsed in the work of researchers who developed a multidimensional scale on social support (Goldsmith, McDermott, & Alexander, 2000). Their work involved three studies. The first study asked a sample of more than 100 participants to interpret the meaning of the terms "helpful," "supportive," and "sensitive." The second study involved almost 400 participants rating 30 semantic differential items derived from the first study. The third study was conducted to ascertain the scale reliability, validity, and conceptual distinctiveness of the terms. The work on this instrument is typical of the time, resources, and effort needed to design quality scales, and underscores the value of carefully selecting valid, reliable instruments.

When human service providers select scales for use in practice or research, they need to assess whether research is methodologically sound. In scale construction, this requires considering how rigorous the investigator was in developing items, whether pretesting was conducted, and whether validity and reliability were tested. In some cases, after reviewing a piece of research, the practitioner may decide that, although the results are tantalizing, the study lacks the methodological rigor necessary to convince him or her to incorporate those results into practice.

REVIEW AND CRITICAL THINKING

Main Points

- Multiple-item scales are particularly valuable for measuring complex variables, because they enhance validity and reliability, increase the level of measurement, and improve the efficiency of data handling.

- The five basic steps common to most scaling techniques are as follows: Develop many preliminary items; eliminate obviously bad items; pretest the remaining items; eliminate bad items on the basis of pretest results; and select items for the final scale.

- The Likert scale is a popular scale format that involves a series of statements, each followed by a number of ordered response alternatives ranging from, for example, strongly disagree to strongly agree, or from excellent to poor; most Likert scales have four to seven response alternatives.

- An important consideration in selecting items for inclusion in a Likert scale is discriminatory power—that is, the ability of each item to differentiate between those who score high and those who score low on the overall measurement scale.

- Thurstone scales use judges to assign a value from 1 to 11 to each item in the scale, which results in a scale capable of producing interval-level data.

- Items for inclusion in a Thurstone scale have scale scores that cover the full 1 to 11 range and were most agreed on by the judges.

- The semantic differential (SD) scaling format presents respondents with a concept to be rated and a series of opposite adjective pairs separated by a seven-point scale that is used to evaluate the concept.

- Semantic differentials are a convenient scaling format, because they are considerably easier to construct than the alternatives.

- Guttman scales have the unique characteristic of reproducibility, meaning that a given total

score reflects one—and only one—pattern of responses to the items in the scale.
- Multidimensional scaling uses two or more dimensions or components of a complex variable to locate people with regard to the various components of the variable.
- The use of scales or the results of research based on measurement scales should be approached cautiously, with careful consideration given to whether adequate development has gone into the scale, particularly in terms of assessing its validity and reliability.

Important Terms for Review

discriminatory power score
Guttman scale
Likert scale
multidimensional scale
response bias
response pattern anxiety
response set
scale
semantic differential
social desirability effect
summated rating scale
Thurstone scales
unidimensional scale

Critical Thinking

As an extension of Chapter 5, this chapter is all about measurement or being careful and precise. This chapter provides some of the nuts and bolts of how researchers design valid questions, indexes, and scales, which are used to measure much social phenomena. Much can be learned from how scientists do these things and translated into tips for critically analyzing any information that you might confront in practice or policy settings or in your everyday life:

1. If a series of questions or statements are used to measure something, is that something appropriately measured by a multiple-item measuring device?
2. Where did the items for the multiple-item measuring device come from? Is there any evidence available as to the validity or reliability of the individual items or the multiple-item measure?
3. If a multiple-item measuring device is used, is it properly constructed to support the conclusions drawn? Can you identify ways in which its design could lead to misinterpretation or bias in the conclusions?

Exploring the Internet

Information about a potential scale for a research project and, sometimes, copies of the scale itself can be found at various Internet sites. For example, the scales that Walter Hudson developed can be found at http://www.walmyr.com/perscales.html. From this site, you can download samples of scales to view with Acrobat Reader, along with information about ordering scales and other products for professional and educational purposes.

Another way of using the Internet to learn more about scaling is to use such key terms as "Guttman" or "Likert" with a specialized search engine, such as the one provided in conjunction with the General Social Survey Internet site (http://www3.norc.org/GSS+website). This search engine returns bibliographic citations and full-text reports related to the General Social Survey. Many different scales have been used in the General Social Survey, making this site an excellent source of research articles about scaling issues.

Another excellent source for locating information on scales is the Buros Institute of Mental Measurements (http://buros.unl.edu/buros/jsp/search.jsp), which includes a Test Reviews Online. Not only can you search for scales, but you can also find review information on tests and scales. While exploring these sites or others related to scaling, pay attention to whether and in what ways the sites include information about the methods of assessing scales discussed in this chapter: validity, reliability, reproducibility, discriminatory power, and so on.

For Further Reading

Albarracin, D., Johnson, B. T., & Zanna, M. P., Eds. (2005). *The Handbook of Attitudes*. Mahwah, N.J.: Lawrence Erlbaum Associates. This handbook presents, synthesizes, and integrates the existing knowledge of methods, theories, and data in the study of attitudes. The book is relevant to the topic of measurement in general and attitude scaling in particular.

DeVellis, R. F. (2012). *Scale Development: Theory and Applications*, 3rd ed. Thousand Oaks, Calif.: Sage. This is an understandable guide to all the various stages in developing good scales. It includes discussions of how to generate items, how long scales should be, and other useful topics.

Fischer, J., & Corcoran, K. (2007). *Measures for Clinical Practice and Research: A Sourcebook*, 4th ed. New York: Oxford University Press. A two-volume set that includes actual scales as well as reliability and validity data. Volume I covers instruments for couples, families, and children. Volume II is devoted to instruments for adults.

McDowell, I. (2006). *Measuring Health: A Guide to Rating Scales and Questionnaires*, 3rd ed. New York: Oxford University Press. This volume discusses the theoretical and technical aspects of constructing and evaluating scales relating to such health issues as social health, psychological well-being, and depression. It presents and evaluates many actual scales.

Miller, D. C., & Salkind, N. J. (2002). *Handbook of Research Design and Social Measurement*, 6th ed. Thousand Oaks, Calif.: Sage. The latest edition of a classic in the field of measurement. Miller's book provides an overview of the various types of scale construction along with many examples of proven scales.

Netemeyer, R. G., Bearden, W. O., & Sharma, S. (2003). *Scaling Procedures: Issues and Applications*. Thousand Oaks, Calif.: Sage. This current resource on scaling examines the issues involved in developing and validating multi-item, self-report scales. The authors present a four-step approach for multi-indicator scale development. The book includes relevant empirical examples and a review of the concepts of dimensionality, reliability, and validity.

Schutte, N. S., & Malouff, J. M. (1995). *Sourcebook of Adult Assessment Strategies* (Applied Clinical Psychology). New York: Plenum. A text for practitioners, researchers, and instructors in the mental health field. This book presents more than 70 scales on a wide range of adult mental disorders, reviews of their psychometric properties, and user instructions. The scales include self-report, observer-based, and clinician-rating measures.

Streiner, D. L., & Norman, G. R. (2008). *Health Measurement Scales: A Practical Guide to Their Development and Use*, 4th ed. Oxford: Oxford University Press. A thorough discussion of issues related to locating and assessing scales for health-related research is the focus of this book.

Touliatos, J., Perlmutter, B. F., Straus, M. A., & Holden, G. W., Eds. (2001). *Handbook of Family Measurement Techniques*. Thousand Oaks, Calif.: Sage. This three-volume set is intended for researchers, clinicians, and students in the family and related fields. It includes abstracts of family measurement instruments published from 1929 to 1996, as well as full versions and scoring instructions for many instruments.

Class Exercises for Competency Assessment

One point we have made in this chapter on scaling is that the human service professional may not have occasion to construct new scales. In many situations, you can use scales that have already been developed and reported in the literature.

13.1. **[Research & Practice]** For one of the following topics, find one or more scales that are included in the professional literature:

Depression

Life satisfaction

Alcoholism

Stress

Child abuse

Marital satisfaction or adjustment

13.2. We suggest using *Psychological Abstracts, Sociological Abstracts,* and *Social Work Research and Abstracts* as aids in your research. (See also Appendix A on information retrieval and the use of the library.)

13.2. **[Critical Thinking] [Research & Practice]** For each scale that you locate, indicate what kind of scale it is—for example, Likert, Guttman, or semantic differential. Are reliability and validity information available on the scale? If you wanted to use a scale on this topic, what would be the problems with and advantages of using the one you found?

13.3. Among the Personal Adjustment Scales developed by Walter Hudson and colleagues, the WALMYR Assessment Scale Training Package, which contains the 10 most widely used scales, is especially useful. As a class project, have members complete and score the Generalized Contentment Scale. (Scales may be ordered from Walmyr Publishing at http://www.walmyr.com/scales.html)

13.3. **[Critical Thinking] [Research & Practice]** What value does such a scale have over data gathered in interviews?

13.4. **[Critical Thinking] [Research & Practice]** These scales are intended for repeated use with single-subject designs. How do you envision clients might respond to such a scale, especially with repeated applications?

Chapter 14

✸

Data Analysis I: Data Preparation and Presentation

Preparation for Data Analysis
   Coding Schemes
   Preparing and Using a Codebook

Data Entry
   Raw Data Entry
   Data Cleaning
   Creating New Variables

Data Distributions
   Types of Data Distributions
   Constructing Frequency Distributions

Graphical Display of Data Distributions
   Bar Graphs
   Histograms and Frequency Polygons
   Pie Charts

Contingency Tables
   Bivariate Relationships
   Multivariate Analysis

Review and Critical Thinking
   Main Points
   Important Terms for Review
   Critical Thinking
   Exploring the Internet
   For Further Reading
   Class Exercises for Competency Assessment

All research involves some form of **data analysis**, which refers to deriving some meaning from the observations made during a research project. Data analysis can take many forms. In some cases, it is qualitative, such as a summary description of an investigator's field notes from a participant-observation study. The focus of this chapter, however, is on quantitative data analysis, in which observations are put into numerical form and manipulated in some way based on their arithmetic properties. The analysis of quantitative data typically involves the use of **statistics**, which are procedures for assembling, classifying, tabulating, and summarizing numerical data to obtain some meaning or information.

This chapter begins our coverage of common methods of data analysis, which we will continue in Chapter 15. Primarily designed for those who have not taken a course in statistics, these chapters also may serve as a refresher for those who have. To learn to do statistical analysis requires at least a full course devoted solely to that topic, but our goals here are more basic: to introduce the issues of preparing a data set for analysis; guide selection of the most appropriate statistics to accomplish a particular task; and provide guidance in the interpretation of statistical results. This knowledge prepares us to better understand various statistics when we encounter them in research reports and the popular media and to assess whether the statistics are being used properly. This chapter explores some of the fundamentals of preparing and managing data—an often overlooked portion of the research process that falls between the generation of observations by the research design on the one hand and the production of statistical results on the other. Although it may not seem as challenging or intellectually demanding as developing the design or analyzing the data, it is still a critical step that can determine the success of the overall project.

PREPARATION FOR DATA ANALYSIS

In this chapter, we generally assume that the data have already been collected and that the task now is to enter the data into a computer file and begin the data analysis. Recall from Chapter 1 that data analysis is part of the overall research process, and many questions regarding data analysis should be resolved before any data are actually collected. As emphasized in Chapters 2, 4, and 5, theoretical and conceptual considerations are important in determining the nature of the data to be collected, and the nature of the data determines the kinds of statistics that can be applied. Furthermore, as we discussed in Chapter 7 in relation to survey data collection, procedures such as computer-assisted telephone interviewing (CATI) essentially merge the steps of data collection, data coding, and data set creation into one process, because responses of participants are entered directly into a computer file data set. So, even though the actual data analysis occurs toward the end of a research project, many of the issues discussed in this chapter will have been settled—or at least envisioned—*before* any data are actually collected.

Imagine that a researcher has completed a survey with a sample size of 400. The completed questionnaires are neatly stacked on the desk. Presumably, these questionnaires contain much information and data for assessing the hypotheses that the researcher set out to test. But as long as the data are on the questionnaires—or in any other raw form, for that matter—they are useless. The raw data are in a highly inconvenient form from the standpoint of deriving usable meaning from them. Indeed, even if we tediously read through the 400 questionnaires, we would have little idea about the overall contents. The collected data must be reorganized before we can go on and apply the necessary statistics for their analysis.

Coding Schemes

In the current context, *coding* refers to the process by which a researcher transforms raw data into a machine-readable format suitable for data analysis, which requires that each observation be translated into a numerical value or set of letters. The numbers or letters assigned to an observation of a variable are called a *code*. The raw data set may have resulted from an observational study, a survey, an experiment, or an analysis of existing data; and it can be in one of several forms, including completed written questionnaires, survey interview schedules, observation notes, or agency records. In the following discussion, we used survey data to illustrate the coding process, but the basic principles apply to other research methods as well.

Coding data requires adapting the data as collected to the constraints of the program used for statistical analysis. On the one hand, the researcher must consider the data source, such as a completed questionnaire, and determine how to translate the data into coded form. On the other hand, the researcher also must be cognizant of the capabilities and restrictions of the computer program that will analyze the data. Although we present these perspectives somewhat independently, in practice the researcher must give simultaneous attention to both. The plan by which the researcher organizes responses to a variable or an item, together with how the variable is defined for computerization, constitutes the **coding scheme** for a variable. The initial purpose of the coding scheme is to provide the rules and directions for converting the observations into code. Referring to our example of the 400 completed questionnaires, the researcher's first task is to convert the responses into numbers and letters for computer entry.

As explained in Chapters 8 and 9, coding refers to categorizing a variable into a limited number of categories. Sometimes, this coding is built into the way a question is asked and answered (see Chapter 7). This is the case with the following question format:

Which of the following best describes where you live? (Circle the number of your choice.)

1. Large city.
2. Suburb of a large city.
3. City of 50,000 or less.
4. Rural but nonfarm.
5. Rural farm.

In this case, the circled number is the code for how a particular respondent answered a question. This example also illustrates one reason issues of coding and data analysis need to be considered before data collection is initiated. The number of options in the question predetermines the maximum number of response categories that can be used later to look at possible relationships between "residential area" and other variables. Because we did not provide a separate option for "City of 50,000 to 300,000," however, we could not use this as a category in our data analysis.

With some variables, the actual value of the response is a number and can be used to code the data. Family size, income, and number of arrests are variables of this type. When the data take the form of responses to open-ended survey questions, field notes, or other non-numerical entities, however, the data must be translated into numbers for quantitative analysis. This process is essential for most data analysis, because the substitution of numbers for observations greatly reduces the volume of data that must be stored and facilitates its analysis, especially by computer. (As we noted in Chapter 9, qualitative analysis often does not involve the substitution of numbers for the actual observations.) Many computer programs permit the use of words or letters to stand for categories, but these generally are more cumbersome, and thus are used only infrequently. (Recall from Chapter 5, however, that assigning a number to coding categories does not necessarily mean we can perform the various mathematical functions, such as addition and subtraction, on them. Whether we can do this depends on the level of measurement.)

When establishing coding categories, the researcher should follow two general rules. First, the categories should be *mutually exclusive*—that is, a given observation is coded into one, and only one, category for each variable. The universal practice of categorizing people by sex as either male or female exemplifies mutually exclusive categories. Second, the coding categories should be *exhaustive,* which means that a coding category exists for every possible observation that was made. For example, it might be tempting not to bother to code the "no opinion" response with Likert-type questions, on the grounds that those responses probably will not be included in the data analysis. A researcher might well decide not to analyze those responses in the end, but the coding stage is not the time to make such decisions. If the researcher fails to code a response and later decides to include it in the analysis, it becomes necessary to develop a new coding scheme and reenter the data into the computer. A good rule of thumb when coding is to do it in such a way that *all* information is coded.

FIGURE 14.1 Data Entry Screen Commonly Used in Statistical Software

Today, virtually all quantitative—and much qualitative—data analysis is done with computers. In its most basic form, a computerized data set can be conceptualized as a rectangular table of cells where the columns represent variables and the rows designate individual cases. Figure 14.1 illustrates a portion of a simulated data set showing how it would appear on a typical computer program data entry screen. The first column consists of respondent last names; the remaining columns designate first names, birthdates, prior arrests, date of offense, relationship to victim, and annual income. Notice that the top of each column displays the variable name (lname, fname, and so on). The variable names and other variable attributes, together with information about the position of the variable in the data set, also are vital elements of the coding scheme for computerized data. At a minimum, a computer-coding scheme identifies a variable name and a variable format.

For variable names, computer program data entry screens typically use a default designation, such as C1, C2, and C3 (in the case of Minitab) or var001, var002, and var003 (in SPSS), to identify variables. Spreadsheet programs, such as Lotus, Excel, and Quattro, label them a, b, c, ..., aa, ab, and so on. Obviously, such designations convey little information about the meaning of a particular variable. With even a few variables, relying on such default designations for variable names quickly becomes confusing, so the researcher needs to provide more recognizable variable names. A variable name should be an indicator of the content of that variable. A common practice is to use a mnemonic device when naming variables. Thus, "lname" and "fname" clue the user that the variable names stand for last name and first name, respectively.

Variable names also may be selected to help group variables together. For example, a data set on domestic violence may include similar variables on both the suspect and the victim, such as date of birth, age, and alcohol use. Beginning each variable related to victims with the letter "v" and each suspect-related variable with an "s" helps the researcher quickly distinguish to which party a given variable refers. Another benefit of this approach is that data analysis programs commonly display variable lists alphabetically. Beginning all victim-related variables with the letter "v" causes them to be grouped together whenever the computer displays a variable list. This reduces the need to scroll through a long list of variables when selecting variables for inclusion in a data-analysis procedure. When a variable is measured by combining responses to a number of separate items, it often is helpful to use a number as part of the name to identify the variable's position in the set. Variables representing individual items of a 10-item self-esteem scale, for example, might be designated se1, se2, se3, and so on through se10. Such a designation can reduce the amount of work involved when combining the items into a single score. Thus, a total score on self-esteem can be generated by a computer command like "Sum se1 to se10" instead of requiring a listing of all 10 individual items.

In addition to the variable name, a coding scheme specifies the *variable format,* which determines how many characters a coded entry may have, whether it is non-numeric or some form of numeric variable, and where identifiers, such as decimals, commas, or dollar signs, should be placed. Figure 14.1 displays several types of variables: Some consist of letters, others include letters and numbers, and some are only numbers.

Data-analysis programs vary in terms of the kinds of variables that they accept, but the two major types are *numeric* and *alphanumeric.* **Numeric variables** sometimes are called "values," because they have the property of a quantitative value. **Alphanumeric variables**, on the other hand, consist simply of type characters; they sometimes also are referred to as "string" variables or labels. An alphanumeric variable has no quantitative meaning and cannot be used in mathematical computations. Thus, the variable "lname" is clearly an alphanumeric variable, because its field (column) consists of text, such as "Smith" and "Hernandez." What makes a variable alphanumeric, however, is determined by how the variable is defined in the coding scheme, not simply by what characters are displayed on the computer monitor. For example, we could enter Social Security numbers in a data set and designate these as alphanumerical values. Even though the entire column consists of numerical characters, such as 375426174, a statistical program would not compute the mean, standard deviation, or other statistics on this variable, because it is designated as an alphanumeric or string variable. Data-analysis programs commonly accept almost any keyboard character in a variable designated as alphanumeric. Although one can enter numeric characters in an alphanumeric variable, statistical packages such as SPSS and Minitab only accept numerical symbols in a variable designated as numeric.

In addition to string and numeric variables, many programs also permit the specification of other types of variables, such as currency and date or time. Although the format code is not visible on the screen, it is stored with the data file and tells the program how much space to reserve for a given variable in the data set, as well as how to display it. In the case of the variable LNAME, when defining it as an alphanumeric variable, you have to specify the maximum number of characters possible (specified as 12 characters in Table 14.1). Similarly, the date-of-birth variable would have to be identified as a date with 11 characters in it. When defining a numeric variable, such as PRIORS, you have to specify the number of decimal places, if any, permitted. With currency variables you can specify a range of display options, such as $9 (one character, no decimals, maximum value of nine dollars) to $99,999,999.99 (ten characters, two decimal places, maximum value ninety-nine million and change)—all depending on how precisely you measure the variable. In Table 14.1, the variables DOB and CRDATE are defined as date variables. If we want to determine how old each suspect was at the time of the offense, we can enter a computer command that will subtract DOB from CRDATE and then display the result in years. Although different computer programs use their own conventions for designating variable types, the important point is that how the variable is defined before data entry determines its type, and the researcher must plan how variables will need to be used in the analysis and define them accordingly.

Additional elements may be added to a coding scheme to enhance its usefulness. Besides a brief variable name, the researcher may specify a variable label, which is an extended description of a variable that the data-analysis program will display, in addition to the variable name whenever output is generated for that variable. Thus in a table using the variable CRDATE, the designation "crime date" can be printed to make the table more understandable. Similarly, the coding scheme may include "value labels," which designate in words what a

TABLE 14.1 Domestic Violence Study Codebook

Item	Variable Name	Variable Label	Variable Type and Value Labels	Number of Characters	Number of Decimals	Missing Values	Level of Measurement
1. List offender last name	LNAME	last name	alphanumeric	12	0	999	nominal
2. List offender first name	FNAME	first name	alphanumeric	10	0	999	nominal
3. Enter date of birth	DOB	date of birth	date	11	0	999	ordinal
4. How many prior arrests for domestic violence?	PRIORS	number of prior arrests	numeric	8	0	999	ratio
5. What was the date of offense?	CRDATE	crime date	date	11	0	999	ordinal
6. What was offender's relationship with victim?	RELATION	relation to victim	numeric Value Label: 1 = married 2 = cohabiting 3 = separated 4 = divorced 5 = dating 6 = other	8	0	999	nominal
7. What was offender's adjusted gross income reported to IRS for 2010?	INCOME	2010 income	dollars	7	0	999	ratio

given value represents. For example, in Table 14.1, numbers are used to designate the following relationship possibilities between offender and victim: 1 = married, 2 = cohabitating, 3 = separated, 4 = divorced, 5 = dating, and 6 = other. Because this is a nominal variable, and thus, without an inherent quantitative meaning to the numbers, the value labels are displayed on outputs to help clarify what quality each number represents.

Finally, the coding scheme also should show how to interpret special codes, such as *missing values*.

Missing values arise when no response is recorded for a particular item. Depending on why the item is a nonresponse, the researcher may either leave the variable blank in the data set or enter a value that signifies why the item was missing. For example, an item might be coded "−1" if the respondent refused to answer the question or "99" if the item does not apply to a particular respondent. This could be an important distinction for some types of analysis, so the coding scheme must specify how these various entries should be handled in computations.

Preparing and Using a Codebook

The coding scheme results in a specification of the variable name, variable format, range of permissible response codes, location of the variable in the data set, and optional features, such as variable labels, value labels, and missing value codes. Researchers commonly develop a *codebook* for the data set, which is an inventory of all the individual items in the data collection instrument together with the coding schemes (see Table 14.1). The codebook provides lasting documentation on how the data set is constructed. Whenever a question exists about how a variable is constructed or can be used in analysis, the researcher can turn to the codebook for help. Not only does the researcher who collected the data need the codebook, it would be impossible to conduct a replication study on a previously collected data set or to explore new hypotheses with existing data without such documentation. Finally, the codebook is invaluable for data file management. A data set may consist of hundreds of variables, so to make the analysis more efficient, researchers commonly create subfiles containing only the variables needed for a particular analysis. The codebook plays an essential role in selecting the variables and creating new files.

The preliminary codebook normally is prepared before data are entered into the computer and then used as a guide for data entry; however, the codebook is not a static document. Researchers often recode original variables and compute new ones. It is critical that these manipulations of the original data also be documented in the codebook so any researcher can determine how these new variables were derived, what they mean, and where they are located in the data set.

DATA ENTRY

The goal of the data entry process is to produce a complete data set, free from errors, that the data-analysis applications can access and process. Significant strides have been made in recent years in both minimizing data entry error and increasing the speed of transforming raw data into a data set that is ready for analysis.

Raw Data Entry

When the raw data must be extracted from existing documents, such as court records, or from printed questionnaires or survey schedules, the data must be entered manually into the computer. Several options exist for this process. Sometimes, the questionnaire data are coded onto pages known as "transfer sheets," which consist of numbered rows and columns that look much like the computer screen in Figure 14.1. In other cases, questionnaires have space along the border for writing the code, referred to as "edge coding." Whether one uses a transfer sheet, edge coding, or simply the raw questionnaires themselves, the next step is to enter the data using the data entry facility of the statistical application that will eventually analyze the data.

Conventions and individual features vary from one statistical application to another, but the basic process of data entry is similar in all of them. The data entry screen is laid out in columns and rows (see Figure 14.1). Each column represents one variable (field), and each row represents one case (record). Assuming that the variable names, labels, and other specifications have already been entered during the preparation of the codebook, the value for each variable is simply typed into the respective cell in the row corresponding to the individual case. Errors can be corrected by reentering the correct code in a cell. If the coding scheme's data definition for the computer has not already been entered into the computer file, this step can be completed as data are entered into each variable.

Often the data a researcher is interested in is already in an electronic form: A human service agency has already computerized the data into a spreadsheet or database program as part of its administrative or management functions, or the data was collected via an online survey or a handheld computer. In these cases, the data can usually be imported directly into a statistical application, such as SPSS or Minitab, often with the variable definition information included.

Another innovation in data entry is the use of optical scanning technology. A data-collection instrument is designed using a special program. Respondents either mark a circle corresponding to their choice or, in more sophisticated programs, write a response. Then the questionnaire is read by a scanning machine or faxed into the computer, and the coded values are entered directly into the database for analysis. Whether one uses specialized data entry like this or relies on manual entry into the data-analysis program depends on several factors. The specialized equipment is cost-effective for large projects, where a staff of data entry personnel would otherwise be needed. For a small data set, however, designing, setting up, and testing an automated data entry program may be prohibitively expensive. Researchers today have many options to choose from. The most important issue is to select the process that yields the most accurate, usable data set.

Data Cleaning

No matter how much care one takes during the data entry process, errors can be expected, such as skipping variables for certain cases, entering the wrong value, or entering the value in the wrong location. If uncorrected, some errors can cause the analysis program to abort a statistical procedure, or, at least, seriously distort the findings of the analysis. Thus, before the analysis begins, the researcher should examine the data set carefully and make any corrections that are needed. Although no system is foolproof, researchers have developed a variety of techniques for locating errors.

If the data set is small, he or she may be able to detect some errors simply by scanning the data with the data editor screen. Scrolling through the rows and columns of data on the screen can turn up obvious errors, such as blank cells, unusually large numbers, or stray alphanumeric characters. It is best, however, to rely on a more systematic approach. One simple technique with a statistical package, spreadsheet, or database is to use a sort procedure. Sorting rearranges the order of all cases in the data set on the basis of the values of the variable selected as the sort key. Alphanumeric variables are sorted alphabetically, and numerical variables are sorted in numerical order. Scanning the sorted data on the monitor, the researcher can detect misspellings and missing or out-of-range values. For example, if the variable used in the sort procedure is a scale item where expected values are integers from 1 to 5, blank entries and entries of "0" would be at the top of the list, decimals such as 1.5 would show up between "1" and "2," and values of 6 or more would be at the end of the list. This can be a cumbersome process with large data sets, but for only 50 or so variables, sorting the data works well.

With a statistical package such as SPSS, another option is to generate a frequency distribution on all variables. This produces a list of every value that actually occurs in the data set for each variable in ascending order and the number of cases for each respective value. This helps detect variables with out-of-range values or values that should not be present. Of course, knowing that some cases exist somewhere with the wrong entries for a variable and finding those cases are very different things, especially when the data set may contain a thousand or more cases. Having identified a variable with one or more suspect cases, the researcher can use a conditional selection process. The exact command differs from program to program, but basically the researcher enters a command to select those cases for which the value for the variable in question meets a certain condition. For example, if no one in the data set should have an age greater than 18, execute a command to select all cases where AGE > 18, then include a second command to list the case numbers or the last and first names of all cases meeting that condition. Armed with this information, scroll through the data set to the identified cases and correct them. The researcher may edit the entry by replacing it with the correct value, enter a missing value code if the correct value is not available, or in really serious cases, eliminate the case entirely.

These techniques help find data entries that are too large or too small, but sometimes the data are within the acceptable range, but simply wrong for that case. Some of these errors can be detected by looking for logical inconsistencies. For example, if the value in a month variable is April, June, September, or November, then the value in a day variable associated with that month should not be greater than 30. If the variable entry for the number of adults in the household is 2 and the number of children is 4, then the entry for total household size should be 6. Depending on the software program, it is possible to build queries that detect cases in which such inconsistencies are present. Large-scale professional surveys have the benefit of specialized software to help detect errors and employ supervisory personnel who review data entry to detect problems, but most human service practitioners are unlikely to have access to such services. Rigorous application of these procedures, however, can locate many errors. Finally, error detection underscores the importance of numbering the questionnaires or other raw data sources and keeping the raw data in a safe, accessible location so you can compare the original data to the computer file when needed.

Creating New Variables

At this point, the data have all been entered and checked for error, but one task remains before proceeding to the data analysis: The variables as recorded may not be in the final form for the desired analysis procedures. If this is the case, the researcher needs to modify the variables—or generate usable new ones. Such data manipulation may sound unusual, but it is a legitimate and necessary part of the research process.

Here is one example of how and why this is done. Recall from Chapter 13 that some scale items are stated in positive terms and other items in negative terms to avoid problems such as response set. With a 10-item Likert scale for depression, for instance, having choices ranging from 1 to 5, half the items would be stated such that a positive response, such as "strongly agree" or "1," would indicate low depression. The other items would be stated such that a negative response, such as "strongly disagree" or "5," would indicate low depression. To conduct statistical analysis, some items need to be reverse-scored so that a score of 1 on all items signifies a low value on the concept being measured and a 5 signifies a high value. This can be accomplished by use of a *recode* procedure in statistical programs. A recode statement specifies the existing values in a given variable and what the new values should be. In our example, for the five items in which a negative response (a "5") indicated low depression, we would change the values as follows:

Old Item Value	Revised Item Value
1 →	5
2 →	4
3 →	3
4 →	2
5 →	1

Having recoded the negative items, we now have 10 consistent items where low values indicate low levels of depression, and high values indicate high levels of depression. What we really need, however, is a total scale score on depression. This can be obtained by using a *compute* procedure in the data-analysis program. A compute procedure creates a new variable by performing mathematical computations using one or more existing variables. Depending on the conventions of the particular software, we enter a formula like this:

DEPSCORE = sum (DEP1 to DEP10)

With this formula, a new variable called DEPSCORE is created. Its value is computed for each case by summing all 10 individual items that make up the depression scale (DEP1 through DEP10). The new variable—the total depression scale score—is added to the data file. As with the existing variables, the researcher can attach a variable label and value labels to such newly created variables. Whenever the researcher modifies the data set, whether by recoding or by computing new variables, the steps

DATA ANALYSIS I: DATA PREPARATION AND PRESENTATION

EYE ON ETHICS — Out of Sight, Out of Mind: The Ethics of Data Editing

Data editing includes adding, dropping, or changing variables, values, or cases. Although it is an essential element of the research process, data editing is difficult for gatekeepers to police and fraught with potential for ethical abuse (Leahey, 2008). Although much research can be portrayed as an orderly and transparent process, one researcher has argued that data editing belongs to "the underbelly of social research—those thoughts, actions, constraints, and choices that lurk beneath the surface of our well-dressed research publications." (Staw, 1981, p. 225). Overseeing standardized practices such as sampling and statistical analysis is comparatively easy, but practices for which fewer consensual norms and standards exist—like data editing—pose greater challenges. Before research commences, IRBs review proposals to assure that human subjects are protected. Funding organizations scrutinize proposed methods to determine whether a study should be funded, and journals employ peer reviewers to judge if a study is worthy of publication.

But tasks like managing and cleaning data are less likely to be shared with people outside the research team. The way researchers edit their data can affect research findings, and if data edits are not reported, or if they lend more support to researchers' hypotheses, ethical issues may arise. The case of Lenore Weitzman's research presented in Chapter 4 is an example; the disparity in findings between the original study and the reanalysis was largely due to data editing procedures.

So, data editing is one phase of the research process that relies heavily on the integrity of the researcher to do the right thing rather than expecting that outside organizations will provide the safeguard. One means by which the quality and integrity of the data editing process can be reviewed is through replication. Maintaining complete, thorough, and detailed records of data editing aids in replication and makes the researcher's work transparent in the event that ethical questions are raised about the study.

used in the data manipulation must be recorded and added to the codebook. Fortunately this is easy to do, because statistical programs typically record all executed data transformations in a special file. Documenting these transformations ensures that any researcher using the data file will be able to confirm how the new variables were generated. Recoding and computing new variables is an essential step in the process of unlocking the findings contained in the data set. And, as the Eye on Ethics section shows, ethical considerations are involved in the proper organization, documentation, and manipulation of data.

DATA DISTRIBUTIONS

Once the data have been stored as a computer file, systematically inspected for error, cleaned, and possibly revised through recoding and variable creation, we are ready to begin actual data analysis. Data analysis is the process of seeking out patterns within individual variables or the patterns in relationships between variables. The term *univariate analysis* refers to the process of describing individual variables. Even when our ultimate goal in a research project is to determine how two or more variables are related, the process of describing the data by specifying the characteristics of individual variables is critical to a research project. Learning how individual variables are distributed can help determine which variables to use in studying relationships and which data-analysis procedures we should use.

Types of Data Distributions

One of the first steps usually taken with a data set is to look at the range of values for each variable. To accomplish this, a *frequency distribution* is constructed. In Table 14.2, the variable is the grade for a college class, with the traditional five categories. The frequency column shows the number of class members who received each grade. Of particular interest is the *shape* of a frequency distribution. A distribution's shape derives from the pattern that

TABLE 14.2 Hypothetical Grade Distribution for a Social Science Research Class

Grade	Frequency
A	4
B	7
C	10
D	5
F	3
	N = 29

the frequencies produce among the various categories of the variable. A number of labels are used to describe the shapes of distributions. First, distributions may be symmetrical or asymmetrical (see Figure 14.2). *Symmetrical distributions* are balanced, with one half of the distribution being a mirror image of the other half. In reality, most distributions only approach perfect symmetry. *Asymmetrical distributions* have cases bunched toward one end of the scale, with a long "tail" caused by a small number of extreme cases trailing off in the other direction. Asymmetrical distributions are said to be *skewed,* with positively skewed distributions having long tails extending in the direction of the higher values and negatively skewed distributions having tails going in the direction of the lower values. (Note that the concepts of positive and negative skewness apply only to distributions involving data of the ordinal level of measurement or higher. Because the categories of nominal data have no inherent order, the shape of a distribution of nominal data is purely an arbitrary matter of how we choose to arrange the categories.) Determining the amount of skewness is an important preliminary

FIGURE 14.2 Symmetrical and Asymmetrical Distributions

step for later analysis. Certain inferential statistics, for example, are based on the assumption that the variables are normally distributed. One of the basic properties of a normal distribution is that of being symmetrical. Therefore, our analysis at this stage may be critical to help decide later which inferential procedures are appropriate.

Constructing Frequency Distributions

Simple Frequency Distributions. When data are collected, they are in the form of a *raw data distribution,* which means that the distribution contains all the different values that were observed on a variable. Table 14.3 displays a raw data distribution

TABLE 14.3 Two Types of Data Distributions of Patients' Ages

A. Raw Data Distribution

98	82	78	70	68	60
96	81	76	70	68	60
95	80	76	70	68	59
92	80	75	70	68	59
91	79	74	70	68	59
89	79	73	70	67	58
87	79	72	70	66	56
85	79	72	70	66	54
85	79	71	70	66	52
84	79	71	69	64	51
82	79	71	69	63	50
82	79	71	69	63	

Total $N = 71$

B. Simple Frequency Distribution

X	f	X	f	X	f
98	1	76	2	59	3
96	1	75	1	58	1
95	1	74	1	56	1
92	1	73	1	54	1
91	1	72	2	52	1
89	1	71	4	51	1
87	1	70	9	50	1
85	2	69	3		
84	1	68	5		
82	3	67	1		
81	1	66	3		
80	2	64	1		
79	8	63	2		
78	1	60	2		

of the ages of a sample of 71 residents in a veterans' facility. A first step in data analysis might be to construct a *simple frequency distribution,* in which each value of a variable is listed only once, along with the number of cases that have that value. Table 14.3 includes a simple frequency distribution of the ages of the people in the facility. The X column refers to the values or categories of the variable, while the *f* column indicates the frequency, or the number of cases, that have each value.

Simple frequency distributions can be constructed on variables at any level of measurement. In Table 14.3 it is much easier to gain some sense of the age distribution of the residents from the simple frequency distribution in comparison to the raw data distribution. Sometimes, however, simple frequency distributions are too cumbersome. Table 14.3 shows a lot of categories to look at, and many categories have either no or only a few cases. In these situations, it often is preferable to collapse a distribution further by creating a grouped frequency distribution.

Grouped Frequency Distributions. At its core, data analysis is basically a search for patterns in data. Sometimes, however, searching for patterns in raw data is akin to the old adage of not being able to see the forest for the trees. Even if we order the observations with a simple frequency distribution, the large number of observations, the small variations between some observations, and large gaps between others combine to hide the pattern inherent in the data.

Grouping is the process of combining a large number of individual variable categories into a smaller number of larger categories. It permits us to step back from the data and see the big picture by ignoring minor variations between cases and focusing our attention on larger patterns. One reason for grouping is to summarize the data into a manageable number of categories; a table or graph may be unreadable if it has too many categories. Another purpose is to eliminate categories with either no or few cases in them. In addition to making it easier to see patterns in the data, grouping often is necessary for certain data-analysis procedures. For example, a statistical computation may require enough cases so that each cell in a table could, theoretically, have at least five cases in it. Grouping helps meet this requirement, because reducing the number of categories increases the number of cases falling into the newer, larger categories.

The manner in which grouping is done depends, in large part, on the level of measurement of the data. Table 14.4 shows the hypothetical results of a small survey that includes the variable "religious affiliation." This frequency distribution clearly is in need of grouping: Some categories have no cases at all; others have few cases. The coding scheme also has a large number of categories. When grouping nominal data like these, we rely on logic and common sense to group categories that, in some way, fit with each other. For example, it is logical to group all Protestant denominations into a new category called "Protestant" because they all share some core beliefs and practices. On the other hand, those categories with few or no frequencies could reasonably be grouped into a category called "other," simply because none of them contain a sufficient number of cases. The difference in reasoning behind each group is important to note, because it may be significant for later analysis. For example, if we are evaluating how religious affiliation relates to attitudes toward volunteering for community service, then "Catholic," "Jewish," and "Protestant" are meaningful categories, whereas "other" is a hodgepodge of cases that we really cannot describe in terms of common theology. For purposes of analysis, we may want to classify these latter cases as "missing" and exclude them from analysis.

Grouping ordinal data can be a very straightforward process of merging adjacent categories. For example, if we decide that the nine social-class categories in Table 14.5 are too many, it is easy to collapse them down to the conventional three shown in the table. In this illustration, going from nine to three categories makes logical sense, because the nine small categories are gradations of the three larger groupings.

This is not always the case, however. A survey may include an item that asks for years of education

TABLE 14.4 Illustration of Grouping a Nominal Variable

	Original Code Scheme RELIGION religious affiliation			Recoding Scheme RELIG2 religious affiliation groups	
Value	Label	Frequency	Value	Label	Frequency
1	Roman Catholic	10	1	Roman Catholic	10
2	Methodist	3	2	Protestant	20
3	Presbyterian	2	3	Jewish	10
4	Lutheran	5	4	Other	5
5	Baptist	4			
6	Unitarian	3			
7	Episcopalian	3			
8	Jewish	10			
9	Moslem	1			
10	Eastern Orthodox	0			
11	Hindu	1			
12	Buddhist	1			
13	Shintoist	0			
14	Atheist	2			
15	Other	0			

Total $N = 45$

TABLE 14.5 Grouping Ordinal Data

Social Class	f	Social Class	f
Upper-upper	8		
Middle-upper	14	upper	57
Lower-upper	35		
Upper-middle	56		
Middle-middle	92	middle	212
Lower-middle	64		
Upper-lower	44		
Middle-lower	32	lower	87
Lower-lower	11		
Total (N) = 356		Total (N) = 356	

but it may not have a variable for the highest degree attained. In this case, the desired variable could be approximated by grouping the existing variable. Although years of education could, conceivably, be construed of as a ratio-level variable, if it is applied as an indicator of preparation for employment, then it might better be treated as an ordinal. In terms of getting a job, having a high school diploma, an associate degree, or a bachelor's degree may be the critical determinants. People who dropped out without completing the 12th grade are all dropouts whether they completed 9, 10, or 11 years. People who have 13 to 15 years of education probably have some college but not a bachelor's degree. Rather than using equal multiples, as in the social class example, a researcher might approximate employment preparation by grouping years of education into the following categories:

1 = <9 years (no high school)
2 = 9–11 years (some high school)
3 = 12 years (high school graduate)
4 = 13–15 years (some college)
5 = 16+ years (college graduate)

This scheme would not be perfect, of course, because not everyone with 12 years of schooling graduated, but it would approximate the desired variable. As this example illustrates, the fact that the original categories are ordered is a starting point for grouping a variable, but the researcher must still rely on logic and knowledge of the application to which the grouped variable will be put to decide on the boundaries of the intervals.

Grouping interval-level data is a fairly direct process. Unlike ordinal data, the distance between units of interval-level data are, by definition, equal, so one general principle is to use equal-width intervals when grouping data. Nevertheless, common sense and knowledge of the use to which the grouped data will be put are essential to planning the group intervals. Intervals of $10 might make perfect sense if grouping data on the weekly earnings of high school students, but these intervals are completely inappropriate if the data concern the annual income of single-parent households. All raw frequency distributions of interval data have units of 1, such as length of jail sentence in days, earnings in dollars, or live births per year. In grouping, we merely increase the number of units in each new interval from 1 to 3, 10, 1,000, or whatever amount both makes logical sense given the data and provides the desired number of intervals for describing that data and doing data analysis. The size of the grouped intervals is called the *interval width*. Consider the distribution of ungrouped ages for the residents of the veterans' residential facility in Table 14.3. Clearly, these scores are in need of grouping, because they are so spread out that any pattern is difficult to see.

To illustrate grouping interval data, we will group the scores in Table 14.3 into 10 new intervals. We want enough intervals so we do not obscure significant variation in the data, but we also want to reduce the clutter of too many categories. Once the decision regarding the number of intervals is made, we must determine the number of measurement units that will go into each new interval—that is, the interval width. In this example, with a range of 48 years in the age variable and the number of grouped intervals set at 10, it is quite obvious that the interval width should be 5. In other situations, however, the interval width may not be so easy to determine, so there is a formula that one can apply to find the interval width:

$$\text{Interval Width} = \frac{H_s - L_s}{N_i}$$

where H_s is the highest actual score in the distribution, L_s is the lowest actual score in the distribution, and N_i is the number of desired intervals. Now, if we applied this equation to the data in Table 14.3, we would have

$$\text{Internal Width} = \frac{98 - 50}{10} = \frac{48}{10} = 4.8$$

In many cases, the result of this formula is a decimal of some sort that one merely adjusts upward or downward to the nearest convenient interval width. In our case, we would adjust upward for an interval width of 5. The resulting frequency distribution is displayed in Table 14.6.

When selecting interval widths, we suggest that the width be an odd number, such as 3, 5, or 7, because intervals with an odd-numbered width have a whole number for their *midpoints*. For example, with an interval of size 5, 50–54 has a midpoint of 52, but with an interval of sized 4, 46–49 has a midpoint of 47.5. When working with grouped interval data, the midpoints have a number of uses; for example, they could be used as category labels in Table 14.6, and it is far more convenient to work with midpoints that do not have decimals.

Compare the grouped data in Table 14.6 with the ungrouped and simple frequency distributions in Table 14.3. Do you notice anything in the grouped distribution that you did not see when you first looked at those distributions, especially the ungrouped distribution? The grouped distribution clearly shows the characteristic accumulation of people in the middle of a distribution with the frequencies tapering off

TABLE 14.6 Patient Age Data Grouped by Intervals of 5 Years

Interval Width	Value	Frequency	Percent	Valid Percent	Cum Percent
50–54	52	4	5.6	5.6	5.6
55–59	57	5	7.0	7.0	12.7
60–64	62	5	7.0	7.0	19.7
65–69	67	12	16.9	16.9	36.6
70–74	72	17	23.9	23.9	60.6
75–79	77	12	16.9	16.9	77.5
80–84	82	7	9.9	9.9	87.3
85–89	87	4	5.6	5.6	93.0
90–94	92	2	2.8	2.8	95.8
95–99	97	3	4.2	4.2	100.0
	Total	71	100.0	100.0	
Valid cases 71	Missing cases 0				

toward both tails of the distribution. Such a distribution is commonly referred to as a "normal curve," and is an important characteristic of data distributions that will be used in choosing some statistics in Chapter 15.

GRAPHICAL DISPLAY OF DATA DISTRIBUTIONS

In addition to describing variables by means of a frequency distribution, another common procedure is to use a graph. The visual impact of a graph can help identify and summarize patterns in data that might not be detected as readily by perusing frequency distribution tables. Today statistical software can produce a diverse array of graphs that can be enhanced with color and editing capabilities. Used correctly, graphs are a powerful tool for communicating information about data; used incorrectly, they can confuse and even mislead viewers about the meaning of a distribution. One situation in which graphs are popular occurs when the results of a frequency distribution must be presented to an audience unfamiliar with reading such tables.

Here we present a few of the more common ways to graph individual variables. Basically, these graphs are visual representations of a frequency distribution. Earlier we discussed ways of grouping data for presentation in a frequency distribution table. Many of these same issues apply to graphing data. For example, a graph is more effective if there are a manageable number of categories. If several categories have a very low frequency, they will be hard to see on a graph. An effective graph, then, begins with organizing the data appropriately, just as one would for a frequency distribution table.

Bar Graphs

One of the most commonly used types of graphs is the **bar graph**. A distinguishing feature of the bar graph is the space between the bars. These spaces illustrate that the categories of the variable being represented are separate, or *discrete*. In Chapter 5, we pointed out that only certain categories are theoretically possible in a discrete variable, such as sex, religious affiliation, and household size. Nominal and ordinal variables are, by definition, discrete variables, so bar graphs are especially useful for these levels of

Noncitizens Serving a Sentence in a Federal Prison, 1990–1994

Year	Number of noncitizens in prison
1990	12,349
1991	14,046
1992	16,117
1993	18,218
1994	18,929

FIGURE 14.3 Example of a Bar Graph

SOURCE: Based on Bureau of Justice Statistics, (1996). *Noncitizens in the Federal Criminal Justice System 1984–1994* (Washington, D.C.: U.S. Department of Justice), p. 9.

data. Figure 14.3 illustrates a typical bar graph, with the height of the bars representing the frequencies in each category of the variable. As can be seen from the figure, a bar graph makes it easy to note trends, such as the upward one in Figure 14.3.

When constructing a bar graph—and most other types of graphs, for that matter—care should be taken when establishing the dimensions of the graph. The vertical axis, which represents the frequencies, and the horizontal axis, which represents the categories of the variable, should be about equal, with reasonably equal spacing of the categories on both axes. Again, Figure 14.3 illustrates this. The concern for roughly equal dimensions is important because it is possible to accidentally—or purposely—construct a graph that gives a false impression. For example, by expanding the dimensions of the vertical axis, a graph can be constructed that makes small differences among categories appear to be large, at least to the casual observer. On the other hand, expanding the horizontal dimension has the opposite effect; a graph can be constructed that appears to minimize differences among the categories. Purposeful manipulation of graph dimensions in an attempt to deceive viewers is considered unethical. It should be noted, however, that misleading graphs are produced all the time, so anyone reading a research report should always carefully inspect any graph to be sure that viewers are not being misled by its initial appearance.

Histograms and Frequency Polygons

Although some variables, such as household size or a frequency count of a behavior, are discrete variables, the variables at the interval or ratio level of

FIGURE 14.4 Histogram and Frequency Polygon of Hypothetical Exam Scores

measurement are conceived of as *continuous,* meaning that, unlike the discrete variables, there are no gaps or spaces between the categories. Thus age is a continuous variable. This continuous nature of interval and ratio data should be reflected in graphs used to present them. The researcher wishing to graph interval or ratio data has a choice of two popular methods.

The **histogram** bears a considerable resemblance to the preceding bar graph. Once again, as we see in Figure 14.4, bars of various lengths represent the magnitude of the frequencies from a frequency distribution. The only difference between a bar graph and a histogram is that the bars in a histogram touch, signifying the continuous nature of the data.

Figure 14.4 also illustrates the alternative technique of graphing interval or ratio data, the **frequency polygon**, which is simply a line graph that connects the midpoints of each category of the variable. The choice of either a histogram or a frequency polygon is purely a matter of personal preference, because they are interchangeable.

Pie Charts

The **pie chart** is another type of commonly used graph that is particularly good for showing how some whole amount is divided. As such, pie charts often are used to illustrate how budgets are distributed for varying functions. Anyone who has occasion to prepare a grant proposal will most likely have to create one or more pie charts indicating how the money would be spent. Figure 14.5 is a pie chart based on projected revenue to the federal government for the 1997 fiscal year.

A pie chart gets its name from its resemblance to the slices of a pie. The size of each slice visually depicts the percentage of the whole that each category represents. Preparing a pie chart via a computer program now involves simply choosing a

FIGURE 14.5 Example of a Pie Chart
SOURCE: *Budget Supplement Fiscal Year 1997.* (1996). Washington, D.C.: U.S. Government Printing Office, p. 2.

variable and the pie chart option from the graphing menu. However, the process that the graphing program uses involves determining how many of the 360 degrees of an entire circle are to be allocated to each of the categories. For example, Figure 14.5 indicates that 11 percent of revenues are expected to come from corporate income taxes. To determine how large a slice to allocate to corporate income taxes, the data-analysis software multiplies 360 by 11 percent, obtaining a value of 39.6 degrees. So, the slice devoted to corporate income taxes is drawn such that it occupies 39.6 degrees of the 360 degrees of the circle.

CONTINGENCY TABLES

Thus far, we have discussed ways of describing the distribution of cases on a single variable and of presenting single variable data in the form of frequency distributions and graphs. Now we turn our attention to ways of describing and exploring how two or more variables are distributed together. That is, given the values in a data set on one variable, how are values distributed on one or more other variables? Classifying or organizing the data on one variable according to values on a second variable is the basis for contingency table analysis.

Bivariate Relationships

The statistics we have considered so far describe the distribution of a single variable and, therefore, are called **univariate statistics**. Most data analysis in research involves dealing with two or more variables simultaneously. Statistical procedures that describe the relationship between two variables are called **bivariate statistics**, and **multivariate statistics** deal with three or more variables. When two or more variables are analyzed with descriptive statistics, the major feature of interest is the relationship between the variables, especially the extent to which they covary, or vary together. If two variables are related, then a change in one of the variables is associated with a change in the other.

A convenient way of investigating bivariate relationships is to cross-tabulate the data in the form of a table. A *contingency table* contains raw frequencies, percentages, or both. Here, we discuss the construction of such tables for only two variables; however, contingency table analysis can be applied to three or more variables.

Table 14.7 illustrates the general form of a contingency table. We use two conventions to standardize the construction of contingency tables. First, when we have an independent variable and a dependent variable, the vertical *columns* represent categories of the independent variable, and the horizontal *rows* represent categories of the dependent variable. In Table 14.7, the variable *Income* is the independent variable, and *Hours of Television Watched* is the dependent variable. Second, when ordinal- or higher-level data are cross-tabulated, the categories should be ordered as illustrated in Table 14.7, with columns running from lowest on the left to highest on the right, and rows from lowest at the bottom to highest at the top. These conventions are not universally applied, however. Some tables are constructed differently, but following the conventions does contribute to consistency and ease of interpretation. Furthermore, the

TABLE 14.7 A Contingency Table with Frequencies and Percentages

(dependent variable)   *(independent variable)*

NUMBER OF HOURS OF TELEVISION WATCHED

		INCOME	
	Low	Medium	High
High	49 (19.2%)	19 (8.6%)	10 (6.7%)
Medium	164 (64.3%)	136 (61.5%)	86 (57.5%)
Low	42 (16.5%)	66 (29.9%)	53 (35.6%)
Totals	255 (100%)	221 (100%)	149 (100%)

(cell frequency)   *(cell percentage)*   *(column marginals)*

SOURCE: Davis, J. A., & Smith, T. W. (1972–1994). General Social Surveys. Chicago: National Opinion Research Center; Storrs, CT: The Roper Center for Public Opinion Research, University of Connecticut.

computational routines for some statistics assume that tables are constructed according to this convention, and therefore must be modified to produce correct results with differently structured tables.

Several labels refer to the various parts of tables. The squares of the table are called *cells,* with the frequencies within the cells labeled *cell frequencies.* Values in the "Totals" column or row are called *marginals* (only the column marginal is shown in Table 14.7). Tables often are identified according to the number of rows and columns they contain. A table with two rows and two columns becomes a 2 × 2 (read "2 by 2") table. A table such as Table 14.7 is a 3 × 3 table. In addition, because the number of rows is always designated first, a 2 × 3 table is not the same as a 3 × 2.

Contingency tables almost always include *cell percentages,* because by themselves, cell frequencies are difficult to interpret if the number of cases varies in each column and row. Converting frequencies to percentages makes interpretation much easier, and can be done by dividing each cell frequency by the appropriate marginal total and then multiplying the result by 100. We would use column marginals if we wanted to see how the dependent variable was distributed across categories of the independent variable. Percentages in the first column of Table 14.7 were obtained by dividing the cell frequencies 49, 164, and 42 by the column marginal 255, with the result multiplied by 100. Below each column, the percentages are totaled and indicated as equaling 100 percent. This informs the reader that the column marginals were used to compute the percentages. Sometimes the cells in a contingency table contain only percentages and no frequencies. In this case, the marginal frequencies should always be included, because they supply valuable information regarding the number of cases on which the percentages are based and enable the reader to compute the cell frequencies if needed.

Reading percentage tables is a straightforward process similar to constructing them. Whereas we computed the percentages down the columns, we read percentage tables by comparing percentages along the rows. Of particular interest is the *percentage difference* (% d) between any two categories within a given row. For example, in Table 14.7, the difference between the low-income column and the high-income column in the top row is

12.5 percent, meaning that substantially more low-income people watch high levels of television. The % d suggests that high levels of television watching are less common among high-income groups. Note that, with a 2 × 2 table, a single % d summarizes the complete table. As the number of rows and columns in a table increases, the number of % d's that can be calculated increases rapidly.

The magnitude of % d's is a crude indicator of the strength of the relationship between two variables: Small differences of 1 or 2 percent indicate weak and, possibly, meaningless relationships, while % d's of 15 percent or more usually indicate substantial relationships. Unfortunately, no hard-and-fast rules concerning evaluation of the magnitude of % d's can be offered because of the complicating factor of sample size. For example, if we are dealing with employment data for the entire nation, a difference of 1 percent or less could represent a million more workers with or without jobs. With large samples, smaller % d's are more important. Alternatively, with small samples, % d's must be large before they indicate a substantial relationship. (We will discuss other statistics for assessing the strength of relationships in contingency tables in Chapter 15.)

Multivariate Analysis

As noted in Chapter 2, analyzing an independent and a dependent variable and finding a bivariate relationship between them does not prove that the independent variable actually *causes* variation in the dependent variable. To infer causality, the possible effects of extraneous variables must be investigated. Although research projects may focus primary attention on two variables, they typically consider others to assess the full complexity of social phenomena. A set of procedures for conducting this kind of multivariate analysis is called either **table elaboration**, or **contingency control**. Contingency control involves examining a relationship between an independent and a dependent variable while holding a third variable (also called a *test factor*) constant. Three variable tables are constructed such that the relationship between the independent and dependent variable can be examined within each category of that third variable. The general format of contingency control is illustrated in Figure 14.6.

The original table with which the researcher begins the analysis is called the *zero-order table,* and the relationship contained within it is known as a *zero-order relationship*. The *zero* in these labels indicates that no control or test variables are being used. As we introduce test variables, the tables produced are called *partial tables,* and the relationships within them are known as *partial relationships*. A partial relationship is a relationship between an independent and a dependent variable within one category of the test or control variable.

Partial tables are referred to by the number of test variables being controlled at one time. If we are controlling one test variable in our partial tables, these tables are referred to as *first-order partials,* indicating that the number of variables being controlled is one. If more variables than one are being simultaneously controlled, the tables are called

FIGURE 14.6 General Format for Partialing Tables

second-order partials, third-order partials, and so on. Often, research does not go beyond the first order with contingency control. One reason is that as we add more test variables, the number of partial tables generated increases rapidly, and interpreting all these tables becomes difficult. The other reason table elaboration often is not taken much beyond the first order is that the sample gets divided quickly, to the point that individual cell frequencies may become too small and reduce our confidence in the results. In other words, we literally run out of cases. This effect can be seen in Figure 14.6, where in the zero-order case the sample is divided among the four cells of the zero-order table; but when we move to the partials, the same number of cases is spread among the eight cells of the two tables, thus reducing the magnitude of the cell frequencies. For analyzing multivariate relationships beyond the first order, we normally use techniques other than table elaboration.

A number of outcomes can occur when a test variable is introduced and partial tables are created. Describing some of these outcomes offers an idea of the basic logic behind multivariate analysis. First, the partial tables may show *no effect.* This also is called *replication,* because the results in the partial tables replicate, or repeat, the results in the zero-order table: The relationship in the partial tables is approximately the same in terms of strength and direction as it was in the zero-order table. In this case we have tested a variable that is unrelated to either the independent or the dependent variable; therefore, it could not affect the relationship between those variables. We have illustrated this in Figure 14.7, where the zero-order table shows the relationship between *gender* and *whether people believe life to be exciting, routine, or dull.* You can see in the zero-order table that about 10 percent more of the males believe that life is exciting. It is possible, however, that *marital status* might influence whether men and women perceive life to be exciting. So, in the partial tables, we look at the relationship between the two variables separately for married and single people (to

Zero-Order Table

Is Life Exciting?

	Gender Male	Gender Female
Exciting	213 (50.1%)	221 (39.8%)
Routine/Dull	212 (49.9%)	334 (60.2%)
Totals	425 (100%)	555 (100%)

First-Order Partial Tables

Single — Is Life Exciting?

	Gender Male	Gender Female
Exciting	69 (54.3%)	48 (46.2%)
Routine/Dull	58 (45.6%)	56 (53.8%)
Totals	127 (100%)	104 (100%)

Married — Is Life Exciting?

	Gender Male	Gender Female
Exciting	114 (47.7%)	107 (40.4%)
Routine/Dull	125 (52.3%)	158 (59.7%)
Totals	239 (100%)	265 (100%)

FIGURE 14.7 Table Elaboration Showing "No Effect" of the Test Variable (Replication)

SOURCE: Davis, J. A., & Smith, T. W. (1972–1994). *General Social Surveys.* Chicago: National Opinion Research Center; Storrs, CT: The Roper Center for Public Opinion Research, University of Connecticut.

Zero-Order Table

		Person Reads Report	
		Yes	No
Person Quits Smoking	Yes	200 (50%)	135 (27%)
	No	200 (50%)	365 (73%)
	Totals	400 (100%)	500 (100%)

First-Order Partial Tables

Less Than High School Education

		Person Reads Report		Totals
		Yes	No	
Person Quits Smoking	Yes	20 (20%)	75 (19%)	95 (19%)
	No	80 (80%)	325 (81%)	405 (81%)
	Totals	100 (100%)	400 (100%)	500

High School Education or More

		Person Reads Report		Totals
		Yes	No	
Person Quits Smoking	Yes	180 (60%)	60 (60%)	240 (60%)
	No	120 (40%)	40 (40%)	160 (40%)
	Totals	300 (100%)	100 (100%)	400

FIGURE 14.8 Relationship between Reading Smoking Reports and Smoking Cessation, with Level of Education as a Control Variable

simplify the example, we have left out the other possible marital statuses). You can see that this third variable has almost no effect on the original relationship. In each of the categories of marital status, about 7 to 8 percent more men than women see life as exciting.

A second possibility when doing table elaboration is that the strength of the relationship found in the zero-order table may be substantially reduced—or even disappear entirely—in the partials. We described this kind of situation in the discussion of causality in Chapter 2, but without calling it by these names. We have reproduced that data in Figure 14.8. The zero-order table shows how reading reports about the health consequences of smoking impacted on whether people quit smoking. The table shows that people who read such reports are substantially more likely to quit smoking (% d = 23%). When we control for education, however, the original relationship disappears. In each educational grouping, quitting smoking is as common among those who have not read the report as it is among those who have.

This result can be difficult to interpret, because there are two possibilities and we need more information, which may or may not be available, to choose between the two. One possibility is that in terms of temporal order, the test variable intervenes between the independent and the dependent variables (see Figure 14.9). When such an intervening variable is controlled, it is called *interpretation*. The independent variable is changing the test variable, which in turn is changing the dependent variable; in other words, a causal sequencing is being specified. When there is such a causal chain, the relationship between the independent variable and the dependent variable is effectively blocked in the partial tables. In our example, an intervening variable relationship means that reading the report is what produces their level of education and that level of education, in turn, causes them to quit smoking. This probably is not an appropriate assessment of these variables, however, because there is no logical or theoretical reason to assume that reading a health

Intervening Variable Relationship

Independent Variable → Test Variable → Dependent Variable
Read Report → Level of Education → Quit Smoking

Antecedent Variable Relationship

Test Variable → Independent Variable
              → Dependent Variable

Level of Education → Read Report
                   → Quit Smoking

FIGURE 14.9 Comparison of Intervening and Antecedent Variable Relationships

report would change people's level of education. So interpretation probably is not what is going on in this table.

This brings us to the other possibility—namely, that the zero-order relationship is either all or partly *spurious*. In this case, which is called *explanation*, the test variable is temporally located before either the independent or the dependent variable and is related directly to both. This is called an *antecedent variable relationship*. When the effects of the test variable are controlled, the apparent relationship between the independent variable and the dependent variable is reduced or eliminated because the operation of the test variable was to inflate the actual relationship between the other two variables in the zero-order table. In other words, the relationship shown in the zero-order table was a false reading. In Figure 14.8, we know that people's educational levels are antecedent: Their educational levels were established before they had a chance to read the report or quit smoking. In addition, theoretical reasons allow us to conclude that level of education can influence both whether people read the report and whether they quit smoking. This tells us that the relationship in the zero-order table is spurious.

So when a relationship disappears in a partial table, we need to establish the appropriate temporal location of the test variable or use some theoretical or logical considerations to determine whether interpretation or explanation is the proper assessment of what is going on. If that cannot be done, as might occur with survey data, then we cannot be sure whether the partials are indicating the presence of an intervening variable or a spurious relationship. (As noted in Chapter 2, determining temporal order is crucial in sorting out causal relationships among variables.)

Yet another possibility can be discovered in table elaboration. *Specification* refers to a situation where the relationship between the independent and dependent variables is found in the zero-order table, but the partial tables show different relationships from one table to another. One partial table may show no relationship or only a weak relationship, while the other shows a strong relationship. In other words, the table elaboration specifies the categories of the test variable in which the relationship occurs or does not occur.

Figure 14.10 shows one example of what specification can look like. The figure shows the relationship found in one study between social class and self-esteem among adolescents. The zero-order table shows a fairly strong relationship, with adolescents of higher social classes being more likely to have high self-esteem (% d = 13% in the high self-esteem category). When gender is introduced as a test factor,

Zero-Order Table

		Social Class		
		Lower	Middle	Upper
Self Esteem	High	38%	46%	51%
	Medium	26%	25%	23%
	Low	35%	29%	26%
	Total	340 (100%)	2686 (100%)	195 (100%)

First-Order Partial Tables

Males

		Social Class		
		Lower	Middle	Upper
Self Esteem	High	36%	47%	55%
	Medium	26%	25%	17%
	Low	39%	28%	28%
	Total	168 (100%)	1383 (100%)	89 (100%)

Females

		Social Class		
		Lower	Middle	Upper
Self Esteem	High	41%	46%	47%
	Medium	27%	25%	28%
	Low	32%	29%	24%
	Total	172 (100%)	1311 (100%)	106 (100%)

FIGURE 14.10 Table Elaboration Showing Specification: Relationship between Social Class and Self-Esteem, Controlling for Gender. *Society and the Adolescent Self-Image* by Morris Rosenberg (Princeton, NJ: Princeton University Press, 1965), pp. 40–41.

SOURCE: Davis, J. A., & Smith, T. W. (1972-1994). *General Social Surveys.* Chicago: National Opinion Research Center; Storrs, CT: The Roper Center for Public Opinion Research, University of Connecticut.

however, the original relationship gets dramatically specified: Upper-class boys are substantially more likely to have high self-esteem than lower-class boys are (% d = 19% in the high self-esteem category). The relationship is much weaker, although still in the same direction, among girls (% d = 6% in the high self-esteem category). So the introduction of the test factor enables us to specify that social class is a fairly powerful factor in shaping self-esteem among boys, but much less so among girls.

We want to mention one final possibility that can be found in table elaboration: The partial tables may show an even stronger relationship between the independent and dependent variables than was indicated by the zero-order table. This outcome occurs because the action of the uncontrolled test variable in the zero-order table is to suppress the relationship between the independent and the dependent variables. In fact, variables that produce this result are called *suppressor variables,* and the result itself is known as *suppression.* This occurs when the test variable and the independent variable exert forces on the dependent variable that are at least partly offsetting. In other words, as values of the independent variable increase, they influence the dependent variable to increase; but as the test variable increases, it influences the dependent variable to decrease, thus masking part of the relationship between the independent and the dependent variables. When the influence of the test variable is controlled, this masking effect is removed, and the relationship between the independent variable and the dependent variable is revealed to be stronger than in the zero-order table.

A number of other possibilities can occur in table elaboration, but these examples illustrate the importance and difficulty of this kind of multivariate analysis. It is important because it enables us to discover the complexity of social reality where dependent variables are influenced by a number of factors at the same time. It is difficult because it requires time, patience, and creativity to tease out what can sometimes be hard-to-discover relationships.

REVIEW AND CRITICAL THINKING

Main Points

- Data analysis refers to deriving some meaning from the observations that have been made as part of a research project. Quantitative data analysis involves putting observations into numerical form and manipulating them based on their arithmetical properties.
- Data preparation and organization is an essential part of the research process, including knowing the best way to enter data into an electronic file and manipulate that data.
- Data analysis begins by developing a coding scheme and a codebook, which is a set of mutually exclusive and exhaustive numerical codes into which the raw data are categorized.
- After the data have been entered into a computer file, they must be carefully checked for coding or input errors.
- New or revised variables may be created by recoding existing variables or computing new variables based on existing variables.
- Frequency distributions may be effectively communicated with bar graphs, histograms, frequency polygons, and pie charts.
- Frequency distributions reveal the pattern that the frequencies produce among the various categories of the variable, and may be symmetrical or asymmetrical.
- Contingency tables and percentage tables are particularly useful for analyzing bivariate and multivariate relationships with categorical or partially ordered data.

Important Terms for Review

alphanumeric variables	contingency control	multivariate statistics	table elaboration
bar graph	data analysis	numeric variables	univariate statistics
bivariate statistics	frequency polygon	pie chart	
coding scheme	histogram	statistics	

Critical Thinking

Today we are confronted with massive amounts of numerical information in our daily lives, due in part to modern communications technologies. This makes it especially important to develop critical thinking skills that will enable you to evaluate this deluge of information and separate what is legitimate and useful from what is meaningless or deceptive. The material presented in this chapter can serve as a guideline for this critical thinking.

When confronted with statistical information, ask the following questions:

1. Was some kind of coding or other data reduction strategies used in preparing the data for analysis? If so, does this introduce any distortions or oversimplifications into the data?
2. Is the raw data presented? Or does the analysis involve some summarization of the data into a simple frequency distribution, a grouped frequency distribution, or a contingency table? If so, does this introduce anything distorting or misleading into the analysis?
3. Are the data displayed in any graphical form? If so, are the graphs chosen

appropriate? Are the graphs designed in a way that the visual impression communicates a different conclusion than the numerical data seem to suggest?

Exploring the Internet

One of the better sites on the Internet related to designing and using graphs to display data is Michael Friendly's site, Data Visualization: Looking Back, Going Forward (http://datavis.ca). This site provides a topic-based collection of available resources for statistics, statistical graphics, and computation related to research, data analysis, and teaching. An interesting feature of this site is a page devoted to illustrating some of the best and worst examples of graphs to depict data. Examining these graphical depictions of data will show you the value of using graphs—and some of the pitfalls to avoid as well. Access the Data Visualization Gallery at http://datavis.ca/gallery. Google for other web pages that offer similar kinds of instructions for and examples of the visual presentation of data.

For Further Reading

Craft, J. L. (1990). *Statistics and Data Analysis for Social Workers,* 2nd ed. Itasca, Ill.: Peacock. This brief introduction to statistical analysis provides many good illustrations of the kinds of statistical analysis that involve human service workers.

Gravetter, F. J., & Wallnau, L. B. (2013). *Statistics for the Behavioral Sciences,* 9th ed. Belmont, Calif.: Cengage Learning/Wadsworth. This is a standard but well-written introductory textbook in statistics. It covers all the topics discussed in this and the next chapter, going into more detail and including additional topics.

Green, S. B., & Salkind, N. J. (2011). *Using SPSS for Windows and Macintosh: Analyzing and Understanding Data,* 6th ed. Upper Saddle River, N.J.: Pearson. This book provides an introduction to utilizing the most widely used statistical package today, SPSS. This handbook will show you how to do all the things discussed in this and the next chapter.

Healey, J. F. (2012). *Statistics: A Tool for Social Research,* 9th ed. Belmont, Calif.: Cengage Learning/Wadsworth. This is another standard but well-written introductory textbook in statistics. Along with the Gravetter and Wallnau book, it can help you understand all the material in this and the next chapter.

Jones, G. E. (2007). *How to Lie with Charts,* 2d ed. Santa Monica, Calif.: LaPuerta. An ideal guide for all who want to understand how presenters can use charts to deceive an audience. Readers will learn how to make their presentations more effective.

Journal of Technology in Human Services. New York: Haworth, quarterly. A journal that began publication in 1984, focusing on the potential of computer technology to help us deal with mental health, developmental disabilities, and other human problems. It provides a timely contribution to this area.

Wallgren, A., Wallgren, B., Persson, R., & Jorner, U. (1996). *Graphing Statistics and Data: Creating Better Charts.* Walnut Creek, Calif.: Altamira Press. This book suggests how to create graphs and charts that make viewers aware of the qualities of data. It introduces the elements of charts, such as axes, scales, and patterns; describes steps to make charts clearer, using real data for examples; and walks through the entire process from data to finished chart.

Zeisel, H. (1984). *Say It with Figures,* 6th ed. New York: Harper & Row. A classic analysis of how to present data with statistics. It is very useful for policymakers who wish to improve their understanding of the statistics presented to them.

Class Exercises for Competency Assessment

Assume you have just completed the data collection on a needs assessment regarding a volunteer visitation program for the elderly in your community. You have a random sample of 500 questionnaires completed by people 55 years and older that must now be analyzed. Variables included in the survey are sex, age, annual income, proximity to family members, a scale score on perception of neighbors' capacity to help, and a scale indicating desirability of a visitation program. Finally, the question was asked, "If this program were implemented, would you use it?" The question could be answered yes or no.

14.1. [Research & Practice] Describe the general process you would follow in analyzing the data by listing the main steps to be completed.

14.2. [Research & Practice] Develop a hypothetical coding scheme for the following variables: age, sex, income, and desirability scale score (assume the scale scores can range from 0 to 30).

14.3. [Research & Practice] In terms of bivariate relationships, using the final question as the dependent variable, show which indicators would be appropriate for each of the independent variables. What if the dependent variable is the scale score?

14.4. [Research & Practice] Use the final question as the dependent variable and assume you have recoded age into a bivariate variable: under 65 and 65 or older. Diagram a contingency table for "use program yes or no" versus age group. Now diagram a zero order and first order partial table with sex as the first order variable.

Chapter 15

Data Analysis II: Descriptive and Inferential Statistics

Considerations in Choosing Statistics
   Level of Measurement
   Goals of the Data Analysis
   Number of Variables
   Properties of the Data
   Audience

Descriptive Statistics
   Measures of Central Tendency
   Measures of Dispersion
   Measures of Association
   The Normal Distribution

Inferential Statistics
   Probability Theory
   Sampling Distributions
   Statistical Hypothesis Testing
   Statistical Procedures

Review and Critical Thinking
   Main Points
   Important Terms for Review
   Critical Thinking
   Exploring the Internet
   For Further Reading
   Class Exercises for Competency Assessment

This chapter is a continuation of the introduction to data analysis that began in Chapter 14. Recall that data analysis is the process of deriving some meaning from the observations that are made during the research process. Thus far, the focus has been on describing data using relatively simple procedures such as frequency distributions, data plots, and contingency tables. Although these means of summarizing and displaying data are useful, researchers often rely on more sophisticated statistics to describe data precisely and examine relationships between variables.

Statistics have become common to the lexicon of modern living. We often hear people casually referring to something being "above the norm," "below average," or "correlated" with something else. Tune in to the evening news and you might assume that death from cancer is imminent, because research has shown a "statistically significant correlation" between your favorite food and the dreaded disease. Or you might hear a report stating that the relationship between underage drinking and traffic-related injuries to adolescents is "statistically significant." Because statistics are ubiquitous in our modern world, people often use statistical terms, such as "correlation" or "statistical significance," without fully comprehending what they mean. It is imperative to have a basic understanding of statistical concepts to be an informed consumer of both the popular media and the professional literature in the social sciences and human services.

It is also very likely that, as a human service professional, you will need to compile data, analyze it, and present the findings as part of a needs assessment, funding proposal, or documentation of program outcome. This requires knowing not only how to interpret a statistic, but also which statistics to use and how to compute them. We believe it is especially important to emphasize choosing the correct statistic. Computer technology has made statistical computation relatively easy, but the proper selection of statistical procedures and interpretation of statistical results cannot be done by the computer—it requires an intellect informed about statistical analysis.

This chapter is not intended as a thorough coverage of statistical procedures; to provide such coverage requires a book devoted solely to the subject. We do, however, provide a basic introduction to the fundamentals of statistical analysis in order to draw conclusions from the data and understand their broader implications.

CONSIDERATIONS IN CHOOSING STATISTICS

Once the data are coded and in a computer file, the researcher is ready to begin the data analysis that will unlock the information that the data contain. One of the major errors that can occur in data analysis is selecting a statistic that is inappropriate for the kind of data gathered in a research project. Although many factors need to be taken into account in choosing statistics appropriately, five major considerations are especially important.

Level of Measurement

One consideration is the level of measurement of the data collected. Chapter 5 addressed the four levels of measurement: nominal, ordinal, interval, and ratio. Each level of measurement involves different rules of permissible mathematical operations that can be performed on the numbers produced while measuring variables at that level (see Table 5.3, p. 112). The nominal level involves merely classifying observations into categories. The categories have no order, and the numbers associated with a category only serve as a label for the category. In other words, the numbers have no mathematical value, and performing any arithmetic operation on them is inappropriate. On the other hand, a ratio level of measurement has a true zero point, making all mathematical operations permissible.

Each statistical procedure involves mathematical operations that are appropriate at one of the levels of measurement. For example, a nominal statistic assumes that the data have only mutually exclusive and exhaustive categories and none of the mathematical properties of the other levels of measurement. Likewise, a ratio statistic assumes that the data have a true zero point and requires mathematical operations appropriate to that.

The basic rule is that variables measured at a given level can be analyzed either with a statistic designed for that level of measurement or with a statistic designed for a lower level of measurement. As Table 15.1 illustrates, nominal, ordinal, interval, or ratio data can be treated as nominal and used with a statistical procedure designed for nominal data. For example, a frequency distribution (as described in Chapter 14) can be used with a nominal-level variable such as religious affiliation; however, a frequency distribution also can be used to classify data at higher levels of measurement, such as levels of agreement to Likert scale items (ordinal level) or annual income in dollars (ratio level). Because it

TABLE 15.1 Relationship between Statistics and Level of Measurement

Level of Measurement Statistic Is Designed For	Nominal	Ordinal	Interval	Ratio
Ratio	No	No	No	Yes
Interval	No	No	Yes	Yes
Ordinal	No	Yes	Yes	Yes
Nominal	Yes	Yes	Yes	Yes

No = Inappropriate to use the statistic with this data
Yes = Appropriate to use the statistic with this data

can handle data at all levels of measurement, a frequency distribution is a good statistical procedure with which to begin data analysis.

Even though data measured at higher levels can be analyzed with lower-level statistics, a trade-off results in terms of the kind of information and relationships we can discover about the data based on the statistics. With annual income, for example, it is much more informative to be able to say that the people in the upper 10 percent of the income distribution range earn eight times more money than people in the bottom 50 percent than to simply report the number or percentage of people who are in a particular income category. Therefore, researchers generally prefer to use the highest level of statistic that is appropriate for a particular variable. In addition, it is definitely inappropriate to use a statistic designed for a level of measurement higher than the level of measurement of the data being analyzed.

Thus far, we have discussed the role of levels of measurement in selecting a statistic on the basis of individual variables. Many research questions, however, involve examining relationships between two or more variables simultaneously, and these may involve different levels of measurement. For example, we might study whether substance abusers abstain or use drugs (nominal) after attending one of several treatment programs (nominal) while also taking into account religious affiliation (nominal), age (interval), and severity of addiction (ordinal). One reason why so many different statistical procedures exist is that they address different possible combinations of levels of measurement among variables. For any data-analysis problem, then, the researcher must be able to classify each variable in terms of its level of measurement.

Goals of the Data Analysis

The second consideration in assessing the appropriateness of statistics is to determine what goals the statistic is meant to accomplish. Each statistical technique performs a particular function, revealing certain information about the data. A clear conception of the analytical goals of the data analysis is a prerequisite for selecting the best statistics for achieving those goals. Statistical techniques have one of two goals: *description* or *inference*. **Descriptive statistics** assist in organizing, summarizing, and interpreting data. The data might be from a sample or from a whole population (see Chapter 6); in either case, descriptive statistics organize and summarize the body of data. **Inferential statistics** allow us to make generalizations from sample data to the populations from which the samples were drawn. Recall from Chapter 6 that the ultimate reason for making observations on samples is to draw conclusions regarding the populations from which those samples were drawn. We make observations on a sample of clients in an agency because it is too expensive, time-consuming, or impractical to observe all the clients, yet we want to draw conclusions about all the clients. Inferential statistics are based on probability theory, and they basically tell us the probability of being wrong if we extend the results found in a sample to the population from which the sample was taken.

Statistics must be chosen that are appropriate to the goals of the data analysis. In some cases, we use both descriptive and inferential statistics, because the analysis intends to accomplish both goals. If, however, a population were small enough that the data could be collected from every element in the population, inferential statistics would not be necessary and would be inappropriate. In addition, inferential statistics should not be used if the goals of the analysis are descriptive, and descriptive statistics should not be used if the goal of the analysis is inference.

Number of Variables

A third consideration in choosing an appropriate statistic is the number of variables to be analyzed: **Univariate statistics** are those that analyze only one variable, **bivariate statistics** analyze two variables, and **multivariate statistics** analyze three or more variables. An example of a univariate statistical problem would be an investigation of the average income paid to correctional officers in a particular correctional facility. The only variable in this problem is "amount of income." The correctional facility is not a variable, but rather a constant; that is, it has only one value or category. This problem could be changed into a bivariate problem by introducing a second variable: How does gender affect the average income paid to the correctional officers in the facility? Now, the problem has two variables—namely, gender and amount of income. A multivariate problem could be hypothesized by adding additional variables: How do gender, race, and seniority influence levels of income in the facility?

Each statistic is designed to be used on either a univariate, bivariate, or multivariate problem. A point of clarification, however, is warranted: Some univariate statistics also are calculated as *part* of some bivariate or multivariate statistics. For example, among the statistics to be discussed in this chapter, the mean is a univariate statistic, but it is also calculated as a part of some bivariate statistics, such as Student's *t*, and some multivariate statistics, such as multivariate analysis of variance (MANOVA). In these cases, however, the univariate statistic is only one step in the more complex and lengthy calculation of the bivariate and multivariate statistics.

Properties of the Data

To be properly used, some statistics require that the data to be analyzed have certain mathematical or other properties. We have already discussed an example of this as levels of measurement, which involves the mathematical properties required for particular statistical tests. This is discussed separately, because it is of paramount importance and relates to every statistical procedure. Other assumptions about the properties of the data, however, also need to be considered.

One important assumption of many statistical procedures is that the observations on the dependent variable are independent of one another. For example, if we are evaluating the effectiveness of a counseling program for men who batter their partners, we might randomly assign 20 men to receive treatment and 20 men to the control group. Upon completion of the program, each man participates in a videotaped simulation exercise where an observer rates the subject's use of controlling tactics with his partner. The 20 control tapes are graded first, and then the 20 treatment tapes are graded. The grading process is a complex task, and the observer becomes more skilled in grading as he or she gains practice and counts more controlling behaviors as a consequence. In this situation, subjects who are scored later are likely to have higher scores than those who are rated first, so the scores are correlated with—that is, are "dependent" on—rating order. This condition is referred to as *serial dependence*, because the scores are dependent on their position in the series of measurements. Serial dependence often is hard to detect. It can be a serious problem, however, because one may reach erroneous conclusions when comparing the average rating for the treatment group with the average rating of the control group. (Statistical procedures exist to detect such a correlation with serial position and estimate how much of the difference between groups results from it.)

In other situations, it is more obvious that observations are not independent; in fact, some research problems call for designs that include related observations. This is particularly the case when we want to study change over time. For example, perhaps we classified homeless shelters by funding source in 1986 and again by funding source in 1996 to determine if there was a trend. A similar situation occurs when the same group of people is given a pretest and a posttest, or possibly several tests over the course of an intervention. Single-system designs (discussed in Chapter 11) are another example of a research design that often fails to satisfy the assumption of independence. In these three examples, because the same organizations or individuals are being observed at different points in time, the observations are not independent, and we would consider this fact when selecting statistical procedures.

Another important assumption for some statistics concerns the shape of the distribution of observations on a variable. Some statistics require that this distribution be normal or symmetrical. If the distribution is not normal, then the statistic that is calculated on the data may be misleading.

As a part of the process of selecting an appropriate statistic, researchers review these various assumptions about the nature of the data they are analyzing and assess the risk of using a statistic that requires assumptions not met (or not fully met) by the data. The more the data violate these assumptions, the greater the risk of producing a misleading result.

Audience

If all the preceding considerations are weighed and more than one statistic can appropriately be used, we next consider the audience for whom the data analysis is intended. If that audience has limited statistical expertise, then a relatively simple, easily understood statistic is preferred over a more complex, possibly confusing statistic. Among the simpler statistics are the visual forms of presenting data (discussed in Chapter 14) and univariate statistics. Some bivariate statistics—and, especially, the multivariate statistics—may be beyond the comprehension of most audiences without at least an elementary introduction to statistics.

With these considerations in mind, we now turn to the descriptive statistics that are most commonly used in the social sciences and human services.

DESCRIPTIVE STATISTICS

Imagine that we are selected to spend a year studying abroad. We say good-bye to our friends and family and board a plane for Europe, Asia, or another far-off locale. During the course of our stay, we will likely be asked by our hosts to describe what Americans are like. For example, we might be asked to describe American college students. We might talk about what is typical or common among American college students: American college students are middle-class kids who like to attend sporting events such as football, basketball, and hockey. They head south during Spring Break to party, eat junk food, and pay for school by relying on their parents and taking out loans. They love to use texting, email, and the Internet to communicate, and they watch a lot of television.

That's not a complete description, however, and hardly a fair one. Many students don't attend athletic events at all, nor do they get to sport a tan after Spring Break. Some do not get any financial aid, and although a majority of freshmen may be 18, some are in their 50s! So in trying to describe what American college students are like, we really need to talk about the diversity among students, not just what is most common. Beyond describing similarities and differences, we also might discuss the characteristics of particular groups. So we might say, for example, that women at our school are more likely to major in social work and men in criminal justice. As we engage in this process of describing what students are like, we would be using, albeit casually, the basic principles of descriptive statistics. Descriptive statistics provide quantitative indicators of what is common or typical about a variable, how much diversity or difference there is in the variable, and how values on one variable are associated with values on one or more other variables.

Measures of Central Tendency

Although valuable for revealing patterns within the data and the shape of the distribution, frequency distributions (discussed in Chapter 14) can be cumbersome. In fact, with variables that can take on many values, such as age or income, a frequency distribution can become so massive that it is difficult to detect patterns in it. **Measures of central tendency**, more commonly known as *averages*, summarize distributions by identifying the "typical," or "average," value and are one of the most commonly used statistics. The three most widely used measures of central tendency are the *mode, median*, and *mean*, each of which has unique qualities and is designed for use with a particular level of measurement.

The *mode* is the category in a frequency distribution that contains the largest number of cases. The mode for the grade distribution in Table 14.2 on page 380 is C, because more people received that grade than any other. Although the mode can be determined for data of any level of measurement, such as the grade distribution, which is ordinal, the mode usually is used with data of the nominal level for two reasons. First, the mode is the least stable of the three measures—that is, its value can be changed substantially by rather minor additions, deletions, or changes in the values that make up the distribution. With the other measures of central tendency, adding more cases produces less dramatic shifts in their values. Second, if two or more categories are tied with the largest number of cases, we could have two, three, or more modes, none of which would necessarily be very typical of the distribution. The presence of several modes also undermines its utility as a summary statistic to describe the average case.

With ordinal data, the *median* is the appropriate measure of central tendency. The median is the point in a distribution below which 50 percent of the observations occur. For example, a distribution of six scores—10, 14, 15, 17, 18, 25—results in a median of 16. Note that when the distribution contains an even number of values, an observed score may not fall on the median; then the median is the value halfway between the two central scores. If we add another score greater than 16 to the preceding distribution so it contains seven cases, the median is 17, an observed score. Because the median does not take into account the actual value of the scores but only the number of observations, whether the score we add is 17, 100, or 1,000 makes no difference—the median is still 17. This makes the median very stable, because the presence of extremely high or low scores in a distribution has little effect on the value of the median.

The *mean* is the measure of central tendency that most people think of when they hear the word "average," and it is calculated by summing all the values in a distribution and dividing by the number of cases. The mean, however, is only suitable for interval- or ratio-level data, where there is equal spacing along a scale and various mathematical functions can be performed (see Chapter 5). There is one exception to this—namely, dichotomous nominal- or ordinal-level variables that have only two values. Many interval-level statistics, such as the mean, can be meaningfully computed on such variables. This is called *dummy variable analysis* and is beyond the scope of this chapter.

Because the mean takes into account the actual value of all the scores in a distribution, it is less stable than the median. The presence of a few extreme scores will pull the mean in that direction. Because of this, the median often is the preferred average when summarizing skewed distributions, even with interval-level data, because it more accurately reflects the central value. For example, although the mean could be used to summarize income data, the U.S. Census Bureau typically reports median income, because the relatively few wealthy people tend to pull the mean to such a high level that it overstates typical family income. Because it is less affected by extreme scores, the median also often is preferred in clinical practice research, where treatment and control groups usually are small and violate the assumptions required for statistics based on the mean.

Selecting the most appropriate measure of central tendency for a given set of data is not difficult. Level of measurement and skewness are the primary considerations. With relatively symmetrical distributions, the only factor is level of measurement.

Measures of Dispersion

Like measures of central tendency, measures of dispersion describe and summarize distributions. Whereas central tendency indicators describe the middle or average of the distribution, **measures of dispersion** indicate how dispersed or spread out the values are in a distribution. Measures of dispersion add valuable information about distributions. On the basis of central tendency measures alone, we might assume that two distributions with similar averages are basically alike. Such an assumption would be erroneous, however, if the spread of the distributions were different. As illustrated in Figure 15.1, distribution A is more dispersed, with values deviating widely from the central value; the values in distribution B are more tightly clustered near the average. To avoid possible erroneous assumptions about the spread of distributions, researchers report a measure of dispersion along with a measure of central tendency.

The three commonly used measures of dispersion are *range, semi-interquartile range,* and *standard deviation*. The *range* is the simplest of these, referring merely to the difference between the highest and lowest scores in the distribution. As such, the range indicates the total spread of a distribution. Knowing the end points of a distribution, however, tells us nothing about how the remainder of the values are dispersed within the distribution. Furthermore, because the range is based on only two values, it is unstable. Adding or deleting extreme scores causes the range to vary widely, whereas the bulk of the distribution may change little. Moreover, despite its simplicity, the range is suitable only for interval data. The operation of subtraction used to obtain the range assumes that the values of the scores in a distribution have meaning; however, this is true only for interval- and ratio-level data. Because of these limitations, the range usually is used as an adjunct to other measures of dispersion and not reported alone.

The *semi-interquartile range* (sometimes called the *quartile deviation*) is symbolized by the letter Q; it is closely related to the median and is the measure of dispersion usually reported with it. The semi-interquartile range is obtained by first dividing a frequency distribution into fourths or *quartiles*. The first quartile (Q_1) is the score below which 25 percent of the scores occur, and the third quartile (Q_3) is the score below which 75 percent of the scores occur. (The median is the second quartile [Q_2] and is the point below which 50 percent of the scores occur.) The semi-interquartile range is equal to half the difference between the third quartile and the first quartile. The larger the value of the semi-interquartile range, the more dispersed the scores are from the median. The value of Q is calculated as

$$Q = \frac{Q_3 - Q_1}{2}$$

The *standard deviation*, symbolized by the letter s, indicates the average (or mean) spread of the scores from the mean, and therefore is the measure of dispersion usually reported along with the mean. The larger the value of the standard deviation, the more dispersed the scores are from the mean. Actual calculation of the standard deviation is relatively

FIGURE 15.1 Two Distributions with the Same Average but Different Dispersions complex and beyond the scope of this chapter. In addition to its use as a descriptive statistic, the standard deviation has important applications in inferential statistics.

One final note on measures of dispersion: Although their overall purpose is to assist in the description of distributions, a single dispersion value from a single distribution is not particularly revealing. The major utility of dispersion indicators is in comparing several distributions, because they enable us to tell at a glance which has more or less spread.

Measures of Association

Measures of association describe the nature of relationships between variables, particularly the *strength* of the relationship or how closely the variables are related. The strongest relationship is a *perfect* one, in which a given change in one variable is *always* associated with a given change in the other variable. Rarely, however, are perfect relationships found in human service research. A less-than-perfect relationship indicates only a tendency for the variables to vary together. With ordinal- or higher-level data, relationships between variables also can be positive, negative, or curvilinear. Recall from Chapter 2 (p. 32) that a positive relationship is one in which the change in value of the variables is in the same direction—that is, both increase or both decrease. A negative relationship is one in which one variable increases while the other decreases, and a curvilinear relationship is one in which the direction of change in one variable is not consistent with changes in the other. For example, in a U-shaped curvilinear relationship, both low and high values of the independent variable may be associated with high values of the dependent variable. In this case, a negative relationship exists between the two variables for low values on the independent variable and a positive relationship with high values on the independent variable. Most measures of association indicate a perfect positive relationship by +1.00 and a perfect negative one by −1.00. The closer the value of the measure is to −1.00 or +1.00, the stronger the relationship is. Likewise, the closer the value is to 0, the weaker the relationship is.

The overriding determinant in selecting a measure of association is the level of measurement of the data at hand. Therefore, we will consider measures of association according to the level of measurement for which each was designed.

Nominal Data. Some data are dichotomous in form—that is, the variables have only two values, such as yes/no or male/female. A useful measure of association for two dichotomous variables is the *phi* (pronounced *phee*) coefficient (φ). The data are cast into a 2 × 2 table, as illustrated by Table 15.2. The value of phi indicates the strength of the relationship between variables by yielding a value between −1.00 and 1.00. Although phi may yield negative values, the negative sign is simply ignored, because it has no meaning in the case of nominal data.

The value of phi is considered a good measure of association for three reasons. First, it is easy to compute. Second, it is mathematically related to measures of association that are suitable for other levels of measurement, which makes comparing the strength of different relationships possible. Measures of association that are not mathematically related have different operating characteristics and produce values that are not comparable, precluding

TABLE 15.2   Nominal Data Suitable for Phi

	Gender	
Is Life Exciting?	Male	Female
Exciting	213	221
	(50.1%)	(39.8%)
Routine/Dull	212	334
	(49.9%)	(60.2%)
Totals	425	555
	(100%)	(100%)
	Phi = 0.11	

SOURCE: Davis, J. A. & Smith, T. W. (1972–1994). *General Social Survey.* Chicago: National Opinion Research Center; Storrs, CT: The Roper Center for Public Opinion Research, University of Connecticut.

TABLE 15.3 Nominal Data Suitable for Lambda and Goodman and Kruskal's Tau

		Region			
		Northeast	Midwest	South	West
Religious Preference	Protestant	54 (41.2%)	140 (64.5%)	206 (84.8%)	80 (53.3%)
	Catholic	55 (42.0%)	56 (25.8%)	28 (11.5%)	43 (28.7%)
	Jewish	10 (7.6%)	1 (0.5%)	1 (0.4%)	3 (2.0%)
	None	12 (9.2%)	20 (9.2%)	8 (3.3%)	24 (16.0%)
	Totals	131 (100%)	217 (100%)	243 (100%)	150 (100%)

Lambda = 0.07

Goodman and Kruskal's tau = 0.07

SOURCE: Davis, J. A. & Smith, T. W. (1972–1994). *General Social Survey*. Chicago: National Opinion Research Center; Storrs, CT: The Roper Center for Public Opinion Research, University of Connecticut.

meaningful comparisons. Third, phi is a member of a group of measures of association that can be given what is called a **proportional reduction in error** (PRE) interpretation. The PRE interpretation means that the measure shows how much the independent variable helps reduce error in predicting values of the dependent variable. To interpret phi in this way, it is first necessary to square it (φ^2). For example, $\varphi = 0.11$ is squared to become $\varphi^2 = 0.01$. This latter value is treated as a percentage and interpreted to mean that the independent variable reduced the error in predicting values of the dependent variable by 1 percent. All PRE statistics are interpreted in this way.

Because phi is suitable only for two dichotomous variables, a different measure of association must be used for nominal data with more categories. The most generally useful measure for data of this type is *lambda* (λ). As with phi, the data are cast into tabular form, as illustrated in Table 15.3.

Lambda is a bit different from most measures of association in that its value can range only from 0 to 1.00. Lambda is never negative, but this is not a disadvantage since the negative sign is meaningless with nominal data anyway. Lambda is always positive because it is a direct-reading PRE statistic. In other words, lambda indicates the proportional reduction in error as calculated and need not be squared (as with phi). This is an important point to remember, because the values that lambda produces usually look rather small. The reason is not that lambda understates relationships, but rather that the lambda values are "presquared," which makes them appear to be small.

Although phi and lambda are the most common nominal measures of association, several others are available. For two dichotomous variables, an alternative to phi is Yule's Q. However, Q cannot be given the PRE interpretation, and tends to make relationships appear stronger than they actually are. For nominal data with more categories, Goodman and Kruskal's *tau* (τ) is often used. Sometimes, tau is preferred to lambda, because the former uses data from all cells in the table while the latter only includes data from some of the cells. The value of tau, however, does not always vary from 0 to 1.00, especially when the dependent variable has more categories than the independent variable.

Ordinal Data. Many commonly used measures of association exist for ordinal data. A major consideration in selecting one has to do with whether the data are *fully ordered*. In situations where every—or nearly every—case has its own unique rank and there are no or few ties, the data are said to be fully ordered. Table 15.4 illustrates fully ordered data. The most popular measure of association for fully ordered data is Spearman's rho (r_s). Like phi, Spearman's rho is mathematically related to other measures, and thus facilitates comparisons of relationships. It also has the desirable characteristic of varying between +1.00 and −1.00. Note that now, with ordinal data, the negative sign has meaning and indicates a negative relationship. Also, rho may be squared (r_s^2) and given the PRE interpretation.

When we have only a few ordered categories and many cases to place into them, the data will contain many ties—far too many for Spearman's rho to be usable. Data of this type are called *partially ordered* and are handled in tabular form, as illustrated in Table 15.5. Several alternative measures of association are available for data of this type; for example, gamma (γ), Somer's *D*, and Kendall's tau (τ) are all suitable and vary between −1.00 and +1.00.

TABLE 15.4 Ordinal Data Suitable for Spearman's Rho

Independent Variable	Dependent Variable
Ranks	Ranks
10	9
8	10
1	1
3	5
2	2
9	6
4	7
6	3
5	4
7	8
	$r_s = 0.77$

Some subtle differences among them, however, make one or another most appropriate in a given situation.

The value of gamma is the easiest of the three to compute, but unfortunately, it does not take into

TABLE 15.5 Ordinal Data Suitable for Gamma, Somer's *D*, or Kendall's Tau

		Income		
		Low	Medium	High
Number of Hours Television is Watched	High	49 (19.2%)	19 (8.6%)	10 (6.7%)
	Medium	164 (64.3)	136 (61.5)	86 (57.5)
	Low	42 (16.5)	66 (29.9)	53 (35.6)
	Totals	225 100%	221 100%	149 100%

Gamma = 0.33
Somer's *D* = 0.18
Kendall's tau = 0.20

SOURCE: Davis, J. A. & Smith, T. W. (1972–1994). *General Social Survey.* Chicago: National Opinion Research Center; Storrs, CT: The Roper Center for Public Opinion Research, University of Connecticut.

account any of the tied scores and tends to overstate the strength of the relationship. Indeed, on the basis of a positive gamma alone, we cannot safely assume that as X increases, Y also increases, which is a normal assumption of a positive relationship. Because of its failure to consider ties, all that a positive gamma allows us to conclude is that as X increases, Y does not decrease, which is a much weaker conclusion.

Somer's D is used when we are only interested in our ability to predict a dependent variable from an independent variable. When predicting Y from X, Somer's D takes into account ties on the dependent variable. This has the effect of reducing the value of D in comparison with gamma when the two are computed on the same data. Somer's D, however, gives a more accurate indication of how much the independent variable reduces error in predicting the dependent variable.

Finally, Kendall's tau takes into account all the tied scores. It indicates the degree to which the independent variable reduces error in predicting the dependent variable, and also how much the latter reduces error in predicting the former. Because it considers the relationship both ways, Kendall's tau is particularly appropriate when we do not have a clearly identifiable independent and dependent variable and merely wish to determine if two variables are related. By including all the ties, a positive tau allows us to conclude—correctly—that as X increases, Y also increases. This is the type of statement we expect to make on the basis of a positive result, so Kendall's tau is more generally useful than gamma is.

Interval Data. The most used measure of association for interval data is the *correlation coefficient* or *Pearson's r*. The correlation coefficient is mathematically related to both phi and Spearman's rho, making comparisons among them possible. As with the other two, Pearson's r varies between -1.00 and $+1.00$ and may be squared (r^2) and given the PRE interpretation. When squared, this value is called the *coefficient of determination*.

The correlation coefficient has a unique characteristic that is important to remember when applying or interpreting it. Pearson's r indicates the degree to which the relationship between two interval-level variables can be described by a straight line when plotted on a scattergram, as in Figure 15.2. The formula for r mathematically determines the best-fitting line, and then considers the amount by which the scores deviate from perfect linearity. This feature of Pearson's r means that, if the relationship between the two variables is curvilinear, r will understate the actual strength of the relationship, producing a coefficient that is smaller than it should be. Therefore, it is advisable to plot a *scattergram* or a table with the scores of both variables plotted on it. The scattergram provides a visual indication of the relationship between the two variables and is useful for uncovering curvilinearity. Figure 15.2 illustrates three typical scattergrams. For those instances in which curvilinearity is discovered, a measure of association other than Pearson's r should be selected. Curvilinear measures of association do exist, but these are beyond the scope of this discussion.

Before we leave measures of association, one important matter requires emphasis: Association or correlation does not imply causality! Just because one variable is labeled independent and another dependent and a relationship is found between them does not prove that changes in one variable cause changes in the other. Correlation is only one step toward inferring causality. In addition, it is necessary to affirm the appropriate temporal sequence and rule out rival causal variables.

The Normal Distribution

Chapter 14 discussed frequency distributions as descriptive statistical procedures that transform a raw data distribution into a more meaningful form. There is another way to transform raw data to derive additional meaning from it, and this transformation also will serve as our transition from descriptive to inferential statistics. A transformation is a set of arithmetical operations executed on a variable to obtain a new variable. One common transformation is known as *standardizing*. Raw scores are transformed into *standard scores*, also

FIGURE 15.2 Three Typical Scattergrams

known as *z-scores*. Symbolically, a standardized score, *z*, is given by

$$z = \frac{x - \bar{x}}{s}$$

Standard scores are obtained by following these two steps:

1. Subtract the mean, $\bar{x}$, from each raw score, *x*.
2. Divide the $x - \bar{x}$ difference by the standard deviation, *s*, of the distribution.

If all the raw scores in a distribution are transformed to *z*-scores, a new distribution is obtained that will always have $\bar{x} = 0$ and $s = 1$. This is called a *standard normal distribution*, and as it turns out, this distribution has some quite convenient properties.

One way to think about the z-transformation is that it expresses raw scores in a distribution in units of standard deviation rather than the original unit of measurement. A z-score of 1.5 indicates a score point that is 1.5 standard deviations greater than the mean, whereas a z-score of -1.5 indicates a score point 1.5 standard deviations below the mean. In other words, a standard score, z, is a number indicating the distance that a raw score deviates from the mean as measured in standard deviation units. Furthermore, the sign of a z-score indicates whether the score point is above (+) or below (−) the mean of the distribution.

On first encounter, it may seem strange to express raw scores in terms of standard deviation units, but doing so allows us to make comparisons between distributions that otherwise would be difficult to make because their original units of measurement differ. Standardizing equalizes the units so a meaningful comparison can be made. For example, the comparison of a person's raw scores on two different IQ tests would not be legitimate unless the IQ tests have a common unit of measurement and operate on the same scale. Therefore, mental testers commonly employ the z-transformation as a way of making different IQ tests comparable.

Consider the data in Table 15.6. In both tests, someone received a score of 99; but are both scores really equal? In terms of raw scores, they certainly appear to be, but in relative terms—that is, compared to the other scores in the distribution—the 99 on Test 2 is far more remarkable, and a z-score transformation will reveal this. On Test 1, with a relatively high mean and small standard deviation, the 99 transforms to a z-score of 1.46, which means it is 1.46 standard deviations above the mean of 94.6. The 99 on Test 2, with a low mean and high standard deviation, transforms to a z-score of 2.47, which means it is 2.47 standard deviations above the mean of 49.6. The comparison of z-scores shows that the two scores of 99 are, in fact, far from equal compared to the other scores in their respective distributions. Allowing these types of comparisons to be made is one important use of z-scores.

Another important use of z-scores has to do with what is called the normal distribution. The normal distribution is a continuous, bell-shaped distribution, as shown in Figure 15.3. The **normal distribution** is a symmetrical, unimodal distribution in which the mode, median, and mean are identical. Actually, there is not just a single normal distribution; there are many. Normal distributions may, for example, have different means and different standard deviations. What makes them all normal is that they all are symmetrical and unimodal and have the three measures of central tendency at the same point. In addition, all normal distributions have the same proportion of cases between the same two ordinates. This statement means that between, say, −1 and +1 standard deviations from the mean for any normal distribution, the proportion of the total cases bounded by those points is the same for all those normal distributions.

In Figure 15.3, the shaded area is the proportion of the total area under the curve bounded by points that are 1 standard deviation on either side of the mean. For any normal distribution, no matter what the mean and standard deviation happen to be, the area bounded by $\bar{x} - s$ and $\bar{x} + s$ is always equal to 68.26 percent of the total area under the curve, whereas 95.46 percent of the total area is between $\bar{x} - 2s$ and $\bar{x} + 2s$. In place of $\bar{x} - s$ and $\bar{x} + s$, one may substitute any two points one wishes and carve out a proportion of the total area that will be the same for all normal distributions. Figure 15.3 shows selected points and the

TABLE 15.6   **Two Sets of Hypothetical Test Scores**

	Test 1	Test 2	
	99	99	
	98	45	
$\bar{X} = 94.6$	96	44	$\bar{X} = 49.6$
	95	44	
$s = 3$	95	43	$s = 20$
	93	41	
	91	41	
	90	40	

FIGURE 15.3 Proportions of the Area Under the Normal Curve between Selected Points

proportions of the total area that fall between them for any and all normal distributions.

This indicates another use of z-transformations—namely, to assess the relative position of a score in a distribution of scores. For example, suppose a female student took a national merit exam and received a score of 580. How well did she do compared with the others who took it? If she knows that the scores on this exam are normally distributed and if she knows the values of the mean score and the standard deviation, she can calculate her position relative to the others who took the exam. Suppose the mean was 490 and the standard deviation 72. She could then use the z-formula to transform her exam score of 580 into a z-score as follows:

$$z = \frac{x - \bar{x}}{s} = \frac{580 - 490}{72} = +1.25$$

So her score is +1.25 standard deviations above the mean for all the students who took the test. By looking at Figure 15.3, she can determine that she scored better than at least 84 percent of the students who took the exam. She can figure this out because 50 percent of the students scored below the mean and another 34.13 percent scored between the mean and +1.00 standard deviation above the mean. To figure out what additional percentage is included between +1.00 and +1.25 standard deviations, she can refer to tables that tell what proportion of cases fall between any two points in a normal distribution. (These tables can be found in any introductory statistics text.) From those tables, she can determine that 89.44 percent of all cases in a normal distribution fall below +1.25 standard deviations above the mean. So she did better than more than 89 percent of all the people who took that examination! Transforming her test score into a z-score enabled her to make a precise statement about her place in the distribution relative to others in the distribution.

The standard normal distribution is useful for comparing distributions with different means and standard deviations, and it helps us make precise statements about relative position in a distribution. A third important use of this distribution is that it serves as the foundation for inferential statistics.

The Eye On Ethics section addresses some important ethical issues relating to statistical analysis in research.

INFERENTIAL STATISTICS

As noted in Chapter 6, most social research is conducted on relatively small samples that are drawn from much larger populations, and all the statistical procedures discussed so far are designed to assist in describing, summarizing, and interpreting data from samples. Findings from sample data, however, are of little scientific value if they cannot be generalized beyond the members of the sample to the larger population from which the samples were drawn. For example, it would do other practitioners little good to learn that a researcher had successfully raised the school performance of 50 underachievers unless they could reasonably expect the new approach to work on children who were not in the researcher's sample. In other words, for the new technique to be worthwhile, it must be generalizable to members of the population of underachievers.

Probability Theory

How do we know when research findings are generalizable? Generalization is always an uncertain business, but inferential statistics can reduce the uncertainty to the point where reasonably safe generalizations can be made and the probability of a given amount of error can be estimated. Inferential statistics are based on probability theory—the same probability theory that works to make probability samples representative. Because of this, inferential statistics can be meaningfully applied only to data based on probability samples or experiments in which random assignment has been implemented.

Probability theory allows the mathematical calculation of the likelihood, or probability, that random events or outcomes will occur. For example, if 10,000 raffle tickets are issued and the winning ticket is chosen in such a way that each ticket has an equal chance of being selected, then each person who purchases one ticket has 1 in 10,000 chances of winning. If you buy 10 tickets, then you have 10 in 10,000 (or 1 in 1,000) chances of winning. You have increased the probability of your winning even though the mechanism for selecting the winner is unchanged. This does not mean, of course, that you *will* win. Less likely events do occur, although with less frequency than more likely ones, and a person who purchased only one ticket could certainly win the raffle. In other words, probability theory tells us the *likelihood* of something occurring, but not what *will* occur. For this reason, inferential statistics can tell us whether the odds are on our side that a particular generalization is accurate, but they do not make it a sure bet.

As noted in Chapter 6, probability samples are supposed to represent the populations from which they are drawn, but we can expect differences between a sample and its population because of chance alone. Because these differences are the result of the random process used in the selection of samples, their probability can be readily calculated. For example, suppose a researcher draws a probability sample of 50 delinquent boys and applies a special intervention designed to reduce future involvement in delinquency. At the end of one year, the success rate of the sample is 75 percent, whereas for the population of untreated delinquents, the rate is 60 percent. Can we conclude that the experimental intervention was a success? At the level of the sample alone, it is clear that the treated boys had a better rate, but the differences could have resulted, either in part or completely, from sampling error. Even with random sampling, the researcher might have obtained a sample of boys who were better risks, on average, than those in the general population of delinquent boys. The question that inferential statistics answers is whether the difference between the sample results and the population results is too great to be likely on the basis of chance alone. In the example, running the appropriate inferential statistic would tell us what the chances are of obtaining, through random error, a 15 percent difference between a population and a probability sample drawn from that population. If such a difference were highly probable, then we would conclude that the seeming effect of the experimental treatment was the result of chance differences between the sample and the population. On the other hand, if the result indicated only a small likelihood that a 15 percent differential resulted from chance, then we would reject chance variation as the explanation and conclude that there is a generalizable effect associated with the treatment group.

Sampling Distributions

Our ability to determine the likelihood that a sample difference is the result of chance derives from the properties of the normal distribution, discussed earlier in this chapter, and what are called *sampling distributions*. To explain sampling distributions, let us return to the example of the 50 delinquents with the 75 percent success rate. If we had selected 10 samples of size 50 and computed a success rate on each sample, then we would have found that the success rate differed somewhat from sample to sample, because each sample would have consisted of a different set of 50 boys. For the 10 samples, we might have found the following success rates: 72 percent, 71 percent, 73 percent, 69 percent, 66 percent, 70 percent, 73 percent, 69 percent, 71 percent, and 67 percent. The success rate for these 10 samples is distributed over the range of possible sample results. If we took many more samples of size 50, then we would see a pattern emerge as the number of samples approached infinity. We would find the occasional extremely high or low value, but most frequently, the samples would lie in the middle of this range. A **sampling distribution** is a theoretical distribution of a statistic from all possible samples of a certain size drawn from a population; the distribution shows the probability of occurrence of each value of the statistic. If we actually knew the success rate among all delinquent boys in the population from which these samples were taken, this would be referred to as the *population parameter*, and it is this population parameter around which all the sample success rates are distributed in a statistically predictable pattern.

This sampling distribution has certain properties that are very important in inferential statistics. In particular, the **central limit theorem** from mathematics tells us that when a large number of large, random samples are selected from a population, the resulting distribution of sample statistics has two key properties: First, the sampling distribution approximates a normal distribution; and second, the population parameter is equal to the mean of the sampling distribution. In our example, the distribution of all sample success rates is normal, and the success rate in the population is equal to the average of all those sample success rates. This means we can determine the probability that a sample result will fall between any two points in the sampling distribution, just as we did with z-scores and the normal distribution. It also means we can determine the probability that a sample result will fall far away from the population parameter. Recall from the earlier discussion that approximately 68 percent of all cases in a normal distribution fall within 1 standard deviation above and below the mean of the distribution, and approximately 95 percent of cases fall within 2 standard deviations. Likewise, in a distribution of samples, 95 percent of the sample results will fall within 2 standard deviations of the mean of the sampling distribution, which also is the population parameter. Only 5 percent of samples will fall more than 2 standard deviations away from the population parameter.

Going back to our example, we can choose one of two alternatives: First, the treatment did not work, and we have selected a sample of boys that, by chance, is very different from the boys in the population (sampling error). Second, the treatment worked, and this is what makes the treated boys different from the nontreated boys in the population. If, however, the success rate in the population is 60 percent and the sample success rate of 75 percent is more than 2 standard deviations away from 60 percent, the z-transformation tells us that 75 percent is way out in one of the tails of the normal distribution, and the probability of obtaining such a sample by chance would be highly unusual. Therefore, we are on safer grounds, just in terms of probabilities, to conclude that the sample success rate of 75 percent probably is not the result of sampling error, but rather is showing that the treatment had an effect on this group of boys.

Although many different kinds of inferential statistics are used, they all follow the basic logic involving sampling distributions and normal distributions. The formal process by which researchers decide whether the results of data analysis could be caused by chance or are better explained by relationships between variables is called *statistical hypothesis testing*.

Eye on Ethics — Thou Shalt Not Lie (or Even Mislead) with Statistics!

Many people mistrust statistics. Mark Twain is alleged to have said: "There are three kinds of lies: lies, damned lies, and statistics." Another sentiment regarding statistics was expressed by Mrs. Robert A. Taft:

> I always find that statistics are hard to swallow and impossible to digest. The only one I can remember is that if all the people who go to sleep in church were laid end to end they would be a lot more comfortable. (Patton, 1982, p. 243)

Such sentiments suggest that statistics can be manipulated to reach any conclusion you want. And it is possible to manipulate statistics to support misleading or inaccurate conclusions. That, however, is not the fault of statistics but of the person who uses them unethically. The ethical researcher follows the fundamental principle that one must always give a thoroughly accurate representation of research and statistical data.

Researchers rarely present all of the data they have; usually, they report some sort of summary or distillation that purports to be an accurate characterization of the data. While many ways exist to misrepresent data, one example will illustrate how this can be done with graphical representations. Figure 15.4 presents data on the infant mortality rate in the United States for each year from 1990 to 2000. The data are presented in two separate graphs, although the data are exactly the same. The actual data on infant mortality for that period suggest a modest decline over that period: 22 percent fewer infant deaths in 2000 than in 1990. Now if we look at the visual impression given by the two figures, Figure 15.4A seems to imply a much more sizeable decline than Figure 15.4B, with far less infant mortality at the end of the period. The reason is that the vertical axis in Figure 15.4A is designed so each measurement unit (each additional infant death) takes up a lot of space on the axis. The vertical axis also doesn't show the whole range of measurement units. When we lengthen that axis and add in all the measurement values, as in Figure 15.4B, the visual impression given by the graph is of a much more modest decline, which is a more accurate representation of what the data actually say.

Now, a number of good reasons can be found to shorten one or another axis on a graph, such as saving space, but it must not be done in a way that produces a misleading visual impression of the patterns actually found in the data. And certainly it must never be done to deliberately distort the data. What is said regarding this illustration is true of all statistical analysis in the social sciences: Data analysis can distort results, but social science researchers consider it highly unethical to do so. The prime responsibility of the researcher is to give a complete and accurate representation of the data and conclusions.

Statistical Hypothesis Testing

When we use inferential statistics, we are engaging in a special form of hypothesis testing in which we develop two hypotheses that are precisely the opposite of each other. Then the outcome of a statistical test is used to determine which hypothesis most likely is correct. The first hypothesis, called the **null hypothesis**, states that no relationship exists between two variables in the population or that there is no difference between a sample statistic and a population parameter. "There is *no* relationship between variable X and variable Y in the population" or "There is *no* difference between the success rate of the sample and the success rate of the population" are two examples of null hypotheses. Alternatives to null hypotheses are called **research hypotheses**. Suitable research hypotheses to go with the two preceding null hypotheses are: "There *is* a relationship between variable X and variable Y at the level of the population" and "There *is* a difference between the sample success rate and the population success rate." In each application of a statistical test, we assess the research

Perinatal Mortality Rate

Graph A — Infant Deaths < 28 Days Per 1000 Live Births (y-axis: 6.00 to 10.00), years 1990, 1995, 1996, 1997, 1998, 1999, 2000.

Graph B — Infant Deaths < 28 Days Per 1000 Live Births (y-axis: 0.00 to 10.00), years 1990, 1995, 1996, 1997, 1998, 1999, 2000.

FIGURE 15.4 Two Graphs Showing the Rate of Infant Mortality, 1990–2000
SOURCE: Data Adapted from The 2009 Statistical Abstract, The National Data Book. Table 109. (http://www.census.gov/compendia/statab/cats/births_deaths_marriages_divorces/deaths.html)

hypothesis by determining whether the opposite null hypothesis is probable or improbable.

On first exposure to statistical hypothesis testing, it is not uncommon to question the utility of null hypotheses. If we believe the research hypothesis is true, why not just test that hypothesis? The need for null hypotheses stems from the fact that it is not possible with inferential statistics to prove research hypotheses directly; however, by determining the likelihood that the null hypotheses are false, we indirectly provide evidence that their opposites, the research hypotheses, probably are true. To illustrate this point we will use an example with a clear criterion to use in testing a hypothesis.

Imagine attempting to determine whether a die is unbiased. If it is, then each side should appear an approximately equal number of times—that is, about one sixth of the times the die is thrown. If the die is biased, however, one or more outcomes will occur a disproportionate number of times—that is, one or more numbers will occur substantially more than one sixth of the time. Suppose the die is tossed 12 times,

TABLE 15.7 Illustration of Type I and Type II Errors

Decision	Condition in Population	
	Null Hypothesis Is True	Null Hypothesis Is False
Reject null hypothesis	Type I (alpha) error prob. = alpha	Correct decision (power of test) prob. = 1 − beta
Fail to reject null hypothesis	Correct decision prob. = 1 − alpha	Type II (beta) error prob. = beta

with each outcome occurring twice, or one sixth of the time. Would this prove the die is unbiased? The answer is no. The bias, if it exists, might be too slight to appear after only 12 trials. What if the die is tossed 144 times and each outcome occurs one sixth of the time? Such a result would still not make it certain that the die is unbiased, because a slight bias might be revealed by even more trials. Indeed, no number of trials would provide absolute assurance that the die is unbiased; however, a large number of trials with no evidence of bias would make the hypothesis of a biased die so unlikely that it would be reasonable to reject it. By finding no evidence of support for one hypothesis, we indirectly obtain support for its alternative. In all applications of statistical hypothesis testing, if the evidence fails to support the null hypothesis, then the opposing research hypothesis is accepted as probably true.

Although their computational routines vary, all inferential statistical tests use the properties of sampling distributions and normal curves to yield a result indicating the probability that the null hypothesis is true. In choosing between the competing hypotheses, we ask, "How unlikely must it be for the null hypothesis to be true before we are willing to reject it as false and accept the research hypothesis?" This is determined by the **alpha level**: the probability at which the null hypothesis will be rejected (see Table 15.7). Researchers have some discretion in setting alpha levels, but they must guard against the two types of inferential errors that can be made. **Type I error**, or **alpha error**, is the probability of rejecting a null hypothesis that is actually true. The alpha level selected determines the amount of alpha error we are willing to tolerate, so the researcher directly controls Type I error by setting the alpha level. Usually, alpha levels are written as "$p < .20$" and are read as "a probability of less than 20 percent."

Alpha levels can be understood in the following way: Suppose the null hypothesis is that "no relationship exists between variable X and variable Y in the population." We draw a sample from that population to test the hypothesis and, indeed, find a relationship in the sample data. An alpha level of .20 means that we would find a relationship as large as we did in 20 percent of the samples we draw, even though the null hypothesis actually is true and there is no relationship between the variables in the population. We are now faced with a difficult dilemma: "Is the null hypothesis true and our sample an unusual one, or is the null hypothesis false?" Inferential statistics cannot answer that question for us. It can, however, tell us that, in the long run and by testing many hypotheses, we would be correct 80 percent of the time in rejecting null hypotheses when differences of a given size have an alpha level of .20.

Setting an alpha level as low as .20 makes it easy to reject the null hypothesis, but we are also assured of frequently rejecting a true null hypothesis. To avoid so much Type I error, we might establish a very stringent alpha, such as .001, meaning we would reject the null hypothesis only if its odds of being true were less than 1 in 1,000. If the null hypothesis can be rejected at such an alpha level, we would be quite confident that it was false and we were not committing a Type I error.

Setting extremely rigorous alpha levels, however, raises the probability of making the other possible inferential error. **Type II error**, or **beta error**, is the probability of failing to reject null hypotheses that actually are false. Alpha levels such as .001 make it so difficult to reject null hypotheses that many false ones that should be rejected are not. Thus, in selecting suitable alpha levels, we face a dilemma: Guarding against one type of error increases the chances of making the other type.

Fortunately, conventions regarding appropriate alpha levels have been developed. In general, social researchers operate with alpha levels of .05, .01, or .001. Although these levels are the most common ones in research reports, there is nothing sacred about them. The researcher must consider the purpose of the research and the alternative risks in selecting a given level. For example, medical research into the safety and effectiveness of new drugs or treatments typically operates with very stringent alpha levels, because life-and-death issues are at stake. If the null hypothesis in a research project is "Drug X is not safe," then we want to reject it only if we are very sure it is false. If it is wrongly rejected, people will be exposed to an unsafe product. On the other hand, a practitioner with a null hypothesis of "Reminder phone calls do not reduce the number of no-shows for clinic appointments" might select an alpha level as low as .10. If the procedure shows any chance of working, the clinic may want to try it. In this case, the consequences of rejecting a true null hypothesis are not severe. Some additional issues related to hypothesis testing as well as alpha and beta errors are discussed in Research in Practice 15.1.

A common way of expressing that the null hypothesis was rejected is to indicate that a given result is "statistically significant" at some specified alpha level. Unfortunately, the use of the word "significant" can cause some confusion. In popular usage, "significant" means important or notable. Its meaning in statistics, however, does not have the same connotation. Whether a set of research findings is important or notable depends far more on the topic, theory, sample, and quality of measurement than it does on statistically rejecting null hypotheses. Research on trivial matters or that is procedurally flawed cannot produce important results no matter how many "statistically significant" findings it might contain. Be sure to remember that the meaning of "significant" in statistics is simply that a null hypothesis has been successfully rejected.

Statistical Procedures

Some of the basic considerations for selecting inferential statistical procedures are much like those for selecting descriptive statistics. One important consideration is the nature of the dependent variable. For nominal dependent variables, the commonly used procedures, such as chi-square, are discussed later. Many additional procedures, such as log-linear analysis, go beyond the scope of this book, but are prominent in the research literature. With ordinal dependent variables, many procedures are, in addition to being applicable to ordered data, compatible with small clinical samples. Furthermore, many procedures that are technically appropriate for interval-level data also are used with ordinal variables, because they are "robust"—that is, not readily affected by violation of their theoretical assumptions. Finally, many procedures have been developed to handle interval-level data, such as Student's t, analysis of variance (ANOVA), and regression.

Beyond the level of measurement in the dependent variable, another consideration is the character of the independent variable. Some procedures are designed for single independent variables with only two levels. Other procedures handle two or more independent variables simultaneously and estimate combined effects.

Finally, another issue concerns how the data were generated. Some procedures, such as ANOVA, are intended for data generated by an experiment in which one or more control groups are compared with one or more treatment groups. Other procedures, such as regression analysis, are well suited for analyzing large samples, such as surveys, to estimate effects. Still other procedures, such as MANOVA, are suitable for both statistical control of nonexperimental variables and analysis of experimentally generated variables at the same time. Many of these procedures are highly complex and beyond the scope of this text. The point is that

Research in Practice 15.1   Program Evaluation: Designed For Failure: Statistical Power In Human Service Research

Although much attention is given to the issue of statistical significance or alpha levels in evaluation research, a related and equally important issue—statistical power—often is overlooked. *Statistical power* refers to the probability of *correctly* rejecting a null hypothesis in a research study (see Table 15.7). Another way of looking at statistical power is to conceptualize a study designed with low power as being a study with a high probability of failure, because it cannot detect an intervention that works. If the number of cases in the treatment and control groups is small, and the variation within each group is large, there may be insufficient difference between the groups to generate a statistically significant result.

In technical terms, the problem is that the study has insufficient effect size. The concept of effect size has been receiving increasing attention among researchers (Bloom, Fischer, & Orme, 2009; Prentice & Miller, 1998; Schmidt, 1998). Although various ways exist to measure effect size, for illustration purposes, we will use a simplified version:

$$ES = \frac{\bar{X}_t - \bar{X}_c}{S}$$

where

ES = Effect size
$\bar{X}_t$ = Treatment mean
$\bar{X}_c$ = Control mean
S = Standard deviation of both groups combined

The effect size coefficient is basically a standardized indicator of how big a difference exists between the treatment and control groups. Compare this formula to the one for standardized scores, or z-scores, on page 409; they are almost identical—both are formulas to transform raw scores into standardized scores. Basically, the formula shows that the larger the standardized difference between groups, the larger the effect size. Other things being equal, a larger effect size is more likely to generate a significant statistic. For example, assume we conduct a test of a family intervention program using a treatment group of 15 families that receive the intervention and a control group of another 15 families that do not. Assume also that the intervention program does work, although the effect is modest. If we perform a statistical test on the difference between the two groups, the results may not be statistically significant, despite the fact that the intervention works.

This is a quite real problem, as evidenced by examinations of published human service research indicating that almost half the studies reviewed could not detect even a medium-sized effect (Orme & Combs-Orme, 1986; West, Biesanz, & Pitts, 2000). A consequence of this shortcoming is that policy decisions may be made to curtail or not implement potentially useful innovations. Another important consideration is that a research effort is wasted if it is unable to detect a program effect when one is present.

In the typical evaluation of a human service program, the investigator formulates a null hypothesis such as "There is no difference between the treatment group and the control group," expecting to reject it at the specified level of statistical significance or alpha level. The sample data are analyzed, and the null hypothesis is rejected if the difference between the experimental group and the control group is sufficiently large to be considered an improbable event at the preselected alpha level such as .05, .01, or .001. An unfortunate error of interpretation is to assume that failure to reject the null hypothesis is equivalent to proving the treatment had no effect. A more correct assessment is that the data generated from this study, *as designed*, failed to detect a difference between the treatment and the control conditions. Unless care is taken in the design of the study, that study might not be able to detect an effect even if one is present.

Statistical power is determined quantitatively as

$$1 - beta$$

or

$$1 - \text{(the probability of a Type II error)}$$

The beta level is complex to calculate and beyond the scope of this book. For a particular research

---

specific factors favor the use of some statistical procedures over others, so it is important to select the appropriate procedures. Through other courses, you may learn to use and select the procedures yourself; or as a human service professional, you may rely on outside consultants to assist you with this aspect of your research.

In experimentation, researchers often make comparisons between a control group and a treatment group. If these two groups are comparable in problem, beta can be looked up in a reference work, such as Cohen (1988), or calculated by appropriate computer software. Once this is done, the adequacy of beta can be assessed by the following rule of thumb: The minimum acceptable ratio of Type II errors to Type I errors should be about 4 to 1. Thus, if alpha is set at .05, beta should be 4 X .05 or .20. Because power equals 1−beta, power equals 1 −.20 or .80. (This means we have an 80 percent chance to correctly reject the null hypothesis.) Similarly, if alpha is .01, power should be a minimum of .96, and if alpha is .001, power should be a minimum of .996. The 4-to-1 rule is only a general guideline, however. The power level that is acceptable in a particular research project should be determined by the nature of the research project and its implications.

Reviews of published research studies in the human services and other fields have consistently reported that the actual power of a large proportion of studies is well below these standards of .80, .96, and .996 (Orme & Tolman, 1986). What can be done to improve the power of a research project? Although the concept of power is complex, it has three major determinants: sample size, alpha level, and effect size. By manipulating them, one can improve statistical power.

The larger the sample, the greater the statistical power of a research project. Using the rule of thumb described above with an alpha level of .05 and power equal to .80, it can be shown that (with participants evenly divided between treatment and control groups) a total of 52 participants are needed to detect a large effect, 126 participants to detect a moderate effect, and 786 to detect a small effect (West, Biesanz, & Pitts, 2000). Therefore, a straightforward solution to increase power may be to increase sample size. Going back to our illustration of the family intervention program, it would obviously make sense to increase the size of our groups from 15 each to 30 each. It is also apparent, however, that going to about 800 participants to detect a small effect could greatly complicate a research project and make it prohibitively expensive. Another option is to consider reducing the alpha level. Because Type I and Type II errors are related, it may be an acceptable trade-off to set alpha at .1 with beta at .40, according to the rule of thumb of 4 times alpha. Under this scenario, power is equal to 1 − 40 = .60. This would make it easier to detect an effect, but it does increase the risk of a Type I error.

Of course, neither of these solutions is without drawbacks. Fortunately, a researcher may use additional steps in an effort to increase statistical power (Lipsey, 1997). The best approach may be to increase the effect size of the independent variable in the sample (or increase the difference between $\bar{X}_t$ and $\bar{X}_c$ in the *ES* formula). Other things being equal, the larger the effect of the independent variable relative to other factors, the more likely the null hypothesis will be rejected. One way to increase effect size is to select samples that minimize measurement error and ensure a high proportion of the difference between treatment and control groups is the result of the independent variable (see Chapters 6 and 10). Another solution lies in taking steps to eliminate as much extraneous variation as possible. Thorough training of service providers, careful rehearsal of procedures, and attention to program detail can all serve to eliminate variation caused by factors other than the program effect (or reduce the size of the denominator, or variation, in the *ES* formula).

We don't often think of social interventions in terms of dosage, but the evaluation researcher should make sure the participants receive a sufficient dose of the independent variable to make a difference. If the program is financial aid, then it might be better to give a small sample large amounts of aid instead of a little aid to many. If the program is counseling, then the program should provide an intensive counseling experience. Using the most valid and reliable measurement tools can help detect a difference that exists between groups.

all respects except for the treatment received, a commonly used statistic is Student's *t*. This statistic compares the mean of one group against the mean of the other. Recall from Chapter 6 that the groups may have different means by chance alone. Large differences, however, suggest a treatment effect, but what is a large difference? The answer depends on the scale of the variable being measured and the size of the samples. The Student's *t* test results in a statistical value that is referred to a table for samples of different sizes. This table indicates the probability of obtaining a value that is as large or larger by chance. If the table value is less probable than the alpha level, one rejects the null hypothesis and concludes that the difference is significant. Tables indicating the value of t and other inferential statistics necessary for rejecting null hypotheses at various alpha levels may be found in any introductory statistics textbook. Computer packages, such as SPSS, provide the significant value.

In many experimental situations, the research involves more than two groups. The researcher also may want to measure the difference between groups. For example, if four treatment groups each receive different amounts of tutorial help, the researcher might be interested in the effect each level of help has on the number of problems the members of the different groups can solve. For this situation, which involves an experimental design and an interval-level dependent variable (number of problems solved), a commonly applied statistical procedure is *analysis of variance*, or *ANOVA*, which compares the variability in the scores of members within each group (within-group variance) with the variability between treatment groups. We do not expect all members of a treatment group to do equally well. In fact, even if one level of treatment works better than another, some members of a group receiving a lower-level tutorial program might do better than some members receiving a better tutorial program. Use of ANOVA permits the researcher to estimate how much of the variance in performance between groups results from the treatment.

Another commonly used statistical procedure is *multiple-regression analysis*. Multiple regression is used for a variety of purposes, but a typical application involves estimating the effect of multiple independent variables. For example, we might be interested in determining if a person's income is influenced by gender, race, and age—plus *how much* each of these variables affects income. As discussed earlier, correlation indicates whether two variables are associated, but regression permits the researcher to estimate how much change in the dependent variable is produced by a given change in an independent variable. Multiple regression is especially useful in that it can handle a large number of independent variables simultaneously, permitting researchers to estimate the effects of one variable while controlling for others. We know, for example, that income is correlated with race, education, age, and occupation—among many other variables. If we collect these data from a number of respondents, regression permits us to estimate the contribution of each independent variable to income. Multiple regression produces coefficients that indicate the direction and amount of change in the dependent variable to be expected from a unit change in the independent variables. Thus if the dependent variable is dollars of income, a regression coefficient of $580 for the variable "years of education" indicates that one more year of education is worth an additional $580 per year in income, assuming the other independent variables are held constant. In our illustration, regression would produce an equation as follows:

$$Y'(\text{income}) = a + b_1(\text{race}) + b_2(\text{education}) + b_3(\text{age}) + b_4(\text{gender})$$

where a is the value of Y before other factors' effects are considered, b_1 is an estimate of the effect of race on income, b_2 is the estimated effect of education, b_3 is the estimated effect of age, and b_4 is the estimated effect of gender. Y' is the estimated change in income produced by the combination of all these factors.

A widely used inferential statistic suitable for nominal data is chi-square (χ^2), which is applied to data in tabular form. The several versions of chi-square allow its application to data of different types. All versions, however, operate by comparing the number of cases that are actually found in the cross-classification of two or more variables with the number of cases that would be expected by chance. For example, Table 15.8 shows the relationship between region and religious preference in a sample of 741 people in the United States. The null hypothesis for this table would be that there is no relationship between the two variables. Chi-square compares the actual values in a table like this with what would be expected if the variables

TABLE 15.8 Nominal Data from Table 15.3. Suitable for Chi-Square, Showing Observed and Expected Values

		Region				
		Northeast	Midwest	South	West	Totals
Religious Preference	Protestant	54 (exp = 85)	140 (exp = 141)	206 (exp = 157)	80 (exp = 97)	480
	Catholic	55 (exp = 32)	56 (exp = 53)	28 (exp = 60)	43 (exp = 37)	182
	Jewish	10 (exp = 3)	1 (exp = 4)	1 (exp = 5)	3 (exp = 3)	15
	None	12 (exp = 11)	20 (exp = 19)	8 (exp = 21)	24 (exp = 13)	64
	Totals	131	217	243	150	N = 741

Chi-Square = 107, $p < 0.001$

SOURCE: Davis, J. A. & Smith, T. W. (1972–1994). *General Social Survey*. Chicago: National Opinion Research Center; Storrs, CT: The Roper Center for Public Opinion Research, University of Connecticut.

were unrelated. Table 15.8 also contains these expected values (given within parentheses in each cell). Expected values can be calculated from the marginals in the table. The expected proportion of cases in each cell is what would be found in the population if there were no relationship between the two variables. For example, because people in the Northeast make up 17.7 percent of the whole sample, we expect 17.7 percent of all Protestants in the sample, or 85 out of 480, to be from the Northeast if the variables of religious preference and region are unrelated. Because of random variation, we would expect that the actual values in the sample would not be exactly the same as the expected values in the population, even when there is no relationship. The more the actual cell frequencies in a sample diverge from the expected frequencies, however, the more likely it is that the null hypothesis is false and an association does exist between the two variables in the population. In Table 15.8, "Chi-Square = 107" shows the actual chi square coefficient calculated for the table, and "$p < 0.001$" means that the likelihood of having differences between expected and observed values as large as we found in this table when the null hypothesis actually is true in the population (meaning there are no differences between expected and observed values in the population) is 1 out of 1,000.

Small values of chi-square indicate little or no association, whereas large values indicate an association is likely. With chi-square, the value of the statistic is influenced by the sample size and the number of categories on each variable. Computer data-analysis packages automatically take this into account in reporting significance level; however, when doing hand calculations, researchers must refer the statistical value to a special table that states the probability of obtaining a chi-square value of that magnitude by chance, given the sample size and number of variable categories. Chi-square does not indicate the strength of the association, but rather whether one exists at the level of the population.

For the consumer of research, this introduction provides some basic guidelines for interpreting statistical analyses encountered in reading research. Those who will conduct research and engage in statistical analysis themselves need to go beyond the materials presented here and to books such as those mentioned later in *For Further Reading*.

INFORMATION TECHNOLOGY IN RESEARCH — Statistical Software

Although computing statistics by hand or by calculator is possible, virtually all data analysis today is done on a computer. Personal computers are sufficiently powerful that they can run sophisticated statistical packages, such as SPSS, SAS, and MINITAB, which have placed state-of-the-art statistical capabilities at the disposal of virtually everyone—and at a relatively low price. At the same time, the bewildering array of software has made software selection a complicated choice.

Because researchers now use computers for so many different tasks, we no longer can evaluate statistical software solely on the basis of the number of statistical procedures it can run—we also must consider the other applications of the software. Fortunately, several excellent sources are available for assistance in selecting statistical software. Many popular periodicals about computers, such as *PC Magazine*, *PC World*, and *InfoWorld*, publish articles evaluating software. In addition, many professional journals publish articles on statistical software. One of the better sources for social research applications is *Social Science Computer Review*.

As for selecting the correct statistic to use for a set of data, computer software is available to help the researcher identify key issues and systematically put that knowledge to use. One example is the program Methodologist's Toolchest (Brent & Thompson, 2000). This program does not analyze data; rather it presents options for data analysis from more than 200 statistical procedures and a description of how well each option fits the stated objectives and assumptions of the research. Methodologist's Toolchest is an example of a so-called expert system in that the program contains information for decision making. The software leads the user through an interview by presenting questions on the screen. The answer to one set of questions determines the next set of questions to appear. Through these questions, the researcher tells the program whether the data analysis is descriptive or inferential, how many variables are involved, and so on—basically, the kind of information discussed in this chapter. It should be emphasized that the program does not select the statistic for the user; rather it guides the user through the steps necessary for choosing a proper statistic. The program prepares a report that includes as many as four statistical procedures, rated by how well they match the assumptions and objectives of the researcher as well as the expectations of the intended audience. The report also includes a comprehensive description of each selected test, complete with references and a list of statistical software packages that include the test.

Using a computer program like this does not ensure that a researcher will always select the appropriate statistic. Nor can one expect it to replace knowledge of research methods and data analysis. The program does, however, systematize the selection process, make a large amount of technical information immediately accessible, and encourage the researcher to consider design options that might otherwise be overlooked.

REVIEW AND CRITICAL THINKING

Main Points

- The major considerations in choosing statistics properly are level of measurement of the variables, goals of the research, number of variables involved, properties of the data, and audience.
- Descriptive statistics are procedures that assist in organizing, summarizing, and interpreting sample data.
- Measures of central tendency, or averages, summarize distributions by locating the central value of frequency distributions.
- Measures of dispersion indicate how dispersed or spread out the values are in a distribution, with most indicators revealing the average spread of the scores around the central value.
- Measures of association indicate the strength of relationships and, with ordinal- or higher-level data, the direction of relationships.
- Sometimes data are transformed into z-scores or standard normal distributions. These distributions enable us to compare distributions with one another, assess the relative position of cases in a distribution, and conduct inferential statistics. The properties of the normal distribution are important in this regard.

- Inferential statistics allow generalizations to be made from sample data to the populations from which those samples were drawn. Inferential statistics derive from the properties of the normal distribution, sampling distributions, and central limit theorem.
- In inferential statistics, a research hypothesis is paired with an opposite null hypothesis, and the results of a statistical test are used to decide which is most likely to be correct.
- Particular inferential statistics are linked to level of measurement. Among the inferential statistics are Student's t, analysis of variance, regression, and chi-square.

Important Terms for Review

alpha error
alpha level
beta error
bivariate statistics
central limit theorem
descriptive statistics
inferential statistics
measures of association
measures of central tendency
measures of dispersion
multivariate statistics
normal distribution
null hypothesis
proportional reduction in error (PRE)
research hypothesis
sampling distribution
Type I error
Type II error
univariate statistics

Critical Thinking

Information in professional journals will use much of the technical jargon used in this chapter, such as alpha levels, statistical significance, or chi square. Information from other sources, however, such as in a newspaper, magazine, or on a website, may not discuss these matters, even though the conclusions they arrive at relate to them. Whether explicitly mentioned or not, you still need to ask questions relating to statistical description and inference:

1. What is the level of measurement of the variables being considered?
2. Do the conclusions drawn have to do with goals of description or inference? In other words, are conclusions being drawn about a population on the basis of sample data?
3. If any statistics are presented, are they properly used and interpreted?
4. If the conclusions involve an inferential goal, is there any statement about a probability level (that is, an alpha level)? Is there any discussion of "statistical significance" or "margins of error"? Is enough information presented to use this information properly?

Exploring the Internet

Some websites can help you actually carry out data analysis. For example, we have discussed the issue of statistical power in Research in Practice 15.1. Some Internet sites permit you to enter parameters about your data set and receive statistical power calculations as output. One such site is available at the University of Iowa (http://homepage.stat.uiowa.edu/~rlenth/Power), which permits you to determine power statistics for several different kinds of data-analysis problems.

Finally, we have mentioned several different data-analysis software programs in the course of this chapter. You can learn more about such software by contacting software firms at their Internet addresses. Many social science research–related sites also include links to these sites.

For Further Reading

Aron, A., Coups, E. & Aron, E. N. (2011). *Statistics for the Behavioral and Social Sciences*, 5th ed. Upper Saddle River, N.J.: Pearson. This readable introduction to statistics explains the issues clearly and minimizes the use of formulas.

Cuzzort, R. P., & Vrettos, J. S. (1996). *Elementary Statistical Reasoning*. New York: St. Martin's. This fairly brief textbook introduces statistical analysis to the student. It focuses more on the logic of statistics and how to reason through problems than on computational issues.

Frankfort-Nachmias, C., & Leon-Guerrero, A. (2011). *Social Statistics for a Diverse Society*, 6th ed. Thousand Oaks, Calif.: Pine Forge Press. This book provides a comprehensive overview of descriptive and inferential statistics and the applications of statistics by using them to elaborate on issues of race, class, and gender diversity.

See also the books listed in *For Further Reading* in Chapter 14.

Class Exercises for Competency Assessment

A community mental health agency operates a program called Assertive Community Treatment for those with chronic mental illness. The goal of the program is to enable the mentally ill to live in their own community with as few restrictions as possible, and to prevent rehospitalization, which is extremely expensive. In addition to providing and monitoring medications, the program offers a drop-in center, therapy groups, arts and crafts, a 24-hour emergency service, and regular contact with a case management team. The agency converted its record keeping to computer databases several years ago, but has not used the data in any systematic way to evaluate program effectiveness. The agency asks your help in deciding which of several hundred variables they should use and what statistical procedures would be appropriate. The table on page 425 presents a selection of some of the variables available, together with coding information.

15.1. [Research & Practice] Classify each of the variables in this data set as nominal, ordinal, interval, or ratio. Compare your classification with those of the other students, and discuss cases that are difficult to classify.

15.2. [Critical Thinking] [Research & Practice] You run a frequency distribution procedure on all the variables. There are 120 total cases. You notice that *HOSPDAYS* range from 0 to 57. However, 117 of the cases had 15 days or less of hospitalization, whereas the remaining three cases had 35, 48, and 57 days, respectively. Which measures of central tendency and dispersion would you use with this variable, and why?

15.3. [Critical Thinking] [Research & Practice] Which measure(s) of association would be appropriate for examining each of the following relationships?
HOSPDAYS–CMANHRAL
HYESNO1–MEDUSE
MEDUSE–GAS1
CRISIS1–HYESNO1
HYESNO1–CMANHR1
CRISIS1–GAS1
GAS1–GAS2

15.4. [Critical Thinking] [Research & Practice] Similar programs are used throughout the state with approximately 15,000 patients. Assume that the same data are available from other programs and a random sample of 600 patients is selected. Identify three research questions you could ask from these data. For each question, state the research and null hypotheses, and indicate the alpha level to use for Type I error.

Variable Name	Description	Permissible Range of Values
HOSPDAYS	Number of days hospitalized during fiscal year	Integer values from 0 to 366
HYESNO1 to HYESNO12	Was patient hospitalized at all during a given month? (HYESNO1 = January, HYESNO2 = February, etc.)	0 = No, 1 = Yes
CMANHR1 to CMANHR12, CMANHRAL	Case manager hours devoted to the case each month (CMANHR1 = January, CMANHR2 = February, CMANHRAL = sum for year)	Any value from 0 to 200
GAS1 to GAS12	Goal attainment rating score; completed by case manager on each client each month on client progress toward treatment goals	1 = low, 2 = medium, 3 = high
RESSTAT	Residential status: living alone, with roommate, in group home, or with family member	1 = alone, 2 = roommate, 3 = group home, 4 = family, 5 = other
MEDUSE1 to MEDUSE12	Case manager estimate about patient compliance with medication regime	1 = poor, 2 = good, 3 = excellent
CRISIS1 to CRISIS12	Did the patient have an emergency contact with center during month?	0 = No, 1 = Yes

Chapter 16

✺

Analysis of Qualitative Data

Goals of Qualitative Data Analysis

Data Reduction and Analysis
  Codes and Coding
  Reflective Remarks and Memos
  Contextualizing Strategies

Displaying Data
  Narrative Text
  Visual Displays

Conclusions and Verification

Using Computers in Qualitative Research
  Coding and Retrieving Data

  Data Analysis and Hypothesis Testing
  Conceptualization and Theory Building

Review and Critical Thinking
  Main Points
  Important Terms for Review
  Critical Thinking
  Exploring the Internet
  For Further Reading
  Class Exercises for Competency Assessment

The parallels and linkages between practice and research are most readily apparent in qualitative approaches to research. In fact, it has been argued that many traditional social work methods for evaluating and assessing practice also are traditional qualitative methods for collecting and analyzing data (Smith, 1998). So as we present the ways by which qualitative researchers make sense of their data, it should help the student of the human services to see that the techniques used for drawing meaning from qualitative research data lend themselves equally well to making sense of practice information.

For example, process recording, a technique long used in social work for training students in clinical methods and for documenting case progress, is closely related to the case study method used by qualitative researchers. Social workers commonly are required to write case summaries, and these reports closely parallel a qualitative researcher's report that analyzes, interprets, and integrates data from a qualitative study. Human service students in internships or field placements often are required to maintain a log or journal of their experiences. Again, the student's task of synthesizing and summarizing the content of such a journal is similar to the qualitative researcher's task of analyzing field notes. Students who have covered the use of such techniques as genograms, sociograms, and timelines to graphically represent practice phenomena will find themselves on familiar ground as we present some of the same approaches here (although sometimes with different labels). What differentiates these approaches in research and in practice is the greater emphasis on systematic and rigorous application found in research.

The raw material for qualitative data analysis often is in the form of field notes and in-depth interviews (discussed in Chapter 9). Qualitative data, however, also may come in the form of diaries, narratives, video recordings, and other sorts of texts that are nonquantitative. In qualitative data analysis, the researcher attempts to transform these raw data and extract some meaning from it, mostly without quantifying the data. (We pointed out in Chapter 9 that field research can produce some quantitative data; when it does, these data are analyzed using the procedures discussed in Chapters 14 and 15.)

GOALS OF QUALITATIVE DATA ANALYSIS

The goals of qualitative data analysis are both similar to and different from the goals of quantitative data analysis. The specific strategies used in qualitative data analysis are different from those used in quantitative data analysis, but nonetheless, it is still data analysis—that is, extracting meaning from observations. The goals of a qualitative research project might be the same as those discussed in Chapter 1, especially description, explanation, and evaluation. In addition, qualitative research often strives for understanding by generalizing beyond the data to more abstract and general concepts or theories. In some cases, the ultimate end may be to generalize the results to people, groups, or organizations beyond those observed. Thus qualitative data analysis creates meaning, in part, by using raw data to learn something more abstract and general. In this respect, qualitative and quantitative data analyses are similar.

Beyond the similarities, however, qualitative and quantitative approaches have obvious differences. First, qualitative research recognizes that abstraction and generalization are matters of degree and may be of less importance in some studies. Second, qualitative research gives more emphasis to the effort to contextualize—to understand people, groups, and organizations within the full context or situation in which they act. In fact, some qualitative data-analysis strategies devote more effort to contextualizing than to abstracting or generalizing. This is based on the position that scientific knowledge is found not only in abstracting and generalizing, but also can derive from a deep and full description of a context. In other words, some qualitative research focuses on idiographic explanations rather than nomothetic ones (see Chapter 2). Third, qualitative research tends to place more emphasis on inductive reasoning than deductive reasoning. Qualitative researchers stress the value of letting concepts and abstract ideas emerge from the data rather than using the data to provide evidence for preexisting concepts and theories.

As a part of the goal of stressing the contextual, qualitative research maintains a close, interactive link between data collection and data analysis. In Chapter 1, we presented the stages in the research process as a sequence in which one stage is mostly completed before the next stage is begun. In particular, we suggested that the data-collection stage be completed before the data-analysis stage begins, and that data analysis should be largely finished before conclusions are drawn (see Figure 1.1). This is the way many quantitative and positivist researchers describe the process. One major reason for this sequencing is to ensure that the data-collection procedures used are the same over time; if the measurement procedures change from the beginning to the end of the data-collection phase, then researchers

```
                    ┌─────────────────────┐
                    │ Problem formulation │
                    └──────────┬──────────┘
                               │
                               ▼
                ┌──────────────────────────────┐
                │ Research design and development │
                └──────────────┬───────────────┘
                               │
          ┌────────────────────┼────────────────────┐
          │    ┌─────────────┐ │ ┌───────────────┐  │
          │    │ Data collection │◄──►│ Data analysis │  │
          │    └──────┬──────┘   └───────┬───────┘  │
          │           │                  │          │
          │           ▼                  ▼          │
          │          ┌─────────────────────┐        │
          │          │ Drawing conclusions │        │
          │          └──────────┬──────────┘        │
          └─────────────────────┼───────────────────┘
                                │
                                ▼
                 ┌───────────────────────────────┐
                 │ Public dissemination of results │
                 └───────────────────────────────┘
```

FIGURE 16.1 The Stages of Social Research as Conceptualized by Some Qualitative Researchers

may be measuring different variables (see Chapters 5 and 13). This is an important consideration in research, where there are clearly stated and quantifiable variables and hypotheses and where quantitative measurement procedures are used.

For many qualitative researchers, on the other hand, the process looks more like Figure 16.1: The stages of data collection, data analysis, and drawing conclusions are more simultaneous and interactive (Maxwell, 2012; Seidman, 2006). The researcher begins to analyze and draw conclusions almost as soon as data collection begins, and these analyses and conclusions provide direction for whatever additional data collection needs to occur. Unlike the positivists, for whom comparability over time is essential, many qualitative researchers see that aspect of data collection as problematic, in the sense that it is a decision to be weighed given the particulars of a research project. In many cases, the advantages gained by adjusting and refocusing the data-collection efforts as they proceed outweigh the disadvantages of changing the manner in which the data are collected. One of the advantages gained when data collection and analysis overlap is **theoretical sensitivity**: having data collection and analysis closely guided by emerging theoretical issues (Glaser, 1978; Strauss, 1987). Now, data collection and analysis are guided by theoretical issues in all research but in a different way. In most research, theoretical issues are used to create measuring devices before collecting the data, and what occurs during the process of data collection does not lead to changes in the measuring devices. Because many qualitative researchers do not see a rigid separation between data collection and data analysis, however, their stance opens the door for the possibility of theoretical issues arising *during* data collection to change what kind of data are collected or from whom. So theoretical sensitivity involves a constant interaction between theory and data collection. Data collected in one interview, for example, may raise some theoretical issues for the researcher such that later interviews are modified to collect data addressing those issues.

Following Miles and Huberman (1994), we find it helpful to organize qualitative data analysis into three categories: data reduction and analysis, data displays, and drawing conclusions and verifying theories. Keep in mind that these are not sequential steps, but rather overlapping activities that mutually support one another. As Miles and Huberman (1994, p. 12) state, "The three types of analysis activity [data reduction, data displays, and conclusion drawing] and the activity of data collection itself form an interactive, cyclical process." All three activities occur, at least in part, during the process of data collection and may influence and change that process.

DATA REDUCTION AND ANALYSIS

As we describe different kinds of qualitative data analysis, it may seem at times as if we are talking again about the process of data collection in the field (the topic of Chapter 9). That confusion can arise because in qualitative research, data collection and data analysis often occur simultaneously. In qualitative field research, for example, the data-collection phase involves collecting field notes and other materials. *Data analysis* refers to the application of coding schemes and other procedures to those field notes that are described in this section. So the analysis is sometimes occurring as the data are being collected.

The data-analysis strategies discussed in this section tend to be of two types. **Categorizing strategies** attempt to generalize and abstract by generating concepts and even theories from the raw data. **Contextualizing strategies** attempt to treat the data as a coherent whole and retain as much of the raw data as possible to capture the whole context (Maxwell, 2012). Actually, however, many specific qualitative data analyses can involve elements of both.

We will first review categorizing strategies in the form of coding, reflective remarks, and memos. Then, we will discuss the contextualizing strategies.

Codes and Coding

We have talked about the process of *coding* at a number of points in this textbook—as a part of doing content analysis of available data in Chapter 8, of making structured field observations in Chapter 9, and of quantitative data analysis in Chapter 14.

Coding is also a form of data analysis with qualitative data and has similarities to coding done in other contexts.

Coding refers to the categorizing of observations into a limited number of categories. In most qualitative data analyses, however, coding is distinct from other forms of coding in at least three important ways. First, it is not an effort to quantify the data or to create a set of numerical categories, as often is the case with other types of coding. Coding in qualitative analysis reduces and simplifies the data, but it does so by retaining words and their essential meanings. Second, in qualitative analysis, codes and coding schemes are created, at least in part, from the data themselves during the process of data collection; in other words, the data create the codes. Quantitative coding schemes are more typically derived from some preexisting theoretical stance, and then an effort is made to see if the data fit the coding scheme. Third, the purpose of coding in qualitative analysis is different. In quantitative research, coding usually is a part of the process of measurement: The coding categories constitute the operational definition of the underlying variable. Although this principle applies, to an extent, in coding for qualitative research, qualitative coding goes beyond measurement: It is also an integral part of conceptual development and theory building. So the process of coding in qualitative research spans the realms of both measurement and the more abstract process of developing concepts and theories.

In qualitative research, then, the data are in the form of field notes—narratives produced by respondents, or possibly written documents or archival material. Coding is the process of categorizing sections of that data—a phrase, a sentence, a paragraph. Coding is a way to see which parts of the data are connected to one another in terms of some issue, concept, theme, or hypothesis. Some researchers use different terms, such as *thematic analysis*, for strategies of data analysis that basically involve categorizing the data (Seidman, 2006). Table 16.1 is an example, with a few sections of the transcript of an in-depth interview on the right-hand side and the codes that the researcher applied to each section on

TABLE 16.1 A Section of Transcribed In-Depth Interview, with Codes

Codes	Interview Statements
Self-perception Awareness of difference Identifying self through ill health Comparing health to others'	A 29-year-old man with renal failure was discussing his high school years and events that occurred long before he was diagnosed. … I knew I was different. I caught colds very easily and my resistance was very low, and so I knew that, generally speaking, my health wasn't as good as everybody else's, but I tried to do all the things that everybody else was doing.

Normalizing the context of illness
Self-esteem:
    feelings of failure
    failure of self
Reality contradicts idealized
    experience
	A 29-year-old woman with colitis was recounting her first episode of illness.
	… I was under a great deal of stress as a result of all this bouncing around and trying to get a job and trying not to have to go home to my parents and admit that I had failed. [I] failed at life. I had left college, and left there saying, "Gee, I can do it on my own," so I was trying this exciting existence I read about and there was something wrong; I had all this pain. I didn't know what to do about it.

Self in retrospect Self-esteem Outcome of timed struggle Improving self-esteem as treatment goal	A 54-year-old woman who had had cancer and currently had a crippling collagen disease was explaining her view on why she had had a recurrence of cancer. … When I look back on my second bout of cancer, I was not feeling good about myself and the whole struggle of the last three years put me into X (a cancer institute) to try and get me to feel better about myself.

SOURCE: Reprinted by permission of Kathy Charmaz, from Charmaz, K. (1983 [reissued 1988]). "The Grounded Theory Method: An Explication and Interpretation." In Emerson, R. M., Ed., *Contemporary Field Research: A Collection of Readings*. Prospect Heights, IL: Waveland Press.

the left. These interviews were conducted as part of a study about how people with chronic illnesses experience time and personal identity. Many of the conceptual codes the researcher identified have to do with self-esteem and feelings about oneself—the concepts this researcher identified as important in each part of what was said in the interview.

Approaches to Coding. Three approaches exist to developing the coding schemes used by qualitative researchers. One is to create a fairly complete coding scheme before going out into the field to collect observations (Miles & Huberman, 1994). This would be based on theoretical considerations regarding what will be observed in the field and what are the important variables, social mechanisms, and causal processes. This approach might rely on prior research or preexisting coding schemes developed by others and used in research on similar topics. For example, a qualitative evaluation of a high-school mental health program involved coding focus-group responses according to four topics: (1) positive aspects of the program, (2) suggestions for improving services, (3) how to reach youth in need of mental health services, and (4) ideas for measuring treatment outcomes (Nabors, Reynolds, & Weist, 2000). Examples of coding categories included therapist behaviors and academic, personal, and neighborhood changes.

This coding scheme can be readily adapted to studies of similar programs. When using this approach, the list of coding categories should be fairly complete in terms of what the observer expects to see in the field, and may be quite detailed and lengthy. One thing that distinguishes this approach to coding, however, from what most quantitative researchers do is that the qualitative researcher still expects to change and adapt the coding scheme as observations are made in the field. With almost any coding scheme, some categories prove more useful and others less so. Some categories might not be used at all, whereas others get used too much—that is, so many observations fall into the category that it needs to be divided into subcategories based on differences among the various observations. Thus the coding scheme continues to develop as the data are collected.

The second approach to developing coding schemes is the reverse of the first: Observers enter the field with no preestablished coding scheme (Strauss, 1987). Coding categories are developed as observations are made in the field context. One example of this is the grounded theory approach (described in Chapter 9), a data-driven, contextualized approach to data analysis. Without the restrictions of a preexisting coding scheme, the observer describes what happens, tries to identify relevant variables, and searches for explanations of what is observed. Beginning with these concrete observations, the researcher then develops a coding scheme that points toward more abstract concepts, propositions, and theoretical explanations that would be plausible given those observations. In this way, preexisting theory does not limit the kind of data collection that occurs.

This general approach was used in a qualitative study of the role of the family in the achievement of African-American males (Maton, Hrabowski, & Greif, 1998). The researchers interviewed sons and parents in 60 African-American families, generating more than 800 single-spaced pages of text data. Through reading the transcripts, the research team developed initial coding categories related to things that might influence achievement such as discipline, high expectations, love, and community resources. The researchers then moved back from the coding categories to the original text and developed a final set of categories. Eventually, the process resulted in a formal coding system of the 20 most salient factors contributing to outstanding academic achievement.

Even this open approach to coding is given some structure, however, by some proponents of grounded theory, such as Anselm Strauss. These proponents argue that coding should address four general categories of phenomena:

- conditions or causes
- interaction among people
- strategies and tactics
- consequences

A third approach to developing coding schemes falls in between the first two: A general coding scheme is developed that identifies domains of observation rather than referring to specific content within those domains. Then, coding schemes are inductively developed within those domains (Bogdan & Biklen, 1992; Lofland et al., 2006). These domains are more specific and detailed than the four general categories just mentioned that are used by some grounded theory researchers. A possible list of such domains might include the following:

- actions/events
- activities (actions of some duration)
- meaning (what people say and do to define a situation)
- perspectives (ways of thinking or orientations)
- relationships
- setting/context
- social structure (status, roles, and their relationships)

Most—or all—of these domains are likely to be relevant in a field setting, yet the categories are so general that context still plays a strong part in shaping the observations made and the specific coding scheme that emerges.

To show more concretely how coding is done, we can use an example from a qualitative study of rural homelessness that used ethnographic interviews as a source of data (Hilton & DeJong, 2010). The study focuses on coping behaviors and felt experiences of homeless adults in a rural area while identifying behavioral patterns and strategies for meeting basic necessities. Relying on audio recordings of interviews, the researchers identified major concepts and themes related to coping behaviors and dilemmas faced by those struggling to survive while homeless. The researchers identified areas in the interviews where these concepts and themes were prominent by listening for certain phrases and words indicative of these concepts and

TABLE 16.2 Excepts from Ethnographic Interviews with Homeless Adults, with Suggested Coding

Abstract Concept	More Specific Behaviors	Excerpts from Ethnographic Interview
Possessions Dilemma	Storage Issues	"I have **stored things with friends**, but I learned that friends can't be responsible for your things, ya know. Friends move and you can't keep track of them all the time, so you're like "Well, I lost this or that. Over time I learned that I got what I got."
		"If you're sleeping in the woods you have to **worry about your stuff**—because someone could come by steal things."
	Transporting Issues	When you need to go in town, you **don't want to carry everything**, but if you leave it someone could take your things, or an animal could get at it too."
		"**I carry 75 to 80 lbs of stuff in a backpack on wheels**. I load it on and off the bus. I carry it across town so a day really wears on you. I tried **storing some things in a friend's car** and going with the bare minimum, but I ended up in the rain, soaking wet and cold."

SOURCE: Hilton, T. & DeJong, C. (2010). Homeless in God's Country: Coping Behaviors and Felt Experiences of the Rural Homeless. *Journal of Qualitative and Ethnographic Research* 5: 12–30.

themes. Table 16.2 presents some excerpts from interviews, with the key words highlighted that indicate a particular abstract coding category. The homeless adults interviewed were asked about their possessions and how they managed them without a permanent home. Issues related to storing and transporting items were common, so the researchers created codes for these concepts. The researchers used these codes to assess hypotheses related to difficulties associated with managing possessions.

Notice a couple of characteristics in the coding in both Tables 16.1 and 16.2. First, the coding does not focus on counts of how often things happen, but rather on descriptions of what is applicable to a particular person or context. The data analysis produces words, phrases, and descriptions as meaning, rather than as numbers, to extract meaning. Second, there is a close link between the codes and the data: When a code is applied, it is linked to a particular section (word, phrase, sentence, or paragraph) of the raw data. This is important in terms of assessing validity.

Descriptive versus Abstract Coding. Coding schemes vary in terms of how general or abstract the coding categories are. Different qualitative researchers have developed different descriptions of this. Miles and Huberman (1994), for example, suggest three different types of coding.

Descriptive codes are coding categories that involve fairly directly observed behaviors or events; the coder need not do a great deal of interpretation to place a statement in the field notes into these categories. So field notes that say "Jane left the room" or "Jim shook hands with the nurse" can be fairly directly coded as "departure" and "greeting," respectively.

Interpretive codes are coding categories that require field researchers to use some of their deep understanding of the social context to place a section of the field notes into a category; in other words, they must interpret the meaning of a particular entry in the field notes. Interpretive codes might involve assessing people's motivations or moods or the meanings that people attach to things. So if the field notes say that "Jane left the room angrily" or "Jim gave the nurse a cool greeting," the words "angry" and "cool" are interpretive in nature—that is, they involve a judgment or interpretation by the researcher. Thus placing these parts of the field notes into categories of "angry" and "distant" is more interpretive and subjective than are the descriptive codes.

The third type of coding involves *pattern codes*, which are "explanatory or inferential codes, ones that identify an emergent theme, configuration, or explanation. They pull together a lot of material into more meaningful and parsimonious units of analysis" (Miles & Huberman, 1994, p. 69). Pattern codes reduce the amount of data into more manageable amounts and help focus later data collection on data that assist in better understanding the patterns or themes. A section of field notes is identified as representing some abstract or theoretical theme or pattern in the events that are occurring. An explanatory code may refer to an abstract social process. So "Jane left the room angrily" might be coded as exemplifying the social process of "rejection of deviant," whereas "Jim gave the nurse a cool greeting" might be coded as the social process of "role distance."

Pattern codes usually focus on one of four general categories of phenomenon: themes, causes or explanations, relationships among people, and theoretical constructs. The danger with pattern coding is that the researcher might prematurely impose a certain meaning on the data and then try to fit everything else into that pattern. To prevent this, Miles and Huberman recommend that the researcher remain tentative and flexible:

> The trick here is to work with loosely held chunks of meaning, to be ready to unfreeze and reconfigure them as the data shape up otherwise, to subject the most compelling themes to merciless cross-checking, and to lay aside the more tenuous ones until other informants and observations give them better empirical grounding. (Miles & Huberman, 1994, p. 70)

Keep in mind that a single section of a text or field notes can be given more than one type of code; in fact, it might be given a descriptive, an interpretive, and a pattern code.

Going back to Table 16.2, notice that it is fairly straightforward to give a descriptive code to some segments, such as "stored things with friends"; however, it is more difficult—requires more interpretation and judgment—to give interpretive codes. For example, it requires some judgment to say that "worry about your stuff" is an instance of the code "storage issues." It is even more inferential to assign a pattern code, such as "worry about your stuff as a possessions dilemma." Such abstract coding might be based on things said in other parts of the interview or on the researchers' deep knowledge of the field setting in which the interviewees live and the interviews occurred. This is why Miles and Huberman caution against settling on pattern codes too quickly.

Open versus Focused Coding. Another approach to coding is to begin by looking for any types of codes that might emerge from the data, and then focus on a limited number of codes to see how well they fit various parts of the data (Charmaz, 2006; Glaser, 1978). The initial coding of field notes, interviews, or other documents is called *open coding*, and involves unrestricted coding to produce concepts and dimensions that seem to fit the data fairly well. These codes can be linked to the various dimensions mentioned above (conditions, causes, etc.), and the coding categories are provisional and tentative. The point of open coding is to open up the data—to open up possibilities—rather than to finalize anything. Anything that is wrong or unclear at this stage will be rectified and clarified at later stages of coding. As Strauss (1987, p. 29) puts it, at this stage of coding, researchers "play the game of believing everything and believing nothing." Whereas in quantitative research the goal of coding is to produce counts (how many cases fall into each category), the point of open coding, according to Strauss (1987, p. 29), is to "fracture, break the data apart analytically"—in other words, to create new categories and to split apart and rearrange existing categories. There is nothing fixed about the category system, at least, at this stage; it is emerging out of the data, and therefore is in flux. Especially early in the process, open coding is likely to be more of the descriptive variety, but it also may include some interpretive and pattern codes.

After open coding has proceeded for a while, the field researcher can turn to *focused coding*, or what Strauss calls *axial coding*: intense analysis around one or a few of the coding categories. (Each of the general coding categories is called an "axis," hence the name "axial coding.") Focused coding is more selective and conceptual; it involves applying a limited set of codes to a large amount of data. Focused coding enables the researcher to assess how extensively a set of codes applies and discover the various forms in which the categories appear. This enables the researcher to explore one of these dimensions of social reality throughout the field notes, and thus expose relationships that may not have been obvious with open coding. Focused coding cannot be done until open coding has already provided a plethora of potential concepts; but after a period of open coding, focused coding can be done periodically. In open coding, the center of attention is the raw data; in focused coding, the focus of attention is the emerging coding categories. Focused coding begins to expose the core concepts and categories as well as the relationships among them that emerge from the data. Focused coding, however, is still strongly linked to the data, because the researcher must constantly go back to the original texts to validate decisions about what the core concepts are and what the relationships appear to be among them. Furthermore, focused coding may lead to revisions in the coding that are done during open coding, as new concepts emerge from the data. What occurs at this stage is essentially conceptual development (discussed in Chapter 4), but here, conceptual development grows out of the process of data analysis rather than occurring before research design development.

Selective coding is a term used by Strauss (1987) to describe coding that focuses on the core concepts and categories that emerged during focused coding. It is, in a sense, a more intense form of focused coding. All elements of the text are coded in terms of how they relate—or do not relate—to the core concepts and theories that emerge from the data. This is similar to Miles and Huberman's pattern coding. Selective coding builds on open and focused coding and can begin only after some of those forms of coding have been accomplished. As data analysis proceeds, selective coding comes to predominate in the process. In addition, as core concepts and theories emerge from selective coding, they can point toward what additional data need to be collected to provide further tests and comparisons for the theory.

Operational Definitions and Reliability. However as a coding scheme is developed, each category within it must have a good operational definition to ensure that all observers use the coding scheme both properly and consistently. The *operational definition* is a verbal statement of the kind of observations that should be placed in a particular category. The definition might emerge from an existing theoretical framework or out of the observations, as in grounded theory. Nevertheless, it is critical that the definition be clearly specified and understood by all observers. Otherwise observations that are placed in one category by one observer might be placed in another category by another observer—or even ignored altogether. One way to clarify these operational definitions is through *double coding*: Two observers code the same set of field notes, and then cases where these observers disagree on the coding can be evaluated. Discussion about their disagreements usually produces a sharper, clearer operational definition or a revision in the coding scheme that takes the difficulty into account.

Reliability of coding schemes can be assessed in a number of different ways. As discussed in Chapter 8, one way is double coding, and then the degree of agreement between the two coders can be assessed. One simple way to do this is to calculate the percentage of judgments on which coders agree out of the total number of judgments that they must make:

$$\text{percentage of agreement} = \frac{2 \times (\text{number of agreements})}{\text{total number of observations recorded by both observers}}$$

Some disagreement exists about what level of agreement is acceptable, but many researchers argue that, after revisions and adjustments, the final coding scheme should achieve at least 85 to 90 percent agreement. Another way to check the reliability of a coding scheme is to have each observer code the same set of field notes twice, separated by a period of at least a few days. Again, the ultimate code–recode reliability should achieve at least 85 to 90 percent.

Reflective Remarks and Memos

In performing qualitative data analysis, researchers need some mechanisms for moving away from the immediate, raw data toward the general and abstract. Pattern coding and selective coding are two ways to achieve this, but field researchers have identified other methods as well. One is **reflective remarks** on field notes: reflections, interpretations, connections, or other thoughts that occur to the researcher while transcribing the field notes or coding the data. This can take many different forms: questioning the original interpretation of some events in the field notes; a recollection of something about the relationship between two people that was not put into the field notes; an elaboration on something that was only sketchily described in the field notes; or a new hypothesis to explain something that happened in the field. All these might be useful in understanding and coding the field notes, and they should be committed to writing.

If the field notes are being transcribed when the reflective thoughts occur, such thoughts can be incorporated directly into the field notes. It is a good idea, however, to keep the data recorded in the field separate from the reflective remarks, because the latter could be influenced by selective recall or retrospective interpretation. One way to keep the field notes separate from the reflective remarks is to set the remarks apart from the notes with some device—a different font, double parentheses, brackets, or any other device not used anywhere else in the field notes—that clearly identifies these remarks. If the reflective thoughts occur during coding, they can be written into a margin of the field notes but not in the margin where the codes are placed.

Another significant step away from the raw data is provided through what are variously called *memos, analytical memos*, or *theoretical memos*. **Memos** refer to attempts at theorizing: The researcher writes down ideas about the meanings of the codes that are emerging from the data and the relationships between the various codes (Glaser, 1978; Strauss, 1987). Memos do not just describe the data, however; they are more conceptual and abstract in nature, showing that a particular part of the data is an instance of a particular concept or social process. Or a memo might link various pieces of data together as sharing some abstract property in common. Whatever form they take, memos represent a move beyond the raw data toward more abstract theorizing. Memoing can be done as the data collection and data analysis proceed. In fact, memoing can begin as soon as abstract ideas begin to occur to the researcher, which may be fairly early in the data-collection process. This is quite different from quantitative research, in which data collection and analysis must be pretty much complete before the theoretical implications begin to emerge.

Memos can be short or long, from a few sentences to a few pages. Most researchers identify on the memo exactly what parts of the field notes are referred to by the memo. This is theoretically important for such approaches as grounded theory because of their stance about the close link between raw data and abstract theory: All abstract ideas should be tied to specific parts of the data. In these approaches to qualitative data analysis, it is not adequate for researchers to report on general impressions from the data; this has low validity. Instead, memos should identify the lines in the field notes or other memos to which they relate so there is a clear link between bits of data and abstract conclusions. Memos also should identify what codes or concepts they refer to, and be dated so it is clear when the thoughts occurred during the research process. Some of the memos, or at least parts of them, may later be incorporated into the final research report.

Beyond saying that memos are abstract and general, it is difficult to specify their content, because it is so highly variable. A memo might clarify an idea or an existing coding category, suggest some new coding categories or subcategories, or link data from different parts of the field notes,

FIGURE 16.2 The Data Analysis Process in Some Types of Qualitative Research

or, possibly, even from other research projects. A memo might propose a hypothesis or a new pattern code, or it might identify something puzzling that does not fit in with the conceptual framework emerging in other memos. As the memoing process continues, what begins to emerge is a more formalized, coherent set of propositions or explanations of what is found in the data. (We discussed the development of propositions and theories at length in Chapter 2.) The propositions in qualitative data analysis emerge out of the data in an inductive process. In fact, some qualitative researchers eventually force themselves to state some tentative propositions that they can then review in light of all the memos, codes, and data to see if the propositions have any validity. In some cases, propositions may emerge early in the process of data analysis. Some propositions will eventually be discarded as they are shown to be inconsistent with much of the data; but at some point, a set of propositions emerges that seems to be consistent with all or most of the observations. Propositions can take a number of different forms such as:

When A happens, B is also found.

A causes B to occur.

A is found when B, C, and D exist.

A is found when B and C but not D occur.

In whatever form they take, however, the propositions are abstract explanations of phenomena. In qualitative research, these explanations are viewed as tentative; another sweep through the data by the same or different researchers could produce different coding, memoing, and proposition development. In addition, field observations of different groups or different locations could produce different outcomes. Figure 16.2 diagrams these categorizing strategies; the double arrows illustrate, once again, how interactive this process is. As the analysis proceeds, the researcher constantly goes back and forth among the memos, reflective remarks, and coding; in addition, he or she goes back and forth between these three elements and the data and conclusions.

Contextualizing Strategies

Qualitative researchers, in general, stress the importance of context and of viewing and analyzing data with an appreciation for the complete context in which the data were produced. The categorizing strategies that we have just discussed, however, tend, to a greater or a lesser degree, to move the researcher and the analysis away from the concrete data and toward more abstract categories and propositions. Some qualitative researchers argue that something is lost using this strategy (Maxwell, 2012; Seidman, 2006). They argue for *contextualizing strategies*: approaches to data analysis that treat the data as a coherent whole and retain as much of the raw data as possible to capture the whole context. Contextualizing strategies are less concerned with abstracting from one set of data to generalize to other people or circumstances, and are more interested in a deep, rich appreciation of the individuals from whom or situations from which the data were collected. In other words, these contextualizing strategies focus more on idiographic than on nomothetic explanations (see Chapter 2).

One type of contextualizing strategy is the use of *profiles*, as promoted by Irving Seidman (2006). **Profiles** refer to vignettes of a person's experience, usually taken from in-depth interviews, stated largely in the person's own words, with relatively little interpretation or analysis by the researcher. Profiles are, fundamentally, narratives that tell a story. Telling stories is a key way for people to make sense of themselves and their world, and hearing others' stories is a valuable way to learn about those people's lives. Profiles are constructed by transcribing in-depth interviews and then identifying parts of the interviews that seem especially important, to the researcher, in telling the person's story. Then, the parts of the interview are put together into a preliminary profile. This profile is then reviewed with a critical eye to see if any passages are redundant or irrelevant, and whether the passages are sequenced properly to tell the most effective story. This review process continues until the researcher is satisfied with the profile. The final profile is mostly in the person's own words, although the researcher might include some comments to clarify or provide transitions. Any comments of the researcher should be clearly identified as such.

The researcher has to exercise considerable judgment about what to include in the story and how to sequence passages, and the possibility exists that some bias might enter into this selection process. Yet, Seidman (2006) argues that the researcher is in the best position to make these judgments. It is, after all, the researcher more than anyone who is most intimately familiar with the interviewee, the transcripts of the interview, and the literature on the topic. Certainly, the researcher might consult with those interviewed to see if they concur with the researcher's judgment, but ultimately the researcher needs to be confident that his or her intuitive and professional judgments about how to shape the best profile are the right ones. The final step in developing a profile is analogous to the conceptualizing or theorizing of other researchers: The researcher spells out what he or she has learned from the whole process of collecting data, reviewing data, and developing the profile. Undoubtedly, some abstracting and conceptualizing are part of this conclusion, but it is probably grandiose to call it theory building.

An approach similar to profiling is **narrative analysis**, in which interviews, autobiographies, life histories, letters, and other personal materials are used to form a descriptive narrative of a person's life or circumstances (Clandinin & Connelly, 2000; Merriam, 1998). As with the profile, this narrative tells a story and relies heavily on the person's own words as taken from their letters, autobiography, or other sources. Narrative analysis does not rely so heavily on interviews, however; it uses a broader range of data sources than profiles.

A similar contextualizing strategy, but one that doesn't rely so heavily on the subject's own words, is the **case study**: a detailed, descriptive account of one individual, situation, organization, group, or other entity (Merriam, 1998; Patton, 2002). As with profiles, data analysis in case studies focuses on description and narrative rather than on categorizing strategies. Furthermore, the description in case studies is detailed and what sometimes is called "thick"— that is, a complete and literal accounting of the person or setting under study. Some quantitative data might be presented as a part of a case study, but the emphasis is on telling a story in prose or narrative, although not completely in the words of the people being studied, as in the profile or narrative. The idea, however, is the same: The researcher describes people's lives and experiences in great detail.

In addition to the researcher's description, the case study might use quotations from those being studied, along with photos, videos, artifacts, and any other materials that help provide an in-depth description of the subject of the case study. Social work students who have to complete a process recording as part of their practice methods training find the case study method familiar, because the two methods have many features in common. By way of illustration, Katherine Tyson (1999) essentially used process recording from therapy with a three-year-old boy in presenting a qualitative study demonstrating the effectiveness of an empowering approach to crisis intervention. Her presentation of the research interspersed quotations of interchanges between the therapist and child with analysis and discussion of the principles of the therapeutic approach.

Case studies can be based on direct observation, interviews, document analysis, organizational records, or some combination of these—basically, any data that would contribute to a description of the case under study. Historical research often focuses on a case study and might use a wide variety of materials as data, such as historical accounts, published newspapers and magazines, biographies, letters, government statistics, official records, and so on.

The primary goal of the case study and the other contextualizing strategies is an idiographic explanation that focuses on an in-depth understanding of this particular case. Such an understanding might enhance one's comprehension of other cases and situations, but the primary focus is description, not generalization. The advantage of profiles, narratives, and case studies is the rich and detailed descriptions they provide of people's lives, experiences, and circumstances. A disadvantage of these contextualizing strategies is that they depend heavily on the subjective and intuitive judgments of the researchers who are closest to the data. Another researcher producing a case study or profile of the same person or situation might come up with quite a different story. Yet another disadvantage is the limited ability to generalize beyond the individual case.

DISPLAYING DATA

A **data display** is an organized presentation of data that enables researchers and their audiences to draw some conclusions from that data and move on to the next stage of the research (Miles & Huberman, 1994; Strauss, 1987). In any data analysis, the researcher must display the data so that a convincing argument can be made to support the conclusions drawn in the research. In science, we don't take the researcher's word in regard to conclusions: We need to be convinced by a display of the data. In quantitative data analysis, an important part of the display of data is the numbers, in the form of contingency tables, charts, or descriptive and inferential statistics (see Chapters 14 and 15). Some narrative is required to explain how the numbers were arrived at and to explain clearly their interpretation, but the core of the argument is the display of the numbers. In qualitative data analysis, however, the core of the argument is not numbers. Although the qualitative researcher may have some numbers to show, he or she uses different kinds of data displays. Creating data displays is very much a part of data analysis; creating the displays assists the researcher in identifying and clarifying the concepts and categories that are emerging from the coding and other strategies being used on the data.

Narrative Text

One key type of data display in qualitative research is the description, narrative, or verbal argument, which is made by the researcher. In the contextualizing strategies, the narrative provides as full a description as possible to give an in-depth picture of the field, interview, or person that is the center of attention. The narrative attempts to be true to the meaning of the original experience—as interpreted by the researcher. The anthropologist Philippe Bourgois (1995, p. 341), in his study of street drug dealers, points out "the impossibility of rendering into print the performance dimension of street speech. Without the complex, stylized punctuation provided by body language, facial expression, and intonation, many of the transcribed narratives of crack dealers appear flat, and sometimes even inarticulate." The challenge for Bourgois was to produce a narrative that conveyed the rich, detailed meanings he perceived in the field setting based on all the linguistic and nonlinguistic cues available to him.

In the categorizing strategies, the researcher's narrative describes the concepts and propositions that emerged from the research, along with excerpts from the field notes or other data sources that illustrate these concepts and propositions and that corroborate the conclusions drawn (see Tables 16.1 and 16.2). In neither quantitative nor qualitative research do researchers report *all* the data, which would mean the raw data. A research report is always a summarization of the data, and it is ethically incumbent on the researcher to give an accurate summarization. For the qualitative researcher, this means the illustrations presented to corroborate the conclusions are representative illustrations, and not selective or distorted.

Visual Displays

Qualitative researchers also use a variety of visual formats to display data, just as quantitative researchers use contingency tables, graphs, and charts in their data analysis (Miles & Huberman, 1994; Patton, 1981; Strauss, 1987). These visual data displays are considered part of the data analysis, because the process of their development serves as an assist in conceptualization and theory development. By summarizing what is found in the data, these displays help clarify conceptual categories and give further insight concerning relationships between categories. They also enable the researcher to see weaknesses in the analysis, and thus to suggest areas where additional data analysis is needed. Of course, visual data displays also are an effective adjunct to the narrative text in communicating results to a variety of audiences. Although these visual displays can take a variety of formats, there generally are two types. One is a figure that serves as a visual mapping of some physical or conceptual terrain. The second is a table, chart, or matrix into which some text, phrases, or other materials are placed. Although the specific form that these visual displays can take is highly variable and dependent on the specific data and concepts, we can provide a few illustrations to offer a sense of their nature, function, and development.

One type of visual display is a **context map**, which describes in graphic form the physical or social setting that is the context of the observations. Qualitative researchers stress the centrality of the context in understanding people's behavior; they are fond of pointing out that everything must be contextualized or situated. Positivist, quantitative research, however, often collects and analyzes data without regard to the context. A survey researcher, for example, will collect data on a questionnaire without regard to whether those attitudes might be important, different, or possibly irrelevant *depending on the context in which the person is behaving*. Many nonpositivists refer to this as "decontextualized" data collection and analysis, and argue that those attitudes only take on a life—that is, become important—in a particular context. Just as a percentage table informs the audience about some of the meaning in the data, a context map provides meaning to the data by describing the context in which the behaviors occurred.

In some cases, the context map is a drawing of the physical or geographic setting in which the observations are made. In Chapter 9, we suggested that each session of field observation might begin by drawing a map of the setting. This map might be a drawing of a room, building, street, or neighborhood, and it might include physical objects, entrances and exits, the locations of people or groups, and whatever else is relevant to understanding the social interaction described in the narrative. In other cases, the context map describes the social setting: the individuals, statuses, roles, groups, or organizations that are relevant to the observations. It would also show connections and relationships between these elements using lines and arrows. Some forms of this are called **sociograms** or **network analysis**. Figure 16.3 gives an example of what this might look like by showing the friendship choices made among a group of people. Network analysis may be the primary analytical approach used in a study, as was the case in a research project on the role that social networks play in the daily survival of homeless Latino and African-American men (Molina, 2000).

A common strategy for developing a sociogram is to conduct a sociometric interview with each member of a group. Each member is asked questions such as these:

- Whom of your group would you like to always be beside you during classes (or work or other relevant activity)?
- Who do you think can get the group organized best of all?

FIGURE 16.3 A Sociogram as an Example of a Context Map

- Whom of your group would you invite to a party at your home?
- Whom would you not invite?
- Whom do you work with if you have to, but really don't like very much?

The resulting visual representation helps us better see certain social phenomena such as particular patterns of relationships. Figure 16.3 provides evidence for certain social phenomena such as the clique (a group of people who all make mutual friendship choices) or the star (a person who is selected as a friend by a large number of people). Figure 16.3 is based on friendship or attraction choices, but it could map other aspects of relationships, such as deference, submission, dominance, or giving and receiving help. As with other context maps, the specifics depend on the particular observational setting and the concepts that emerge from it.

Another type of visual display in qualitative research is called a **matrix display**, which looks very much like a contingency table with rows and columns. The difference is that, whereas the cells of a contingency table contain numbers or percentages, the cells of a matrix contain text, quotations, phrases, or symbols from the field notes or other sources of qualitative data. The rows in the matrix may represent the categories of a variable (as in contingency tables) or different concepts that emerged from the field notes or different points in time. The columns also may represent such a range of possibilities. Table 16.3 is a matrix used to analyze data in a study of homelessness in rural communities. The rows represent different strategies to secure shelter utilized by the homeless, whereas the columns represent different kinds of family circumstances of the homeless. Notice that the material in the cells is not an attempt to quantify how many people felt or acted a certain way, but rather to give an overall assessment or judgment of each group's housing strategies and some quotes from the field notes to support that judgment. In this study, for example, the matrix display suggests the very different considerations made by the attached adults with children when assessing housing strategies as compared with the unattached adults. Sometimes in matrix analysis the rows might

TABLE 16.3 Example of a Matrix Display: The Housing Strategies Utilized by Homeless People and Their Family Circumstances

	Homeless Person's Family Circumstances	
Housing Strategy	**Unattached Adults**	**Attached Adults w/ children**
Camping	Freedom—"I can come and go as I please." Outdoor life—"August is the best month up here cause there's no bugs." Avoid societal sanctions—"I got a record, so this way I don't have to deal with them."	Fear of Child Protection Services—"The worker said, 'If you can't provide for your son, CPS will take him' So I was afraid to ask for help." Survival Parenting—"All we do is walk. A child needs a schedule, but we never know from one day to the next."
Shelter Living	Rigidity—"I'm a sex offender, so I can't stay anywhere near kids." Homeless label—"Nobody will hire you when they see you're living at the shelter." Occupying time—"They kick you out at 7:00 a.m. and don't let you in until 4:00 p.m. All I do is walk."	Stability—"At least we know where we're staying but my partner can't be here because we're not married." Homeless label helps—"When you have kids, they try to help you more. They put us at the top of the list to get a place." Safety—"Sometimes I'm more afraid of the other residents than being out in the woods."
Couch Hopping	Independence—"I'll stay with one friend for a while and any time I want I can just take off." Excitement—"We party a lot." Minimal space needs—"I just crash. I keep most of my stuff at a friend's place, so I don't need much." Network Rationing—"I share my food stamps, and I don't stay too long; don't want to wear out my welcome."	Dependence—"It makes you feel obligated, because it's a real burden on my mom. They don't have much themselves." Lack own space—"We had to sleep in the laundry room. Anytime she wanted to do wash, we had to be out of there." Network exhaustion—"My mom has a boyfriend and they have a life of their own. He doesn't want the little kids around."

SOURCE: Constructed from the field notes of Cornell R. DeJong and Timothy P. Hilton from the research project "Homeless in God's Country."

represent each individual observed and the columns different categories from the data.

Thus matrix displays are a good way to summarize data from the field notes. It is possible to summarize as many as 20 pages of field notes into one matrix, which makes this a much easier and more effective way to communicate the results to an audience. Matrix displays also are used as an assist in the data analysis, because the researcher can review the matrix in an effort to detect patterns, themes, or trends, which may be difficult or impossible to detect by reading and rereading the field notes or other texts. This is analogous to what a quantitative data analyst would do in looking at a contingency table rather than the raw numerical data.

Beyond what we have said here, there are few fixed rules about creating matrices. It is a creative process, and the exact nature of the matrix is very much driven by the data. If, however, we begin qualitative data analysis thinking in terms of matrices, then it may be easier to discover in the data how possible matrices can be created.

The Eye on Ethics section discusses some ethical considerations that can arise when analyzing data from qualitative research.

CONCLUSIONS AND VERIFICATION

Data analysis involves discovering meaning in the data. In qualitative research, this means identifying themes, patterns, and regularities and, in some cases,

Eye on Ethics — When the Truth Hurts—Seeing Unflattering Data

That the participants in research should benefit from the research and not simply avoid being harmed is a tenet of feminist research introduced in Chapter 3. Empowering women who are disadvantaged in a male-dominated, sexist society is a fundamental means of assuring that participants do benefit. But at times, researchers are forced to deal with data that may cast their research participants in a negative light and make empowering them more problematic (Buchbinder & Eisikovits, 2004).

This issue came up in a qualitative study based on in-depth interviews of Israeli battered women. The study focused on the turning point—that is, the point at which women came to refuse to live with violence and took active steps to stop it while staying with the perpetrator. The researchers employed coding and content analysis and used the approach of Gilligan to identify the different voices in the text (see Research in Practice 4.2). This approach involved examining both the superficial text and searching for deeper, underlying meanings. An important part of the accounts the women constructed concerned the role of children in a life immersed in violence. On the surface level, women described the "best interests of the children" as an important rationale for what they did. But a more detailed examination of the subtext in the interviews in some cases called into question this assertion. At this deeper level, the interviews revealed that the children's interests sometimes became secondary to those of the mothers', who apparently did not see the use of child-related justifications and the need to protect their children from harm as being mutually exclusive. For the researchers, this raised the ethical question of how to interpret these unanticipated findings, which present the informants of the study in a negative light.

For the qualitative researcher, remaining ethical during data analysis requires avoiding the simplicity of "formula stories" (Loseke, 2001), which locate abusive men and abused women in fixed roles such as "villain versus victim." The actual life experiences of abused women are often complex, ambiguous in meaning, and fundamentally conflictual in nature. So although much more difficult to carry out and more subject to criticism from advocates, the authors concluded that presenting this complexity is the ethically correct and factually honest approach. The authors concluded that glossing over the uncomplimentary data in an effort to defend abused women while expecting that they be both martyrs and "mothers of the year" was both unethical and unrealistic, and may do more harm than good to the cause of abused women in the long run.

---

stating propositions, causal connections, and developing theories. In this regard, qualitative research is identical to quantitative research; however, the differences between the two are important to emphasize. One difference is that drawing conclusions in qualitative research occurs, at least in part, during the process of data collection and analysis, whereas in quantitative research, this stage usually occurs after the data have been collected and analyzed (compare Figure 1.1 on page 11 and Figure 16.1 in this chapter). Second, most qualitative researchers hold their conclusions more tentatively, or "lightly," especially during early stages of the analysis, because they recognize that additional analysis could lead to reinterpretations or reconceptualizations of the data. As the analysis proceeds, however, conclusions become more complete and certain.

Third, the conclusions in qualitative research are more grounded in the data, which means the conclusions are more clearly allowed to flow out of the data rather than being imposed on that data by measurement devices created before the data were collected. In a grounded approach, the data analysis and conclusions are allowed to adapt to what is discovered in the data. Finally, in qualitative research, more than in quantitative research, the primary data-gathering instrument is the researcher herself or himself, and that raises concerns about the many ways in which the instrument/observer may bias the observations. This also is a problem in quantitative research; we have discussed ways in which a researcher might build a bias into, for example, a question or a multiple-item scale used during survey research. When the observer is the data-gathering instrument, however, his or her own personal values or biases can seriously compromise the collection of data and must be taken into account when assessing conclusions.

Qualitative researchers not only draw conclusions but also make efforts to verify those conclusions by finding evidence of their truth and validity. Are the conclusions reasonable and plausible? Without verification, one researcher's conclusions are simply his or her own account of what is going on. This verification is part of the overall argument that a researcher makes to convince himself or herself, along with any relevant audiences, that the conclusions are both reasonable and justified. In Chapter 5, we discussed some of the procedures used to assess validity in quantitative research, such as criterion and construct validity. In Chapter 9, we discussed ways to assess the validity of observations made in qualitative research. Here, we are discussing the validity of the data analysis and conclusions, but some of the points made about the observations also apply to the conclusions. Some additional points also can be made:

1. *Assess whether the conclusions are based on a thorough description and interpretation of the situation, including competing interpretations and explanations.* As soon as something resembling a pattern, generalization, or conclusion seems to be emerging from the data, researchers need to ask what rival explanations or conclusions are possible. This serves as a check against bias, misinterpretation, or laziness; and it will likely require additional passes through the data to see what evidence supports the rival explanations. It can be helpful to enlist other researchers in this process, because the researcher's own bias may prevent him or her from recognizing and clearly evaluating alternatives. If the conclusions are justifiable, then the rival explanations will find considerably less support in the data, thus providing more verification for the conclusions.

2. *Consider negative evidence and deviant cases.* Although much data analysis is a search for evidence to support a theme or a conclusion, it is also important to search for evidence that does not support it. Especially in qualitative research, it can be easy to miss negative evidence because the researcher is so focused on developing evidence to support a conclusion. (As one example of how this can occur, recall the "big man bias" in the discussion of research on minorities in Chapter 9.) If possible, have other researchers go back to the raw data—namely, the field notes—to see if they can find any negative evidence. If they don't, then the researcher has fairly powerful support for the conclusions. A part of this is to search for *deviant cases* or *outliers*—that is, cases that don't follow the themes or patterns that are being discovered in the data. Deviant cases may be difficult to find, but the search for them is important and can be assisted by some of the data displays discussed in this chapter. It is important not only to discover the deviant cases, but also to explain them. Can their deviation be understood within the context of the overall themes and propositions of the research? Explaining deviant cases may call for modification in the concepts and propositions or, in extreme cases, a total revamp of the theoretical approach.

3. *Carefully assess the desires, values, and expectations of the person analyzing the data to see if these might bias the conclusions drawn.* People's perceptions are drastically shaped by their expectations—or lack of them. If we expect something to occur we are much more likely to observe it—whether it actually occurs or not. If we expect welfare recipients to be lazy, then we become acutely aware of all those entries in field notes that might be interpreted as laziness. Thus, the validity of conclusions is reduced to the extent that expectations—whether recognized or unrecognized—mold interpretations of data. On the other side of the coin, a lack of expectations may lead us to miss entirely something of importance in the data.

4. *Have other researchers analyze the data to see if they come to the same conclusion.* There are problems with this method, because these other researchers probably were not involved in collecting the data in the field. That experience of being in the field provides all kinds of information and insights which may not appear in the raw data (the field notes). Nonetheless if these other researchers do come to the same conclusions, they provide corroboration that the conclusions are valid.

5. *Compare the conclusions reached through field observations with the conclusions reached through other research methodologies.* These other research methodologies include observational research in other settings or survey data, available data, or experimental research. This is a variation on criterion validity (discussed in Chapter 5). Sometimes, it is also called *triangulation*; that is, approaching the problem from a number of different directions. If various methodologies yield the same conclusions we have greater confidence that the field observations have validity. Field research whose conclusions are at wide variance with the results of other research should be accepted with caution, especially if none of the other checks on validity are available.

6. *Consider how the condition of the observer might influence both observations and conclusions.* Hunger, fatigue, stress, or personal problems can lead to distorted perceptions and interpretations. Likewise, physical characteristics, such as the lighting in an establishment, may lead to invalid observations. (This is another good reason for keeping complete field notes—field conditions affecting validity can be assessed at a later point.) If a number of these conditions exist, it may be judicious to terminate observation and then resume when conditions are more favorable.

7. *Look for behavior that is illegal, stigmatizing, potentially embarrassing, or that risks punishment.* If people engage in these kinds of behaviors when they know they are being observed they probably are acting naturally and not putting on a performance for the benefit of the observer. For example, in his study of a sexually transmitted diseases clinic, Joseph Sheley (1976, p. 116) argued that the validity of his data was quite strong, because "staff members dropped their professional masks and displayed quite unprofessional behavior and ideas in the company of the researcher." Under such conditions, we can assume people are reacting to environmental stimuli that normally guide their behavior rather than shaping a performance for the benefit of the investigator. When these kinds of behaviors constitute the evidence for the conclusions we can have added confidence in those conclusions.

8. *If possible, make a video or audio recording of the scene.* Although such recordings have their weaknesses as records of what occurred, they do provide another way for observers to check and validate their observations and conclusions. These recordings can also be reviewed by others, offering further checks on possible bias or misinterpretation.

9. *Assess the representativeness of the individuals, groups, informants, and observational sites.* Qualitative researchers do not typically use probability samples, but this does not absolve them from addressing the issue of how representative their observations are and how valid their generalizations. (We already addressed this issue in Chapter 6 when talking about some types of nonprobability samples.) To generalize beyond the individuals, groups, or sites observed, we need to make a case that those individuals, groups, or sites are representative of other individuals, groups, or sites. We do this by showing that the characteristics of those observed are similar to the characteristics of other individuals, groups, or sites that were not observed. If we cannot make claims of representativeness, this does not completely invalidate the research, but it does throw into question any conclusion we claim to be generalizable. Of course, with some qualitative methodologies, especially the

contextualizing strategies, generalization may be of secondary importance in the research.

10. *Evaluate whether the subjects of the research agree with or support the conclusions.* Who knows the field better than those whose field it is? This is poignantly illustrated by Sarah, a developmentally disabled young woman participating in a qualitative study. At one point, posters that displayed the themes found in the data by the researchers were presented to the group. Sarah walked to a poster that displayed the theme of "sense of belonging" at school and work. In response to a question, she smiled broadly and swung her arms out as far as she could reach to communicate just how much she agreed (Mactavish, Mahon, & Lutfiyya, 2000).

Thus, an important clarifying and validating step in qualitative research is to assess the reactions of those being observed to the conclusions. Do they agree with the themes, patterns, and propositions that form the conclusions? Depending on who is being observed, they may or may not understand the more abstract and theoretical parts of the conclusions, but many of the patterns and themes will be comprehensible to them, or possibly require only a little explanation. If they generally agree with the conclusions, then this provides additional evidence for the validity of those conclusions. If they disagree with some or all of the conclusions, then this can have two positive effects. One effect is to stimulate the researcher to consider changing or clarifying the conclusions to take into account the objections. Of course, it is possible that the researcher will conclude that no change or clarification is necessary. This can lead to the second positive effect—namely, explaining why the people disagree with the conclusions. In other words, their objections become further observations to be described and explained by the research. This may, in fact, provide more support for the conclusions.

As many of these guidelines as possible should be followed in verifying the conclusions that are drawn in qualitative data analysis. No single guideline, of course, is the key to having confidence in the conclusions; the key is the more that are incorporated, the more confidence we can have.

USING COMPUTERS IN QUALITATIVE RESEARCH

Most people are at least somewhat familiar with what computers do with quantitative data: They "crunch the numbers" by performing various statistical procedures on the numerical data. When the data take a more qualitative form, however, such as field notes, audio and video recordings, or the text of a magazine article, the manner in which computers analyze the data is less widely understood. As early as the 1960s, computer programs could perform some content analysis tasks, at least on text files. Since then, advances in computer hardware and software, artificial intelligence, and optical scanning technologies have expanded dramatically the kinds of tasks that computers can do in qualitative research (Bazeley, 2007; Fielding, 2002; Flick, 2009). Computer application to qualitative data ranges on a continuum from such basic tasks as using a word processor program to organize, store, and search text to software programs dedicated to qualitative analysis. We won't discuss specific software programs here but, rather, the general capabilities of what is now called **computer-assisted qualitative data analysis** (CAQDA).

There is no substitute for the creative insight of the researcher, but CAQDA software provides a wide array of tools to help the researcher organize the data, sift through it, identify concepts, and communicate the findings. Consider a qualitative study of eating disorders among people referred to an addiction treatment center. The data in this study might consist of open-ended interviews with the clients, client social histories and treatment plans, and chart logs taken from client records. There also might be videotapes of meetings where the staff discusses cases. Many of these "documents" would be in narrative form, but others could be photographs of the clients or video and audio recordings of interviews. CAQDA software permits the researcher to organize these diverse data sources into one project. Although it is common to convert most data into text files, some CAQDA programs enable the researcher to work directly with image and audio files. This has the advantage of saving time in comparison to conversion to text; but in addition, working directly with audio or video recordings preserves the richness of the data, including such things as voice inflection and facial expression that might be lost in the transcription process.

Coding and Retrieving Data

At a very elementary level, computer software can provide counts of how often particular words or phrases appear in a text or in field notes, as well as indicate which words and phrases tend to appear together or near one another in the text. Most qualitative data analyses, however, go far beyond this. A more important use for CAQDA software is to assist the researcher in creating and using a coding scheme and in coding the qualitative data. When working with data as text files, the researcher displays the text on the screen and selects a portion of interest. In some software, this is done by blocking the section of text on the screen in much the same way that you block a section of text in a word processor to copy or cut it. Other software automatically divides the text into sections based on lines, sentences, or paragraphs, and the researcher then places a marker at the beginning or end of the section to code. For example, a section of text describing the way in which a mother disapproved of her daughter's behavior could be selected and marked with a code for "Mother disapproval of daughter behavior." Then, the CAQDA software could search through the text, identifying and counting the number of times various codes appear in the field notes. Advanced software also can analyze whether certain words, phrases, or codes tend to be used together, how far apart from one another they tend to be, whether words or codes in a text tend to be positively or negatively evaluated, and whether certain words or codes tend to be associated with certain other words or codes (Kelle, 2004; Seale, 2010). Audio or video data coding follows a similar pattern. The recording may be displayed as a line across the screen. As the researcher listens to or watches the video, key sections of the recording are identified, and the researcher designates one or more codes for that segment of the recording. The researcher can also append notes or memos linked to the recording segment. As the researcher progresses through the various data sources, new code designations may be created and organized. Research in Practice 16.1 suggests some new doors that are opened for qualitative data analysis by technological advances in CAQDA software.

One of the advantages of this computerized system is that the researcher can quickly locate and pull together all the data elements, whether official records, interview notes, or audio recordings where a particular code was applied. In this hypothetical study, we begin by locating all cases that contain the codes "Mother pressured" or "Father pressured." This process is similar to conducting a computerized literature search by entering combinations of key words. Using these codes joined by the key term "OR," we can identify a subset of all cases where parental pressure was indicated and then save that group of files for further analysis. Having selected a subset of cases based on one or more codes, the program can produce a report with whatever information the researcher wishes: the individual's name, the name given to various codes, the frequency of use of various codes, and which source material the data were taken from. Conversely, for the coding category "Mother pressured," the researcher can quickly review all locations in the data where that code was applied. This aids the researcher in honing and revising the concepts as they emerge from the data.

Most CAQDA software programs store the codes for a given case in a special file, sometimes called an "index card." After coding the material for one case, the index card file contains all the codes the researcher used for all the materials pertaining to that individual. Thus, the computer program follows a logical procedure much like the traditional practice of manually preparing note cards for cross-referencing cases. To help with coding, the program provides a code list containing all the codes used thus far for all the cases in the study. Some programs also can "autocode," which means to give the same code to all identical words or phrases in a document. For example, if one data source for the eating disorder study were case intake forms stored as text files, the researcher can import these files into the CAQDA software program, which can then automatically apply the heading sections of the form as coding categories. In addition, we can store information about each case or individual in the study, such as age, gender, or whatever else is available in the data, and the software allows us to give more than one code to a given segment of text. We can revise the coding scheme in a variety of ways as well. For example, we can create different levels of codes. If a number of codes all share something in common, then we can group them under a higher level or more abstract code. The program retains all levels of coding, and the data can be retrieved using any level of code. Or we can go the opposite way: A single coding category can be elaborated into a series of more specific or concrete categories.

Data Analysis and Hypothesis Testing

Some content analysis software can test hypotheses by performing searches for all cases containing particular combinations of codes. Suppose our hypothesis is that "mothers who are critical of their daughter's body image have a negative effect on their daughter's self-image." The software could search for all cases that include the codes "Mother critical of daughter's body image," "Mother–daughter relationship strained," and "Daughter experiencing weight loss." To each of those cases, it then adds the code "Mother negative influence on daughter self-image," indicating that these cases confirm the hypothesis. Only cases meeting all three conditions have the new code added to their files. In a similar way, we can construct codes for other combinations of interest.

Some content analysis software can perform statistical analyses regarding the frequency of occurrence of various codes and display the data using some of the graphs and matrices discussed in this chapter. Some software also can import data from and export data to statistical programs and spreadsheets. In addition, beyond merely automating content analysis procedures, some programs provide important advances in the validation, reliability, and generalizability of qualitative data analysis. For example, an independent researcher can code the same data with the codes already developed and stored, and thus determine inter-rater reliability. To assess validity, an independent researcher might code the same material blindly—that is, without benefit of the existing coding scheme—to determine if the second coder develops the same or similar meanings as the first coder.

Conceptualization and Theory Building

Some CAQDA software is designed to assist in the tasks of conceptualization and theory building (Dohan & Sánchez-Jankowski, 1998; Fielding, 2002). Of course the software doesn't actually create coding schemes or build theories, but it can assist the researcher in these tasks by showing links in the data between concepts, coding categories, and observations that he or she might not have observed without such assistance. In fact, this type of CAQDA software has been used heavily by some proponents of grounded theory methodology, because the software assists in going back and forth from data to concepts, a key feature of grounded theory.

One way the software supports theory building is by providing opportunities for the process of memoing (discussed earlier in this chapter): Researchers can write their own comments and the software will link those comments/memos to sections of identified text. The memos can be stored separately from the field notes or inserted as annotations directly into the field notes or other text. Annotations to field notes are identified as such by the software, and the annotations themselves can be coded. As explained earlier in this chapter, these memos and annotations are expressions of conceptual and theoretical ideas, and the software assists in this process by enabling the researcher to build a conceptual scheme and theory

RESEARCH IN PRACTICE 16.1 Behavior and Social Environments: Technology Advances the Analysis of Qualitative Interviews

New technologies have given researchers greater flexibility in analyzing qualitative data. NVivo and Atlas.TI software packages, for example, allow researchers to directly code audio, video and even digital photographic data without having to first create transcripts or summaries of data content. Timothy Hilton and Cornell DeJong, both coauthors of this textbook, and their colleague at Northern Michigan University, Deanna Trella (2011), use NVivo in their research on rural homelessness. According to Hilton, "I first looked into NVivo because we were working on a limited budget. We had more than 50 hours of audio recordings and did not have the resources or time to have them transcribed. I had heard that NVivo allowed researchers to code interview data directly from audio files, so we tried it."

Coding interview data using NVivo is relatively simple. After creating links to audio or video files researchers can pull up each interview. The interview appears as a timeline on the screen, and the researchers can play the interview as they would when using any audio software. The coder can highlight sections of the timeline and assign a "node" (NVivo's term for a code) to that section. Researchers can view which sections have been coded and see their assigned codes by viewing coding stripes. Each node is represented by a different color. The program also allows researchers to attach annotations (or short notes) to interview segments. This can be helpful in research using grounded theory. Researchers' notes may contain ideas for new codes, hypotheses, or frameworks that emerge during the course of reviewing interviews. Hilton, DeJong, and Trella have used the annotations feature to transcribe short interview segments that may be used as quotes in presentations and reports.

According to Trella, the benefits to directly coding audio files are not limited to time and costs. "When I hear an interview I get a much more complete picture of what is happening than when I read an interview transcript. I get a much better sense of one's emotional state. We miss the importance and meaning of things like pauses, uncomfortable silences, and even sarcastic tones when we read transcripts. We also miss things like crying children and other background noises. In our research we try to understand felt experiences of people in some very dire situations. If we miss emotion or context, we miss a whole lot."

Another technology used by the research team was an audio file editing program called Audacity. As DeJong explains, "I was looking for a program to help me create short audio clips of interview segments so we could play them when presenting our research. One of the features we found most helpful was the ability to mask voices by slightly modifying the tone, pitch, or speed at which the clip is played. This was important for us, especially when we presented the research to local community groups or agencies. We wanted to make sure no one could identify our participants. To that end, the program lets you delete very short pieces of these clips where participants mention a proper name or specific place."

The team has presented their research numerous times, both locally and nationally, and played several audio clips at each presentation. As one audience member remarked, "It is really powerful to hear the homeless speaking in their own voice. You really get a sense of what they are feeling and experiencing. It also helped me to better understand the researchers' hypotheses about how the homeless cope in rural areas." Another remarked on a presentation evaluation form,

that gradually provides a more abstract understanding of the data while remaining closely linked to the data. Also, by being able to code these memos, the researcher is helped with noticing linkages that might have escaped his or her attention otherwise. Some software also provides maps that give a visual representation of links between concepts and other concepts and between concepts and data. This visual picture can be of substantial assistance in theory building: "Maps may help the analyst picture the project's theoretical shape, the concepts in use, the relationships between those concepts, and the ethnographic data that have been collected regarding each of those concepts and links. Theory-building software facilitates experiments with different concepts and links within the research process" (Dohan & Sánchez-Jankowski, 1998, p. 490).

"The clips were amazing. Sad and gripping. I don't recall ever having such feelings from an academic presentation. I will remember them for sure."

One of Hilton's bachelor's of social work students, Joseph Masters, also used NVivo in his research on Native Americans returning to reservations in Michigan's Upper Peninsula after jail or prison (Masters & Hilton, forthcoming). As he explained, "This has been a great tool. Listening to the interviews I conducted really helped jog my memory. I could remember what I was thinking during the interview and what was happening around us—where we were, who was nearby, the circumstances surrounding how we set up the interview. Without this I would probably have lost some of these important details."

Masters, himself a Native American, focuses on reintegration into tribal communities and subjective experiences of this process. As he explained, "When I hear participants' talk about coming home I know this means much more than returning to a house and family. Home is the "rez," a place where many of them never left until going to prison. They are comfortable there unlike anywhere else. This is where they are accepted unconditionally. Everywhere on the reservation is home and everyone there is family. The interview recordings convey that. You hear it in their voices—differences between how they talk about life on reservations versus life outside, in prison or anywhere else. It is very difficult to explain to other people, but when I play interview clips I do not necessarily have to explain it. It comes through in their tone, their attitude, their spirit."

An important concept that emerged from Masters's data is "nnmino-yaa", an Anishinabek or Native American word that expresses the idea of defining success internally, being content and living in harmony with one's community and the surrounding environment. One of Masters's initial goals was to understand whether those who returned to reservations believed they successfully reintegrated into society. "People I spoke with laughed a lot about this issue" he explained. "They understand what researchers mean when they talk about 'reintegration successes,' that it means having a job and a place to live. The people I met think differently about life after prison. Reintegration into the community is easier because they know they will be accepted by others simply because they are all members of the same tribe, the same people. People do not necessarily see having their own home or apartment, and a job as success. As long as other people on the reservation have homes, then so do they. Jobs are seen as helpful, of course, but they are not as important as being happy and tribal membership." Success for many Native Americans, Masters explains, "Is more about belonging and what one gives to others as opposed to what one possesses. Their perception of success has little to do with how outsiders might view them."

Masters explained that direct coding of the audio recordings allowed him to more fully capture cultural variations in attitudes and felt experiences. "Deciphering meanings from discussions based on a simple question about reintegration success requires sifting through many layers. At times this means interpreting what is spoken based on tones and attitudes. I might have missed this or forgotten much of it if I had relied on my notes or transcripts."

(Based on personal interviews conducted in June 2012.)

REVIEW AND CRITICAL THINKING

Main Points

- Qualitative data analysis focuses on extracting meaning from nonnumerical data without transforming those data into numbers. Though nonpositivist paradigms have been receptive to qualitative approaches, a one-to-one link does not exist between a particular paradigm and a tendency to use qualitative rather than quantitative research.

- In qualitative research, the stages of data collection, data analysis, and drawing conclusions tend to overlap. One of the advantages of this overlap is greater theoretical sensitivity. Qualitative research pursues goals of description, explanation, and evaluation as well as attempts to abstract and generalize; it also seeks to contextualize the analysis.

- Qualitative data analysis can pursue a categorizing strategy or a contextualizing strategy. One approach to the former is to code the data. One approach to coding is to create a fairly complete and detailed coding scheme before gathering data; other approaches let the coding scheme emerge as the data are collected and analyzed.
- Specific types of coding can focus on the concrete versus the abstract, or on open versus more focused coding. Coding schemes should have clear operational definitions and should be tested for reliability.
- Reflective remarks and memos can assist in coding, conceptualization, and theory building.
- Contextualizing strategies include profiles, narrative analysis, and case studies. Their primary goal is idiographic—that is, to understand a particular case rather than to generalize from other cases.
- Data displays are important in helping the researcher develop coding schemes and conceptual categories, as well as in communicating his or her conclusions to audiences. Data displays come in the form of narrative texts and visual displays, such as context maps and matrix displays.
- Qualitative data analysis produces conclusions that must be verified. A variety of guidelines are applied to assess the validity of conclusions, and confidence in the conclusions increases as more of the guidelines are satisfied.
- Qualitative data analysis often is accomplished with computers, which can assist in coding and retrieving data, analyzing data, testing hypotheses, and engaging in memoing and other strategies that help in conceptualization and theory building.

Important Terms for Review

case study
categorizing strategies
coding
computer-assisted qualitative data analysis
context map
contextualizing strategies
data display
matrix display
memos
narrative analysis
network analysis
profiles
reflective remarks
sociograms
theoretical sensitivity

Critical Thinking

Much of the information that practitioners and policymakers confront is not quantitative in nature, but rather what social scientists would call qualitative: narratives and descriptions, either written or oral. Some of the issues addressed in this chapter can assist practitioners and policymakers in evaluating this qualitative information:

1. What is the context for the information? As presented, has the information been removed from its context and, if so, might that change the meaning of the information?
2. Is the information you are presented with the raw data? Or has the information been abstracted or summarized in some fashion (i.e., the equivalent of coding, reflective remarks, or memos)?
3. What abstract or conceptual conclusions are inferred from the information? Are they justified on the basis of the criteria for assessing validity discussed in this chapter?

Exploring the Internet

The Internet is a useful resource for learning about qualitative data analysis. As you try various search strategies, pay attention to the number of different fields in the social sciences and human services that show an interest in this topic. A good way to begin (as mentioned in Chapter 9) is to search under such terms as "qualitative methods," "participant observation," or "field research." The last will produce many sites relating to the natural sciences, because they also conduct field research. This, however, can produce an important learning exercise: Can you identify the ways in which the research or science discussed at the natural science websites is similar to or different from that done by social scientists and discussed in this book? For example, do the natural scientists appear to be concerned with the positivist versus nonpositivist debate? Beyond these terms, you can search for various terms discussed in this chapter, such as computer-assisted qualitative data analysis, coding, narrative, case studies, and so on. Look for websites that deal with qualitative data *analysis*, not with how to conduct field research.

A number of websites contain useful information and/or links to other valuable sites. For example, at the School of Social and Systemic Studies at the Nova Southeastern University website, "The Qualitative Report" (http://www.nova.edu/ssss/QR/web.html) is an online journal dedicated to qualitative research. The same site also has a comprehensive section on ethics in qualitative research (http://www.nova.edu/ssss/QR/nhmrc.html). Two other comprehensive sites are Forum: Qualitative Social Research (http://www.qualitative-research.net) and QualPage: Resources for Qualitative Researchers (http://www.qualitativeresearch.uga.edu/QualPage). Another good website, the CAQDAS Networking Project (http://www.surrey.ac.uk/sociology/research/researchcentres/caqdas/index.htm), includes an extensive bibliography as well as opportunities to review qualitative data-analysis software.

For Further Reading

Bazeley, P. (2007). *Qualitative Data Analysis With NVivo*, 2nd ed. Thousand Oaks, Calif.: Sage. This book provides a good overview of how CAQDA is done and focuses on how to use one fairly popular CAQDA software package.

Corbin, J., & Strauss, A. (2008). *Basics of Qualitative Research: Techniques and Procedures for Developing Grounded Theory*, 3rd ed. Thousand Oaks, Calif.: Sage. This book offers a complete introduction to the data-analysis techniques developed to support the grounded theory approach. It is both readable and practical.

Fielding, N. G., & Lee, R. M. (1998). *Computer Analysis and Qualitative Research*. Thousand Oaks, Calif.: Sage. This book focuses on the ways computers can be used in qualitative data collection and analysis, including discussions of available software and how qualitative research might change to adapt to computer capabilities.

Flick, U. (2009). *An Introduction to Qualitative Research*, 4th ed. Thousand Oaks, Calif.: Sage. This book covers all aspects of qualitative research, including how to analyze data and how to present the data visually.

Merriam, S. B., Ed. (2002). *Qualitative Research in Practice: Examples for Discussion and Analysis*. San Francisco: Jossey-Bass. Qualitative research has been popular in human service fields, such as education, for decades, and this book gives a good introduction on how to collect and analyze qualitative data in such practice settings.

Richards, L., & Morse, J. M. (2012). *README FIRST for a User's Guide to Qualitative Methods*, 3rd ed. Thousand Oaks, Calif.: Sage. This provides a general overview of qualitative methods, but also focuses on issues of data analysis.

Rossman, G. B., & Rallis, S. F. (2012). *Learning in the Field: An Introduction to Qualitative Research*, 3rd ed. Thousand Oaks, Calif.: Sage. These authors describe the complexity of doing field research while still making the basic data-analysis tools accessible to the student.

Sandelowski, M., & Barroso, J. (2007). *Handbook for Synthesizing Qualitative Research*. New York: Springer. Evidence-based practice often relies on synthesizing data from randomized controlled trials, but these authors argue that such synthesis can also be done with qualitative studies. The authors identify ways to optimize the validity of qualitative research synthesis studies and present the results of qualitative research synthesis studies in effective, audience-appropriate ways.

Class Exercises for Competency Assessment

16.1. **[Evidence-Based Evaluation] [Research & Practice]** One approach to coding is to enter the field with no preestablished coding scheme. This chapter suggests that four general categories of phenomena should be addressed when doing this kind of field observation: conditions or causes, interactions among people, strategies and tactics, and consequences. Have teams of students conduct observations in various settings for about an hour each. When recording observations, identify examples that would fit each of these four categories. Here are some suggested observational opportunities:

   a. Children, parents, officials, and spectators at a youth sporting event, such as a soccer, junior hockey, or Little League game
   b. Supermarket checkout area
   c. Traffic court or misdemeanor court arraignment or sentencing
   d. Student campus organization meeting
   e. Local government commission meeting or public hearing on a controversial issue

16.2. **[Evidence-Based Evaluation] [Research & Practice]** Another approach to coding suggested in the chapter is to develop a coding scheme that identifies domains of observation. The text provides an illustration of a listing of possible domains on page 431. Using the observation experiences suggested in Exercise 16.1, develop examples that would fit each of the seven domains.

16.3. **[Critical Thinking] [Research & Practice]** One of the ways that qualitative researchers visually display data is through sociograms. Construct a sociogram, for yourself, based on a social network in which you function, such as fellow employees in a work group, students in your housing unit, or a voluntary organization to which you belong.

Chapter 17

✳

Writing for Research: Grant Proposals and Report Writing

The Grant-Funding Process
   Federal Government Funding Sources
   State Government Grants
   Private Funding Sources
   Learning about Funding Opportunities

Grant Proposal Planning
   Proposal Development as a Process
   Identifying the Topic
   Needs Assessment
   Specifying the Organization's Mission
   Developing a Program
   Targeting a Funding Source
   Contacting and Visiting Funding Sources

Writing the Grant Proposal
   Appearance and Writing Style
   Components of the Proposal
   Submitting the Proposal

Writing a Research Report
   Consideration of the Audience
   Organization of the Report
   The Process of Writing

Review and Critical Thinking
   Main Points
   Important Terms for Review
   Critical Thinking
   Exploring the Internet
   For Further Reading
   Class Exercises for Competency Assessment

This chapter focuses on two important elements of applied research that often are neglected in introductory texts on research methods—namely, the role of grants in research and human service practice and the importance of good writing. The term **grant** refers to the provision of money or other resources to be used for research or service delivery. Grants are an important funding source for social research and the provision of human services. In fact, the amount of grant monies awarded each year is truly staggering. Among the agencies of the federal government that dispense funds, the National Institute of Justice awarded $97 million in 2002 (National Institute of Justice, 2003) and the U.S. Department of Health and Human Services' research, demonstration, and evaluation budget (RD&E) for 2003 totaled almost $2 billion (U.S. Department of Health and Human Services, 2002). Private foundations give out grants worth well over $1 billion each year for projects in the social sciences and human services (U.S. Census Bureau, 2011). Given the large role that grants play in funding research, demonstration projects, and some activities of nonprofit human service organizations, it is highly likely that most future human service practitioners will be directly involved in grant-funded projects during their careers.

Despite the pervasiveness of grants, preparing a grant proposal without previous experience can feel overwhelming. Grant writing sometimes is perceived as a mystical process, with strange jargon and convoluted procedures through which only seasoned professionals having an inside track succeed in receiving funds. Grants, however, range from complex, multimillion-dollar undertakings to fairly modest projects for small agencies. Some universities offer small research grants specifically for undergraduate student research. So preparing a successful funding proposal is an attainable goal even for the beginning human service professional. A neophyte understandably has many questions: What do I do first? Whom do I contact? What do they want to know? Although the prospect of writing the first grant proposal can be daunting, preparing a fundable proposal involves many of the principles of sound practice and research that are part of a professional education. If approached systematically, writing grant proposals can be an interesting challenge rather than something to be feared.

In this chapter, we can neither explore all aspects of grantsmanship nor go into much detail. Instead we will focus on obtaining grants for agency functions, including both service delivery and research purposes. In fact, grants for service delivery typically include a call for needs assessment data and an evaluation of the service delivery; therefore, many grants combine practice and research activities. Depending on the demands of the funding source, minor differences may arise between preparing a proposal for a research project, service delivery, or a combination of the two. Those who are serious about seeking grants should consult the listings in *For Further Reading* at the end of this chapter.

THE GRANT-FUNDING PROCESS

Sources of grant money fall into three general categories: governmental agencies, private foundations, and corporations (Bauer, 2011; Smith & McLean, 1988). Of these, government agencies are by far the largest source of grant monies; they also are about the only sources of grants for more than a few thousand dollars. Even in the case of smaller grants, it often pays to start first with governmental sources, because many private foundations refuse funding automatically unless the researcher can prove that efforts to obtain governmental funding have failed. Among governmental agencies, branches of the federal government are the largest source for grant money.

Federal Government Funding Sources

The *Catalog of Federal Domestic Assistance* (which we will discuss in more detail at the end of this section) is a key governmental publication for communicating information about funding opportunities. The catalog identifies seven types of financial assistance provided by the federal government. One of the most important types of federal support is the *project grant* or *categorical grant* (the terms are synonymous). **Project grants** or **categorical grants** provide funding, for fixed or known periods of time, to specific projects, including research grants, training grants, experimental and demonstration grants, evaluation grants, and planning grants, among others. Grant seekers design approaches, within specified guidelines provided by the governmental agency, to meet the need or ameliorate the problem specified by the government agency. The agencies make their requests for programs or research opportunities known through what is called a **Request for Proposals** (RFPs): a formal request for people or agencies to submit proposals on how they would conduct some research or establish and run some program. Agencies or researchers then submit proposals in a competition to obtain the grant money. Because these grants are awarded selectively, on a competitive basis, to those submitting the best proposals within the guidelines established by the granting agency, they also are known as **discretionary grants**.

Another type of grant generally is dispensed to all eligible units. A **formula grant** is an allocation of federal money to states or their subdivisions in accordance with distribution formulas prescribed by law or administrative regulations, for activities of a continuing nature not confined to a specific project. For example, at times of high unemployment, the federal government commonly sponsors various job creating activities through formula grants. Because various places in the country experience unemployment in varying levels of severity, the money is allocated by a "formula" (hence the name) that provides most of the funds to those areas hardest hit and prorates the remaining funds to other areas as needed. Normally, formula grants are channeled through state and local governments until they reach the agency level. This allows each state and locality to tailor its approach to the problems of its particular situation. For example, unemployment may be concentrated among displaced factory workers in one locale and among minority teenagers in another. The most effective approach in the first locale may be retraining programs, but the second locale may benefit more from having its teenagers taught basic job skills, such as showing up for work regularly and on time.

The term *block grant* sometimes is used interchangeably with *formula grant*, but it generally refers to a package of funding that is created by consolidating several existing programs into one. **Block grants** are awards that are allocated to states by formula and funded by annual congressional appropriations. A block grant often is a fixed or capped alternative to more open-ended funding approaches. The state government does the final allocating to state agencies and nonprofit service providers. Block grants are special in that they cover broad areas, such as maternal and child health or elementary and secondary education, and they are ongoing, year after year. For example, the Community Mental Health Services Block Grant is authorized by the Public Health Service Act for the purpose of improving mental health service systems across the country. A stated goal of the program is to promote cost-effective systems of community-based care for people with serious mental disorders (Substance Abuse and Mental Health Services Administration, 2003). Although individual human service agencies do not receive federal block grants directly, this type of grant is still important to human service providers, because they may be able to access the funds by submitting proposals to the state or local government office that does receive them.

Though not strictly grants, **federal government contracts** also can be an important source of funds. With contracts, the government decides precisely what it wants and how it wants it done, leaving little flexibility to the researcher or the service provider. The government then looks for agencies that can perform the desired tasks at the lowest price. Sources of information about contracts and the rules under which they are awarded are different from grants. Also the number and variety of contracts is vast, so considerable research may be needed to get involved with the contract side of the federal government. Despite the obstacles, however, nonprofit agencies are moving into contracts as a new way to fund both research and services.

State Government Grants

Although states have always dispersed some of their own tax revenue through the granting process, the rise of federal block grants and the occasional formula grant have greatly expanded the dispersal of funds at the state level. Because each state disperses these monies differently, we cannot make any blanket statements about how to bid successfully for such funds. Regarding block grants, however, something consistent across all states is a federally mandated series of open meetings to discuss how the grant money should be used. The Community Mental Health Services Block Grant follows this procedure. Although showing up and speaking at these meetings will not ensure that a practitioner or an agency will get a grant, it will help ensure that some money is allocated for the area of greatest concern to that practitioner or agency. Another way to increase the chances of getting state grant monies is to keep in contact with the state departments and agencies that oversee and fund research and services related to the human services, such as the department of corrections, the department of mental health, and the department of social services. These state agencies may also publish RFPs to solicit grant proposals.

Private Funding Sources

A **foundation** is a nonprofit, legally incorporated entity that is organized for the purpose of dispersing funds to projects that meet the guidelines of its charter. The number of private foundations is staggering—upwards of 35,000 (Bauer, 2011). Not all foundations, however, are created equal. The largest 20 percent of foundations control 97 percent of all foundation assets, so this narrows the number of likely prospects considerably. Most foundations also award only small grants; only about 500 foundations typically give grants in excess of $5,000 each.

Submitting a proposal—no matter how noble the purpose or how well prepared the paperwork—that calls for a grant of $20,000 to a foundation that has never awarded more than $5,000 in any one grant is a waste of time. The person looking for a small grant must begin looking at some of the other characteristics of foundations to sort through the possibilities and find those few that are most likely to fund the proposal. In general, private funding sources are good places to seek grants for agency activities or applied research, because they prefer to fund action programs that produce immediate results rather than research projects that, at best, have some long-term payoff. Also, the complexity of proposal preparation and submission is much less than that encountered with federal agencies.

There are five distinct types of foundations. These are community foundations, general-purpose foundations, special-purpose foundations, family foundations, and corporate foundations.

Community foundations exist to serve their immediate local area. Therefore, if a project is modest in scale and serves some local need, a community foundation may be a good choice.

General-purpose foundations often are large, such as the Ford Foundation, and operate nationwide. If a project is large in scope, with the potential for having an impact broader than just the local community, these large foundations may be ideal. These foundations particularly like innovative demonstration projects that show the way for other communities to solve various problems.

Special-purpose foundations carve out a particular area of interest and award grants only to projects that deal directly with that area of specialization. Successful funding from these sources requires some research into which foundations fund what kinds of projects. Fortunately, large foundations usually publish annual reports, much as corporations do, outlining recently funded projects (Krathwohl, 1988); from these, we can tell what issues and projects various foundations are interested in and willing to support.

Family foundations are the most difficult to categorize, both because there are so many—more than 30,000, according to Bauer (2011)—and because they are so different. Some are large and have the resources to award fairly substantial grants, whereas others have a cap on grant size of a few thousand dollars. Some are quite general in the projects they fund, whereas others have very narrow interests. For example, some only fund projects that benefit a particular religious or ethnic group, whereas others only fund projects that address a particular problem, such as alcoholism or child abuse.

Corporate foundations are used by some companies as the conduit for corporate philanthropy.

Other corporations engage in philanthropy but do not use the foundation mechanism. In either case, nonprofit agencies are common recipients of corporate giving. To maximize the chances for sharing some of this corporate wealth, grant seekers must understand a few things about corporate giving. As investor-owned, profit-making enterprises, corporations are giving away stockholders' money. As such, the directors who make the philanthropic decisions are careful to fund only those activities that they can justify to their stockholders. This tends to mean that the corporation or its employees must stand to benefit in some way from the projects that are funded. For example, a nonprofit child care facility used by many corporate employees might receive a corporate grant or other corporate support. Also, because of this need to benefit, corporate giving is concentrated largely in areas where the corporations have their offices, headquarters, or manufacturing facilities.

Learning about Funding Opportunities

Given all the separate agencies and organizations that disperse grants, how do we find specific funding opportunities? Publications and computer databases can help. The *Catalog of Federal Domestic Assistance* (CFDA), for example, is available on the web (http://www.cfda.gov), and it describes all federal government programs. Detailed information is provided for a vast array of programs. The CFDA explains the objectives of each program, eligibility requirements, steps in the application process, examples of funded projects, and criteria for selecting proposals. The http://USAspending.gov website can help search the CFDA by providing information on people and organizations that have successfully applied for grants from programs listed in the CFDA (information about older grants is made available by the National Archives and Records Administration at http://www.archives.gov).

Grant seekers can search for funding opportunities with the "Grants" database prepared by the Dialog Corporation and Oryx Publishing on the web (http://library.dialog.com) or on a CD-ROM.

Oryx Press also has a printed version available, titled *Directory of Research Grants*. This is the most comprehensive source of current information on grants offered by government, corporate, and private funding sources. In addition to its convenience, the database has the advantage of monthly updates and contains an extensive and useful list of websites related to obtaining funding for research.

Another useful publication is the *Federal Register*. This daily, magazine-sized volume reports on the activities of the federal government and also is available online (http://www.gpoaccess.gov/fr/index.html). Although the *Federal Register* includes a lot of information of little use to grant seekers, new programs are announced first in it, so this is a good resource for the ever changing opportunities to obtain federal funding. Guidelines for obtaining funds under the new programs also are first provided in the *Federal Register*. Eventually, this information gets into the CFDA, but because that is only published annually, many months can pass before a new program gets listed there.

Many funding agencies publish periodic newsletters or bulletins describing their latest activities and programs. It is easy to get on these mailing lists, which often contain RFPs that may unveil a funding opportunity.

An organization called the Foundation Center (http://www.foundationcenter.org) produces a huge amount of material to help in searching for grants. One of its primary publications is *The Foundation Directory* (print version) or *Foundation Directory Online*, which contains information on foundations of all types that fund research. The online version has a guided tour that shows you how to search the *Directory* for foundations that provide grants. (The print version is available in libraries, but you must subscribe to the online version in order to fully use its capabilities.) The *Directory* supplies a considerable amount of information about each foundation or organization it includes—information that is useful in sorting out to whom to make a grant request. For example, financial information about each organization gives some idea about the size of grants that a foundation typically makes. It also provides information on a foundation's purpose and activities, types of support, and limitations to further screen potential funders. In these sections, you can learn whether a particular foundation provides grants for research purposes (some do not). Also procedures for making applications are described and memberships of the boards of directors provided. For those in the business of seeking grants, *The Foundation Directory* is an essential tool.

Another publication from the Foundation Center, *Foundation Fundamentals,* is particularly useful for beginners. It outlines the services of the center, along with information on locating foundations and preparing and submitting proposals to private foundations. A special guide to corporate foundations, *Corporate Foundations Profiles,* also is offered by the Foundation Center. This useful volume presents detailed descriptions of the largest 250 corporate foundations and less detailed information on 470 more. This directory shows which corporations have operations in which areas, and therefore, which ones might be likely prospects for funding. In addition, the Foundation Center publishes *The Foundation Center's Guide to Grantseeking on the Web* and provides a wide variety of other center materials online.

The Annual Register of Grant Support: A Directory of Funding Sources, like *The Foundation Directory,* is an excellent source of information on grant sources. Of particular interest to human service professionals is that funding sources are organized according to funding purposes. One category is "Special Populations," and includes subcategories for African Americans, Native Americans, Spanish-speaking people, and women. Additional listings for children and youth, community development, crime prevention, and public health and social welfare are covered under "Urban and Regional Affairs." Another good source is *The Grants Register* (Palgrave Macmillan).

GRANT PROPOSAL PLANNING

The grant-funding process involves two players: the funding sources, who sift through proposals seeking worthy projects in which to invest, and the agencies with project ideas that deserve funding. Getting the two together is the heart of the granting enterprise. Having described the funding sources, we now turn to the second process—namely, the development of a fundable proposal (Locke, Spirduso, & Silverman, 2007; Miner & Miner, 2003).

Proposal Development as a Process

Let's explode one myth about obtaining grants: Successful proposals are not started and finished in short order. Rather, they are developed in detail and carefully honed over time. The preparation of grant proposals should be considered an ongoing, continuing function within an agency rather than a sporadic event. All too often, grants are begun in haste and rushed to partial completion to meet some fast approaching deadline. The result, frequently, is rejection.

When conceptualized as a process instead of as a single event, grant development has many principles in common with the research process introduced in Chapter 1. When the grant is for the purpose of conducting a research project, the connection with the research process is obvious, but a sound understanding of research principles also is directly applicable to grants for service delivery. In seeking funds, the prospective grantee must identify a problem, hone it into a well-defined and manageable topic, develop objectives for the project, search the literature to devise a method of intervention, and plan an evaluation strategy. Furthermore, just as one research study leads to new questions for study, the lessons learned in one grant-funded project lead to new ideas for further projects.

In this section, we describe a number of key elements of the grant-funding process. These are not a series of sequential steps, but rather a number of separate and interconnected elements that can be accomplished in different orders at different times. Some are ongoing agency activities; others are specific things that must be done at a particular point. Together they culminate in and make possible the actual writing of the grant proposal.

To promote the concept of the generation of grant proposals as an ongoing part of agency activities, the use of a *proposal development workbook* (PDW) is recommended (Bauer, 2011). This loose-leaf binder becomes the mortar that holds the building blocks of a proposal together. As the proposal develops from a vague idea to a full-blown project—complete with a demonstration of need, evidence of community support, funding source possibilities, and much more—the PDW organizes everything that goes into a successful proposal as the various components are obtained or completed. Agency staff should be encouraged to watch for items to contribute. For example, favorable news stories about the proposed project are effective demonstrations of community support that help influence funding decision makers. Some of the materials in the PDW for one project also might be useful for a later project.

Identifying the Topic

Before we can begin filling our PDW, of course, we need an idea that can be developed into a fundable proposal. Problems that need to be solved exist in abundance, and many sources of research problems are discussed in Chapter 4. What tends to be in short supply, however, are innovative ways of attacking them. One approach is to organize brainstorming sessions (Bauer, 2011) where members of the staff divide into small groups and develop as many possible solutions or approaches to the selected problem as they can. All the proposed solutions are recorded for further consideration. The goal is to generate ideas, not to reach a consensus regarding which solution is best. In fact, it is desirable to maintain alternative approaches to the problem. One or another of these alternatives may be more palatable politically to a particular funding source, and the chances of obtaining a grant can be significantly enhanced by choosing a solution favored by a funding source.

After brainstorming, the next step is evaluation. Thanks to group dynamics, wildly impractical or just plain stupid ideas usually never make it out of the group. Realistically, however, some ideas will be better than others. We want to sort the best few ideas to save for building into a proposal. One important part of this evaluation is to work out cost–benefit or cost-effectiveness analyses (see Chapter 12). The cost–benefit analyses reveal whether the suggested solutions are economically viable. With any luck, one or more of the considered approaches will show benefits outweighing costs. The cost–benefit analyses of the chosen approach also will be important later, when they become one of the arguments for funding the proposal. Cost-effectiveness analyses, of course, allow selecting the approaches that produce the greatest effect for the least cost. Being able to argue that the project for which an applicant is seeking funds is the most cost-effective of the several projects being considered can only be looked on favorably by decision makers at the funding source.

Needs Assessment

One of the most important components of a successful grant application is establishing the existence of some problem or need that requires amelioration. All funding sources must operate within their annual budgets, so the competition for available funds is fierce. If an agency can make the case that the problem or need it wishes to address is the most pressing, that agency greatly increases its chances of being funded.

There are a variety of ways to make a case for your proposal, and those who are successful include information from more than one source. The core of the evidence supporting the existence of need will likely come from a *needs assessment survey*. With a properly drawn sample, it is possible to make quite accurate estimates concerning the extent of some need within a given population. Additional supporting evidence can come from *key informants*, or people who are particularly close to and knowledgeable about the problem at issue. *Community forums* can gather testimony about the problem, and examples of individuals suffering from the problem can be used as *case studies*, which illustrate the problem in more human terms than abstract statistics can. Finally, data from *public records* may be used as additional evidence of need. Bauer (2011) makes the useful analogy between the grant seeker and a lawyer preparing a case for trial. Each wishes to prepare as persuasive a case as possible to influence a set of decision makers (a jury or review panel) to reach the desired conclusion. In the case of obtaining grants, documenting need is a crucial part of the process. Just as it is not enough for a defendant to be innocent of the crime to be found not guilty by a jury, it is not enough for a need to actually exist to convince a funding source to approve a relevant proposal. In both situations, evidence must be gathered and the case presented to the decision makers with great care to generate a favorable verdict.

In some cases, it may be possible to obtain a grant to conduct needs assessment research. Especially with problems about which we know little, funding agencies sometimes are willing to fund a survey to obtain more information. In other cases, a funding agency may require that a needs assessment survey be included as part of a larger funding proposal, which may include a service delivery program that affects the problem. In any event, needs assessment often plays an important part in the grant-funding process.

Specifying the Organization's Mission

Not only must the need for services or research be documented, the funding source must be convinced that a particular organization is the proper site for a program to address that problem. This entails demonstrating to the funding source that the problem described in the needs assessment is within the applicant's domain or mission. Many organizations, such as universities, have formal mission statements that appear in official publications. Often, however, such statements are global in nature and may not be adequate for such a purpose. At a minimum, the mission statement should include both how and why the organization was started, and detail its primary goals. Generally, funding sources look more favorably on organizations with a history and track record of accomplishment related to the project to be funded; a new organization might have to work hard to prove its viability. The mission statement also should address the current activities of the agency, because organizations change with the changing needs of society—an organization that originated for one purpose may be doing something else today. Finally, the mission statement should include the organization's future plans. Funding sources like organizations that appear to be serious and well managed. One way of demonstrating this is by showing careful plans for the future.

Another way to convince a funding source that an applicant is best suited for a particular project is to focus on the uniqueness of that agency. The goal here is to stand apart from other agencies. There is a tendency to think that agencies providing similar services are not very different, but with some thought—and, perhaps, another brainstorming session—the staff should be able to come up with some characteristics that make it special. Perhaps it is the geographical location, such as a particularly remote area or proximity to a large minority population. Possibly something is unusual about the clientele or staff. Or maybe the problem-solving approach is different and uniquely successful. With a little careful consideration, the grant seeker should be able to develop unique qualifications to address the documented need.

Developing a Program

The most crucial component of any proposal is the research or service project itself. Having established a need, it is necessary to translate that need into specific outcomes for the project and develop a plan by which those objectives can be achieved. In the case of a research grant, such as a proposal to evaluate the effectiveness of a client advocacy program in a state department of mental health, the task is fundamentally one of preparing a detailed blueprint of the stages of the research process (presented in Chapter 1). Hypotheses must be developed and a method of testing these hypotheses devised. Issues of subject selection, study design, and data collection and analysis must be taken into account. A service delivery grant requires specification of exactly what will be done to address the need. Direct connections between the goals of the project and the content of the program must be explicated. Even though service delivery may be the primary emphasis of the proposal, most grants require an evaluation component, so a strategy for monitoring the program and securing data for evaluation purposes must be included.

An important consideration is the time sequencing of the project. Before subjects can be interviewed, interviewers must be trained, and instruments need to be selected or developed. How long will each of these steps take? Must certain staff be hired before the activities can take place? Accounting for all these details requires developing a work plan that shows the flow of procedures from the beginning to the end of the project, and that identifies how the various activities coordinate. Although a simple time schedule with beginning and ending dates for various phases may suffice for some projects, the use of graphics, such as a flow chart, often is convincing—and may even be preferred. Such charts can clearly portray the relationships between elements of the project, when each element begins and ends, and which elements overlap. Planning the steps of the project and determining the amount of time for each require a great deal of effort, but this is effort well spent. For one, it forces the agency to analyze how the various parts of the program fit and function together. It also serves to uncover difficulties before the proposal is written and approved, avoiding, for example, the discovery midway through the project that some significant and expensive component was overlooked. Finally, when the time comes to develop the budget and ask for dollars, the plan serves as a justification for the resources.

A number of tools have been created to aid in developing the work plan. Two of the most common are PERT (Program Evaluation Review Technique) and CPM (Critical Path Method). With these techniques, a collection of tasks is specified that results in a final outcome, which in this case is the completed project. Circles, rectangles, and arrows graphically illustrate the progression of events. The technical details of PERT and CPM are beyond the scope of this text, but a variety of computer applications are available that employ these program-planning principles. A major advantage of these applications is that we can readily see the budgetary impact of changing situations by manipulating the variables that affect the budget when we play "what if." For example, we can readily determine how much an extra full- or part-time employee would cost over the life of the program by inputting a single number. Likewise, all other costs can be easily evaluated and a final, accurate budget prepared.

Targeting a Funding Source

By this point, the raw material of a proposal—including a clear idea of the problem, data regarding the need, the preferred program alternative, and cost estimates for the components of that alternative—have been amassed. Before organizing the final proposal, however, consideration must be given to potential funding sources. As a first step, the most appropriate organizations should be identified from among the myriad governmental agencies and private foundations. Sending numerous duplicate proposals to whichever funding sources appear to be most receptive, however, probably will not work. Each proposal must be fine-tuned specifically for each funding source, because each funding source has different rules and needs. This requires research into the various funding sources—their rules of submission, project areas they have funded in the past, and their particular political viewpoints. Having created a list of possible funding agencies, the grant seeker then begins to narrow the list. One consideration is whether the organization has any advocates who are associated with the funding agency or can make contact with it.

By *advocates*, we refer to individuals who will not only speak on the agency's behalf to funding sources, but also offer guidance and advice throughout the funding process. Previously, we described the grant seeker preparing a proposal as being analogous to a lawyer preparing a case for trial. This analogy applies once again in the area of advocates to help make the case for the grant. The lawyer uses witnesses to help convince a jury, and advocates are the grant seeker's witnesses, supplying favorable testimony about the proposal to funding sources.

Like an attorney, grant seekers need to envision how advocates might be viewed and select those who can make the most favorable impression, because advocates can play a key role in the final outcome.

The best advocates are people who are favorably disposed toward the agency and the proposed project and who have some influence on the funding source. In this respect, securing grant funding is a political process, requiring strategies similar to those used by practitioners in community practice. The range of people who can help influence a funding source is vast and difficult to discuss in general terms, but some possibilities include people with membership on both the agency's and the funding source's governing boards, members of the agency's staff (don't forget their spouses) with special contacts at funding sources, politicians at all levels who support the agency's efforts, and agency volunteers who may have useful contacts.

Once the advocates are identified, along with the funding sources with which they can help, it is time to put them to use. Advocates can be helpful in a variety of ways. At the initial stage, they can help contact representatives of the funding sources to establish a working relationship. They can set up appointments with funding sources. They may even accompany grant seekers when visiting a funding source; and they may know someone at the funding source who can help ensure that the proposal receives a fair and complete review. When the proposal has actually been written, advocates also can provide letters of support. All these efforts are intended to increase the likelihood that a proposal will receive attention. Funding agencies have limited resources, and they receive many more proposals than they can possibly fund. No matter how numerous or powerful, no collection of advocates can substitute for a worthy project and a well-prepared proposal, so in all of this, we are assuming that those two conditions are met. Advocates are important because a meritorious proposal is in competition with others that are also deserving. It is when decision makers are forced to choose from among numerous worthy proposals that advocates come into play.

Contacting and Visiting Funding Sources

Having identified a few agencies or foundations as likely funding sources, contacting them may be the next step. Doing so can sometimes substantially increase the chances of funding (Collins, 2008; Miner & Miner, 2003). Today, most agencies and organizations maintain a website, and visiting it is a good start to gathering information—sometimes even including funding guidelines and applications. If the research organization has advocates who are associated with the funding agency or can make contact with it, then they could make the first contact. Otherwise, contact the funding source by letter. Such a contact letter has a number of purposes: to inform the granting organization of your agency's intent to apply for a grant and to obtain some much-needed forms and other information. Assuming that the agency's initial response is not negative, such as "no funds available," it may be worthwhile to arrange for a personal or telephone contact to explore research plans and gather more information about the source. Some funding agencies also will review drafts of a grant proposal and make suggestions for revision and improvement.

In some cases, it may be possible to make an actual visit to the funding agency. This is especially feasible with local agencies, such as a county social service department or school district office, and can accomplish three general purposes. First, it will confirm or reject the selection of the organization as a likely source of funding. With large federal agencies that offer funding under numerous special programs, information gained during this visit ensures that the grant seeker is applying to the most appropriate agency for the project. For example, a research proposal submitted to a program designed to fund action-oriented projects probably would be rejected, even though it might have been funded under some other program controlled by the same agency. Second, the visit supplies additional information on how best to tailor the proposal to the funder's special needs, thus increasing the chances for funding. Third, the visit provides a personal touch for the proposal when it is submitted. Instead of representing a faceless organization, the proposal will be presented by people who are known personally and who made an impressive presentation about a serious need and their plans to fill it. Whether the grant seeker calls, writes, or visits the organization, he or she should check Table 17.1 for suggestions about what to learn about an agency.

TABLE 17.1 What to Learn about a Granting Agency

- Does the funding agency have a real commitment to funding in the area of the proposed project, as evidenced by previous grants funded?
- Does the amount of funds requested in the proposed grant fit within the granting agency's typical range of funding?
- What proportion of agency grants go to new projects, as opposed to the continuation of currently running projects? Will this proportion change in the coming year?
- Does a new grant from an agency like ours have a chance for funding, especially when competing against those requesting a continuation of funding?
- To see what has worked in the past, can we review grant proposals that have received funding from this agency in the past?
- What are the most common reasons for rejecting a grant proposal submitted to this agency?
- What is the most common mistake people make when submitting a grant request to this agency?
- Can we submit a draft of our grant proposal to this agency and receive feedback before submitting the final proposal?
- Are there any packaging guidelines that must be followed or the proposal will not be seriously considered (e.g., length, number of copies, binding, format, etc.)?
- What is the deadline for submitting a grant proposal?

Note that one thing that should be acquired, whether through letter contact or personal visit, is a list of last year's grant recipients. Before finalizing the grant proposal, the grant seeker should contact one or more of these successful organizations, because the range of useful information that they can supply is vast. They have experience with the agency, and there is no substitute for that in learning the ins and outs of successful grantsmanship with that particular agency. Each agency develops its own particular style of operating as well as its own perspective on problems and ways to solve them. It is important to learn about these bureaucratic idiosyncrasies from past grant recipients to tailor the proposal to best fit what the agency is looking for.

WRITING THE GRANT PROPOSAL

Having identified a topic, collected supporting documentation that confirms the need for action or research, formulated a method for addressing the problem, and targeted a funding source, you have completed the groundwork. Actually writing the proposal, with the information gleaned from these earlier steps, should be a relatively straightforward endeavor—but it still requires a great deal of care (Miner & Miner, 2003). In a number of places in this book we emphasize that a very important part of both research and practice is to communicate to others about plans and accomplishments. Such communication can occur at a number of different points in the research process, of which we emphasize two in this chapter—namely, preparing a grant proposal and writing a research report. Anyone who cannot prepare a comprehensible and convincing grant proposal will not gain the financial support needed to complete a research project. In turn, the research findings of anyone who cannot write a clear and thorough research report—no matter how important—cannot be translated into policies and practices by practitioners. We do not pretend that we can create accomplished writers here, but we do hope to offer some useful suggestions and resources.

Appearance and Writing Style

The old adage that you cannot judge a book by its cover may be true, but people routinely make such superficial judgments. Because of this, both outward appearance and style of presentation in a grant proposal are crucial to success. Demand for grant monies is great, so funding agencies may look for any excuse to reject proposals and thus reduce the number that will require a full review. Failure to follow any guideline may be seized on as a reason not to consider a proposal further. So to begin with, follow the guidelines to the letter—even if they appear senseless. In particular, be careful about length restrictions. Submitting an overly long proposal, no matter how worthy, may result in rejection.

Reviewers have a limited amount of time to review many proposals, so a proposal should be attractive and capable of being skimmed easily. Uncomplicated sentences and short paragraphs work toward this end. Emphasizing key phrases or the use of bullets (solid dots or other symbols used to set off a series of points in a text) for highlighting purposes helps, too. Different type styles, boldface headings, and variable margins and spacing further contribute to overall appearance and readability. Include charts and graphs to enhance visual impact and convey information in a small space. For example, use of a graph depicting the increasing incidence of some problem is often far more effective at making the point than use of a simple reference to that fact in the text. The graph also is less likely to be unintentionally passed over by busy reviewers.

Not long ago, great effort and a professional printing company were required to produce a proposal with these desirable features. The advent of word processing and computerized desktop publishing systems, however, has placed the ability to produce high-quality documents within easy reach of most agencies and many individuals. Such systems are strongly recommended for producing grant proposals—the competing grant applicants will likely produce a slick and attractive grant request using such technology. Beyond appearance, the style of the text is important. A dull, lifeless proposal, regardless of its merit, has less chance of being funded than one that exudes interest and excitement. Use action words and express emotions wherever appropriate. Interest the reviewers in the problem and in the proposed innovative approach to it by reaching them at an emotional level. Citing dialogue is one effective approach: Presenting possible future clients describing their problems in their *own words* is better received than a third-party description. As a general rule, try to maintain a fairly light, readable style.

As in all writing, a sense of one's audience is crucial to preparing a successful grant proposal. Of particular importance is the fact that review panels for both federal agencies and private foundations may contain at least some nonspecialists (Krathwohl, 1988). This means grant seekers must be careful to communicate their intentions in language that is clear to someone who is not a professional in the field. More specifically, jargon should be avoided, or, if unavoidable, should be explained. Beyond that, no assumptions can be made regarding prior knowledge of the problem, its importance, previous approaches, measurement devices, or analytical techniques. Explain everything in detail—and in terms a layperson can understand. Doing so and, at the same time, not boring the specialists requires a difficult balancing act in writing.

Writing a proposal requires such extreme care because the proposal represents the agency to the funding source and is an indicator of the quality of the agency's personnel and their work. A great idea presented in a sloppy proposal will not get the funding it deserves. A worthy idea deserves proper presentation so that funding can be obtained to implement it. The ultimate goal, after all, is not just to get grant money but, rather, to finance programs that accomplish some good.

After a draft of the proposal is completed and before the proposal is submitted, it is a good idea to have several members of the agency who were not directly involved in its production proofread it. This step is important because people who are unfamiliar with the proposal will approach it more like a reviewer—that is, with no prior knowledge of its content. The proposal will have to stand on its own, just as it will during the review by the funding source. In addition to looking for the usual typographical and grammatical errors, proofreaders should assess the total package for content and presentation. Is all the needed information included? Is the problem adequately documented by the needs assessment? Does the proposed project logically address the problem identified in the needs assessment? Is the budget adequately detailed to justify the requested funds? These and many other questions regarding the content of the proposal should be addressed during this final proofreading stage.

All these suggestions regarding the appearance, style, and presentation of a proposal should not distract from the central importance of the proposed project itself. No amount of fancy wrappings will make up for an ill-conceived idea. The importance of these matters is to separate one agency's deserving proposal from all the other deserving proposals to the point that yours gets funding.

Components of the Proposal

A typical proposal to a government agency or major foundation will contain most or all of the components shown in Table 17.2, probably in the order listed. The precise components depend on the requirements of the specific agency or organization and whether the proposal is intended to fund research, service delivery, or both. Notice that the order in Table 17.2 is quite different from the grant development sequence because the proposal is organized according to the needs of the reader, and not necessarily according to the order in which one prepares the parts.

TABLE 17.2 Typical Proposal Contents and Sequence

1. Cover letter	6. Methods
2. Title page	7. Evaluation
3. Summary	8. Future funding
4. Problem/Need	9. Dissemination
5. Objectives	10. Budget
	11. Attachments

TABLE 17.3 Title Page Specifications

1. Title of project
2. Program being applied to
3. Grant program contact person
4. Name, position, and institutional affiliation of principal investigator
5. Name of other sources, if any, to which you have applied for funding for this project
6. Proposed start-up date and anticipated completion date

The Cover Letter. The cover letter probably is the last item to be completed, but because it is the first thing read by those who will evaluate your proposal, it is crucial. One important function of the cover letter is to remind the agency personnel of who the grant seeker is and that he or she bothered to visit the funder and take into account their suggestions when designing the proposal. The idea is to show that everything has been done correctly (according to the funder's views) so that, now, the proposal deserves careful consideration.

Title Page. The title page often is a standard form supplied by the granting organization. Table 17.3 illustrates the common elements of a title page. A good title is one that describes the project and communicates the anticipated results. Thus the title "Reducing Homicide in Family Disputes" is preferable to "Applying Mental Health Crisis Intervention Techniques to Family Violence": The first title indicates what the project plans to achieve with the funds, whereas the second title merely describes a service. Beyond serving as a label for the proposal, the title page will route the application to the various officials who must process it. The page should clearly identify the applicant's name and address as well as the specific program being applied for and the granting organization contact person.

Summary. Most granting agencies request a brief summary of the proposal so agency administrators can quickly assess who should receive a copy. This should be no more than a paragraph and should briefly mention all elements of the proposal: research problem or service to be delivered, methods used, and anticipated results.

Problem or Needs Statement. This is where the applicant really begins to make the case. What should go here has already been discussed in the previous section while analyzing the needs assessment and mission of the organization. What must be done is put clearly and coherently into prose, describing the problem and why this agency can help solve it.

Objectives. Objectives state very clearly and precisely what the proposal will achieve—that is, exactly what research will be done or what service will be delivered—in concrete and achievable terms. No funding agency will be impressed if the objective is "to discover the real truth about spousal abuse." A more concrete objective would be to learn about the role of economic independence in the ability of women to avoid such abuse. List all the objectives with no more than a sentence or two devoted to each, and present them in the order of their potential importance and contribution, with the most important first. In a research proposal, this section should contain theoretical considerations and the development of hypotheses.

Methods. The proposal should include a complete description of how the applicant plans to conduct research or provide a service. In a research proposal, this section should contain all the mechanics of carrying out the research: sample size, sampling technique, research design, and statistical procedures to be used in analyzing the data.

Evaluation. Federal funding sources place particular emphasis on evaluation. It is politically (as well as practically) important to gather evidence that shows the funded activities are achieving the objectives claimed for them. Therefore, virtually all proposals must contain adequate methods for assessing both whether and how well the program is achieving its goals. In a service delivery grant, this typically involves conducting research to assess whether the program resulted in the improvements or changes intended. (A review of Chapter 12, along with some of the suggested readings, should be helpful in preparing this part of the proposal.)

Future Funding. A grant, by its very nature, is a one-time dispersal of funds. Human service organizations, on the other hand, typically support ongoing programs that require continuous funding. The disjunction between the one-time grant and the ongoing needs of the program should be addressed in the proposal. What happens when the grant money ends? The agency will want to see that this problem has been thought through and plans have been made to deal with it. Plans for local funding, other grants, fund-raisers, telethons, and so on should be included. Agencies like to see lasting and successful programs develop out of their seed money. Inclusion of money in the budget for future fund-raising efforts is perfectly appropriate.

Dissemination. Dissemination refers to spreading the word about the research, service delivery program, grant, funding source, and we hope, successes. Inclusion of comments regarding dissemination of results is looked on as an indicator of confidence. Agencies like positive publicity about the good they do and tend to look favorably on opportunities to obtain it. This is a small item. Alone it will not secure funding, but successful grantsmanship ultimately is a result of doing a lot of little things right—and better than the competition.

Budget. A carefully detailed budget is an important part of any grant proposal because granting agencies are punctilious in their accounting demands of grant recipients. Table 4.3 on page 94 provides an example of a research budget for a survey interview, showing the major elements that would be included in a budget. Essentially, every dollar requested must be accounted for. The methods section of the proposal, which spells out precisely what the program will do, provides the guide for developing the budget. All costs that will be incurred must be identified and included. Novice grant seekers often underestimate costs or leave out expenses. Because the developers of the project usually are researchers or practitioners and not financial officers, it is important to seek consultation in determining costs. The grant seeker's agency may have standard formulas for fixing fringe benefit costs, travel, and overhead, and it may require bidding procedures for purchasing equipment. The budget, however, must be realistic. Promising the moon on a shoestring budget will not endear the proposal to a funding source. It will merely be seen as the amateurish effort that it is. If costs are reasonable and well justified, however, it may be possible to negotiate reductions if the total amount is too high.

Attachments. The attachments section provides important supporting evidence for claims made elsewhere in the proposal. Bauer (2011) suggests the following as appropriate for inclusion in the attachments section: needs assessment and supporting research, résumés of key personnel, minutes of advisory committee meetings, names of board members, auditor's financial statement, letters of support from advocates, evidence of tax-exempt status from the Internal Revenue Service, any pictures or diagrams, and copies of any organization publications.

Documentation of community support also is important. Some funding sources demand a demonstration that the community is behind a project, but this should be provided even for those who do not. Evidence of community support generally comes from two sources—namely, advisory board minutes and newspaper articles. Many agencies of the type we are discussing here have advisory boards that oversee their operations. These boards, which are comprised primarily of other professional service providers, former consumers of the agency's services, and people whose expertise lies in the area of fund-raising, hold regular meetings to discuss the activities of the agencies they oversee. Minutes from meetings when the project for which funding is being sought was discussed can be used as evidence of community support. Newspaper articles that reflect positively on the project form the other major source of evidence for community support. Grant seekers can actively seek publicity for the agency and the project they are trying to get funded.

Submitting the Proposal

Public funding sources have quite rigid guidelines—not to mention firm deadlines—that govern the submission process. Applicants, of course, have to obtain these along with all other relevant information from the funding agency. Because deadlines are involved, the proposal should be submitted either electronically, in person, or by registered mail so that time of submission can be verified. In either case, it is a good idea to telephone the funding source to verify receipt (unless they request no phone calls).

With many of the private foundations, generalizing about submission procedures is difficult, because each foundation has its own peculiar way of doing business. This places an added burden on the grant seeker. In some cases private foundations do not require the lengthy and detailed proposals that we have described. They do not have the resources, in the form of reviewers, to evaluate such complex documents. Instead, they rely on what is called the *letter proposal* (Miner & Miner, 2003). As the name suggests, the letter proposal outlines the need, the plans to meet that need, and the grant request, all in a fairly brief letter of no more than a few pages in length. Even something as important as the budget is abbreviated. Usually, the estimated total cost is all that is required. Rather than the voluminous detail characteristic of a federal proposal, each important issue in the letter proposal must fit into a paragraph. Brevity and clarity are the watchwords.

Because the applicant has done the homework, chances are good that the grant will be approved, but what if it is not? Understandable disappointment aside, rejection is an opportunity to learn. The applicant may contact the funding source and inquire about what was wrong (and right) about the proposal. He or she can learn from them how to do a better job the next time. The only grant seekers who are never turned down are those who never submit a proposal. It is the nature of the game.

Grantsmanship is an exciting and increasingly essential element of human service research and practice. We hope that this chapter has made the prospect of preparing a grant proposal less daunting. Remember, however, that we have been able to present only a limited amount of material on obtaining grants. We strongly recommend that you read carefully a complete book devoted to grantsmanship.

WRITING A RESEARCH REPORT

One of the strengths of the scientific method is the public character of scientific results. Publicizing scientific findings accomplishes several important functions. First, unless research findings are made public, they accomplish little social good. How can others learn from the findings of research if those findings are withheld? Clearly, publication of research findings is necessary to be able to apply those findings in developing programs and policies.

Second, publication allows the process of replication to ferret out the errors, frauds, and falsehoods that inevitably creep into the products of human endeavor. This self-correcting nature of science, which has contributed so much to its success, depends on the wide dissemination of research results.

Third, publication of research findings makes attempted suppression of those findings more difficult. In Chapter 12, we noted that, historically, this had been a problem for evaluation research reports. A few copies were supplied to a sponsor, who then had complete control over what was—or was not—done with the results. Broader publicity concerning research findings makes it more likely that such findings will come to the attention of someone who will use them.

Finally, the publication of research findings, like any written publication, is an effort at persuasion, an attempt to influence the readers to accept specific ideas or conclusions. Chapter 3 discussed the idea of advocacy in research and showed that human service researchers are especially likely to advocate some particular use for their research findings. To be effective, advocates must communicate positions to others, and one major mode of communication is through the written word. An interesting, well-written, and smooth presentation is more likely to be persuasive.

Given the central role that communication of research results plays in the entire scientific enterprise, proper preparation of the research report is vital. In this section, we assume knowledge of appropriate English grammar and usage. The complexity of the English language being what it is, however, we strongly recommend consulting one or more of the style manuals listed in *For Further Reading*. No matter how well we think we write, our writing always benefits from regular application of a style manual. The Eye on Ethics section explores some of the ethical considerations in the publishing of research.

Consideration of the Audience

An important consideration before beginning any writing assignment is the intended audience. For the writing to be most effective, it must be tailored to its specific audience. Although it is possible to identify several distinct audiences for research reports, the most significant distinction is between a *professional audience* and a *lay audience*. Of course, within these two broad categories are several more specific audiences that may require special consideration. Not all professionals are created equal. Even in the social sciences and human services, those pursuing research careers develop a different expertise and professional jargon than those following a more practice-oriented career. Likewise, those concentrating on clinical practice gain different expertise from those dealing with administration or community practice. They may all be professionals within the same discipline, but they do not share the same knowledge. It is important to keep these distinctions in mind when writing reports.

When a report is aimed at an audience of other professionals, we can make certain assumptions,

> **EYE ON ETHICS**   **Ethical Issues in Publishing Research**
>
> "The only ethical principle which has made science possible is that the truth shall be told all the time. If we do not penalize false statements made in error, we open up the way, don't you see, for false statements by intention. And of course a false statement of fact, made deliberately, is the most serious crime a scientist can commit."
> —C. P. Snow, *The Search*
>
> A major ethical issue that arises at the dissemination-of-results stage of research is how the research will be published. Researchers' jobs and livelihoods depend on their research getting published in professional journals. Yet in the world of social science research, about four out of five papers submitted for journal publication are rejected (Kimmel, 2007). Given the high stakes, scholars may be tempted to cut corners on the path to career security. One frowned-upon activity is multiple submissions—submitting essentially the same article to multiple journals with only slight modifications in the hope of securing multiple publications for one's résumé. But padding a résumé comes at a price. Print space in journals is limited, and multiple publications of essentially the same content means that other new knowledge is left out and other researchers' opportunities to publish are limited.
>
> A related issue concerns rightful authorship. On the one hand, someone who has contributed to a scientific project may fail to receive credit because a senior author may want sole credit for the work. This situation may arise when a faculty member takes credit for research actually conducted by graduate students. On the other hand, out of a desire to promote junior research careers, authorship may be padded with extra names of individuals who really contributed little to the research. In either case, it is an unethical distortion: Authorship should accurately reflect who made significant contributions to the research.
>
> Finally, there is a practice closely aligned with plagiarism for which the editor of a major journal coined the term, "paraphragiarism" (Levin, 1993), by which he means the "extended paraphrases of others' words, one-to-one idea correspondences, structural similarities, etc." (Levin, p. 5) This is an unethical passing off of someone else's writing as your own. Advances in computer technology have made this practice especially tempting, given the ease of cutting, pasting, and substituting a few words of one's own. Science advances through the rigorous testing of and building upon the ideas of those who have gone before, so it is imperative that an idea can be traced to its rightful source.

such as familiarity with basic concepts of the discipline and knowledge of common statistical terms. Although these assumptions make writing for other professionals easier, such an audience is likely to be more critical of such things as following proper format, elements of style, and substantive content.

If the intended audience is the lay public or others who are less familiar with research and the human services, we cannot make those assumptions. Instead, we must minimize the use of professional jargon, which is likely to be meaningless, or possibly misleading to such an audience. Occasionally, jargon cannot be avoided. Social science disciplines do not make up jargon for its own sake, but rather to enhance precision or to describe phenomena that everyday language does not have words for. When used, professional jargon should be carefully explained to lay readers. Presentation of data to a lay audience also must be simplified. They probably will not know what a probability coefficient is, and they may even have difficulty grasping the importance of a percentage table. Instead, the visual impact of graphs and charts helps get the message across. Also, explain fully what each statistic used accomplishes and what the result means. Professionals who do not routinely work with statistics and data analysis also may need some assistance of this sort. If we believe in the importance of our research and want it to be useful, careful attention to our audience will further that goal immensely.

Because different journals are read by different audiences, requirements of professional periodicals vary from one publication to another. If a research report is being prepared for possible publication, care must be taken to follow the specifications of the particular journal to which the manuscript will be submitted. A helpful resource toward this end is *An Author's Guide to Social Work Journals* (NASW Press Staff, 2009). Published by the National Association of Social Workers, the guide includes more than 130 social work, social welfare, and human service journals. Readers will find information on the journal's review process, editorial focus, format, and suggested style guide. In addition, the guide indicates where each journal is abstracted and indexed.

Organization of the Report

Despite the variation depending on the audience, research reports usually include most or all of the following elements: title, abstract, introduction and problem statement, methods, results, discussion, and references.

Title. The title is an important part of a report and the first element a reader sees. The major function of the title is to give prospective readers an idea of what the study is about so they can decide whether they are interested in reading more. Therefore, a good title informs the reader about the major independent and dependent variables and, possibly, the major findings. A second reason to develop a good title is that online library searches, as discussed in Appendix A, use key words in titles as one means of selecting articles. Therefore, a report with a misleading or poor title may be lost from these searches. The following examples are from a recent issue of a social work journal:

- Socialization and the Belief Systems of Traditional-Age and Nontraditional-Age Social Work Students
- The Korean Protestant Church: The Role in Service Delivery for Korean Immigrants
- The Effect of Short-Term Family Therapy on the Social Functioning of the Chronic Schizophrenic and His Family

Note that each of these titles provides sufficient information for a reader to decide whether to pursue the article further and for a computer retrieval system to identify key words.

Abstract. Most scientific journals and reports contain an abstract, which is a brief summary of the study that allows the reader to learn enough to decide whether to read the whole report. (Some examples of this type of abstract are presented in Chapter 4.) Abstracts also often are published in reference volumes or online in searchable databases, some of which are discussed in Appendix A. In these collections, the abstracts allow the reader to decide whether to locate the complete articles. Because of their importance and brevity (125–175 words), abstracts must be carefully written. The first sentence should be a clear statement of the problem investigated by the study. The research methodology and sampling techniques are then indicated. Finally, a brief summary of the findings and conclusions completes the abstract. Figure 17.1 shows an abstract with its component parts identified.

Introduction and Problem Statement. The first part of the body of the report states the research problem and its importance, including a literature review of the history of the problem in previous research and theory. This material indicates how the current study flows from what has gone before. Presentation of the theoretical material sets the stage for presenting the hypotheses that were tested in the study. Of necessity, this section must be kept relatively brief. For example, the literature review typically consists of numerous citations of previous work in the topic area, with comments on only the most relevant aspects of each study. This emphasis on brevity, however, should not be overdone. Clarity of presentation in this section is a must—without it, the remainder of the report loses its meaning.

Methods. The methods section describes the sample that was studied and the research techniques employed. It also shows how concepts were operationalized and what measurement devices, such as scales, were used. This section is important because it provides the basis on which the validity and generalizability of the conclusions will be judged. It also is the basis for any future replication efforts.

> **1** { This research examines homelessness in Michigan's Upper Peninsula, a remote area in the northern Midwest, while comparing coping tactics, felt experiences, and unmet needs of homeless single adults and families. A major goal of the study was to understand how the homeless use family, friends, and services to secure food, shelter, and other basic necessities. //
>
> **2** { The authors recruited 116 homeless persons, 58 single adults and 58 adults with children, throughout the Upper Peninsula for the study. Participants were recruited through social service agencies, flyers, and snowball sampling. //
>
> **3** { Data include audio recordings of in-depth, semi-structured interviews focused on: methods of securing basic necessities; relationships with family, friends, and human service organizations; and the felt experiences of homelessness, including the social and psychological impacts of homelessness. Directly coding audio recordings using NVivo software, the authors employed a grounded theory approach to reveal coping patterns; identify relationships between personal, family, and community factors and help-seeking behaviors; and create hypotheses related to differential homeless experiences. //
>
> **4** { Adults with children tended to have greater access to social services than single adults and reported that providers were more willing to accommodate them. Some avoided social services, however, because they feared being reported to child protection services. Services for singles were very limited, especially in smaller communities and many homeless individuals were reluctant to use available services, especially shelters, as these were associated with decreased freedom. Assistance from non-homeless family members was often limited to a portion of the homeless family, and in many cases there were social, psychological and financial costs associated with help from non-homeless family members. These costs often limited homeless families' seeking help within the extended family. Singles were more likely to report receiving assistance from non-homeless family members, although help received was often limited, especially for those with substance abuse histories. Help from friends was limited for many homeless families due to space and financial constraints (it is more costly to house an entire family than a single person). Almost all homeless individuals received help from friends and many maintained an extensive and diverse network of friends. Overall data suggests that while there are more services available for homeless families than singles, the psychological toll of homelessness is far worse for those with children. Available help from family and friends (and costs associated with receiving this help) and the fear of losing children to child protection services helps explain differences between homeless singles' and families' felt experiences.

FIGURE 17.1 Example of an Abstract, with Its Component Parts Identified: 1 = Statement of Problem, 2 = Sample Selection, 3 = Method of Study, 4 = Results

SOURCE: Hilton, T., DeJong, C., & Trella, D. (2012). *Experiences of Homelessness among Singles and Families in a Rural Area: Comparing Coping, Felt Experiences and Unmet Needs.* Unpublished paper.

As such, this section must be written with sufficient detail so that it can perform both of these functions. Readers must be able to tell precisely what was done in the study and who participated.

Results. This section is a straightforward presentation of the findings of the study, devoid of any editorializing or comment as to the meaning of the results—that comes later. Typically, the presentation of results involves the use of tables, graphs, and statistics. The one exception to this is the results section from a participant observation study, which is likely to have little quantitative data. As noted previously, consider your audience, and fashion your presentation so the data can be readily understood.

Discussion. In this section, conclusions are drawn regarding the implications of the data that are presented in the results section. Each tested hypothesis should be related to relevant data and a conclusion stated about the degree of support (or nonsupport) that the data provide for it. Beyond that, any broader implications of the findings for research, practice, or social policy should be noted. Any limitations or weaknesses of any of the results should be noted honestly as well. Often research results raise new questions as they answer others. Therefore, it is common practice to identify opportunities for future research.

References. A list of all works cited in the report usually is presented as the last element of the report. A variety of formats can be used, but the one known as the *Harvard method* is common in the social sciences. As sources are cited in the body of the text, the author's last name and date of publication are placed in parentheses at the end of the sentence. The references are then listed in alphabetical order by the first author's last name at the end of the report. An alternative format is called the *serial method,* in which the citations are indicated numerically in the body of the text. The references are then presented in the reference section, with each reference identified by the number associated with it in the text.

Preparing a list of references or a bibliography for a grant or research report generally is difficult and not a very pleasant task. All the names of the authors must be spelled correctly, and the page numbers and dates must be correct. In addition, the punctuation is not like that used anywhere else. Computer software, however, can take some of the drudgery out of preparing bibliographies. Bibliography formatting software creates a file of references with all the required information for each reference (still a lot of work). Once the file is complete, the program reformats and prints the information in a variety of popular bibliographic styles. In addition, some programs interface with word-processing programs, search documents for citations, and make up a correct bibliography from the file of references. It also flags any citations not in the file and any references in the file that are not cited. When revising a long document, such as a book or a grant proposal, this feature can save a lot of work and reduce errors. Bibliographic software does not do all the busywork, but it can reduce the drudgery considerably and greatly enhance the accuracy of the finished product.

The Process of Writing

It is not possible, of course, to cover in a brief chapter all the elements involved in writing. This is done in writing courses and through writing practice. A few points, however, are of special importance.

First, writing is a process rather than a product. We never finish writing, although we may finish a paper or a report because it has to be submitted by a deadline. This, however, doesn't mean that we couldn't write and revise further. Writing aims at the expression and communication of clear thought. It is difficult to write because, in some respects, language is a poor mechanism for communicating the subjective reality of our thoughts. If we hear that someone was almost hit by a car on the way to school this morning, words like "car" and "hit" seem straightforward and comprehensible, but do those words actually encompass the experienced reality? It was a bright red car, and it was speeding, and the driver seemed not to notice, and.... How much detail communicates an experience? We say that we were frightened by the close call and then realize we cannot make clear the wrenching terror, so we repeat that we were "really" frightened, using qualifiers, emphasis, and inflection to make our point. The words seem inadequate to communicate the experience, but this is precisely the challenge that any writer confronts: using words to describe a very complex and confusing reality. Researchers face the challenge of using words to describe a very complex theoretical and methodological reality to various audiences.

A second point, which really flows from the first, is that rewriting and revision are an inherent part of the writing process. Few writers are capable of making the first draft the final draft. Most writers, especially professional writers, must rewrite their material several times before they consider it to be clear, comprehensible, and smooth. (The term "smooth" in this context simply means the writing contains few errors or awkward constructions that distract the reader from the content.) One of the keys to revision is to be able to read the prose through the eyes of the intended audience. Would they understand a particular word, phrase, or sentence? Can they follow the sequential organization in the report? Do they grasp the transitions that move the reader from one sentence to another, from one paragraph to another? What is perfectly clear from the writer's perspective may be muddled and unclear from the reader's. The writer's talent is to perceive his or her writing from that other perspective.

Rewriting is an essential—if sometimes tedious—task, but it also is creative. As with other creative efforts, the energy and attention needed to create is greater at some times than at others. This means that the best writing usually is not produced in one sitting. Most writers find it useful to approach revisions after they have been away from a paper for some time. This enables them to work on it with fresh insight and attention. For this reason, words written at the last minute, with a deadline rapidly approaching, may not be the best words after all.

REVIEW AND CRITICAL THINKING

Main Points

- Grants have become a very important source of funding for both social research and human services. To gain funding successfully, grant proposals must be written well.

- Sources of grant money fall into three categories: governmental agencies, private foundations, and corporations. Governmental agencies are the largest source.

- Government funds come in a number of different forms: project (categorical or discretionary) grants, formula grants, block grants, federal contracts, and state government grants.

- Although many foundations fund grants, most fund only small projects, and some fund research only on limited subject areas. Corporations tend to fund grants that can be justified to the stockholders, such as for services or improvements from which the corporation or its employees will benefit.

- Many funding sources can be located through online computerized search services.

- The preparation of grant proposals should be considered an ongoing, continuing function of a human service agency. The steps in the grant development process are analogous to the steps in the research process.

- The first step in grant development is to identify a fundable topic. Conducting a needs assessment can assist with this task.

- Once the project has been identified, the next step is to target a funding source that will be interested in the project. This might call for visits to potential funding sources to assess their interest.

- To be successful, grant proposals must be written well, and this requires paying attention to the appearance and the writing style. Proposals must be neat, interesting to read, and addressed to the audience that will read them.

- A grant proposal should contain all the components necessary to provide a funding source with adequate information to assess it.

- Research reports also should be well written, because the communication and publication of scientific results accomplish important functions for science.

- A research report should be written at the level of the audience for whom it is intended. These might be researchers who are conversant with the jargon of research and statistics, practitioners who are unfamiliar with such jargon, or the lay public.

- Most research reports include the following elements: title, abstract, introduction and statement of the problem, description of the methods and results, discussion of the implications of the findings, and a list of references.

Important Terms for Review

block grants
categorical grants
discretionary grants
federal government contracts
formula grant
foundation
grant
project grants
Request for Proposals

Critical Thinking

This chapter has to do, in part, with convincing other people of the worth of your analysis and conclusions. You are trying to convince someone to fund your research through a grant proposal or someone else to accept your conclusions as summarized in a research report. This persuasive process is another exercise in critical thinking, and really involves an overview of the scientific process elaborated on in all the chapters preceding this one:

1. Of all the critical thinking elements discussed in earlier chapters, which ones can most readily advance this persuasive effort?
2. Does the persuasive effort reflect and include the key criteria that make scientific research a distinctive way of understanding the world, in comparison to tradition, experience, common sense, or journalism?
3. Knowing how to write proposals and research reports should also make one a more critical consumer of reports. Assuming that you are working or interning in a human service setting, you may be able to review a current program funding proposal or recent submission from your agency. In so doing, ask:
   - Why should this intervention be expected to work?
   - Is there a clear linkage between the intervention/program and the anticipated outcomes?

Exploring the Internet

Some of the major governmental human service sites have extensive material on grants, including abstracts of funded projects and RFPs that you can examine to better understand the issues of writing successful proposals. For example, the National Criminal Justice Reference Service (https://www.ncjrs.gov) has extensive information available on grants from the National Institute of Justice, the Office of Juvenile Justice and Delinquency Prevention, the Office for Victims of Crime, the Bureau of Justice Assistance, and other grant opportunities from the U.S. Department of Justice. Click on the "Grants & Funding" tab.

You also can go to the web page for the *Catalog of Federal Domestic Assistance* (http://www.cfda.gov), which, as pointed out in this chapter, is a government-wide compendium of federal programs, projects, services, and activities that provide assistance or benefits to the public. It contains financial and nonfinancial assistance programs administered by departments and agencies of the federal government. This website has a search engine where you can query the catalog. By entering terms for human service issues, you can quickly locate information about related grant opportunities.

A good way to get a better sense of how to write grant reports is to read some completed studies. One source you might try is the U.S. Department of Justice (http://www.ovw.usdoj.gov). You can easily search their databases and review abstracts of completed projects. The references indicate both where and how to obtain complete reports. Another excellent location is the National Science Foundation (http://www.nsf.gov).

For Further Reading

Brown, L. G., & Brown, M. J. (2001). *Demystifying Grant Seeking: What You Really Need to Do to Get Grants.* San Francisco: Jossey-Bass. This book takes the reader through the steps of setting up a usable office, making matches between agencies and foundations, writing grant applications, and evaluating the process. The authors use one agency as an example, taking the reader through the entire process.

Chicago Manual of Style. Chicago: University of Chicago Press, http://www.chicagomanualofstyle.org/home.html. Prepared by the editorial staff of the University of Chicago Press, the *Chicago Manual* has long been considered the definitive writing reference work. If you take your writing seriously, you should have a copy.

Cuba, L. (2002). *A Short Guide to Writing about Social Science,* 4th ed. New York: Longman. This book is a good review of what you need to know about writing research papers and preparing presentations on topics in the social sciences.

Hall, D., & Birkerts, S. (2006). *Writing Well,* 9th ed. Reading, Mass.: Longman. Hall, the author of dozens of books, brings his experience and expertise to a book that can help anyone improve his or her writing. Unlike many such books that present the rules in a rather stiff and direct fashion, Hall makes learning to write interesting.

Henson, K. T. (2004). *Grant Writing in Higher Education: A Step-by-Step Guide.* Boston: Allyn & Bacon. This is a practical resource for developing effective grant proposals. Specific strengths of this resource are sections on preparing budgets and locating funding sources.

Miner, J. T., & Miner, L. E. (2005). *Models of Proposal Planning and Writing.* Westport, CT: Praeger. This is another excellent guide to developing grant proposals for research or other types of grants.

Ogden, T. E., & Goldberg, I. A. (2002). *Research Proposals: A Guide to Success,* 3rd ed. San Diego: Academic Press. This book focuses on research grants and includes topics not found in more general works. It covers the National Institutes of Health and other sources of research support. The book addresses the various components of a research proposal, such as preliminary studies, research design and methods, and human subjects.

Thyer, B. A. (2008). *Preparing Research Articles.* New York: Oxford University Press. Aimed at the profession of social work, this book is written by an experienced author and journal editor. Its topics include selecting an appropriate journal, handling rejections and revisions, understanding confusing concepts like impact factors and electronic publishing, and avoiding common methodological and formatting pitfalls.

Yuen, F. K. O., & Terao, K. L. (2003). *Practical Grant Writing and Program Evaluation.* Belmont, Calif.: Wadsworth. This brief and practical text covers program planning, grant writing, and program evaluation, with emphasis on the interrelationship between these components. Readers will learn both the development and the implementation of grant proposals, program evaluation plans, data collection and analysis, and report writing.

Class Exercises for Competency Assessment

Portage Bay is a resort-oriented, medium-sized city of about 40,000 persons. Recently, the city council has received numerous complaints from downtown merchants about vagrants and homeless people taking over the parks and public areas along the waterfront mall. A large mental health institution is located near the city, and deinstitutionalized patients are accused of driving tourists away and hurting sales. Representatives of several organizations, such as the Community Mental Health Center and Community Action Agency, counter that the mentally ill also are residents and are being unfairly blamed for the problem. The advocates for the patients contend that the services are inadequate to meet the needs of the homeless in the community. A task force is formed to study the problem and develop a plan to resolve the conflict with the merchants while meeting the community's desire to be compassionate and meet the needs of the homeless. It becomes immediately clear that outside funding will be necessary to do a comprehensive study and implement a plan of action.

17.1. **[Critical Thinking] [Research & Practice]** As a first step, the task force considers possible funding alternatives.
   a. Make a list of resources to which the task force might turn to locate funding sources. Do you think government grants or foundation grants would be more appropriate?
   b. By using the *Catalog of Federal Domestic Assistance* and the *Catalog of U.S. Government Publications (CGP)* websites, identify a list of several potential grant sources related to the problem faced by the city of Portage Bay.

17.2. **[Critical Thinking] [Research & Practice]** Request sample grant application forms from organizations in your state that fund human service research projects. Your college or university probably has an office of research and development that can provide the guidelines; or you might contact such agencies as the state departments of mental health, social services, or corrections.
   a. Compare the grant applications in terms of the kind and detail of information that each requires.
   b. For each application, determine the problems for which the granting organization dispenses funding. What special priorities, if any, does the granting organization specify? Who is eligible to apply for the grant?

17.3. **[Critical Thinking] [Research & Practice]** Select a human service–related research article from a recent professional publication, and review it from the standpoint of the criteria presented in the discussion of writing a research report.
   a. To what audience does the article appear to be addressed—professional social workers, researchers, the general public?
   b. Is the title effective?
   c. Is there an abstract? If so, does it communicate the necessary information?
   d. Examine the organization of the study to determine if it contains the basic components described in the text. How are the problem statement, methods description, results, and discussion handled by the author(s)?

Appendix A

A Guide to Library Use and Information Retrieval

Organization of the Library
   Library Departments
   Accessing Library Materials and Other Information

Books
   The Classification System
   The Library Catalog

Periodicals
   The Classification System
   Journals Important to the Human Services

Online Databases

Reference Books for the Human Services

Government Documents

Information Literacy and Critical Thinking Skills

For Further Reading

A key part of all scientific research is information retrieval—that is, finding the information to conduct sound research. Information retrieval is central to virtually all the steps in the research process: reviewing existing literature to see what has been done on a particular topic, gaining help in developing a research design, locating existing scales, and so on. Good information retrieval today requires two types of knowledge: how to use the physical library and how to search for information online.

   A library is both a repository of information and a gateway for accessing information stored at other sites. Libraries own some of the information products that they make available to customers and assist customers in locating and accessing information resources at other libraries or locations. Because of the proliferation of information retrieval technologies, however, finding pertinent information can be a daunting task for those who are unfamiliar with modern technologies of information retrieval and processing. Effective information retrieval requires a number of things: first, a precise definition of what is needed; second, a determination of the best strategy for locating that information; and third, an evaluation of the information found. This appendix focuses primarily on the second step by providing a basic introduction to library usage and online information retrieval technologies. In addition, we point to some specific resources in the library and online that are especially useful to researchers and practitioners in the human services.

ORGANIZATION OF THE LIBRARY

Two key elements in the organization of a library must be understood for effective library use. First, the library contains certain *departments* that perform special functions in the search for information. Second, the library contains a number of important mechanisms for *accessing information*.

Library Departments

For students seeking materials, one of the most valuable departments in the library is the *reference department*. In most libraries, the reference department contains the basic tools for searching for information: encyclopedias, indexes, abstracts, dictionaries, handbooks, yearbooks, government documents that summarize statistical data, and an array of other such resources. Familiarity with this department is critical. In addition to its materials, this department's reference librarians are a valuable asset. Librarians are highly trained and knowledgeable about how to locate materials; one of their major duties is to help patrons. Working closely with a reference librarian enables students not only to locate a specific item, but also to learn the techniques of thorough and efficient searching for materials. Students probably should try to locate materials themselves first, but should not hesitate to consult a reference librarian if they have difficulties.

Without access to a very large library, such as at Harvard University or the University of California–Berkeley, we undoubtedly find that some needed books or resource materials are not readily available. This is where the *interlibrary loan department* comes in. Most libraries participate in an interlibrary loan program that permits them to borrow books, copies of journal articles, or other materials from other libraries. Libraries use computers to locate materials in libraries in their region, around the nation, and in some cases, around the world. All participating libraries benefit because they can provide a greater range of materials and services to patrons than their own budgets allow. Books usually are sent by mail from one library to another, with the borrower often paying a fee for each item. As part of their interlibrary loan service, libraries also participate in a periodical reprint service through which library patrons can request a copy of an article from a periodical.

Libraries also provide *copy machines* for photocopying certain library materials for a nominal fee. Many libraries have collections of older journals and newspapers on microforms, especially microfilm and microfiche, to save space. Most libraries have stopped placing new material on microfilm and microfiche because online databases offer easier access; however, microforms are an important option for researchers interested in reading older journal and newspaper entries. Copying materials is important because it gives the researcher a permanent copy of any materials that cannot be removed from the library. In using copying equipment, however, researchers should be familiar enough with federal copyright laws to avoid violating them. Normally, reproducing one copy of a journal article or book chapter for private use is permissible.

The *documents division* of the library houses government publications, magazines, pamphlets, and sometimes collections of special books. In a small library, the documents division might be integrated with the reference department. Libraries still house many government documents, but today most government documents are available online as well.

Another library service that gives patrons greater access to materials is the table-of-contents and document-delivery services. *Table-of-contents services* make available the tables of contents of thousands of periodicals, providing authors and titles as well as other information relevant to accessing the articles. This means a user can rapidly review the contents of many journals—even those not owned by the library being used. Two online table-of-contents services are Infotrieve (http://www.infotrieve.com) and Ingenta (http://www.ingentaconnect.com). *Document-delivery services*, which often are a part of table-of-contents services, actually deliver copies of articles to patrons. For example, British Library Inside (http://www.bl.uk/index.shtml) is a product of the British Library and has a searchable database of more than 20,000 journals and magazines and 100,000 conference proceedings. However, you may wish to check with a reference librarian before purchasing an article directly through a document-delivery service as libraries often have licenses to use these services and can access documents for you. Reference librarians may also be able to access the same material for you using an online database or through an interlibrary loan.

The stacks are the part of the library where most books and periodicals are stored. Large universities may have more than one library, so all the books and journals will not necessarily be housed in the same building. Some libraries permit anyone to roam the stacks, whereas others are more restrictive, distributing "stack passes" to a limited number of people, such as university faculty, graduate students, or other serious researchers. Access to the stacks is always desirable because browsing in them is a valuable adjunct to the other ways of finding appropriate resource materials. In the stacks we can review the table of contents and the index of a book, which provide more information about how useful it will be than the brief description in the library catalog. In addition, because books on similar topics normally are placed near one another in the stacks, browsing for other, similar books once you are in the right area of the stacks can be extremely helpful.

Accessing Library Materials and Other Information

Having a library available with ample materials and services is of little use unless we know how to access the materials we want. Those who are unfamiliar with the library can easily feel overwhelmed because there seem to be so many nooks and crannies, both physical and electronic, in which relevant resources can hide. Three basic strategies for locating materials, however, can make the search easier:

1. Use the online library catalog (or OPAC: Online Public Access Catalog).
2. Use a variety of online databases to search for books, journal articles, government documents, abstracts, indexes, and other materials.
3. Use the Internet and the web, which have become increasingly important in the search for information.

These three strategies provide a good start to discovering the information available in the library and at other locations. A thorough search that locates the most up-to-date sources requires familiarity with all the three strategies for accessing information.

Many of these library services are operated by the patrons themselves, although some require assistance from library personnel. Some library services are free or provided at low cost, but other services can be expensive. Some of the document-delivery services, for example, can get rather costly. Check with library personnel to determine precisely which services are available and what costs might be incurred.

BOOKS

The Classification System

Small, local libraries might contain a few thousand books. Small to medium-sized universities have libraries with hundreds of thousands of volumes. Large university and public libraries contain millions of books. Despite the tremendous variations in library size, the systems to classify books within them are so flexible that the system used in the smallest library also can be used in the largest; and despite the tremendous size of some libraries, we can easily retrieve a book if we know how the book is classified.

Most classification systems arrange books according to *subject matter*—first into very general categories, such as humanities, science, or social sciences, and then, within each general category, into more precise subcategories. The category of social sciences, for example, is divided into economics, sociology, and so on. In this fashion, the subject matter of a book can be narrowed until it fits into a fairly specific category. Then each book is given a unique *call number*, which contains all the necessary information from the classification system to identify that particular book. Two classification systems are used in the United States: the *Library of Congress System* and the *Dewey Decimal System*. Most college and university libraries use the Library of Congress System (or some variation of it), whereas many smaller public and school libraries use the Dewey Decimal System.

The Library of Congress System uses a combination of letters and numbers to classify books (see Table A.1). The first letter in the call number is one of 21 letters of the alphabet used to classify books into the most general categories. The letter *H*, for example, indicates the general category of the social sciences. The second letter—if there is a second letter—further narrows the subject matter within the social sciences. The letter *Q*, for example, indicates that the book falls in the more specific social science subject matter of "Family, Marriage, Women," whereas the letter *V* refers to the subject of "Social Pathology." The letters of the call number are followed by a number that further narrows the subject matter. Within the classification *HV*, for example, numbers 701–1420 refer to works on the topic of "protection, assistance, and relief of children," whereas numbers 5001–5840 refer to books on "alcoholism." This number is followed by a letter, which is the first letter of the last name of the author of the book (in cases of multiple authors, it is by the first author's last name). This letter is followed by a number that further identifies the author. These sets of letters and numbers of the call number provide an identification that is unique to that book; no other

TABLE A.1 Library of Congress Classification System

A	General Works	
B	Philosophy and Religion	
C	History (General—Civilization, Genealogy)	
D	History—Old World	
E	American History and General U.S. History	
F	American History (Local) and Latin America	
G	Geography, Anthropology, Folklore, Sports, and Other	
H	Social Sciences	
	HA	Statistics
	HB–HD	Economics
	HF	Commerce
	HG–HJ	Finance
	HM	Sociology
	HQ	Family, Marriage, Women
	HV	Social Pathology
J	Political Science	
K	Law	
L	Education	
M	Music	
N	Fine Arts	
P	Language and Literature	
Q	Science	
R	Medicine	
S	Agriculture, Forestry, Animal Culture, Fish Culture, Hunting	
T	Technology	
U	Military Science	
V	Naval Science	
Z	Bibliography and Library Science	
Example:	HV	
	875	
	F6	

book has exactly the same call number. Books are placed on the shelves in the order of their call numbers. All the *H*s are placed together, and within the *H*s all the *HM*s go together. Within the *HM*s, books are arranged according to the other letters and numbers.

The Dewey Decimal System arranges books into 10 general categories based on a three-digit number on the top row of the call number (see Table A.2). Numbers in the 300 range make up the social science category. The second and third digits of this top row further narrow the classification within the social sciences. For example, the 360s deal with "Welfare and Association."

TABLE A.2 Dewey Decimal Classification System

Broad subject areas or classes:

000	Generalities
100	Philosophy and Related Disciplines
200	Religion
300	The Social Sciences
400	Language
500	Pure Sciences
600	Technology (Applied Sciences)
700	The Arts
800	Literature and Rhetoric
900	General Geography and History

Each class can be subdivided into smaller classes or subclasses:

300	The Social Sciences
310	Statistical Method and Statistics
320	Political Science
330	Economics
340	Law
350	Public Administration
360	Welfare and Association
370	Education
380	Commerce
390	Customs and Folklore
Example:	362.7
	N34

The three-digit number is followed by a decimal point and numbers that indicate narrower classifications. In the second row of the Dewey call number is a letter, which, again, is the first letter of the author's last name, followed by a number that further identifies the author. This may be followed by a lowercase letter that is the first letter in the first word of the title of the book (excluding "a," "an," and "the"). The Dewey Decimal System also provides each book with its own unique call number.

The Library Catalog

With knowledge of the classification system in use at a particular library, anybody can locate any book. To do so, first find the *online library catalog*, which is a listing of all the holdings in the library. In some cases, the library catalog can say not only whether the library owns a particular item but also its status: whether it is checked out and, when it will be returned, if it is at the bindery, if it is lost, and so on. Some libraries in regional networks will share an online catalog. Thus if a book is not available at one library, the catalog shows in which library it can be found.

In the library catalog, each library holding has a separate entry or record that can be viewed on a computer. To locate a book or other item in the library, find the record of the book, make note of the location (reference, documents, or stacks) and the call number, and find it on the library shelves. (Remember that books with similar call numbers will be about similar topics, so it is a good practice to browse through books in the immediate vicinity as well.) The record for each book shows the author and title of the book, the subject headings under which it can be found in the library catalog, the library where the book is located, and so on.

To find a record in the catalog, look it up under the author's name, the title of the work, and the subject heading under which it is listed, or by key words that appear in the record. Author and title searches are fairly straightforward. Searching by subject can be a little more problematic, however, because it sometimes is difficult to find useful subject headings for the topic. To assist in this task, refer to the *Library of Congress Subject Headings* if the library uses the Library of Congress System. If the library uses the Dewey Decimal System, the equivalent is the *Sears List of Subject Headings*. Both volumes list headings acceptable for use in a library catalog, cross-referencing a number of different topics. These volumes are located in the library and can be found online as well. Often, however, it is easiest to conduct a key word search first using terms you are familiar with; then you can look at the records of books returned and use the subject headings in the records during a future search. When using the library catalog to locate books, determine from the title of the book and the brief description of the contents contained in the record whether a book will be useful. It is better to err on the side of jotting down too many call numbers rather than too few.

You are not limited to searching your own library because online catalogs of other libraries across the country and around the world can be viewed easily. This is especially useful for those who have access only to small libraries with limited holdings. Exploring other libraries unveils other resources, particularly books and journals, that simply would be unavailable otherwise. The Library of Congress website (http://www.loc.gov), in addition to locating published materials, provides webcasts, online exhibitions, and other audiovisual resources. Another website that provides access to many libraries is LIBDEX (http://www.libdex.com), which contains links to the catalogs of more than 18,000 libraries. The University of Saskatchewan website (http://library.usask.ca/catalogs/world.html) provides links to library catalogs around the world. Finally, OCLC WorldCat (the OCLC Online Union Catalog), which may be accessible through a library's online database system, provides a catalog of books and other materials in libraries worldwide.

PERIODICALS

One of the most valuable—and heavily used—resources of the library, in addition to the books, is the *periodicals* (also called *serials*). Periodicals are published periodically, such as weekly or monthly (hence the name "periodicals"), and usually contain articles by a number of different authors on a variety of topics. Periodicals come in two basic types, although some are a blend of both. *Magazines* are directed at the general public, written in a light and popular style, and often are commercial ventures. *Journals* are professional periodicals that publish articles primarily intended for members of a particular profession. The *American Sociological Review*, the *Journal of Social Service Research*, and the *Journal of the American Medical Association* are examples of journals.

Here, we will focus primarily on journals, but both magazines and journals can be helpful in researching a problem. Periodicals tend to be more current than books, especially in reporting research findings, in part because the production process for books is longer than that for periodicals. In addition, in many scientific fields, including the human services, much research is reported first in journals. In fact, many books contain summaries primarily or assessments of research that has already appeared in journals. The articles in periodicals are brief and specific as well, offering more information about a particular topic in a shorter form.

The Classification System

Periodicals, like books, can have call numbers, although not all libraries classify their periodicals this way. When periodicals are given a call number, they can be housed in the library in two ways: along with the books in the library by call number, or separately from the books by call number. When periodicals are classified by call number, you will need to look in the library catalog or some other location to find the call number of the periodical you want. The advantage of classifying periodicals by call number is that periodicals on a similar topic will be near one another. Some libraries, however, do not use periodical call numbers, but instead arrange periodicals separately from books and in alphabetical order by the title of the journal (excluding the first "the" or "a" in the title). Once we see how the periodicals are stored in a particular library, we can find any periodical, because no two have the same title or call number.

Each issue of a journal is further identified by a volume number, the year of its publication, and an issue number indicating its place in the sequence of issues making up a particular volume. Some journals also identify their issues with the month or season—for example, "Summer"—in which it was published. To locate an issue of a journal, then, requires the following information: the call number or name of the journal, year of publication, volume number, and issue number (or month or season of publication).

Libraries' periodicals have changed substantially in recent years. While access to periodicals has increased considerably in most libraries, the number of periodicals available in hard copy has decreased dramatically. Many publishers have stopped producing hard copies of periodicals. Some periodicals are available in hard copy, but at a very high cost. Electronic versions are more affordable and preferred by many users. Where hard copies of periodicals are available in the library, they tend to be stored in one of three locations. First, most libraries store *current periodicals*, the most recent issues, in a separate place where users can browse through them. Typically, the most recent one or two years are kept there. Second, *bound periodicals* contain several issues that have been bound together in one hardcover volume for extended storage. Each bound volume normally contains one year's worth of issues. Third, old volumes are sometimes stored on *microfilm, microfiche,* or some other space-saving device for long-term storage, and generally are kept in large cabinets near the machines that magnify them for viewing.

A problem can arise when accessing periodicals that, even if minor, is irksome to both patrons and librarians—namely, the binding of separate issues that make up a volume of a journal. This means the volume has to be sent to a bindery, which in turn means the issues in that volume are temporarily unavailable to library patrons. Usually this period is brief, but these periodicals also usually are recent ones (the binding is done within the first few years of publication). Students need to be aware that this problem can occur. It is one reason to begin library research on a project early, because some recent journals that are available now may be gone to the bindery in another month.

Journals Important to the Human Services

Literally hundreds of journals in the library or online contain materials of use to human service researchers and practitioners. Although no one can read all these journals, awareness and occasional perusal of them can uncover much valuable source material. One way to spend free time is to browse through some of these journals, either online or in the current periodicals section of the library. Numerous journals are published primarily for human service professionals. Among the more important are these:

Administration in Social Work
British Journal of Social Work
Child Welfare
Children and Schools: A Journal of Social Work Practice
Clinical Social Work Journal
Exceptional Children
Families in Society
Federal Probation
Health & Social Work
International Journal of Aging and Human Development
International Social Work
Journal of Social Work Education
Journal of Social Service Research
Journal of Sociology and Social Welfare
Policy and Practice of Public Human Services
School Social Work Journal
Smith College Studies in Social Work
Social Security Bulletin
Social Service Review
Social Work
Social Work Abstracts
Social Work in Health Care

Social Work Research
Social Work with Groups
Substance Use and Misuse

Because the human service professions use knowledge developed by several of the behavioral sciences, many journals not published directly for human service providers also can be of great value. Among the more useful are these:

Administration and Policy in Mental Health
American Journal of Orthopsychiatry
American Journal of Public Health
American Journal of Sociology
American Sociological Review
Applied Social Science (formerly *Journal of Applied Sociology* and *Sociological Practice*)
Archives of General Psychiatry
Behavior Therapy
Child Development
Child Psychiatry and Human Development
Community Mental Health Journal
Crime and Delinquency
Criminology
Gerontologist
International Journal of Group Psychotherapy
Journal of Abnormal Psychology
Journal of Applied Behavioral Science
Journal of Clinical Psychology
Journal of Consulting and Clinical Psychology
Journal of Counseling Psychology
Journal of Criminal Law and Criminology
Journal of Drug Issues
Journal of General Psychology
Journals of Gerontology (Series A and B)
Journal of Health and Social Behavior
Journal of Marital and Family Therapy
Journal of Marriage and the Family
Journal of Personality and Social Psychology
Journal of Research in Crime and Delinquency
Journal of Studies on Alcohol and Drugs
Merrill-Palmer Quarterly
Psychological Bulletin
The Public Interest
Social Forces
Social Policy
Social Problems
Social Psychology Quarterly
Sociological Quarterly

Given this diversity in periodicals, how do we find those articles that relate to a particular topic? A variety of online databases are available to assist in this search.

ONLINE DATABASES

A variety of online information retrieval systems are available to locate professional literature on particular topics. Some services are available to individual users, but the most common approach to searching available articles is to use what is known as a unified index. Many libraries purchase a unified index service such as OCLC First Search or ProQuest that allows patrons to search multiple databases at once.

If using individual databases, the first consideration is which specific database to use. Choices vary from one library to another, but library database systems such as FirstSearch or ProQuest even suggest which databases are best for a particular subject area. Table A.3 summarizes some popular databases that human service professionals should consider. Although there is overlap between them, it is a good idea to try several.

A second consideration is the type of search term to use. The search terms might be key words, subject headings, authors' names, titles of articles, and so on. For a basic search, the user specifies only a few types of search terms, such as a key word, author, or title. An advanced search permits the user to refine the search process by entering various combinations of search terms.

TABLE A.3 **Summary of Database Choices**

Database	Topics
Cumulative Index to Nursing and Allied Health Literature (CINAHL)	nursing, allied health
ERIC (ERIC) Journal articles and reports in education	adult, career, and vocational education; assessment and evaluation; disabilities and gifted education; educational management; elementary and early childhood education; higher education; information and technology; language and linguistics; reading and communication; teachers and teacher education; urban education
MEDLINE (MEDLINE) All areas of medicine, including dentistry and nursing	clinical medicine, dentistry, education, experimental medicine, health services administration, nursing, nutrition, pathology, psychiatry, toxicology, veterinary medicine
National Criminal Justice Reference Service (NCJRS) Summaries of more than 180,000 criminal justice publications	crime and justice information, research, statistics, funding opportunities
PsycINFO 1887 (PsycINFO_1887) Psychology and related fields since 1887	anthropology, business, education, law, linguistics, medicine, nursing, pharmacology, physiology, psychiatry, sociology
Sociological Abstracts (SocAbs) Abstracts on all aspects of sociology	community development, culture and social structure, demography and human biology, environmental interactions, family and social welfare, health and medicine and law, religion and science, social psychology and group interactions, welfare services, women's studies
Social Sciences Abstracts (SocialSciAbs)	anthropology, economics, geography, law, political science, psychology, sociology
JSTOR (jstor.org)	provides access to full-text articles from more than 1,300 journals in 50 academic disciplines, including most social and behavioral sciences.
Resource Discovery Network (http://www.intute.ac.uk)	a collaboration of over 70 educational and research organizations, including the British Library
WWW Virtual Library (http://vlib.org)	widely recognized as among the highest-quality guides to particular sections of the web
BUBL Link (http://bubl.ac.uk/link)	selected Internet resources covering all academic subject areas and cataloged according to DDC (Dewey Decimal Classification)

Even a basic search needs to be approached carefully. For example, assume that a researcher is interested in locating articles about the effectiveness of intervention programs on child abuse. Table A.4 illustrates the consequences of using various strategies. Consider the difference between searching for child abuse as a key word or as a title term. Key words are found in titles, abstracts, and descriptors (different databases may call these "subjects," and some database providers include other fields, such as notes and summaries, with a key word search). Key words also are names of people and places that

TABLE A.4 Sample Database Search Results

Database	Type Search	Term(s)	Records Found
PsycINFO_1887	Key word	kw: child and kw: abuse.	18,694
PsycINFO_1887	Key word	kw: child w abuse.	14,462
PsycINFO_1887	Title	ti: child w abuse.	1,905
PsycINFO_1887	Key word and title	kw: outcome and (ti: child w abuse).	68
Sociological Abstracts	Key word	kw: child and kw: abuse.	7,884
Sociological Abstracts	Key word	ti: child w abuse.	6,135
Sociological Abstracts	Title	ti: child w abuse.	733
Sociological Abstracts	Key word and title	kw: outcome and (ti: child w abuse).	23

are the subjects of a library resource or a listing in a directory. Consequently, a key word search will return many more citations than a title search. (The number of citations is something to consider if there is a fee for this search service based, in part, on the number of references provided. Also, the longer list will include many sources that are not directly relevant and could waste valuable time.) The search engine also distinguishes between entering the words "child" and "abuse" (key word: child, and key word: abuse) and entering "child abuse" (key word: child with abuse). The former locates articles about children and various types of abuses, such as drug abuse, spouse abuse, and so on, as well as child abuse, whereas the latter only returns child abuse articles. Presumably, really important descriptors will appear in the title, but using the title for a search also misses many potentially good articles. So a key word search generally is preferred. If the title of the article or at least some terms in it are known, however, then a title search is best for pinpointing a specific study. A final point about searching for key words or subject terms is that some search services provide a dictionary of the terms used in the database. One such database, for example, is ERIC, or Educational Resources Information Center. If a library subscribes to this database, then it also has a volume titled *Thesaurus of ERIC Descriptors* that contains all the subject terms used in the ERIC database. In addition, the ERIC thesaurus is available online through the database.

Other databases, such as PsycINFO and Social Science Abstracts, now have an online thesaurus feature to help in your search. We noted earlier that other volumes of subject headings can be used as well when searching the online library catalog.

Another consideration is to move from a basic to an advanced search, which offers the user control over a wide array of search variables beyond key word, author, and title. One also may broaden or restrict searches by using special features such as "wildcards," which substitute for letters in the search term, and Boolean operators like the words "and," "or," and "not." Before commencing a search, one can consult the extensive help service available on the main menu of the online database program as well as with a reference librarian for guidance on conducting an effective search. Finally, many libraries provide short courses that can improve these skills.

Searching online databases generally is a two-stage process. First, the search program returns a list of identified sources (articles or books) in summary form. Second, by clicking on a selection, the user is taken to a detailed record that includes a variety of information about the source, including an abstract and descriptors. An *abstract* is a brief description, usually no more than a paragraph, of the contents of a book or an article. A good abstract provides a complete summary of the work, including thesis, description of any data collected, conclusions drawn, and study limitations. Abstracts help you locate relevant research and decide whether it is sufficiently useful to warrant reading the entire work. Abstracts also frequently provide the list of key words (descriptors) under which each book or article is cataloged, and this is an important assist in searching for other materials on the same topic.

REFERENCE BOOKS FOR THE HUMAN SERVICES

One group of useful books that are often overlooked, unfortunately, is general reference books. Included in this rather broad category are encyclopedias, directories, and bibliographies. Although such works do not substitute for a thorough library search, they can save time and efficiently answer many routine questions. The following is only a partial listing of common reference works:

An Author's Guide to Social Work Journals
Encyclopedia of Adolescence
Encyclopedia of Aging
Encyclopedia of Alcoholism
Encyclopedia of Associations
Encyclopedia of Drug Abuse
Encyclopedia of Psychology
Encyclopedia of Social Work
Encyclopedia of Sociology
National Directory of State Agencies
Public Welfare Directory
The Social Sciences Encyclopedia
Social Service Organizations and Agencies Directory
Social Work Almanac
State Executive Directory Annual

GOVERNMENT DOCUMENTS

The U.S. government is one of the largest publishers in the world, pouring forth mountains of books, bulletins, circulars, reports, and the like. Practitioners and researchers in the human service field find government documents especially important because the government sponsors much of the research done in this area. The government, for example, commonly funds demonstration projects, program evaluations, and needs assessments, and then publishes the resulting research reports. -Government documents also include information on model programs, funding sources, and bibliographies for topics of interest to human service professionals.

Locating pertinent government documents may, at first, seem a daunting endeavor. With the aid of a few basic tools, however, the task can be done quickly, thoroughly, and with relatively little pain. The first step is to look in the online library catalog. Most libraries list government documents along with other books in the library catalog, and the documents can be identified through name, title, subject, or key word search in the library catalog—just as for any publication. The search for government documents can then go to other online sites. The three best are USA.gov, which is the U.S. Government's Official Web Portal (http://www.usa.gov), the U.S. Government Printing Office (http://www.gpo.gov), and the web page of the *Catalog of U.S. Government Publications* (http://catalog.gpo.gov/F). USA.gov, for example, offers a variety of areas to explore, such as "A–Z List of Agencies" or "Family, Home, & Community," and an advanced search feature in which we can enter key words and use various drop-down menus to specify the kind of search we want. We also can specify whether we want to search for federal government documents only or for state government documents as well. The web pages of Government Printing Office use similar search procedures. The *Catalog of U.S. Government Publications* looks and acts like an online library catalog, with publications dating back to 1976.

In addition to these three government websites, other government agencies have their own websites where documents, reports, and data of various kinds can be found. The following agencies and their websites are among the most useful to researchers and practitioners in the social sciences and human services:

Bureau of the Census (http://www.census.gov)

Department of Health and Human Services (http://www.hhs.gov)

Department of Justice (http://www.justice.gov)

Bureau of Justice Statistics, Department of Justice (http://bjs.ojp.usdoj.gov)

Department of Education (http://www.ed.gov)

Department of Labor (http://www.dol.gov)

Women's Bureau, Department of Labor (http://www.dol.gov/wb)

Commission on Civil Rights (http://www.usccr.gov)

Users of government documents find that more and more such documents are becoming available directly over the web, with no need for locating a hard copy. Many government documents are available as PDF files directly from individual agencies; the files can be viewed online or downloaded to the user's computer for later viewing or printing. In addition, some documents are available for purchase through government websites.

To find government documents in the library, we need to know how and where they are located. Which government documents a particular library possesses depends, in part, on whether it is a *depository library*, a designation made by the Superintendent of Documents at the U.S. Government Printing Office (GPO). A *regional depository library*, of which there can be up to two in any state, receives everything published by the GPO. *Selective depositories* receive only some government publications (see *List of Classes of U.S. Government Publications Available for Selection by Depository Libraries*). Nondepository libraries have some government documents, depending on what they choose to purchase. A listing of depository libraries and more information about the federal depository library program can be found online at the GPO site (http://www.gpo.gov/libraries).

The *Catalog of U.S. Government Publications* includes a listing of most government publications and the information necessary to locate them in a library or purchase them from the office of the Superintendent of Documents. This publication is now online (http://catalog.gpo.gov/F), and contains records dating back to 1976. Any publication you find in the *Catalog* with an electronic presence will have a link to it. Every government document submitted to the office of the Superintendent of Documents is given a *Catalog* entry number, and documents are listed in the printed *Catalog* in order of this number, which has two components. The first two digits indicate the year in which the document was published (an entry number of 88-5280 was published in 1988). The second group of digits locates the record in the printed version of the *Catalog*. This second number is derived from sequencing the publications alphanumerically according to the classification number of the Superintendent of Documents, or SUDOCS number.

The SUDOCS number is like the call number in the library catalog for locating books. Libraries that obtain government documents often classify them according to the SUDOCS number instead of the Dewey Decimal System or Library of Congress System. Whereas the Dewey Decimal and Library of Congress systems classify entries according to subject matter, the SUDOCS system classifies materials according to the agency issuing the materials. In the SUDOCS number "HE 20.7009/a:Ac 7/2/982-87," for example, *HE* means the document was issued by the U.S. Department of Health and Human Services. Thus, the *Catalog* entry number helps locate the document in the printed version of the *Catalog*, and the SUDOCS number helps locate where the document is shelved in the library. Many libraries shelve government documents in a separate location from other books and periodicals, but some also mix them together so that the Library of Congress or Dewey Decimal numbers of books are mixed in with the SUDOCS number of government documents. A rule of thumb is to look for the colon (:) in the classification number—that tells you that it's a government publication and probably kept in a separate location.

INFORMATION LITERACY AND CRITICAL THINKING SKILLS

A library is a veritable cornucopia of information, and we have tried to provide basic information on how to access that information. The best way to learn about any library, however, is to use it. Roam around the stacks, browse through the online library catalog, delve into government documents, and explore the Internet. Here we have emphasized the ways to systematically access information in the library, but much useful material also can appear in random and casual rovings through the library. Above all, consult with the reference librarians who are trained to help students and faculty devise programs and strategies for finding, analyzing, synthesizing, and evaluating information. Such informational literacy is increasingly essential in the modern world. Informational literacy is an important part of critical thinking, which is the ability to judge the authenticity, accuracy, and worth of information.

This guide to the library has emphasized the library's utility to human service practitioners. A library, however, is not meant solely to help write a term paper or complete a research project. A library is a repository of cultural knowledge. It houses research reports on alcoholics along with the epic myths of Homer and the ancient and sacred literature of Hinduism and the Vedas. Literature, philosophy, and theology accompany engineering and celestial mechanics—and the daily newspaper!

Our point is that a library, in a sense, is the storehouse of a culture, and we hope that you use it to its fullest extent throughout your life as a source of enrichment and fulfillment. The search programs and strategies devised for college students with the help of reference librarians are useful long after those years to help find and analyze information about social issues or personal problems, and to help people keep current in their chosen fields of endeavor.

FOR FURTHER READING

Bolner, M. S., & Poirier, G. A. (2006). *The Research Process: Books & Beyond*, 4th ed. Dubuque, Iowa: Kendall/Hunt. This book provides a comprehensive overview of how to do research in the library and online.

Cuba, L. (2002). *A Short Guide to Writing about Social Science*, 4th ed. New York: Longman. This book is mostly about writing term papers and research reports, but also includes a significant amount of material on using the library and the Internet.

Hahn, H. (2003). *Harley Hahn's Internet Yellow Pages*. Emeryville, Calif.: McGraw-Hill Osborne Media. As the name implies, this book is an excellent resource for finding materials on the Internet.

Lenburg, J. (2010). *Facts on File Guide to Research*. Chicago: University of Chicago Press. This volume contains detailed and extensive lists of research resources and easy to use guides for several style manuals.

Reed, J. G., & Baxter, P. M. (2003). *Library Use: A Handbook for Psychology*, 3rd ed. Washington, D.C.: American Psychological Association. Focused as it is on psychology, this book is nonetheless a valuable guide to the library for someone preparing to conduct a social research project. Among other things, it covers using abstracting services, doing computer searches, and locating various scales and measurement devices.

Schneider, G., & Evans, J. (2013). *New Perspectives on the Internet*, 9th ed. Boston: Course Technology/Cengage Learning. This book is an excellent introduction to the Internet, providing all the information needed to use that online source of information.

The Sociology Writing Group. (2013). *A Guide to Writing Sociology Papers*, 7th ed. New York: Worth.

This book provides useful guidance in terms of doing library research in the social sciences, organizing time and materials, and preparing and writing analyses based on both quantitative and qualitative data.

Weissman, J. (2006). *The Research Virtuoso: Brilliant Methods for Normal Brains*. New York: Annick Press. This is a useful resource for learning to obtain research materials and sort through both electronic and print resources to identify relevant sources.

Appendix B

Generating Random Numbers

Random numbers have many purposes in social research. For example, they often are used in constructing a probability sample in which elements are selected from a population and then placed in the sample on a random basis. In some cases, we do this with a table of random numbers. Tables of random numbers can be found in many places, including textbooks on statistics; a few volumes contain nothing but random numbers. Figure B.1 contains a spreadsheet-generated table of random numbers.

Spreadsheet software, such as Microsoft Excel, makes generating random numbers easy. Although the specific procedures vary from program to program, the basic approach is the same. Using Excel, the following command is entered into a cell of a spreadsheet to generate a random number from 0 to 10,000:

$$= INT(RAND \times 0001)$$

The formula contains two subcommands. "RAND" returns a decimal value consisting of an evenly distributed random number greater than or equal to 0 and less than 1. The formula multiplies this random decimal by 10,001, resulting in a number that ranges from a low of less than 1.0000 to a high of less than 10,001.0000. The "INT" command drops the decimal portion and displays the integer portion. Hence, the resulting random number ranges from 0 to 10,000. For example, if the random decimal is 0.00002, the result is

$$= INT(0.00002 \times 10001) = INT(0.20002) = 0$$

If the random decimal is 0.99999, the result is

$$= INT(.99999 \times 10001) = INT(10000.899) = 10000$$

We can adjust the range of random numbers by substituting a different value for 10,001. To generate a list of random numbers, copy the formula into as many cells as needed, using the "Copy" and "Paste" commands. Figure B.1 illustrates 200 random numbers generated by this procedure with Excel. Note that the numbers are displayed in the table with leading zeros, using the "Format Cells" > "Numbers" > "Custom" option found on the Format menu.

APPENDIX B

8473	6469	0023	1284	7224
8942	2464	4716	2969	7263
0483	1714	5849	8958	5386
2149	5816	3700	9948	7455
7453	6909	9577	0492	6852
3122	3299	9818	3816	0147
9852	6862	8790	7899	4399
5501	1995	4117	8482	4002
6969	9006	4146	9040	7428
1374	2614	4006	1365	4388
6454	9996	3058	0393	6331
1859	8391	0248	4116	5107
0964	0824	7381	4105	2046
9787	5866	5979	5099	5007
5314	1390	6447	9694	0161
0786	4317	0927	5093	2017
8012	7434	0633	4440	8431
8035	4707	4235	5832	6368
5954	6540	1745	8472	2485
9846	4691	7976	4018	4088
5214	9309	9049	8558	8203
5238	3653	5350	9468	9199
1143	8013	8016	0706	7169
6014	7212	5308	3707	8973
9352	9680	8359	4905	7620
0661	4566	2770	9675	3599
7735	2633	1237	2176	6353
5568	6770	6900	8182	1006
8759	0209	5726	7022	1945
7844	5681	1323	3519	9542
6310	4024	8095	9248	1715
9114	8417	0360	9554	7951
6276	8759	5863	0888	5439
8415	9510	5243	4901	4480
8937	0400	0181	8841	8829
4965	0216	4428	8468	9285
6722	1994	8732	9902	4732
8914	6150	9054	4557	8645
6085	0677	8324	4685	3131
1767	6983	4181	5552	5760

Random starting point

Sample of 6: 29 04 13 03 07 21

FIGURE B.1 Random Numbers Generated by Microsoft Excel

An advantage of a spreadsheet is that we can easily order the random numbers from lowest to highest, a convenient feature for such tasks as selecting a random sample from an ordered sampling frame. Note that spreadsheets typically return a new random number every time the worksheet is calculated. So reordering the numbers requires first converting the cell formulas to values. To accomplish this, scroll over the cells containing the random numbers, use "Copy" from the Edit menu, and then paste the selection elsewhere in the worksheet by selecting the "Values" option from "Paste Special" on the Edit menu. Next, select the "Sort" option from the Data menu. The result is a list of random numbers in rank order.

Finally, standard statistical packages, such as Minitab, also generate random numbers. In addition, programs such as SPSS and Minitab have menu commands for selecting a sample of cases from a file. For example, a census data set may contain several thousand cases, so this feature enables the researcher to conveniently select a smaller, random subset of cases for analysis.

If we are drawing a random sample by hand, using a table of random numbers to do so is straightforward. First we note the size of the population to determine how many of the random digits we need when selecting each element. For example, if the population does not exceed 9,999 elements, we use four columns of random digits for each of the selections from the sampling frame. If the population exceeds 9,999 elements but not 99,999, we take random digits five columns at a time.

The second step is to select a starting point in the table of random numbers. It is important that we not always start from the same place in the table, such as the upper left corner. If we did, every sample, assuming that we used the same number of digits, would select the same elements from the population and, of course, violate the randomness we seek. This problem can be easily avoided, however, by starting in the table at some point that is itself randomly determined (close your eyes and point).

Figure B.1 implements this process by showing the selection of a sample of size 6 from a population of size 30. Each case in the population is given a number between 1 and 30. Then, we proceed through the table from the randomly selected starting point, taking each set of two digits that is between 1 and 30 until we reach the desired sample size. We just ignore any number between 31 and 99 and any number that is a repeat. We then use this list of random numbers to identify the elements to be included in the sample. When using computers instead of tables to select random samples, each element in a sampling frame is assigned a number, and then the program generates a set of random numbers the size of the sample needed. If there are 2,798 elements in the sampling frame and we need a sample size of 300, the computer generates 300 random numbers between 1 and 2,798. Those 300 cases are our sample. If the whole sampling frame is in a computer file, the computer may be able to both assign the numbers to the sampling frame and select the 300 random cases.

Glossary

Accidental Sampling: samples composed of those elements that are readily available or convenient to the researcher.

Alpha Error: the probability of rejecting a null hypothesis when it is actually true.

Alpha Level: the probability at which the null hypothesis will be rejected; the amount of Type I error (probability of rejecting a true null hypothesis) that is acceptable in a research design, typically $p=.05$ or $p=.01$.

Alphanumeric Variables: variables consisting only of type characters, being without the property of quantitative value, and treated as labels or strings by data-analysis programs.

Anonymity: a situation in which no one, including the researcher, can link individuals' identities to their responses or behaviors that serve as research data.

Applied Research: research designed with a practical outcome in mind, and with the assumption that some group or society as a whole will gain specific benefits from it.

Area Sampling: a multistage sampling technique that involves moving from larger clusters of units to smaller and smaller ones until the unit of analysis, such as the household or the individual, is reached.

Availability Sampling: samples composed of those elements that are readily available or convenient to the researcher.

Available Data: observations collected by someone other than the investigator for purposes that differ from those of the investigator, but that are available to be analyzed.

Bar Graph: a frequency distribution graph for variables treated as nominal or ordinal in which each value is plotted on the X axis as a separate bar whose height signifies the frequency of the value.

Baseline: a series of measurements of a client's condition before treatment that is used as a basis for comparison with the client's condition after treatment is implemented.

Basic Research: research conducted for the purpose of advancing knowledge about human behavior, with little concern for any immediate or practical benefits that might result.

Beta Error: the probability of failing to reject a null hypothesis that is actually false.

Bivariate Statistics: statistics that describe the relationship between two variables.

Block Grants: awards allocated to states according to a formula and funded by annual congressional appropriations.

Blocking: a two-stage system of assigning subjects to experimental and control groups whereby subjects are first aggregated into blocks according to one or more key variables and then members of each block are randomly assigned to experimental and control conditions.

Case Study: a detailed, descriptive account of one individual, situation, organization, group, or other entity.

Categorical Grants: grants that provide funding, for fixed or known periods of time, to specific projects, including research grants, training grants, experimental and demonstration grants, evaluation grants, and planning grants, among others.

Categorizing Strategies: attempts in qualitative data analysis to generalize and abstract by generating concepts and even theories from the raw data.

Causality: the situation where an independent variable is the factor—or one of several factors—that produces variation in a dependent variable.

Central Limit Theorem: if random samples are taken from any population with a given mean and standard deviation, the sampling distribution of sample means will be approximately normally distributed, and the mean of the sampling distribution will be equal to the population parameter.

Clinical Research Model: the merger of clinical practice and research through the use of single-subject designs.

Closed-Ended Questions: questions that provide respondents with a fixed set of alternatives from which they are to choose.

Cluster Sampling: a multistage sampling technique that involves moving from larger clusters of units to smaller and smaller ones until the unit of analysis, such as the household or the individual, is reached.

Coding: the categorizing of behavior into a limited number of categories.

Coding Scheme: a plan by which the researcher organizes responses to a variable, together with specifications for including the variable in a computer data file.

Common Sense: practical judgments based on the experiences, wisdom, and prejudices of a people.

Computer-Assisted Interviewing: using computer technology to assist in the completion of questionnaires and interviews.

Computer-Assisted Qualitative Data Analysis: using computers to do coding, hypothesis testing, and theory building in qualitative data analysis.

Computer-Assisted Telephone Interviewing: conducting an interview over the telephone, with the interviewer reading questions from the computer monitor and recording answers directly into the computer.

Concepts: mental constructs or images developed to symbolize ideas, persons, things, or events.

Concurrent Validity: a type of criterion validity in which the results of a newly developed measure are correlated with the results of an existing measure.

Confidentiality: ensuring that information or responses will not be publicly linked to specific individuals who participate in research.

Construct Validity: a complex approach to establishing the validity of measures that involves relating the measure to a complete theoretical framework, including all the concepts and propositions that the theory comprises.

Content Analysis: a method of transforming the contents of documents from a qualitative, unsystematic form to a quantitative, systematic form.

Content Validity: the extent to which a measuring device covers the full range of meanings or forms included in a variable being measured.

Context Map: one type of visual display in qualitative data analysis that describes, in graphic form, the physical or social setting that is the context of the observations.

Contextualizing Strategies: attempts in qualitative data analysis to treat the data as a coherent whole and retain as much of the raw data as possible to capture the whole context.

Contingency Control: a multivariate analysis that examines the relationship between an independent variable and a dependent variable in each of the categories of a third, or test, variable.

Contingency Question: a question that is answered only if certain responses were given to a previous question.

Continuous Variables: variables that, theoretically, have an infinite number of values.

Control Condition: the condition in an experiment that does not receive the experimental stimulus.

Control Group: the subjects in an experiment who are not exposed to the experimental stimulus.

Control Variables: variables that have their values held constant in all conditions of an experiment.

Convenience Sampling: samples composed of those elements that are readily available or convenient to the researcher.

Cost–Benefit Analysis: an approach to program evaluation wherein program costs are related to program benefits expressed in terms of dollars.

Cost-Effective Analysis: an approach to program evaluation wherein program costs are related to program effects, with effects measured in terms of the units in which they naturally occur.

Cover Letter: a letter that accompanies a mailed questionnaire and serves to introduce and explain it to the recipient.

Criterion Validity: a technique for establishing the validity of measures that involves demonstrating a correlation between the measure and some other standard.

Cross-Sectional Research: research based on data collected at one point in time.

Data Analysis: the process of placing observations in numerical form and manipulating them according to their arithmetic properties to derive meaning from them.

Data Archives: a national system of data libraries that lend sets of data, much as ordinary libraries lend books.

Data Display: an organized presentation of data in qualitative data analysis that enables researchers and their audiences to draw some conclusions from the data and move on to the next stage of the research.

Deductive Reasoning: inferring a conclusion from more abstract premises or propositions.

Demand Characteristics: subtle, unprogrammed cues in an experiment that communicate to experimental subjects something about how they should behave.

Dependent Variable: the passive variable in a relationship, or the one being affected by an independent variable.

Descriptive Research: research that attempts to discover facts or describe reality.

Descriptive Statistics: procedures that assist in organizing, summarizing, and interpreting the sample data on hand.

Dimensional Sampling: a sampling technique designed to enhance the representativeness of small samples by specifying all important variables and choosing a sample that contains at least one case to represent all possible combinations of variables.

Direct Costs: a proposed program budget or actual program expenditures.

Direct Replication: the repeated application of the same treatment by the same clinician to other clients suffering from the same basic problem.

Discrete Variables: variables with a finite number of distinct and separate values.

Discretionary Grants: grants that provide funding, for fixed or known periods of time, to specific projects, including research grants, training grants, experimental and demonstration grants, evaluation grants, and planning grants, among others.

Discriminatory Power Score: a value calculated during construction of a Likert scale that indicates the degree to which each item discriminates between high scorers and low scorers on the entire scale.

Double-Blind Experiment: an experiment conducted in such a way that neither the subjects nor the experimenters know which groups are in the experimental condition and which are in the control condition.

Ecological Fallacy: inferring something about individuals from data collected about groups.

Empirical Practice Model: the merger of clinical practice and research through the use of single-subject designs.

Ethics: the responsibilities that researchers bear toward those who participate in research, those who sponsor research, and those who are potential beneficiaries of research.

Ethnographic Interview: informal and unstructured interviews that can explore a wide range of topics, last for a long time, and involve a nondirective interviewer.

Evaluability Assessment: a preliminary investigation into a program before its evaluation to determine those aspects of the program that are evaluable.

Evaluation Research: the use of scientific research methods to plan intervention programs, monitor the implementation of new programs and the operation of existing programs, and determine how effectively programs or clinical practices achieve their goals.

Evidence-Based Practice: the conscientious, explicit, and judicious use of the best evidence in making decisions about human service assessment and intervention.

Experiential Knowledge: knowledge gained through firsthand observation of events and based on the assumption that truth can be achieved through personal experience.

Experiment: a controlled method of observation in which the value of one or more independent variables is changed to assess its causal effect on one or more dependent variables.

Experimental Condition: the condition in an experiment that receives the experimental stimulus.

Experimental Group: those subjects who are exposed to the experimental stimulus.

Experimental Stimulus: the independent variable in an experiment that is manipulated by the experimenter to assess its effect on behavior.

Experimental Treatment: the independent variable in an experiment that is manipulated by the experimenter to assess its effect on a dependent variable.

Experimental Variability: variation in a dependent variable that is produced by an independent variable.

Experimenter's Expectations: expectations of experimenters about how they wish an experiment to come out that may be inadvertently communicated to experimental subjects.

Explanatory Research: research with the goal of determining why or how something occurs.

External Validity: the extent to which causal inferences made in an experiment can be generalized to other times, settings, or people.

Extraneous Variability: variation in a dependent variable from any source other than an experimental stimulus.

Face Validity: the degree to which a logical relationship exists between the variable and the proposed measure.

Federal Government Contracts: an important source of research and practice funds other than through grants; with contracts, it is the government that decides precisely what it wants and how it wants it done.

Field Experiments: experiments conducted in naturally occurring settings as people go about their everyday lives.

Field Notes: detailed, descriptive accounts of observations made in a given setting.

Field Research: a type of qualitative research that involves observations of people in their natural settings as they go about their everyday lives.

Filter Question: a question whose answer determines which question a survey respondent will answer next.

Focus Group: an interview with a whole group of people at the same time, especially for the purpose of seeking people's subjective reactions and levels of meaning that are important to people's behavior.

Formative Evaluation Research: evaluation research that focuses on the planning, development, and implementation of a program.

Formula Grant: an allocation of federal money to states or their subdivisions, in accordance with distribution formulas prescribed by law or administrative regulation, for activities of a continuing nature not confined to a specific project.

Foundation: a nonprofit, legally incorporated entity organized for the purpose of dispersing funds to projects that meet the guidelines of its charter.

Fraud (Scientific): the deliberate falsification, misrepresentation, or plagiarizing of data, findings, or the ideas of others.

Frequency Polygon: a frequency distribution graph of an interval- or ratio-level variable in which interval midpoints are plotted on the X axis, the corresponding frequencies are plotted on the Y axis, and the resulting points are connected by a line.

Grant: the provision of money or other resources either for research or service delivery purposes.

Grounded Theory: a research methodology for developing theory by letting the theory emerge from the data, or be "grounded" in the data.

Group Depth Interview: an interview with a whole group of people at the same time, especially for the purpose of seeking people's subjective reactions and levels of meaning that are important to people's behavior.

Guttman Scale: a measurement scale in which the items have a fixed, progressive order and that has the characteristic of reproducibility.

Histogram: a graph for depicting the frequency distribution of an interval- or ratio-level variable in which intervals of the variable are plotted on the X axis and frequencies are depicted as bars on the Y axis.

Human Services: professions with the primary goal of enhancing the relationship between people and societal institutions so that people may maximize their potential.

Hypotheses: testable statements of presumed relationships between two or more concepts.

Idiographic Explanations: explanations that focus on a single person, event, or situation and attempt to specify all the conditions that helped produce it.

Independent Variable: the presumed active or causal variable in a relationship.

In-Depth Interview: informal and unstructured interviews that can explore a wide range of topics, last for a long time, and involve a nondirective interviewer.

Index: a measurement technique that combines a number of items into a composite score.

Indicator: an observation assumed to be evidence of the attributes or properties of some phenomenon.

Inductive Reasoning: inferring something about a whole group or class of objects from knowledge of one or a few members of that group or class.

Inferential Statistics: procedures that allow us to make generalizations from sample data to the populations from which the samples were drawn.

Informed Consent: telling potential research participants about all aspects of the research that might reasonably influence their decision to participate.

Internal Validity: an issue in experimentation concerning whether the independent variable actually produces the effect it appears to have on the dependent variable.

Interpretive Approaches: the perspective that social reality has a subjective component to it, , that social reality arises out of social interaction and the exchange of social meanings, and that science must gain knowledge of that subjective dimension.

Interval Measures: measures that classify observations into mutually exclusive and exhaustive categories with an inherent order and equal spacing between the categories.

Interview: a technique in which an interviewer reads questions to respondents and records their verbal responses.

Interview Schedule: a document used in interviewing, similar to a questionnaire, that contains instructions for the interviewer, specific questions to be asked in a fixed order, and transition phrases for the interviewer.

Interviewer Falsification: the intentional departure from the designed interviewer instructions, unreported by the interviewer, that can result in the contamination of data.

Item: a single indicator of a variable, such as an answer to a question or an observation of some behavior or characteristic.

Judgmental Sampling: a nonprobability sampling technique in which investigators use their judgment and prior knowledge to choose people for the sample who best serve the purposes of the study.

Jury Opinion: an extension of face or content validity that uses the opinions of other investigators, especially those who are knowledgeable about the variables involved, to assess whether particular operational definitions are logical measures of a variable.

Laboratory Experiments: experiments conducted in artificial settings and constructed in such a way that selected elements of the natural environment are simulated and features of the investigation are controlled.

Latent Coding: coding of more abstract or implicit meanings in a document or medium in which the coder must infer whether a representation in a document is an instance of some broader phenomenon.

Level of Measurement: rules that define permissible mathematical operations on a given set of numbers produced by a measure.

Likert Scale: a measurement scale consisting of a series of statements, each followed by a number of ordered response alternatives, such as "strongly agree," "agree," "disagree," or "strongly disagree."

Logical Empiricism: the perspective that the world exists independently of people's perceptions of it, and that science uses objective techniques to discover what exists in the world.

Logic Model: a visual or verbal description of how you think a program should or does work; it provides a framework for deciding whether a program can be evaluated and how to go about evaluating it.

Longitudinal Research: research based on data gathered over an extended period of time.

Manifest Coding: coding the more objective or surface content of a document or medium.

Matching: a process of assigning subjects to experimental and control groups in which each subject is paired with a similar subject in the other group.

Matrix Display: a visual display in qualitative data analysis that looks very much like a contingency table with its rows and columns, but contains text rather than numerical quantities in the cells of the table.

Matrix Question: a question designed so that response alternatives are listed only once and each question or statement is followed by a box to check or a number or letter to circle.

Measurement: the process of describing abstract concepts in terms of specific indicators by the assignment of numbers or other symbols to these indicants, in accordance with rules.

Measures of Association: statistics that describe the strength of relationships between variables.

Measures of Central Tendency: statistics, also known as averages, which summarize distributions of data by locating the "typical" or "average" value.

Measures of Dispersion: statistics that indicate how dispersed or spread out the values of a distribution are.

Memos: attempts at theorizing in qualitative data analysis in which the researcher writes down ideas about the meanings of the codes that are emerging from the data and the relationships between the various codes.

Misconduct (Scientific): scientific fraud, plus activities such as carelessness or bias in recording or reporting data, mishandling data, and incomplete reporting of results.

Missing Data: incomplete data found in available data sets.

Multidimensional Scale: a scale designed to measure complex variables composed of more than one dimension.

Multistage Sampling: a multiple-tiered sampling technique that involves moving from larger clusters of units to smaller and smaller ones until the unit of analysis, such as the household or the individual, is reached.

Multitrait–Multimethod Approach: a particularly complex form of construct validity involving the simultaneous assessment of numerous measures and concepts through the computation of intercorrelations.

Multivariate Statistics: statistics that describe the relationships among three or more variables.

Narrative Analysis: similar to profiles, but with interviews, autobiographies, life histories, letters, and other personal materials used to form a descriptive narrative of a person's life or circumstances.

Needs Assessment: the collection of data to determine how many people need particular services and to assess the level of services or personnel that already exist to fill that need.

Network Analysis: a context map using lines and arrows that shows connections and relationships between individuals, groups, statuses, or organizations.

Nominal Definitions: verbal definitions in which one set of words or symbols is used to stand for another set of words or symbols.

Nominal Measures: measures that classify observations into mutually exclusive and exhaustive categories but with no ordering to the categories.

Nomothetic Explanations: explanations that focus on a class of events and attempt to specify the conditions that seem common to all those events.

Nonprobability Samples: samples in which the probability of each population element's being included in the sample is unknown.

Nonreactive Observation: observation in which those under study are not aware that they are being studied, and the investigator does not change their behavior by his or her presence.

Normal Distribution: a symmetrical, unimodal distribution in which the mode, median, and mean are identical and have the same proportion of cases between the same two ordinates.

Null Hypothesis: a statement in statistical hypothesis testing that states no relationship exists between two variables in the population or there is no difference between a sample statistic and a population parameter.

Numeric Variable: a variable that has the property of quantitative value, or a variable in a computer data file that can be used in computations.

Observational Techniques: the collection of data through direct visual or auditory experience of behavior.

Open-Ended Questions: questions without a fixed set of alternatives, leaving respondents completely free to formulate their own responses.

Operational Definitions: definitions that indicate the precise procedures or operations to be followed in measuring a concept.

Opportunity Costs: the value of forgone opportunities incurred by funding one program as opposed to some other program.

Ordinal Measures: measures that classify observations into mutually exclusive and exhaustive categories that have an inherent order to them.

Panel Study: research in which data are gathered from the same people at different times.

Paradigms: general ways of thinking about how the world works and how we gain knowledge about the world.

Participant Observation: a method in which the researcher is a part of, and participates in, the activities of the people, group, or situation being studied.

Pie Chart: a circular graph depicting the frequency distribution of a variable, with the number of degrees of the circle for each section or slice representing the proportionate number of cases for each value of the variable.

Pilot Study: a trial run on a small scale of all procedures planned for a research project.

Population: all possible cases of what one is interested in studying.

Positivism: the perspective that the world exists independently of people's perceptions of it, and that science uses objective techniques to discover what exists in the world.

Predictive Research: research that attempts to make projections about what will occur in the future or in other settings.

Predictive Validity: a type of criterion validity wherein scores on a measure are used to predict some future state of affairs.

Preexperimental Designs: crude experimental designs that lack the necessary controls of the threats to internal validity.

Pretest: a preliminary application of the data-gathering technique to assess the adequacy of that technique.

Privacy: the ability to control when and under what conditions others will have access to your beliefs, values, or behavior.

Probability Samples: samples in which each element in the population has a known chance of being selected into the sample.

Probes: follow-up questions used during an interview to elicit clearer and more complete responses.

Profiles: vignettes of a person's experience, usually taken from in-depth interviews, that are stated largely in the person's own words with relatively little interpretation or analysis by the researcher.

Project Grants: grants that provide funding of specific projects for fixed or known periods, including research grants, training grants, experimental and demonstration grants, evaluation grants, and planning grants, among others.

Proportional Reduction in Error: a property of a measure of association that permits estimation of how much the independent variable contributes to reducing error in predicting values of the dependent variable.

Propositions: statements about the relationship between elements in a theory.

Pure Research: research conducted for the purpose of advancing our knowledge about human behavior with little concern for any immediate or practical benefits that might result.

Purposive Sampling: a nonprobability sampling technique wherein investigators use their judgment and prior knowledge to choose people for the sample who best serve the purposes of the study.

Qualitative Research: research that focuses on data in the form of words, pictures, descriptions, or narratives.

Quantitative Research: research that uses numbers, counts, and measures of things.

Quasi-Experimental Designs: designs that approximate experimental control in nonexperimental settings.

Questionnaire: a set of written questions that people respond to directly on the form itself without the aid of an interviewer.

Quota Sampling: a type of nonprobability sampling that involves dividing the population into various categories and determining the number of elements to be selected from each category.

Random Assignment: a process for assigning subjects to experimental and control groups that relies on probability theory to equalize the groups.

Random Errors: measurement errors that are neither consistent nor patterned.

Ratio Measures: measures that classify observations into mutually exclusive and exhaustive categories with an inherent order, equal spacing between the categories, and an absolute zero point.

Reactivity: the degree to which the presence of a researcher influences the behavior being observed.

Reductionist Fallacy: inferring something about groups, or other macro levels of analysis, based on data collected from individuals.

Reflective Remarks: reflections, interpretations, connections, or other thoughts that occur to the researcher and are added to field notes while transcribing those notes or coding the data.

Reliability: the ability of a measure to yield consistent results each time it is applied.

Representative Sample: a sample that accurately reflects the distribution of relevant variables in the target population.

Request for Proposals: a formal request for people or agencies to submit proposals on how they would conduct some research or establish and run some program.

Research Design: a detailed plan outlining how a research project will be conducted.

Research Hypothesis: the alternative statement to the null hypothesis, stating that a relationship is present between variables at the population level or that there is a difference between a sample statistic and a population parameter.

Respondent-Driven Sampling: a variation of snowball sampling.

Response Bias: responses to questions that are shaped by factors other than the person's true feelings, intentions, and beliefs.

Response Pattern Anxiety: the tendency for people to become anxious if they have to repeat the same response all the time and to change their responses to avoid doing so.

Response Rate: the percentage of a sample that completes and returns a questionnaire or agrees to be interviewed.

Response Set: the tendency for people to agree or disagree with statements regardless of the content of the statements.

Sample: one or more elements selected from a population.

Sampling Distribution: a theoretical distribution of all possible values of a sample statistic, which is distinguished by being a normal distribution whose mean is the population parameter.

Sampling Error: the extent to which the values of a sample differ from those of the population from which it was drawn.

Sampling Frame: a listing of all the elements in a population.

Sampling Validity: an approach to establishing validity of measures through determining whether a measuring device covers the full range of meanings that should be included in the variable being measured.

Scale: a measurement technique, similar to an index, that combines a number of items into a composite score.

Science: a method of obtaining objective knowledge about the world through systematic observation.

Secondary Analysis: the reanalysis of data previously collected for some other research project.

Semantic Differential: a scaling technique that involves respondents rating a concept on a scale between a series of polar-opposite adjectives.

Simple Random Sampling: a sampling technique wherein the target population is treated as a unitary whole and each element has an equal probability of being selected for the sample.

Single-System Designs: quasi-experimental designs featuring continuous or nearly continuous measurement of the dependent variable on a single research subject over a time interval that is divided into a baseline phase, and one or more additional phases during which the independent variable is manipulated; experimental effects are inferred by comparing the subject's responses across baseline and intervention phases.

Snowball Sampling: a type of nonprobability sampling characterized by a few cases of the type that we wish to study, which lead to more cases, and which, in turn, lead to still more cases, until a sufficient sample is achieved.

Social Desirability Effect: people's tendency to give socially desirable, popular answers to questions to present themselves in a good light.

Social Research: a systematic examination (or reexamination) of empirical data, collected by someone firsthand, concerning the social or psychological forces operating in a situation.

Sociograms: context maps using lines and arrows that show connections and relationships between individuals, groups, statuses, or organizations.

Stakeholders: all the people who have an interest in whether a social program operates or how well it does so.

Statistics: procedures for assembling, classifying, and tabulating numerical data so some meaning or information is derived.

Stratified Sampling: a sampling technique wherein the population is subdivided into strata, with separate subsamples drawn from each strata.

Summated Rating Scale: a scale in which a respondent's score is determined by summing the numbers of questions answered.

Summative Evaluation Research: evaluation research that assesses the effectiveness and efficiency of programs and the extent to which program effects are generalizable to other settings and populations.

Survey: a term used both to designate a specific way of collecting data and to identify a broad research strategy; survey data collection involves gathering information from individuals (called respondents) by having them respond to questions.

Survey Research: a broad research strategy that involves asking questions of a sample of people in a fairly short period of time, and testing hypotheses or describing a situation based on their answers.

Systematic Errors: measurement errors that are consistent and patterned.

Systematic Replication: an attempt to extend a treatment to different settings, practitioners, client disorders, or any combination of these conditions.

Systematic Sampling: a type of simple random sampling wherein every nth element of the sampling frame is selected for the sample.

Table Elaboration: a multivariate analysis that examines the relationship between an independent variable and a dependent variable in each of the categories of a third, or test, variable.

Targeted Sampling: a variation on quota and purposive sampling in which procedures are used to ensure that people or groups with specified characteristics will appear in the sample.

Theoretical Sensitivity: having data collection and analysis closely guided by emerging theoretical issues.

Theory: a set of interrelated propositions or statements, organized into a deductive system, that offers an explanation of some phenomenon.

Thurstone Scales: measurement scales consisting of a series of items with a predetermined scale value to which respondents indicate their agreement or disagreement.

Time Sampling: a sampling technique used in observational research in which observations are made only during specified, preselected times.

Traditional Knowledge: knowledge based on custom, habit, and repetition.

Trend Study: research in which data are gathered from different people at different times.

True Experimental Designs: experimental designs that use randomization, control groups, and other techniques to control threats to internal validity.

Type I Error: the probability of rejecting a null hypothesis when it is actually true.

Type II Error: the probability of failing to reject a null hypothesis that is actually false.

Unidimensional Scale: a multiple-item scale that measures one, and only one, variable.

Units of Analysis: the specific objects or elements whose characteristics we wish to describe or explain and about which data are collected.

Univariate Statistics: statistics that describe the distribution of a single variable.

Unobtrusive Observation: observation in which those under study are not aware they are being studied, and the investigator does not change their behavior by his or her presence.

Validity: the degree to which a measure accurately reflects the theoretical meaning of a variable.

Variables: operationally defined concepts that can take on more than one value.

Verification: the process of subjecting hypotheses to empirical tests to determine whether a theory is supported or refuted.

Verstehen: the effort to view and understand a situation from the perspective of the people who are actually in that situation.

References

Achen, C. H. (1986). *The Statistical Analysis of Quasi-Experiments*. Berkeley, CA: University of California Press.

Adams, S., & Orgel, M. (1975). *Through the Mental Health Maze: A Consumer's Guide to Finding a Psychotherapist*. Washington, DC: Health Research Group, Public Citizen.

Alfonso, S. D., & Dziegielewski, S. F. (2001). Self-Directed Treatment of Panic Disorder: A Holistic Approach. *Journal of Social Work Research and Evaluation, 2,* 5–18.

Alford, R. R. (1998). *The Craft of Inquiry: Theories, Methods, Evidence*. New York, NY: Oxford University Press.

Allen-Meares, P. (1984). Content Analysis: It Does Have a Place in Social Work Research. *Journal of Social Service Research, 7* (Summer, 1984), 51–68.

Altman, L. (1996, October 30). Falsified Data Found in Gene Studies. *The New York Times*. Retrieved from http://www.nytimes.com.

Alwin, D. F. (2007). *Margins of Error: A Study of Reliability in Survey Measurement*. Hoboken, N. J.: John Wiley & Sons, Inc.

Amato, P. R., & Booth, A. (1997). *A Generation at Risk: Growing Up in an Era of Family Upheaval*. Cambridge, MA: Harvard University Press.

American Association for Public Opinion Research Standards Committee. (2003). *Interviewer Falsification in Survey Research: Current Best Methods for Prevention, Detection, and Repair of Its Effects* (3rd draft). Retrieved from http://www.aapor.org/uploads/falsification.pdf.

American Sociological Association. *Code of Ethics*. (1999). (Approved by ASA Membership in June 1997). Retrieved from http://www.asanet.org/about/ethics.cfm.

Anderson, B., Silver, B., & Abramson, P. (1988). The Effects of the Race of the Interviewer on Race-Related Attitudes of Black Respondents in SRC/CPS National Election Studies. *Public Opinion Quarterly, 52,* 289–324.

Anderson, J. E., & Stall, R. (2002). Increased Reporting of Male-to-Male Sexual Activity in a National Survey. *Sexually Transmitted Diseases, 29* (November, 2002), 643–646.

Anderson, T., & Kanuka, H. (2003). *e-Research: Strategies and Issues*. Boston, MA: Allyn & Bacon.

Annis, R. C., & Corenblum B. (1986). Effect of Test Language and Experimenter Race on Canadian Indian Children's Racial and Self-Identity. *Journal of Social Psychology, 126* (December, 1986), 761–773.

Antonucci, T. (1986). Hierarchical Mapping Technique. *Generations: The Journal of the Western Gerontological Society, 10,* 10–12.

Arches, J. (1991). Social Structure, Burnout, and Job Satisfaction. *Social Work, 36* (May 1991), 202–206.

Arean, P. A., Alvidrez, J., Nery, R., Estes, C., & Linkins, K. (2003). Recruitment and Retention of Older Minorities in Mental Health Services Research. *The Gerontologist 43* (February, 2003), 36–44.

Armstrong, G. (1993).... Like That Desmond Morris? In D. Hobbs & T. May (Eds.), *Interpreting the Field*. Oxford: Oxford University Press.

Armstrong, J. S., & Luck, E. J. (1987). Return Postage in Mail Surveys: A Meta-Analysis. *Public Opinion Quarterly, 51* (Summer, 1987), 233–248.

Arnold, D. O. (1970). Dimensional Sampling: An Approach for Studying a Small Number of Cases. *American Sociologist, 5*, 147–150.

Aronson, E., Brewer, M. B., & Carlsmith, J. (1985). Experimentation in Social Psychology. In G. Lindzey & E. Aronson (Eds.), *The Handbook of Social Psychology*, 3rd ed., New York, NY: Random House.

Bachman, J. G., & O'Malley, P. M. (1984). Yea-Saying, Nay-Saying, and Going to Extremes: Black–White Differences in Response Styles. *Public Opinion Quarterly, 48*, 491–501.

Backstrom, C. H., & Hursh-Cesar, G. D. (1981). *Survey Research*, 2nd ed. New York, NY: Macmillan.

Bahl, A. B., Spaulding, S. A., & McNeil, C. B. (1999). Treatment of Noncompliance Using Parent–Child Interaction Therapy: A Data-Driven Approach. *Education and Treatment of Children Special Issue: Level 1 Research: Improving Our Education and Treatment through Simple Accountability Procedures, 22* (May, 1999), 146–156

Bailey, K. (1987). *Methods of Social Research*, 3rd ed. New York, NY: Free Press.

Bailey, R. C., Hser, Y., Hsieh, S., & Anglin, M. D. (1994). Influences Affecting Maintenance and Cessation of Narcotics Addiction. *Journal of Drug Issues, 24*, 249–272.

Bales, R. F. (1950). *Interaction Process Analysis*. Cambridge, MA: Addison-Wesley.

Barlow, D., & Hersen, M. (1973). Single-Case Experimental Designs: Uses in Applied Clinical Research. *Archives of General Psychiatry, 29*, 319–325.

Barlow, D., Nock, M., & Hersen, M. (2009). *Single Case Experimental Designs: Strategies for Studying Behavior Change*, 3rd ed. Boston, MA: Pearson.

Barlow, H. (1996). *Introduction to Criminology*, 7th ed. New York, NY: HarperCollins.

Barnes, H. E., (Ed.), (1948). *An Introduction to the History of Sociology*. Chicago, IL: University of Chicago Press.

Bauer, D. G. (2011). *The "How To" Grants Manual: Successful Grantseeking Techniques for Obtaining Public and Private Grants*, 7th ed. Lanham, MD: Rowman and Littlefield.

Baumrind, D. (1985). Research Using Intentional Deception. *American Psychologist, 40*(2), (February, 1985), 165–174.

Bazeley, P. (2007). *Qualitative Data Analysis with NVivo*, 2nd ed. Thousand Oaks, CA: Sage.

Beauchamp, T. L., Faden, R. R., Wallace, R. J., Jr., & Walters, L., (Eds.). (1982). *Ethical Issues in Social Science Research*. Baltimore, MD: Johns Hopkins University Press.

Becerra, R.M. & DeAnda, D. (1999). Can Valid Research on Ethnic Minority Populations only be Conducted by Researchers from the Same Group? In D. DeAnda (Ed.). *Controversial Issues in Multiculturalism*, Boston, MA: Allyn and Bacon.

Becerra, R. M., & Zambrana, R. E. (1985). Methodological Approaches to Research on Hispanics. *Social Work Research and Abstracts, 21*(Summer, 1985), 42–49.

Bell, A. P., & Weinberg, M. S. (1978). *Homosexualities: A Study of Diversity among Men and Women*. New York: Simon & Schuster.

Bell, W. (1987). *Contemporary Social Welfare*, 2nd ed. New York, NY: Macmillan.

Benton, T. (1977). *Philosophical Foundations of the Three Sociologies*. Boston, MA: Routledge & Kegan Paul.

Berg, B. L., & Lune, H. (2012). *Qualitative Research Methods for the Social Sciences*, 8th ed. Boston, MA: Pearson.

Berger, R. L. (1994). Ethics in Scientific Communication: Study of a Problem Case. *Journal of Medical Ethics, 20*, 207–211.

Berk, R., & Rossi, P. (1990). *Thinking about Program Evaluation*. Newbury Park, CA: Sage.

Bernard, H. R. (2006). *Research Methods in Anthropology: Qualitative and Quantitative Approaches*, 4th ed. Walnut Creek, CA: AltaMira Press.

Berry, S. H., & Kanouse, D. E. (1987). Physician Response to a Mailed Survey: An Experiment in Timing of Payment. *Public Opinion Quarterly, 51* (Spring, 1987), 102–114.

Beskow, L. M., Dame, L., & Costello, E. J. (2008). Research Ethics: Certificates of Confidentiality and Compelled Disclosure of Data. *Science, 322* (November, 14, 2008), 1054–1055.

Billups, J. O., & Julia, M. C. (1987). Changing Profile of Social Work Practice. *Social Work Research and Abstracts, 23* (Winter, 1987), 17–22.

Binder, A., Geis, G., & Bruce, D. (1988). *Juvenile Delinquency: Historical, Cultural, and Legal Perspectives.* New York, NY: Macmillan.

Birkeland, S., Murphy-Graham, E., & Weiss, C. (2005). Good Reasons for Ignoring Good Evaluations: The Case of the Drug Abuse Resistance Education (D.A.R.E.) Program. *Evaluation and Program Planning, 28,* 247–256.

Black, M. M., & Ponirakis, A. (2000). Computer-Administered Interviews with Children about Maltreatment: Methodological, Developmental, and Ethical Issues. *Journal of Interpersonal Violence, 15* (July, 2000), 682–695.

Blaikie, N. (1993). *Approaches to Social Enquiry.* Cambridge, MA: Polity.

Bloom, M., Fischer, J., & Orme, J. G. (2009). *Evaluating Practice: Guidelines for the Accountable Professional,* 6th ed. Boston, MA: Pearson.

Blumberg, S. J., & Luke, J. V. (2011). *Wireless Substitution: Early Release of Estimates From the National Health Interview Survey, July–December 2010.* National Center for Health Statistics. Retrieved from http://www.cdc.gov/nchs/data/nhis/earlyrelease/wireless201106.pdf.

Bogdan, R., & Taylor, S. J. (1975). *Introduction to Qualitative Research Methods.* New York, NY: Wiley.

Bogdan, R. C., & Biklen, S. K. (1992). *Qualitative Research for Education: An Introduction to Theory and Methods,* 2nd ed. Boston, MA: Allyn & Bacon.

Bohrnstedt, G. W. (1983). Measurement. In P. H. Rossi, J. D. Wright, & A. B. Anderson (Eds.). *Handbook of Survey Research.* New York, NY: Academic Press.

Bonacich, E. (1990). Community Forum Discussion: What Next? *ASA Footnotes, 18.*

Bonnie, R. J., & Wallace, R. B. (Eds.). (2003). *Elder Mistreatment: Abuse, Neglect, and Exploitation in an Aging America.* Washington, DC: National Academy Press.

Borgatta, E., & Bohrnstedt, G. (1981). Levels of Measurement: Once Over Again. In G. Bohrnstedt & E. Borgatta (Eds.). *Social Measurement: Current Issues.* Beverly Hills, CA: Sage.

Bourgois, P. (1995). *In Search of Respect: Selling Crack in El Barrio.* Cambridge: Cambridge University Press.

Bourgois, P., Lettiere, M., & Quesada, J. (1997). Social Misery and the Sanction of Substance Abuse: Confronting HIV Risk among Homeless Heroin Addicts in San Francisco. *Social Problems, 44,* (May, 1997). 155–173.

Boynton, P. M. (2003). I'm Just a Girl Who Can't Say No?: Women, Consent, and Sex Research. *Journal of Sex and Marital Therapy, 29* (1), 23–32.

Bradburn, N. M. (1983). Response Effects. In P. H. Rossi, J. D. Wright, & A. B. Anderson (Eds.). *Handbook of Survey Research.* New York, NY: Academic Press.

Brajuha, M., & Hallowell, L. (1986). Legal Intrusion and the Politics of Fieldwork. *Urban Life, 14,* 454–479.

Brent, E. E., & Thompson, A. (2000). *Methodologist's Toolchest Version 3.0.* Columbia, Mo.: Idea Works.

Bronowski, J. (1978). *The Origins of Knowledge and Imagination.* New Haven, Conn.: Yale University Press.

Browne, M. N., & Keeley, S. M. (2012). *Asking the Right Questions: A Guide to Critical Thinking,* 10th ed. Boston, MA: Longman.

Brunner, G. A., & Carroll, S. J. (1967). Effect of Prior Telephone Appointments on Completion Rates and Response Content. *Public Opinion Quarterly, 31,* 652–654.

Brunswick-Heineman, M. (1981). The Obsolete Scientific Imperative in Social Work Research. *Social Service Review, 55,* 371–397.

Buchbinder, E., & Eisikovits, Z. (2004). Reporting Bad Results: The Ethical Responsibility of Presenting Abused Women's Parenting Practices in a Negative Light. *Child and Family Social Work, 9,* 359–367.

Burch, G., & Mohr, V. (1980). Evaluating a Child Abuse Intervention Program. *Social Casework, 61,* 90–99.

Burger, J. M. (2009). Replicating Milgram: Would People Still Obey Today? *American Psychologist, 64* (January, 2009), 1–11.

Burgess, R., & Youngblade, L. (1988). Social Incompetence and the Intergenerational Transmission of Abusive Parental Practices. In G. Hotaling, D. Finkelhor, J. Kirkpatrick, & M. Strauss (Eds.). *Family Abuse and Its Consequences: New Directions in Research*, Newbury Park, CA: Sage.

Bushery, J. M., Reichert, J. W., Albright, K. A., & Rossiter, J. C. (1999). Using Date and Time Stamps to Detect Interviewer Falsification. Retrieved from http://www.amstat.org/sections/srms/proceedings/papers/1999_053.pdf. Washington, DC: U.S. Census Bureau.

Cahalan, D. (1989). The *Digest* Poll Rides Again! *Public Opinion Quarterly*, 53, 129–133.

Calvey, D. (2008). The Art and Politics of Covert Research: Doing 'Situated Ethics' in the Field. *Sociology*, 42(5), 905–918.

Campbell, D. T., & Fiske, D. W. (1959). Convergent and Discriminant Validity by the Multitrait–Multimethod Matrix. *Psychological Bulletin*, 56, 81–105.

Campbell, D. T., & Stanley, J. C. (1963). *Experimental and Quasi-Experimental Designs for Research*. Chicago, IL: Rand McNally.

Cannell, C. F., & Kahn, R. L. (1968). Interviewing. In G. Lindzey & E. Aronson (Eds.). *The Handbook of Social Psychology*, 2nd ed., Vol. 2., Reading, MA: Addison-Wesley.

Card, J. J., & Kuhn, T. (2006). Development of Online Suites of Social Science-Based Resources for Health Researchers and Practitioners. *Social Science Computer Review*, 24, (Summer, 2006), 255–261.

Carise, D., Cornely, W., & Gurel, O. (2002). A Successful Researcher–Practitioner Collaboration in Substance Abuse Treatment. *Journal of Substance Abuse Treatment*, 23, 157–162.

Carlock, C. J., & Martin, P. Y. (1977). Sex Composition and the Intensive Group Experience. *Social Work*, 22, 27–32.

Carroll, L. (1946). *Through the Looking Glass*. New York, NY: Random House.

Cartwright, A., & Tucker, W. (1967). An Attempt to Reduce the Number of Calls on an Interview Inquiry. *Public Opinion Quarterly*, 31, 299–302.

Catley, D., & Grobe, J. E. (2008). Using Basic Laboratory Research to Understand Scheduled Smoking: A Field Investigation of the Effects of Manipulating Controllability on Subjective Responses to Smoking. *Health Psychology*, 27, 189–196.

Cavan, S. (1966). *Liquor License*. Chicago, IL: Aldine.

Ceci, S. J., Peters, D., & Plotkin, J. (1985). Human Subjects Review, Personal Values, and the Regulation of Social Science Research. *American Psychologist*, 40 (September, 1985), 994–1002.

Centers for Disease Control and Prevention. (2003). HIPAA Privacy Rule and Public Health: Guidance from CDC and the U. S. Department of Health and Human Services. *Morbidity and Mortality Weekly Review*, 52, 1–12. Retrieved from http://www.cdc.gov/mmwr/preview/mmwrhtml/m2e411a1.htm.

Centers for Disease Control and Prevention. (Sept. 7, 2005). CDC/ATSDR Policy on Releasing and Sharing Data. *Manual GUIDE: General Administration*, CDC-GA-2005-14. Retrieved from http://www.cdc.gov/maso/policy/releasingdata.pdf. Atlanta, GA: Centers for Disease Control.

Centers for Disease Control and Prevention. (February, 2011). Diagnoses of HIV Infection and AIDS in the United States and Dependent Areas, 2009. HIV Surveillance Report, 2009. Vol. 21. Retrieved from http://www.cdc.gov/hiv/topics/surveillance/resources/reports. Atlanta, GA: U. S. Department of Health and Human Services.

Chaiken, M. R., & Chaiken, J. M. (1984). Offender Types and Public Policy. *Crime and Delinquency*, 30 (April, 1984), 195–226.

Champion, D. J. (1981). *Basic Statistics for Social Research*, 2nd ed. Scranton, PA: Chandler.

Charmaz, K. (2006). *Constructing Grounded Theory: A Practical Guide Through Qualitative Analysis*. Thousand Oaks, CA: Sage.

Chen, H., & Rossi, P. H. (1980). The Multi-Goal, Theory-Driven Approach to Evaluation: A Model Linking Basic and Applied Social Science. *Social Forces*, 59, 106–122.

Children's Research Center. (1999). *The Improvement of Child Protective Services with Structured Decision Making: The CRC Model*. San Francisco, CA: National Council on Crime and Delinquency.

Cho, H., & Wilke D. J. (2005). How Has the Violence Against Women Act Affected the Response of the Criminal Justice System to Domestic Violence?

Journal of Sociology and Social Welfare, 32 (December, 2005), 125–139.

Christie, R., & Geis, F. L. (1970). *Studies in Machiavellianism.* New York, NY: Academic Press.

Clandinin, D. J., & Connelly, F. M. (2000). *Narrative Inquiry: Experience and Story in Qualitative Research.* San Francisco, CA: Jossey-Bass.

Clark, H. W. (2002). Bridging the Gap between Substance Abuse Practice and Research: The National Treatment Plan Initiative. *Journal of Drug Issues, 32* (Summer, 2002), 757–768.

Clark, J. (2006). Field Research Methods in the Middle East. *PS: Political Science and Politics, 39,* 417–424.

Clum, G. A. (1990). *Coping with Panic: A Drug-Free Approach to Dealing with Anxiety Attacks.* Belmont, CA: Brooks/Cole.

Cochrane Collaboration. (2003). *The Cochrane Library.* Retrieved from http://www.thecochranelibrary.com.

Coe, R. D., & Hill, D. H. (1998). Food Stamp Participation and Reasons for Nonparticipation: 1986. *Journal of Family and Economic Issues, 19* (Summer, 1998), 107–130.

Coehlo, R. J. (1983). *An Experimental Investigation of Two Multi-Component Approaches on Smoking Cessation* (Doctoral dissertation, Michigan State University).

Cohen, J. (1988). *Statistical Power Analysis for Behavioral Sciences,* 2nd ed. Hillsdale, NJ: Lawrence Erlbaum Associates.

Cohen, M. R., & Nagel, E. (1934). *An Introduction to Logic and Scientific Method.* New York, NY: Harcourt.

Collins, S. (2008). *Foundation Fundamentals: Fundraising Guides,* 8th ed. New York, NY: Foundation Center.

Committee on the Status of Women in Sociology. (1986). *The Treatment of Gender in Research.* Washington, DC: American Sociological Association.

Cook, T. D. (1985). Postpositivist Critical Multiplism. In L. Shotland & M. M. Mark (Eds.). *Social Science and Social Policy.* Beverly Hills, CA: Sage, 1985.

Cook, T. D., Cook, F. L., & Mark, M. M. (1977). Randomized and Quasi-Experimental Designs in Evaluation Research: An Introduction. In L. Rutman (Ed.). *Evaluation Research Methods.* Beverly Hills, CA: Sage.

Corry, J. (1982, July 15). Children's TV Found Dominated by White Men. *New York Times,* p. 14.

Coulton, C. J. (1979). Developing an Instrument to Measure Person–Environment Fit. *Journal of Social Service Research, 3,* 159–174.

Council on Social Work Education. (2010). *Educational Policy and Accreditation Standards.* Washington, DC: Council on Social Work Education. Retrieved from http:// www.cswe.org/Accreditation /2008EPASDescription.aspx.

Couper, M. P., Tourangeau, R., & Kenyon, K. (2004). Picture This! Exploring Visual Effects in Web Surveys. *Public Opinion Quarterly, 68* (Summer, 2004), 255–266.

Cournoyer, B. R., & Powers, G. L. (2002). Evidence-Based Social Work: The Quiet Revolution Continues. In A. R. Roberts & G. J. Greene (Eds.). *Social Workers' Desk Reference.* Oxford: Oxford University Press.

Couvalis, G. (1997). *The Philosophy of Science: Science and Objectivity.* London, England: Sage.

Cox, D. E., & Sipprelle, C. N. (1971). Coercion in Participation as a Research Subject. *American Psychologist, 26,* 726–728.

Crabb, P. B., & Bielawski, D. (1994). The Social Representation of Material Culture and Gender in Children's Books. *Sex Roles, 30,* 69–79.

Cronbach, L. J.(1951). Coefficient Alpha and the Internal Structure of Tests. *Psychometrica, 16,* 197–334.

Cronbach, L. J., & Meehl, P. (1955). Construct Validity in Psychological Tests. *Psychological Bulletin, 52,* 281–302.

Dailey, R. M., & Claus, R. E. (2001). The Relationship between Interviewer Characteristics and Physical and Sexual Abuse Disclosures among Substance Users: A Multilevel Analysis. *Journal of Drug Issues, 31,* 867–888.

Davis, D. W. (1997). Nonrandom Measurement Error and Race of Interviewer Effects among African Americans. *Public Opinion Quarterly, 61,* 183–207.

Davis, L. V. (1984). Beliefs of Social Service Providers about Abused Women and Abusing Men. *Social Work, 29* (May/June, 1984), 243–250.

Dawson, J. A., & D'Amico, J. J. (1985). Involving Program Staff in Evaluation Studies: A Strategy for Increasing Information Use and Enriching the Data Base. *Evaluation Review*, 9 (April, 1985), 173–188.

DeKeseredy, W. S. (2000). Current Controversies on Defining Nonlethal Violence against Women in Intimate Heterosexual Relationships. *Violence Against Women*, 6 (July, 2000), 728–746.

DeKeseredy, W. S., & MacLeod, L. (1997). *Woman Abuse: A Sociological Story*. Toronto, Canada: Harcourt Brace.

Dekker-van Weering, M. G. H., VollenBroek-Hutten, M. M. R., & Hermens, H. J. (2012). Do Personalized Feedback Messages about Activity Patterns Stimulate Patients With Chronic Low Back Pain to Change Their Activity on a Short Term Notice? *Applied Psychophysiological Biofeedback*, 37, 81–89.

DeMaio, T. J. (1984). Social Desirability and Survey Measurement: A Review. In C. F. Turner & E. Martin (Eds.), *Surveying Subjective Phenomena*, 2nd ed., New York, NY: Russell Sage Foundation.

DeMartini, J. (1982). Basic and Applied Sociological Work: Divergence, Convergence, or Peaceful Coexistence? *Journal of Applied Behavioral Science*, 18, 203–215.

Denzin, N. (1989). *The Research Act: A Theoretical Introduction to Sociological Methods*, 3rd ed. Englewood Cliffs, NJ: Prentice Hall.

DeSena, A. D. (2005). SAFE Homes: Is It Worth the Costs? An Evaluation of a Group Home Permanency Planning Program for Children Who First Enter Out-of-Home Care. *Child Abuse & Neglect*, 29, 627–643.

DeVault, M. L. (1999). *Liberating Method: Feminism and Social Research*. Philadelphia, PA: Temple University Press.

DeVellis, R. F. (2012). *Scale Development: Theory and Applications*, 3rd ed. Thousand Oaks, CA: Sage.

DeWalt, K. M., & DeWalt, B. R. (2011). *Participant Observation: A Guide for Fieldworkers*, 2nd ed. Walnut Creek, CA: AltaMira Press.

Dignan, M., Michielutte, R., Sharp, P., Bahnson, J., Young, L. & Beal, P. (1990). The Role of Focus Groups in Health Education for Cervical Cancer among Minority Women. *Journal of Community Health*, 15, 369–375.

Dobratz, B. A., & Shanks-Meile, S. L. (1997). *"White Power, White Pride!" The White Separatist Movement in the United States*. New York, NY: Twayne Publishers.

Doerner, W. G., & Hunter, R. D. (2006). Post-FTO Performance Evaluations of Rookie Police Officers. *Journal of Ethnicity in Criminal Justice*, 4, 113–128.

Dohan, D., & Sánchez-Jankowski, M. (1998). Using Computers to Analyze Ethnographic Field Data: Theoretical and Practical Considerations. *Annual Review of Sociology*, 24, 477–516.

Dotson, L. E., & Summers, G. F. (1970). Elaboration of Guttman Scaling Techniques. In G. F. Summers (Ed.), *Attitude Measurement*. Chicago, IL: Rand McNally.

Drewry, S. (2004). The Ethics of Human Subjects Protection in Research. *The Journal of Baccalaureate Social Work*, 10, 105–117.

Duehn, W. D., & Proctor, E. K. (1977). Initial Clinical Interaction and Premature Discontinuance in Treatment. *American Journal of Orthopsychiatry*, 47, 284–290.

Duffy, B., Smith, K., Terhanian, G., & Bremer, J. (2005). Comparing Data from Online and Face-to-Face Surveys. *International Journal of Market Research*, 47, 615–639.

Dunford, F., Huizinga, D., & Elliott, D. (1989). *The Omaha Domestic Violence Police Experiment*. Washington, DC: National Institute of Justice.

Durkheim, E. (1938). *Rules of the Sociological Method*, trans. S. Solovay & J. Mueller. Chicago, IL: University of Chicago Press.

Earnest, C. (1999). Single Case Study of EEG Asymmetry Biofeedback for Depression: An Independent Replication in an Adolescent. *Journal of Neurotherapy*, 3 (Spring, 1999), 28–35.

Eckenwiler, L. A. (1999). Pursuing Reform in Clinical Research: Lessons from Women's Experience. *Journal of Law, Medicine & Ethics*, 27, 158–70.

Edlesen, J. L. (1985). Rapid Assessment Instruments for Evaluating Practice with Children and Youth. *Journal of Social Service Research*, 8, 17–31.

Edwards, A. L., & Kilpatrick, F. P. (1948). A Technique for the Construction of Attitude Scales. *Journal of Applied Psychology*, 32, 374–384.

Eichler, M. (1988). *Nonsexist Research Methods: A Practical Guide.* Boston, MA: Allen & Unwin.

Elliott, D. S., & Huizinga, D. (1983). Social Class and Delinquent Behavior in a National Youth Panel: 1976–1980. *Criminology, 21,* 149–177.

Elms, A. C. (1982). Keeping Deception Honest: Justifying Conditions for Social Scientific Research Strategies. In T. L. Beauchamp, R. R. Faden, R. J. Wallace, Jr., & L. Walters (Eds.). *Ethical Issues in Social Science Research.* Baltimore, MD: Johns Hopkins University Press.

Engler, R. L., Covell, J. W., Friedman, P. J., Kitcher, P. S. & Peters, R. M. (1987). Misrepresentation and Responsibility in Medical Research. *New England Journal of Medicine, 17,* 1383–1389.

English, N., O'Muircheartaigh, C., Dekker, K., Latterner, M., & Eckman, S. (2009). Coverage Rates and Coverage Bias in Housing Unit Frames. *Proceedings of the Survey Research Methods Section, American Statistical Association,* 595–602.

Epstein, I., & Tripodi, T. (1977). *Research Techniques for Program Planning, Monitoring, and Evaluation.* New York, NY: Columbia University Press.

Erich, S., Leung, P., Kindle, P., & Carter, S. (2005). Gay and Lesbian Adoptive Families: An Exploratory Study of Family Functioning, Adoptive Child's Behavior, and Familial Support Networks. *Journal of Family Social Work, 9,* 17–31.

Erikson, K. T. (1967). A Comment on Disguised Observation in Sociology. *Social Problems, 14,* 366–373.

Ess, C., & AoIR Ethics Working Committee. (2002). *Ethical Decision-Making and Internet Research: Recommendations from the AoIR Ethics Working Committee.* Retrieved from http://www.aoir.org/reports/ethics.pdf. Association of Internet Researchers.

Estroff, S. E. (1981). *Making It Crazy: An Ethnography of Psychiatric Clients in an American Community.* Berkeley, CA: University of California Press.

Eysenbach, G., & Till, J. E. (2001). Ethical Issues in Qualitative Research on Internet Communities. *Information in Practice BMJ,* 1103–1105.

Fahrenberg, J. (1996). Ambulatory Assessment: Issues and Perspectives. In J. Fahrenberg & M. Myrtek (Eds.). *Ambulatory Assessment: Computer-Assisted Psychological and Psychophysiological Methods in Monitoring and Field Studies.* Seattle, Wash.: Hogrefe & Huber.

Farley, R. (1984). *Blacks and Whites: Narrowing the Gap.* Cambridge, MA: Harvard University Press.

Fay, B. (1987). *Critical Social Science: Liberation and Its Limits.* Ithaca, NY: Cornell University Press.

Federal Bureau of Investigation. (2012). *Uniform Crime Reports: Crime in the United States, 2011.* Washington, DC: U.S. Government Printing Office.

Federal Register. (1999). *64* (June 17, 1999), 116.

Feldman, M. S., Bell, J., & Berger, M. T. (2003). *Gaining Access: A Practical Guide for Qualitative Researchers.* Walnut Creek, CA: AltaMira Press.

Feldman, R. A., & Caplinger, T. E. (1977). Social Work Experience and Client Behavioral Change: A Multivariate Analysis of Process and Outcome. *Journal of Social Service Research, 1,* 5–33.

Fernandez, M., & Ruch-Ross, H. S. (1998). Ecological Analysis of Program Impact: A Site Analysis of Programs for Pregnant and Parenting Adolescents in Illinois. *Journal of Applied Sociology, 15,* 104–133.

Ferree, M., & Hall, E. (1990). Visual Images of American Society: Gender and Race in Introductory Sociology Textbooks. *Gender and Society, 4,* 500–533.

Ferrell, K. A. (2000). Growth and Development of Young Children with Visual Impairments. In M. C. Holbrook & A. J. Koenig (Eds.). *Foundations of Education: Volume I. History and Theory of Teaching Children and Youths with Visual Impairments,* 2nd ed. New York, NY: AFB Press.

Festinger, L., Riecken, H., & Schachter, S. (1956). *When Prophecy Fails.* New York, NY: Harper & Row.

Fielding, N. G. (2002). Automating the Ineffable: Qualitative Software and the Meaning of Qualitative Research. In T. May (Ed.). *Qualitative Research in Action.* Thousand Oaks, CA: Sage.

First, M. B., et al. (2004). Clinical Utility as a Criterion for Revising Psychiatric Diagnoses. *American Journal of Psychiatry, 161,* 946–954.

First, R., Toomey, B., & Rife, J. (1990). Preliminary Findings on Rural Homelessness in Ohio. Columbus, OH: The Ohio State University College of Social Work.

Fischer, J., & Corcoran, K. (Eds.). (2007). *Measures for Clinical Practice and Research: A Sourcebook*, 4th ed. New York, NY: Oxford University Press.

Fletcher, L. A., Erickson, D. J., Toomey, T. L., & Wagenaar, A. C. (2003). Handheld Computers: A Feasible Alternative to Paper Forms for Field Data Collection. *Evaluation Review, 27* (April, 2003), 165–178.

Flick, U. (2009). *An Introduction to Qualitative Research*, 4th ed. Thousand Oaks, CA: Sage.

Fontana, A., & Frey, J. H. (1994). Interviewing: The Art of Science. In N. K. Denzin & Y. S. Lincoln (Eds.). *Handbook of Qualitative Research*. Thousand Oaks, CA: Sage.

Fortune, A. E. (1979). Communication in Task-Centered Treatment. *Social Work, 24*, 390–397.

Fowler, F., Jr., & Mangione, T. (1990). *Standardized Survey Interviewing*. Newbury Park, CA: Sage.

Fox, R. J., Crask, M. R., & Kim, J. (1988). Mail Survey Response Rate: A Meta-Analysis of Selected Techniques for Inducing Response. *Public Opinion Quarterly, 52*, 467–491.

Fox, S., & Schwartz, D. (2002). Social Desirability and Controllability in Computerized and Paper-and-Pencil Personality Questionnaires. *Computers in Human Behavior, 18*, (July, 2002), 389–410.

Frankfort-Nachmias, C., & Nachmias, D. (2008). *Research Methods in the Social Sciences*, 7th ed. New York, NY: Worth Publishers.

Franzosi, R. (Ed.) (2008). *Content Analysis*. Thousand Oaks, CA: Sage.

Fredman, N., & Sherman, R. (1987). *Handbook of Measurements for Marriage and Family Therapy*. New York, NY: Brunner/Mazel.

Frey, J. H. (1986). An Experiment with a Confidentiality Reminder in a Telephone Survey. *Public Opinion Quarterly, 50* (Summer, 1986), 267–269.

Fricker, R. D., & Schonlau, M. (2002). Advantages and Disadvantages of Internet Research Surveys: Evidence from the Literature. *Field Methods, 14* (November, 2002), 347–367.

Fricker, S., Galesic, M., Tourangeau, R., & Yan, T. (2005). An Experimental Comparison of Web and Telephone Surveys. *Public Opinion Quarterly, 69*, 370–392.

Frisch, M. B., & Higgins, R. L. (1986). Instructional Demand Effects and the Correspondence among Role-Play, Self-Report, and Naturalistic Measures of Social Skill. *Behavioral Assessment, 8* (Summer, 1986), 221–236.

Galison, P., & Stump, D. (Eds.). (1996). *The Disunity of Science: Boundaries, Contexts, and Power*. Stanford, CA: Stanford University Press.

Galtung, J. (1967). *Theory and Methods of Social Research*. New York, NY: Columbia University Press.

Garfield, E., & Welljams-Dorof, A. (1990). The Impact of Fraudulent Research on the Scientific Literature. *Journal of the American Medical Association, 263*, 1424–1426.

Gelles, R. J. (1978). Methods for Studying Sensitive Family Topics. *American Journal of Orthopsychiatry, 48*, 408–424.

Gelles, R. J. (1987). What to Learn from Cross-Cultural and Historical Research on Child Abuse and Neglect: An Overview. In R. J. Gelles & J. B. Lancaster (Eds.). *Child Abuse and Neglect: Biosocial Dimensions*. New York, NY: Aldine de Gruyter.

Gibbs, L. (1983). Evaluation Researcher: Scientist or Advocate? *Journal of Social Service Research, 7* (Fall, 1983), 81–92.

Gibbs, L. (2003). *Evidence-Based Practice for the Helping Professions: A Practical Guide with Integrated Multimedia*. Pacific Grove, CA: Brooks/Cole–Thomson Learning.

Gibbs, L. (1991). *Scientific Reasoning for Social Workers: Bridging the Gap between Research and Practice*. New York, NY: Macmillan.

Gibelman, M., & Gelman, S. R. (2001). Learning from the Mistakes of Others: A Look at Scientific Misconduct in Research. *Journal of Social Work Education, 37*, 241–254.

Gibson, P., & Abrams, L. (2003). Women in Qualitative Research: Racial Difference in Engaging, Recruiting, and Interviewing African Americans. *Qualitative Social Work, 2*, 457–476.

Gilligan, C. (1982). *In a Different Voice: Psychological Theory and Women's Development*. Cambridge, MA: Harvard University Press.

Gilmore, S., & Crissman, A. (1997). Video Games: Analyzing Gender Identity and Violence in This New Virtual Reality. *Studies in Symbolic Interaction, 2*, 181–199.

Gingerich, W. (1990). Rethinking Single-Case Evaluation. In L. Videka-Sherman & W. Reid (Eds.).

Advances in Clinical Social Work Research. Silver Spring, MD: National Association of Social Workers.

Ginsburg, H., & Opper, S. (1988). *Piaget's Theory of Intellectual Development*, 3rd ed. Englewood Cliffs, NJ: Prentice Hall.

Glaser, B. (1978). *Theoretical Sensitivity.* Mill Valley, CA: Sociology Press.

Glaser, B., & Strauss, A. (1965). *Awareness of Dying.* Chicago, IL.: Aldine.

Gold, R. L. (1958). Roles in Sociological Field Observations. *Social Forces, 36,* 217–223.

Goldberg, A. E. (2009). *Lesbian and Gay Parents and Their Children: Research on the Family Life Cycle.* Washington, DC: American Psychological Association.

Goldfried, M. R., & Wolfe, B. E. (1996). Psychotherapy Practice and Research: Repairing a Strained Alliance. *American Psychologist, 51* (October, 1996), 1007–1016.

Goldsmith, D. J., McDermott, V. M., & Alexander, S. C. (2000). Helpful, Supportive, and Sensitive: Measuring the Evaluation of Enacted Social Support in Personal Relationships. *Journal of Social and Personal Relationships, 17,* 369–391.

Goode, W. J., & Hatt, P. K. (1952). *Methods in Social Research.* New York, NY: McGraw-Hill.

Gorden, R. L. (1987). *Interviewing: Strategies, Techniques, and Tactics,* 4th ed. Chicago, IL.: Dorsey Press.

Gordon, M. M. (1988). *The Scope of Sociology.* New York, NY: Oxford University Press.

Gottman, J. M. (1985). Observational Measures of Behavior Therapy Outcome: A Reply to Jacobson. *Behavioral Assessment, 7* (Fall, 1985), 317–321.

Gottman, J. M. (1981). *Time-Series Analysis: A Comprehensive Introduction for Social Scientists.* New York, NY: Cambridge University Press.

Gottman, J. S. (1990). Children of Gay and Lesbian Parents. In F. W. Bozett & M. B. Sussman (Eds.). *Homosexuality and Family Relationships.* New York, NY: Harrington Park Press.

Gouldner, A. (1976). The Dark Side of the Dialectic: Toward a New Objectivity. *Sociological Inquiry, 46,* 3–16.

Goyder, J. (1985). Face-to-Face Interviews and Mailed Questionnaires: The Net Difference in Response Rate. *Public Opinion Quarterly, 49* (Summer, 1985), 234–252.

Graham, K. R. (1977). *Psychological Research: Controlled Interpersonal Research.* Monterey, CA: Brooks/Cole.

Graham, K., LaRocque, L., Yetman, R., Ross, T. J., & Guistra, E. (1980). Aggression and Barroom Environments. *Journal of Studies on Alcohol, 41,* 277–292.

Gravlee, C. C., Zenk, S. N., Woods, S., Rowe, Z., & Schulz, A. J. (2006). Handheld Computers for Direct Observation of the Social and Physical Environment. *Field Methods, 18,* 382–397.

Gray, B. H. (1982). The Regulatory Context of Social and Behavioral Research. In T. L. Beauchamp, R. R. Faden, R. J. Wallace, Jr., & L. Walters (Eds.). *Ethical Issues in Social Science Research,* ed. Baltimore, MD: Johns Hopkins University Press.

Greene, J. C. (1994). Qualitative Program Evaluation. In N. K. Denzin & Y. S. Lincoln (Eds.). *Handbook of Qualitative Research.* Thousand Oaks, CA: Sage.

Greenley, J. R., & Schoenherr, R. A. (1981). Organization Effects on Client Satisfaction with Humaneness of Service. *Journal of Health and Social Behavior, 22,* 2–18.

Grichting, W. L. (1979). Do Laws Make a Difference? *Journal of Social Service Research, 2,* 245–265.

Griffin, M., Resick, P., Waldrop, A., & Mechanic, M. (2003). Participation in Trauma Research: Is There Evidence of Harm? *Journal of Traumatic Stress, 16* (June, 2003), 221–227.

Grigsby, R. K., & Roof, H. L. (1993). Federal Policy for the Protection of Human Subjects: Applications to Research on Social Work Practice. *Research on Social Work Practice, 3* (October, 1993), 448–461.

Groth-Marnat, G. (2009). *Handbook of Psychological Assessment,* 5th ed. New York, NY: John Wiley & Sons.

Groves, R. M. (2004). *Survey Errors and Survey Costs.* New York, NY: Wiley.

Groze, V. (1991). Adoption and Single Parents: A Review. *Child Welfare, 70,* 321–332.

Groze, V. K., & Rosenthal, J. A. (1991). Single Parents and Their Adopted Children: A Psychosocial Analysis. *Families in Society: The Journal of Contemporary Human Services, 72*(2), 67–77.

Gubrium, J. F., & Holstein, J. A. (1997). *The New Language of Qualitative Methods.* New York, NY: Oxford University Press.

Guttman, L. (1944). A Basis for Scaling Qualitative Data. *American Sociological Review, 9,* 139–150.

Guttman, L. (1950). The Basis for Scalogram Analysis. In S. A. Stouffer et al. (Eds.). *Measurement and Prediction.* Princeton, NJ: Princeton University Press.

Halfpenny, P. (1982). *Positivism and Sociology: Explaining Social Life.* London, England: Allen & Unwin.

Haller, G., Haller, D. M., Courvoisier, D. S., & Lovis, C. (2009). Handheld vs. Laptop Computers for Electronic Data Collection in Clinical Research: A Crossover Randomized Trial. *Journal of the American Medical Informatics Association, 16,* 651–659.

Hannes, K., Claes, L. & the Belgian Campbell Group. (2007). Learn to Read and Write Systematic Reviews: The Belgian Campbell Group. *Research on Social Work Practice, 17,* 748–753.

Harrington, P. E. (2000). *Recruiting and Retaining Women: A Self-Assessment Guide for Law Enforcement.* Los Angeles, CA: National Center for Women and Policing. Retrieved from http://www.womenandpolicing.org.

Harris, A. R., Thomas, S. H., Fisher, G. A., & Hirsch, D. J. (2002). Murder and Medicine: The Lethality of Criminal Assault 1960–1999. *Homicide Studies Journal, 6* (May, 2002), 128–166.

Harris, F. N., & Jenson, W. R. (1985). Comparisons of Multiple-Baseline across Persons Designs and AB Designs with Replication: Issues and Confusions. *Behavioral Assessment, 7* (Spring, 1985), 121–127.

Harrison, W. D. (1980). Role Strain and Burnout in Child-Protective Service Workers. *Social Service Review, 54,* 31–44.

Hayes, S. C., Barlow, D. H., & Nelson-Gray, R. O. (1999). *The Scientist Practitioner: Research and Accountability in the Age of Managed Care* 2nd ed. Boston, MA: Pearson.

Heckathorn, D. D. (1997). Respondent-Driven Sampling: A New Approach to the Study of Hidden Populations. *Social Problems, 44* (May, 1997), 174–199.

Heise, D. R. (1970). The Semantic Differential and Attitude Research. In G. F. Summers (Ed.). *Attitude Measurement.* Chicago, IL: Rand McNally.

Henry, G. (1990). *Practical Sampling.* Newbury Park, CA: Sage.

Hepworth, D. H., & Larsen, J. (1990). *Direct Social Work Practice.* Belmont, CA: Wadsworth.

Herrick, J. M. (2008). Social Policy: Overview. In T. Mizrahi & L. E. Davis (Eds.). *Encyclopedia of Social Work,* 20th ed., Washington, DC: NASW Press, *4,* 61–66.

Higgins, P. C., & Johnson, J. M. (1988). *Personal Sociology.* New York, NY: Praeger.

Hilton, T., & DeJong, C. (2010). Homeless in God's Country: Coping Behaviors and Felt Experiences of the Rural Homeless. *Journal of Qualitative and Ethnographic Research, 5,* 12–30.

Hilton, T., DeJong, C., & Trella, D. (2011, September 16). Homelessness and the Family in the U.P.: Presentation for the Center for Upper Peninsula Studies' Sonderegger Symposium.

Hirschel, J., Hutchison, I. III, & Dean, C. (1992). The Failure of Arrest to Deter Spouse Abuse. *Journal of Research in Crime and Delinquency, 29,* 7–33.

Holstein, J. A., & Gubrium, J. F. (1994). Phenomenology, Ethnomethodology, and Interpretive Practice. In N. Denzin & Y. Lincoln (Eds.). *Handbook of Qualitative Research.* Thousand Oaks, CA: Sage.

Holstein, J. A., & Gubrium, J. F. (1995). *The Active Interview.* Thousand Oaks, CA: Sage.

Holstein, J. A., & Gubrium, J. F. (Eds.). (2003). *Inside Interviewing: Conceptual Issues and Methodological Considerations.* Thousand Oaks, CA: Sage.

Holsti, O. R. (1969). *Content Analysis for the Social Sciences and Humanities.* Reading, MA: Addison-Wesley.

Holtgrave, D. R., (Ed.). (1998). *Handbook of Economic Evaluation of HIV Prevention Programs.* New York, NY: Plenum Press.

Honey, M. (1984). *Creating Rosie the Riveter: Class, Gender, and Propaganda.* Amherst, MA: University of Massachusetts Press.

Hooker, E. (1957). The Adjustment of the Male Overt Homosexual. *Journal of Projective Techniques, 21,* 18–31.

Horner, R. H., Carr, E. G., Halle, J., Odom, S., & Wolery, M. (2005). The Use of Single-Subject Research to Identify Evidence-Based Practice in Special Education. *Exceptional Children, 71,* 165–179.

Horowitz, R. (1987). Community Tolerance of Gang Violence. *Social Problems, 34* (December, 1987), 437–450.

Huber, B. (1981). New Human Subjects Policies Announced; Exemptions Outlined. *ASA Footnotes, 9*, 1.

Hudson, W. W., & McMurtry, S. L. (1997). Comprehensive Assessment in Social Work Practice: The Multi-Problem Screening Inventory. *Research on Social Work Practice, 7* (January, 1997), 79–98.

Hummel-Rossi, B., & Ashdown, J. (2002). The State of Cost-Benefit and Cost-Effectiveness Analyses in Education. *Review of Educational Research, 72* (Spring, 2002), 1–30.

Humphreys, L. (1970). *Tearoom Trade: Impersonal Sex in Public Places.* Chicago, IL: Aldine-Atherton.

Hyman, H. (1954). *Interviewing in Social Research.* Chicago, IL: University of Chicago Press.

Iannacchione, V. G. (2011). Research Synthesis: The Changing Role of Address-Based Sampling in Survey Research. *Public Opinion Quarterly, 75* (Fall, 2011), 556–575.

Innes, R.A. (2009). Wait a Second, Who are you Anyways? The Insider/Outsider Debate of American Indian Studies. *American Indian Quarterly, 33*, 440–461.

Irwin, D. M., & Bushnell, M. M. (1980). *Observational Strategies for Child Study.* New York, NY: Holt, Rinehart & Winston.

Israel, T. (2002). Studying Sexuality: Strategies for Surviving Stigma. *Feminism & Psychology, 12*, 256–260.

James, J., & Bolstein, R. (1990). The Effect of Monetary Incentives and Follow-Up Mailings on the Response Rate and Response Quality in Mail Surveys. *Public Opinion Quarterly, 54*, 346–361.

Janssen, P. P., Schaufeli, W. B., & Houkes, I. (1999). Work-Related and Individual Determinants of the Three Burnout Dimensions. *Work and Stress, 13*, 74–86.

Jayaratne, S., & Levy, R. (1979). *Empirical Clinical Practice.* New York, NY: Columbia University Press.

Jeger, A. M., & Slotnick, R. S. (1982). Community Mental Health: Toward a Behavioral-Ecological Perspective. In A. M. Jeger & R. S. Slotnick (Eds.). *Community Mental Health and Behavioral Ecology.* New York, NY: Plenum.

Jekielek, S. M. (1998). Parental Conflict, Marital Disruption, and Children's Emotional Well-Being. *Social Forces, 76*, 905–935.

Jenkins-Hall, K., & Osborn, C. A. (1994). The Conduct of Socially Sensitive Research: Sex Offenders as Participants. *Criminal Justice and Behavior, 21*, 325–340.

Joe, G. W., Broome, K. M., Rowan-Szal, G. A., & Simpson, D. D. (2002). Measuring Patient Attributes and Engagement in Treatment. *Journal of Substance Abuse Treatment, 22* (June, 2002), 183–196.

Johnson, F. C. (1981). Practice versus Research: Issues in Teaching of Single-Subject Research Skills. *Journal of Education for Social Work, 17*, 62–68.

Joint Initiative of Mental Health Professional Organizations. (2003). *Mental Health Bill of Rights Project: Principles for the Provision of Mental Health and Substance Abuse Treatment Services.* National Association of Social Workers. Retrieved from http://www.naswdc.org/practice/behavioral_health/mental.asp.

Jones, J. H. (1992). *Bad Blood: The Tuskegee Syphilis Experiment.* New York, NY: Free Press.

Jones, N. J., & Bennell, C. (2007). The Development and Validation of Statistical Prediction Rules for Discriminating Between Genuine and Simulated Suicide Notes. *Archives of Suicide Research, 11*, 219–233.

Jonson-Reid, M., & Drake, B. (2008). Multisector Longitudinal Databases: An Indispensable Tool for Evidence-Based Policy for Maltreated Children and Their Families. *Child Maltreatment, 13*, (November, 2008), 392–399.

Jorgensen, D. (1989). *Participant Observation: A Methodology for Human Studies.* Newbury Park, CA: Sage.

Jory, B. (2004). The Intimate Justice Scale: An Instrument to Screen for Psychological Abuse and Physical Violence in Clinical Practice. *Journal of Marital and Family Therapy, 30* (January, 2004), 29–44.

Kadushin, A., & Kadushin, G. (1997). *The Social Work Interview: A Guide for Human Service Professionals*, 4th ed. New York, NY: Columbia University Press, 1997.

Kalra, V. S., Fieldhouse, E. A., & Alam, S. (2001). Avoiding the New Deal: A Case Study of Nonparticipation by Minority Ethnic Young People. *Youth & Policy, 72* (Summer, 2001), 63–79.

Kamerman, J. B. (1988). *Death in the Midst of Life: Social and Cultural Influences on Death, Grief, and Mourning.* Englewood Cliffs, NJ: Prentice Hall.

Kang, M. (1997). The Portrayal of Women's Images in Magazine Advertisements: Goffman's Gender Analysis Revisited. *Sex Roles, 37,* 979–996.

Kaplowitz, M. D., Hadlock, T. D., & Levine, R. (2004). A Comparison of Web and Mail Survey Response Rates. *Public Opinion Quarterly, 68,* 94–101.

Karoly, L. A., et al. (1998). *Investing in Our Children: What We Know and Don't Know about the Costs and Benefits of Early Childhood Interventions.* Santa Monica, CA: Rand.

Katz, J. (1972). *Experimentation with Human Beings.* New York, NY: Russell Sage Foundation.

Kazdin, A. E. (2010). *Single-Case Research Designs,* 2nd ed. New York, NY: Oxford University Press.

Kelle, U. (2004). Computer-Assisted Analysis of Qualitative Data. In U. Flick, E. von Kardoff, & I. Steinke (Eds.). *A Companion to Qualitative Research.* Thousand Oaks, CA: Sage.

Kellogg Foundation. (2004). *Logic Model Development Guide: Using Logic Models to Bring Together Planning, Evaluation, and Action.* Battle Creek, Mich.: W. K. Kellogg Foundation.

Kelly, J. R., & McGrath, J. E. (1988). *On Time and Method.* Beverly Hills, CA: Sage.

Kemeny, J. G. (1959). *A Philosopher Looks at Science.* Princeton, NJ: Van Nostrand.

Kenny, G. K. (1986). The Metric Properties of Rating Scales Employed in Evaluation of Research: An Empirical Examination. *Evaluation Review, 10* (June, 1986), 397–408.

Kimmel, A. (1988). *Ethics and Values in Applied Social Research.* Newbury Park, CA: Sage.

Kimmel, A. J. (2007). *Ethical Issues in Behavioral Research: Basic and Applied Perspectives,* 2nd ed. Malden, MA: Blackwell Publishing.

King, N. M. P., Henderson, G. E., & J. Stein, (Eds.). (1999). *Beyond Regulations: Ethics in Human Subjects Research.* Chapel Hill N.C.: University of North Carolina Press.

Kirk, J., & Miller, M. L. (1986). *Reliability and Validity in Qualitative Research.* Beverly Hills, CA: Sage.

Kirk, S., & Kutchins, H. (1992). *The Selling of DSM: The Rhetoric of Science in Psychiatry.* New York: Aldine de Gruyter.

Kirk, S. A., & Reid, W. J. (2002). *Science and Social Work: A Critical Appraisal.* New York, NY: Columbia University Press.

Kirsch, I. S., et al. (1993). *Adult Literacy in America: A First Look at the Results of the National Adult Literacy Survey.* Washington, DC: U.S. Department of Education, NCES.

Kish, L. (1965). *Survey Sampling.* New York, NY: Wiley.

Kline, D. (1988). The Power of the Placebo. *Hippocrates: The Magazine of Health and Medicine, 2* (May/June, 1988), 24–26.

Klockars, C. B. (1979). Dirty Hands and Deviant Subjects. In C. B. Klockars & F. W. O'Connor (Eds.). *Deviance and Decency: The Ethics of Research with Human Subjects.* Beverly Hills, CA: Sage.

Knorr, K. (1981). *The Manufacture of Knowledge: An Essay on the Constructivist and Contextual Nature of Science.* Oxford: Pergamon Press.

Koch, N. S., & Emrey, J. A. (2001). The Internet and Opinion Measurement: Surveying Marginalized Populations. *Social Science Quarterly, 82,* 131–138.

Kogan, L. S. (1975). Principles of Measurement. In N. A. Polansky (Ed.). *Social Work Research.* Chicago, IL: University of Chicago Press.

Korbin, J. E. (1987). Child Maltreatment in Cross-Cultural Perspective: Vulnerable Children and Circumstances. In R. J. Gelles & J. B. Lancaster (Eds.). *Child Abuse and Neglect: Biosocial Dimensions.* New York, NY: Aldine de Gruyter.

Korn, J. H. (1997). *Illusions of Reality: A History of Deception in Social Psychology.* Albany, NY: State University of New York Press.

Krasucki, C., Ryan, P., Ertan, T., Howard, R., Lindesay, J., & Mann, A. (1999). The FEAR: A Rapid Screening Instrument for Generalized Anxiety in Elderly Primary Care Attenders. *International Journal of Geriatric Psychiatry, 14,* 60–68.

Krathwohl, D. R. (1988). *How to Prepare a Research Proposal: Guidelines for Funding and Dissertations in the Social and Behavioral Sciences,* 3rd ed. New York, NY: Distributed by Syracuse University Press.

Krippendorff, K. (2012). *Content Analysis: An Introduction to Its Methodology*, 3rd ed. Thousand Oaks, CA: Sage.

Krueger, R. A., & Casey, M. A. (2008). *Focus Groups: A Practical Guide for Applied Research*, 4th ed. Thousand Oaks, CA: Sage.

Kuhn, T. (1970). *The Structure of Scientific Revolutions*, 2nd ed. Chicago, IL: University of Chicago Press.

Kuo, W. H., & Tsai, Y. (1986). Social Networking, Hardiness, and Immigrants' Mental Health. *Journal of Health and Social Behavior, 27* (June, 1986), 133–149.

Lally, J. J. (1977). Social Determinants of Differential Allocation of Resources to Disease Research: A Comparative Analysis of Crib Death and Cancer Research. *Journal of Health and Social Behavior, 18*, 125–138.

Landrine, H. (1985). Race and Class Stereotypes of Women. *Sex Roles, 13* (July, 1985), 65–75.

Lane, S. J., Heddle, N. M., Arnold, E., & Walker, I. (2006). A Review of Randomized Controlled Trials Comparing the Effectiveness of Hand Held Computers with Paper Methods for Data Collection. *BMC Medical Informatics and Decision-Making, 6*, 1–10.

Lansford, J. E., Ceballo, R., Abbey, A., & Stewart, A. J. (2001). Does Family Structure Matter? A Comparison of Adoptive, Two-Parent Biological, Single-Mother, Stepfather, and Stepmother Households. *Journal of Marriage and Family, 63*, 840–851.

Lantz, H. R., Schmitt, R., Britton, M., & Snyder, E. C. (1968). Pre-Industrial Patterns in the Colonial Family in America: A Content Analysis of Colonial Magazines. *American Sociological Review, 33*, 413–426.

Lavrakas, P. J., Shuttles, C. D., Steeh, C., & Fienberg, H. (2007). The State of Surveying Cell Phone Numbers in the United States: 2007 and Beyond. *Public Opinion Quarterly, 71*, 840–854.

Lawless, E. J. (1991). Methodology and Research Notes: Women's Life Stories and Reciprocal Ethnography as Feminist and Emergent. *Journal of Folklore Research, 28*, 35–60.

Leahey, E. (2008). Overseeing Research Practice: The Case of Data Editing. *Science, Technology, and Human Values, 33* (September, 2008, 605–630.

Lee, R. M. (2000). *Unobtrusive Methods in Social Research*. Philadelphia, PA: Open University Press.

Lenihan, K. (1977). *Unlocking the Second Gate*. Department of Labor R&D [Monograph] 45. Washington, DC: U.S. Government Printing Office.

Leo, R. A. (1995). Trial and Tribulations: Courts, Ethnography, and the Need for an Evidentiary Privilege for Academic Researchers. *American Sociologist, 26* (Spring, 1995), 113–134.

Leo, R. A. (1996). The Ethics of Deceptive Research Roles Reconsidered: A Response to Kai Erikson. *American Sociologist, 27* (Spring, 1996), 122–128.

Leung, P., Erich, S., & Kanenberg, H. (2005). A Comparison of Family Functioning in Gay/Lesbian, Heterosexual, and Special Needs Adoptions. *Children and Youth Services Review, 27*, (September, 2005), 1031–1044.

Levin, J. (1993). Publishing in the Journal of Educational Psychology: Reflections at Midstream. *Journal of Educational Psychology, 85*, 3–6.

Levin, J. R. (1992). Single-Case Research Design and Analysis: Comments and Concerns. In T.R. Kratochwill & J. R. Levin (Eds.). *Single-Case Research Design and Analysis: New Directions for Psychology and Education*. Hillsdale, NJ: Lawrence Erlbaum.

Levin, J., & Spates, J. L. (1970). Hippie Values: An Analysis of the Underground Press. *Youth and Society, 2*, 59–73.

Lewis, K. G. (1980). Children of Lesbians: Their Point of View. *Social Work, 25*, 198–203.

Likert, R. A. (1932). Technique for the Measurement of Attitudes. *Archives of Psychology, 21*, 140.

Lincoln, Y. S., Lynham, S. A., & Guba, E. G. (2011). Paradigmatic Controversies, Contradictions, and Emerging Confluences, Revisited. In N. K. Denzin & Y. S. Lincoln (Eds.). *Handbook of Qualitative Research*, 4th ed. Thousand Oaks, CA: Sage.

Link, M. W., Battaglia, M. P., Frankel, M. R., Osborn, L., & Mokdad, A. H. (2008). A Comparison of Address-Based Sampling (ABS) Versus Random-Digit Dialing (RDD) For General Population Surveys. *Public Opinion Quarterly, 72*, 6–27.

Lipsey, M. W. (1997). Design Sensitivity: Statistical Power for Applied Experimental Research.

In L. Bickman & D. Rog (Eds.). *Handbook of Applied Social Research Methods*. Thousand Oaks, CA: Sage.

Locke, L. F., Silverman, S. J., & Spirduso, W. W. (2010). *Reading and Understanding Research*, 3rd ed. Thousand Oaks, CA: Sage.

Locke, L. F., Spirduso, W. W., & Silverman, S. J. (2007). *Proposals that Work: A Guide for Planning Dissertations and Grant Proposals*, 5th ed. Thousand Oaks, CA: Sage.

Lockhart, L. L. (1991). Spousal Violence: A Cross-Racial Perspective. In R. L. Hampton (Ed.). *Black Family Violence: Current Research and Theory*. Lexington, MA: Lexington Books.

Lofland, J., Snow, D., Anderson, L., & Lofland, L. H. (2006). *Analyzing Social Settings*, 4th ed. Belmont, CA: Wadsworth/Cengage Learning.

Loseke, D. R. (2001). Lived Realities and Formula Stories of 'Battered Women'. In J. F. Gubrium & J. A. Holstein (Eds.). *Institutional Selves: Troubled Identities in a Postmodern World*. New York, NY: Oxford University Press.

Lynch, K. B., et al. (1998). Successful Program Development Using Implementation Evaluation. *Journal of Prevention and Intervention in the Community*, *17*, 51–64.

Lynch, M., & Bogen, D. (1997). Sociology's Asociological "Core": An Examination of Textbook Sociology in Light of the Sociology of Scientific Knowledge. *American Sociological Review*, *62*, 481–493.

MacGregor, S. (2011). The Impact of Research on Policy in the Drugs Field. *Methodological Innovations Online*, *6*(1), 40–57.

Mactavish, J. B., Mahon, M. J., & Lutfiyya, Z. M. (2000). "I Can Speak for Myself": Involving Individuals with Intellectual Disabilities as Research Participants. *Mental Retardation*, *38* (June, 2000), 216–227.

Magura, S., & Moses, B. S. (1986). *Outcome Measures for Child Welfare Services: Theory and Applications*. Washington, DC: Child Welfare League of America.

Mandell, N. (1988). The Least-Adult Role in Studying Children. *Journal of Contemporary Ethnography*, *16*, 433–467.

Manderson, L., Bennett, E., & Andajani-Sutjahjo, S. (2006). The Social Dynamics of the Interview: Age, Class, and Gender. *Qualitative Health Research*, *16*, 1317–1334.

Manson, S. M. (1986). Recent Advances in American Indian Mental Health Research: Implications for Clinical Research and Training. In M. R. Miranda & H. H. L. Kitano (Eds.). *Mental Health Research and Practice in Minority Communities: Development of Culturally Sensitive Training Programs*. Rockville, MD: U.S. Department of Health and Human Services, DHHS Publication (ADM), 86–1466.

Margolin, G., et al. (2005). Ethical Issues in Couple and Family Research. *Journal of Family Psychology*, *19*, 157–167.

Marin, G., & VanOss Marin, B. (1991). *Research with Hispanic Populations*. Newbury Park, CA: Sage.

Marquart, J. W. (2001). Doing Research in Prison: The Strengths and Weaknesses of Full Participation as a Guard. In J. M. Miller & R. Tewksbury (Eds.). *Extreme Methods: Innovative Approaches to Social Science Research*. Boston, MA: Allyn & Bacon.

Marshall, E. (2000). How Prevalent Is Fraud? That Million-Dollar Question. *Science*, *290* (December, 2000), 1662.

Martinez, T. A. (1997). Popular Culture as Oppositional Culture: Rap as Resistance. *Sociological Perspectives*, *40*, 265–286.

Martini, R., & Polatajko, H. J. (1998). Verbal Self-Guidance as a Treatment Approach for Children with Developmental Coordination Disorder: A Systematic Replication Study. *Occupational Therapy Journal of Research*, *19* (Fall, 1998). 157–181.

Marx, K. (1964 originally published 1848). *Selected Writings in Sociology and Philosophy*. T. B. Bottomore & M. Rubel (Eds.). Baltimore, MD: Penguin.

Maslach, C. (1979). Burned-Out. In J. R. Folta & E. S. Deck (Eds.). *A Sociological Framework for Patient Care*, 2nd ed. New York, NY: Wiley.

Masters, J., & Hilton, T. (Forthcoming). Return to the Rez: Native Americans Transitioning from Prison. In S. W. Bowman (Ed.). *Race, Ethnicity and the Prison System—Critical Perspectives*. Santa Barbara, CA: ABC-CLIO.

Mathios, A., Avery, R., Bisogni, C., & Shanahan, J. (1998). Alcohol Portrayal on Prime-Time Television: Manifest and Latent Messages. *Journal of Studies on Alcohol, 59*, 305–310.

Maton, K. I., Hrabowski, F. A., & Greif, G. L. (1998). Preparing the Way: A Qualitative Study of High-Achieving African American Males and the Role of the Family. *American Journal of Community Psychology, 26*, 639–668.

Matthews, J., & Cramer, E. P. (2008). Using Technology to Enhance Qualitative Research with Hidden Populations. *The Qualitative Report, 13* (June, 2008), 301–315.

Maxwell, C. D., Garner, J. H., & Fagan, J. A. (2001). The Effects of Arrest on Intimate Partner Violence: New Evidence from the Spousal Assault Replication Program. *Research in Brief*. Washington, DC: National Institute of Justice, U. S. Department of Justice.

Maxwell, J. A. (2012). *Qualitative Research Design: An Interactive Approach*, 3rd ed. Thousand Oaks, CA: Sage.

Mayo, J. K., Hornick, R. C., & McAnany, E. G. (1976). *Educational Reform with Television: The El Salvador Experience*. Palo Alto, CA: Stanford University Press.

McClamroch, K. J. (2011). Evaluating the Usability of Personal Digital Assistants to Collect Behavioral Data on Adolescents with Paradata. *Field Methods, 23*, 219–242.

McCord, J. A. (1978). Thirty-Year Follow-Up of Treatment Effects. *American Psychologist, 33*, 284–289.

McDowell, I. (2006). *Measuring Health: A Guide to Rating Scales and Questionnaires*, 3rd ed. New York, NY: Oxford University Press.

McFall, R. M. (1970). Effects of Self-Monitoring on Normal Smoking Behavior. *Journal of Consulting and Clinical Psychology, 35*, 135–142.

McKillip, J. (1987). *Need Analysis: Tools for Human Services and Education*. Beverly Hills, CA: Sage.

McLanahan, S., & Sandefur, G. (1994). *Growing Up with a Single Parent: What Hurts, What Helps*. Cambridge, MA: Harvard University Press.

McLellan, A. T., et al. (1992). The Fifth Edition of the Addiction Severity Index. *Journal of Substance Abuse Treatment, 9*, 199–213.

Mendes, H. A. (1976). Single Fatherhood. *Social Work, 21*, 308–312.

Merriam, S. B. (1998). *Qualitative Research and Case Study Applications in Education*. San Francisco, CA: Jossey-Bass.

Michael, R. T., & O'Muircheartaigh, C. (2008). Design Priorities and Disciplinary Perspectives: The Case of the U.S. National Children's Study. *Journal of the Royal Statistical Society*: Series A, *171*(2), 465–480.

Miles, M. B., & Huberman, A. M. (1994). *Qualitative Data Analysis: An Expanded Sourcebook*, 2nd ed. Thousand Oaks, CA: Sage.

Milgram, S. (1974). *Obedience to Authority: An Experimental View*. New York, NY: Harper & Row.

Miller, D. C., & Salkind, N. J. (2002). *Handbook of Research Design and Social Measurement*, 6th ed. Thousand Oaks, CA: Sage.

Miller, J. M., & Tewksbury, R. (2001). *Extreme Methods: Innovative Approaches to Social Science Research*. Boston, MA: Allyn & Bacon.

Miller, L. P. (1987). The Application of Research to Practice: A Critique. *American Behavioral Scientist, 30* (September/October, 1987), 70–80.

Millum, J., & Emanuel, E. J. (2007). The Ethics of International Research with Abandoned Children. *Science, 318* (December 21, 2007), 1874–1875.

Miner, J. T., & Miner, L. E. (2003). A Guide to Proposal Planning and Writing. In *Directory of Research Grants*, 28th ed. Westport, Conn.: Oryx Press.

Mitsos, S. B. (1961). Personal Constructs and the Semantic Differential. *Journal of Abnormal and Social Psychology, 62*, 433–434.

Moe, K. (1984). Should the Nazi Research Data Be Cited? *Hastings Center Report, 14* (December, 1984), 5–7.

Molina, E. (2000). Informal Non-Kin Networks among Homeless Latino and African-American Men: Form and Functions. *American Behavioral Scientist, 43* (January, 2000),: 663–685.

Mondello, M., Bradley, J., McLaughlin, T., & Shore, N. (2009). Cost of Rural Homelessness: Rural Permanent Supportive Housing Cost Analysis. Corporation for Supportive Housing, Maine

Department of Health and Human Services. Retrieved from http://www.mainehousing.org/data-reports/Housing-Reports.

Montaquila, J., Hsu, V., Brick, J. M., English, N., & O'Muircheartaigh, C. (2009). A Comparative Evaluation of Traditional Listing vs. Address-Based Sampling Frames: Matching With Field Investigation of Discrepancies. *Proceedings of the Survey Research Methods Section*, American Statistical Association, 4855–4862

Moos, M., Bartholomew, N., & Lohr, K. (2003). Counseling in the Clinical Setting to Prevent Unintended Pregnancy: An Evidence-Based Research Agenda. *Contraception*, 67, 115–132.

Morash, M., & Greene, J. R. (1986). Evaluating Women on Patrol: A Critique of Contemporary Wisdom. *Evaluation Review*, 10 (April, 1986), 230–255.

Morgan, D. L. (1996). *Focus Groups as Qualitative Research*, 2nd ed. Thousand Oaks, CA: Sage.

Moser, C. A., & Kalton, G. (1972). *Survey Methods in Social Investigation*, 2nd ed. New York, NY: Basic Books.

Mullen, E. J., Bledsoe, S. E., & Bellamy, J. L. (2008). Implementing Evidence-Based Social Work Practice. *Research on Social Work Practice*, 18 (July 2008), 325–338.

Murray, L., Donovan, R., Kail, B. L., & Medvene L. J. (1980). Protecting Human Subjects during Social Work Research: Researchers' Opinions. *Social Work Research and Abstracts*, 16, 25–30.

Mushquash, C. J., & Bova, D. L. (2007). Cross-Cultural Assessment and Measurement Issues. *Journal of Developmental Disabilities*, 13, 53–65.

Nabors, L. A., Reynolds, M. W., & Weist, M. D. (2000). Qualitative Evaluation of a High School Mental Health Program. *Journal of Youth and Adolescence*, 29 (February, 2000), 1–13.

Nagel, E. (1961). *The Structure of Science*. New York, NY: Harcourt, Brace & World.

NASW Press Staff. (2009). *An Author's Guide to Social Work Journals*, 5th ed. Washington, DC: NASW Press.

National Association of Social Workers. (2008). *Code of Ethics*, rev. ed. Retrieved from http://www.socialworkers.org/pubs/code/code.asp (National Association of Social Workers).

National Cancer Institute. (1998). *Certificates of Confidentiality: Background Information and Application Procedures*. Washington DC: U.S. Department of Health and Human Services.

National Commission for the Protection of Human Subjects of Biomedical and Behavioral Research. (1978). *The Belmont Report: Ethical Principles and Guidelines for the Protection of Human Subjects of Research*. Washington, DC: Department of Health, Education, and Welfare.

National Institute of Justice. (2003). *Funding Opportunities: National Institute of Justice Awards in Fiscal Year 2002*. Retrieved from http://www.nij.gov/funding/awards//2002.htm.

National Institutes of Health. (2012, April 15). *NIH Data Sharing Policy*. Washington, DC: Office of Extramural Research. Retrieved from http://grants.nih.gov/grants/policy/data_sharing.

Navarro, A. E., Wilbur, K. H., Yonashiro, J., & Homeier, D. C. (2010). Do We Really Need Another Meeting? Lessons from the Los Angeles County Elder Abuse Forensic Center. *The Gerontologist*, 50 (5), 702–711.

Neelon, V. J., Champagne, M. T., Carlso, J. R., & Funk, S. G. (1996). The NEECHAN Confusion Scale: Construction, Validation, and Clinical Testing. *Nursing Research*, 45 (November/December, 1996), 324–330.

Nelsen, J. (1994). Ethics, Gender, and Ethnicity in Single-Case Research and Evaluation. *Journal of Social Service Research*, 18, 139–152.

Nelsen, J. C. (1981). Issues in Single-Subject Research for Non-behaviorists. *Social Work Research and Abstracts*, 17, 31–37.

Nelson-Gardell, D. (1997). Child Report of Treatment Issue Resolution: Pilot of a Rapid Assessment Instrument. *Child Abuse and Neglect*, 21, 309–318.

Neuendorf, K. A. (2002). *The Content Analysis Guidebook*. Thousand Oaks, CA: Sage.

Newman, J. C., DesJerlais, D. C., Turner, C. F., & Gribble, J. (2009). The Differential Effects of Face-to-Face and Computer Interview Modes. *American Journal of Public Health*, 92 (February, 2002), 294ff.

Nezu, A. M., & Nezu, C. M. (Eds.) (2008). *Evidence-Based Outcome Research: A Practical Guide to Conducting Randomized Controlled Trials for*

Psychosocial Interventions. New York, NY: Oxford University Press.

Nielson, J. M., (Ed.). (2009). *Feminist Research Methods*. Boulder, Colo.: Westview Press.

Nomaguchi, K. M. (2009). Change in Work-Family Conflict Among Employed Parents Between 1977 and 1997. *Journal of Marriage and Family*, 71 (February, 2009), 15–32.

Norwegian Social Science Data Services. (2012). *About Nesstar*. Bergen, Norway. Retrieved from http://www.nesstar.com.

Nugent, W. R., Sieppert, J. D., & Hudson, W. (2001). *Practice Evaluation for the 21st Century*. Belmont, CA: Wadsworth.

Nyden, P., Figert, A.., Shibley, M., & Burrows D. (1997). *Building Community: Social Science in Action*. Thousand Oaks, CA: Pine Forge Press.

O'Connell, A. A. (2000). Sampling for Evaluation: Issues and Strategies for Community-Based HIV Prevention Programs. *Evaluation and the Health Professions*, 23 (June, 2000), 212–234.

Oeye, C., Bjelland, A. K., & Skorpen, A. (2007). Doing Participant Observation in a Psychiatric Hospital—Research Ethics Resumed. *Social Science & Medicine*, 65, 2296–2306.

Office for Civil Rights. *Health Information Privacy*. Washington, DC: Department of Health and Human Services. Retrieved from http://www.hhs.gov/ocr/hipaa.

Office of Inspector General. (September, 2009). *IHS Contract Health Services Program: Overpayments and Potential Savings*. Washington, DC: Department of Health and Human Services.

Office of Research Integrity. (2010). *Annual Report 2009*. Washington, DC: Department of Health and Human Services. Retrieved from http://ori.hhs.gov.

Ogles, B. M., Lambert, M. J., & Masters, K. S. (1996). *Assessing Outcome in Clinical Practice*. Boston, MA: Allyn & Bacon.

Oksenberg, L., Coleman, L., & Cannell, C. F. (1986). Interviewers' Voices and Refusal Rates in Telephone Surveys. *Public Opinion Quarterly*, 50 (Spring, 1986), 97–111.

Ollendick, T. H. (1995). Cognitive Behavioral Treatment of Panic Disorder with Agoraphobia in Adolescents: A Multiple Baseline Design Analysis. *Behavior Therapy*, 26, 517–553.

Olsen, V. (1994). Feminism and Models of Qualitative Research. In N. Denzin & Y. Lincoln (Eds.). *Handbook of Qualitative Research,*. Thousand Oaks, CA: Sage.

O'Neill, P. (2005). The Ethics of Problem Definition. *Canadian Psychologist*, 46, 13–20.

Orme, J. G., & Tolman, R. M. (1986). The Statistical Power of a Decade of Social Work Education Research. *Social Service Review*, 60, 619–632.

Orme, J. G., & Combs-Orme, T. D. (1986). Statistical Power and Type II Errors in Social Work Research. *Social Work Research and Abstracts*, 22, 3–10.

Orne, M. T. On the Social Psychology of the Psychological Experiment: With Particular Reference to Demand Characteristics and Their Implications. *American Psychologist*, 17, 776–783.

Orr, L. L. (1998). *Social Experimentation: Evaluating Public Programs with Experimental Methods*. Thousand Oaks, CA: Sage.

Ortner, S. B. (1984). The Founding of the First Sherpa Nunnery and the Problem of "Women" as an Analytic Category. In V. Patraka and L. Tilly (Eds.). *Feminist Re-visions.*. Ann Arbor, Mich.: University of Michigan Women's Studies Program.

Osgood, C. E., Suci, G. J., & Tannenbaum, P. H. (1957). *The Measurement of Meaning*. Urbana, IL.: University of Illinois Press.

Parker, A. T., Grimmett, E., & Summers, S. (2008). Evidence-Based Communication Practices for Children with Visual Impairments and Additional Disabilities: An Examination of Single-Subject Design Studies. *Journal of Visual Impairment & Blindness*, 102, 540–552.

Patton, M. Q. (1981). *Creative Evaluation*. Beverly Hills, CA: Sage.

Patton, M. Q. (1987). Evaluation's Political Inherency: Practical Implications for Design and Use. In D. J. Palumbo (Ed.). *The Politics of Program Evaluation.*. Newbury Park, CA: Sage.

Patton, M. Q. (1982). *Practical Evaluation*. Beverly Hills, CA: Sage.

Patton, M. Q. (2002). *Qualitative Research and Evaluation Methods*, 3rd ed. Thousand Oaks, CA: Sage.

Paul, R. (1993). *Critical Thinking: What Every Person Needs to Survive in a Rapidly Changing World*.

Rohnert Park, CA: Foundation for Critical Thinking.

Pepler, D. J., & Craig, W. M. (1995). A Peek behind the Fence: Naturalistic Observations of Aggressive Children with Remote Audiovisual Recording. *Developmental Psychology*, 31, 548–553.

Pescosolido, B. A., Grauerholz, E., & Milkie, M. A. (1997). Culture and Conflict: The Portrayal of Blacks in U.S. Children's Picture Books through the Midand Late-Twentieth Century. *American Sociological Review*, 62, 443–464.

Peterson, R. R. (1996). A Re-evaluation of the Economic Consequences of Divorce. *American Sociological Review*, 61, 528–536.

Peterson, S., & Lach, M. (1990). Gender Stereotypes in Children's Books: Their Prevalence and Influence on Cognitive and Affective Development. *Gender and Education*, 2, 185–197.

Peterson, S., & Kroner, T. (1992). Gender Biases in Textbooks for Introductory Psychology and Human Development. *Psychology of Women Quarterly*, 16, 17–36.

Peyrot, M. (1985). Coerced Voluntarism: The Micropolitics of Drug Treatment. *Urban Life*, 13 (January, 1985), 343–365.

Phillips, K. A., Friedman, M. J., Stein, D. J., & Craske, M. (2010). Special DSM-V Issues on Anxiety, Obsessive-Compulsive Spectrum, Posttraumatic and Dissociative Disorders. *Depression and Anxiety*, 27, 91–92.

Piliavin, I., Masters, S., & Corbett, T. (1977). Factors Influencing Errors in AFDC Payments. *Social Work Research and Abstracts*, 15, 3–17.

Pini, B. (2005). Interviewing Men: Gender and the Collection and Interpretation of Qualitative Data. *Journal of Sociology*, 41, 201–216.

Polsky, N. (1967). *Hustlers, Beats, and Others*. Chicago, IL: Aldine.

Pound, E. T. (2000, July 13). Nurse's Clues Shut Down Research. *USA Today*, 3A.

Powdermaker, H. (1966). *Stranger and Friend: The Way of an Anthropologist*. New York, NY: Norton,.

Prentice, D. A., & Miller, D. T. (1998). When Small Effects Are Impressive. In A. E. Kazdin (Ed.). *Methodological Issues and Strategies in Clinical Research*, 2nd ed. Washington, DC: American Psychological Association.

Prothro, J. W. (1956). Verbal Shifts in the American Presidency: A Content Analysis. *American Political Science Review*, 50, 726–739.

Purcell, P., & Stewart, L. (1990). Dick and Jane in 1989. *Sex Roles*, 22(3–4), 177–185.

Rabinow, P., & Sullivan, W. M. (Eds.). (1987). *Interpretive Social Science: A Second Look*. Berkeley, CA: University of California Press.

Rafferty, J., & Steyaert, J. (2009). Editorial: Social Work in the Digital Age (Special Issue). *British Journal of Social Work*, 39(4), 589–598.

Rapee, R. M., Craske, M. G., & Barlow, D. H. (1990). Subject-Described Features of Panic Attacks Using Self-Monitoring. *Journal of Anxiety Disorders*, 4, 171–181.

Rapp, L. A., Dulmus, C. N., Wodarski, J. S., & Feit, M. D. (1999). Screening of Substance Abuse in Public Welfare and Child Protective Service Clients: A Comparative Study of Rapid Assessment Instruments vs. the SASSI. *Journal of Addictive Diseases*, 18, 83–88.

Ratzan, R. M. (1981). The Experiment that Wasn't: A Case Report in Clinical Geriatric Research. *Gerontologist*, 21, 297–302.

Rea, L., & Parker, R. (2005). *Designing and Conducting Survey Research*, 3rd ed. San Francisco, CA: Jossey-Bass.

Reamer, F. G. (2006). *Social Work Values and Ethics*, 3rd ed. New York, NY: Columbia University Press.

Reece, R., & Siegal, H. (1986). *Studying People: A Primer in the Ethics of Social Research*. Macon, GA: Mercer University Press.

Reinharz, S. (1992). *Feminist Methods in Social Research*. New York, NY: Oxford University Press.

Reiss, A. K., & Rhodes, L. (1967). An Empirical Test of Differential Association Theory. *Journal of Research in Crime and Delinquency*, 4, 28–42.

Reverby, S. M. (Ed.). (2000). *Tuskegee's Truths: Rethinking the Tuskegee Syphilis Study*. Chapel Hill, N.C.: University of North Carolina Press.

Reynolds, P. D. (1979). *Ethical Dilemmas and Social Science Research*. San Francisco, CA: Jossey-Bass.

Ridley, S. M., McWilliam, R. A., & Oates, C. S. (2000). Observed Engagement as an Indicator of Child Care Program Quality. *Early Education and Development*, 11, 133–146.

Riedel, M. (2000). *Research Strategies for Secondary Data: A Perspective for Criminology and Criminal Justice.* Thousand Oaks, CA: Sage.

Robinson, J., Shaver, P., & Wrightsman, L. (Eds.) (1991). *Measures of Personality and Social Psychological Attitudes.* San Diego, CA: Academic Press.

Roscoe, P. B. (1995). The Perils of "Positivism" in Cultural Anthropology. *American Anthropologist, 97,* 492–504.

Rosen, A. (1996). The Scientific Practitioner Revisited: Some Obstacles and Prerequisites for Fuller Implementation in Practice. *Social Work Research, 20* (June, 1996), 105–111.

Rosenhan, D. L. (1973). On Being Sane in Insane Places. *Science, 179,* 250–258.

Rosenthal, R. (1967). Covert Communication in the Psychological Experiment. *Psychological Bulletin, 67,* 356–367.

Rosenthal, R. (1991). Replication in Behavioral Research. In J. Neuliep (Ed.). *Replication Research in the Social Science..* Newbury Park, CA: Sage.

Rosnow, R. L. (1993). The Volunteer Problem Revisited. In P. D. Blanck (Ed.). *Interpersonal Expectations: Theory, Research, and Applications.* New York, NY: Cambridge University Press.

Rossi, P. H., Lipsey, M. W.. & Freeman, H. E. (2004). *Evaluation: A Systematic Approach,* 7th ed. Thousand Oaks, CA: Sage.

Rossi, P. H., Berk, R. A., & Lenihan, K. J. (1980). *Money, Work, and Crime: Experimental Evidence.* New York, NY: Academic Press.

Rudd, M. D., Rajab, M. H., & Orman, D. T. (1996). Effectiveness of an Outpatient Intervention Targeting Suicidal Young Adults: Preliminary Results. *Journal of Consulting and Clinical Psychology, 64,* 179–190.

Ruggles, P. (1990). *Drawing the Line: Alternative Poverty Measures and Their Implications for Public Policy.* Washington, DC: Urban Institute Press.

Runcie, J. F. (1980). *Experiencing Social Research,* rev. ed. Homewood, IL: Dorsey Press.

Russell, B. (1953). On the Notion of Cause, with Applications to the Free-Will Problem. In H. Feigel & M. Brodbeck (Eds.). *Readings in the Philosophy of Science.* New York, NY: Appleton-Century-Crofts.

Sackett, D. L., Straus, S. E., Richardson, W. S., Rosenberg, W., & Haynes, R. B. (2000). *Evidence-Based Medicine: How to Practice and Teach EBM,* 2nd ed. Edinburgh, Scotland: Churchill Livingstone.

Sackett, D. L., Richardson, W. S., Rosenberg, W., & Haynes, R. B. (1997). *Evidence-Based Medicine: How to Practice and Teach EBP.* New York, NY: Churchill Livingstone.

Saltzman, L. E., Fanslow, J. L., McMahon, P. M., & Shelley, G. E. (1999). *Intimate Partner Violence Surveillance: Uniform Definitions and Recommended Data Elements Version 1.0.* Atlanta, GA: Centers for Disease Control and Prevention, National Center for Injury Prevention and Control.

Scarce, R. (2005). *Contempt of Court: A Scholar's Battle for Free Speech From Behind Bars.* Lanham, MD: Altamira Press.

Schafer, A. (1986). On Using Nazi Data: The Case Against. *Dialogue, 25* (Autumn, 1986), 413–419.

Scheaffer, R. L., Mendenhall, W., Ott, R. L., & Gerow, K. G. (2012). *Elementary Survey Sampling,* 7th ed. Belmont, CA: Thomson/Brooks Cole.

Scheper-Hughes, N. (1992). *Death without Weeping: The Violence of Everyday Life in Brazil.* Berkeley, CA: University of California Press.

Schiebinger, L. L. (1999). *Has Feminism Changed Science?* Boston, MA: Harvard University Press.

Schmidt, F. L. (1998). Statistical Significance Testing and Cumulative Knowledge in Psychology: Implications for Training Researchers. In A. E. Kazdin (Ed.). *Methodological Issues and Strategies in Clinical Research,* 2nd ed. Washington, DC: American Psychological Association.

Schonlau, M., et al. (2004). A Comparison Between Responses from a Propensity-Weighted Web Survey and an Identical RDD Survey. *Social Science Computer Review, 22* (Spring, 2004), 128–138.

Schuckit, M.A. (2006). *Drug and Alcohol Abuse: A Clinical Guide to Diagnosis and Treatment,* 6th ed. New York, NY: Springer Verlag.

Schuman, H., & Presser, S. (1979). The Open and Closed Question. *American Sociological Review, 44,* 692–712.

Schutte, N. S., & Malouff, J. M. (1995). *Sourcebook of Adult Assessment Strategies.* New York, NY: Plenum.

Scott, G. (2008). "They Got Their Program, and I Got Mine": A Cautionary Tale Concerning the Ethical Implications of Using Respondent-Driven Sampling to Study Injection Drug Users. *International Journal of Drug Policy, 19,* 42–51.

Scott, J. (1990). *A Matter of Record: Documentary Sources in Social Research.* Oxford, England: Polity Press.

Scott, R. A. (1975). The Selection of Clients by Social Welfare Agencies: The Case of the Blind. In Y. Hasenfeld and R. A. English (Eds.). *Human Service Organizations.* Ann Arbor, Mich.: University of Michigan Press.

Seale, C. (2010). Using Computers to Analyze Qualitative Data. In D. Silverman (Ed.). *Doing Qualitative Research,* 3rd ed.. Thousand Oaks, CA: Sage.

Seidman, I. E. (2006). *Interviewing as Qualitative Research,* 3rd ed. New York, NY: Teachers College Press.

Seiler, L. H., & Hough, R. L. (1970). Empirical Comparisons of the Thurstone and Likert Techniques. In G. F. Summers (Ed.). *Attitude Measurement.* Chicago, IL: Rand McNally.

Semaan, S., Santibanez, S., Garfein, R., Heckathorn, D., & Des Jarlais, D. (2009). Ethical and Regulatory Considerations in HIV Prevention Studies Employing Respondent-Driven Sampling. *International Journal of Drug Policy, 20,* 14–27.

Shadish, W. R., Cook, T. D., & Campbell, D. T. (2002). *Experimental and Quasi-Experimental Designs for Generalized Causal Inference.* Boston, MA: Houghton Mifflin.

Shapin, S. (1995). Here and Everywhere: Sociology of Scientific Knowledge. *Annual Review of Sociology, 21,* 289–321.

Sheafor, B. W., & Horejsi, C. R. (2012). *Techniques and Guidelines for Social Work Practice,* 9th ed. Boston, MA: Pearson.

Sheley, J. F. (1976). A Study in Self-Defeat: The Public Health Venereal Disease Clinic. *Journal of Sociology and Social Welfare, 4,* 114–124.

Sherman, L. (1992). *Policing Domestic Violence: Experiments and Dilemmas.* New York, NY: Free Press.

Sherman, L., & Berk, R. A. (1984). The Specific Deterrent Effects of Arrest for Domestic Assault. *American Sociological Review, 49,* 261–271.

Shilts, R. (1987). *And the Band Played On: Politics, People, and the AIDS Epidemic.* New York, NY: St. Martin's Press.

Shireman, J. F., & Johnson, P. R. (1986). A Longitudinal Study of Black Adoptions: Single Parent, Transracial, and Traditional. *Social Work, 31* (May/June, 1986), 172–176.

Shulman, L. (1978). A Study of Practice Skills. *Social Work, 23,* 274–280.

Shupe, A. D., Jr., & Bromley, D. G. (1980). Walking a Tightrope: Dilemmas of Participant Observation of Groups in Conflict. *Qualitative Sociology, 2,* 3–21.

Sieber, J. (Ed.). (1991). *Sharing Social Science Data: Advantages and Challenges.* Newbury Park, CA: Sage.

Singer, E., VonThurn, D. R., & Miller, E. R. (1995). Confidentiality and Response: A Quantitative Review of the Experimental Literature. *Public Opinion Quarterly, 59,* 446–459.

Skidmore, W. (1979). *Theoretical Thinking in Sociology.* Cambridge, England: Cambridge University Press.

Skinner, H. A. (1981). Benefits of Sequential Assessment. *Social Work Research and Abstracts, 17,* 21–28.

Smart, B. (1976). *Sociology, Phenomenology, and Marxian Analysis: A Critical Discussion of the Theory and Practice of a Science of Society.* Boston, MA: Routledge & Kegan Paul.

Smith, A. W. (1987). Problems and Progress in the Measurement of Black Public Opinion. *American Behavioral Scientist, 30* (March/April, 1987), 441–455.

Smith, C. P. (2000). Content Analysis and Narrative Analysis. In H. T. Reis & C. M. Judd (Eds.). *Handbook of Research Methods in Social and Personality Psychology.* Cambridge, England: Cambridge University Press.

Smith, H. W. (1981). *Strategies of Social Research,* 2nd ed. Englewood Cliffs, NJ: Prentice Hall.

Smith, M. F. (1989). *Evaluability Assessment: A Practical Approach.* Boston, MA: Kluwer Academic Publishers.

Smith, P. R. (1998). How Do We Understand Practice? A Qualitative Approach. *Families in Society: The Journal of Contemporary Human Services, 79* (September, 1998, 543–550.

Smith, S. H., & McLean, D. D. (1988). *ABCs of Grantsmanship.* Reston, Va.: American Alliance for

Health, Physical Education, Recreation, and Dance.

Smith, T. W. (1987). That which We Call Welfare by Any Other Name Would Smell Sweeter: An Analysis of the Impact of Question Wording on Response Patterns. *Public Opinion Quarterly, 51* (Spring, 1987), 75–83.

Smith, T. W. (1995). The Polls—A Review: The Holocaust Denial Controversy. *Public Opinion Quarterly, 59*, 269–295.

Snow, C. P. (1959). *The Search*. New York, NY: Scribner.

Squire, P. (1988). Why the 1936 Literary Digest Poll Failed. *Public Opinion Quarterly, 52*, 125–133.

Spano, R. (2006). Observer Behavior as a Potential Source of Reactivity: Describing and Quantifying Observer Effects in a Large-Scale Observational Study of Police. *Sociological Methods & Research, 34*(4), 521–553.

Spies, R. A., Carlson, J. F., & Geisinger, K. F. (2010). *The Eighteenth Mental Measurements Yearbook*. Lincoln, NE: University of Nebraska Press.

Stacey, J., & Biblarz, T. J. (2001). (How) Does the Sexual Orientation of Parents Matter? *American Sociological Review,* 159–183.

Staw, B. M. (1981). Some Judgments on the Judgment Calls Approach. *American Behavioral Scientist, 25*, 225–232.

Stein, J. (1964). *Fiddler on the Roof*. New York, NY: Crown.

Stevens, S. S. (Ed.). (1951). *Handbook of Experimental Psychology*. New York, NY: Wiley.

Stott, C., & Reicher, S. (1998). How Conflict Escalates: The Inter-Group Dynamics of Collective Football Crowd "Violence." *Sociology, 32*, 353–377.

Straus, M. A., Hamby, S. L., Boney-McCoy, S., & Sugarman, D. B. (1996). The Revised Conflict Tactics Scales (CTS2): Development and Preliminary Data. *Journal of Family Issues, 17* (May, 1996), 283–316.

Straus, M., & Gelles, R. J. (1988). How Violent are American Families? Estimates from the National Family Violence Resurvey and Other Studies. In G. Hotaling, D. Finkelhor, J. Kirkpatrick, & M. Straus (Eds.). *Family Abuse and Its Consequences: New Directions in Research*. Newbury Park, CA: Sage, 1988.

Strauss, A. L. (1987). *Qualitative Analysis for Social Scientists*. Cambridge, England: Cambridge University Press.

Street, D., Vinter, R. D., & Perrow, C. (1966). *Organizations for Treatment: A Comparative Study of Institutions for Delinquents*. New York, NY: Free Press of Glencoe.

Stum, K., & Chu, M. M. (1999). Gang Prevention and Intervention in a Rural Town in California: At-Risk Youth and the Community Policing School Partnership Program. *Journal of Gang Research, 7* (Fall, 1999), 1–12.

Substance Abuse and Mental Health Services Administration. (April, 2003). *Community Mental Health Services Block Grant Program*. Retrieved from http://www.mentalhealth.org/publications/allpubs/KEN95–0022/default.asp.

Sudman, S. (1976). *Applied Sampling*. New York, NY: Academic Press.

Sudman, S. (1985). Mail Surveys of Reluctant Professionals. *Evaluation Research, 9* (June, 1985), 349–360.

Sudman, S. (1965). Time Allocation on Survey Interviews and Other Field Occupations. *Public Opinion Quarterly, 29*, 638–648.

Sudman, S., & Bradburn, N. M. (1982). *Asking Questions*. San Francisco, CA: Jossey-Bass.

Suen, H. K., & Ary, D. (1986). Poisson Cumulative Probabilities of Systematic Errors in Single-Subject and Multiple-Subject Time Sampling. *Behavioral Assessment, 8*, 155–169.

Sullivan, C. (1991). The Provision of Advocacy Services to Women Leaving Abusive Partners. *Journal of Interpersonal Violence, 6*, 41–54.

Sullivan, T. J. (2012). *Introduction to Social Problems*, 9th ed. Boston, MA: Allyn & Bacon.

Sulzer-Azaroff, B., & Mayer, G. (1991). *Behavior Analysis for Lasting Change*. Fort Worth, TX: Holt, Rinehart and Winston.

Sutherland, E. (1939). *Criminology*. Philadelphia, PA: Lippincott.

Sveningsson Elm, M. (2009). How Do Various Notions of Privacy Influence Decisions in Qualitative Internet Research? In A. N. Markham & N. K. Baym (Eds.). *Internet Inquiry: Conversations About Method*. Thousand Oaks, CA: Sage.

Taber, M., & Shapiro, I. (1965). Social Work and Its Knowledge Base: A Content Analysis of the

Periodical Literature. *Social Work*, 10 (October, 1965), 100–107.

Teitelbaum, L., & Mullen, B. (2000). The Validity of the Mast in Psychiatric Settings: A Meta-Analytic Integration. *Journal of Studies on Alcohol*, 61 (March, 2000), 254–261.

Tejani, N., Dresselhaus, T. R., & Weinger, M. B. (2010). Development of a Handheld Computer Platform for Real-time Behavioral Assessment of Physicians and Nurses. *Journal of Biomedical Informatics*, 43, 75–80.

Thorne, B. (1993). *Gender Play: Girls and Boys in School*. New Brunswick, NJ: Rutgers University Press.

Thrasher, E., & Mowbray C. (1995). A Strengths Perspective: An Ethnographic Study of Homeless Women with Children. *Health and Social Work*, 20, 93–101.

Thurstone, L. L., & Chave, E. J. (1929). *The Measurement of Attitudes*. Chicago, IL: University of Chicago Press.

Timberlake, E. M. (1994). Children with No Place to Call Home: Survival in Cars and on the Streets. *Child and Adolescent Social Work Journal* 5(4), 268.

Tinker, C., & Armstrong, N. (2008). From the Outside Looking in: How an Awareness of Difference can Benefit the Qualitative Research Process. *The Qualitative Report*, 13 (March, 2008), 53–60.

Tjaden, P., & Thoennes, N. (1998). Prevalence, Incidence, and Consequences of Violence against Women: Findings from the National Violence against Women Survey. *Research in Brief*. Atlanta, GA: National Institute of Justice, Centers for Disease Control and Prevention.

Tolman, R. (1989). The Development and Validation of a Nonphysical Abuse Scale. *Violence and Victims*, 4, 159–177.

Toseland, R. W., & Reid, W. J. (1985). Using Rapid Assessment Instruments in a Family Service Agency. *Social Casework*, 66, 547–555.

Touliatos, J., Perlmutter, B. F., Strauss, M. A., & Holden, G. W. (Eds.). (2001). *Handbook of Family Measurement Techniques*. Thousand Oaks, CA: Sage.

Tran, T. V., & Williams, L. F. (1994). Effect of Language of Interview on the Validity and Reliability of Psychological Well-Being Scales. *Social Work Research*, 18 (March, 1994), 17–25.

Truman, J. L. (2011). *Criminal Victimization 2010: National Crime Victimization Survey*. Washington, DC: Bureau of Justice Statistics, U. S. Department of Justice, Retrieved from http://bjs.ojp.usdoj.gov/content/pub/pdf/cv10.pdf.

Turnbull, J. E., & Dietz-Uhler, B. (1995). The Boulder Model: Lessons from Clinical Psychology for Social Work Training. *Research on Social Work Practice*, 5 (October, 1995), 411–429.

Tye, M. C. (2003). Lesbian, Gay, Bisexual, and Transgender Parents: Special Considerations for the Custody and Adoption Evaluator. *Family Court Review*, (January, 2003), 92–103.

Tyson, K. (1999). An Empowering Approach to Crisis Intervention and Brief Treatment for Preschool Children. *Families in Society*, 80 (January/February, 1999), 64–77.

U.S. Census Bureau. (2011). *Statistical Abstract of the United States, 2012*, 131st ed. Washington, DC: U.S. Government Printing Office. Retrieved from http://www.census.gov/compendia/statab.

U. S. Department of Health and Human Services. (2005). *Code of Federal Regulations, Title 45 Public Welfare, Part 46 Protection of Human Subjects*. Retrieved from http://www .hhs.gov/ohrp/policy/ohrpregulations.pdf.

U.S. Department of Health and Human Services. (2002). *Research, Demonstration, and Evaluation Activities FY 2003 Plan and Budget*. Retrieved from http://aspe.hhs.gov/progsys/rde/general.htm.

Varmus, H. (1999). Evaluating the Burden of Disease and Spending the Research Dollars of the National Institutes of Health. *New England Journal of Medicine*, 340 (June 17, 1999), 1914–1915.

Vinokur, A., Oksenberg, L., & Cannell, C. (1979). Effects of Feedback and Reinforcement on the Report of Health Information. In C. Cannell, L. Oksenberg, & C. Converse (Eds.). *Experiments in Interviewing Techniques*. Ann Arbor, MI: University of Michigan Institute for Social Research.

Wagenaar, A. C., Murray, D. M., & Toomey, T. L. (2000). Communities Mobilizing for Change on Alcohol (CMCA): Effects of a Randomized Trial on Arrests and Traffic Crashes. *Addiction*, 95, 209–217.

Wakefield, J. C. (1995). When an Irresistible Epistemology Meets an Immovable Ontology. *Social Work Research*, 19, 9–17.

Warriner, K., Goyder, J., Gjertsen, H., Hohner, P., & McSpurren, K. (1996). Charities, No; Lotteries, No; Cash, Yes: Main Effects and Interactions in a Canadian Incentives Experiment. *Public Opinion Quarterly*, 60, 542–562.

Warwick, D. P., & Lininger, C. (1975). *The Sample Survey: Theory and Practice*. New York, NY: McGraw-Hill.

Watters, J. K., & Biernacki, P. (1989). Targeted Sampling: Options for the Study of Hidden Populations. *Social Problems*, 36, 416–430.

Webb, E. J., Campbell, D. T., Schwartz, R. D., Sechrest, L., & Grove, J. B. (1981). *Nonreactive Measures in the Social Sciences*. Boston, MA: Houghton Mifflin.

Weber, M. (1946, originally published 1922). Science as a Vocation. In H. H. Gerth & C. W. Mills (Eds.). *Max Weber, Essays in Sociology*. New York, NY: Free Press.

Weber, M. (1957 originally published 1925). *The Theory of Social and Economic Organization*, trans. A. M. Henderson & T. Parsons. New York, NY: Free Press.

Weinberg, M. (1968). Sexual Modesty, Social Meanings, and the Nudist Camp. In M. Truss (Ed.). *Sociology and Everyday Life*, ed.. Englewood Cliffs, NJ: Prentice Hall.

Weinstein, R. M. (1982). The Mental Hospital from the Patient's Point of View: The Pitfalls of Participant-Observation Research. In W. R. Gove (Ed.). *Deviance and Mental Illness*. Newbury Park, CA: Sage.

Weiss, C. H. (1998). *Evaluation: Method for Studying Programs and Policies*, 2nd ed. Upper Saddle River, NJ: Prentice Hall.

Weiss, R. L., & Frohman, P. E. (1985). Behavioral Observation as Outcome Measures: Not through a Glass Darkly. *Behavioral Assessment*, 7 (Fall, 1985), 309–315.

Wells, G. L., & Olson, E. A. (2003). Eyewitness Identification. In S. T. Fiske, (Ed.). *Annual Review of Psychology*, Vol. 54. Palo Alto, CA: Annual Reviews.

Wells, W. D., & Smith, G. (1960). Four Semantic Rating Scales Compared. *Journal of Applied Psychology*, 44, 393–397.

West, S. G., Biesanz, J. C., & Pitts, S. C. (2000). Causal Inference and Generalization in Field Settings: Experimental and Quasi-Experimental Designs. In H. T. Reis & C. M. Judd (Eds.). *Handbook of Research Methods in Social and Personality Psychology*, Cambridge, England: Cambridge University Press.

Whalen, J., & Zimmerman, D. H. (1998). Observations on the Display and Management of Emotion in Naturally Occurring Activities: The Case of "Hysteria" in Calls to 9-1-1. *Social Psychology Quarterly*, 61, 141–159.

Whyte, W. F. (1958). Freedom and Responsibility in Research: The Springdale Case. *Human Organization*, 17, 1–2.

Whyte, W. F. (1955). *Street Corner Society*, 2nd ed., Chicago, IL: University of Chicago Press.

Wilson, S. R., Brown, N., Mejia, C., & Lavori, P. W. (2002). Effects of Interviews Characteristics on Reported Sexual Behavior of California Latino Couples. *Hispanic Journal of Behavioral Sciences*, 24 (February, 2002), 38–62.

Wilson, T. Normative and Interpretive Paradigms in Sociology. (1970). In . J. Douglas (Ed.). *Understanding Everyday Life: Toward the Reconstruction of Sociological Knowledge*. New York, NY: Aldine.

Wingard, D. (1987). Trends and Characteristics of California Adoptions: 1964–1982. *Child Welfare*, 66 (July/August, 1987), 303–314.

Wolfe, V. V., et al. (1987). Negative Affectivity in Children: A Multitrait-Multimethod Investigation. *Journal of Consulting and Clinical Psychology*, 55 (April, 1987), 245–250.

Wolfgang, M. E. (1981). Confidentiality in Criminological Research and Other Ethical Issues. *Journal of Criminal Law and Criminology*, 72, 345–361.

Wood, J. M., Lilienfeld, S. O., & Garb, H. N. (2000). The Rorschach Test in Clinical Diagnosis: A Critical Review, With a Backward Look at Garfield (1947). *Journal of Clinical Psychology*, 56 (March, 2000), 395–420.

Woodruff, S. I., Conway, T. L., & Edwards, C. C. (2000). Increasing Response Rates to a Smoking

Survey for U.S. Navy Enlisted Women. *Evaluation and the Health Professions, 23* (June, 2000), 172–181.

Yammarino, F. J., Skinner, S. J., & Childers, T. L. (1991). Understanding Mail Survey Response Behavior: A Meta-Analysis. *Public Opinion Quarterly, 55* (Winter, 1991), 613–639.

Yin, R. K. (2009). *Case Study Research: Design and Methods*, 4th ed. Thousand Oaks, CA: Sage.

Zalaquett, C. P., & Wood, R. J. (Eds.). (1997). *Evaluating Stress: A Book of Resources.* Lanham, MD: Rowman & Littlefield.

Zelenski, J. M., Rusting, C. L., & Larsen, R. J. (2003). Consistency in the Time of Experiment Participation and Personality Correlates: A Methodological Note. *Personality and Individual Differences, 34,* 547–558.

Name Index

Abrams, L., 181, 182
Abramson, P., 181
Achen, C. H., 272, 298
Acock, A. C., 47
Adams, S., 7
Alam, S., 321
Albarracin, D., 368
Alexander, S. C., 366
Alfonso, S. D., 363
Alford, R. R., 30, 38, 41
Allen, K. R., 47
Allen-Meares, P., 208
Allison, D. B., 314
Altman, L., 68
Alvidrez, J., 181
Alwin, D. F., 113, 122
Amato, P. R., 25
Andajani-Sutjahjo, S., 181
Anderson, B., 181
Anderson, E., 254
Anderson, J. E., 174
Anderson, T., 339
Annis, R. C., 182
Antonucci, T., 243
Arches, J., 36
Arean, P. A., 181
Armstrong, G., 230
Armstrong, J. S., 171
Armstrong, N., 182
Arnold, D. O., 149
Arnold, E., 284

Aron, A., 424
Aron, E. N., 424
Aronson, E., 279
Ary, D., 244
Ashdown, J., 333

Bachman, J. G., 181
Backstrom, C. H., 144
Bagle, C., 73
Bahl, A. B., 7
Bailey, K., 142, 246
Bailey, R. C., 92
Baker, E. A., 16
Bales, R. F., 204, 236, 237
Barlow, D. H., 16, 25, 290, 291, 295, 296, 298, 303, 305, 306
Barlow, H., 203
Barnes, H. E., 40
Barroso, J., 452
Bartholomew, N., 97
Battaglia, M. P., 133
Bauer, D. G., 454, 456, 459, 467
Baumrind, D., 55
Baxter, P. M., 489
Bazeley, P., 451
Bazeley, P., 445
Bearden, W. O., 368
Beauchamp, T. L., 51
Becerra, R. M., 153
Becerra, R.M., 181
Bell, A. P., 134

Bell, J., 230, 231
Bell, W., 32
Bellamy, J. L., 6
Bengston, V. L., 47
Bennell, C., 208, 213
Bennett, A., 254
Bennett, E., 181
Bensman, J., 57
Benton, T., 38, 220
Berg, B. L., 89, 99, 254
Berger, M. T., 230, 231
Berger, R. L., 54
Berk, R. A., 270, 271, 320, 330, 331, 332
Bernard, H. R., 235
Berry, S. H., 171
Beskow, L. M., 60
Biblarz, T. J., 27
Bielawski, D., 88
Bielawski, D., 214
Biernacki, P., 151
Biesanz, J. C., 418, 419
Biklen, S. K., 235, 431
Billups, J. O., 210
Binder, A., 123
Birkeland, S., 338
Birkerts, S., 475
Bjelland, A. K., 67
Black, M. M., 187
Blaikie, N., 39
Bledsoe, S. E., 6

NAME INDEX

Bloom, M., 115, 294, 313, 418
Blumberg, S. J., 154, 155
Blythe, B. J., 128
Bogdan, R. C., 235, 431
Bogdan, R., 234
Bogen, D., 39
Bohrnstedt, G., 106, 113
Bolner, M. S., 489
Bolstein, R., 171
Bonacich, E., 84
Bonnie, R. J., 60
Booth, A., 25
Borgatta, E., 113
Boruch, R., 342
Bourgois, P., 77, 224, 233, 233, 241, 438
Bova, D. L., 121
Boynton, P. M., 278
Bradburn, N. M., 161, 164, 361
Bradley, J., 86
Brajuha, M., 59
Bransford, J. D., 99
Brent, E. E., 422
Breuning, S., 68, 69
Brewer, M. B., 279
Brick, J. M., 141
Bromley, D. G., 225
Bronowski, J., 24, 25
Brown, L. G., 475
Brown, M. J., 475
Browne, M. N., 15
Brownson, R. C., 16
Bruce, D., 123
Brunner, G. A., 176
Brunswick-Heineman, M., 66
Buchbinder, E., 442
Burch, G., 269
Burger, J. M., 117
Burgess, R., 80
Bush, G. W., 274
Bushery, J. M., 181
Bushnell, M. M., 244

Cahalan, D., 134
Callanan, P., 73
Calvey, D., 225, 232
Camasso, M., 128
Campbell, D. T., 116, 118, 128, 261, 268, 277, 281, 287, 342

Cannell, C. F., 171, 174, 191
Caplan, A. L., 73
Caplinger, T. E., 146
Card, J. J., 14
Carise, D., 125
Carlock, C. J., 264
Carlsmith, J., 279
Carlson, J. F., 295
Carroll, L., 19
Carroll, S. J., 176
Cartwright, A., 176
Casey, M. A., 188, 189, 193
Catley, D., 284
Cavan, S., 235
Cavanaugh, M., 287
Ceci, S. J., 52
Chaiken, J. M., 115
Chaiken, M. R., 115
Champion, D. J., 142
Charmaz, K., 221
Charmaz, K., 430, 433
Chave, E. J., 352, 353, 354
Chen, H., 324
Childers, T. L., 171
Cho, H., 273
Christian, L. M., 193
Christie, R., 346
Chu, M. M., 334
Churchill, W., 23
Claes, L., 96
Clandinin, D. J., 240, 437
Clark, J., 125, 181
Claus, R. E., 181
Clinton, B., 51
Clum, G. A., 306
Coe, R. D., 321
Coehlo, R. J., 71
Cohen, J., 419
Cohen, M. R., 31
Coleman, L., 171
Collins, F., 68
Collins, S., 462
Combs-Orme, T. D., 418
Connelly, F. M., 240, 437
Conway, T. L., 170, 171
Cook, F. L., 329
Cook, T. D., 277, 281, 329, 332, 342
Corbett, T., 199
Corbin, J., 254, 451

Corcoran, K., 115, 124, 295, 364, 368
Corenblum, B., 182
Corey, G., 73
Corey, M. S., 73
Cornely, W., 125
Corry, J., 206
Costello, E. J., 60
Coulton, C. J., 347, 348
Couper, M. P., 186, 365
Coups, E., 424
Cournoyer, B. R., 7
Courvoisier, D. S., 284
Couvalis, G., 38
Cox, D. E., 278
Crabb, P. B., 88
Crabb, P. B., 214
Craft, J. L., 396
Craig, W. M., 228
Cramer, E. P., 339
Crask, M. R., 62
Craske, M. G., 306
Craske, M., 124
Crissman, A., 240
Cronbach, L. J., 116, 121
Crossen, C., 73
Cuba, L., 475, 489
Cuzzort, R. P., 424

Dailey, R. M., 181
Dame, L., 60
D'Amico, J. J., 340
Daniel, J., 158
Davidson, W. S., 287
Davis, D. W., 181
Davis, J. A., 389, 391, 405, 406, 407, 421
Davis, L. V., 21
Dawson, J. A., 340
Dean, C., 271
DeAnda, D., 181
DeJong, C., 86, 431, 432, 441, 448, 471
DeKeseredy, W. S., 108, 109
Dekker, K., 141
Dekker- van Weering, M. G. H., 251
DeMaio, T. J., 181
DeMartini, J., 316
Denzin, N., 147, 249, 254, 332
DeSena, A. D., 329

DeVault, M. L., 90
DeVellis, R. F., 346, 368
DeWalt, B. R., 222
DeWalt, K. M., 222
Dewey, T. E., 148
Dietz-Uhler, B., 7
Dignan, M., 188
Dillman, D. A., 193
Dilthey, W., 40
Dilworth-Anderson, P., 47
Dobratz, B. A., 240
Doerner, W. G., 326
Dohan, D., 447, 448
Donovan, T., 16, 47
Dotson, L. E., 358
Draine, J., 287
Drake, B., 212
Dresselhaus, T. R., 284
Drewry, S., 50
Duehn, W. D., 204
Duffy, B., 187, 365
Dunford, F., 271
Durkheim, E., 39, 220
Dziegielewski, S. F., 363

Earnest, C., 308
Eckenwiler, L. A., 51, 51
Eckman, S., 141
Edlesen, J. L., 364
Edwards, A. L., 358
Edwards, C. C., 170, 171
Eichler, M., 282
Eisikovits, Z., 442
Elliott, D. S., 34
Elliott, D., 271
Ellis, A., 26
Elms, A. C., 55
Emanuel, E. J., 327
Emrey, J. A., 187
Engler, R. L., 64, 65
English, N., 141
Epstein, I., 171
Erich, S., 27
Erikson, E., 21
Erikson, K. T., 56
Ess, C., 70
Estes, C., 181
Estroff, S. E., 223, 224
Evans, J., 489
Eysenbach, G., 70

Fagan, J. A., 272
Fahrenberg, J., 284
Fairweather, G. W., 287
Farley, R., 213
Fay, B., 66
Feldman, M. S., 230, 231
Feldman, R. A., 146
Fernandez, M., 88
Ferree, M., 216
Ferrell, J., 254
Ferrell, K. A., 301
Festinger, L., 247
Field, A., 287
Fieldhouse, E. A., 321
Fielding, N. G., 445, 447, 451
Fink, A., 158
First, M. B., 124
First, R., 86
Fischer, J., 115, 124, 294, 295, 313, 364, 368, 418
Fiske, D. W., 116
Fitzpatrick, J. L., 342
Fletcher, L. A., 251
Flick, U., 445, 451
Fontana, A., 240
Forbes Citro, C., 73
Fortune, A. E., 207
Fowler, F. Jr., 177, 180, 182
Fox, R. J., 62
Fox, S., 295
Frankel, M. R., 133
Frankfort-Nachmias, C., 263, 424
Franklin, R. D., 314
Franzosi, R., 204, 208
Fredman, N., 115, 295
Freeman, H. E., 5, 283, 285, 316, 317, 333, 336, 340
Freud, S., 21, 105
Frey, J. H., 172, 240
Fricker, R. D., 186
Fricker, S., 365
Friedman, M. J., 124
Friendly, M., 396
Frisch, M. B., 296
Frohman, P. E., 294

Gabor, P. A., 287
Galison, P., 39
Galtung, J., 141
Garb, H. N., 124

Garfield, E., 68, 69
Garner, J. H., 272
Gast, D. L., 314
Geis, F. L., 346
Geis, G., 123
Geisinger, K. F., 295
Geismar, L. L., 128
Gelles, R. J., 34, 104, 147
Gelman, S. R., 64
George, A. L., 254
Gerow, K. G., 135, 139, 144, 158
Gibbs, L., 2, 66, 85, 328
Gibelman, M., 64
Gibson, P., 181, 182
Gilligan, C., 90, 442
Gilmore, S., 240
Gingerich, W., 290
Ginsberg, L. H., 342
Ginsberg, P. E., 74
Ginsburg, H., 105
Glaser, B. G., 47, 80, 428, 433, 435
Gold, R. L., 225, 227
Goldberg, A. E., 27
Goldberg, I. A., 475
Goldfried, M. R., 7
Goldsmith, D. J., 366
Goode, W. J., 120
Gorden, R. L., 176, 180, 183, 193
Gordon, M. M., 66
Gorman, B. S., 314
Gottman, J. M., 287, 296, 298
Gottman, J. S., 27
Gouldner, A., 66
Goyder, J., 169, 171
Graham, K. R., 279
Graham, K., 228, 238, 239, 246
Grauerholz, E., 206
Gravetter, F. J., 396
Gravlee, C. C., 284
Gray, B. H., 52
Green, S. B., 396
Greene, J. C., 318, 332
Greene, J. R., 326
Greenley, J. R., 132
Greif, G. L., 431
Grichting, W. L., 88
Griffin, M., 360
Grigsby, R. K., 309
Grinnell, R. M. Jr., 287
Grobe, J. E., 284

Gross, R., 99
Groth-Marnat, G., 295
Groves, R. M., 172
Groze, V. K., 25
Groze, V., 21
Guba, E. G., 220
Gubrium, J. F., 40, 177, 181, 193, 220, 240
Gupta, K., 342
Gurel, O., 125
Guttman, L. A., 356, 359

Hadlock, T. D., 187
Hahn, H., 489
Halfpenny, P., 39, 66, 220
Hall, D., 475
Hall, E., 216
Haller, D. M., 284
Haller, G., 284
Hallowell, L., 59
Hamm, M. S., 254
Hannes, K., 96
Harrington, P. E., 326
Harris, A. R., 262
Harris, F. N., 305
Harrison, W. D., 36
Hatt, P. K., 120
Hayes, S. C., 16, 25, 296
Haynes, S. N., 314
Hazlett, M. H., 357
Healey, J. F., 396
Heckathorn, D. D., 150, 151
Heddle, N. M., 284
Heise, D. R., 355, 356
Henderson, G. E., 62
Henry, G., 137
Henson, K. T., 475
Hepworth, D. H., 30
Hermens, H. J., 251
Herrick, J. M., 5
Hersen, M., 128, 290, 291, 293, 295, 296, 298, 303, 305
Higgins, P. C., 77, 99
Higgins, R. L., 296
Hill, D. H., 321
Hilton, T., 86, 431, 432, 441, 448, 449, 471
Hindelang, M. J., 128
Hirschel, J., 271
Hirschi, T., 128

Hobbs, D., 254
Holden, G. W., 368
Hole, G. J., 287
Holstein, J. A., 40, 177, 181, 193, 220, 240
Holsti, O. R., 205, 206, 208, 209
Holtgrave, D. R., 337
Homeier, D. C., 322
Honey, M., 206
Hooker, E., 134
Hoover, K. R., 16, 47
Horejsi, C. R., 5
Horner, R. H., 301
Hornick, R. C., 330
Horowitz, R., 230
Hough, R. L., 353, 354
Houkes, I., 36
Hout, M., 217
Hrabowski, F. A., 431
Hsu, V., 141
Huber, B., 52
Huberman, A. M., 428, 430, 432, 433, 434, 438, 439
Hudson, W. W., 292, 363, 367, 369
Huizinga, D., 34, 271
Hummel-Rossi, B., 333
Humphreys, L., 57
Hunt, M., 100
Hunter, R. D., 326
Hursh-Cesar, G. D., 144
Hutchison III, I., 271
Hyman, H., 181

Iannacchione, V. G., 133
Ilgen, D. R., 73
Innes, R. A., 181
Irwin, D. M., 244
Israel, T., 77

James, J., 171
Janssen, P. P., 36
Jayaratne, S., 305
Jeger, A. M., 7
Jekielek, S. M., 25
Jenkins-Hall, K., 63
Jenson, W. R., 305
Joe, G. W., 363
Johnson, B. T., 368
Johnson, F. C., 296

Johnson, J. M., 77, 99
Johnson, P. R., 25
Jones, G. E., 396
Jones, J. H., 51
Jones, N. J., 208, 213
Jonson-Reid, M., 212
Jorgensen, D., 230
Jorner, U., 396
Jory, B., 350, 351
Julia, M. C., 210

Kadushin, A., 191, 193
Kadushin, G., 191, 193
Kahn, R. L., 174
Kalra, V. S., 321
Kalton, G., 144, 170, 174, 363
Kamerman, J. B., 263
Kanenberg, H., 27
Kang, M-E., 204
Kanouse, D. E., 171
Kanuka, H., 339
Kaplowitz, M. D., 187
Karoly, L. A., 336, 337
Katz, J., 51
Kazdin, A. E., 292, 298
Keeley, S. M., 15
Kelle, U., 446
Kelly, J. R., 93
Kemeny, J. G., 16, 42
Kenny, G. K., 111
Kenyon, K., 186, 365
Kettner, P. M., 128
Kilpatrick, F. P., 358
Kim, J., 217
Kim, J., 62
Kimmel, A. J., 469
Kimmel, A., 55, 59
King, N. M. P., 62
Kirk, J., 128, 244, 246
Kirk, R. E., 287
Kirk, S. A., 2, 16
Kirk, S., 124
Kirsch, I. S., 165
Kish, L., 132, 139, 144, 158
Klein, D. M., 47
Kline, D., 279
Klockars, C. B., 61, 232
Knorr, K., 41
Koch, N. S., 187
Kogan, L. S., 361

Korbin, J. E., 104
Korn, J. H., 56
Krasucki, C., 364
Krathwohl, D. R., 456, 464
Krippendorff, K., 205
Kroner, T., 216
Krueger, R. A., 188, 189, 193
Kuhn, T., 14, 38
Kuo, W. H., 153
Kutchins, H., 124

Lach, M., 214
Lally, J. J., 81
Lambert, M. J., 364
Landon, A., 134
Landrine, H., 269, 276
Lane, S. J., 284
Lansford, J. E., 25
Lantz, H. R., 205, 213
Larose, D., 217
Larsen, J., 30
Larsen, R. J., 278
Lasorsa, D. L., 47
Latterner, M., 141
Lavrakas, P. J., 186
Lawless, E. J., 241
Leahey, E., 379
Lee, R. M., 217, 227, 246, 451
Lee, R., 74
Leet, T. L., 16
Lenburg, J., 489
Lenihan, K. J., 320, 330
Leo, R. A., 56, 60, 61, 226, 227
Leon-Guerrero, A., 424
Lettiere, M., 77
Leung, P., 27
Levin, J. R., 290
Levin, J., 209, 211, 469
Levine, R., 187
Leviton, L. C., 342
Levy, R., 305
Lewin, C., 17
Lewis, K. G., 27
Liburdy, R. P., 68
Likert, R. A., 349
Lilienfeld, S. O., 124
Lincoln, Y. S., 220
Lincoln, Y. S., 254
Lindsey, D., 17
Lininger, C., 178

Link, M. W., 133
Linkins, K., 181
Lipsey, M. W., 5, 283, 285, 316, 317, 333, 336, 340, 419
Locke, L. F., 83, 100, 458
Lockhart, L. L., 34
Lofland, J., 222, 234, 235, 431
Lohr, K., 97
Loseke, D. R., 442
Lovis, C., 284
Luck, E. J., 171
Luke, J. V., 154, 155
Lune, H., 89, 99, 254
Lutfiyya, Z. M., 445
Lynch, K. B., 321
Lynch, M., 39
Lynham, S. A., 220

MacGregor, S., 338
Machiavelli, N., 346, 347
MacLeod, L., 108
Mactavish, J. B., 445
Magura, S., 115, 295
Mahon, M. J., 445
Maisel, R., 158
Malouff, J. M., 115, 368
Mandell, N., 231
Manderson, L., 181
Mangione, T., 177, 180, 182
Manson, S. M., 121
Margolin, G., 58
Marin, G., 121
Mark, M. M., 329
Marquart, J. W., 226, 227
Marsden, P. V., 217
Marshall, C., 254
Marshall, E., 180
Martin, L. L., 128
Martin, P. Y., 264
Martinez, T. A., 203
Martini, R., 308
Marx, K., 66
Maslach, C., 36
Masters, J., 449
Masters, K. S., 364
Masters, S., 199
Mathios, A., 203, 207, 210
Maton, K. I., 431
Matthews, J., 339
Maxwell, C. D., 272

Maxwell, J. A., 145, 428, 429, 436
Mayer, G., 27
Mayo, J. K., 330
McAnany, E. G., 330
McClamroch, K. J., 251
McCord, J. A., 324
McCulloch, G., 217
McDermott, V. M., 366
McDowell, I., 115, 368
McFall, R. M., 296
McGrath, J. E., 93
McKillip, J., 320
McLanahan, S., 25
McLaughlin, T., 86
McLean, D. D., 454
McLellan, A. T., 125
McMurtry, S. L., 363
McWilliam, R. A., 276
Meehl, P., 116
Menard, S., 100
Mendenhall, W., 135, 139, 144, 158
Mendes, H. A., 146
Merriam, S. B., 437, 451
Mertens, D. M., 74
Merton, R. K., 47
Michael, R. T., 141
Miles, M. B., 428, 430, 432, 433, 434, 438, 439
Milgram, S., 117
Milkie, M. A., 206
Miller, D. C., 115, 128, 172, 295, 356, 368
Miller, D. T., 418
Miller, E. R., 55
Miller, J. M., 77
Miller, L. P., 35, 38, 338
Miller, M. L., 128, 244, 246
Millum, J., 327
Miner, J. T., 458, 462, 463, 467, 475
Miner, L. E., 458, 462, 463, 467, 475
Mitsos, S. B., 355
Moe, K., 53
Mohr, V., 269
Mokdad, A. H., 133
Molina, E., 439
Mondello, M., 86
Montaquila, J., 141
Moos, M., 97
Morash, M., 326

NAME INDEX

Morgan, D. L., 188, 314
Morgan, R. K., 314
Morse, J. M., 451
Moser, C. A., 144, 170, 174, 363
Moses, B. S., 115, 295
Mowbray, C., 178, 179
Mowrer, H., 26
Mullen, B., 124
Mullen, E. J., 6
Murnane, R. J., 217
Murphy-Graham, E., 338
Murray, D. M., 264
Murray, L., 52
Mushquash, C. J., 121

Nabors, L. A., 430
Nachmias, D., 263
Nagel, E., 31, 35
Nas, T. F., 342
Navarro, A. E., 322
Neelon, V. J., 364
Nelsen, J. C., 296
Nelsen, J., 309
Nelson-Gardell, D., 364
Nelson-Gray, R. O., 16, 25, 296
Nery, R., 181
Netemeyer, R. G., 368
Neuendorf, K. A., 204
Newman, J. C., 174
Nezu, A. M., 301
Nezu, C. M., 301
Nielson, J. M., 90
Nock, M., 290, 291, 295, 296, 298, 303, 305
Nomaguchi, K. M., 200
Norman, G. R., 368
Nugent, W. R., 292
Nyden, P., 62

O'Brien, W. H., 314
O'Connell, A. A., 145, 150
O'Malley, P. M., 181
O'Muircheartaigh, C., 141
O'Neill, P., 84
Oates, C. S., 276
Oeye, C., 67
Ogden, T. E., 475
Ogles, B. M., 364
Oksenberg, L., 171, 191
Ollendick, T. H., 306

Olsen, V., 90
Olson, E. A., 244
Opper, S., 105
Orgel, M., 7
Orman, D. T., 69
Orme, J. G., 115, 294, 313, 418, 419
Orne, M. T., 278
Orr, L. L., 328
Orshansky, M., 31, 32
Ortner, S. B., 247
Osborn, C. A., 63
Osborn, L., 133
Osgood, C. E., 354, 355
Ott, L., 135, 139, 144, 158

Padgett, D. K., 254
Parker, A. T., 301
Parker, R., 162, 169, 172, 183
Patton, M. Q., 240, 318, 342, 414, 437, 439
Paul, R., 15
Pepler, D. J., 228
Perlmutter, B. F., 368
Perrow, C., 149
Persell, C. H., 158
Persson, R., 396
Pescosolido, B. A., 206
Peters, D., 52
Peterson, R. R., 65
Peterson, S., 214, 216
Peyrot, M., 278
Phillips, K. A., 124
Piaget, J., 105
Piliavin, I., 199
Pini, B., 182
Pitts, S. C., 418, 419
Plotkin, J., 52
Poirier, G. A., 489
Polatajko, H. J., 308
Polsky, N., 77
Ponirakis, A., 187
Pound, E. T., 68
Powdermaker, H., 233
Powers, G. L., 7
Prentice, D. A., 418
Presser, S., 164, 193
Proctor, E. K., 204
Prothro, J. W., 205
Purcell, P., 214

Quesada, J., 77

Rabinow, P., 40
Rafferty, J., 14
Rajab, M. H., 69
Rallis, S. F., 17, 451
Ramasamy, R., 314
Rapee, R. M., 306
Rapp, L. A., 364
Ratzan, R. M., 56
Rea, L., 162, 169, 172, 183
Reamer, F. G., 26
Reece, R., 59
Reed, J. G., 489
Reicher, S., 229
Reid, W. J., 2, 16, 364
Reid, W., 207
Reinharz, S., 62, 90, 100
Reiss, A. K., 147
Reverby, S. M., 51
Reynolds, M., 430
Reynolds, P. D., 52
Reza, H., 242, 243
Rhodes, L., 147
Richards, L., 451
Richards, R. Y., 314
Richards, S. B., 314
Ridley, S. M., 276
Riecken, H., 247
Riedel, M., 196, 217
Rife, J., 86
Ritter, L. A., 193
Roberts, A. R., 17
Robinson, J., 115
Rogers, C., 26
Roof, H. L., 309
Roosevelt, F., 134
Roscoe, P. B., 40
Rosen, A., 7, 25
Rosenberg, M., 394
Rosenhan, D. L., 225
Rosenthal, J. A., 25
Rosenthal, R., 24, 279
Rosnow, R. L., 278
Rossi, P. H., 5, 283, 285, 316, 317, 320, 324, 330, 332, 333, 336, 340
Rossman, G. B., 17, 254, 451
Rowe, Z., 284
Ruch-Ross, H. S., 88

Rudd, M. D., 69
Ruggles, P., 31
Runcie, J. F., 235
Russ-Eft, D. F., 342
Russell, B., 42
Russo, M. J., 128, 287, 342
Rusting, C. L., 278

Sackett, D. L., 6, 97, 289
Salant, P., 193
Salkind, N. J., 115, 128, 172, 295, 356, 368, 396
Saltzman, L. E., 109
Sánchez-Jankowski, M., 447, 448
Sandefur, G., 25
Sandelowski, M., 452
Sanders, J. R., 342
Scarce, R., 60
Schachter, S., 247
Schafer, A., 53
Schaufeli, W. B., 36
Scheaffer, R. L., 135, 139, 144, 158
Scheper-Hughes, N., 229
Schiebinger, L. L., 90
Schmidt, F. L., 418
Schneider, G., 489
Schoenherr, R. A., 132
Schonlau, M., 186, 187
Schuckit, M., 31
Schulz, A. J., 284
Schuman, H., 164, 193
Schutte, N. S., 115, 368
Schwartz, D., 295
Scott, G., 152
Scott, J., 211
Scott, R. A., 156
Seale, C., 446
Seidman, I. E., 428, 429, 436, 437
Seiler, L. H., 353, 354
Semaan, S., 152
Shadish, W. R., 277, 281, 342
Shanks-Meile, S. L., 240
Shapin, S., 39
Shapiro, I., 209
Sharma, S., 368
Shaver, P., 115
Sheafor, B. W., 5
Sheley, J. F., 230, 245, 444
Sherman, L., 65, 270, 271, 272, 276, 328

Sherman, R., 115, 295
Shilts, R., 82
Shireman, J. F., 25
Shlonsky, A., 17
Shoemaker, P. J., 47
Shore, N., 86
Shulman, L., 115, 118, 120, 121
Shupe, A. D. Jr., 225
Sieber, J., 196
Siegal, H., 59
Sieppert, J. D., 292
Silver, B., 181
Silverman, D., 254
Silverman, S. J., 83, 100, 458
Singer, E., 55
Sipprelle, C. N., 278
Skidmore, W., 27
Skinner, H. A., 364
Skinner, S. J., 171
Skorpen, A., 67
Sleezer, C. M., 342
Slotnick, R. S., 7
Slutsky, R., 64
Smart, B., 38
Smith, A. W., 152
Smith, C. P., 205
Smith, G., 355
Smith, H. W., 52, 59
Smith, M. F., 40, 322, 332
Smith, P. R., 426
Smith, S. H., 454
Smith, T. W., 164, 165, 217, 389, 391, 405, 406, 407, 421
Smyth, J. D., 193
Snow, C. P., 469
Solomon, P., 287
Somekh, B., 17
Spano, R., 231
Spates, J. L., 209, 211
Spies, R. A., 295
Spirduso, W. W., 83, 100, 458
Squire, P., 134
Stacey, J., 27
Stall, R., 174
Stanley, J. C., 118, 261, 269, 277
Staw, B. M., 379
Stein, B. S., 99
Stein, D. J., 124
Stein, J., 20, 62
Stevens, S. S., 106

Stewart, L., 214
Steyaert, J., 14
Stott, C., 229
Straus, M. A., 18, 360, 362, 368
Straus, M., 34
Strauss, A. L., 47, 428, 431, 433, 434, 435, 438, 439
Strauss, A., 80, 254, 451
Street, D., 149
Streiner, D. L., 368
Stuart, A., 158
Stum, K., 334
Stump, D., 39
Suci, G. J., 354
Sudman, S., 137, 158, 161, 162, 164, 169, 170, 176
Sue, V. M., 193
Suen, H. K., 244
Sullivan, C., 95
Sullivan, T. J., 31
Sullivan, W. M., 40
Sulzer-Azaroff, B., 27
Summers, G. F., 358
Sutherland, E., 27
Sveningsson Elm, M., 70

Taber, M., 209
Taft, R. A. Mrs., 414
Tankard, J. W., 47
Tannenbaum, P. H., 354
Taylor, R. L., 234, 314
Teitelbaum, L., 124
Tejani, N., 284
Terao, K. L., 475
Teske, H. C. Jr., 357
Tewksbury, R., 77
Thoennes, N., 108
Thompson, A., 422
Thorne, B., 229, 231, 233, 247, 248
Thrasher, E., 178, 179
Thurstone, L. L., 352, 353, 354
Thyer, B. A., 475
Till, J. E., 70
Timberlake, E. M., 178, 179
Tinker, C., 182
Tjaden, P., 108
Tolman, R. M., 419
Tolman, R., 109
Toomey, B., 86
Toomey, T. L., 264

NAME INDEX

Toseland, R. W., 364
Touliatos, J., 115, 368
Tourangeau, R., 186, 365
Tran, T. V., 121
Trella, D., 448, 471
Tripodi, T., 128, 171
Troeltsch, E., 40
Truman, H. S., 148
Truman, J. L., 123, 202
Tsai, Y., 153
Tucker, W., 176
Turnbull, J. E., 7
Turner, J. H., 47
Twain, M., 414
Tye, M. C., 27
Tyson, K., 437

Van de Ven, A. H., 47
VanOss Marin, B., 121, 182
Varmus, H., 81
Vidich, A., 57
Vinokur, A., 191
Vinter, R. D., 149
Vollenbroek-Hutten, M. M. R., 251
VonThurn, D. R., 55
Vrettos, J. S., 424

Wagenaar, A. C., 264, 265
Wainer, H., 158
Wakefield, J. C., 89
Walker, I., 284

Wallace, R. B., 60
Wallgren, A., 396
Wallgren, B., 396
Wallnau, L. B., 396
Warriner, K., 170
Warwick, D. P., 178
Washington, H. A., 74
Watters, J. K., 151
Watts, D. J., 47
Webb, E. J., 227
Weber, M., 40, 66, 221, 223
Weinberg, M. S., 134
Weinberg, M., 77
Weinger, M. B., 284
Weinstein, R. M., 245
Weis, J. G., 128
Weiss, C. H., 316, 324, 325, 332, 339
Weiss, C., 338
Weiss, R. L., 294
Weissman, J., 490
Weist, M. D., 430
Welljams-Dorof, A., 68, 69
Wells, G. L., 244
Wells, W. D., 355
West, M. D., 218
West, S. G., 418, 419
Whalen, J., 204
Whyte, W. F., 58, 226
Wilbur, K. H., 322
Wilke, D. J., 273

Willett, J. B., 217
Williams, L. F., 121
Wilson, S. R., 182
Wilson, T., 40, 221
Wingard, D., 195, 196
Wolfe, B. E., 7
Wolfe, V. V., 116
Wolfgang, M. E., 62
Wood, J. M., 124
Wood, R. J., 295
Woodruff, S. I., 170, 171
Woods, S., 284
Worthen, B. R., 342
Wright, R., 254
Wrightsman, L., 115

Yammarino, F. J., 171
Yeager, K., 17
Yin, R. K., 240
Yonashiro, J., 322
Youngblade, L., 80
Yuen, F. K. O., 475

Zalaquett, C. P., 295
Zambrana, R. E., 153
Zanna, M. P., 368
Zeisel, H., 396
Zelenski, J. M., 278
Zenk, S. N., 284
Zimbardo, P. G., 74
Zimmerman, D. H., 204

Subject Index

AB design, 300–302
Absolutist, 54–56, 280
Abstraction, 104–105, 427
Abstracts, 470–471, 485–486
Accountability, 7, 290, 312, 332, 333
  See also Cost-benefit analysis.
Addiction Severity Index, 125
Address-based sampling, 133–134, 141, 155
Advocates, 65–66, 82, 442, 461–462, 467–468
African Americans, 34, 151, 181, 206, 213, 282, 458
Alcohol Use Inventory, 364
Alpha error, 416–417
Alpha level, 416–417, 418–419, 420
American Association for Public Opinion Research, 71, 180
American Sociological Association, 70, 71
Analysis of Variance (ANOVA), 401, 417–418, 420
Anonymity, 54, 57–59, 70, 169–170, 186, 212, 246
Applied Research, 4, 14, 68, 188, 316–317, 340, 453, 456
  See also Research; Evaluation research.
Archival records, 105–106, 276
Area sampling, 138–139, 144

Association. *See* Measures of association.
Association for Applied and Clinical Sociology, 340
Association of Internet Researchers, 70
Asymmetrical distributions, 380
Attitude toward Church Scale, 354
Attrition, experimental, 264–265, 266, 273
Audacity, 448
Audience, 402
Authority obedience to, 117
Availability sampling, 146–147
Available data, agencies and, 197–198
  assessment, 211–214
  bias in, 214
  coding of, 203–205
  computers and, 215
  defined, 196
  documents as, 196
  hazards of, 202–203
  longitudinal analysis and, 213–214
  minorities and, 214–216
  reactivity in, 214
  sampling in, 210–211, 213
  sources, 196–200
  statistical, 196–203
  units of analysis in, 205–206

  validity and reliability of, 201–203
Average. *See* Central tendency.
Axial coding, 434

Bar graphs, 385–386
Baseline phase, 6, 265, 290, 293–298, 300, 302–305, 306, 307, 310
Basic research, 4
Behavior modification theory, 27, 30, 130
Belmont Report, 50, 52
Beta error, 416–417
Bias, available data and, 212, 214
  attrition and, 268
  big man, 247, 443
  dissemination and, 317
  field research, 247, 442
  gender, 309
  interviewer, 174, 177, 181, 183
  jury opinion and, 114
  minorities and, 33–34, 181–182
  misconduct and, 64
  nonresponse, 172
  observation and, 234–235, 245, 249
  personal, 24–25
  prior research and, 78
  probes and, 180
  qualitative analysis and, 443, 444
  question order and, 167, 168,

Bias, available data and (continued)
question wording and, 164
quota samples and, 147–148
racial, 309
research and, 24, 415–416
response, 190, 251, 361–363
response pattern anxiety, 362
sampling, 136, 148, 150, 153, 155, 185, 211, 214, 244, 271
self-report and, 265
stakeholders and, 319
survey design, 168–169, 172
training and, 124
unit of analysis and, 89
Big Man bias, 247, 443
Bivariate relationships, 388–390
Block grants, 455
Blocking, 261–262
Budgets, 94–95
Burnout, 36

Campbell Collaboration, 96, 301
Case studies, 23, 57, 240–241, 248, 426, 437–438, 459–460
Casual experiments, 256–257
Catalog of Federal Domestic Assistance, 454
Catalog of U.S. Government Publications, 488
Categorical grants, 454–455
Categorizing data analysis strategies, 429
Causality, criteria for, 42–44, 390, 392, 408
defined, 42, 408
experiments and, 257–259, 282–283, 328
field research and, 249–250
idiographic explanations and, 37
multivariate analysis and, 390–394
practice models and, 25–26
search for, 20, 25
Cell frequencies, 389
Cell phones, ethics, 186
research device, 14, 251
sampling, 133, 154–155, 185
Central limit theorem, 413
Central tendency, 403–404
Certificates of confidentiality, 60, 63
Changing criterion design, 307–309

Children, research on, 4, 7, 20–25, 27, 68, 103–105, 141, 146, 173, 178–179, 182, 195, 228, 238, 242–243, 247, 276, 308, 327, 329, 336–337, 442
Chi-square, 417–421
City directory, 134
Clients, assessment of, 5, 363–364
ethics and, 66–67, 68–69, 309
interviewing, 189–191
program evaluation and, 199
reversal designs and, 302
sampling, 132, 153–156
scale use and, 364
self-report and, 296
Clinical Anxiety Scale, 363
Clinical-research, assessment of, 310–312
defined, 291
model, 290–291
process of, 292–300
Clinician Administered PTSD Scale, 360
Closed-ended questions, defined, 161–164
interview structure and, 176
layout, 167
response recording, 180
Closure, 11–12
Cluster sampling, 138–139, 150
Cochrane Library, 96, 301
Codebook, 375–376, 379
Coding, available data and, 203–205
direct, 448–449
manifest versus latent, 206–207
observation and, 236–239
qualitative research and, 429–435, 446–447
questions and, 162
schemes for, 204–205, 429–435
sheets, 236–239
validity and reliability in, 207–208, 246
Coefficient of determination, 408
Cohort groups, 330–331
Collaboration, 3, 8, 125, 241
Committee on the Status of Women in Sociology, 34
Common sense, 22
Complete participant, 225–226

Computer Assisted Interviewing (CAI), 185, 371
Computer assisted qualitative data analysis (CAQDA), 445–448
Computer mediated communication technology (CMCT), 14
Computerized Delivery Sequence File (CDSF), 134, 141
Computers, agency data and, 14, 215
data analysis by, 373, 445–448
libraries and, 484–487
measurement and, 125, 251
qualitative research and, 445–448
software, 422
surveys and, 186–187
concepts, defined, 30–31
development of, 30–31, 82–83, 229, 429–435, 447–448
literature review and, 83–85
measurement and, 103–105
minorities and, 33–34
Conclusions, 85, 442–445
See also Hypotheses.
Concurrent validity, 115
Confidence interval, 142–143
Confidence level, 142–143
Confidentiality, 52, 54, 55, 57–60, 63, 70, 170, 171–172, 212
Conflict Tactics (CT) Scale, 108–109, 350–351, 360, 362–363
Construct validity, 116–117, 443
Content analysis, coding in, 203–205, 429–430
computers and, 445–448
defined, 204
measurement and, 208–210
minorities and, 214–216
program evaluation and, 334
qualitative analysis and, 442
reliability and, 208
sampling in, 210–211, 214
units of analysis and, 205–206
validity in, 207–208
Content validity, 114, 116–117, 207–208, 347
Context map, 439–440
Contextualizing data analysis strategy, 429, 431, 436–438

SUBJECT INDEX

Contingency control, 390–394
Contingency questions, 167–168, 190
Contingency tables, 390–394
Continuous variables, 113, 386–387
Contravariation, 305
Control, condition of, 259
  experimental, 257–258, 283
  groups, 67–71, 417–418
  statistical, 330–332
  variables, 42–44, 259, 390
Correlation, 408
Cost-benefit analysis, 333–337
Cost-effective analysis, 337–338
Courts and confidentiality, 59–61
Cover letter, 169–171
Crime and criminal justice, research on, 202–203, 324, 331, 334
Crisscross directory, 134
Criterion validity, 114–116, 207–208, 245, 443–444
Critical approaches to science, 41, 241, 333
Critical thinking, 8, 14–15, 489
Cronbach's alpha, 120–121, 352
Cross-sectional research, 42–43, 91–92, 132, 213, 283
Curvilinear relationships, 405, 408–409

Data, analysis, 9–10, 190, 346, 370, 379–385, 399, 427–429, 445–448
  archives, 105–106, 196–197, 215
  cleaning, 377–378
  coding, 371–375
  collection, 9, 196–200, 276–277, 284
  digital storage of, 212
  displays, 438–441
  distributions, 379–388
  entry, 190
  empirical, 3
  ethics and, 379
  fully ordered, 347
  missing, 200
  partially ordered, 346
  properties of, 401
  qualitative and quantitative, 91–92, 178–179, 432
  reduction, 429–438

source vs. unit of analysis, 89
See also Available data.
Databases, 11, 14, 96–97, 190, 199, 212, 264, 376–377, 457, 478–479, 482, 484–486
Debriefing, 56–57, 61, 63, 117, 279, 280
Deception, 52, 54, 55–57, 61, 65, 225, 280, 350
Deduction, 28, 34–35, 200–201
De-identified data set, 212
Demand characteristics, 278–279
Department of Health and Human Services (DHHS), 1, 52–53, 79, 81, 141, 317, 454, 488
Dependent variable, abstraction and, 104
  causality and, 42–44
  coding and, 238
  contingency tables and, 388
  defined, 32
  effect size and, 85
  ethics and, 68–69, 117
  experiments and, 257–262
  history and, 266
  literature review and, 84
  nonprobability samples and, 145
  observation, 238
  practice measures and, 124
  program evaluation and, 323–324
  single-system design and, 290
  statistics and, 417
  stratification and, 138
  tables and, 388–389
Descriptive research, 3, 320
Descriptive statistics, 199, 388, 400–401, 402–411
Deviant behavior, 35–37
Deviant cases, 443
Dewey Decimal System, 480–481
Dichotomous variables, 405, 406
Different group time series design, 273–275
Differential association theory, 27–30
Dimensional sampling, 156, 149–150
Direct replication, 308
Discrete variables, 113, 385–387
Discriminatory power score (DP), 349–352

Disguised observation, 52, 55, 56, 57, 226, 249, 228–229, 238, 246, 249, 251
Dispersion, 404–405
Dissemination of results, 9, 10, 12, 64, 95, 190, 317–318, 339, 466, 468, 469
Distress, 54, 61–62, 63, 117, 360
Distributions, 379–388, 403–405, 408–411
Diversity, concepts, 33–34
  descriptive statistics and, 402–403
  evaluation research and, 325–326
  experiments and, 281–282
  feminist methods and, 90
  field research and, 247–248
  gays and lesbians, 27
  homeless children, 242
  Indian Health Service and, 79
  interview relationship and, 181–182
  measurement and, 121–122, 33–34
  Native Americans, 449
  observational research on, 243, 222–224, 247–248
  operational definitions of, 33–34
  problem selection and, 80–82
  research issue, 8
  sampling and, 151–153
Documentation, 12
Document delivery, 475, 479
Documents, available data as, 196
  inaccessible subjects and, 213
  longitudinal analysis of, 213
  nonreactivity, 211–213
  sample size and, 213
Documents division of library, 478
Domestic violence, codebook, 375
  dependent variable as, 273,
  measuring, 108–109
  program evaluation and, 270–272, 276
  research revictimization, 360
  survey and, 173
Double coding, 434
Drug Evaluation Network System (DENS), 125
Drug use, research on, 150
Dual frame surveys, 155
Dummy variable analysis, 403

SUBJECT INDEX

Ecological fallacy, 88
Educational Resources Information Center (ERIC), 486
Effect size, 85, 418–419
Empirical practice, 291, 292
  See also Clinical research,
Error, data entry and, 376
  measurement and, 106–107, 416–417
  random, 122–123
  systematic, 122–123
  Type I and Type II, 416–417
Ethics, absolutist position, 54–55
  advocacy and, 65–66
  anonymity, 57–58, 170, 186, 246
  audio recording and, 448
  available data and, 212
  cell phones and, 154–155, 186
  clients and, 66–67
  codes of, 7, 71
  concealment, 249
  confidentiality, 59–60, 63, 170
  control groups and, 67–71, 270, 283, 327
  data analysis and, 379, 414
  data storage and, 212
  deception, 65, 55–57, 225, 249, 280
  defined, 50
  de-identifed data set, 212
  disseminating results and, 318, 469
  experiments and, 280
  formula stories, 442
  harm and distress, 61–62, 68–69, 232, 360
  information technologies and, 212
  informed consent, 54–56, 63, 67, 225, 249, 280
  institution review boards (IRB), 52–53, 68, 117, 309
  internet research and, 70
  interviewer falsification, 180–181
  limited data set, 212
  measuring harm, 117, 360
  minorities and, 50–54
  misconduct and fraud, 64–65, 68–69
  Nuremberg trials, 51–52
  participant observation and, 249
  plagiarism, 469
  privacy and, 57–61, 63
  problem selection and, 84
  qualitative analysis and, 442
  random assignment, 327
  research and evaluation compared, 309
  respondent-driven sampling, 152
  risk-benefit doctrine, 52, 55, 71
  sampling and, 152
  scale use trauma, 360
  single-system design and, 298, 302, 309, 310
  sponsors and, 62–64
  statistics and, 414
  values and, 50
  withholding treatment, 67–71, 270, 283, 298, 302, 309
Ethnicity. *See* Minorities.
Ethnography, data analysis in, 448,
  interviews, 178–179, 239, 431–432
  map, 151
  observation, 247–248
  participant relationship, 233
Evaluability assessment, 321–323
Evaluation, in practice, 11
Evaluation research, basic research and, 316–318
  barriers to, 338–340
  cost-benefit analysis, 333–337
  cost-effective analysis, 337–338
  defined, 4, 315
  designs for, 326–338
  evidence-based practice and, 316, 328, 330–331
  goals of, 319
  minorities, 325–326
  nonpositivist, 332–334, 334
  politics, 318–319
  types of, 319
  utilization of, 338–340
Evidence-based practice, accountability and, 7
  dcfincd, 6
  ethics and, 68
  evaluation research and, 316, 328, 330–332
  experiments and, 257
  human services and, 6
  literature search and, 96–97
National Registry of Evidence-Based Programs and Practices, 264
  practice linkage, 8, 25, 27
  program evaluation and, 264–265
  rating study criteria, 330–331
  scaling in, 125, 363
  surveys and, 173
  single-system design and, 289, 301
  steps in, 10–12
Ex ante analysis, 333–335
Ex post analysis, 333–335
Experience, 21–22, 27
Experimental attrition, 264–265, 266
Experimental condition, 258
Experimental effectiveness, 298
Experimental group, 258
Experimental stimulus, 258
Experimental variability, 258–259
Experimenter expectations, 279, 284–285
Experiments, assessment of, 282–285
  causality and, 43
  costs of, 283
  data collection, 276–277, 284
  defined, 257
  designs, 265–269, 272
  double-blind, 279–280
  ethics and, 55, 67–71, 117, 280
  evidence-based practice and, 257
  field, 257, 270
  laboratory, 257
  program evaluation and, 264
  quasi. *See* Quasi-experimental designs.
  scientific explanation and, 38
Explanation, 393, 427
Explanatory research, 4, 10
External validity, defined, 277
  experiments and, 277–281
  threats to, 277–281
Extraneous variability, 259

Face validity, 114–115, 244–245, 331
Factor analysis, 351, 355
Factorial design, 269
Family, research on, 20, 25, 27

Family Educational Rights and
     Privacy Act, 212
Feasibility, 92–97
Federal Bureau of Investigation
     (FBI), 33, 123, 199, 202–203
Federal Register, 457
Feminist. See Women.
Feminist approaches to science, 41,
     62, 90–91, 241, 442
Field experiments. See Experiments.
Field notes, 179, 245, 427, 435,
     440–441
Field research, assessment of,
     248–250
  bias in, 247–248
  defined, 220
  ethics, 56–57, 225, 226–227, 249
  invisibility in, 231
  reactivity in, 246–247
  recording observations in,
     234–236
  sampling in, 242–244
  steps in, 229–234
  types of, 222–229
  validity and reliability in, 244
  See also Participant observation.
Filter questions, 167–168
Financial considerations, 94–95
Focus groups, 187–189, 240, 320,
     334, 339, 430
Focused coding, 433–435
Formative evaluation, 319–321
Formula grants, 455
Foundation Center, 457–458
Foundations, 454, 456–457
Fraud, 10, 54, 64–65, 68–69, 468
Frequency distribution, 381–385, 403
Frequency polygon, 386–387
Funneling, 363

Gamma, 407–408
Gender, 8, 90–91, 182, 240,
     247–248, 281–282
  See also Women.
Generalization, 35–38, 241, 246,
     277–282, 285, 310–312, 413,
     427, 436–438, 443–445
Goals, defined, 324–325
  logic model and, 322–323
  objectives and, 325

proximate, 323–324
research, 3–4
variables as, 323
Going native, 225, 249
Goodman and Kruskal's tau, 406
Government documents, 487–488
Grants, components of, 465–467
  defined, 453
  planning, 458–463
  seeking, 457–458
  submission, 467–468
  types, 454–457
  writing, 463–467
Graphs, 385–388, 469
Grounded theory, 221–222, 239,
     431, 434, 435, 442, 447,
     448–449
Group depth interviews, 187–189
Grouped frequency distribution,
     382–385
Groups, control, 259, 417–418
  experimental, 258, 417–418
  unit of analysis, 85–89
Guttman scales, 356–360
  See also Scales; Scaling.

Harm, 50, 61–62, 63, 70, 187, 232,
     233, 280, 442
Health Insurance Portability and
     Accountability Act (HIPAA),
     212
Histogram, 386–387
History, 262–263, 266, 268, 273,
     302, 305
Holocaust, wording and, 165
Homelessness, 86, 178–179, 242,
     448–449
Human services, defined, 1–2
  problem source, 80
  research and, 66–71
  scaling in, 363–366
  See also Evidence-based practice;
     Practice.
Hypotheses, available data and,
     200–201
  development of, 32–33
  literature review and, 83–85
  null, 414–417
  research, 414–417
  sample size and, 139–142

statistical testing of, 414–417
testing in evaluation, 316
verification, 33

Idiographic explanations, 37, 241,
     427, 436–438
Impact assessment, 316
Implementation, 11
Independence, 401
Independent variable, causality and,
     42–44
  defined, 32
  literature review and, 84
  observation, 238
  statistics and, 417
  tables and, 388–389
Indexes, 104
Indian Health Service (IHS), 79
Indicators, 103–105
Induction, 34–35, 105, 200–201,
     221–222, 427, 436
Inference, 21, 206, 207, 257, 277,
     282, 326, 400
Inferential statistics, 400
Informants, 230
Information Literacy, 489
Informed consent, 54–56, 63, 67,
     225, 249
Institute for Social Research,
     164, 196
Institutional review boards (IRBs),
     52–53, 68, 117, 309
Instrumentation, 263
Interaction effect, 268
Interactive sampling, 147
Intercoder reliability, 246
Interlibrary loan, 478
Internal consistency, 120–121
Internal validity, 261–265, 305, 332
Internet, 70, 186–187
Interpretation, 392–393
Interpretive approaches to science,
     40–41, 221
Interquartile range, 358
Interval measures, 110–111, 346,
     399, 403
Interval midpoints, 384, 387
Interval width, 384
Interviewer falsification, 180–181,
     185

Interviewers, 177–181
Interviews, assessment of, 182–183
  defined, 161
  in-depth, 187–189, 239–240, 242–243, 248, 427, 430, 437–438
  practice and research compared, 189–191
  probes and, 179–180
  recording data in, 180
  respondents in, 176–177
  response rate in, 176–177
  social relationships, 177–180, 181–182
  structure of, 174–176
  types of, 174–175
Intimate Justice Scale, 350–351
Intimate partner violence, 34, 65, 81, 108–109, 272–273, 350–351, 362, 442
  See also Women.
Inverse relationship, 32
Items, 104
  See also Scales

Journalism, 22–23
Journals for human services, 469–470, 483–484
Judges, 353
Judgmental sampling, 148–149, 346–347
Jury opinion, 114, 207–208

Kendall's tau, 407–408
Knowledge, 20–25, 37–41
Known groups, 116

Laboratory experiments, 220, 257, 277, 281
Lambda, 406
Language differences, 182
Lesbians, research on, 27
Levels of measurement, 109–112, 346, 352, 360, 380–381, 399–400, 403–404, 417
Library classification systems, 482–484
Library divisions, 478–479
Library of Congress System, 480–481
Library search strategies, 479

Life histories, 240–241
Likert scales, 210, 349–352, 353–354, 362, 399–400
  See also Scales; Scaling.
Literary Digest, 134
Literature review, 83–85, 229, 470
Logical positivism, 38–41, 90–91, 220
Logic models, 322–323
Longitudinal research, 42–43, 90–91, 213–214, 248

Machiavellianism scale, 347
MANOVA, 401, 417–418
Marginals, 389
Matching, 259–261, 329
Matrix display, 440–441
Matrix questions, 168
Maturation, 263, 266, 267, 268, 273
Mean, 401, 403, 409–411, 413
Measurement, abstraction and, 104–105
  available data and, 201–202
  computers and, 125
  cultural sensitivity and, 121–122
  definition, 103
  error in, 106–107, 122–123, 416–417
  indicators, 31–32, 103–105
  instruments, 125
  items, 104, 344–345
  levels of, 109–112, 126, 346, 349, 352, 360, 380–381, 399–400, 403–404, 417
  minorities and, 33–34
  positivism, 106–109
  problem formulation and, 85–86
  qualitative research and, 108–109
  response bias in, 361–363
  selection, 126
  scales and, 104
  techniques, 105–106
  views, 106–109
Measures of association, 405–408
Measures of central tendency, 403–404
Measures of dispersion, 404–405
Median, 403
Memos, 435–436, 446
  See also Field notes.
Midpoints of intervals, 384, 387

Minorities, available data analysis of, 214–216
  concepts, 33–34
  ethics and, 50–54
  evaluation research and, 325–326
  experiments and, 281–282
  measurement and, 33–34
  operational definitions of, 33–34
  problem selection and, 80–82
  research issue, 8
Misconduct, 54, 64–65, 68
Missing data, 200, 213, 375–376
Mode, 403
Multidimensional scales, 360–361
Multiple baseline design, 302–306
Multiple time series design, 275–276
Multiple treatment design, 305
Multiple treatment interference, 280–281
Multiple-forms reliability, 119–120
Multi-Problem Screening Inventory, 363
Multistage sampling, 138–139, 141, 211
Multitrait-multimethod validity, 116–117
Multivariate statistics. See statistics.

Narrative analysis, 437
Narrative inquiry, 240–241
National Association of Social Workers, available data study, 200
  code of ethics, 7, 71
  journals, 470
  sampling frame, 133
  survey sponsor, 169
National Children's Study (NCS), 141
National Crime Victimization Survey, 123, 202, 270–273
National Registry of Evidence-Based Programs and Practices, 264
National Training Laboratory (NTL), 340
Native Americans, grants, 458
  measurement, 121
  research participants, 181–182
  qualitative research on, 449
  sampling, 151–152

SUBJECT INDEX

Needs assessment, 319–321, 459–460
Negative relationships, 32, 405
Network analysis, 439–440
Nnmino-yaa, 449
Nominal data, 110, 209, 380, 382, 399, 405–406, 420–421
Nominal definitions, 31, 103–104
Nominal measures, 110, 403, 405–406
Nomothetic explanations, 35–38, 41, 427, 436
Nonpositivist approaches to science, 40–41, 220–222, 332–334
Nonprobability samples, 172
Nonreactive observation. *See* Unobtrusive observation.
Nonreactivity, available data and, 211–213
Nonresponse bias, 172, 174, 187
Normal distribution, 381, 402, 408–411
Null hypothesis, 414–417
Nuremberg code, 52
Nvivo, 448

Objectives, 325
Objectivity, 24, 26, 225, 231–233, 249
Observation, disguised, 52, 56–57, 228–229, 249, 251
 diversity and, 247–248
 hidden, 228
 human service practice and, 250
 journalism and, 23
 measurement, 105–106
 minorities and, 247–248
 observer roles, 225–226
 participant, 222–227
 reactivity in, 246–247
 recording, 234–236
 reliability and validity, 244–246
 single-system designs and, 294–295
 techniques, 220
 unobtrusive, 227–229, 239
Observer-as-participant, 225–226
Office of Research Integrity, 64, 68
Online public access catalog (OPAC), 479

Online surveys, 186–187, 339, 365
Open coding, 433–435
Open-ended questions, 161–164, 178
Operational definitions, available data and, 200–201
 defined, 31
 literature review and, 84
 measurement and, 103, 104–105
 minorities and, 34
 qualitative research and, 108–109, 434–435
Opportunity costs, 335
Ordinal data, 110, 360, 380, 382–383, 385, 388, 399–400, 403, 407–708
Organizations, units of analysis and, 87
Outliers, 443

Panel studies, 92, 141, 173
Paradigms in science, 38–41
Partial tables, 392–394
Participant-as-observer, 225–226
Participant observation, bias in, 249
 defined, 222
 ethics of, 225, 249
 examples of, 222–224
 interviews and, 241, 249
 reactivity in, 246–247
 recording observations in, 234–236
 role alternatives, 224–227
 steps in, 229–234
Pearson's r, 408
Peer review, 64–65, 96, 301, 379
Percentage difference, 389–390
Percentage tables, 389–390
Perfect relationship, 405
Periodicals, 482–484
Periodicity, 136, 211
Personal Digital Assistant, 251
Personal interest, 77
Phi, 405–406
Pie charts, 387–388
Pilot study, 9, 93, 96–97, 164
Police, research on, 56, 232, 326, 334
Policy and policy-focused research, 5, 79, 141, 202–203, 242–3

Politics of research, 80–82
Population, defined, 132
 of documents, 211
 hidden, 150
 homogeneity, 143–144
 inferential statistics, 400–401
 probability theory, 412
Positive relationship, 32, 405
Positivist approaches to science, 38–41, 106–109, 220–221, 332–333
Power, 418–419
Practice, available data in, 196
 collaboration with research, 2–3, 125
 competencies, 13
 interviews, 189–191
 linkage to research, 2–3, 12, 426
 parallels to research, 8–12, 250, 189–191, 363–366, 426
 scaling in, 363–366
 scientific, 25–26
 stages of, 10–12
 theories in, 25–26
Precision, 142–143
Predictive research, 3–4
Predictive validity, 115–116
Preexperimental designs, 266
Prejudice. *See* Minorities.
Pretest, 9, 165–166, 320, 346
Primary sampling units, 141
Prisons and prisoners, 226–227, 330–332, 449
Privacy, 50, 57–61
Probability theory, 412
Probes, 176, 179–180
Problem, assessment, 10
 feasibility, 92–97
 formulation, 9, 229
 minorities, 80–82
 selection, 77–82, 84
 shaping, 82–92
 statement of, 470
Process recording, 426, 437
Profiles, 437–438
Profiles of Student Life, 173
Program, as unit of analysis, 88
 program evaluation, defined, 5
 experiments and, 264
 problem formulation, 78–80

542 SUBJECT INDEX

Project grants, 454–455
Proportional reduction in error (PRE), 408
Propositions, 27, 34–35, 436
Public catalog, See Online public access catalog.
Public dissemination of research, 10, 12, 469
Public Health Service (PHS), 51–52
Pure research, 4
  See also Basic research.
Purposive sampling, 148–149, 242–243

Q score, See Interquartile range.
Qualitative data, 108–109, 204–205, 234–236
Qualitative research, assessment of, 248–250
  categorizing strategies in, 429–436
  characteristics of, 220–222
  coding in, 429–435
  computers and, 445–448
  contextual approach, 220, 427, 436–438
  defined, 39
  displaying data in, 438–441
  ethics and, 442
  example of, 242, 108–109
  goals of, 427–429
  practice compared and, 426–427
  quantitative research comparison, 89–91, 178–179, 432, 441–443
  types of, 239–240
  validity and reliability in, 442–445
  See also Observation.
Quality-adjusted life years (QALY), 337
Quantitative data, 93, 179, 189, 220, 236–239, 370, 438
Quantitative research, defined, 39
  data analysis, 370
  qualitative research comparison, 89–91, 178–179, 441–443
Quartiles, 351, 358, 404–405
Quasi-experimental designs, evaluation alternatives, 329
  different groups, 273–275
  multiple time-series, 275–276
  time-series design, 272–273

Questionnaires, advantages of, 172–174
  assessment of, 172–174
  cover letter and, 169–171
  defined, 161
  disadvantages of, 174
  follow-ups, 171
  length, 171
  mailed, 59
  respondent payment, 170–171
  response rate, 168–172
  structure of, 167–168
  questions, order of, 167, 362–363
  sensitive, 173–174
  skip-logic and, 190
  slang avoidance, 165
  types, 161–164, 174–175
  wording, 164–166, 183, 449
Quota sampling, 147–148

Random assignment, 68, 91, 258, 260–261, 265, 266, 267, 268, 270, 271, 275, 276, 283, 326–329, 330–332, 412
Random digit dialing, 133, 155, 185, 186
Random error, 122–123
Random numbers, 136, 491–493
Random samples, 211
Randomization, 260–262
Range, 404
Rapid Assessment Instruments (RAI), 364
  See also Scales.
Ratio measures, 111–112, 403
Reactivity, available data and, 214
  defined, 89
  field research and, 246–247
  human service practice and, 250
  observational research and, 227–229, 246–247
  panel studies and, 92
  problem formulation and, 89
  settings and, 278–280
  self-monitoring and, 296
  testing and, 263, 277
Reanalysis, 78
Reductionist fallacy, 88
Reference department of library, 478

Referencing formats, 472
Reflective remarks, 435–436
Regression, 417–420
Regression discontinuity design, 331–332
Relationships, measures of association and, 405–408
  types of, 32, 405
Reliability, content analysis and, 208
  defined, 117
  equivalence, 118
  field research and, 244–246, 434–435
  improving, 123–126
  intercoder, 246, 434–435
  internal consistency, 120–121
  multiple forms, 119–120
  observation research and, 244–246
  scaling and, 345, 351, 356, 364
  Spearman-Brown correction formula, 120
  split-half, 120
  stability, 118
  test-retest, 118–119
  types of, 118–121
Replication, codebook and, 376
  control variables and, 391–392
  data editing and, 379
  direct, 308
  ethics and, 117
  external validity and, 281
  fraud detection and, 64–65
  grounded theory and, 222
  observational studies and, 249
  problem formulation and, 78, 83
  program evaluation and, 270, 272
  publication and, 468, 470
  sampling and, 143, 145
  science and, 24, 78
  single-system, 301, 305, 308–312
  systematic, 308
  table elaboration, 391
Representative samples, availability sampling and, 146
  cell phones and, 154–155
  defined, 131–132
  diversity and, 151–153, 282
  document analysis and, 210
  experiments and, 278

Representative samples, availability sampling and (*continued*)
  external validity and, 281
  focus groups and, 188
  nonresponse and, 172
  probability sampling, 135–136
  program evaluation and, 326
  proportionate sampling, 137
  qualitative data and, 444–445
  response rate and, 168
  sampling validity and,114
Reproducibility, 357–360
Request for Proposals (RFPs), 455
Research, applied, 4
  basic, 4
  collaboration with practice, 3, 125
  cross-sectional, 89–91
  defined, 3
  designs, 9
  goals of, 3–4
  hypothesis, 414–417
  longitudinal, 90–91
  parallels to practice, 2, 8–12, 29–30, 426
  prior, 78
  qualitative, 40–41, 91–92, 108–109, 178–179
  quantitative, 40–41, 89–91, 178–179
  psychological factors in, 3
  report writing, 468–473
  social factors in, 3
  systematic, 3
  technique, 85
  theories in, 25–26
  types of, 4–5
Respondents, contacting, 176–177
  interviews and, 161
  payment to, 170–171
Response bias, 174, 251, 361–363
  See also Bias.
Response pattern anxiety, 362
Response rate, 52, 55, 85, 167, 168–174, 176–177, 186, 187, 339
Response set, 168
Reversal design, 302, 305, 312
Roper Organization poll, 165

Salk polio vaccine, 329
Sample, defined, 132

population and, 132, 400–401
  See Representative Sample.
sampling area, 138–139
size, 139–145, 213, 419, 421
  See also Representative Sample.
Sampling, address-based, 133–134, 155
  availability, 146–147
  bias, 172, 214, 243
  cell phones and, 133, 154–155
  city directory and, 134
  Computerized Delivery Sequence File and, 134, 141
  content analysis and, 210–211
  criss-cross directory and, 134
  defined, 131
  dimensional, 149–150, 156
  disproportionate, 138
  distributions, 413
  error, 135, 136–137, 139, 145
  fraction, 144
  frame, 132–134, 145, 244
  interactive, 147
  interval, 136
  literature review and, 85
  minority populations, 150
  multistage, 138–139
  nonprobability, 145–149, 242
  practice and, 153–156
  precision, 142–143
  probability, 135–145, 247, 413–416
  proportionate, 137–138
  purposive, 148–149, 242–243
  random digit dialing and, 133, 155, 187
  respondent-driven, 150
  sampling, cell phones and, 133, 154–155
  simple random (SRS), 135
  snowball, 147, 156, 242–243
  stratified, 136–138
  surveys and, 187
  systematic, 136
  targeted, 150
  technique, 144–145
  time, 244
  traditional listing method, 133–134, 141
  validity, 114

Scale discrimination technique, 358
Scale items, 346–349, 350, 351, 353, 356, 364, 377, 378, 399
Scales, Alcohol Use Inventory, 364
  Attitude toward Church, 354
  Conflict Tactics Scale, 108–109, 360, 362
  FEAR, 364
  Hudson Index of Alcohol Involvement, 364
  indexes and, 104
  Intimate Justice Scale, 350–351
  Machiavellianism Scale, 347
  Michigan Alcohol Screening Test, 364
  NEECHAN Confusion, 364
  Rapid assessment instruments, 364
Scaling, advantages of, 345–346
  defined, 345
  development process, 346–348
  ethics and, 360, 365
  evidence-based practice and, 363
  formats for, 349–361
  Guttman, 356–360
  human services and, 363–366
  Likert, 210, 349–352, 353–354, 362, 399–400
  measurement and, 104, 347–348, 356, 360
  multidimensional, 360–361
  online, 365
  reliability and, 345, 351, 354–356, 364
  semantic differential,
  summated rating, 349
  Thurstone, 352–354, 358
  unidimensional, 348, 351
  validity in, 347, 351
Scattergrams, 408–409
Science, defined, 23
  explanation in, 35–38
  features of, 23–25
  paradigms in, 38–41
  perspectives on, 34–41
  public nature of, 468
  values in, 66
  See also Knowledge, Research.
Scientific advocacy, 65–66
Scientific practice, 7, 25–26, 315
  See also Clinical research.

SUBJECT INDEX

Search Institute, 173
Sears List of Subject Headings, 482
Secondary analysis, 196
Selection, validity and, 264–265, 267
Self determination, 50
Semantic differential scales, 354–356
Semi-interquartile range, 404–405
Serial dependence, 401
Single-system designs, assessment of, 310–312
 baselines, 293–296
 clinical-research and, 290–291
 computers and, 310–311
 defined, 6, 290
 design types, 300–308
 ethics and, 58, 309
 generalizability, 309
 measurement and, 363
 See also Clinical research.
Skewed distribution, 380, 403
Skip pattern, 168, 190
Snowball sampling, 147, 156, 242–243
Social artifacts, 88
Social control theory, 35–37
Social desirability, 181, 362
Social distance, 181, 230
Social problems, 77–78
Social Research, *See* Research.
Sociogram, 439–440
Solomon Four-Group Design, 268
Somer's D, 407–408
Spearman-Brown formula, 120
Spearman's rho, 407
Specification, 393–394
Split-half reliability, 120
Sponsored research, 62–64, 169
Spurious relationships, 42–44, 393
Stacks, 479
Stakeholder, 84, 318–319, 324, 332–333, 334
Standard deviation, 404–405, 408–411, 418
Standard normal distribution, 410–411
Standard scores, 408–411
Statistical control, 332
Statistical data, 196–203
Statistical effectiveness, 298, 300

Statistical hypothesis testing, 414–417
Statistical power, 418–419
Statistical regression, 263–264, 267, 332
Statistical significance, 145–146, 399
Statistics, bivariate, 402
 choice of, 399–402
 defined, 370–371, 400
 descriptive, 400
 ethics and, 414
 inferential, 400, 411–421
 multivariate, 390–394, 401
 single-system designs and, 298
 software for, 422
 univariate, 379–388, 401
Stratified samples, 136–138, 139, 141, 144, 147, 210–211
Student's t, 417, 419
Subjectivism, *See* Interpretive approaches to science.
Success rate, 88
Summated rating scales, 349
Summative evaluation, 321–338
Superintendent of Documents (SUDOCS), 488
Suppressor variables, 394
Surveys, causality and, 42–43
 cell phones and, 186
 cost comparisons, 183–184
 defined, 161
 evidence-based practice and, 173
 online, 186–187
 qualitative vs. quantitative, 178–179
 telephone, 171, 183–186
 See also Interviews; Questionnaires.
Symmetrical distributions, 380, 402, 410
Systematic error, 122–123, 362
Systematic replication, 308
Systematic sampling, 211

Table elaboration, 390–394
Table-of-contents services, 479
Tables, kinds of, 388–390
Targeted sampling, 150–151, 242–243
Telephones in research, 133, 154–155, 171–172, 183–186

Testing, validity and, 263
Theoretical sensitivity, 428
Theory, available data and, 200–201
 concepts and, 30–34, 427–428
 deduction and, 28, 34–35, 221
 functions of, 28–30
 grounded, 221–222, 239, 434, 442, 447
 induction and, 105
 problem selection and, 78, 83
 qualitative research and, 437, 447–448
 role and burnout, 36
 testing of, 78
 verification of, 23, 30, 222, 441–445
Therapeutic effectiveness, 298
Thurstone scale, 352–354, 358
 time, project feasibility and, 93–94
 sampling, 244
Time series design, 213
 See also Single-system designs.
Title research report and, 470
Tradition, 20–21
Traditional listing method, 133–134
Treatment, 296–300, 419
Trend studies, 92
Triangulation, 444
Type I and Type II error, 416–417, 418–419

Uniform Crime Reports (UCR), 123, 202–203
Unit of analysis, content analysis and, 205–206
 ecological fallacy and, 88
 groups as, 87
 individuals as, 87
 organizations as, 87
 programs as, 88
 reductionist fallacy and, 88
 social artifacts as, 89
 options for, 85–89
 source of data and, 89
Univariate statistics, 379–388, 401
Unobtrusive observation, 227–229, 239, 246, 250, 251, 277, 294–295

SUBJECT INDEX

Validity, available data and, 201–203, 207–208
  concurrent, 115
  construct, 116–117
  content, 114
  content analysis and, 207–208
  criterion, 114–115, 207–208, 245, 443–444
  definition of, 113–114
  external, 277–281
  face, 114
  field research and, 244–246, 442
  improving, 123–126
  internal, 261–265, 273, 281, 305
  jury opinion, 114
  observation and, 244–246
  predictive, 115–116
  sampling, 114
  scale items and, 347, 351
  types of, 114–117
Values, 21, 24, 50, 66, 443
Variables, alphanumeric versus numeric, 374
  antecedent, 393
  computer formatting of, 373–374
  continuous, 113, 387
  control, 43–44, 259
  creating and transforming, 378–379
  defined, 32
  dependent and independent, 32–33, 388–389, 417–418
  discrete, 113, 386–387
  interval, 110–111, 346
  intervening, 392–393
  naming, 373–374
  nominal, 110
  ordinal, 110
  program evaluation, 323–326
  ratio, 111–112
  suppressor, 394
Verbal reports, 105–106
Verification, 30, 441–445
Verstehen, 40, 221, 223, 225
Violence Against Women Act, 273
Voluntary consent, 67, 152

Welfare, wording and, 164
Wildcards, 486
Withdrawal designs, 302
Withholding treatment, 51, 54, 67–71, 270, 283, 298
  See also Ethics.

Women, available data research on, 214–216
  culture and, 242–243
  divorce and, 65
  experiments and, 263, 281
  female voices, 90–91
  gender insensitivity, 90–91
  images of, 206
  interviews and, 182
  job performance and, 325–326
  measuring abuse of, 21–22, 34, 77, 95, 108–109, 178, 271, 442
  observation and, 247
  operational definitions and, 34
  power and, 205, 325
  problem formulation and, 81
  program evaluation and, 326
  qualitative research on, 447
  sampling and, 146, 150–151
  survey research on, 188–189
  unit of analysis and, 89
  Violence Against Women Act, 270–273
  See also Intimate partner violence, Diversity, Minorities.

Z-scores, 408–411, 418–419